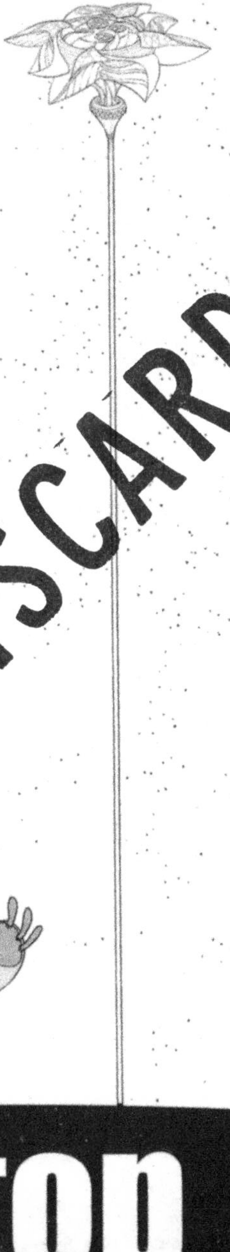

ORSON SCOTT
CARD
EMILY JANICE
CARD
WITH ZINA CARD

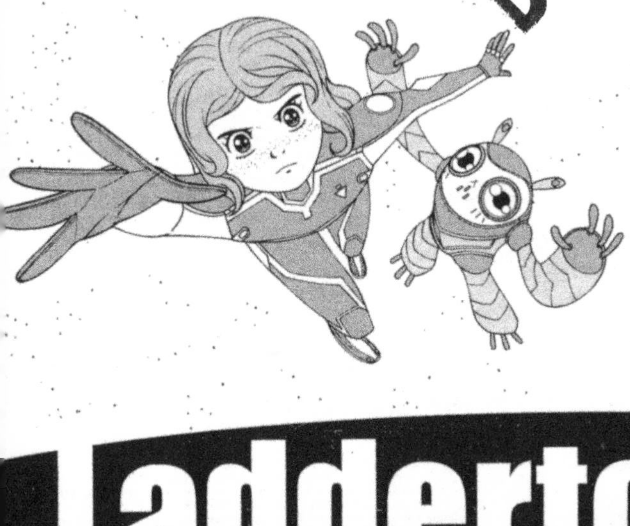

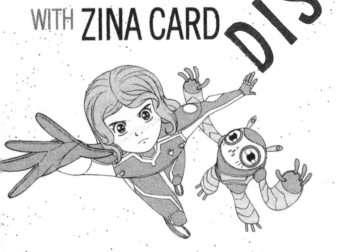

Laddertop

ILLUSTRATED BY HONOEL A. IBARDOLAZA
BOOKS 1-2

Laddertop

Books 1-2

story by **Orson Scott Card & Emily Janice Card**
with **Zina Margaret Card**

art by **Honoel A. Ibardolaza**

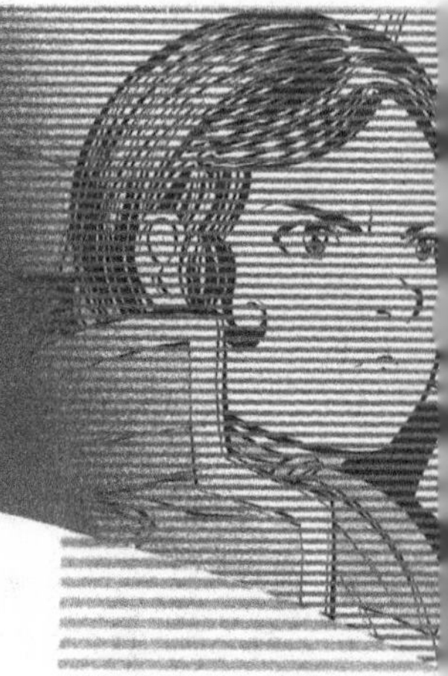

STAFF CREDITS

lettering & interiors	**Nicky Lim**
toning	**Ludwig Sacramento**
layout	**Alexis Roberts**
story consultant	**Jason DeAngelis**
production editor	**Adam Arnold**

LADDERTOP BOOKS 1-2

Copyright © 2013 by Orson Scott Card and Emily Janice Card

All rights reserved.

A Tor/Seven Seas Paperback
Published by Tom Doherty Associates, LLC
175 Fifth Avenue
New York, NY 10010

Visit us online at **www.gomanga.com** and **www.tor-forge.com**.

Seven Seas and the Seven Seas logo are trademarks of Seven Seas Entertainment, LLC. Tor® and the Tor logo are registered trademarks of Tom Doherty Associates, LLC.

ISBN 978-0-7653-2461-0

First Edition: October 2013

P1

TOR®

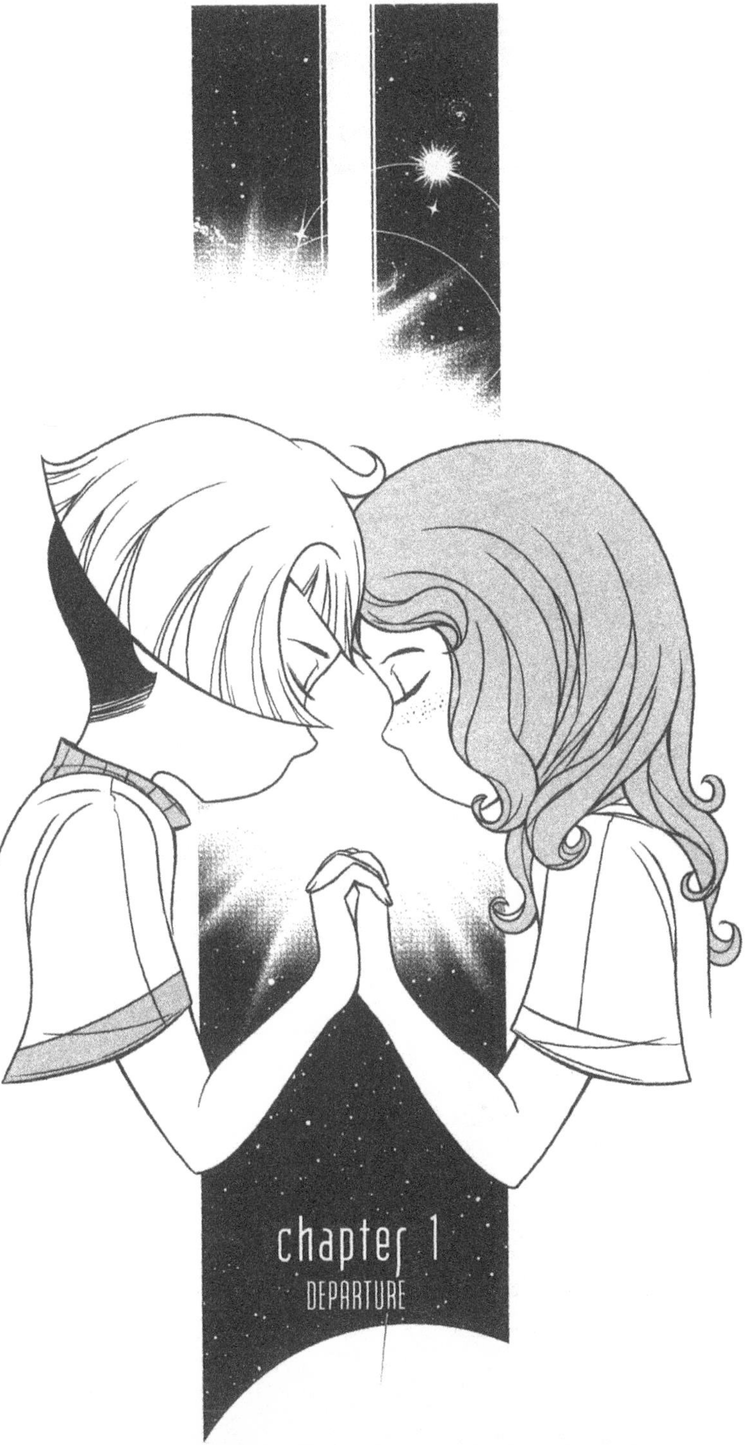
chapter 1
DEPARTURE

Laddertop

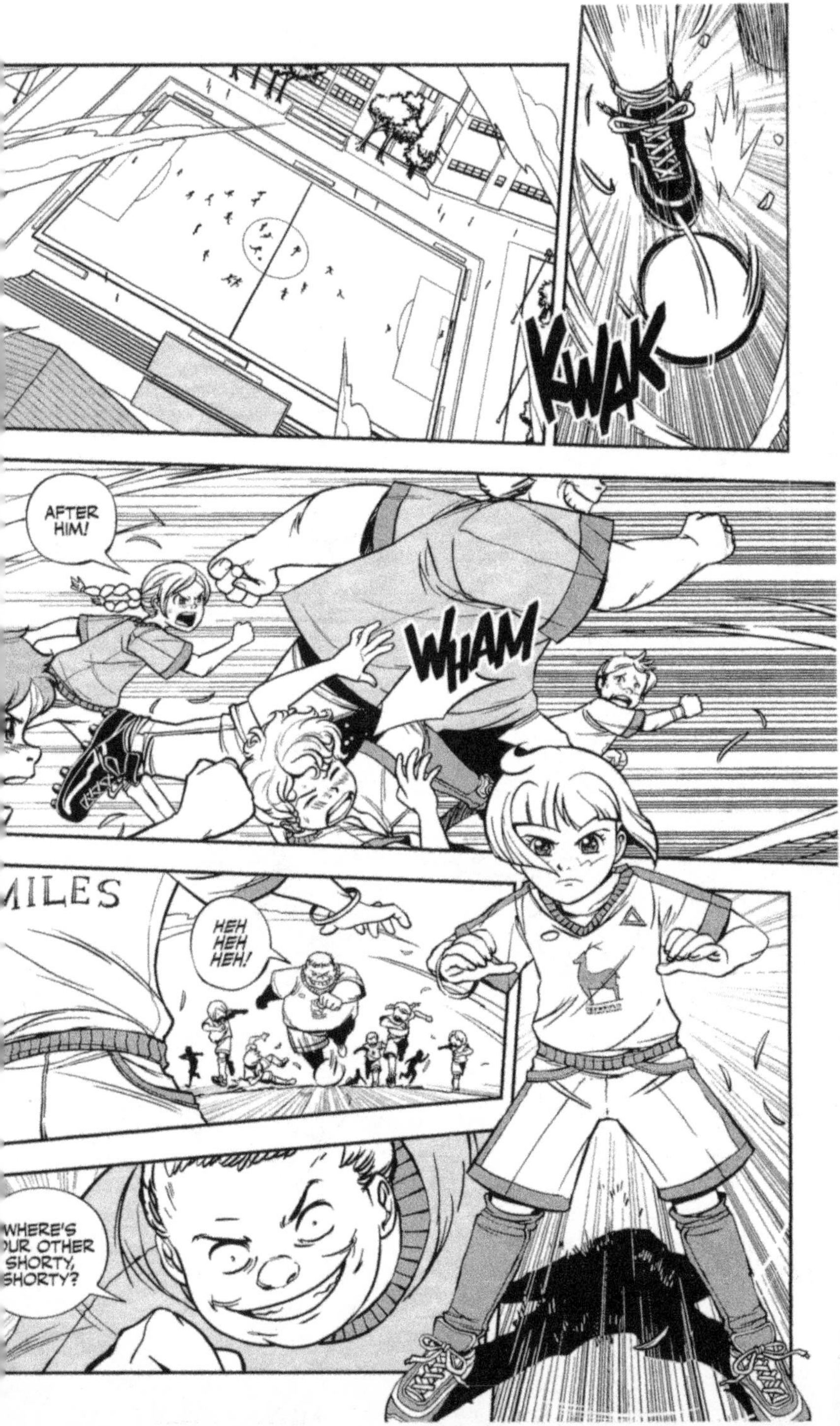
KWAK
AFTER HIM!
WHAM
MILES
HEH HEH HEH!
WHERE'S OUR OTHER SHORTY, SHORTY?

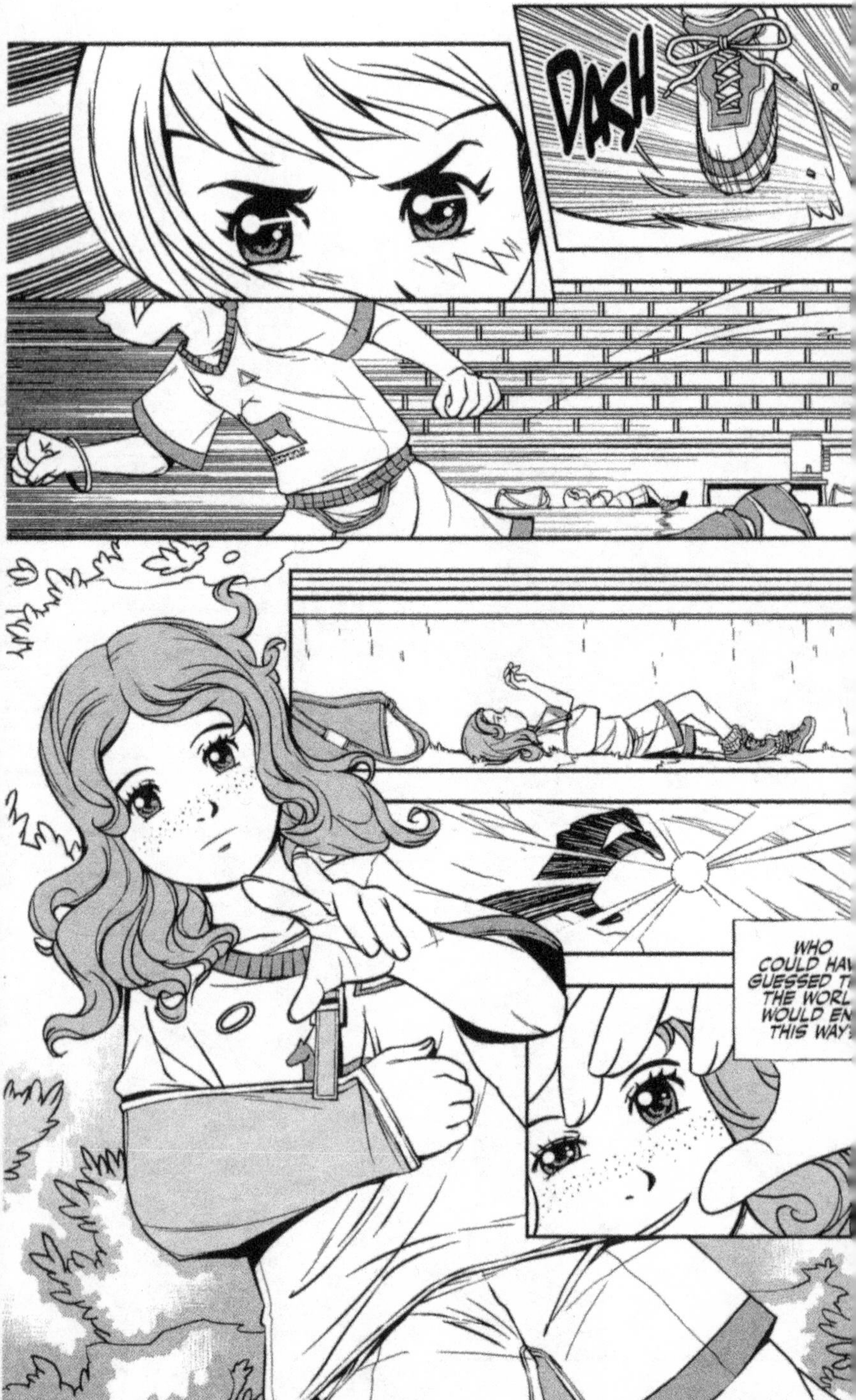
DASH
WHO COULD HAV GUESSED T THE WORL WOULD EN THIS WAY

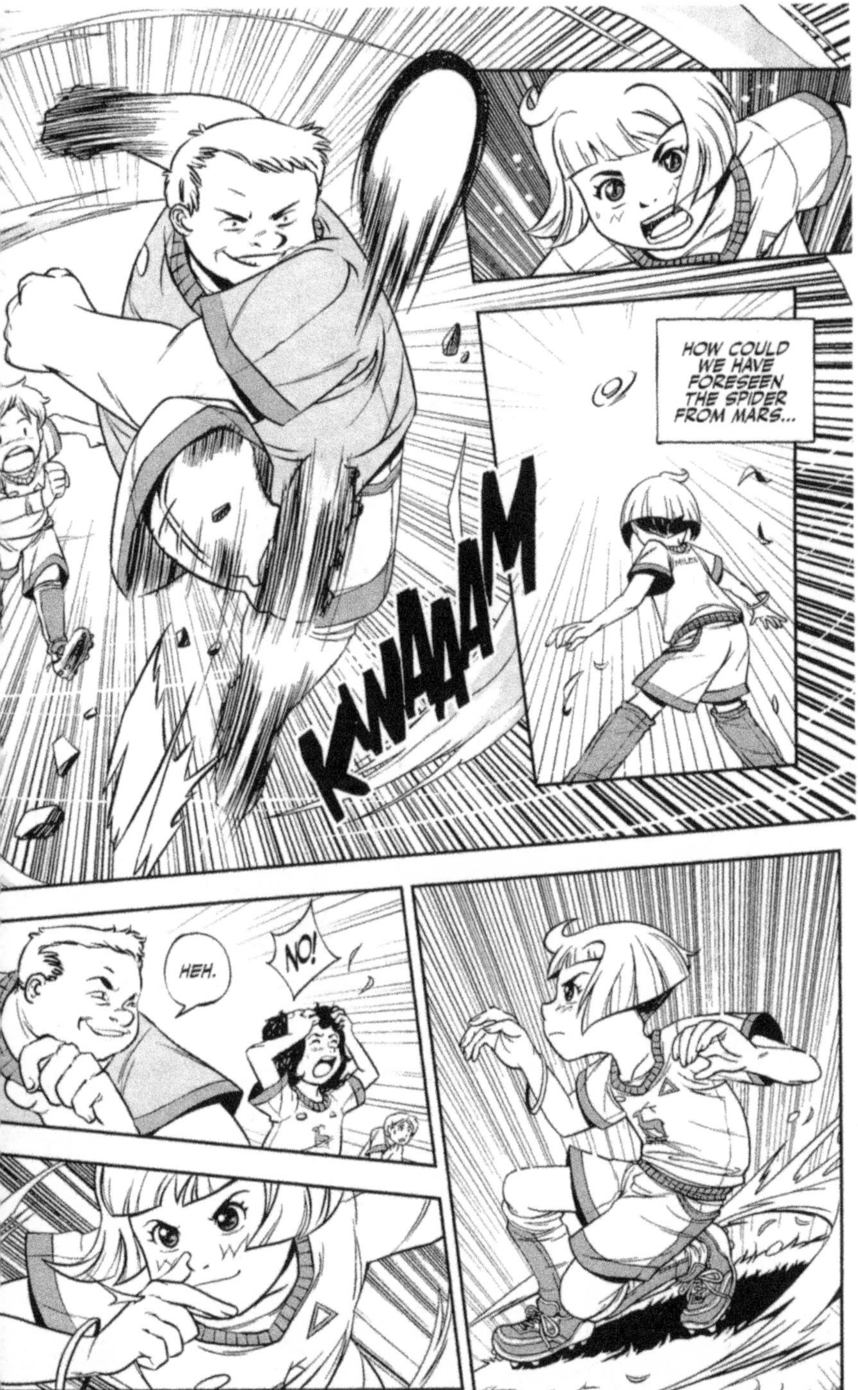
HOW COULD WE HAVE FORESEEN THE SPIDER FROM MARS...
KWAAAAM
HEH.
NO!

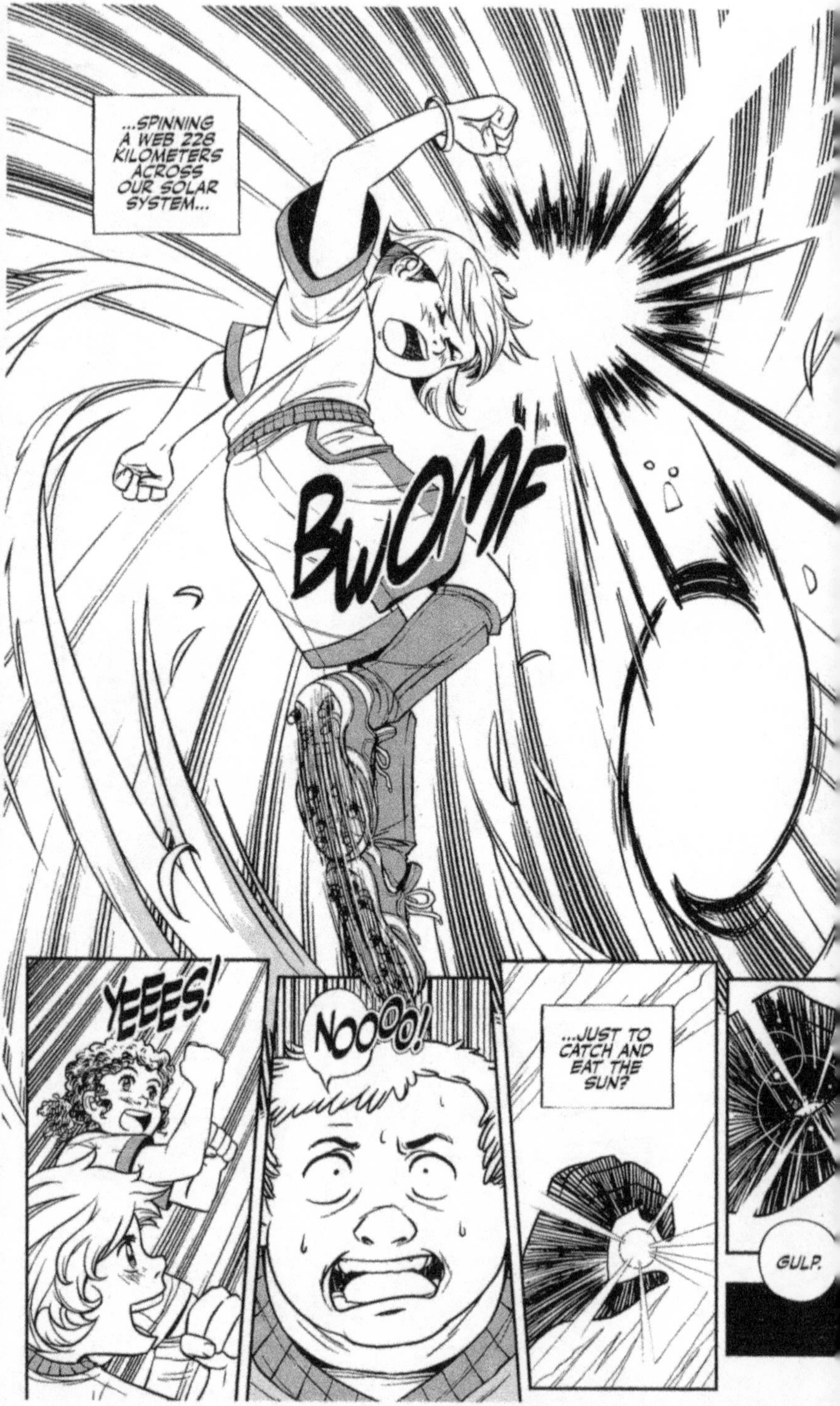
...SPINNING A WEB 228 KILOMETERS ACROSS OUR SOLAR SYSTEM...
BWOMF
YEEES!
NOOOO!
...JUST TO CATCH AND EAT THE SUN?
GULP.

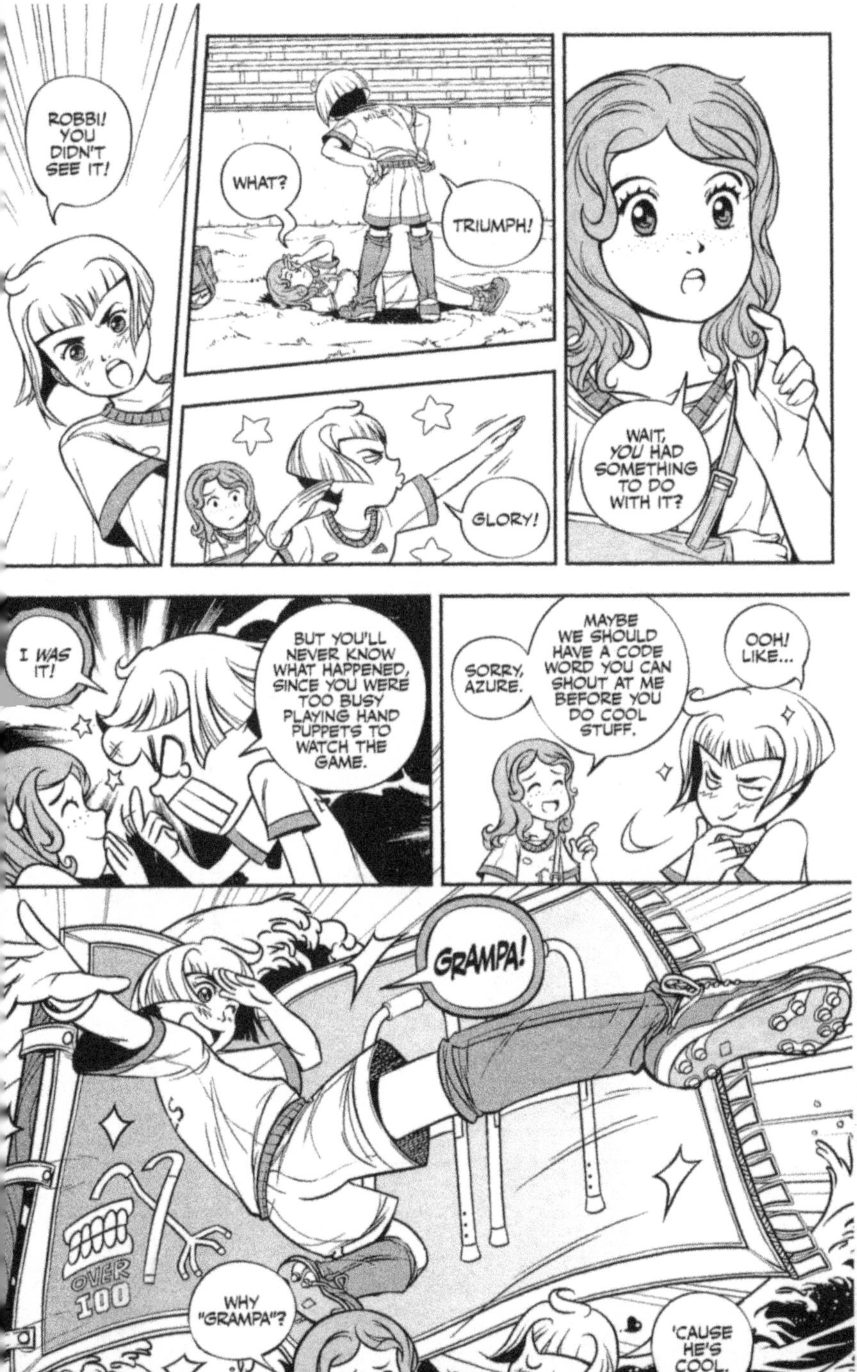
ROBBI! YOU DIDN'T SEE IT!
WHAT?
TRIUMPH!
GLORY!
WAIT, *YOU* HAD SOMETHING TO DO WITH IT?
I *WAS* IT!
BUT YOU'LL NEVER KNOW WHAT HAPPENED, SINCE YOU WERE TOO BUSY PLAYING HAND PUPPETS TO WATCH THE GAME.
SORRY, AZURE.
MAYBE WE SHOULD HAVE A CODE WORD YOU CAN SHOUT AT ME BEFORE YOU DO COOL STUFF.
OOH! LIKE...
GRAMPA!
OVER 100
WHY "GRAMPA"?
'CAUSE HE'S COOL.

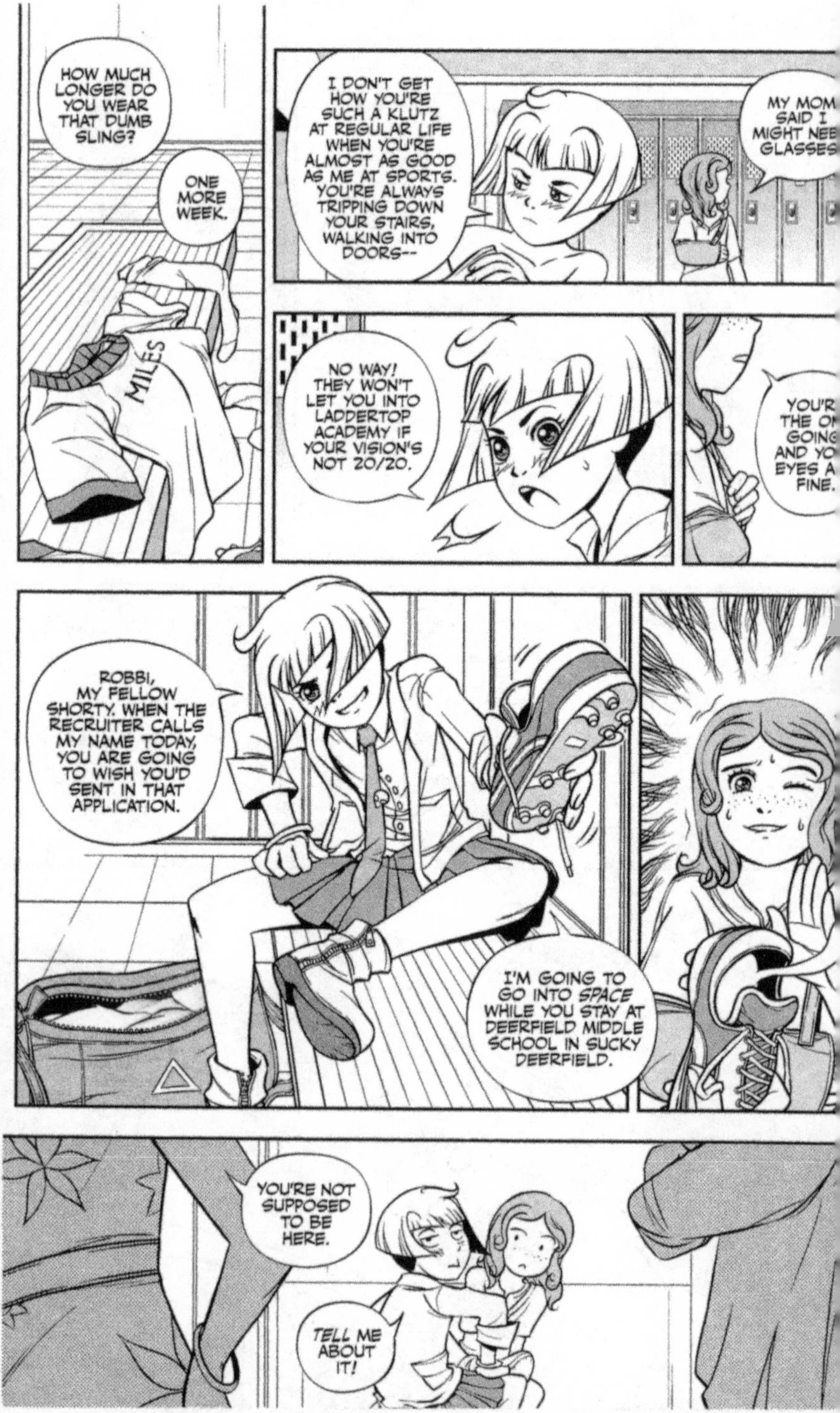
HOW MUCH LONGER DO YOU WEAR THAT DUMB SLING?
ONE MORE WEEK.
MILES
I DON'T GET HOW YOU'RE SUCH A KLUTZ AT REGULAR LIFE WHEN YOU'RE ALMOST AS GOOD AS ME AT SPORTS. YOU'RE ALWAYS TRIPPING DOWN YOUR STAIRS, WALKING INTO DOORS--
MY MOM SAID I MIGHT NEE GLASSES
NO WAY! THEY WON'T LET YOU INTO LADDERTOP ACADEMY IF YOUR VISION'S NOT 20/20.
YOU'R THE O GOING AND YO EYES A FINE.
ROBBI, MY FELLOW SHORTY. WHEN THE RECRUITER CALLS MY NAME TODAY, YOU ARE GOING TO WISH YOU'D SENT IN THAT APPLICATION.
I'M GOING TO GO INTO *SPACE* WHILE YOU STAY AT DEERFIELD MIDDLE SCHOOL IN SUCKY DEERFIELD.
YOU'RE NOT SUPPOSED TO BE HERE.
TELL ME ABOUT IT!

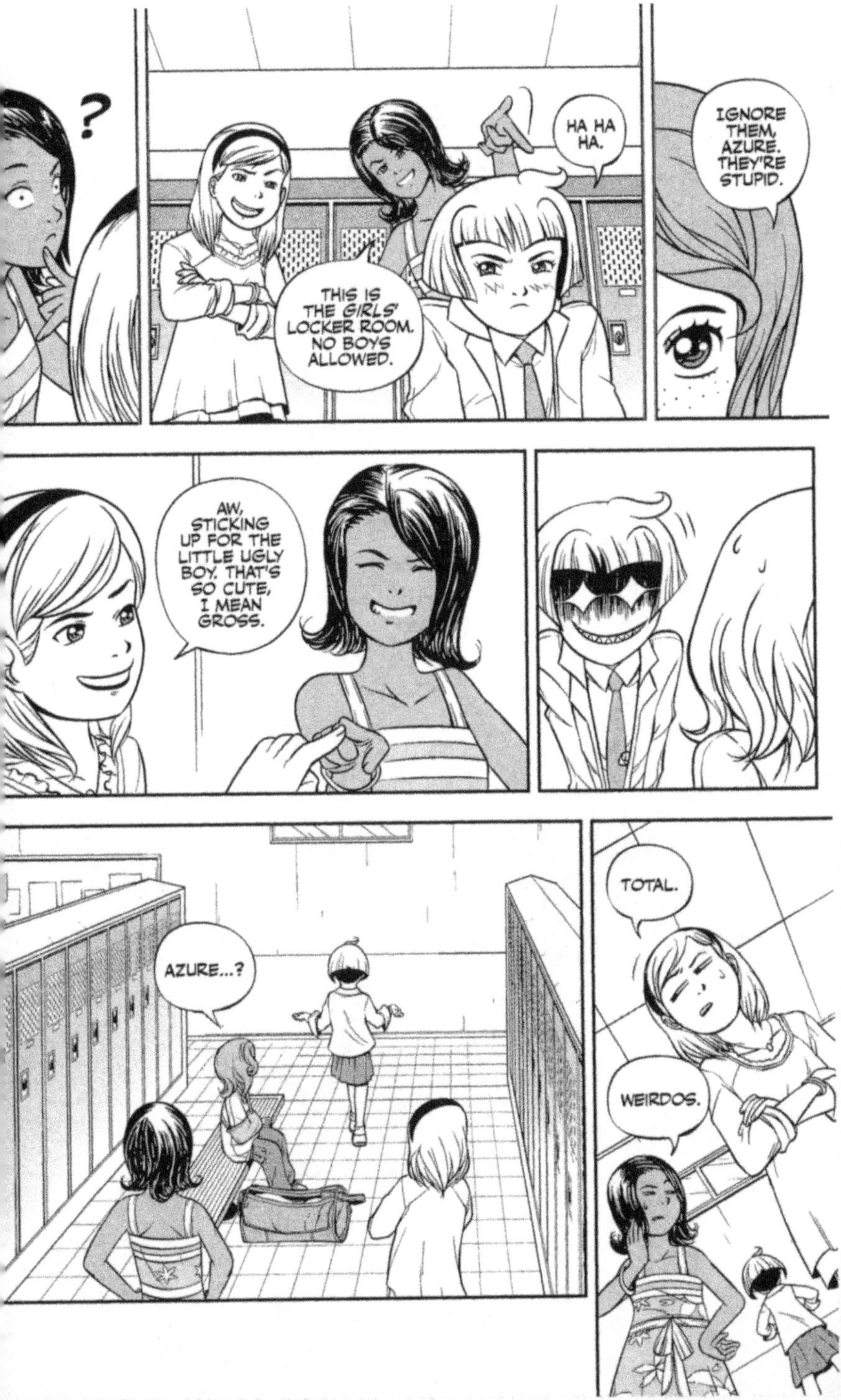
?
THIS IS THE *GIRLS'* LOCKER ROOM. NO BOYS ALLOWED.
HA HA HA.
IGNORE THEM, AZURE. THEY'RE STUPID.
AW, STICKING UP FOR THE LITTLE UGLY BOY. THAT'S SO CUTE, I MEAN GROSS.
AZURE...?
TOTAL.
WEIRDOS.

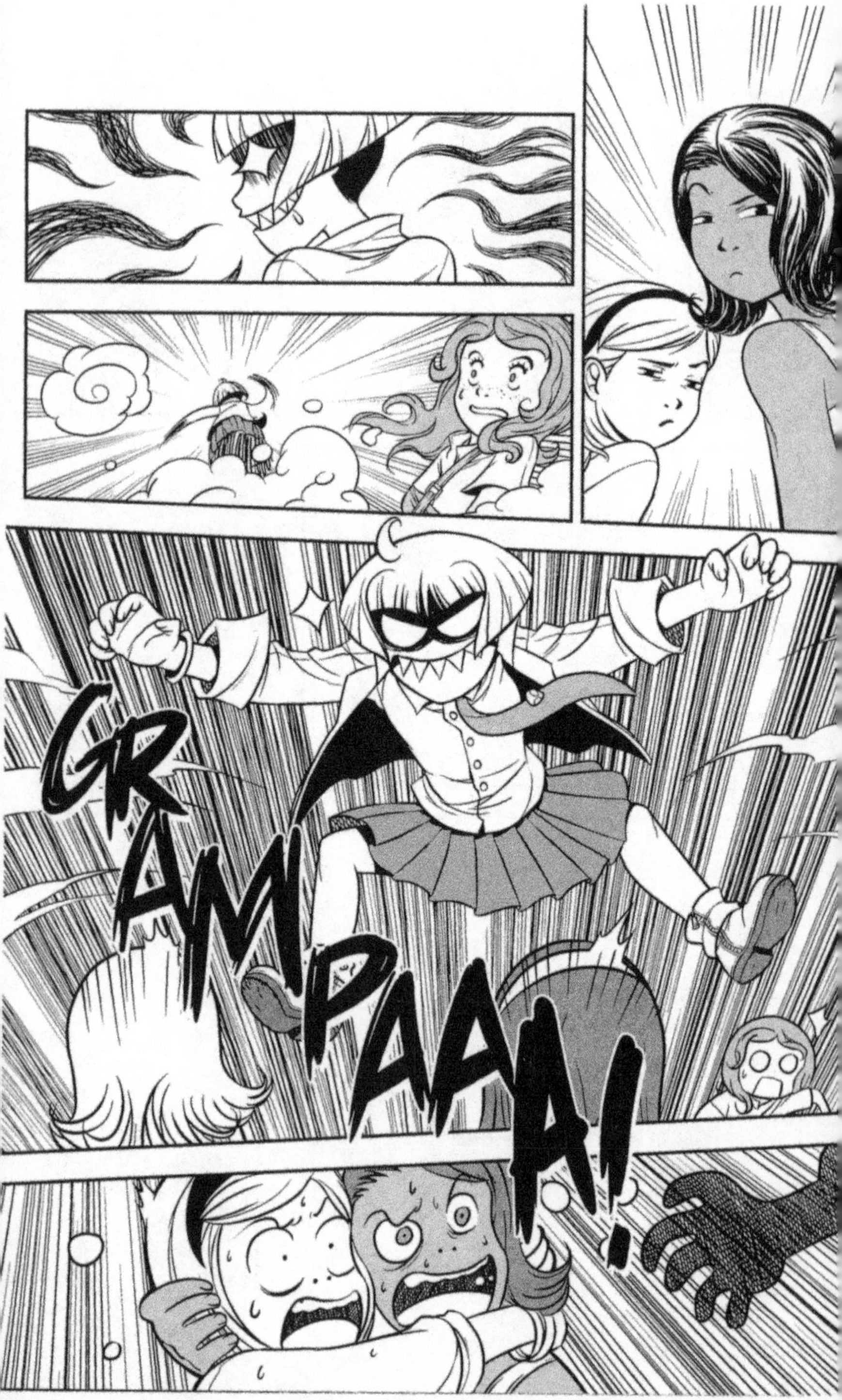
GRAMPAAA!

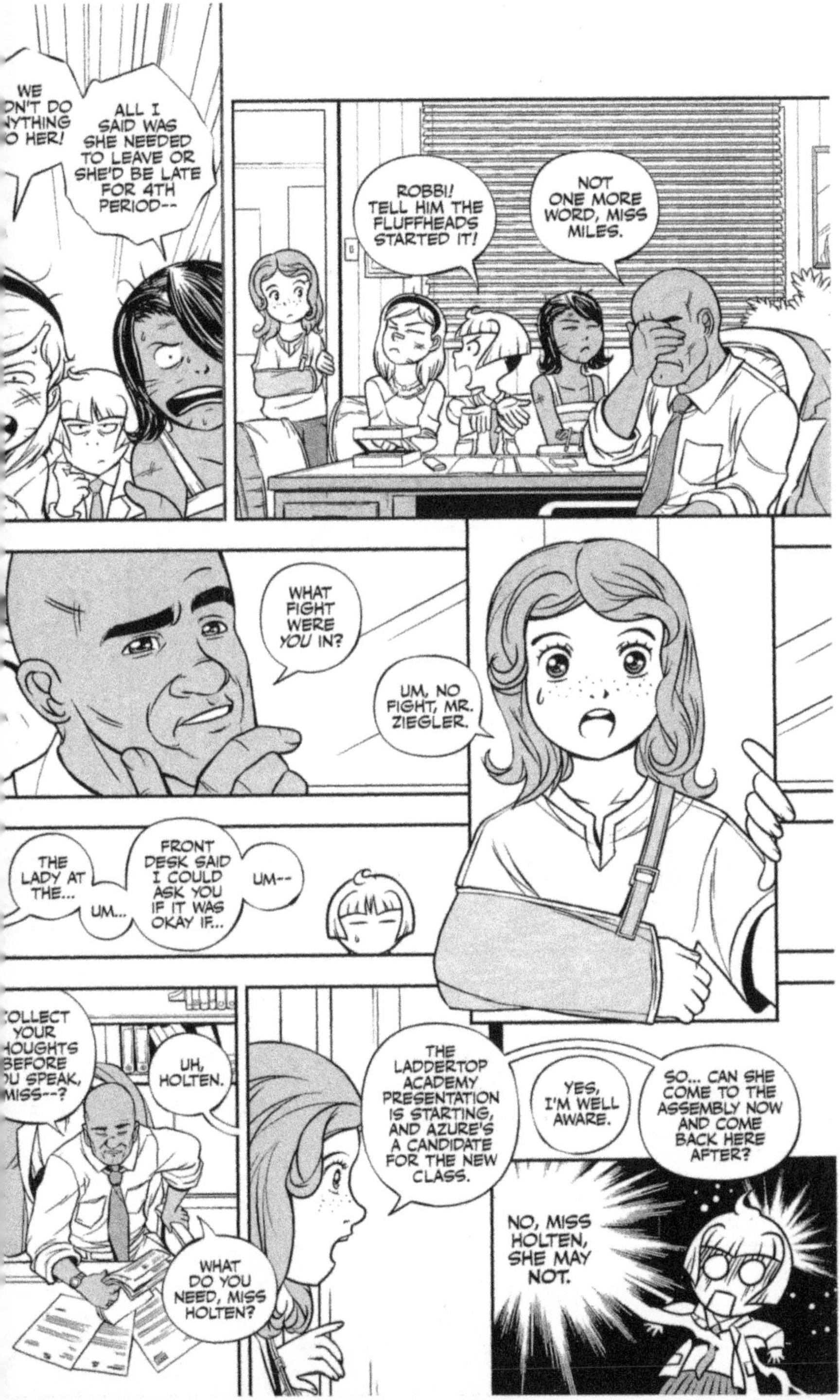
WE DN'T DO NYTHING O HER!
ALL I SAID WAS SHE NEEDED TO LEAVE OR SHE'D BE LATE FOR 4TH PERIOD--
ROBBI! TELL HIM THE FLUFFHEADS STARTED IT!
NOT ONE MORE WORD, MISS MILES.
WHAT FIGHT WERE *YOU* IN?
UM, NO FIGHT, MR. ZIEGLER.
THE LADY AT THE...
UM...
FRONT DESK SAID I COULD ASK YOU IF IT WAS OKAY IF...
UM--
COLLECT YOUR HOUGHTS BEFORE OU SPEAK, MISS--?
UH, HOLTEN.
WHAT DO YOU NEED, MISS HOLTEN?
THE LADDERTOP ACADEMY PRESENTATION IS STARTING, AND AZURE'S A CANDIDATE FOR THE NEW CLASS.
YES, I'M WELL AWARE.
SO... CAN SHE COME TO THE ASSEMBLY NOW AND COME BACK HERE AFTER?
NO, MISS HOLTEN, SHE MAY NOT.

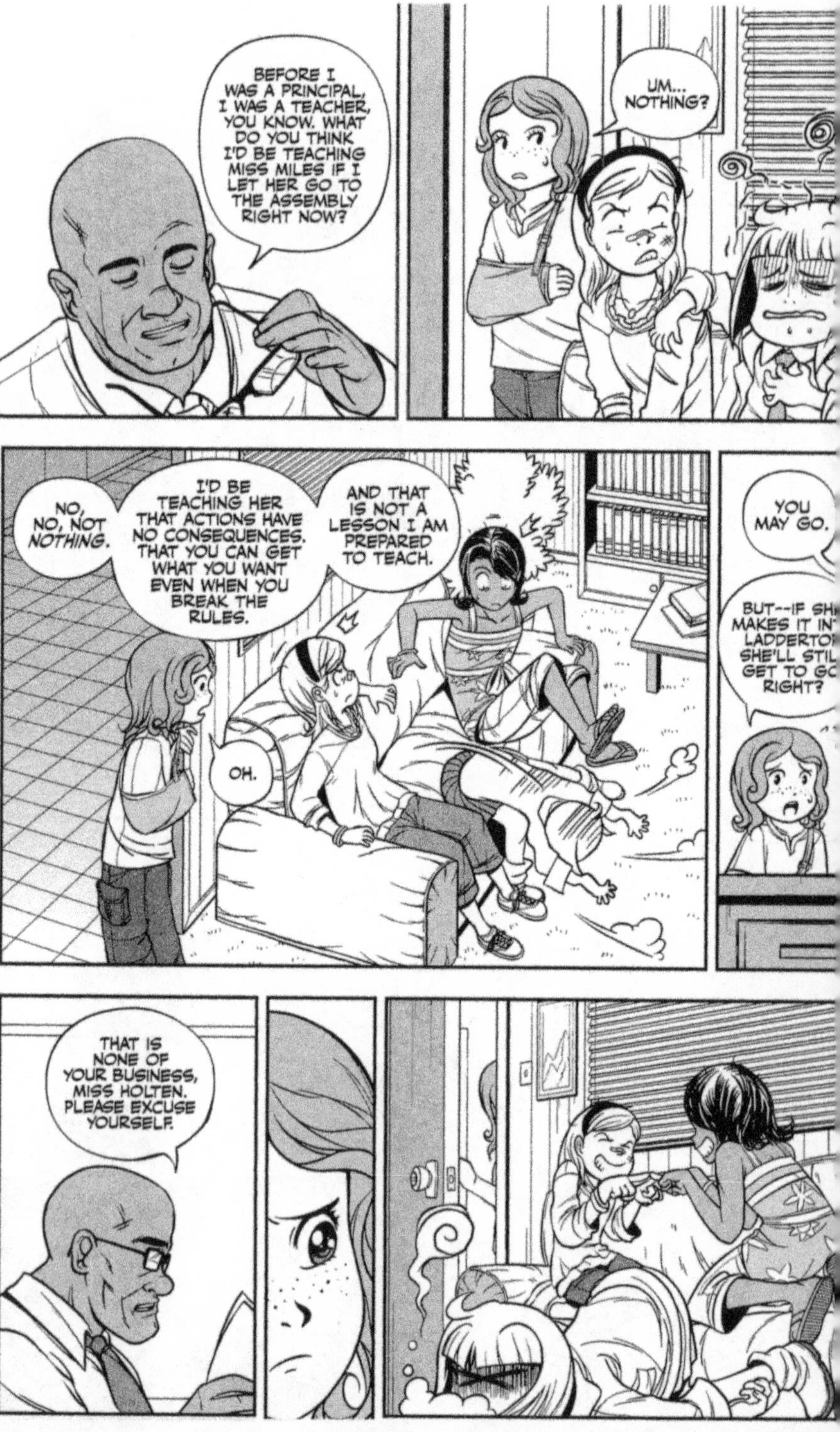
BEFORE I WAS A PRINCIPAL, I WAS A TEACHER, YOU KNOW. WHAT DO YOU THINK I'D BE TEACHING MISS MILES IF I LET HER GO TO THE ASSEMBLY RIGHT NOW?
UM... NOTHING?
NO, NO, NOT *NOTHING*.
I'D BE TEACHING HER THAT ACTIONS HAVE NO CONSEQUENCES. THAT YOU CAN GET WHAT YOU WANT EVEN WHEN YOU BREAK THE RULES.
AND THAT IS NOT A LESSON I AM PREPARED TO TEACH.
OH.
YOU MAY GO.
BUT--IF SH MAKES IT IN LADDERTO SHE'LL STIL GET TO GO RIGHT?
THAT IS NONE OF YOUR BUSINESS, MISS HOLTEN. PLEASE EXCUSE YOURSELF.

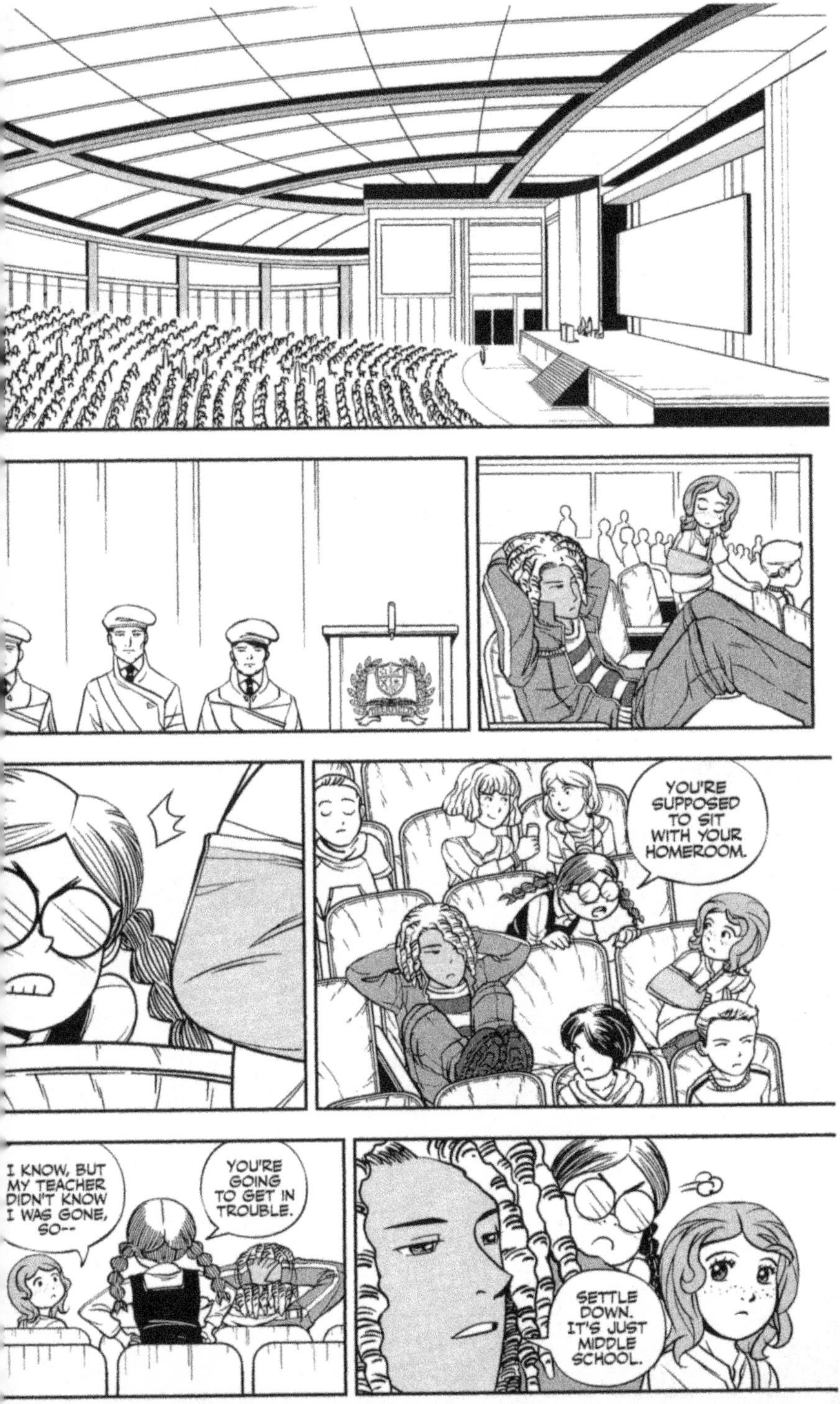
YOU'RE SUPPOSED TO SIT WITH YOUR HOMEROOM.
I KNOW, BUT MY TEACHER DIDN'T KNOW I WAS GONE, SO--
YOU'RE GOING TO GET IN TROUBLE.
SETTLE DOWN. IT'S JUST MIDDLE SCHOOL.

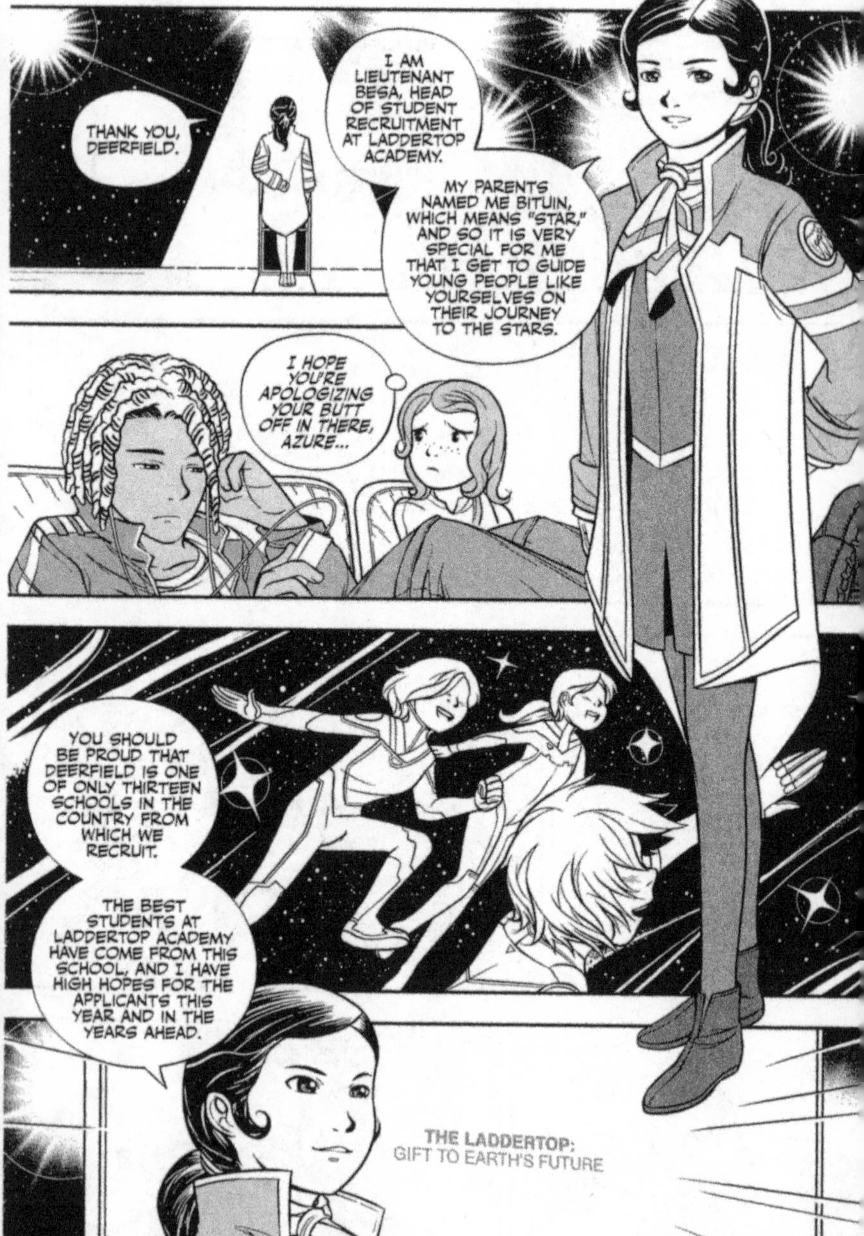
THANK YOU, DEERFIELD.
I AM LIEUTENANT BESA, HEAD OF STUDENT RECRUITMENT AT LADDERTOP ACADEMY.
MY PARENTS NAMED ME BITUIN, WHICH MEANS "STAR," AND SO IT IS VERY SPECIAL FOR ME THAT I GET TO GUIDE YOUNG PEOPLE LIKE YOURSELVES ON THEIR JOURNEY TO THE STARS.
I HOPE YOU'RE APOLOGIZING YOUR BUTT OFF IN THERE, AZURE...
YOU SHOULD BE PROUD THAT DEERFIELD IS ONE OF ONLY THIRTEEN SCHOOLS IN THE COUNTRY FROM WHICH WE RECRUIT.
THE BEST STUDENTS AT LADDERTOP ACADEMY HAVE COME FROM THIS SCHOOL, AND I HAVE HIGH HOPES FOR THE APPLICANTS THIS YEAR AND IN THE YEARS AHEAD.
THE LADDERTOP:
GIFT TO EARTH'S FUTURE

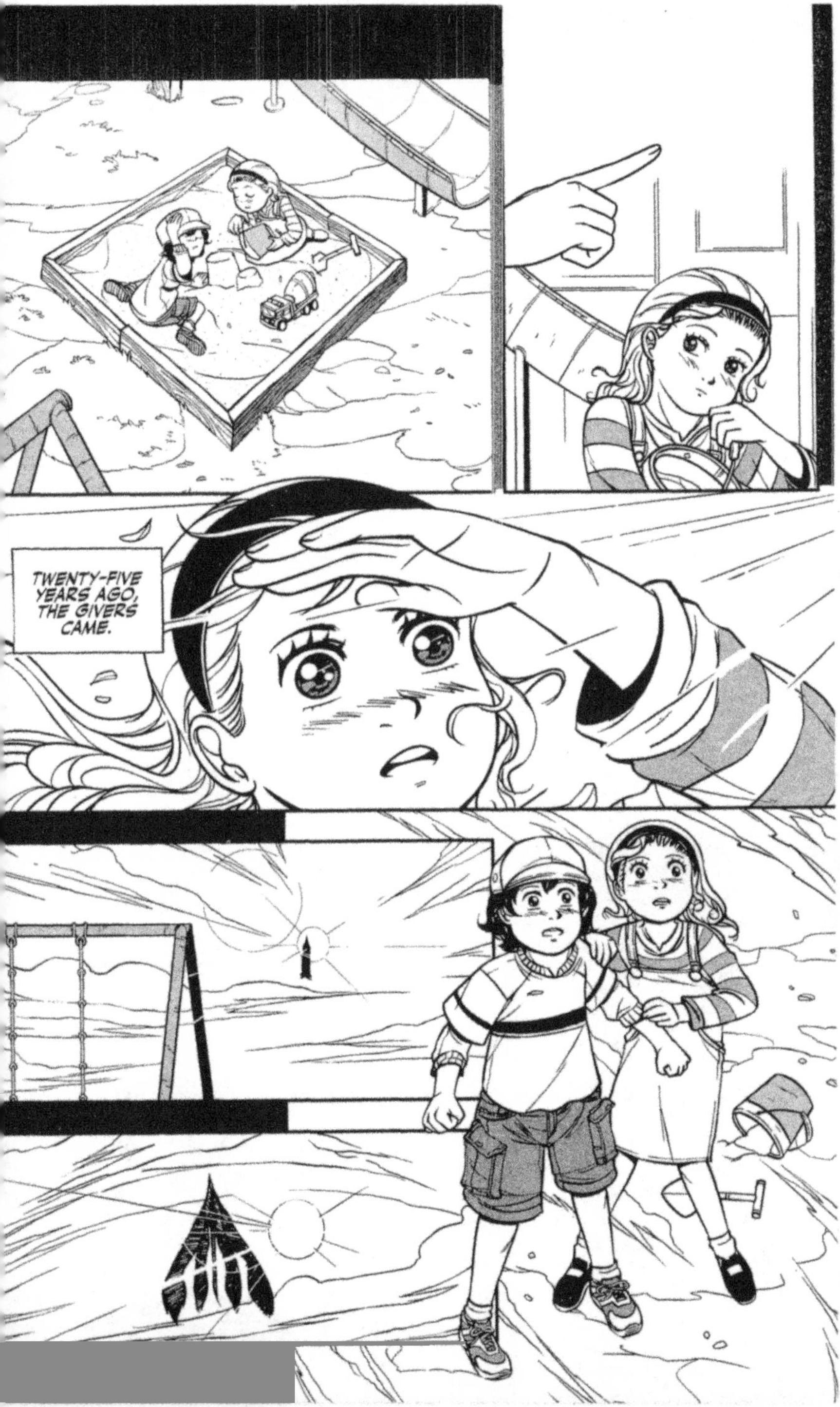
TWENTY-FIVE YEARS AGO, THE GIVERS CAME.

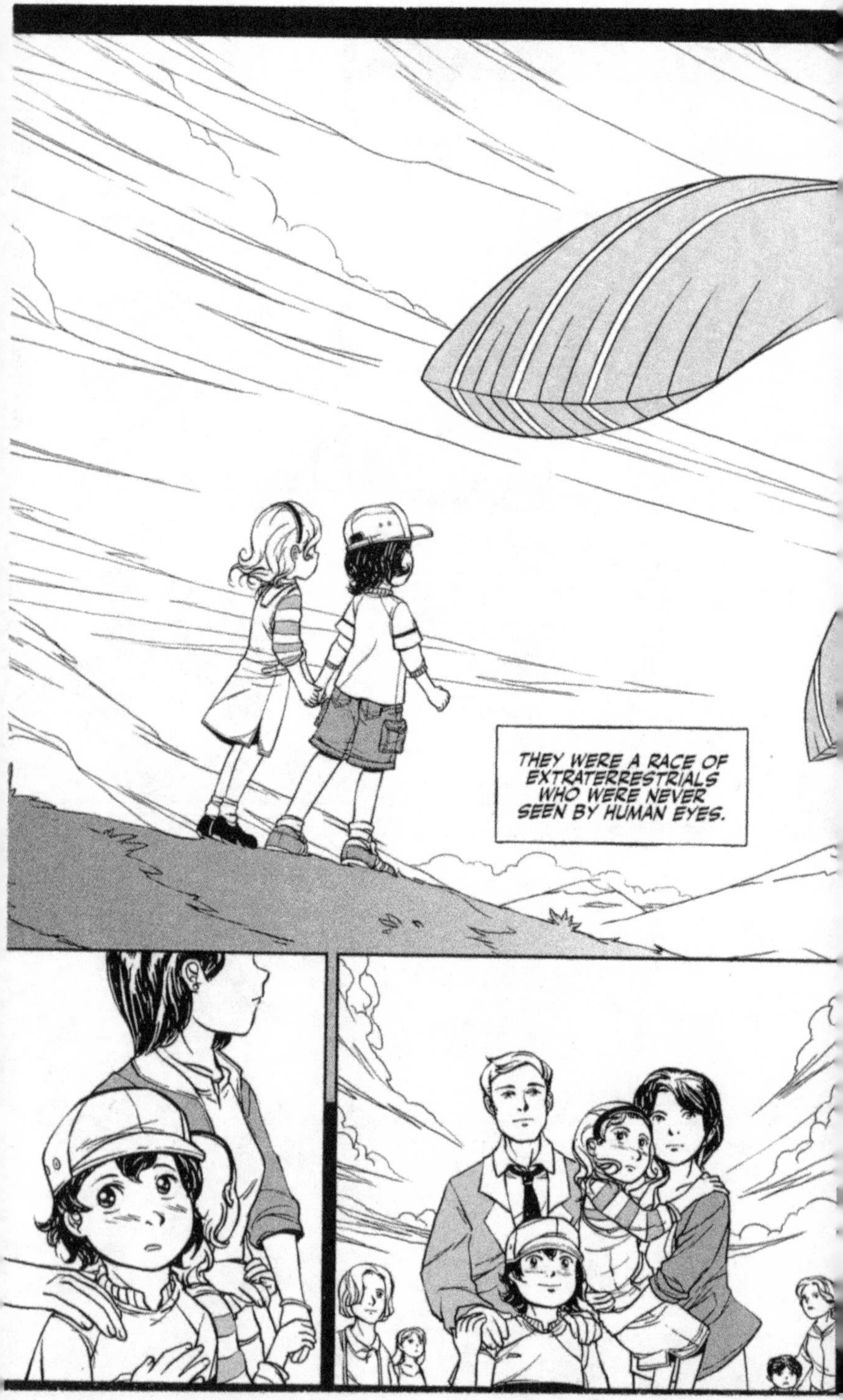
THEY WERE A RACE OF EXTRATERRESTRIALS WHO WERE NEVER SEEN BY HUMAN EYES.

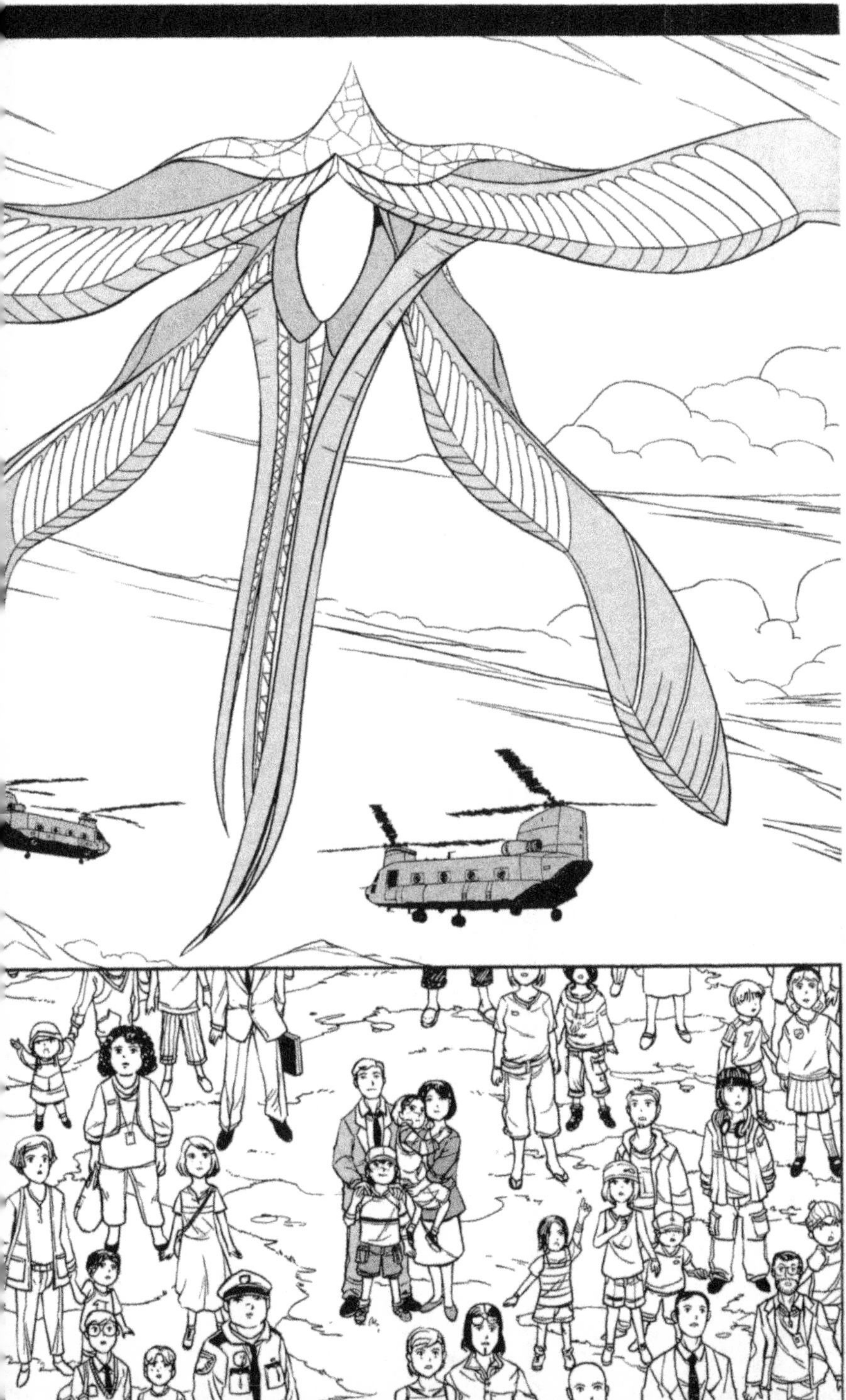

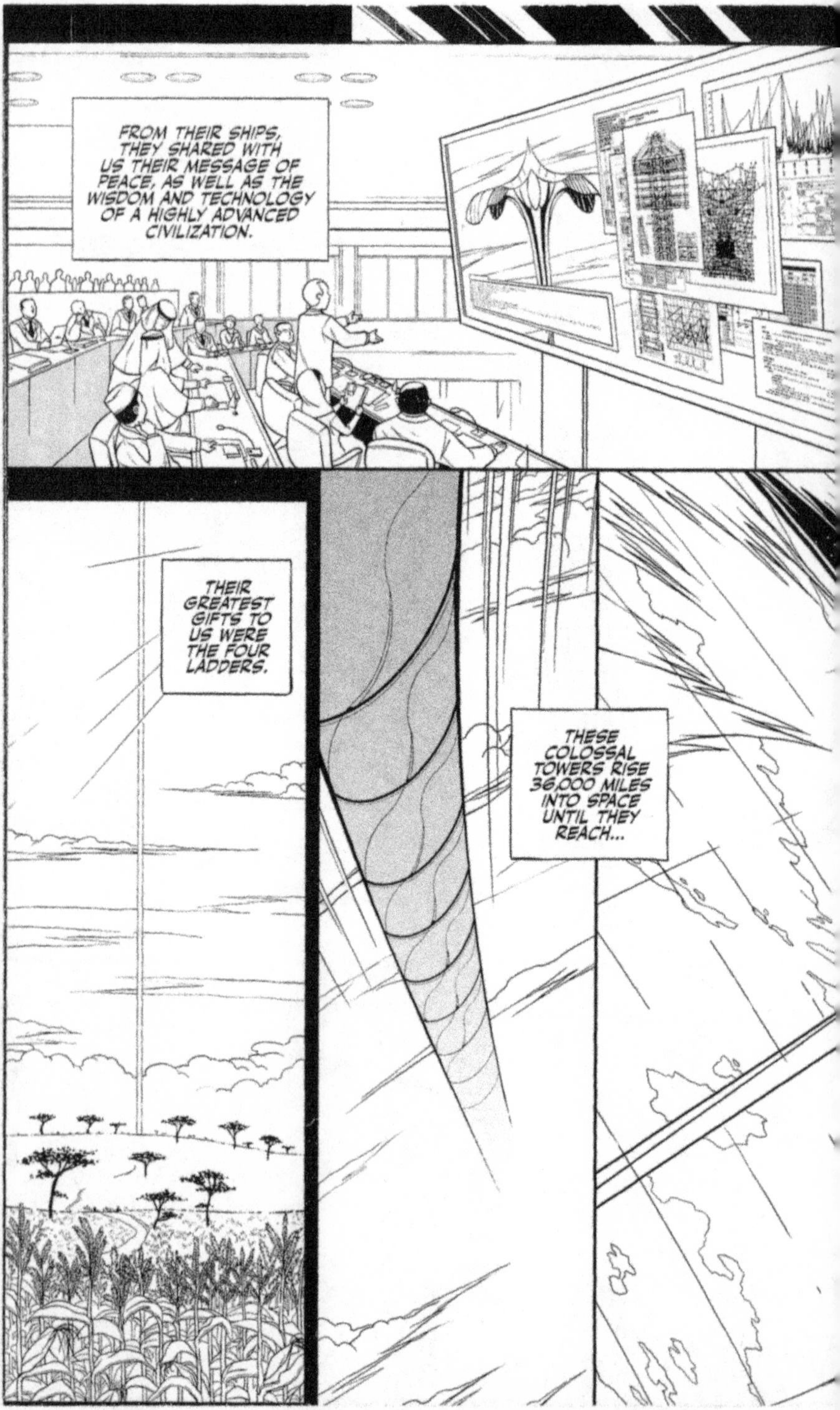
FROM THEIR SHIPS, THEY SHARED WITH US THEIR MESSAGE OF PEACE, AS WELL AS THE WISDOM AND TECHNOLOGY OF A HIGHLY ADVANCED CIVILIZATION.
THEIR GREATEST GIFTS TO US WERE THE FOUR LADDERS.
THESE COLOSSAL TOWERS RISE 36,000 MILES INTO SPACE UNTIL THEY REACH...

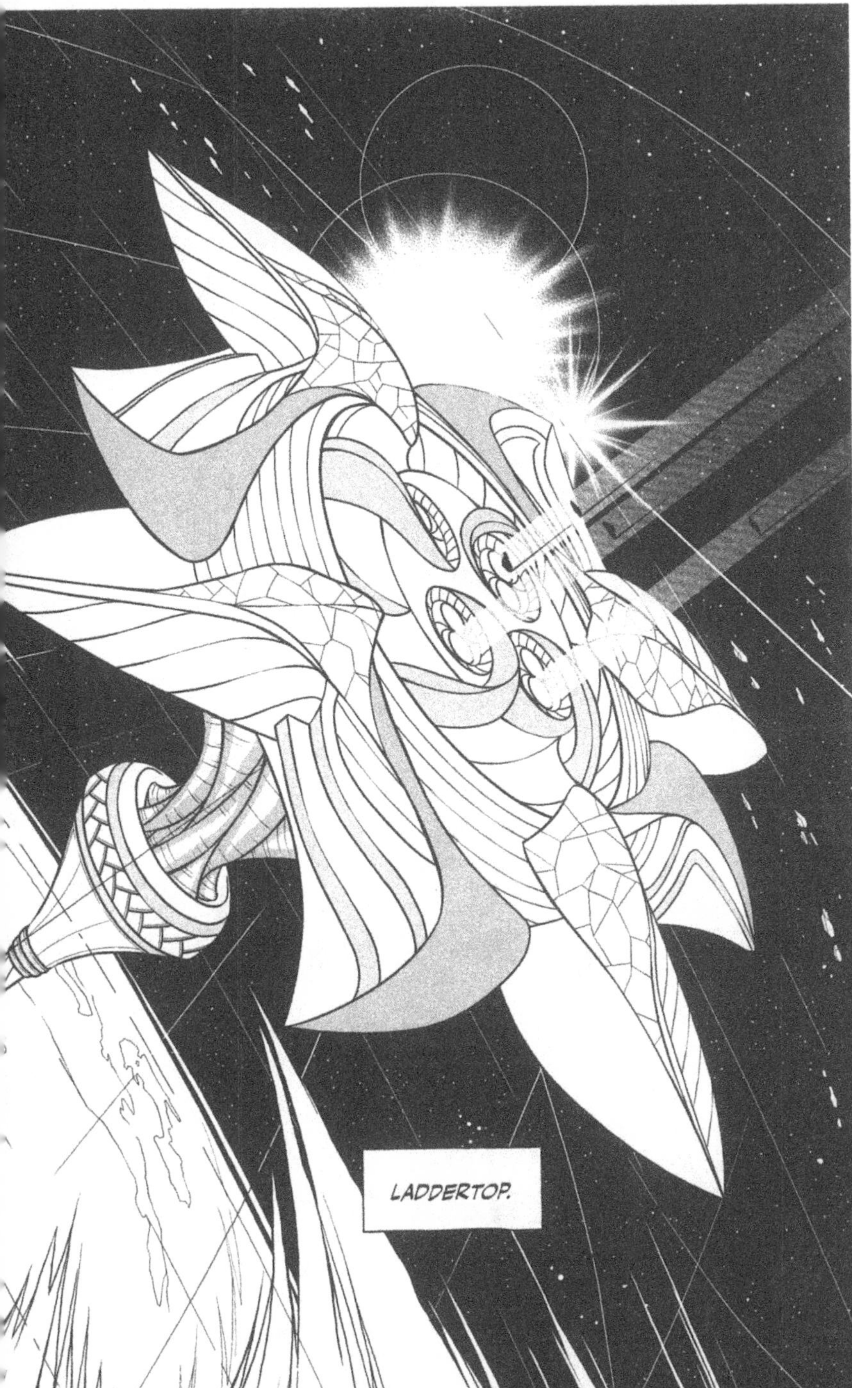
LADDERTOP.

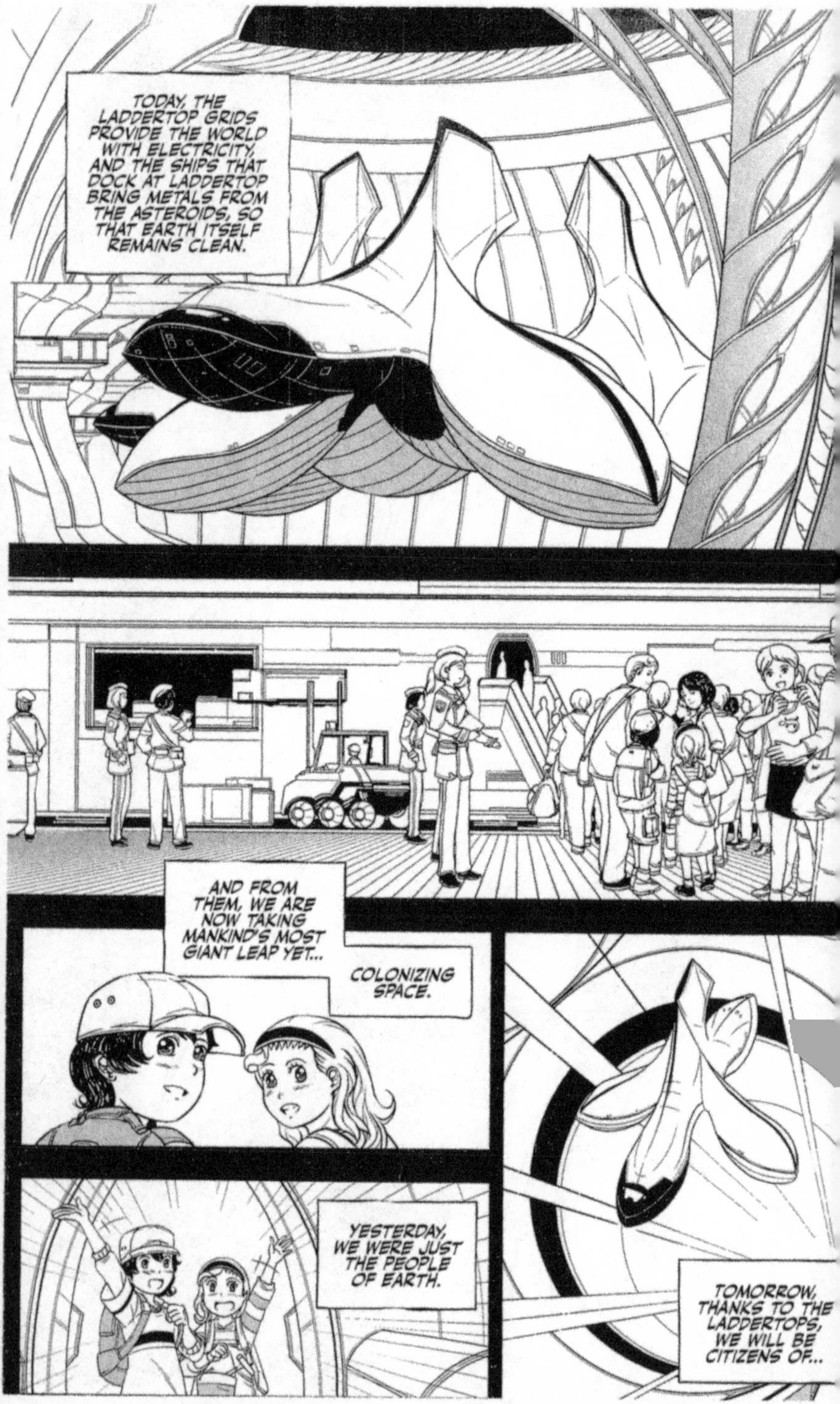
TODAY, THE LADDERTOP GRIDS PROVIDE THE WORLD WITH ELECTRICITY, AND THE SHIPS THAT DOCK AT LADDERTOP BRING METALS FROM THE ASTEROIDS, SO THAT EARTH ITSELF REMAINS CLEAN.
AND FROM THEM, WE ARE NOW TAKING MANKIND'S MOST GIANT LEAP YET...
COLONIZING SPACE.
YESTERDAY, WE WERE JUST THE PEOPLE OF EARTH.
TOMORROW, THANKS TO THE LADDERTOPS, WE WILL BE CITIZENS OF...

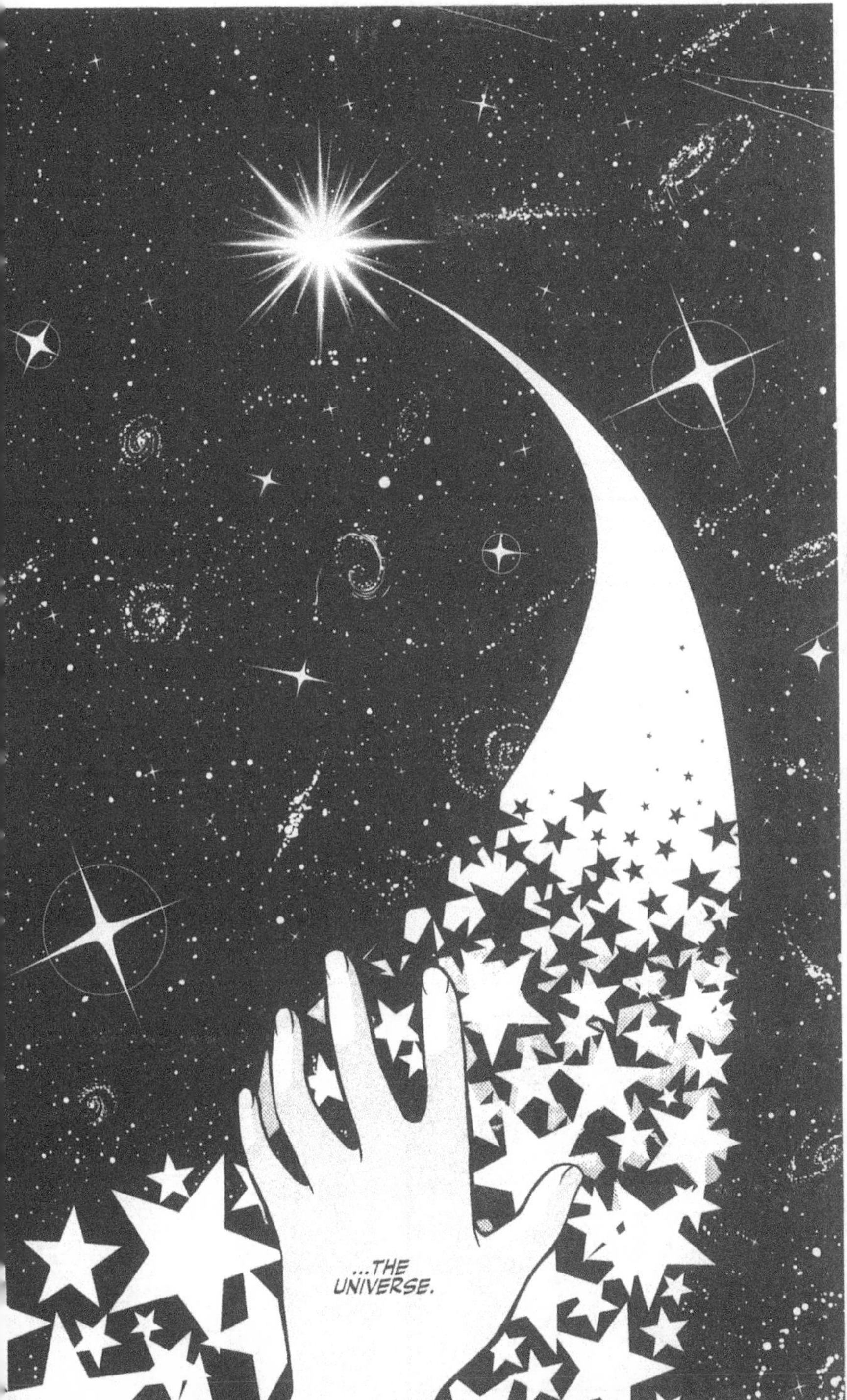
...THE
UNIVERSE.

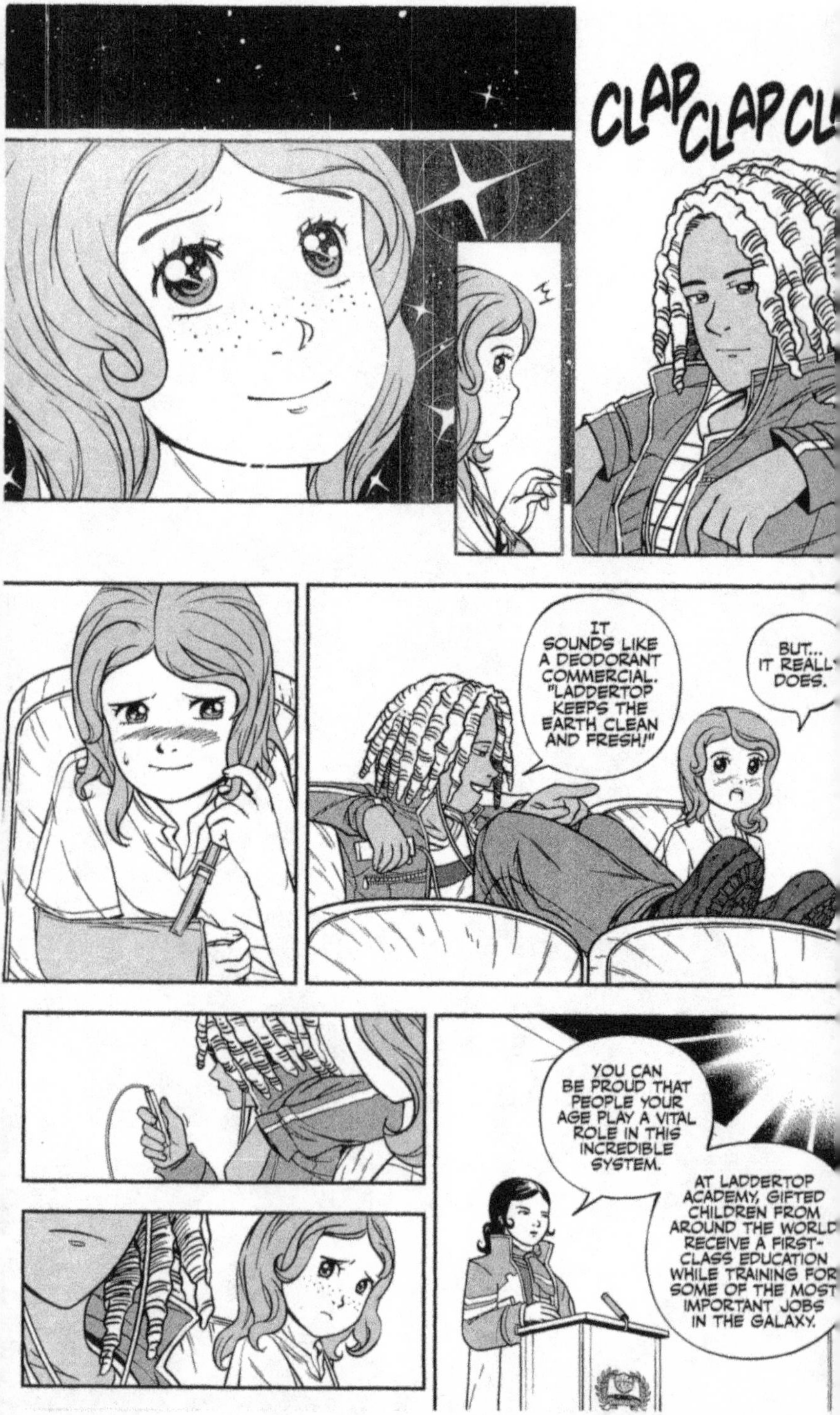
CLAP CLAP CL
IT SOUNDS LIKE A DEODORANT COMMERCIAL. "LADDERTOP KEEPS THE EARTH CLEAN AND FRESH!"
BUT... IT REALL DOES.
YOU CAN BE PROUD THAT PEOPLE YOUR AGE PLAY A VITAL ROLE IN THIS INCREDIBLE SYSTEM.
AT LADDERTOP ACADEMY, GIFTED CHILDREN FROM AROUND THE WORLD RECEIVE A FIRST-CLASS EDUCATION WHILE TRAINING FOR SOME OF THE MOST IMPORTANT JOBS IN THE GALAXY.

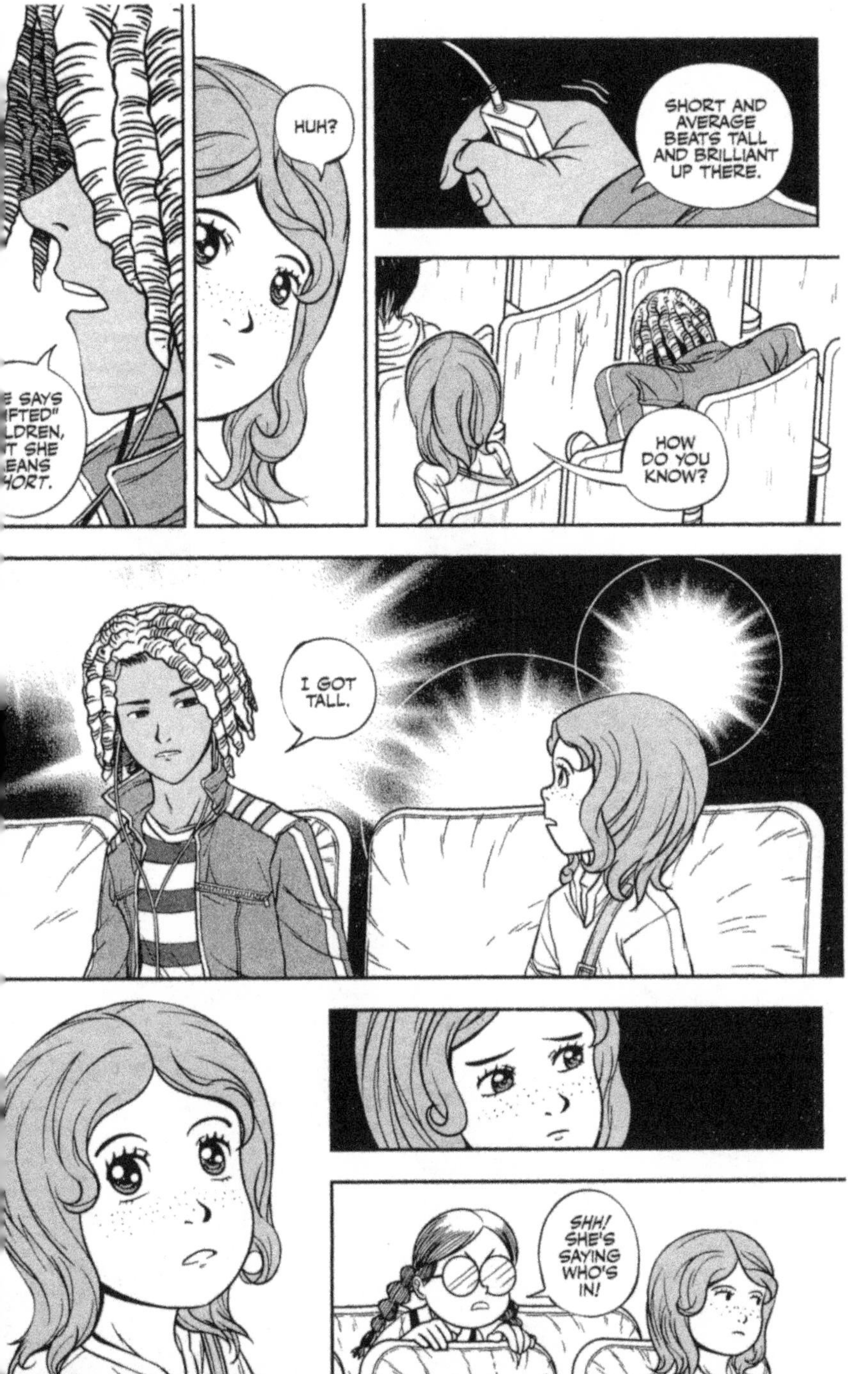
E SAYS "IFTED" LDREN, T SHE EANS HORT.
HUH?
SHORT AND AVERAGE BEATS TALL AND BRILLIANT UP THERE.
HOW DO YOU KNOW?
I GOT TALL.
SHH! SHE'S SAYING WHO'S IN!

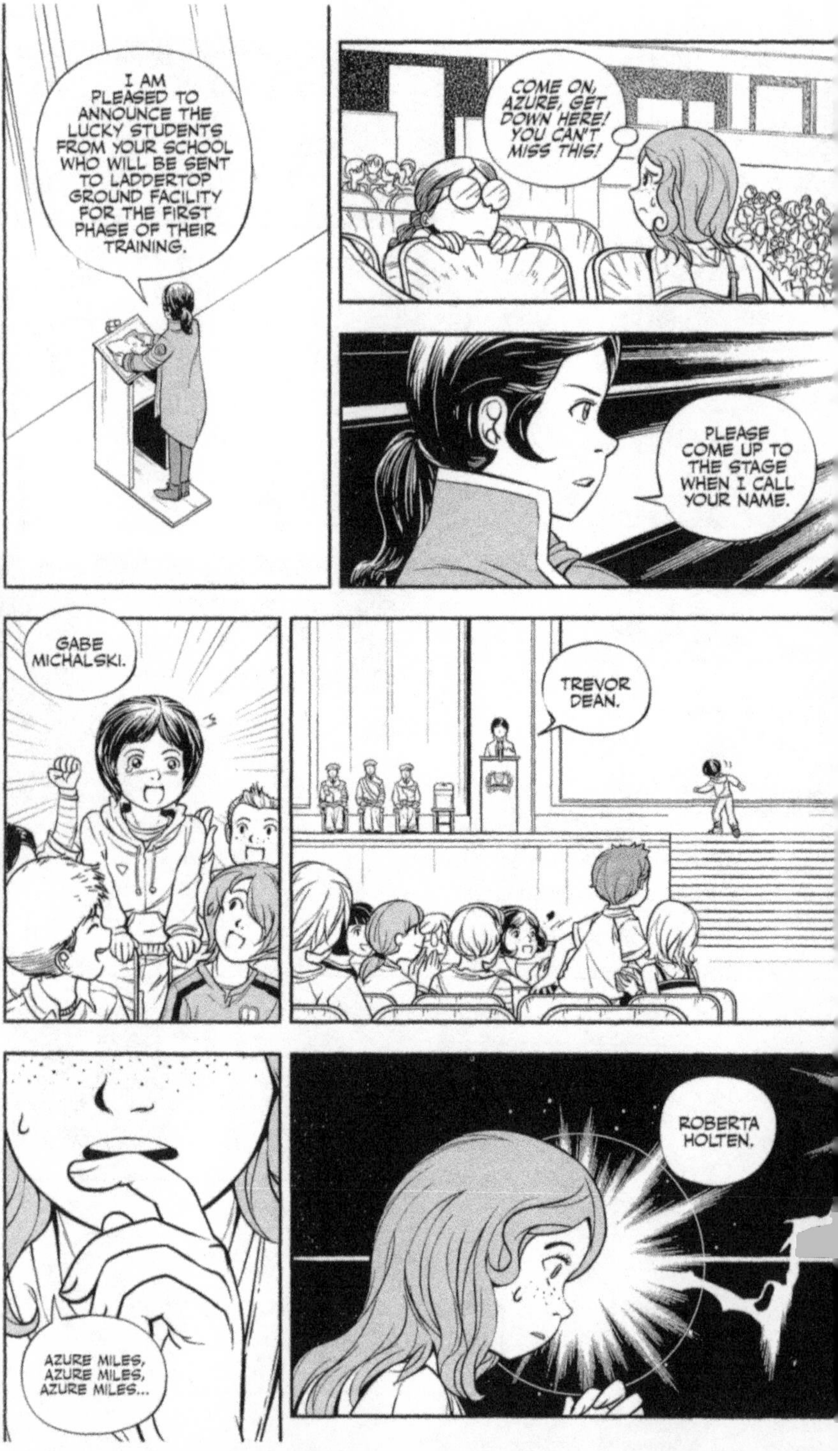
I AM PLEASED TO ANNOUNCE THE LUCKY STUDENTS FROM YOUR SCHOOL WHO WILL BE SENT TO LADDERTOP GROUND FACILITY FOR THE FIRST PHASE OF THEIR TRAINING.
COME ON, AZURE, GET DOWN HERE! YOU CAN'T MISS THIS!
PLEASE COME UP TO THE STAGE WHEN I CALL YOUR NAME.
GABE MICHALSKI.
TREVOR DEAN.
AZURE MILES, AZURE MILES, AZURE MILES...
ROBERTA HOLTEN.

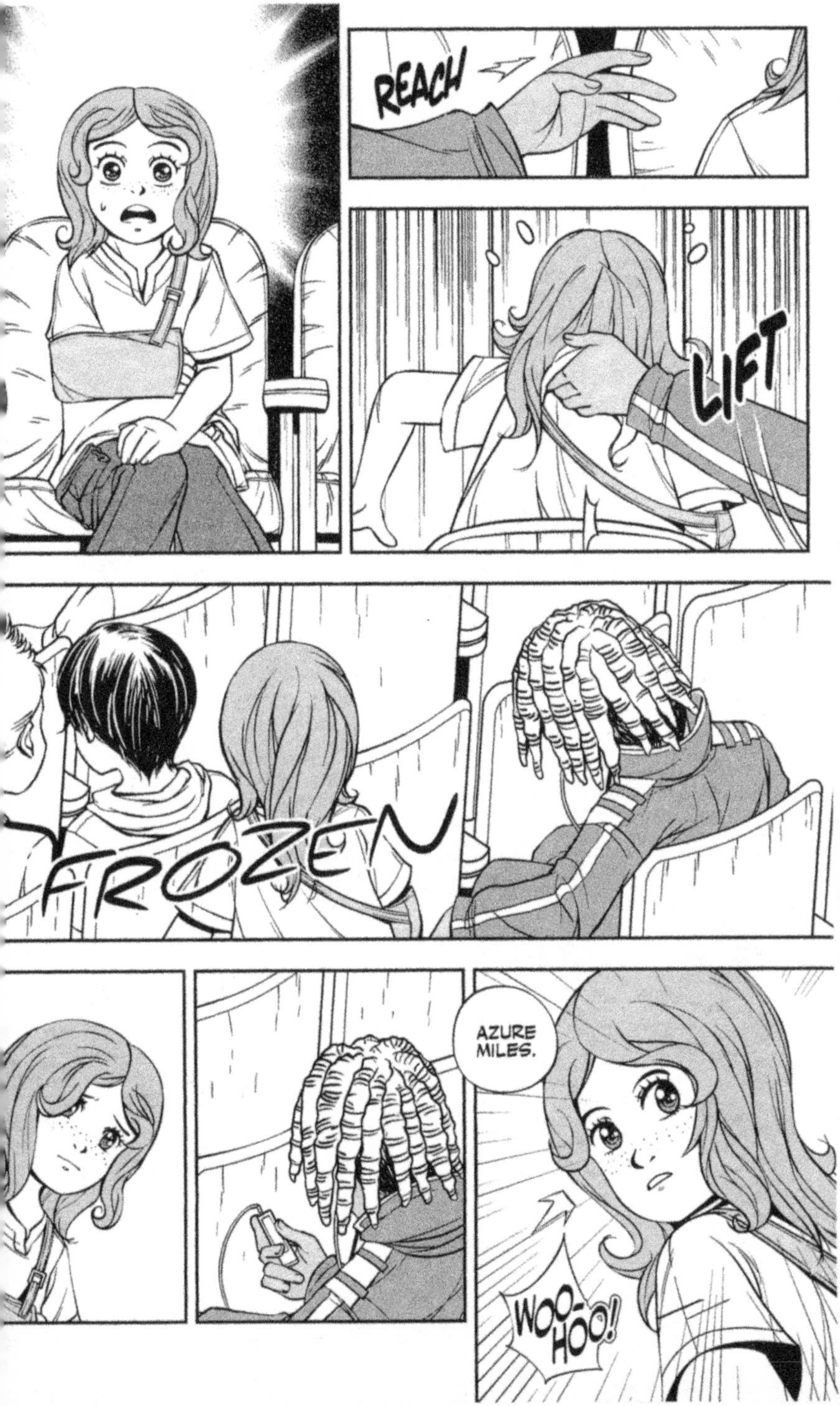
REACH
LIFT
FROZEN
AZURE MILES.
WOO-HOO!

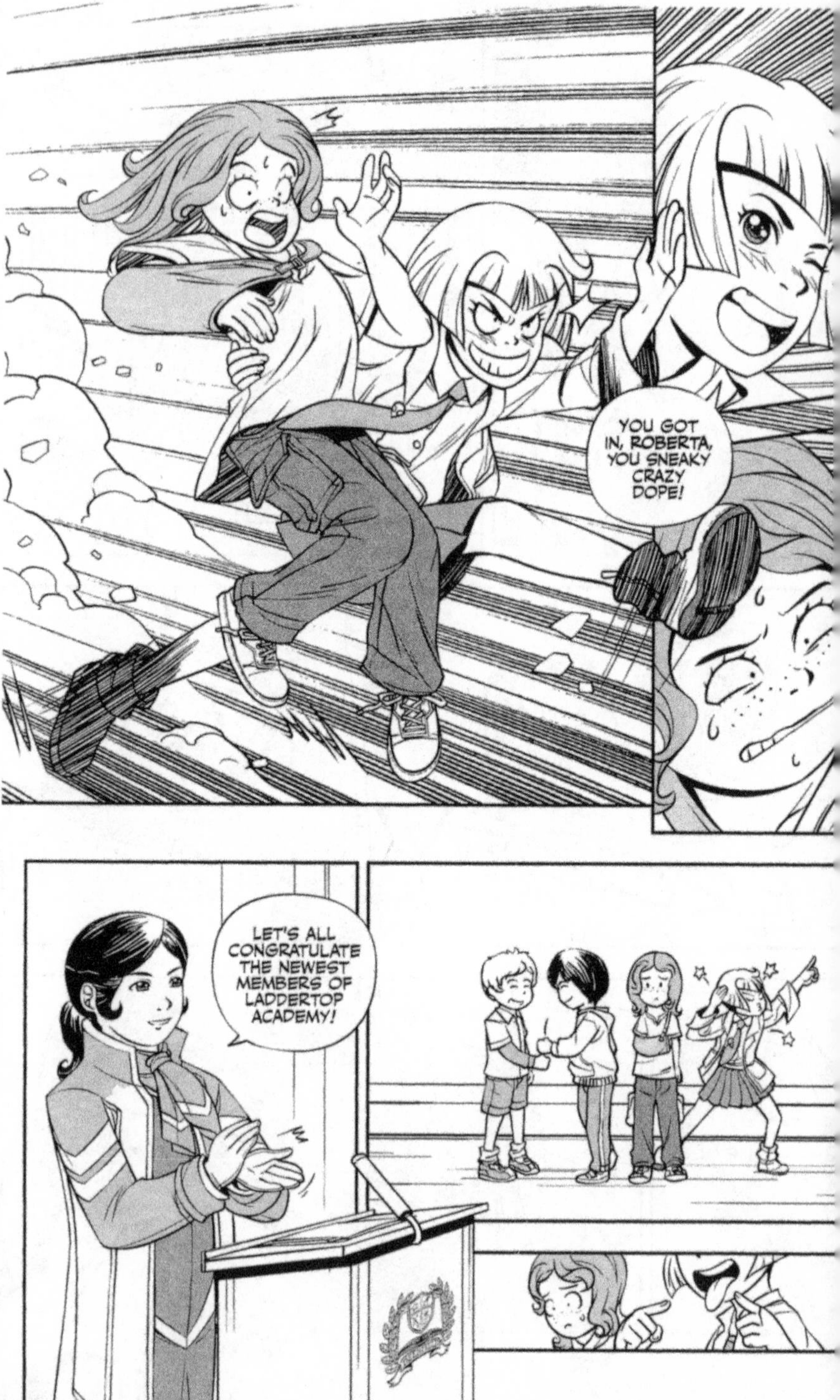
YOU GOT IN, ROBERTA, YOU SNEAKY CRAZY DOPE!
LET'S ALL CONGRATULATE THE NEWEST MEMBERS OF LADDERTOP ACADEMY!

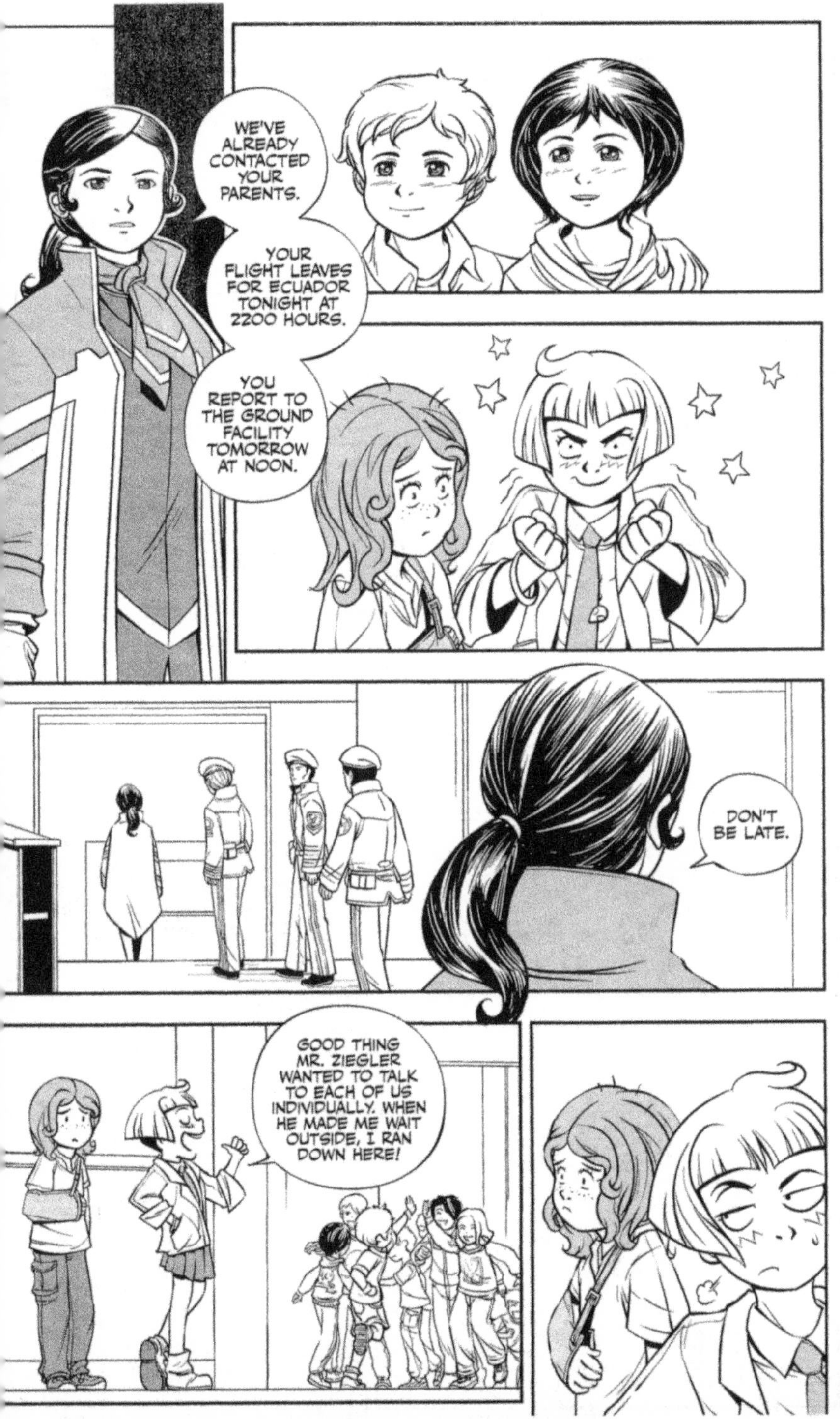
WE'VE ALREADY CONTACTED YOUR PARENTS.
YOUR FLIGHT LEAVES FOR ECUADOR TONIGHT AT 2200 HOURS.
YOU REPORT TO THE GROUND FACILITY TOMORROW AT NOON.
DON'T BE LATE.
GOOD THING MR. ZIEGLER WANTED TO TALK TO EACH OF US INDIVIDUALLY. WHEN HE MADE ME WAIT OUTSIDE, I RAN DOWN HERE!

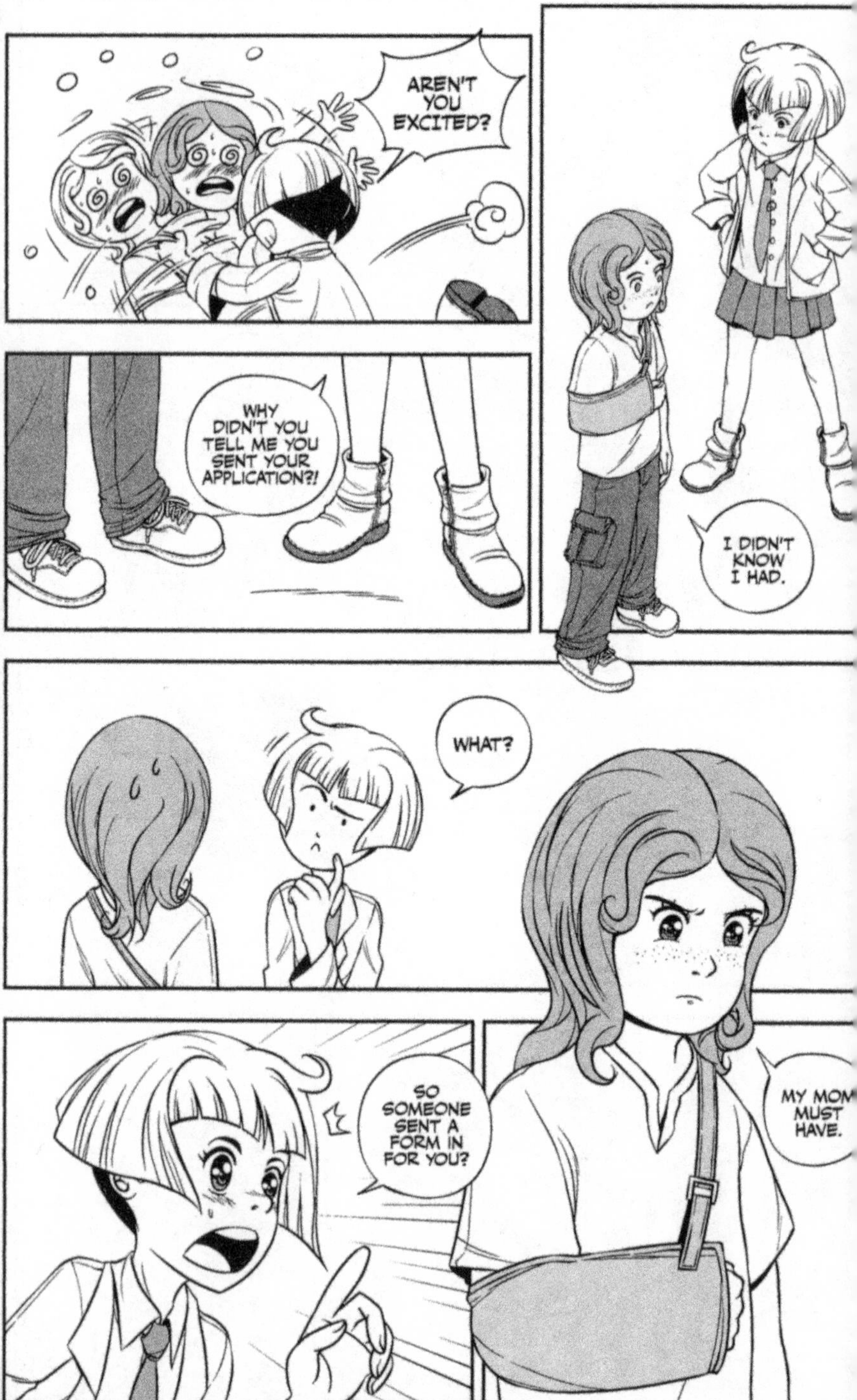
AREN'T YOU EXCITED?
WHY DIDN'T YOU TELL ME YOU SENT YOUR APPLICATION?!
I DIDN'T KNOW I HAD.
WHAT?
SO SOMEONE SENT A FORM IN FOR YOU?
MY MOM MUST HAVE.

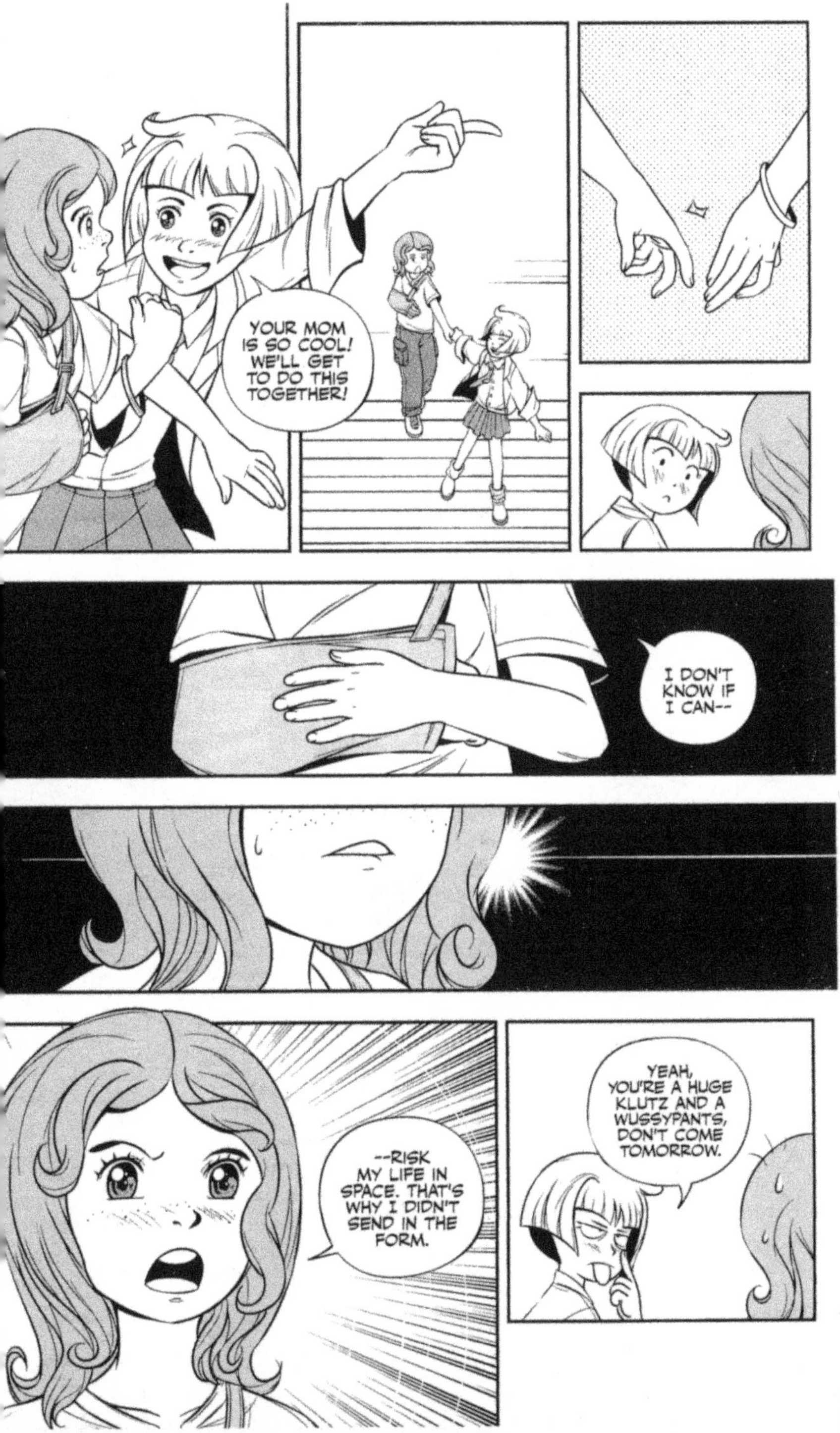
YOUR MOM IS SO COOL! WE'LL GET TO DO THIS TOGETHER!
I DON'T KNOW IF I CAN--
--RISK MY LIFE IN SPACE. THAT'S WHY I DIDN'T SEND IN THE FORM.
YEAH, YOU'RE A HUGE KLUTZ AND A WUSSYPANTS, DON'T COME TOMORROW.

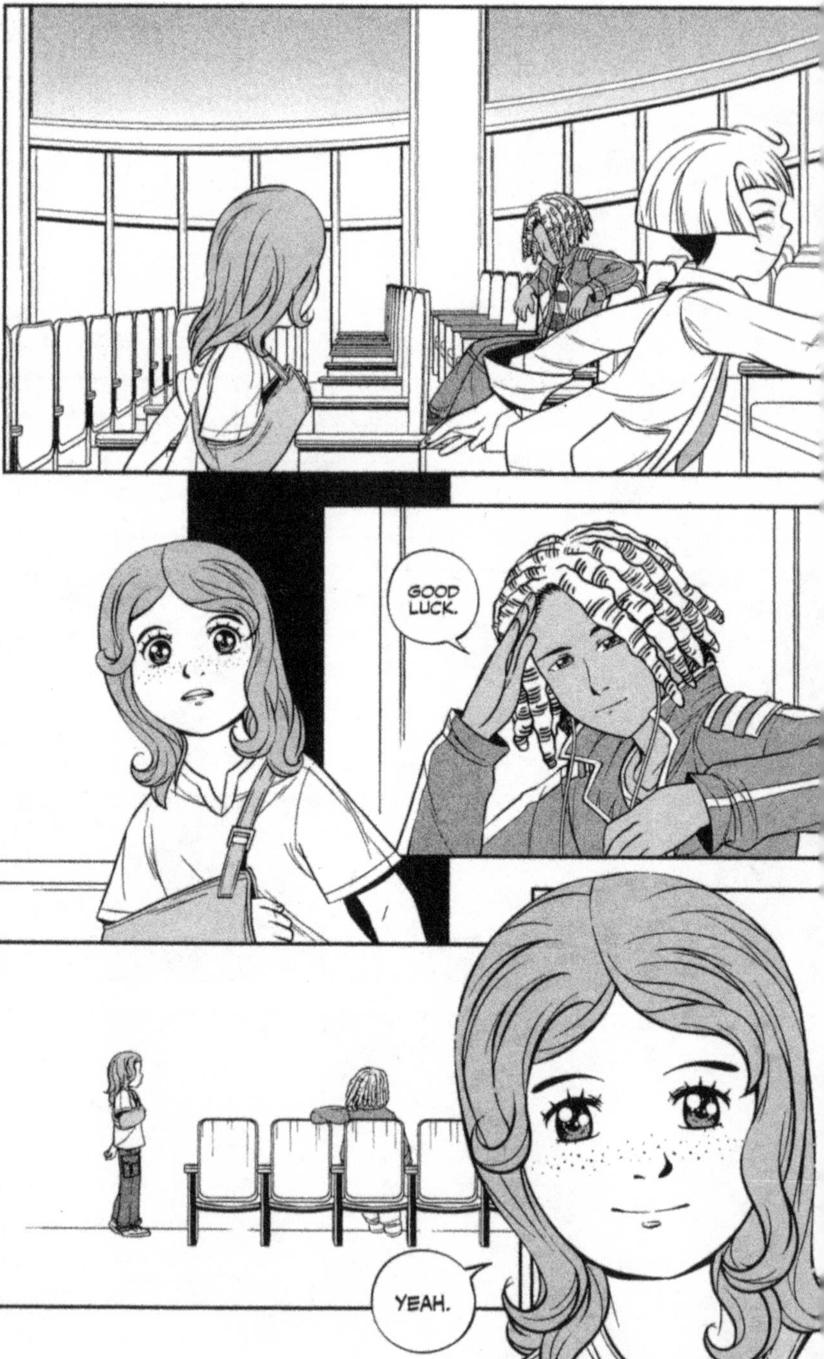
GOOD LUCK.
YEAH.

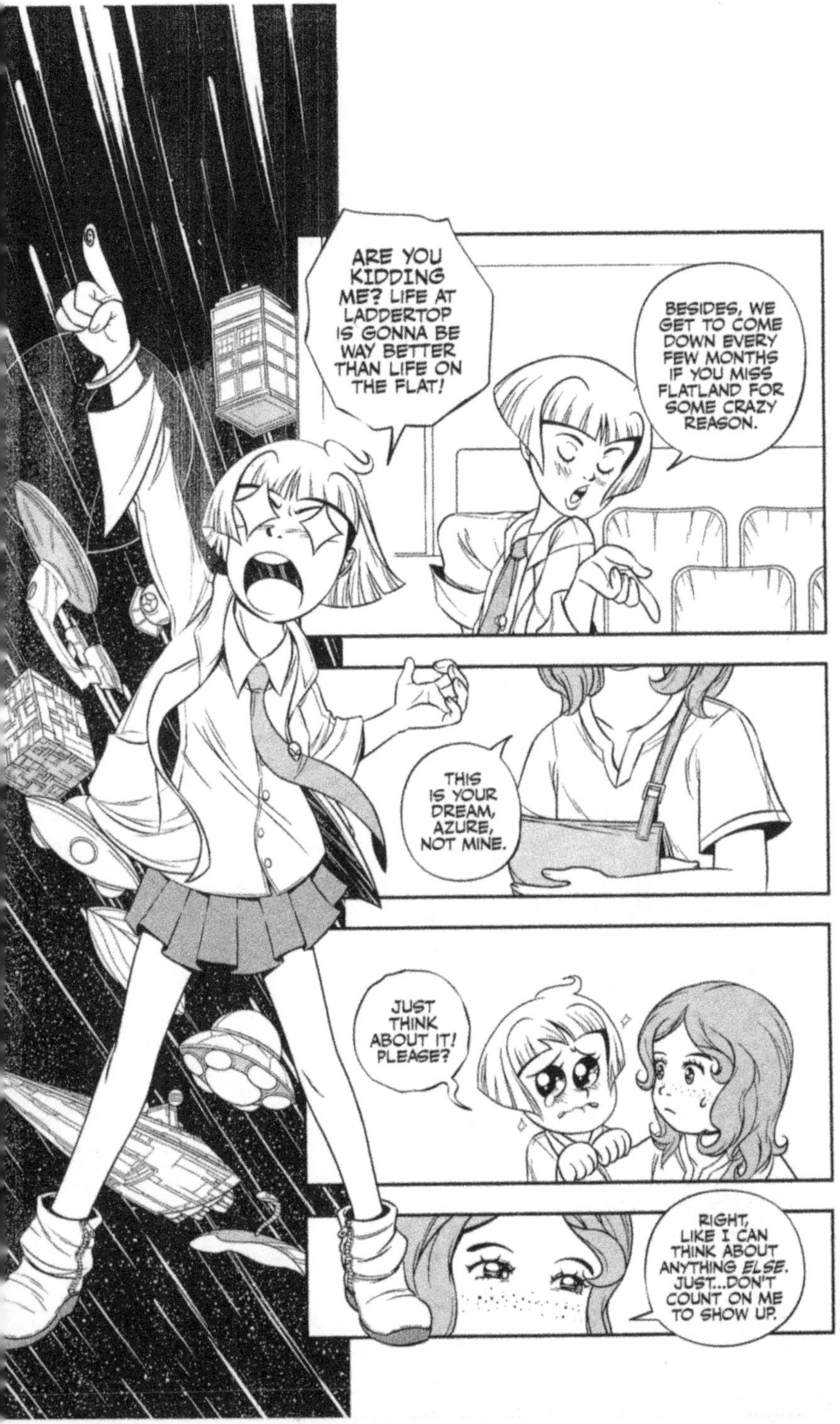
ARE YOU KIDDING ME? LIFE AT LADDERTOP IS GONNA BE WAY BETTER THAN LIFE ON THE FLAT!
BESIDES, WE GET TO COME DOWN EVERY FEW MONTHS IF YOU MISS FLATLAND FOR SOME CRAZY REASON.
THIS IS YOUR DREAM, AZURE, NOT MINE.
JUST THINK ABOUT IT! PLEASE?
RIGHT, LIKE I CAN THINK ABOUT ANYTHING *ELSE*. JUST...DON'T COUNT ON ME TO SHOW UP.

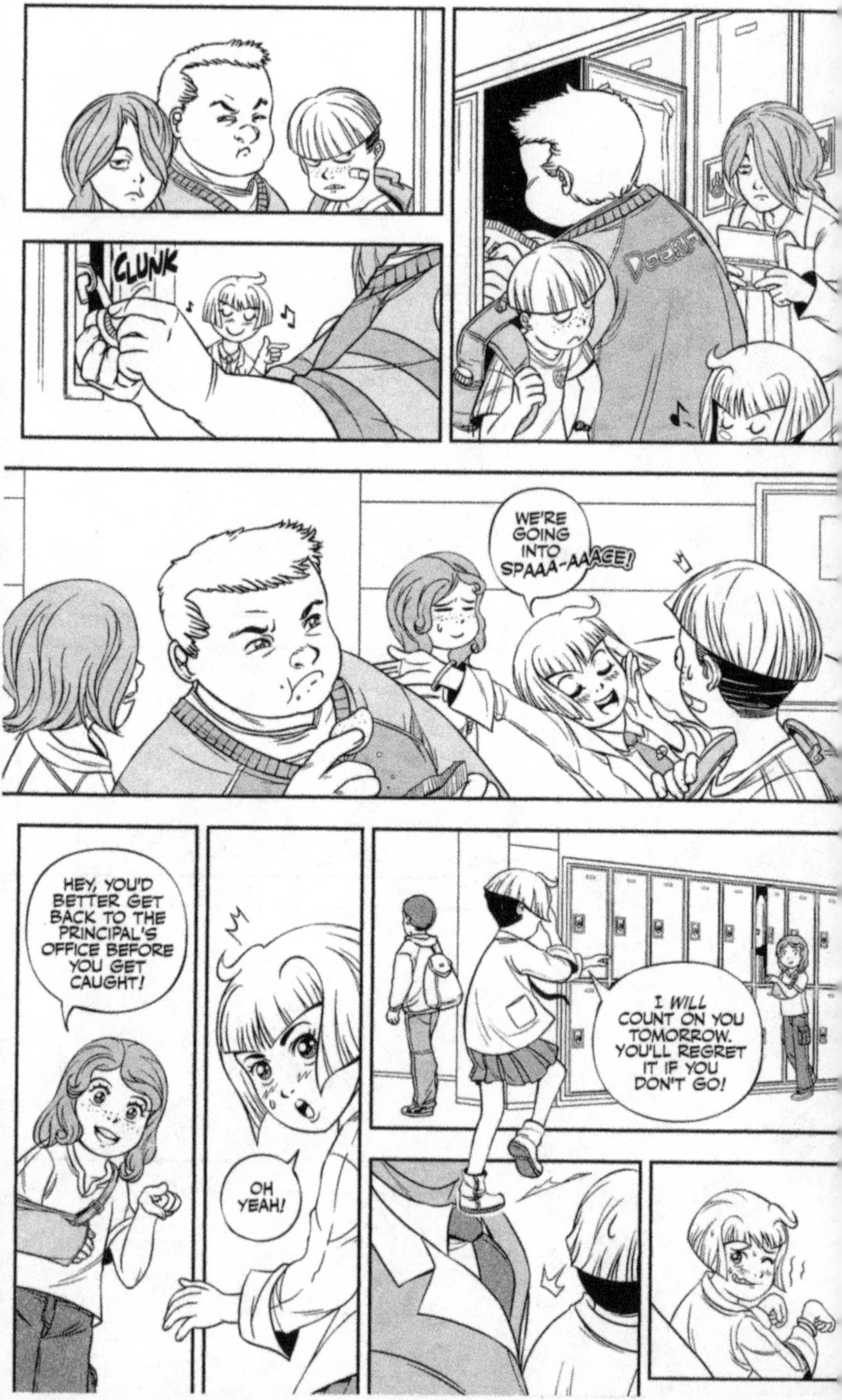
CLUNK
WE'RE GOING INTO SPAAA-AAAACE!
HEY, YOU'D BETTER GET BACK TO THE PRINCIPAL'S OFFICE BEFORE YOU GET CAUGHT!
OH YEAH!
I WILL COUNT ON YOU TOMORROW. YOU'LL REGRET IT IF YOU DON'T GO!

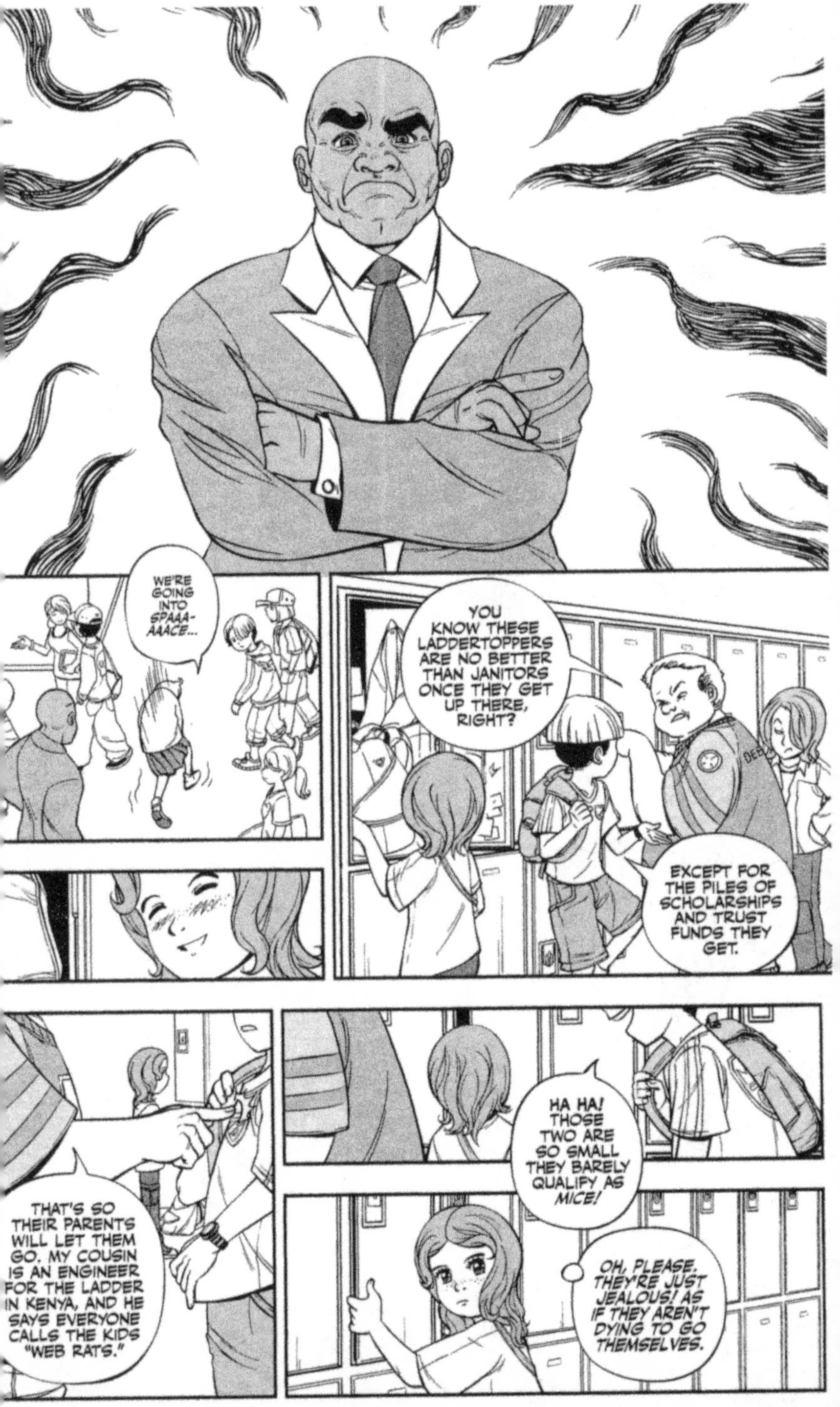
WE'RE GOING INTO SPAAAAAACE...
YOU KNOW THESE LADDERTOPPERS ARE NO BETTER THAN JANITORS ONCE THEY GET UP THERE, RIGHT?
EXCEPT FOR THE PILES OF SCHOLARSHIPS AND TRUST FUNDS THEY GET.
THAT'S SO THEIR PARENTS WILL LET THEM GO. MY COUSIN IS AN ENGINEER FOR THE LADDER IN KENYA, AND HE SAYS EVERYONE CALLS THE KIDS "WEB RATS."
HA HA! THOSE TWO ARE SO SMALL THEY BARELY QUALIFY AS *MICE!*
OH, PLEASE. THEY'RE JUST JEALOUS! AS IF THEY AREN'T DYING TO GO THEMSELVES.

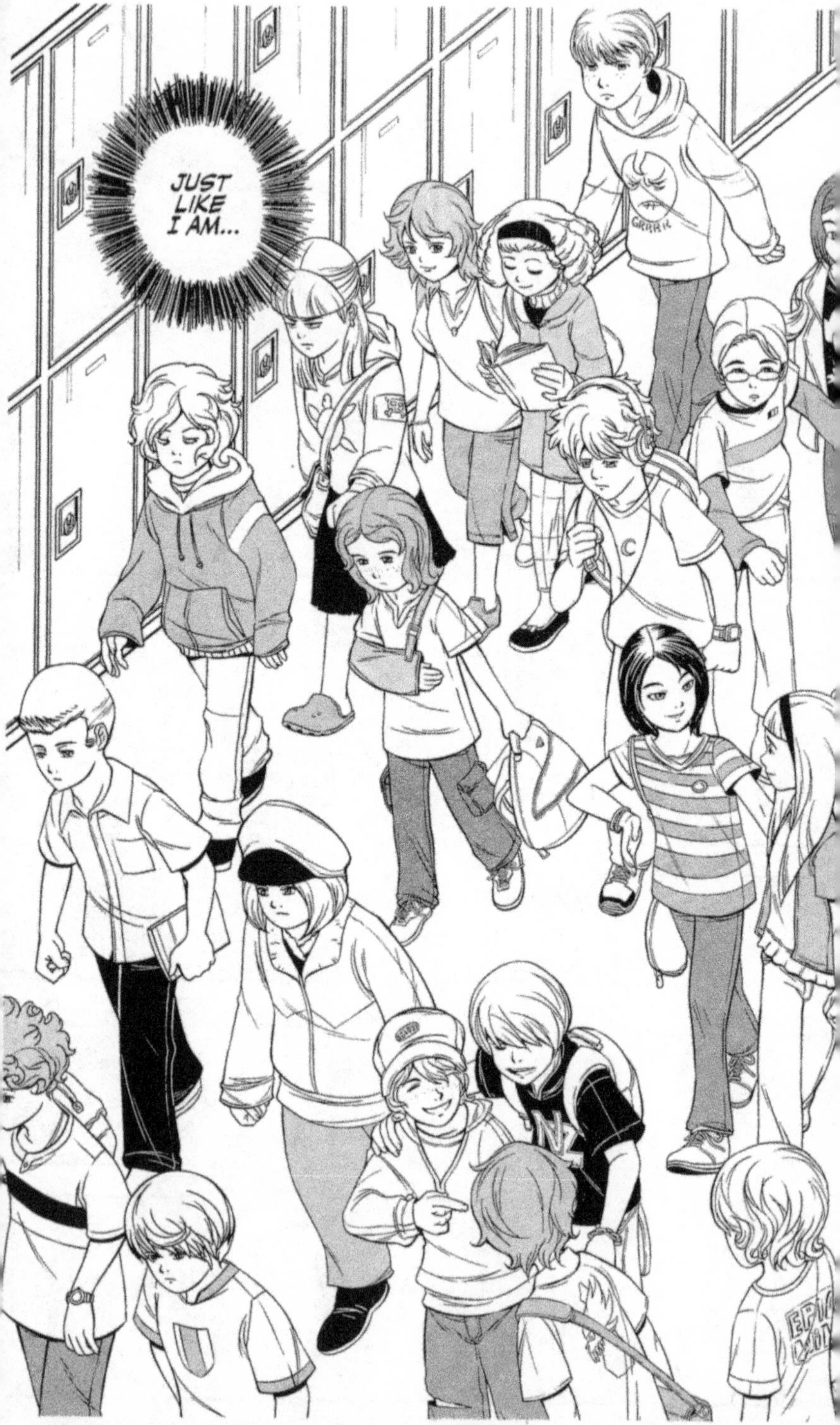
JUST LIKE I AM...

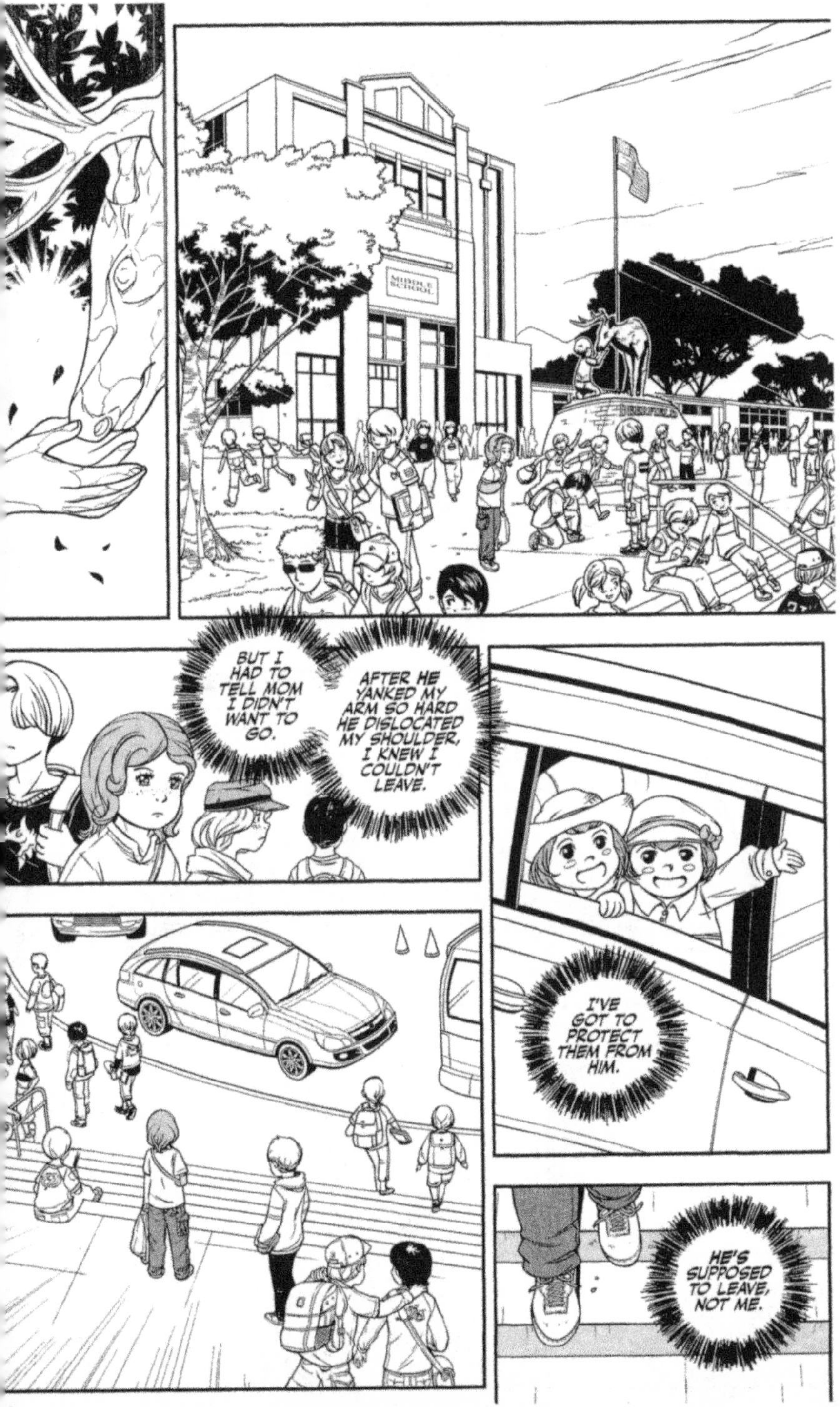
MIDDLE SCHOOL
BUT I HAD TO TELL MOM I DIDN'T WANT TO GO.
AFTER HE YANKED MY ARM SO HARD HE DISLOCATED MY SHOULDER, I KNEW I COULDN'T LEAVE.
I'VE GOT TO PROTECT THEM FROM HIM.
HE'S SUPPOSED TO LEAVE, NOT ME.

GET IN, RINKY-DINK!
DON'T BE SO HAPPY. YOU KNOW WHAT YOU DID.
DIDN'T YOU LIKE YOUR LUNCH?
SOMEHOW, WITHOUT EVEN APPLYING, I GOT ACCEPTED TO LADDERTOP ACADEMY.
I KNOW! I'M SO PROUD OF YOU! I WANTED TO TELL YOU, BUT--
WHEN WILL YOU BE PROUD ENOUGH TO LISTEN TO WHAT I WANT?
PLEASE, FASTEN YOUR SEATBELT AN WE CAN TALK ABOUT THIS A WE DRIVE.

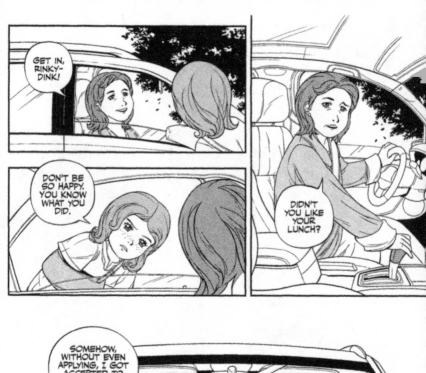

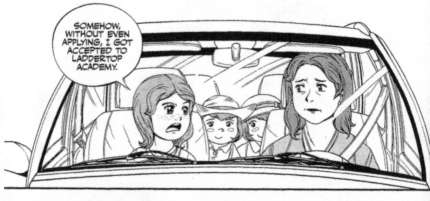

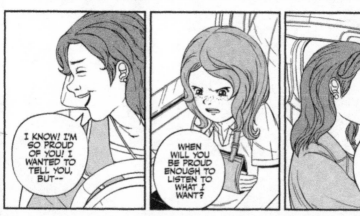

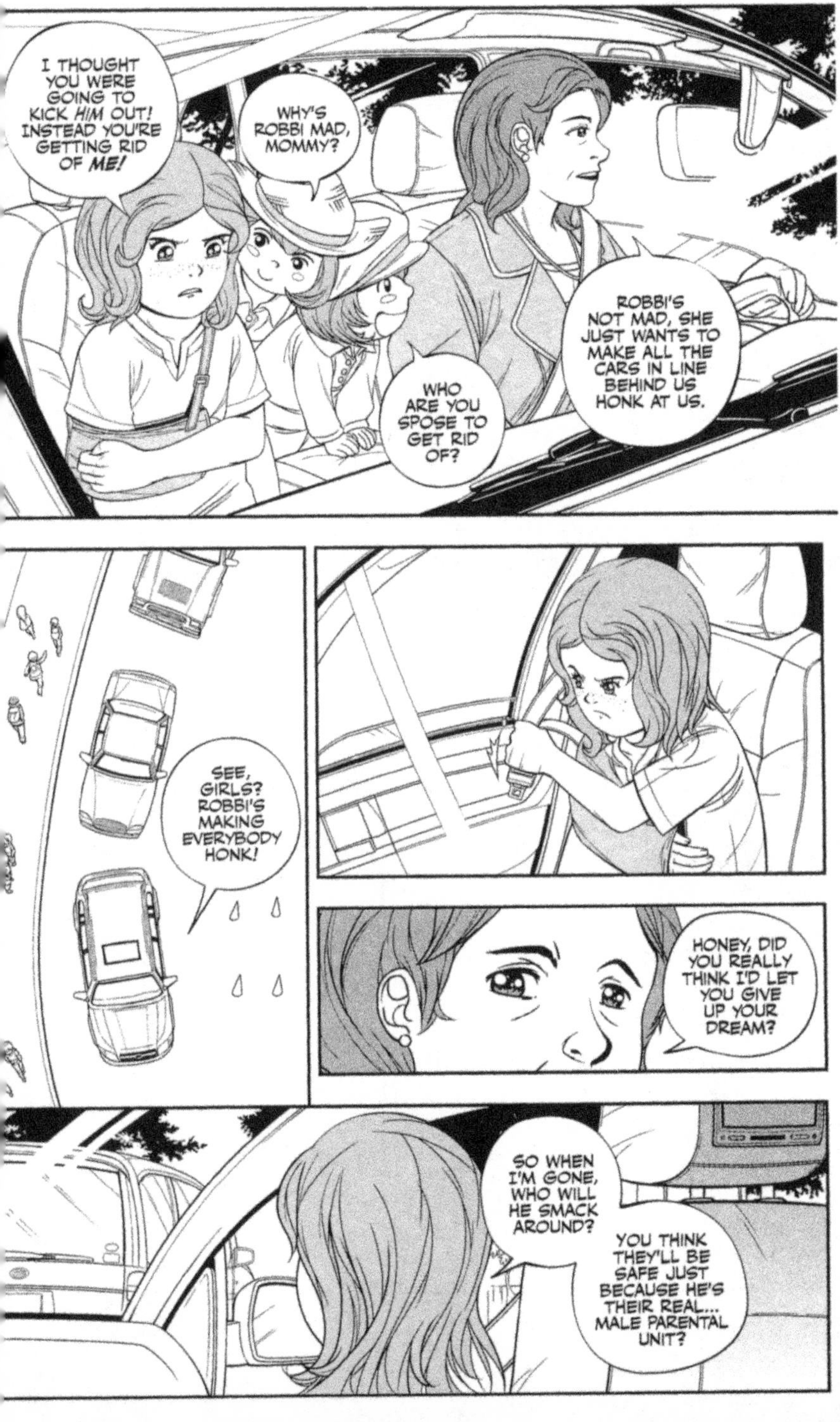
I THOUGHT YOU WERE GOING TO KICK *HIM* OUT! INSTEAD YOU'RE GETTING RID OF *ME!*
WHY'S ROBBI MAD, MOMMY?
ROBBI'S NOT MAD, SHE JUST WANTS TO MAKE ALL THE CARS IN LINE BEHIND US HONK AT US.
WHO ARE YOU SPOSE TO GET RID OF?
SEE, GIRLS? ROBBI'S MAKING EVERYBODY HONK!
HONEY, DID YOU REALLY THINK I'D LET YOU GIVE UP YOUR DREAM?
SO WHEN I'M GONE, WHO WILL HE SMACK AROUND?
YOU THINK THEY'LL BE SAFE JUST BECAUSE HE'S THEIR REAL... MALE PARENTAL UNIT?

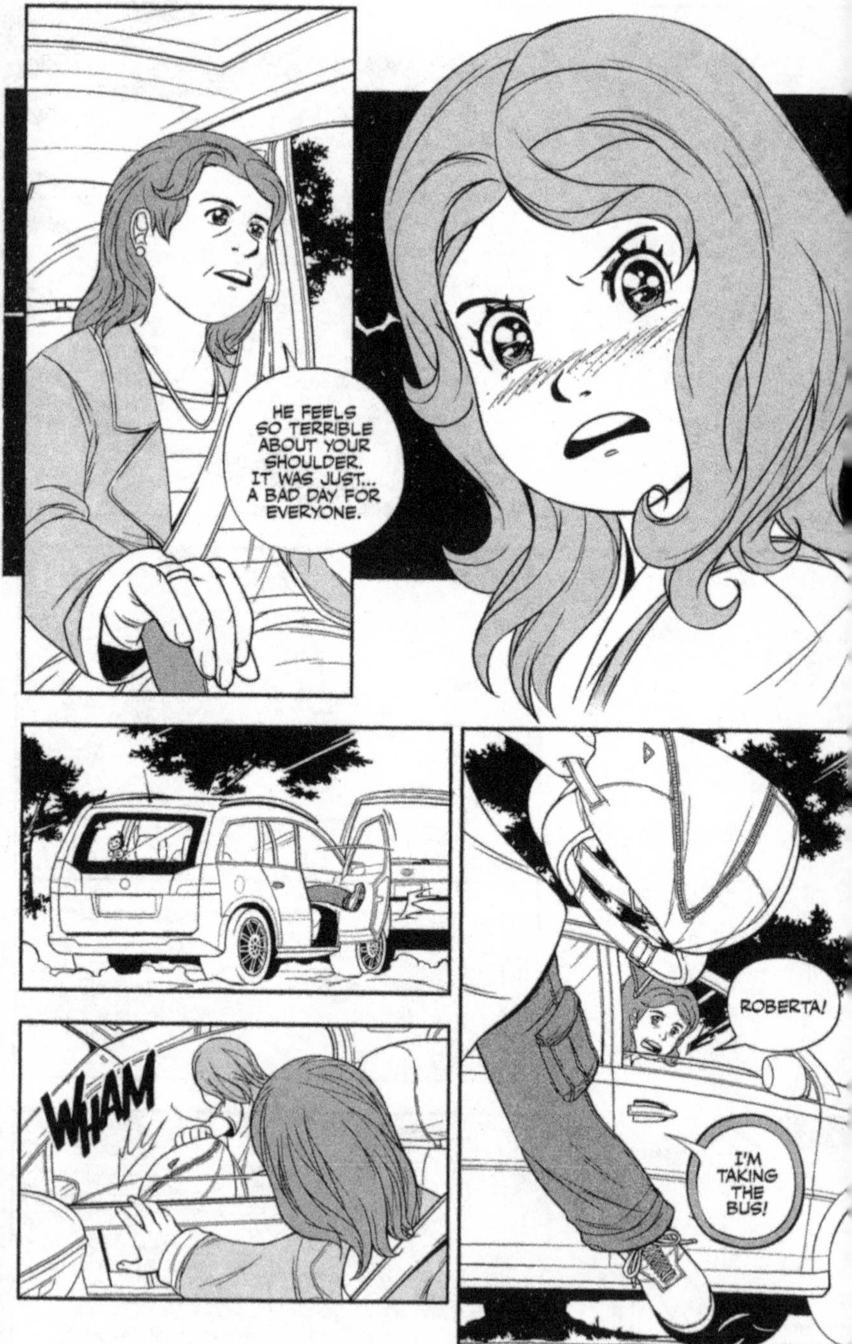
HE FEELS SO TERRIBLE ABOUT YOUR SHOULDER. IT WAS JUST... A BAD DAY FOR EVERYONE.
WHAM
ROBERTA!
I'M TAKING THE BUS!

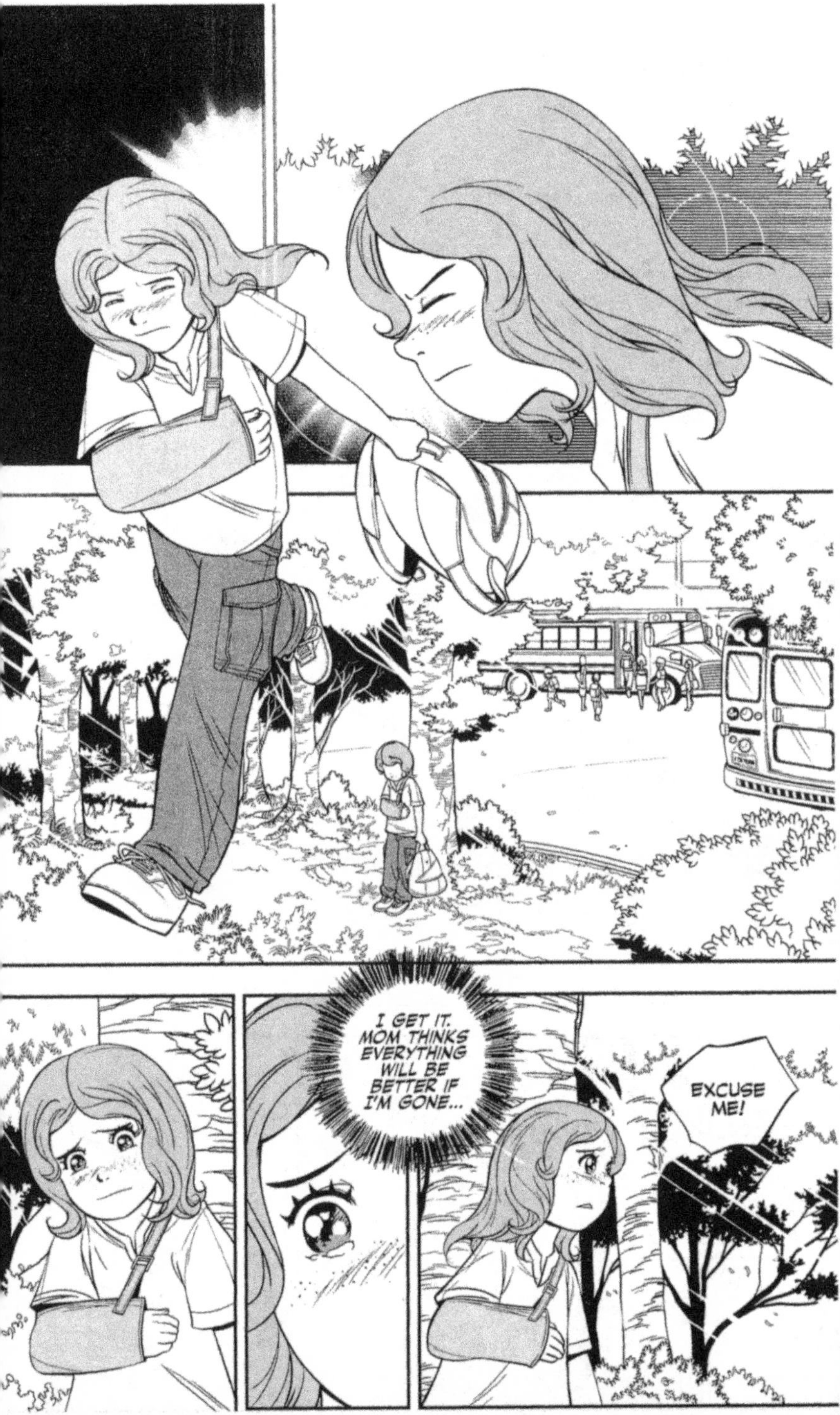
I GET IT. MOM THINKS EVERYTHING WILL BE BETTER IF I'M GONE...
EXCUSE ME!

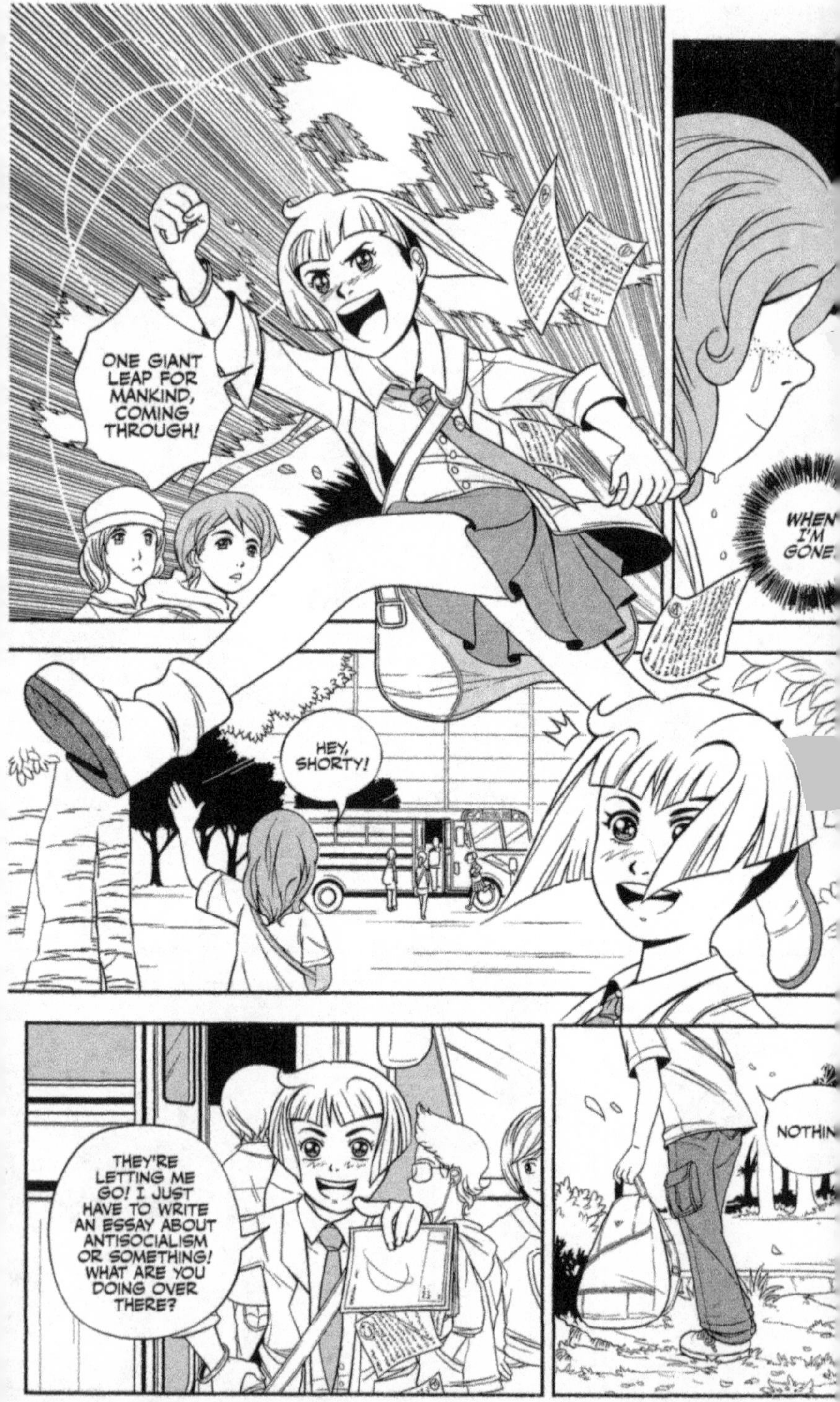
ONE GIANT LEAP FOR MANKIND, COMING THROUGH!
WHEN I'M GONE
HEY, SHORTY!
THEY'RE LETTING ME GO! I JUST HAVE TO WRITE AN ESSAY ABOUT ANTISOCIALISM OR SOMETHING! WHAT ARE YOU DOING OVER THERE?
NOTHIN

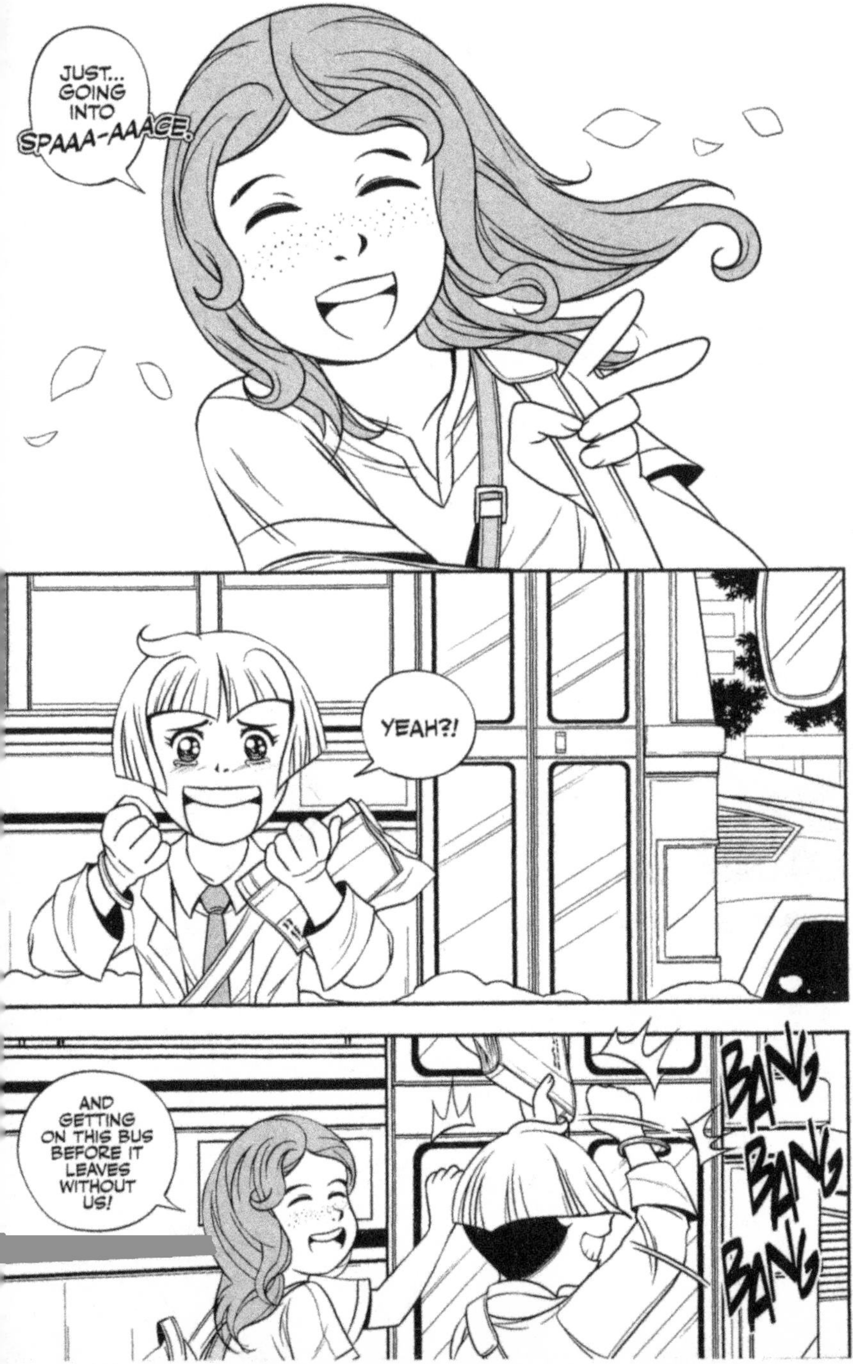
JUST... GOING INTO SPAAA-AAACE.
YEAH?!
AND GETTING ON THIS BUS BEFORE IT LEAVES WITHOUT US!
BANG BANG BANG

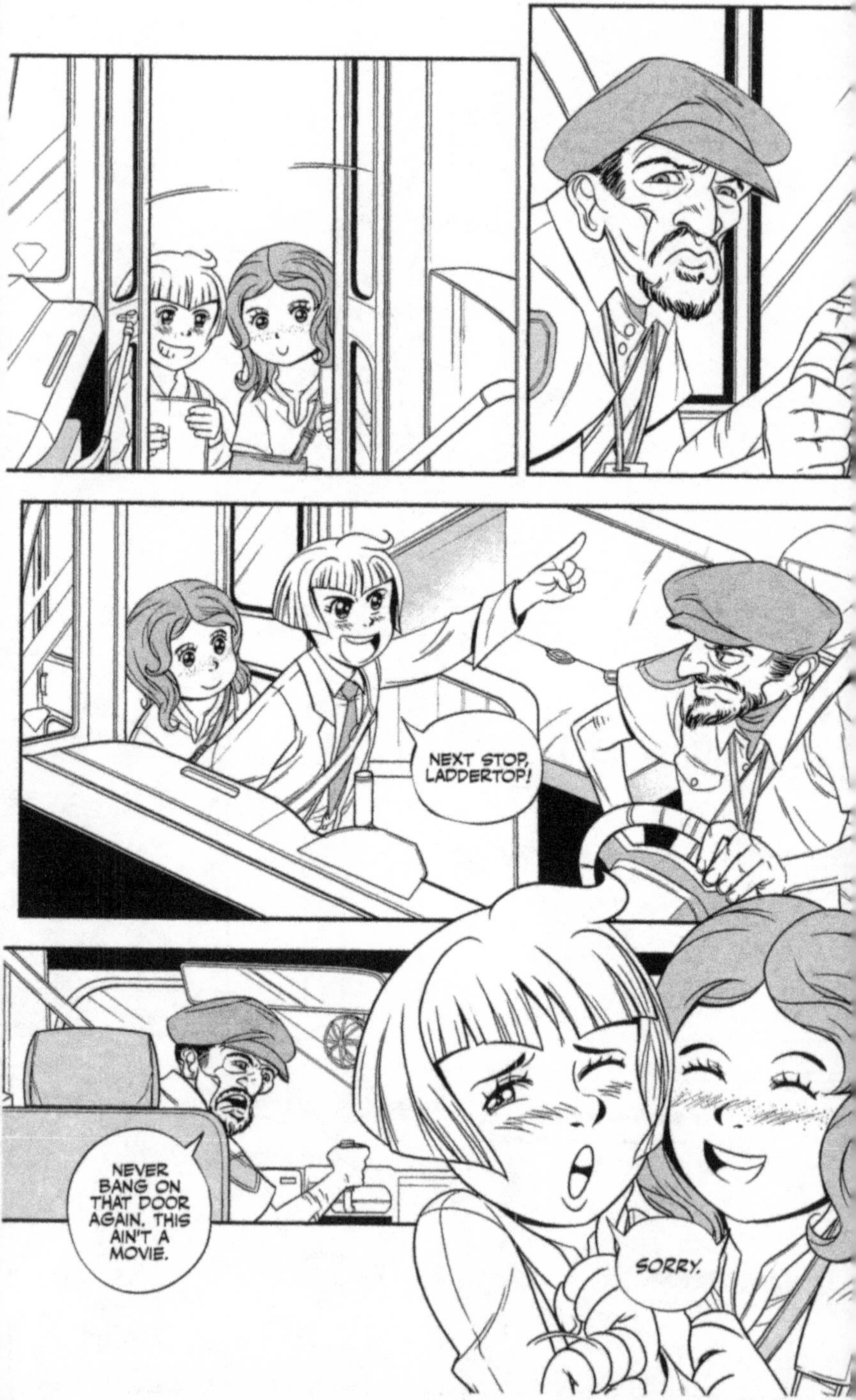
NEXT STOP, LADDERTOP!
NEVER BANG ON THAT DOOR AGAIN. THIS AIN'T A MOVIE.
SORRY.

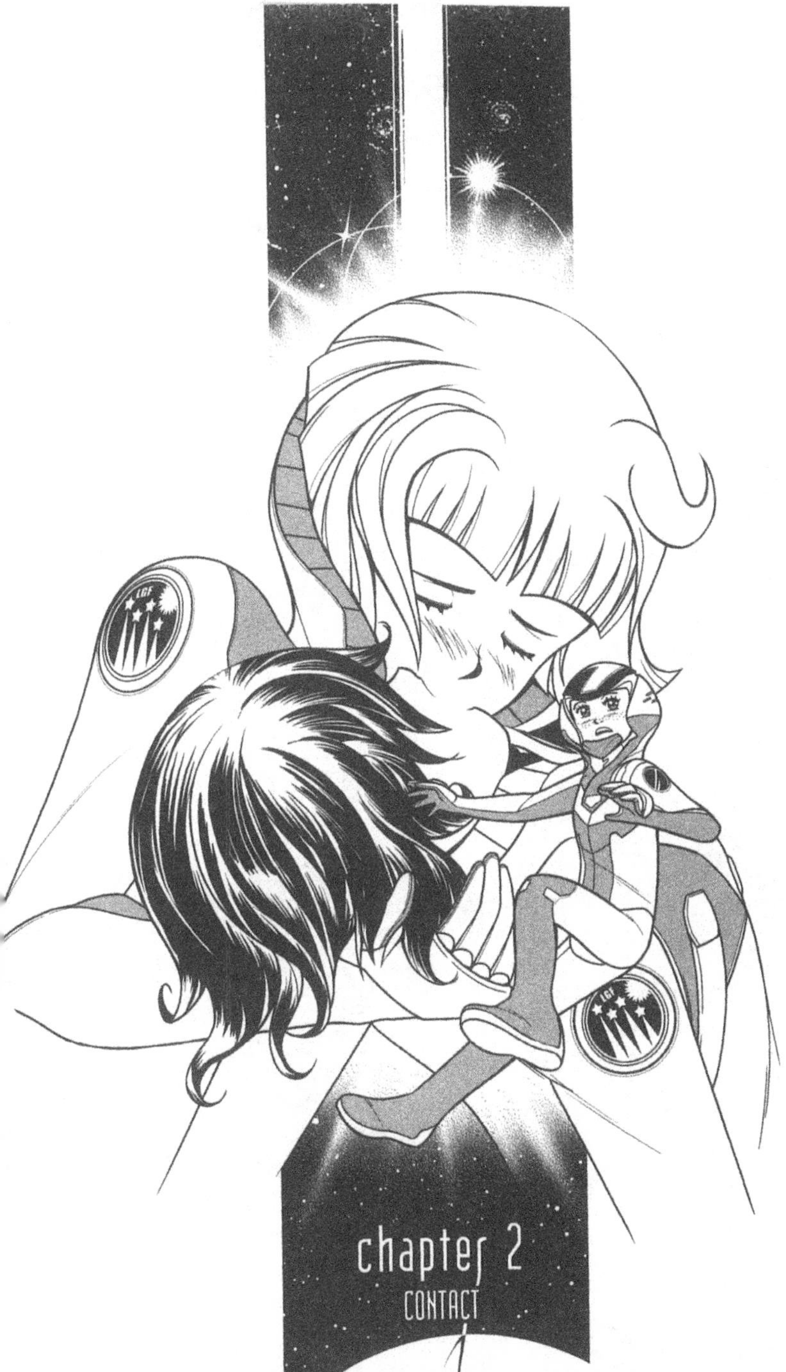chapter 2
CONTACT

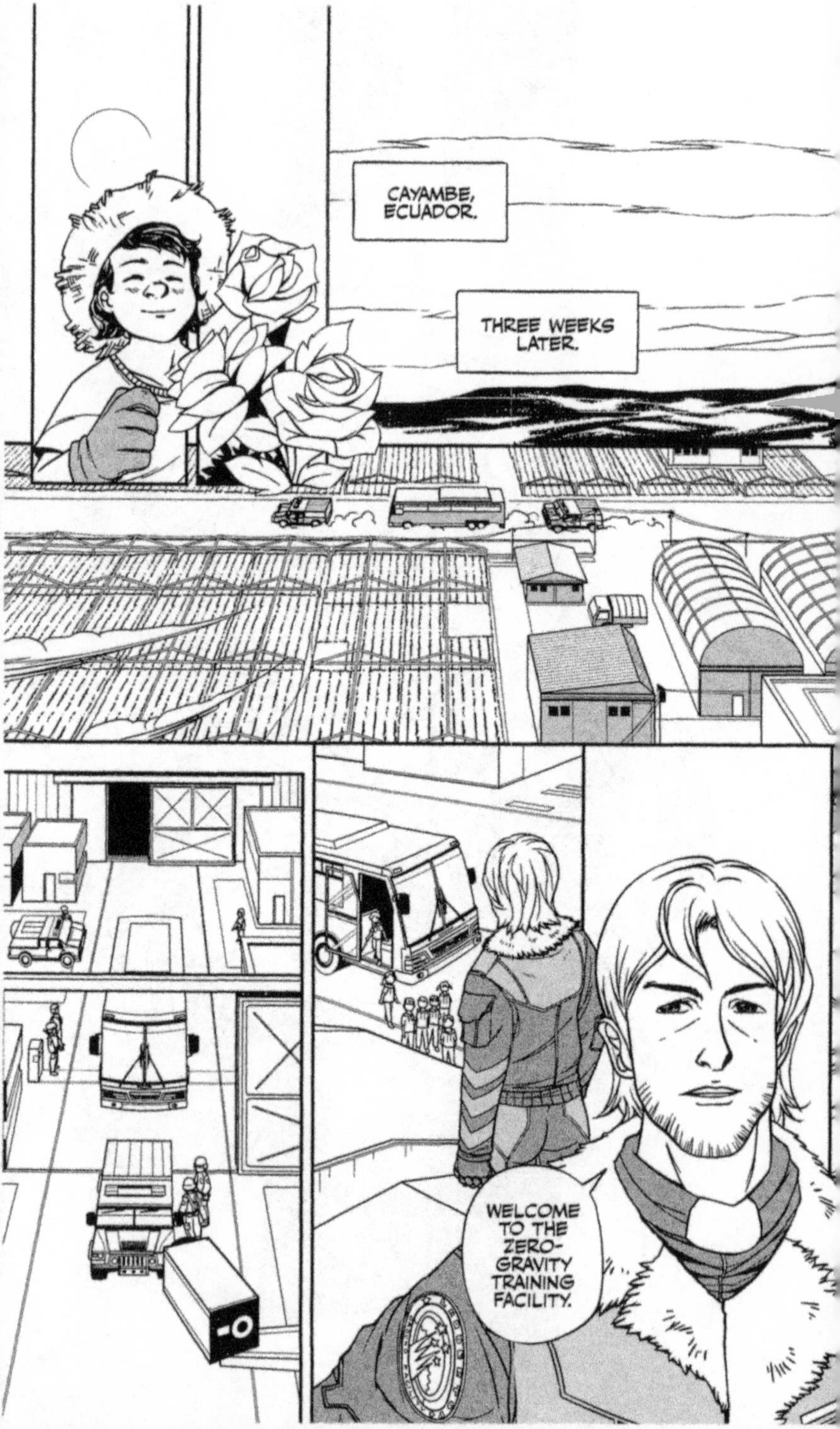
CAYAMBE, ECUADOR.
THREE WEEKS LATER.
WELCOME TO THE ZERO-GRAVITY TRAINING FACILITY.

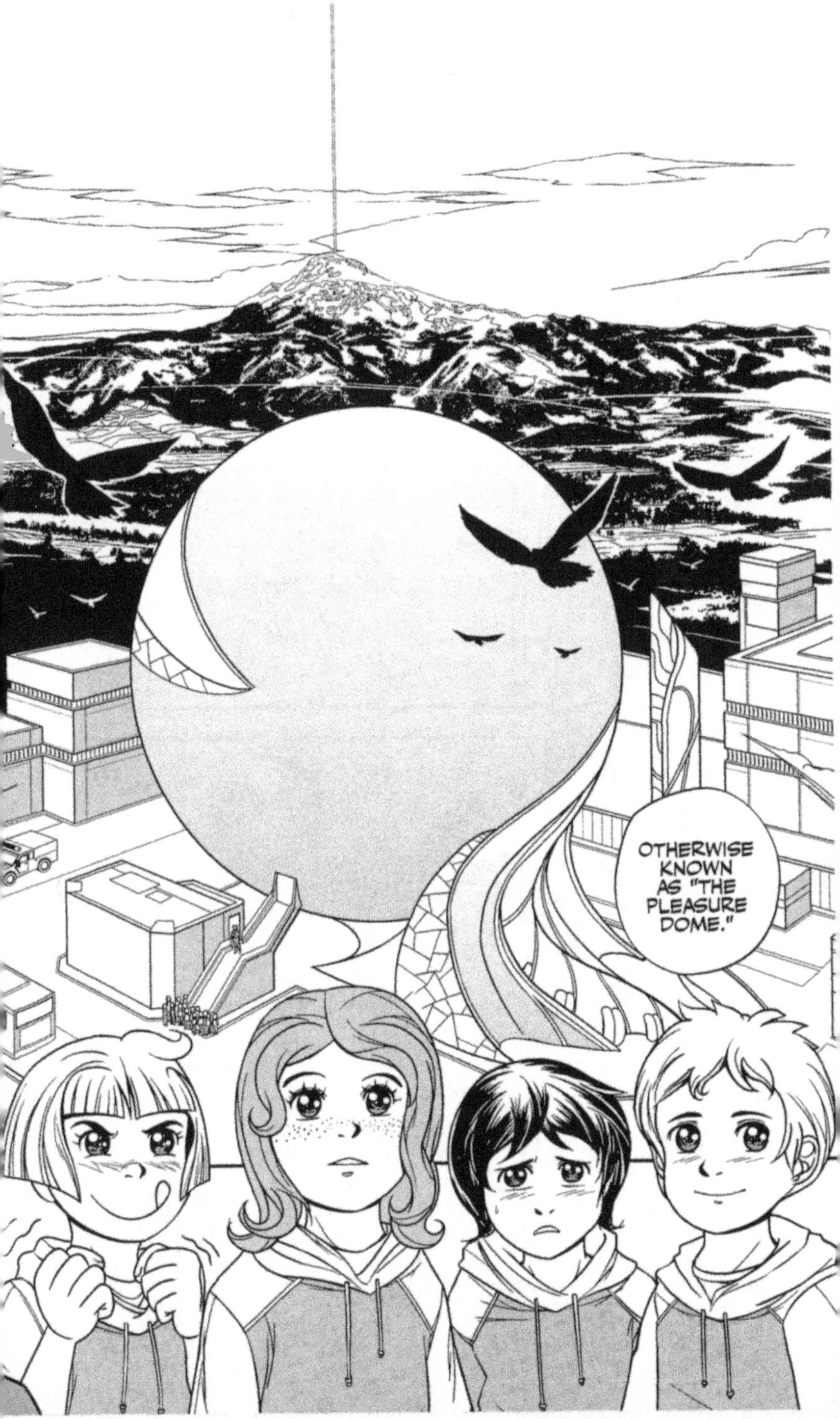
OTHERWISE KNOWN AS "THE PLEASURE DOME."

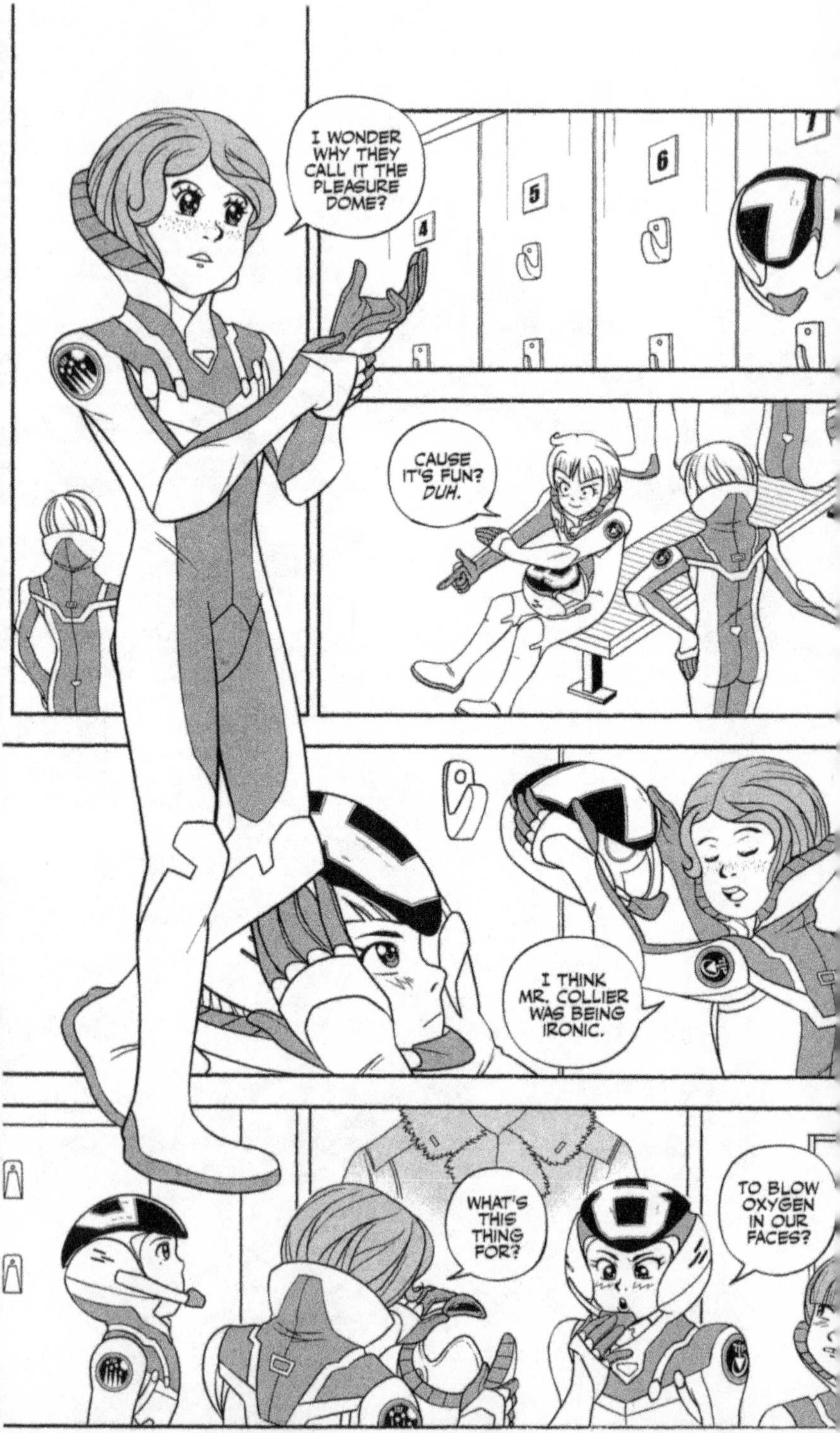
I WONDER WHY THEY CALL IT THE PLEASURE DOME?
4
5
6
7
CAUSE IT'S FUN? *DUH.*
I THINK MR. COLLIER WAS BEING IRONIC.
WHAT'S THIS THING FOR?
TO BLOW OXYGEN IN OUR FACES?

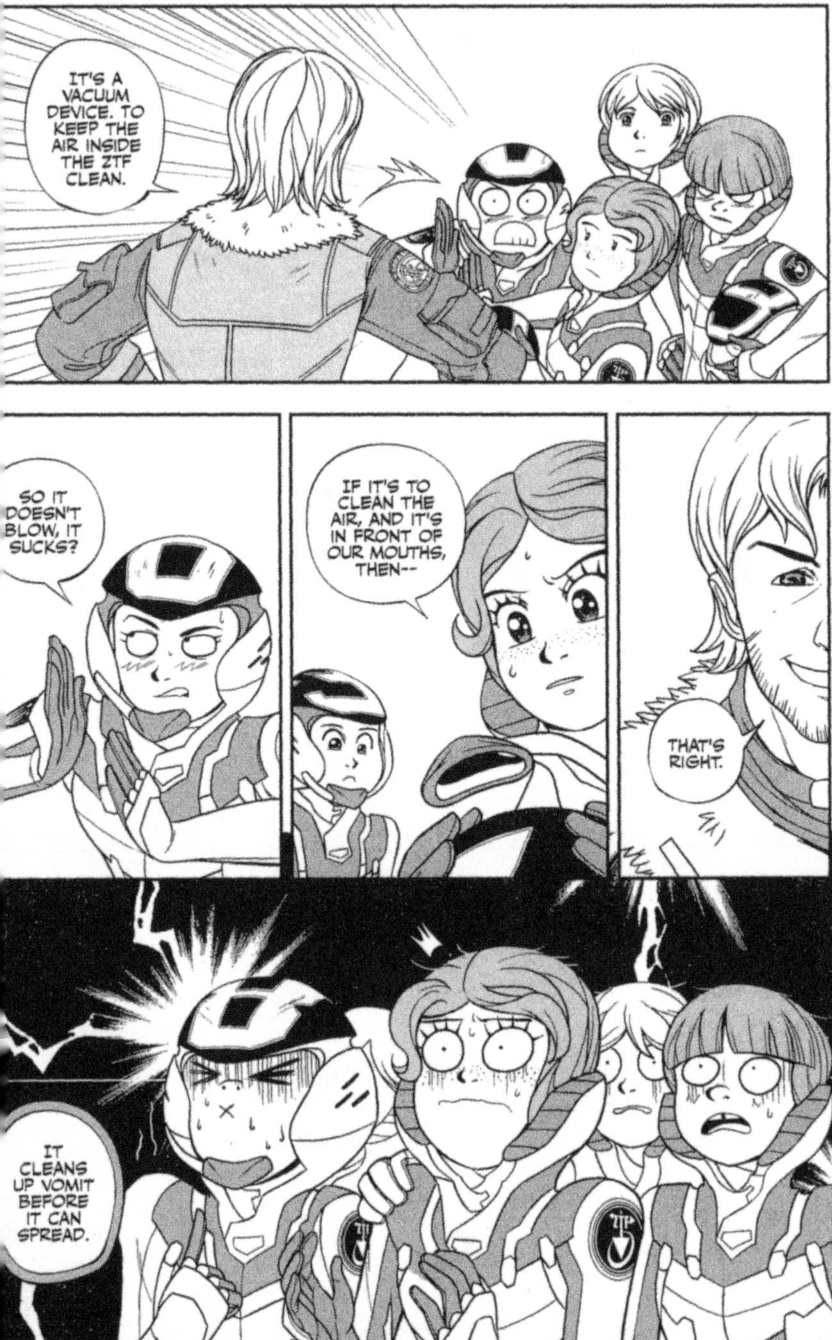
IT'S A VACUUM DEVICE. TO KEEP THE AIR INSIDE THE ZTF CLEAN.
SO IT DOESN'T BLOW, IT SUCKS?
IF IT'S TO CLEAN THE AIR, AND IT'S IN FRONT OF OUR MOUTHS, THEN--
THAT'S RIGHT.
IT CLEANS UP VOMIT BEFORE IT CAN SPREAD.

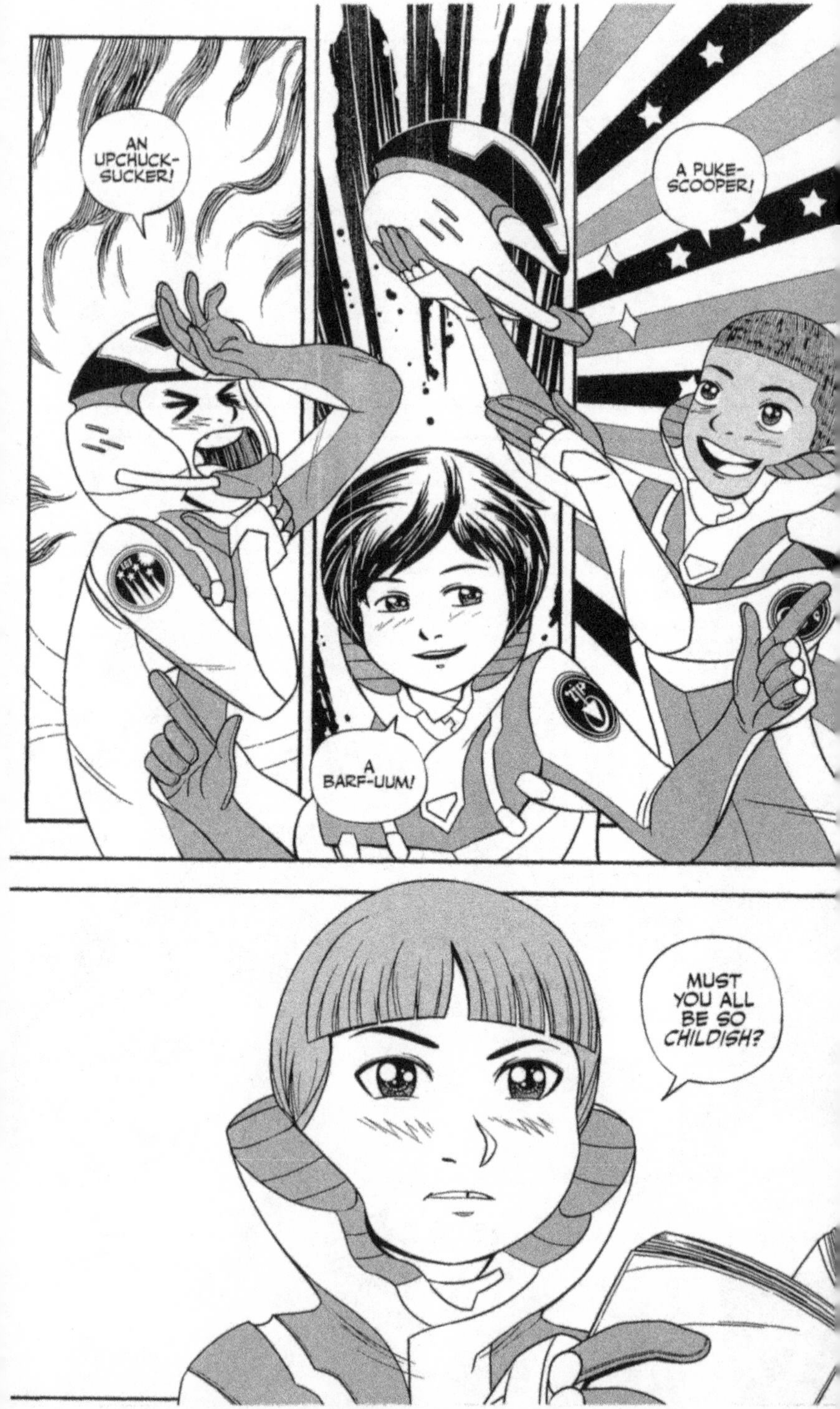
AN UPCHUCK-SUCKER!
A PUKE-SCOOPER!
A BARF-UUM!
MUST YOU ALL BE SO *CHILDISH?*

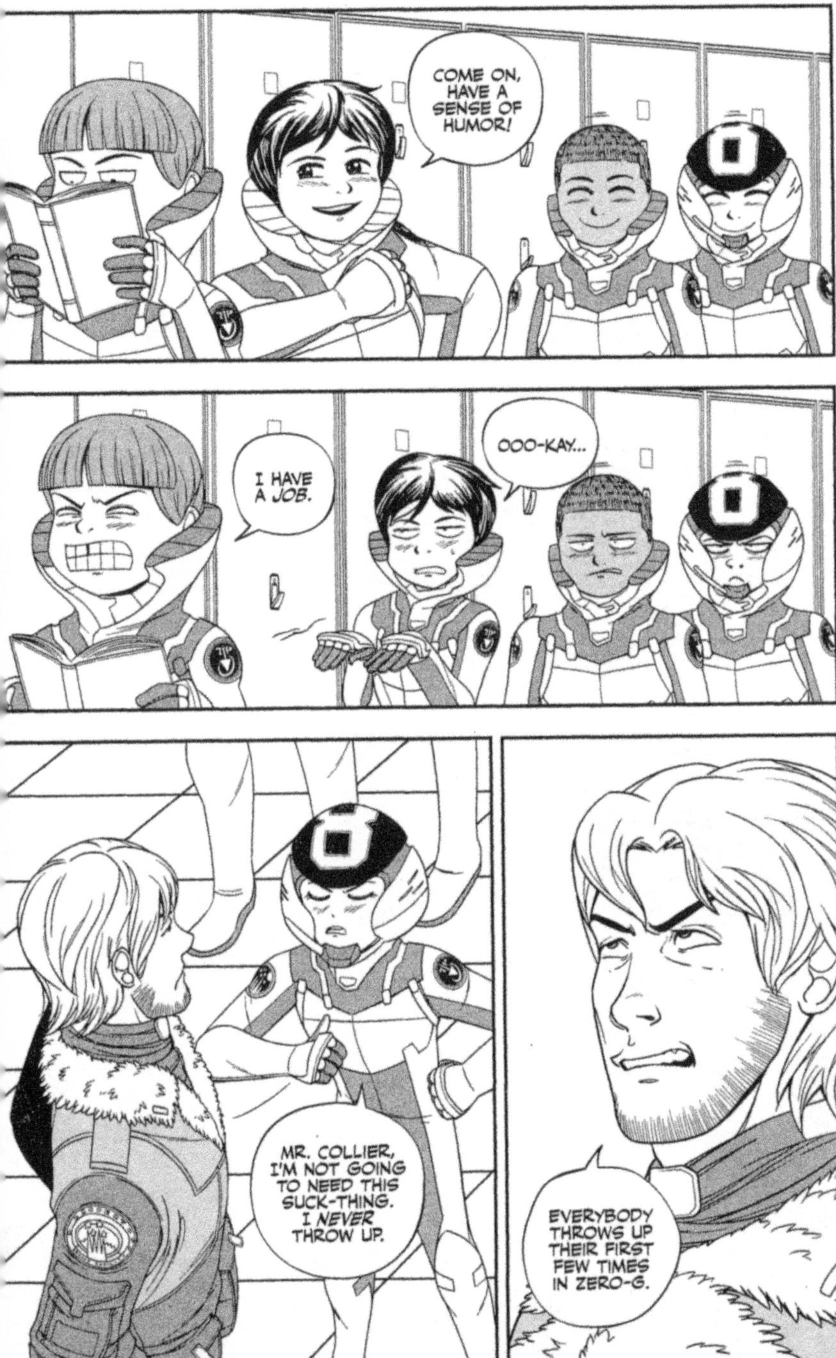
COME ON, HAVE A SENSE OF HUMOR!
I HAVE A *JOB*.
OOO-KAY...
MR. COLLIER, I'M NOT GOING TO NEED THIS SUCK-THING. I *NEVER* THROW UP.
EVERYBODY THROWS UP THEIR FIRST FEW TIMES IN ZERO-G.

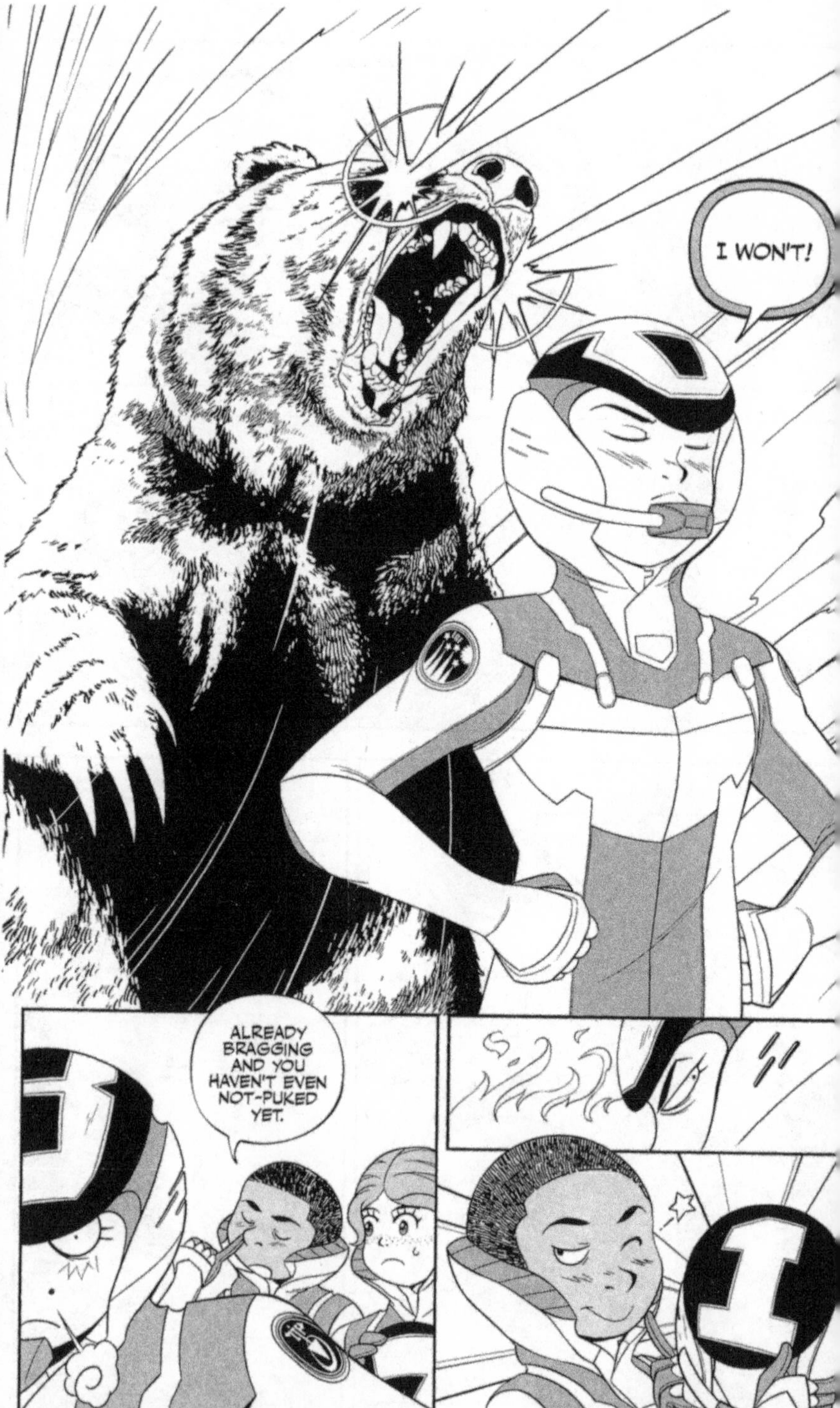
I WON'T!
ALREADY BRAGGING AND YOU HAVEN'T EVEN NOT-PUKED YET.

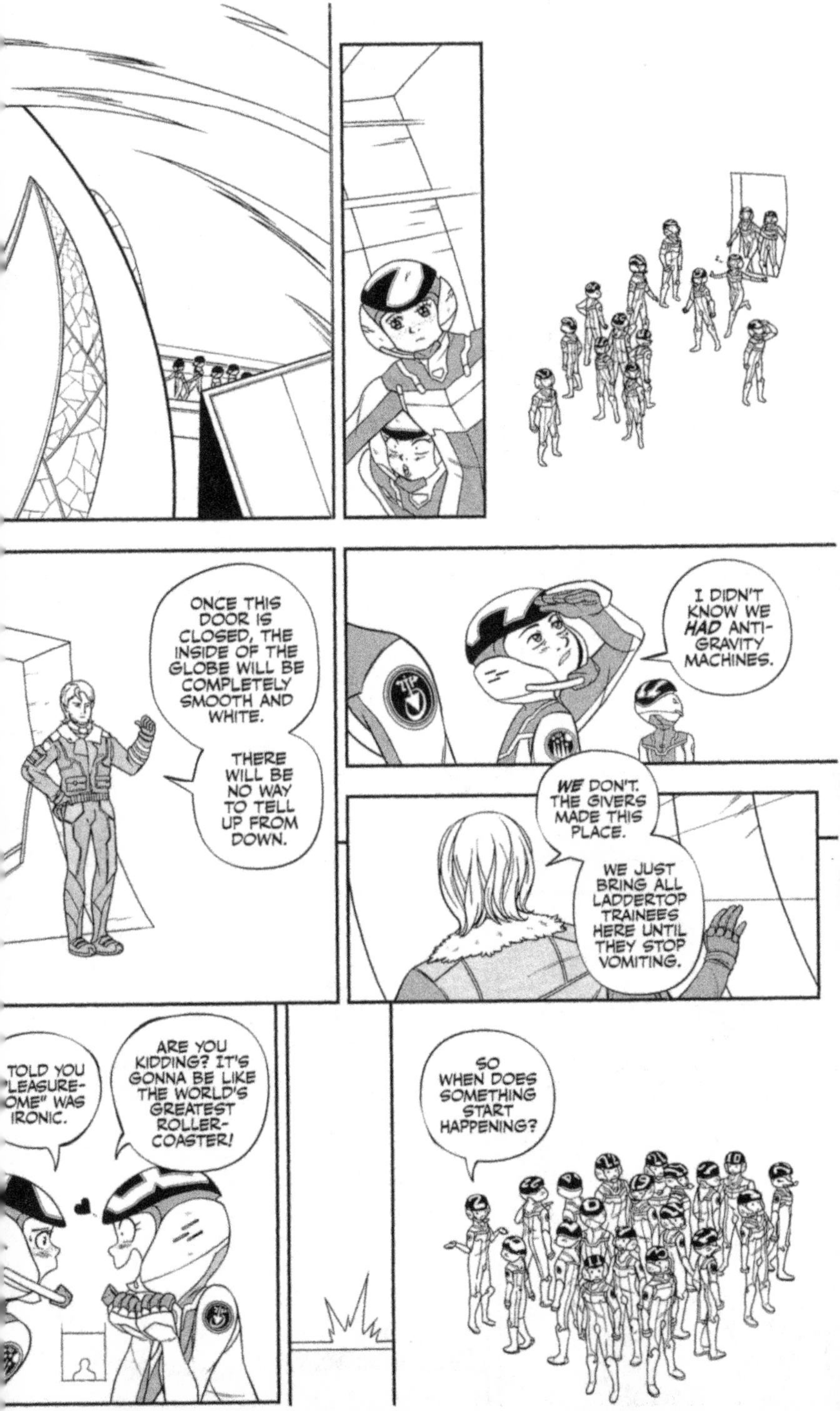
ONCE THIS DOOR IS CLOSED, THE INSIDE OF THE GLOBE WILL BE COMPLETELY SMOOTH AND WHITE.
THERE WILL BE NO WAY TO TELL UP FROM DOWN.
I DIDN'T KNOW WE *HAD* ANTI-GRAVITY MACHINES.
WE DON'T. THE GIVERS MADE THIS PLACE.
WE JUST BRING ALL LADDERTOP TRAINEES HERE UNTIL THEY STOP VOMITING.
TOLD YOU "LEASURE-OME" WAS IRONIC.
ARE YOU KIDDING? IT'S GONNA BE LIKE THE WORLD'S GREATEST ROLLER-COASTER!
SO WHEN DOES SOMETHING START HAPPENING?

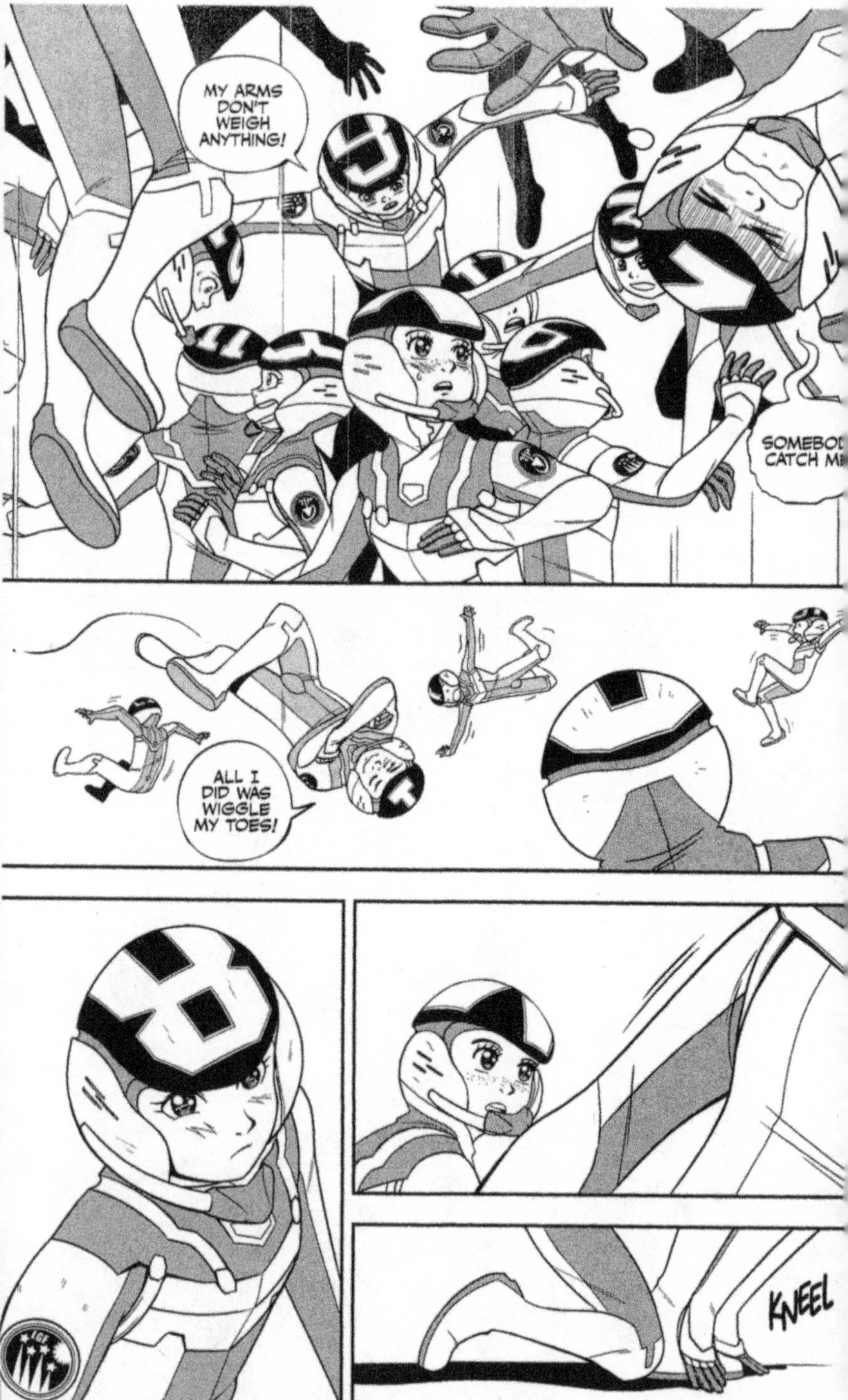
MY ARMS DON'T WEIGH ANYTHING!
SOMEBOD CATCH M
ALL I DID WAS WIGGLE MY TOES!
KNEEL

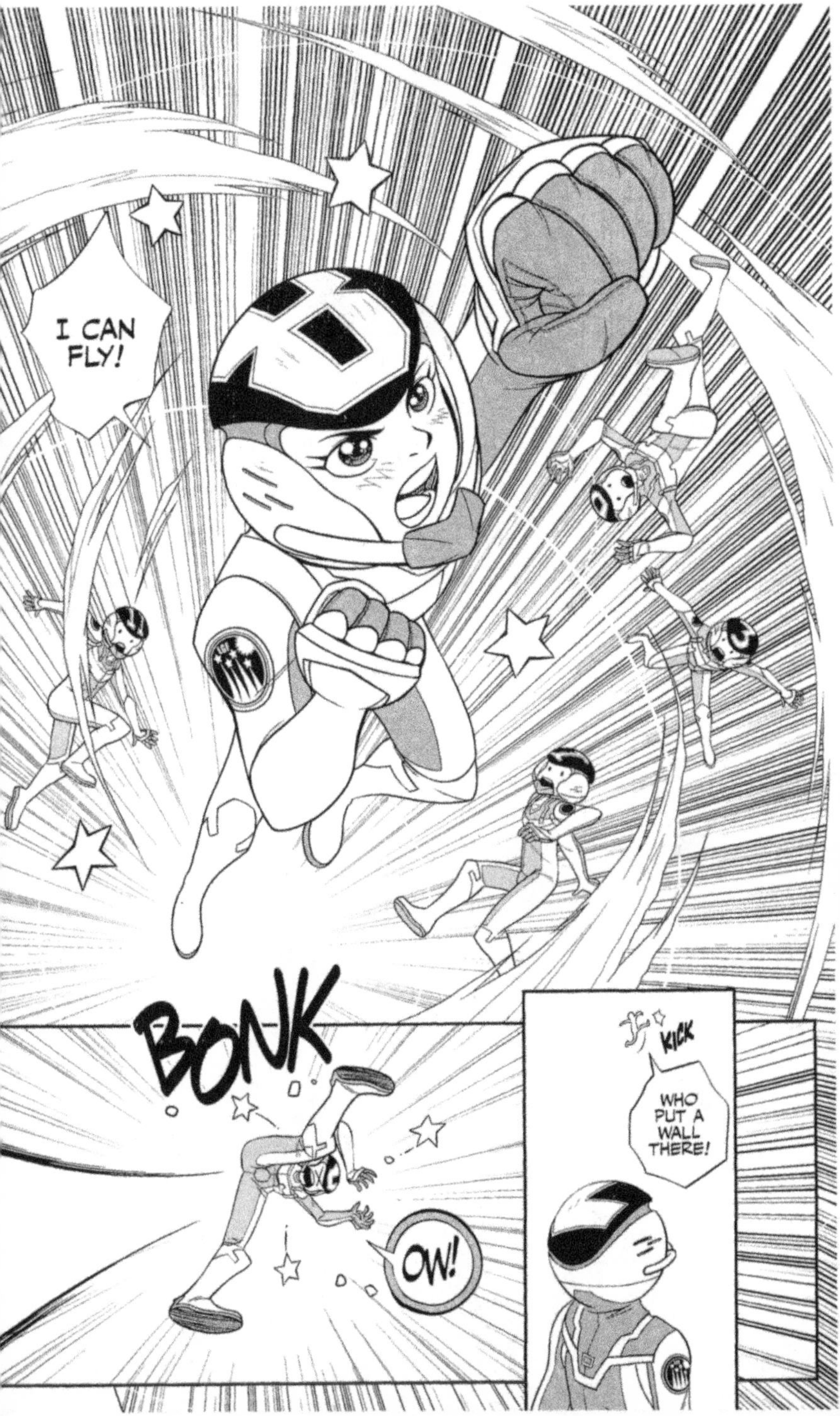
I CAN FLY!
BONK
OW!
KICK
WHO PUT A WALL THERE!

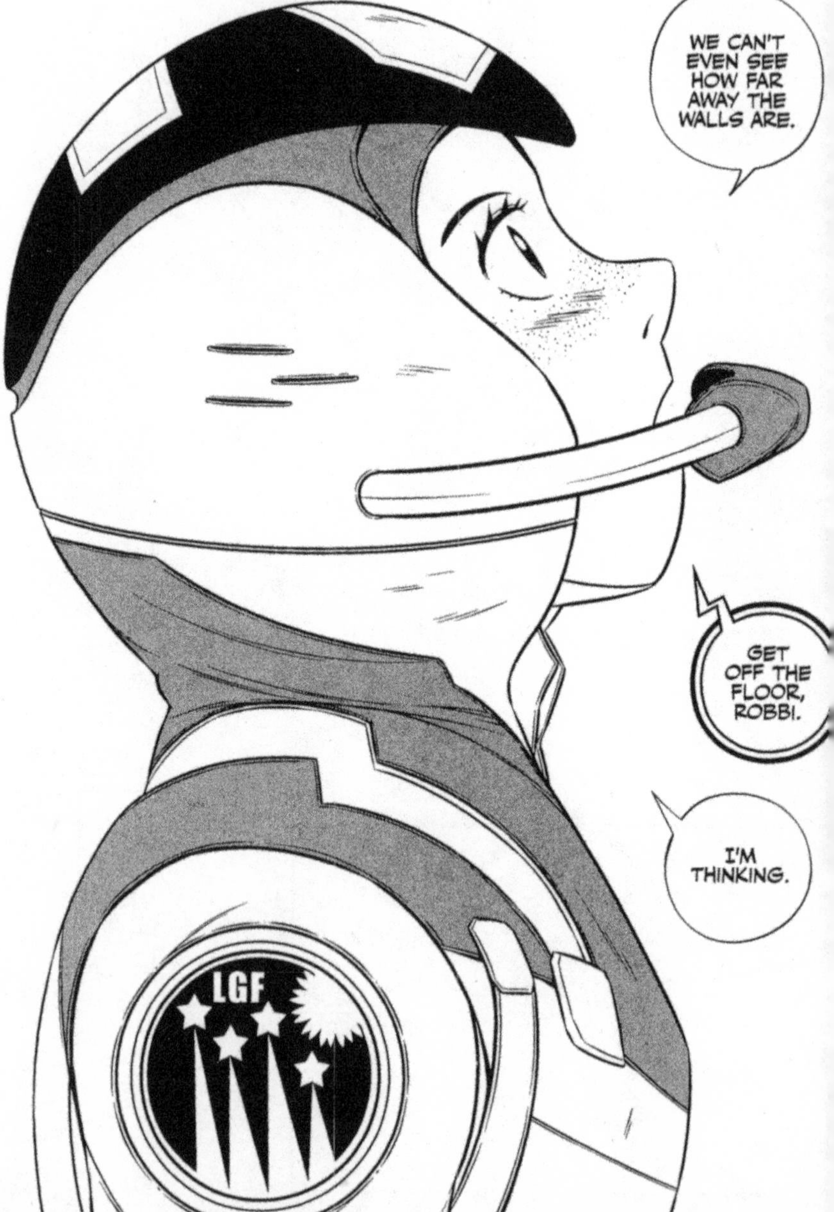
WE CAN'T EVEN SEE HOW FAR AWAY THE WALLS ARE.
GET OFF THE FLOOR, ROBBI.
I'M THINKING.
LGF

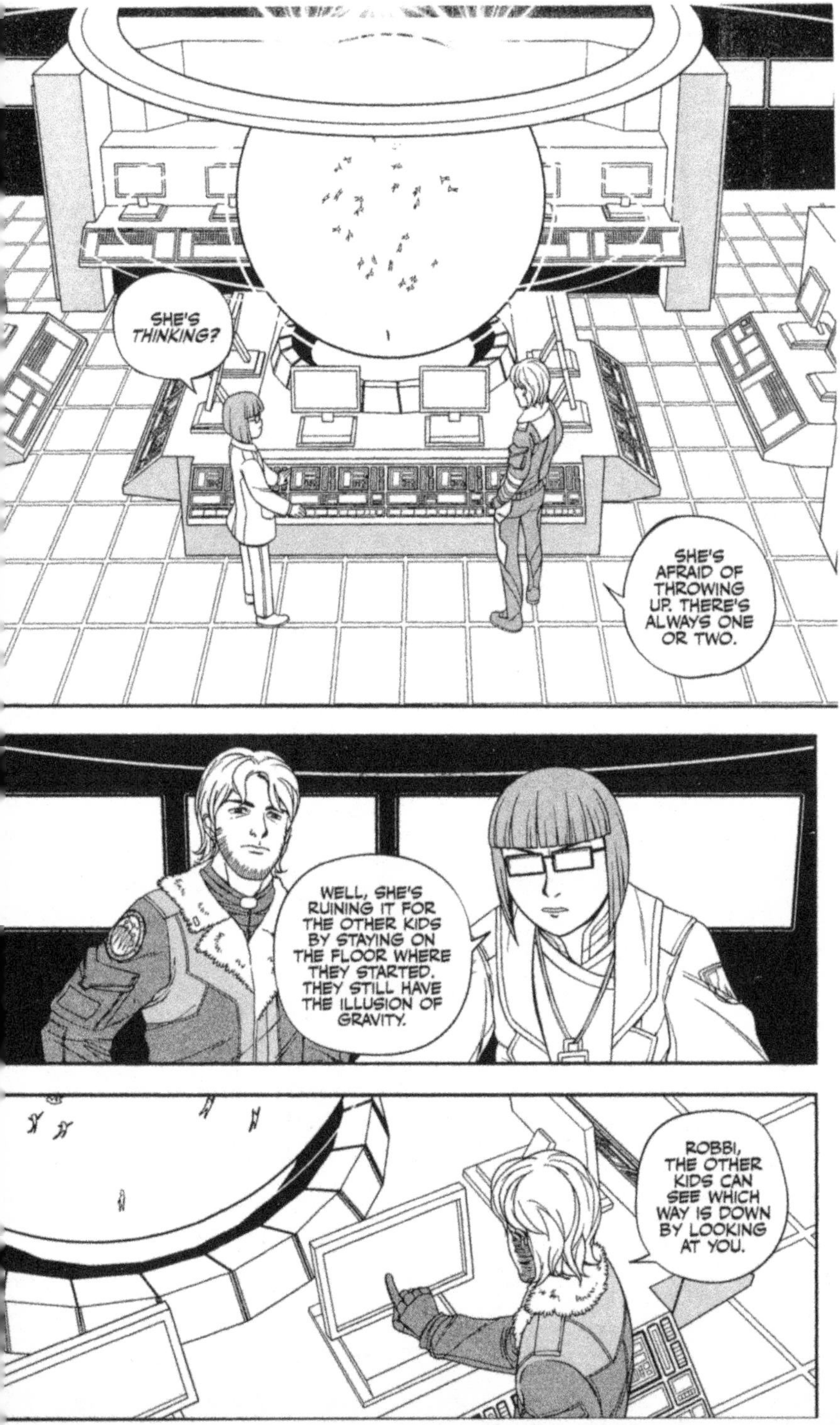
SHE'S THINKING?
SHE'S AFRAID OF THROWING UP. THERE'S ALWAYS ONE OR TWO.
WELL, SHE'S RUINING IT FOR THE OTHER KIDS BY STAYING ON THE FLOOR WHERE THEY STARTED. THEY STILL HAVE THE ILLUSION OF GRAVITY.
ROBBI, THE OTHER KIDS CAN SEE WHICH WAY IS DOWN BY LOOKING AT YOU.

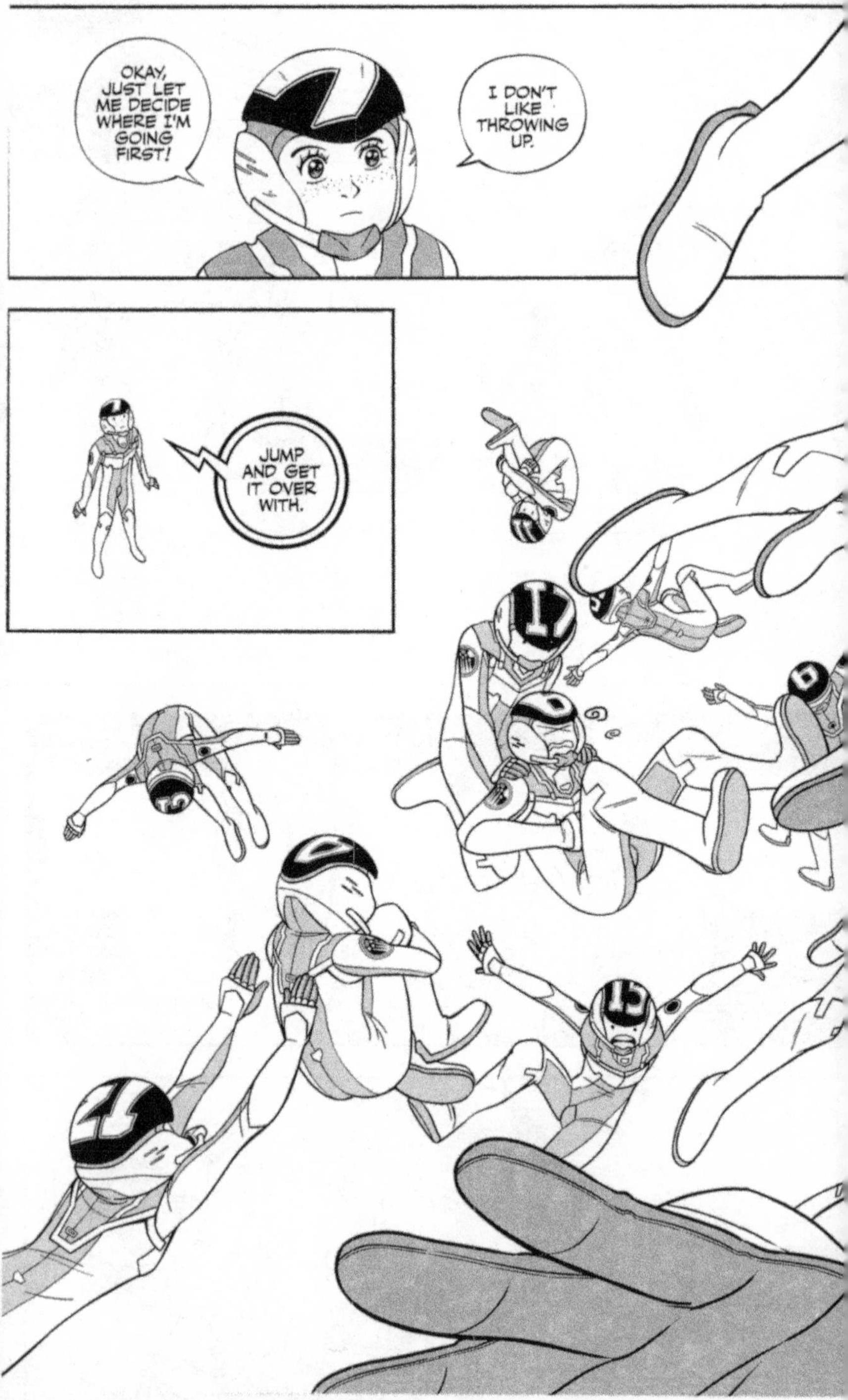
OKAY, JUST LET ME DECIDE WHERE I'M GOING FIRST!
I DON'T LIKE THROWING UP.
JUMP AND GET IT OVER WITH.

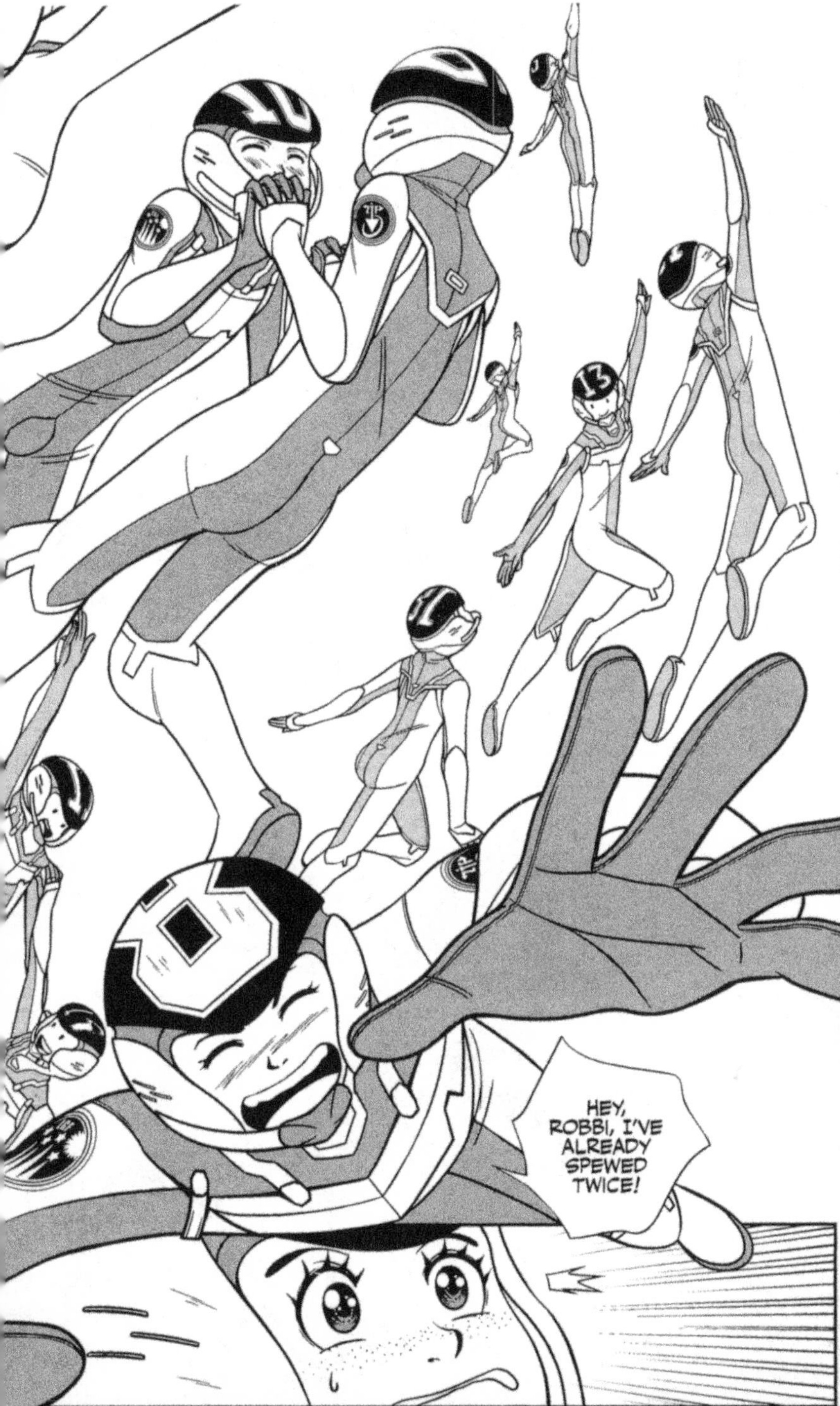
HEY, ROBBI, I'VE ALREADY SPEWED TWICE!

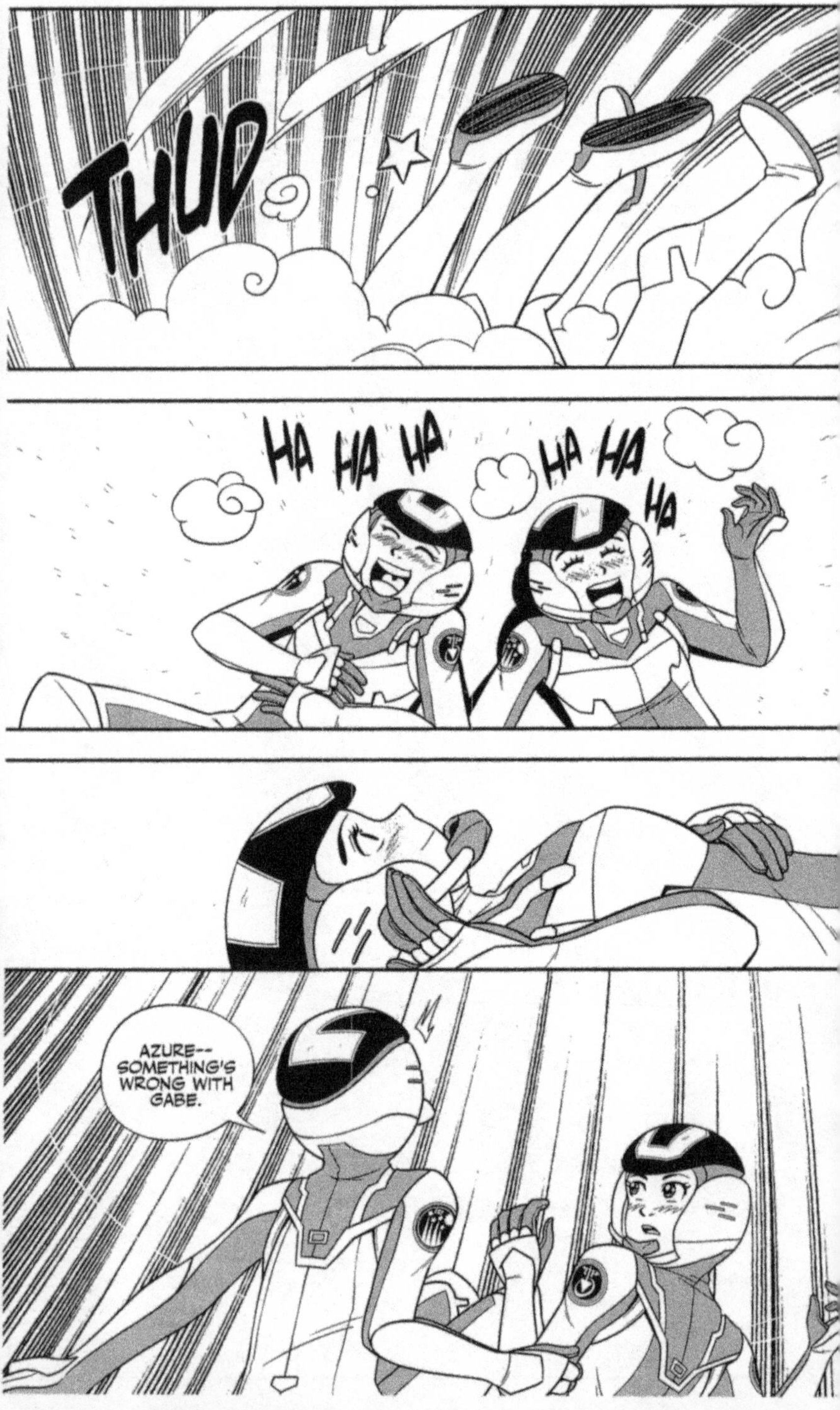
THUD
HA HA HA
HA HA HA
AZURE--SOMETHING'S WRONG WITH GABE.

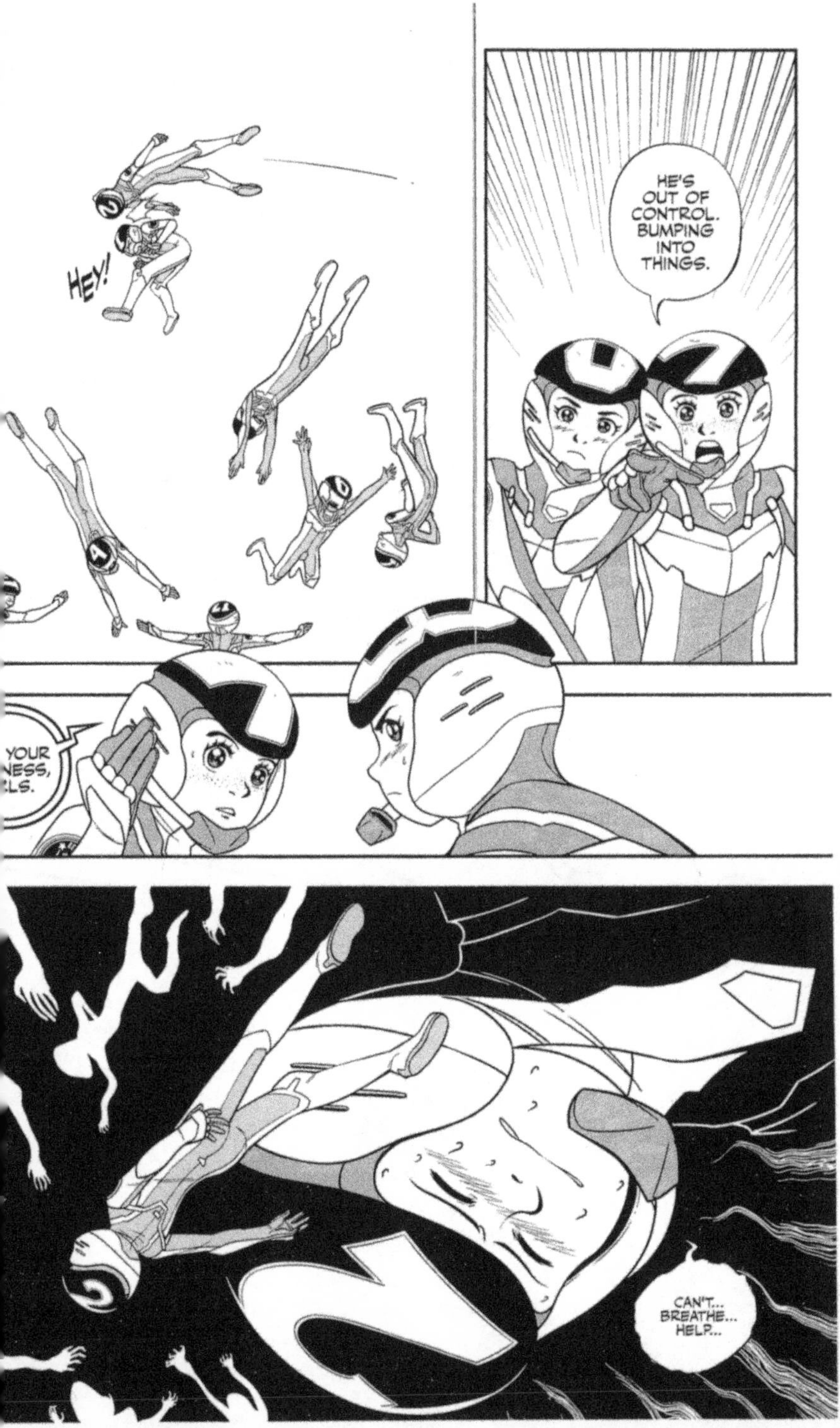
HEY!
HE'S OUT OF CONTROL. BUMPING INTO THINGS.
YOUR
CAN'T... BREATHE... HELP...

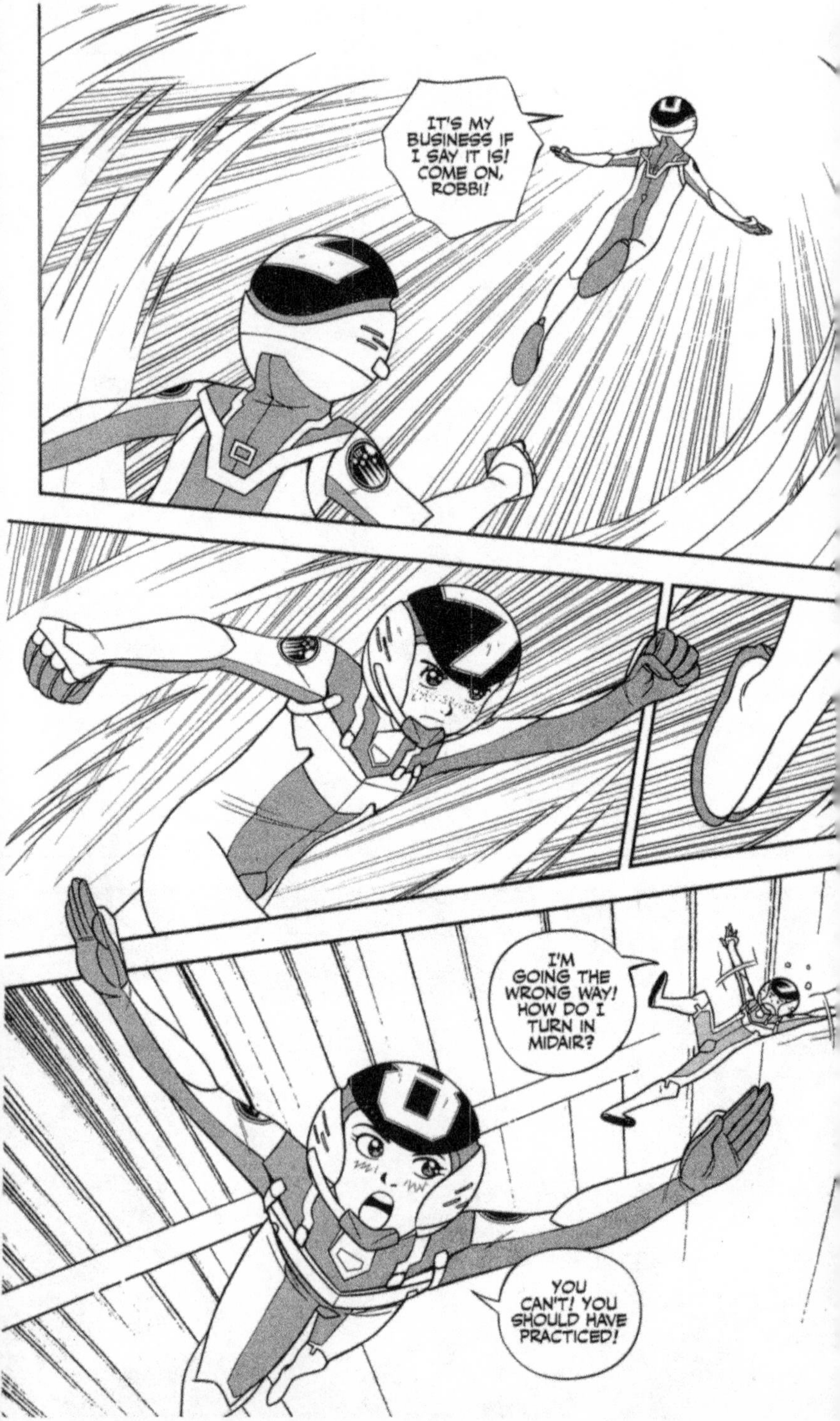
IT'S MY BUSINESS IF I SAY IT IS! COME ON, ROBBI!
I'M GOING THE WRONG WAY! HOW DO I TURN IN MIDAIR?
YOU CAN'T! YOU SHOULD HAVE PRACTICED!

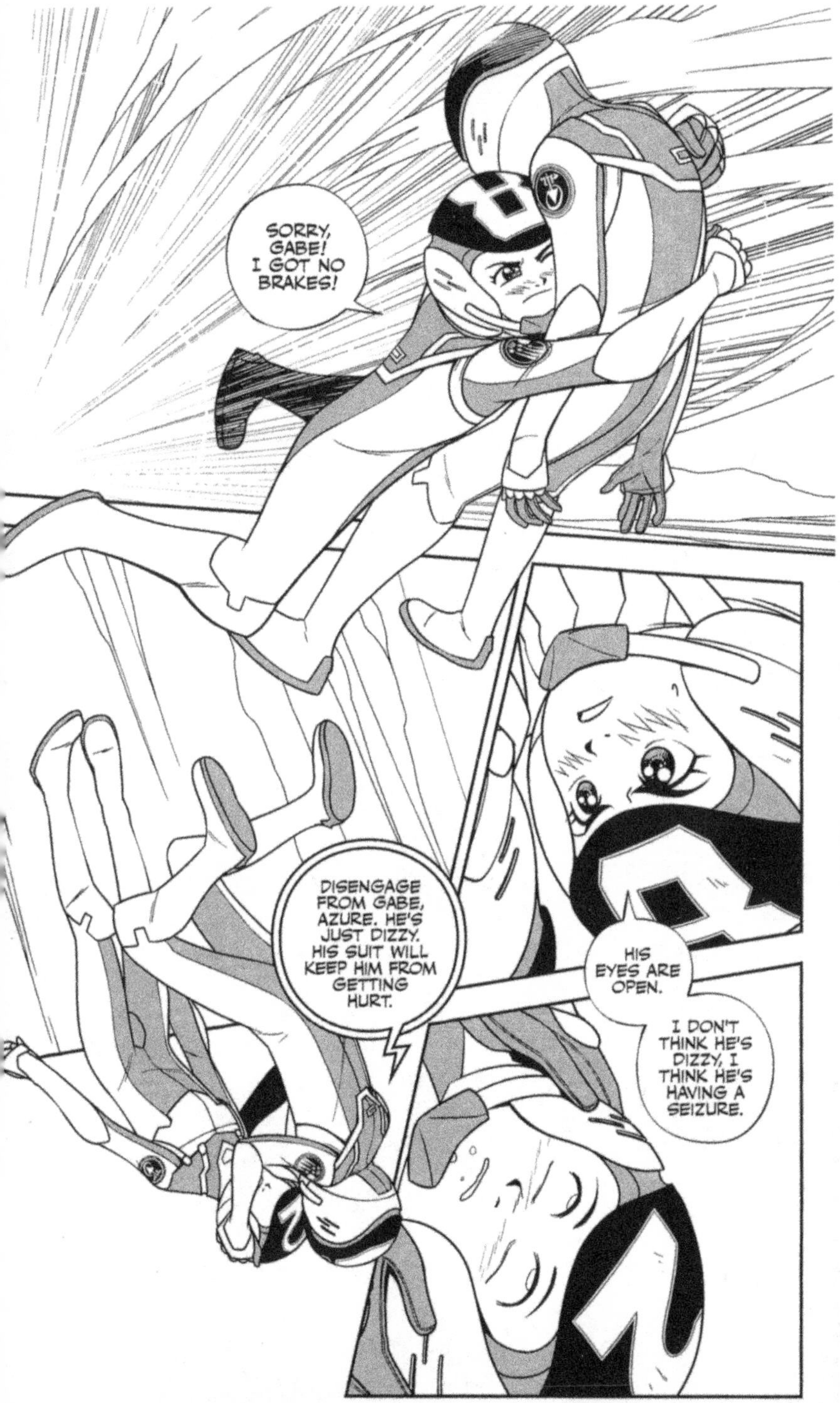
SORRY, GABE! I GOT NO BRAKES!
DISENGAGE FROM GABE, AZURE. HE'S JUST DIZZY. HIS SUIT WILL KEEP HIM FROM GETTING HURT.
HIS EYES ARE OPEN.
I DON'T THINK HE'S DIZZY, I THINK HE'S HAVING A SEIZURE.

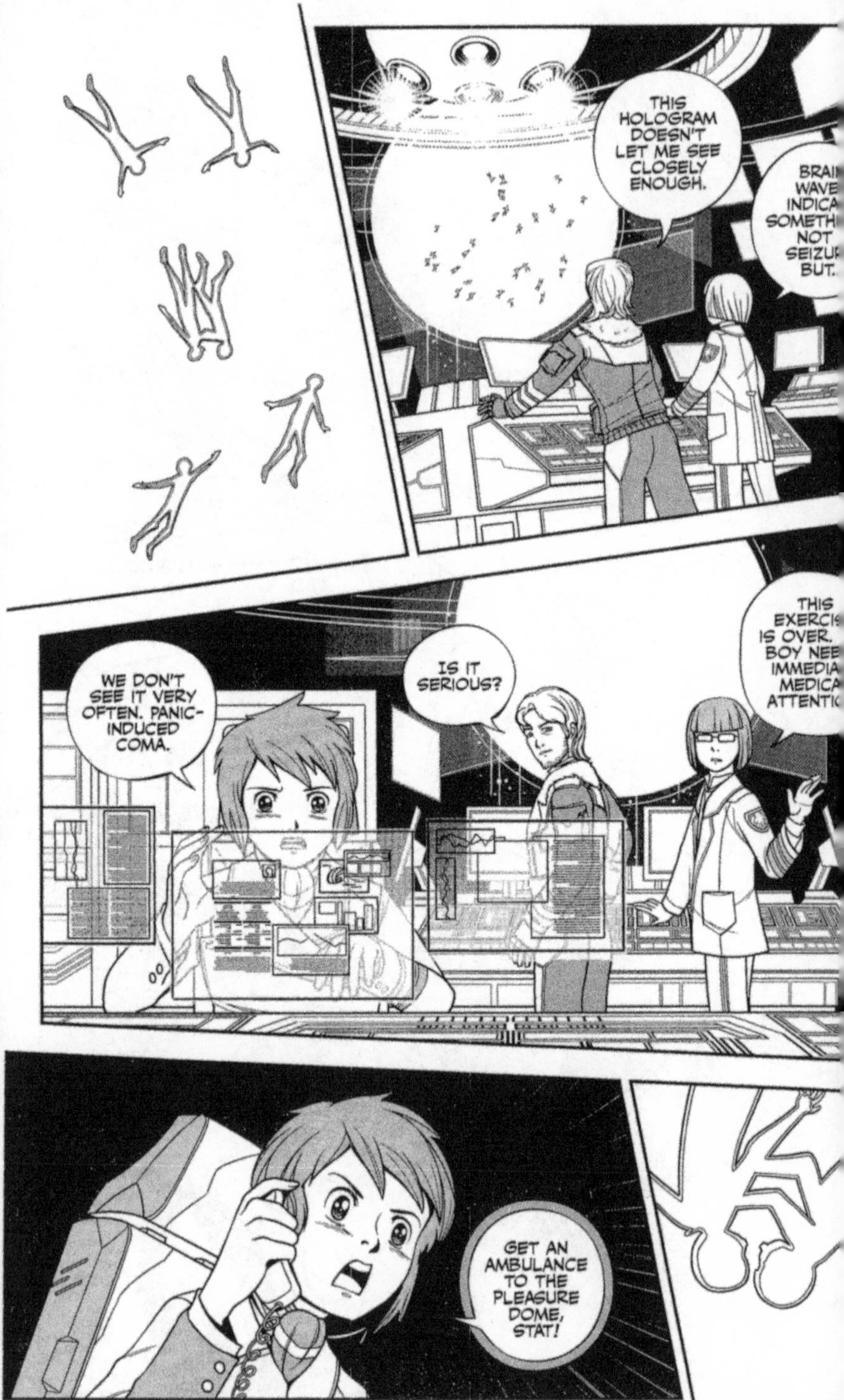
THIS HOLOGRAM DOESN'T LET ME SEE CLOSELY ENOUGH.
BRAI WAVE INDICA SOMETH NOT SEIZUR BUT...
WE DON'T SEE IT VERY OFTEN. PANIC-INDUCED COMA.
IS IT SERIOUS?
THIS EXERCIS IS OVER. BOY NEE IMMEDIA MEDICA ATTENTIC
GET AN AMBULANCE TO THE PLEASURE DOME, STAT!

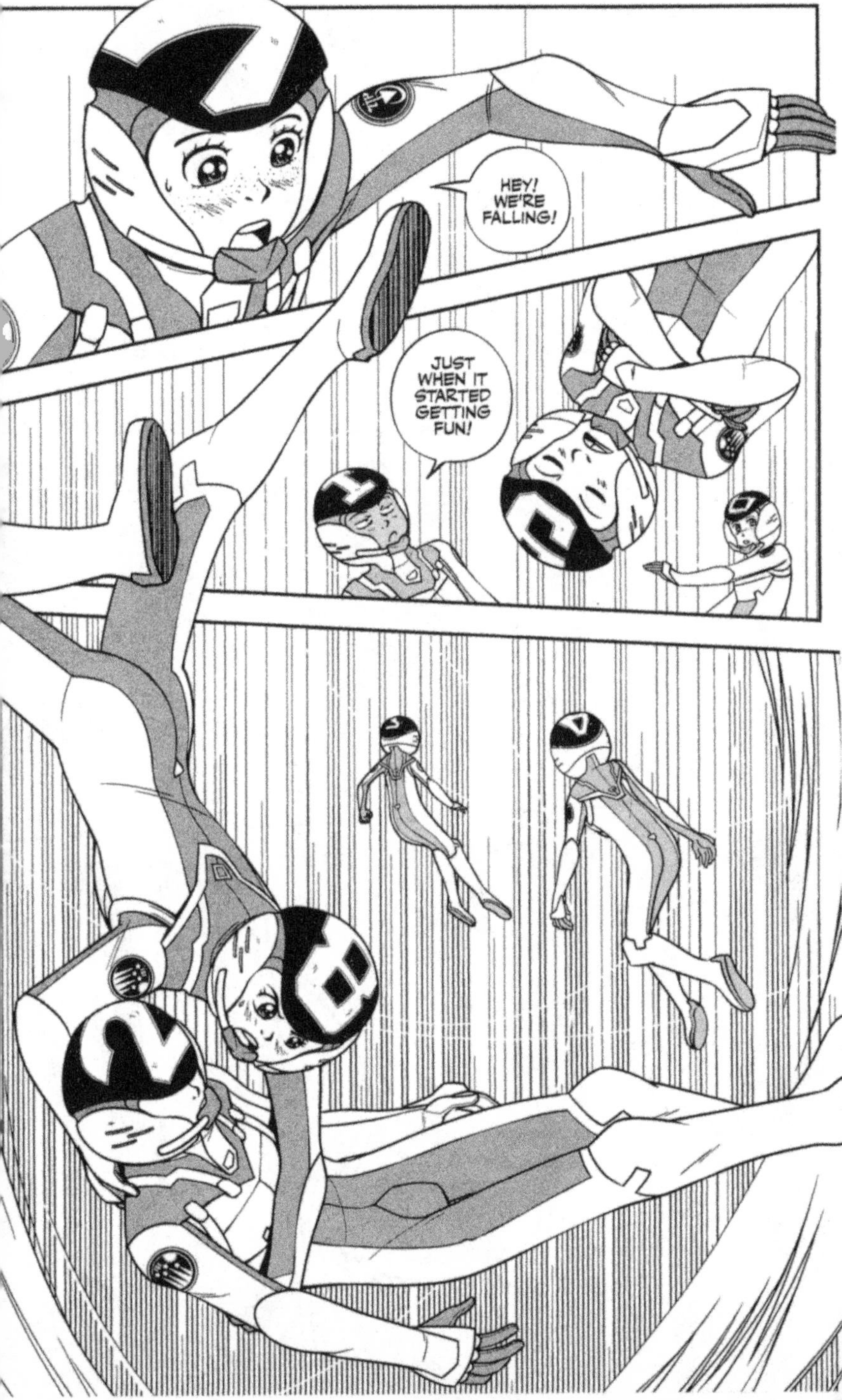
HEY! WE'RE FALLING!
JUST WHEN IT STARTED GETTING FUN!

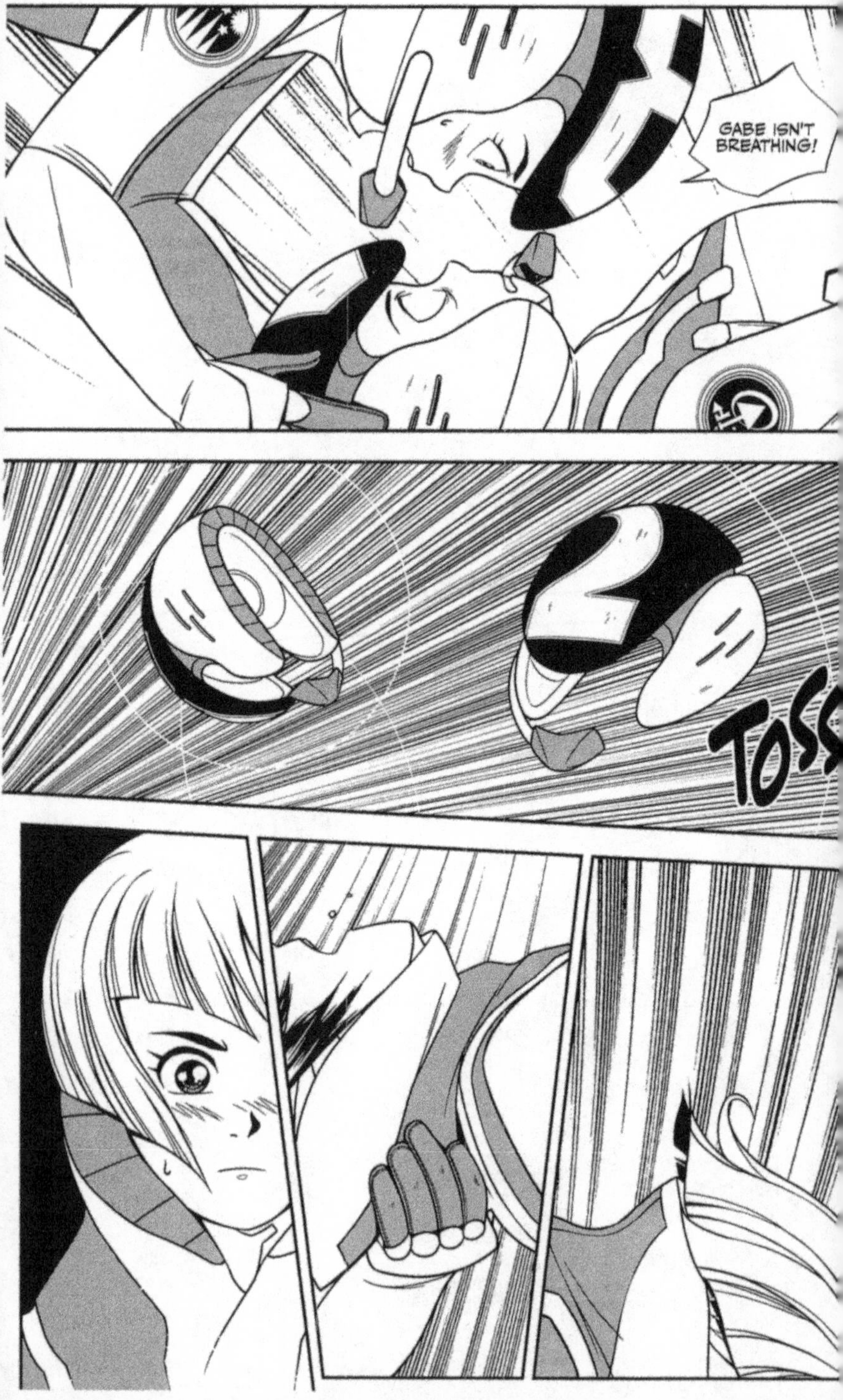
GABE ISN'T BREATHING!
TOSS

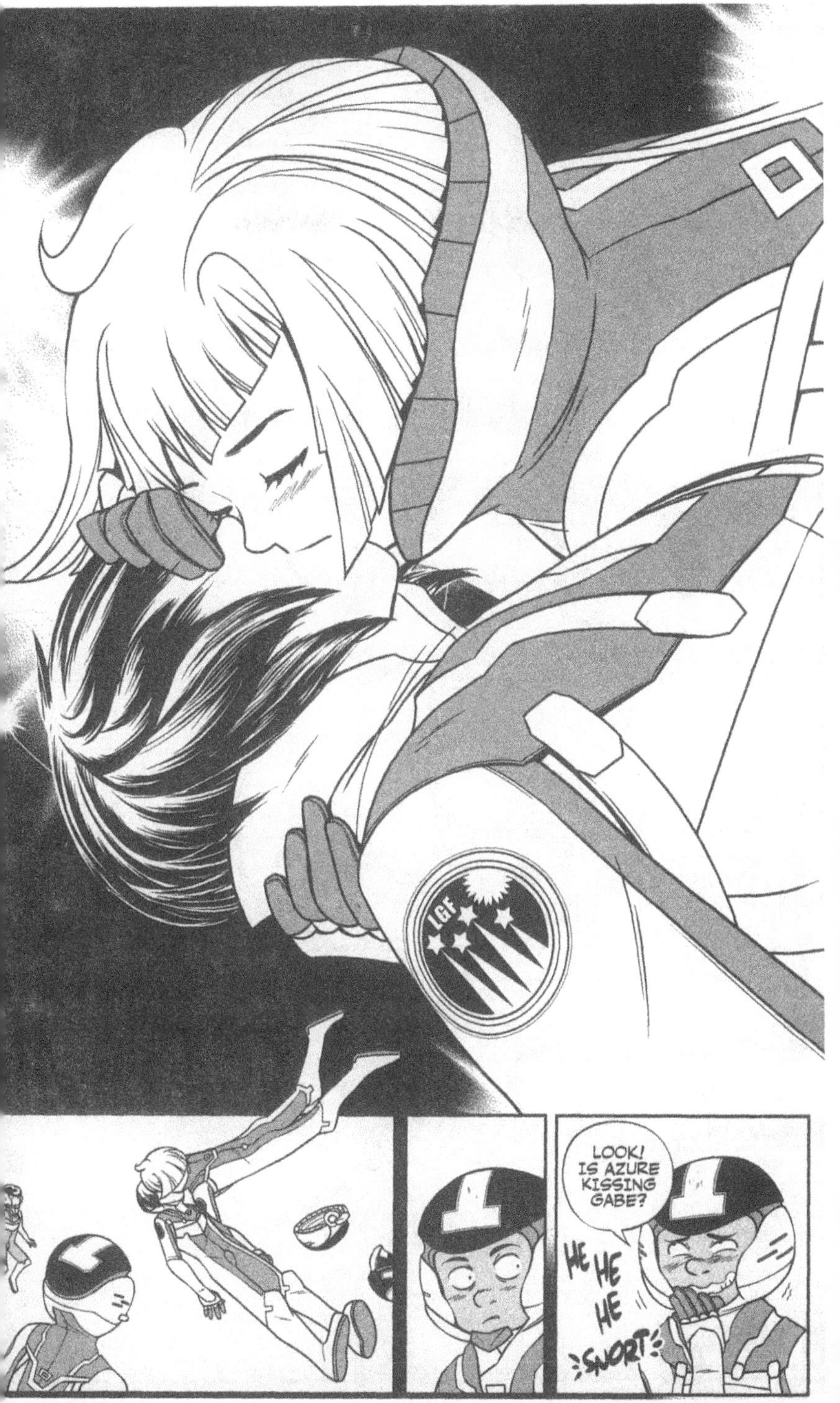
LGF
LOOK! IS AZURE KISSING GABE?
HE HE HE HE
SNORT

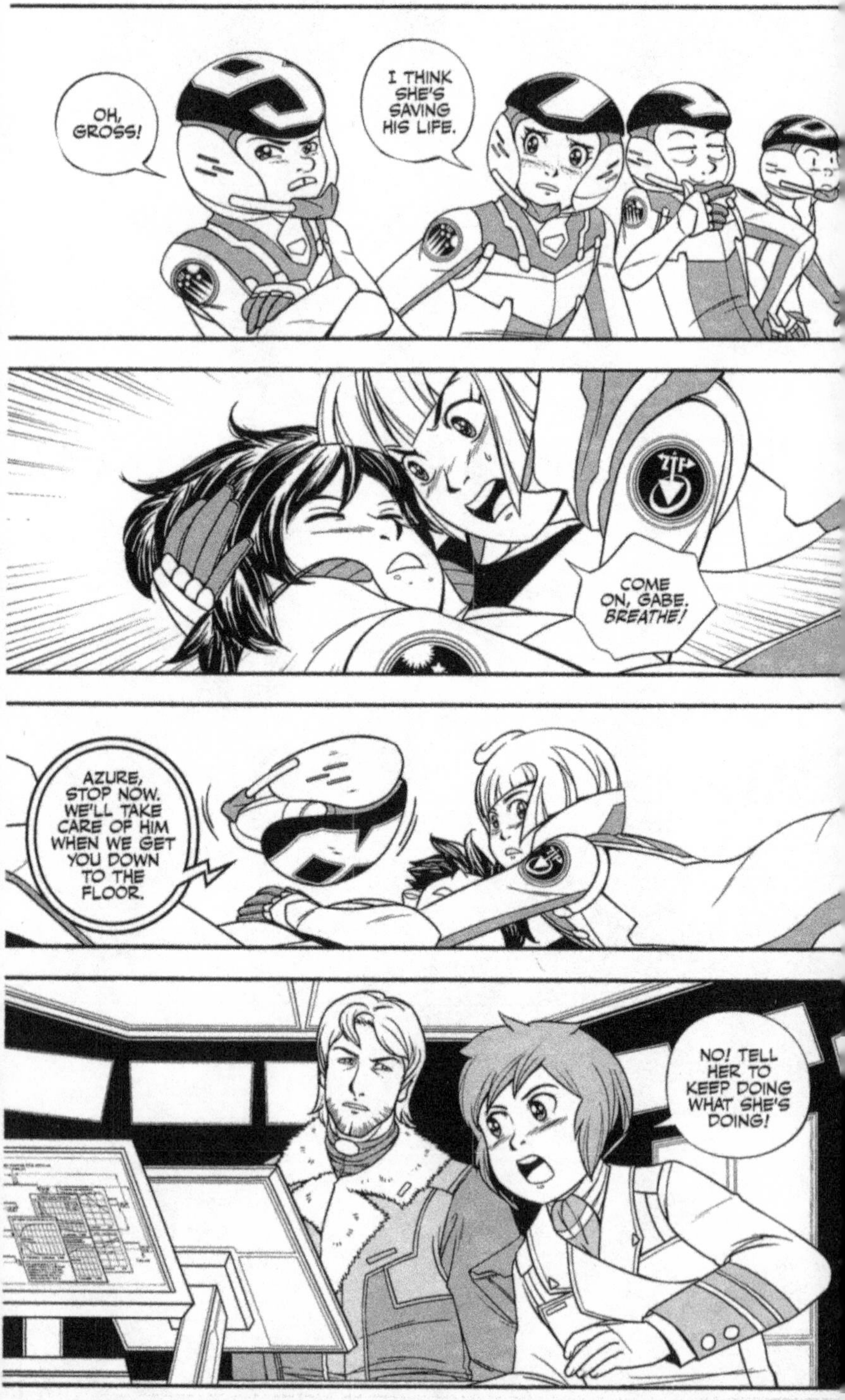
OH, GROSS!
I THINK SHE'S SAVING HIS LIFE.
COME ON, GABE. BREATHE!
AZURE, STOP NOW. WE'LL TAKE CARE OF HIM WHEN WE GET YOU DOWN TO THE FLOOR.
NO! TELL HER TO KEEP DOING WHAT SHE'S DOING!

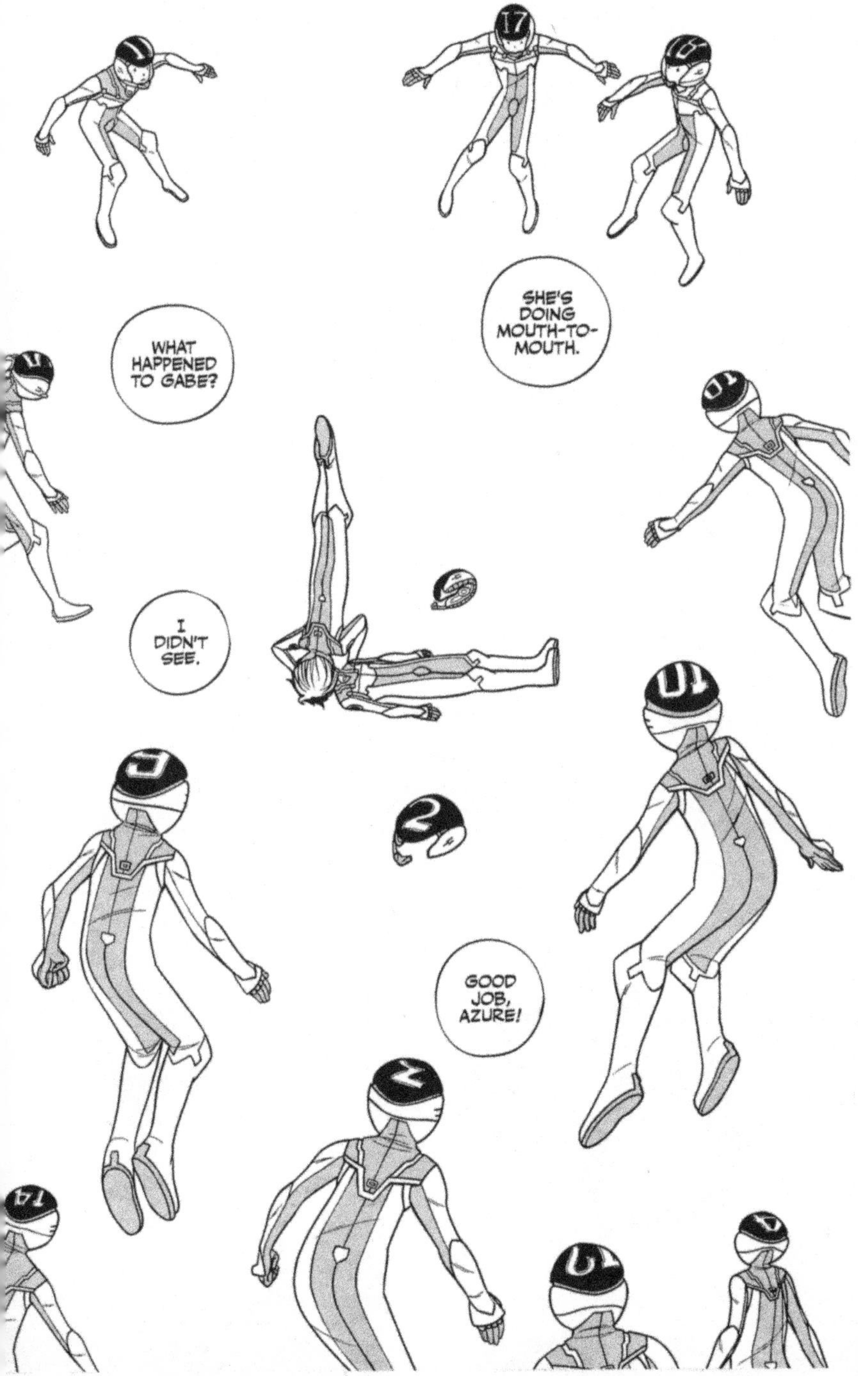
WHAT HAPPENED TO GABE?
SHE'S DOING MOUTH-TO-MOUTH.
I DIDN'T SEE.
GOOD JOB, AZURE!

KLANK
KLANK
KLANK

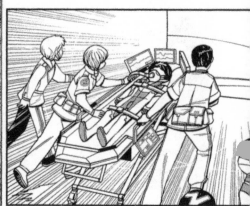

GABE'S GOING TO BE FINE.

SOMEBODY GET HIS HELMET, AND ALL OF YOU GO TAKE OFF THE ZERO-G SUITS.

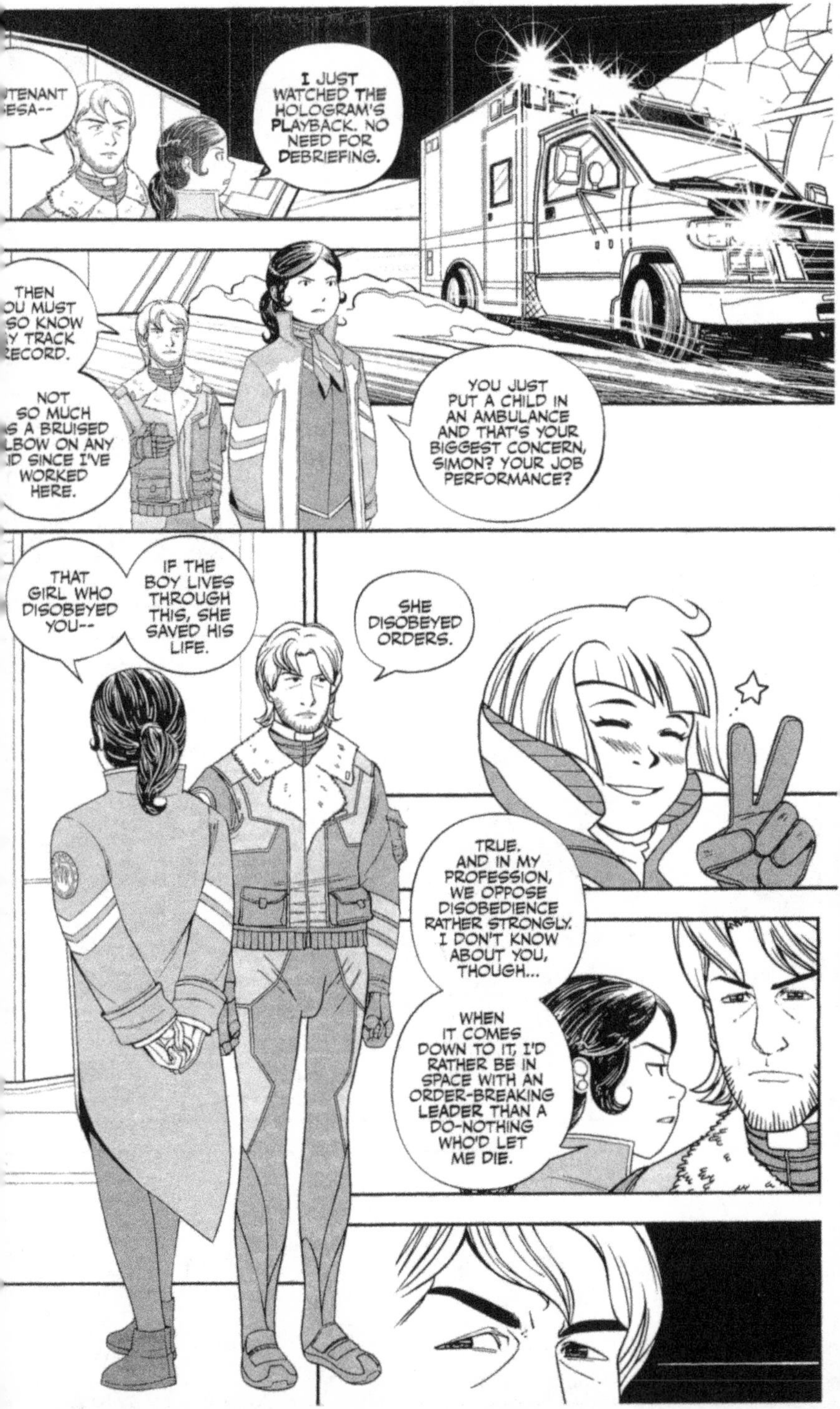
UTENANT ESA--
I JUST WATCHED THE HOLOGRAM'S PLAYBACK. NO NEED FOR DEBRIEFING.
THEN OU MUST SO KNOW Y TRACK ECORD.
NOT SO MUCH S A BRUISED LBOW ON ANY ID SINCE I'VE WORKED HERE.
YOU JUST PUT A CHILD IN AN AMBULANCE AND THAT'S YOUR BIGGEST CONCERN, SIMON? YOUR JOB PERFORMANCE?
THAT GIRL WHO DISOBEYED YOU--
IF THE BOY LIVES THROUGH THIS, SHE SAVED HIS LIFE.
SHE DISOBEYED ORDERS.
TRUE. AND IN MY PROFESSION, WE OPPOSE DISOBEDIENCE RATHER STRONGLY. I DON'T KNOW ABOUT YOU, THOUGH...
WHEN IT COMES DOWN TO IT, I'D RATHER BE IN SPACE WITH AN ORDER-BREAKING LEADER THAN A DO-NOTHING WHO'D LET ME DIE.

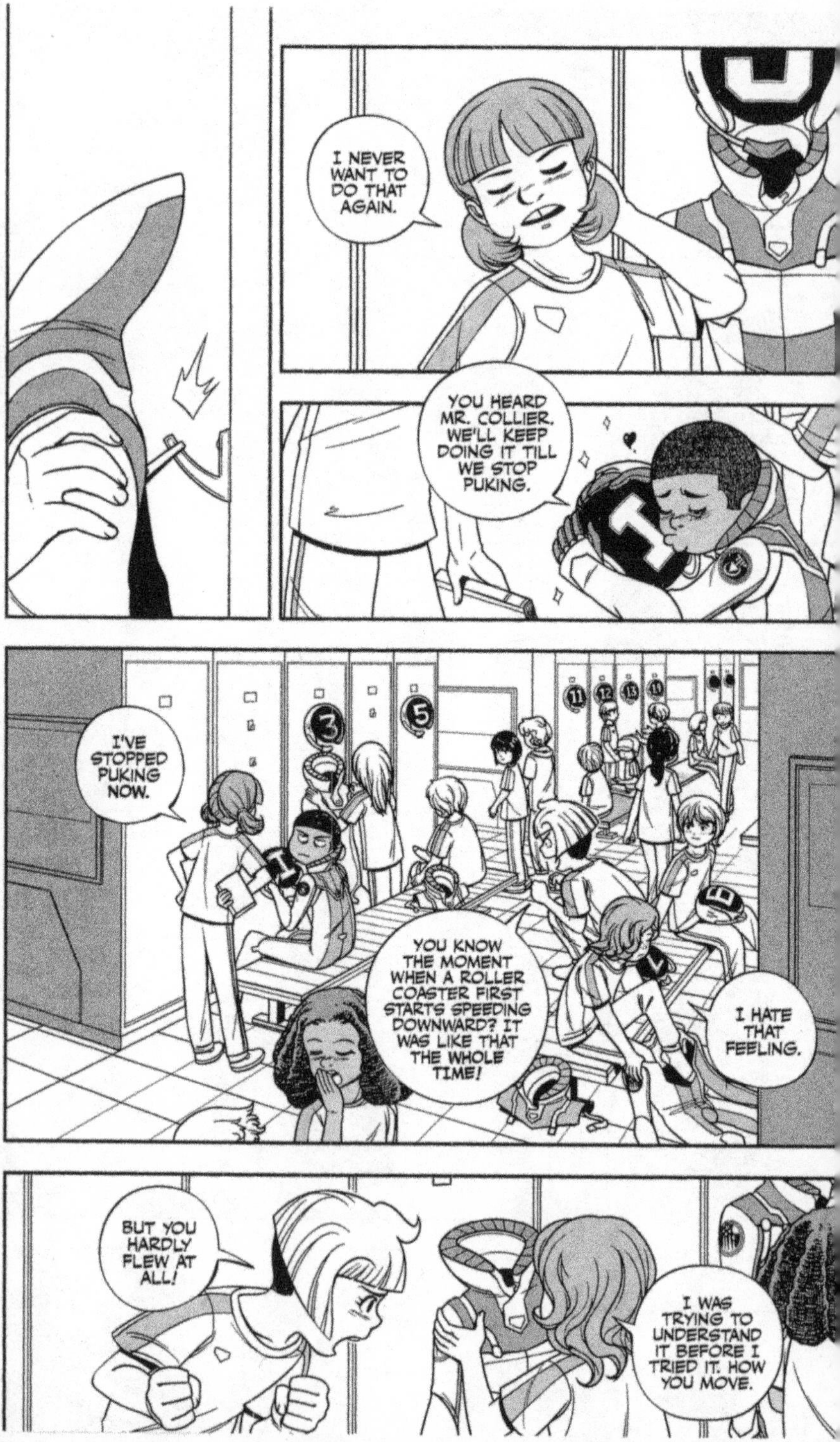
I NEVER WANT TO DO THAT AGAIN.
YOU HEARD MR. COLLIER. WE'LL KEEP DOING IT TILL WE STOP PUKING.
I'VE STOPPED PUKING NOW.
YOU KNOW THE MOMENT WHEN A ROLLER COASTER FIRST STARTS SPEEDING DOWNWARD? IT WAS LIKE THAT THE WHOLE TIME!
I HATE THAT FEELING.
BUT YOU HARDLY FLEW AT ALL!
I WAS TRYING TO UNDERSTAND IT BEFORE I TRIED IT. HOW YOU MOVE.

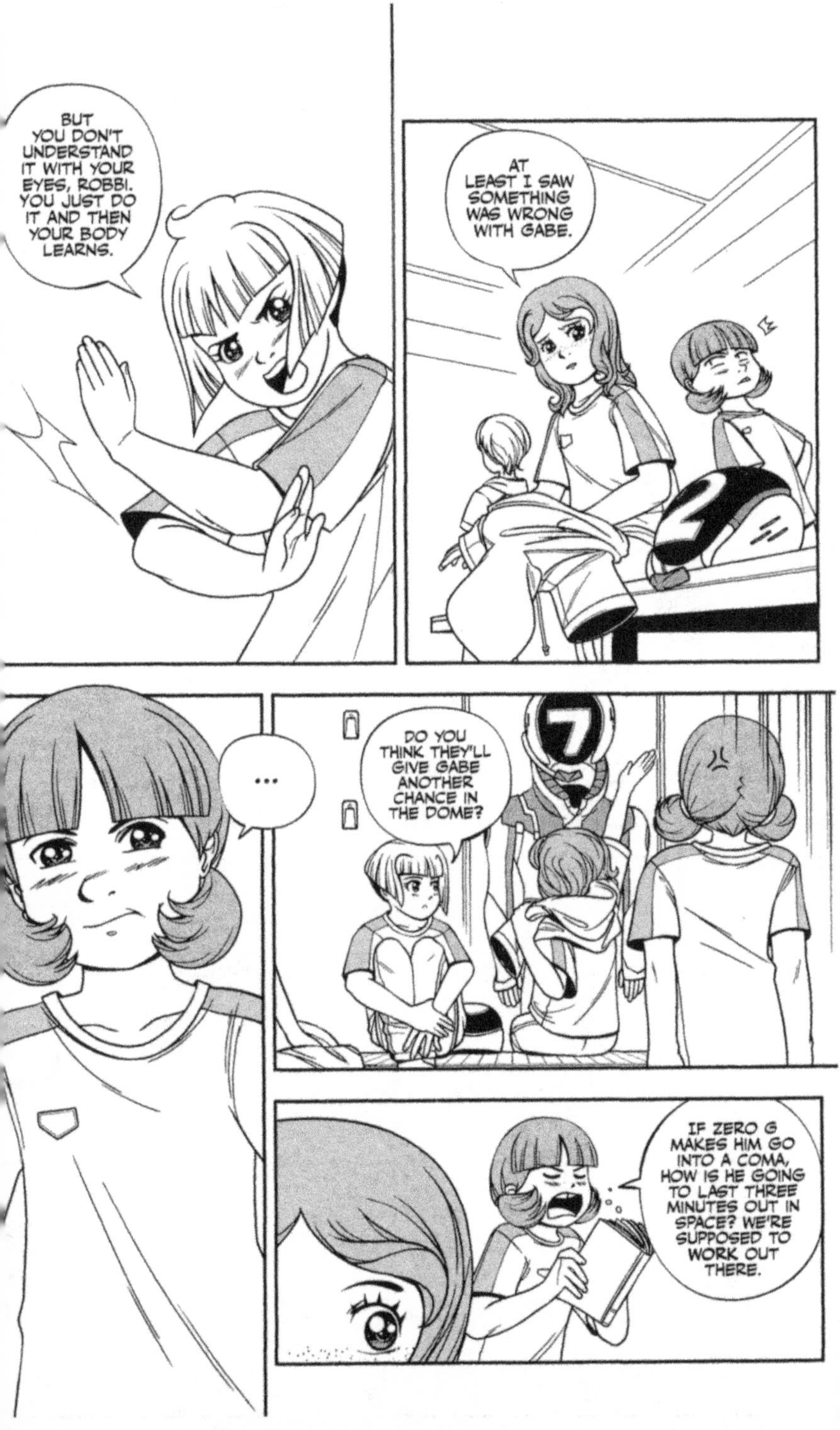
BUT YOU DON'T UNDERSTAND IT WITH YOUR EYES, ROBBI. YOU JUST DO IT AND THEN YOUR BODY LEARNS.
AT LEAST I SAW SOMETHING WAS WRONG WITH GABE.
...
DO YOU THINK THEY'LL GIVE GABE ANOTHER CHANCE IN THE DOME?
IF ZERO G MAKES HIM GO INTO A COMA, HOW IS HE GOING TO LAST THREE MINUTES OUT IN SPACE? WE'RE SUPPOSED TO WORK OUT THERE.

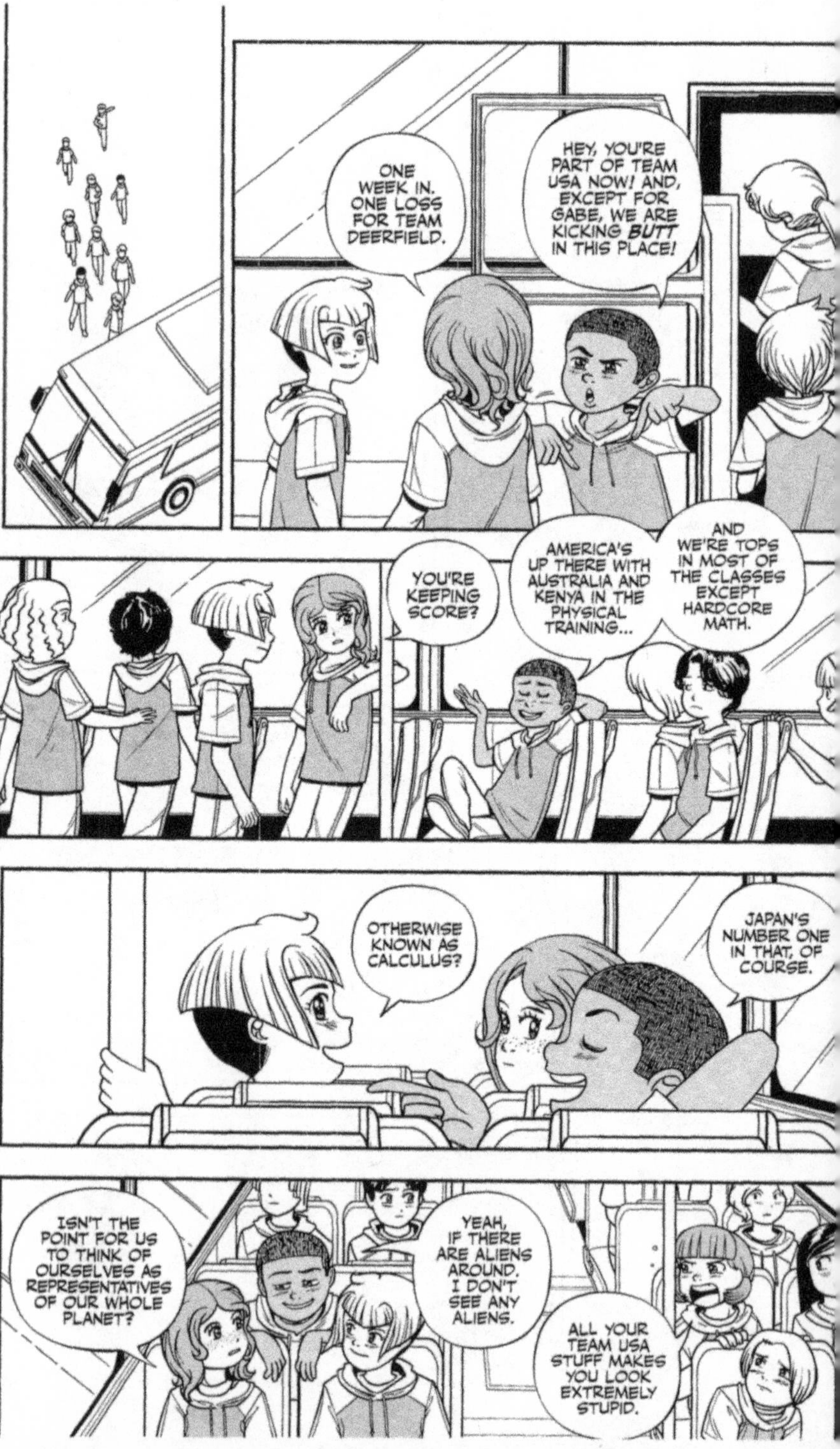
ONE WEEK IN. ONE LOSS FOR TEAM DEERFIELD.
HEY, YOU'RE PART OF TEAM USA NOW! AND, EXCEPT FOR GABE, WE ARE KICKING *BUTT* IN THIS PLACE!
YOU'RE KEEPING SCORE?
AMERICA'S UP THERE WITH AUSTRALIA AND KENYA IN THE PHYSICAL TRAINING...
AND WE'RE TOPS IN MOST OF THE CLASSES EXCEPT HARDCORE MATH.
OTHERWISE KNOWN AS CALCULUS?
JAPAN'S NUMBER ONE IN THAT, OF COURSE.
ISN'T THE POINT FOR US TO THINK OF OURSELVES AS REPRESENTATIVES OF OUR WHOLE PLANET?
YEAH, IF THERE ARE ALIENS AROUND. I DON'T SEE ANY ALIENS.
ALL YOUR TEAM USA STUFF MAKES YOU LOOK EXTREMELY STUPID.

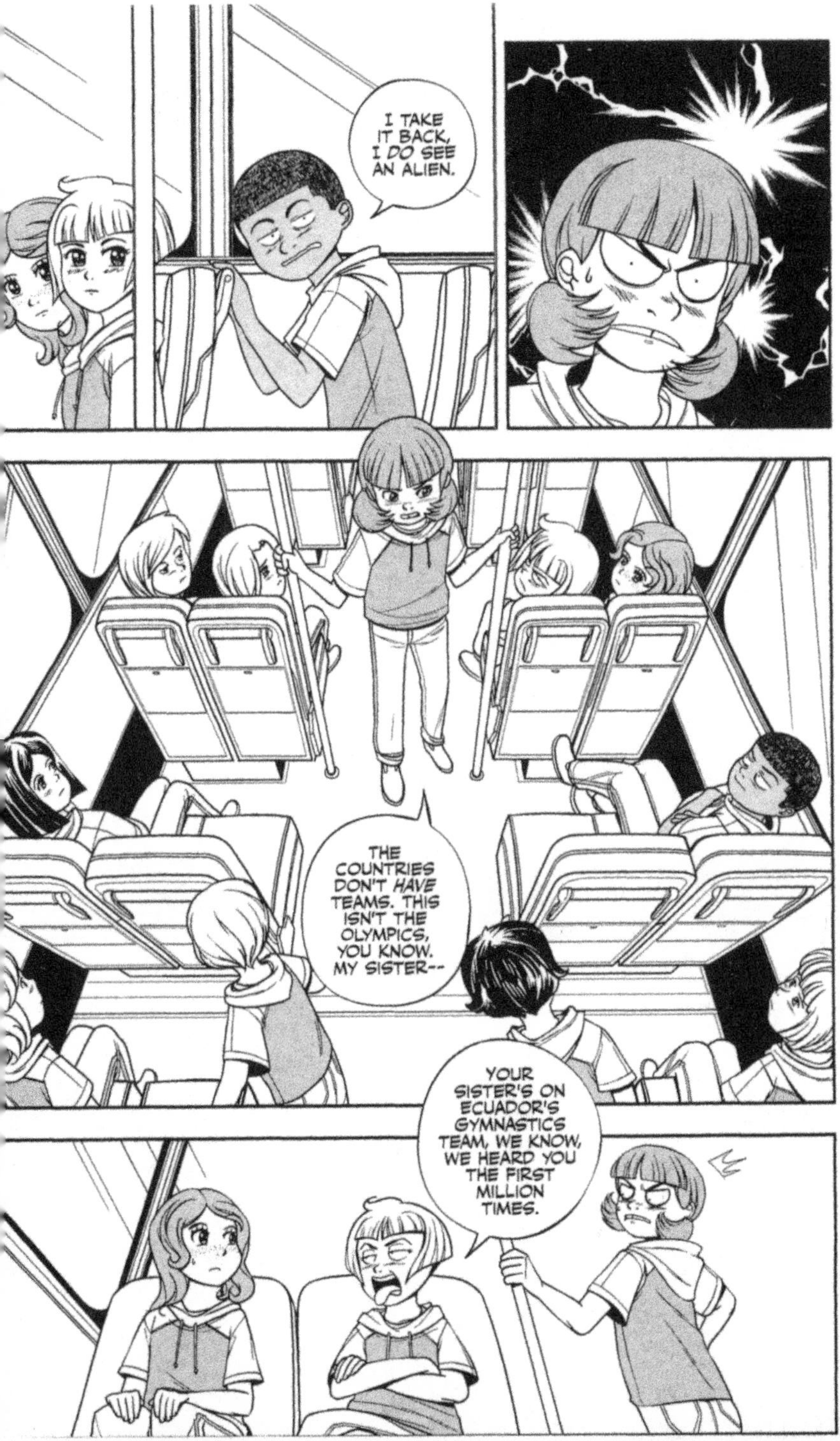
I TAKE IT BACK, I *DO* SEE AN ALIEN.
THE COUNTRIES DON'T *HAVE* TEAMS. THIS ISN'T THE OLYMPICS, YOU KNOW. MY SISTER--
YOUR SISTER'S ON ECUADOR'S GYMNASTICS TEAM, WE KNOW, WE HEARD YOU THE FIRST MILLION TIMES.

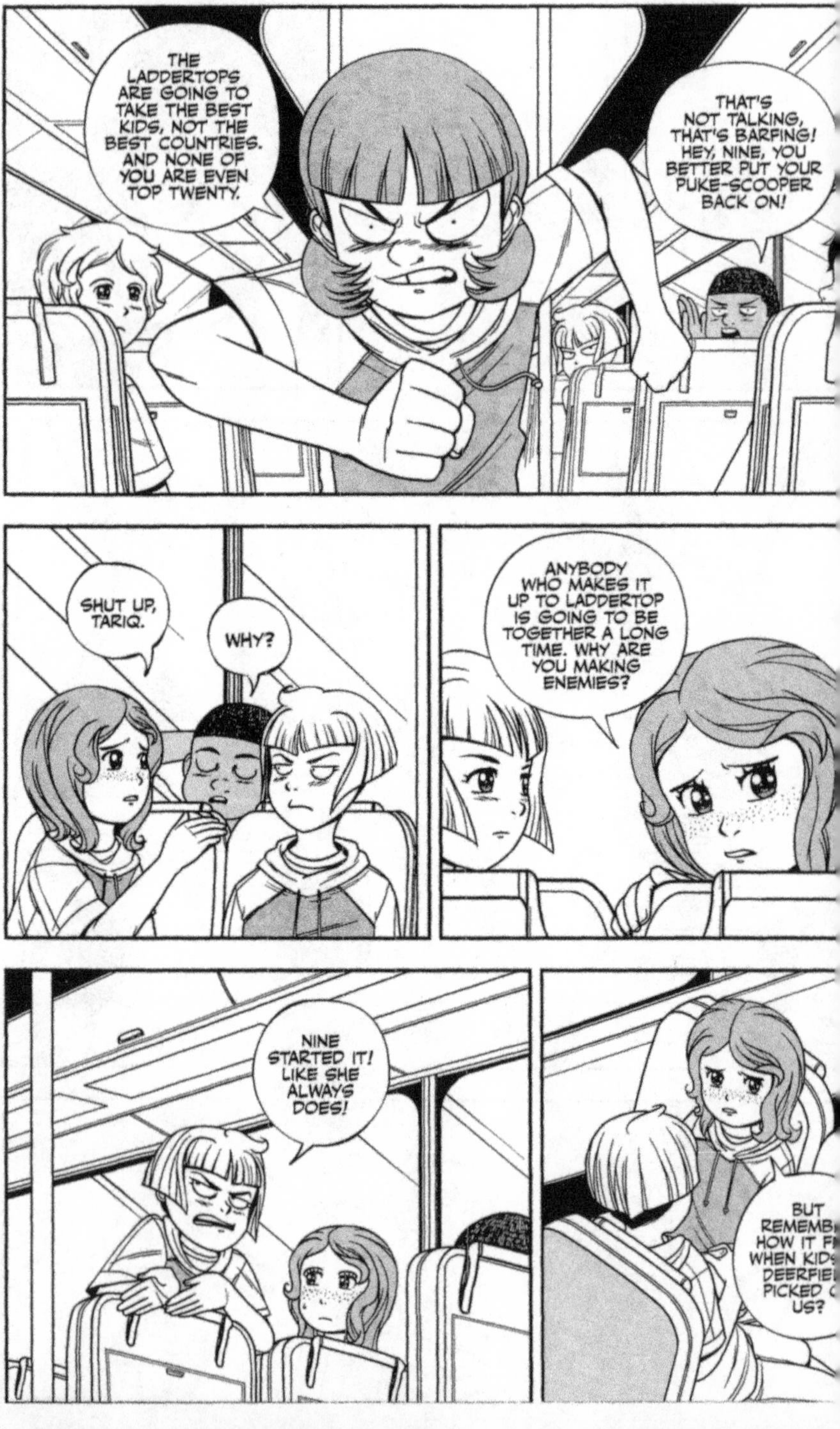
THE LADDERTOPS ARE GOING TO TAKE THE BEST KIDS, NOT THE BEST COUNTRIES. AND NONE OF YOU ARE EVEN TOP TWENTY.
THAT'S NOT TALKING, THAT'S BARFING! HEY, NINE, YOU BETTER PUT YOUR PUKE-SCOOPER BACK ON!
SHUT UP, TARIQ.
WHY?
ANYBODY WHO MAKES IT UP TO LADDERTOP IS GOING TO BE TOGETHER A LONG TIME. WHY ARE YOU MAKING ENEMIES?
NINE STARTED IT! LIKE SHE ALWAYS DOES!
BUT REMEMB HOW IT F WHEN KIDS DEERFIE PICKED US?

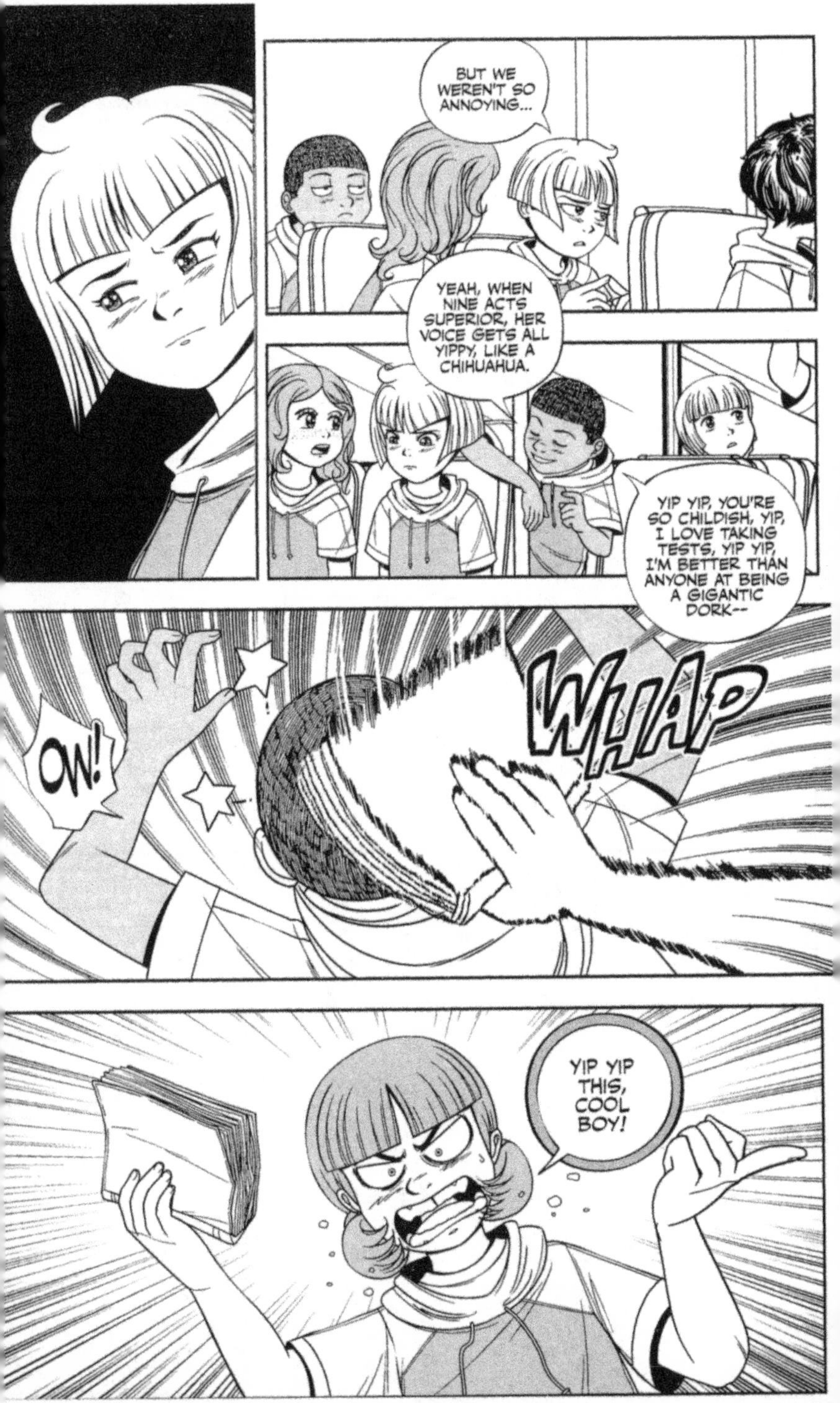
BUT WE WEREN'T SO ANNOYING...
YEAH, WHEN NINE ACTS SUPERIOR, HER VOICE GETS ALL YIPPY, LIKE A CHIHUAHUA.
YIP YIP, YOU'RE SO CHILDISH, YIP, I LOVE TAKING TESTS, YIP YIP, I'M BETTER THAN ANYONE AT BEING A GIGANTIC DORK--
OW!
WHAP
YIP YIP THIS, COOL BOY!

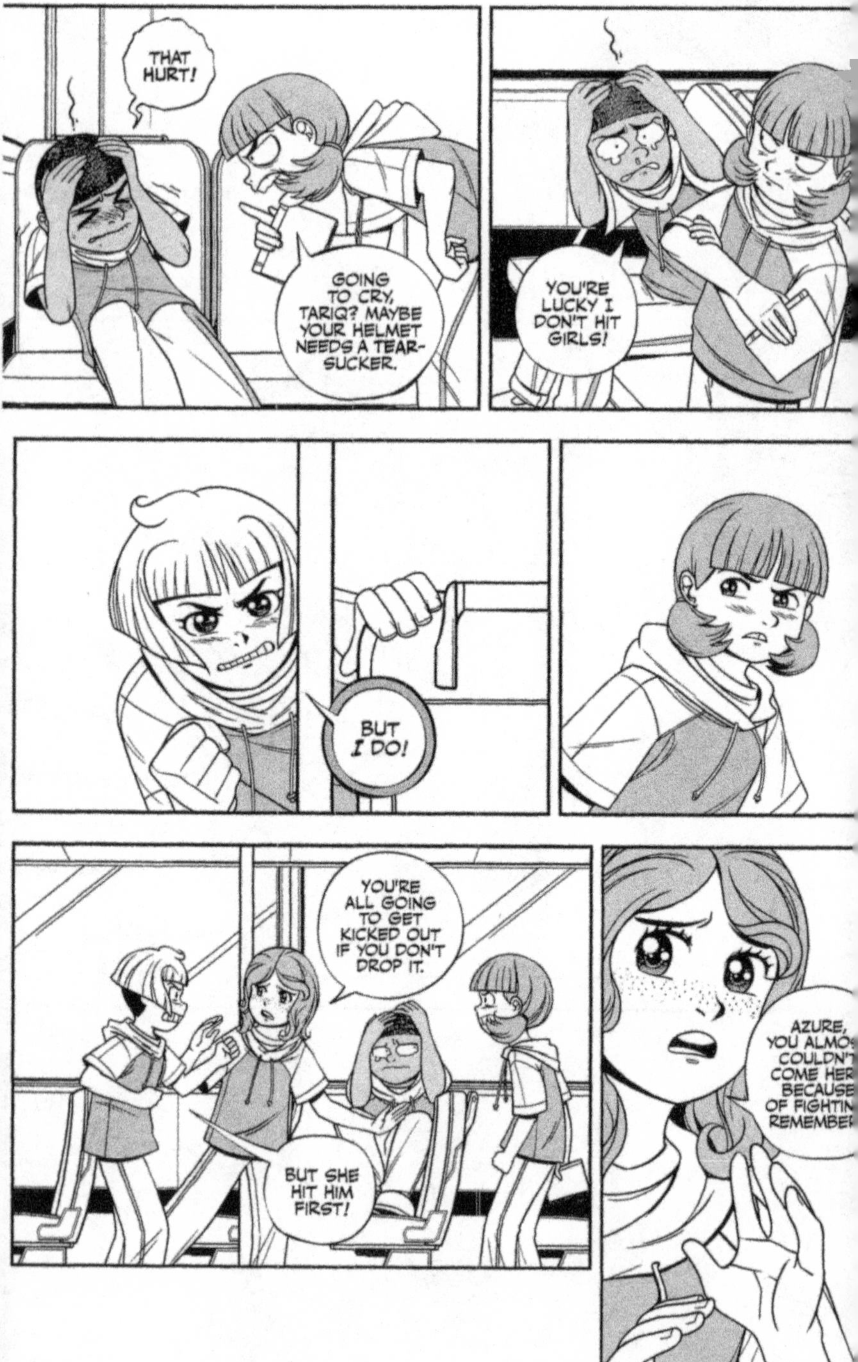
THAT HURT!
GOING TO CRY, TARIQ? MAYBE YOUR HELMET NEEDS A TEAR-SUCKER.
YOU'RE LUCKY I DON'T HIT GIRLS!
BUT I DO!
YOU'RE ALL GOING TO GET KICKED OUT IF YOU DON'T DROP IT.
BUT SHE HIT HIM FIRST!

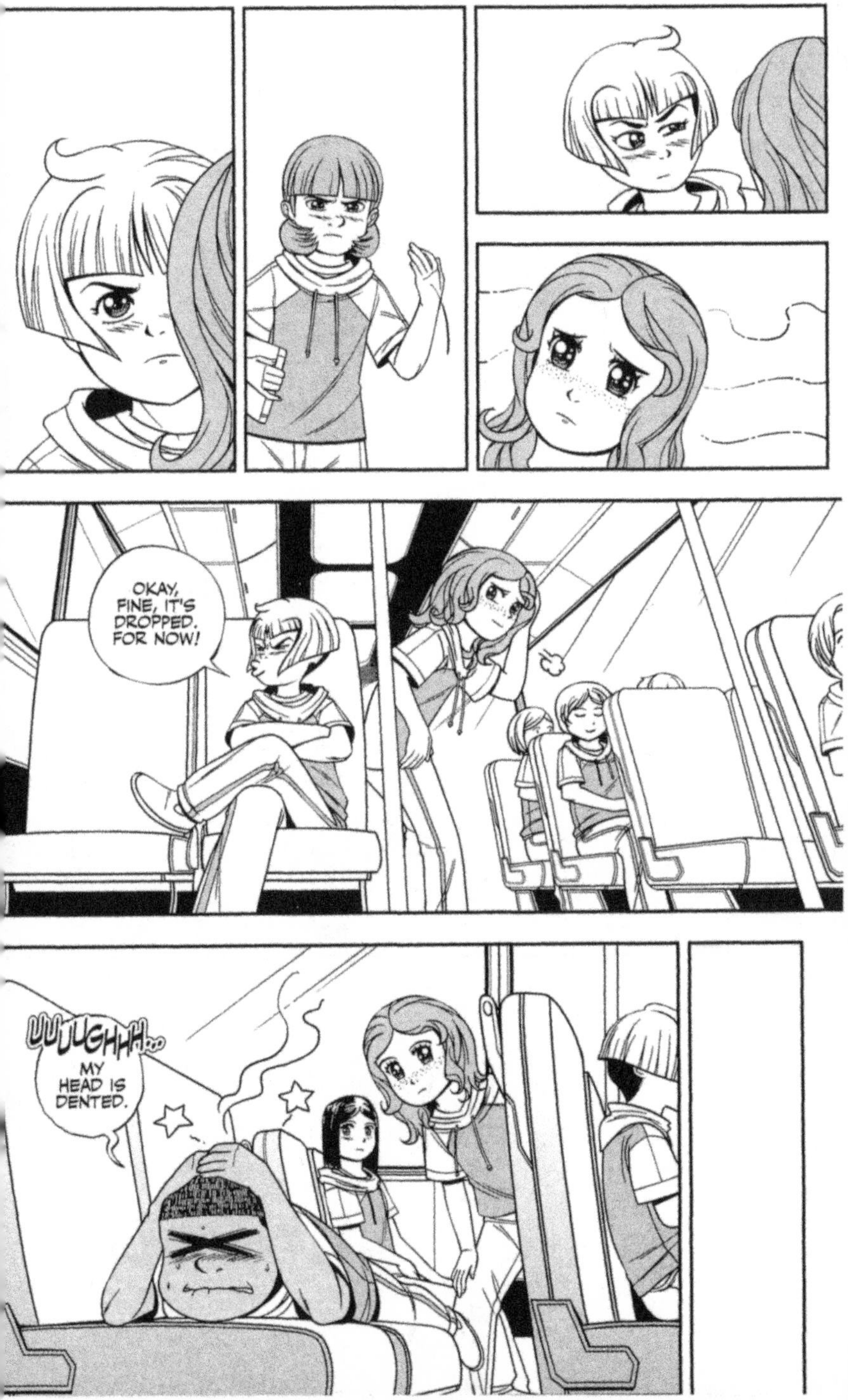
OKAY, FINE, IT'S DROPPED. FOR NOW!
UUUUGHHH...
MY HEAD IS DENTED.

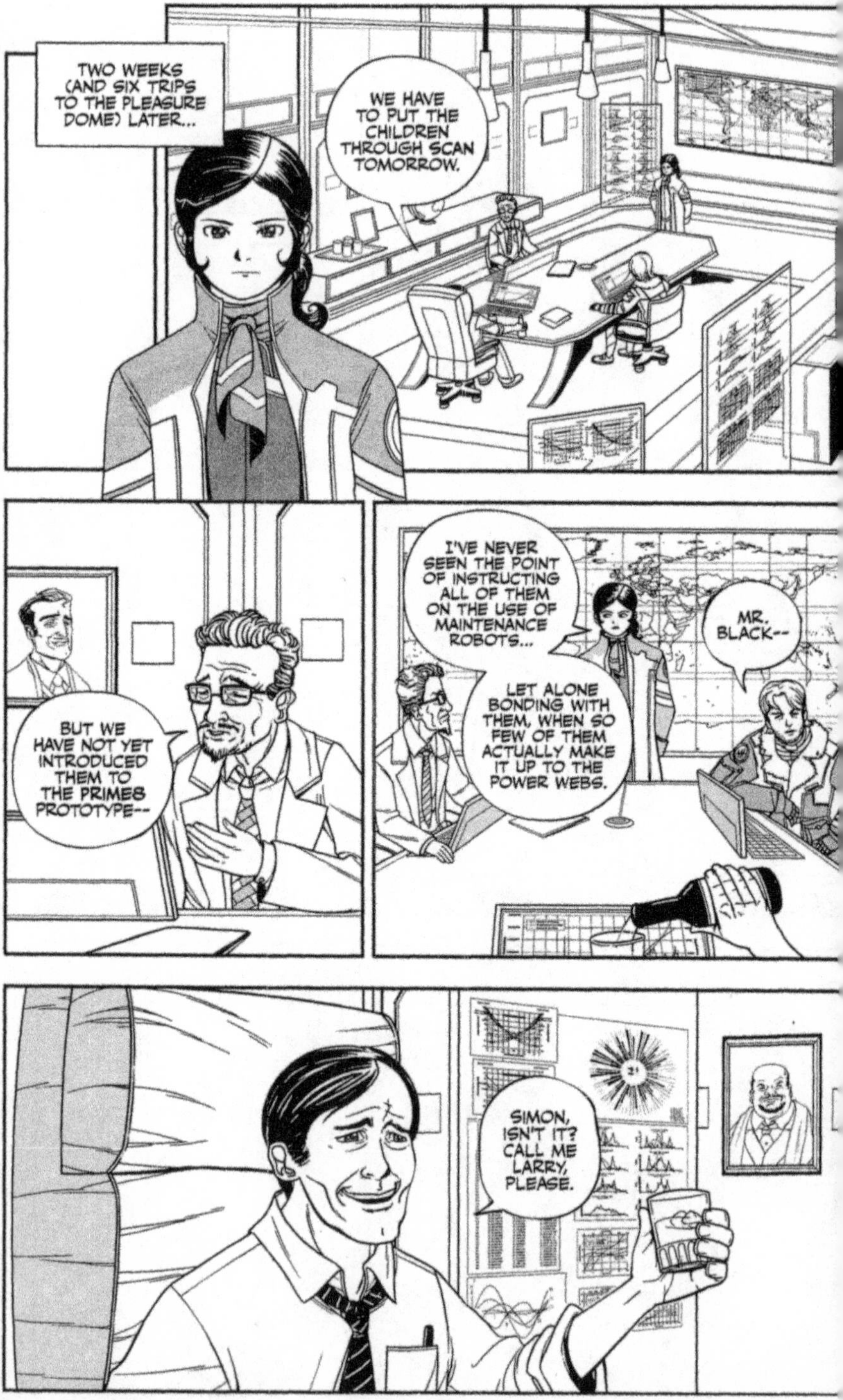
TWO WEEKS (AND SIX TRIPS TO THE PLEASURE DOME) LATER...
WE HAVE TO PUT THE CHILDREN THROUGH SCAN TOMORROW.
BUT WE HAVE NOT YET INTRODUCED THEM TO THE PRIMES PROTOTYPE--
I'VE NEVER SEEN THE POINT OF INSTRUCTING ALL OF THEM ON THE USE OF MAINTENANCE ROBOTS...
LET ALONE BONDING WITH THEM, WHEN SO FEW OF THEM ACTUALLY MAKE IT UP TO THE POWER WEBS.
MR. BLACK--
SIMON, ISN'T IT? CALL ME LARRY, PLEASE.

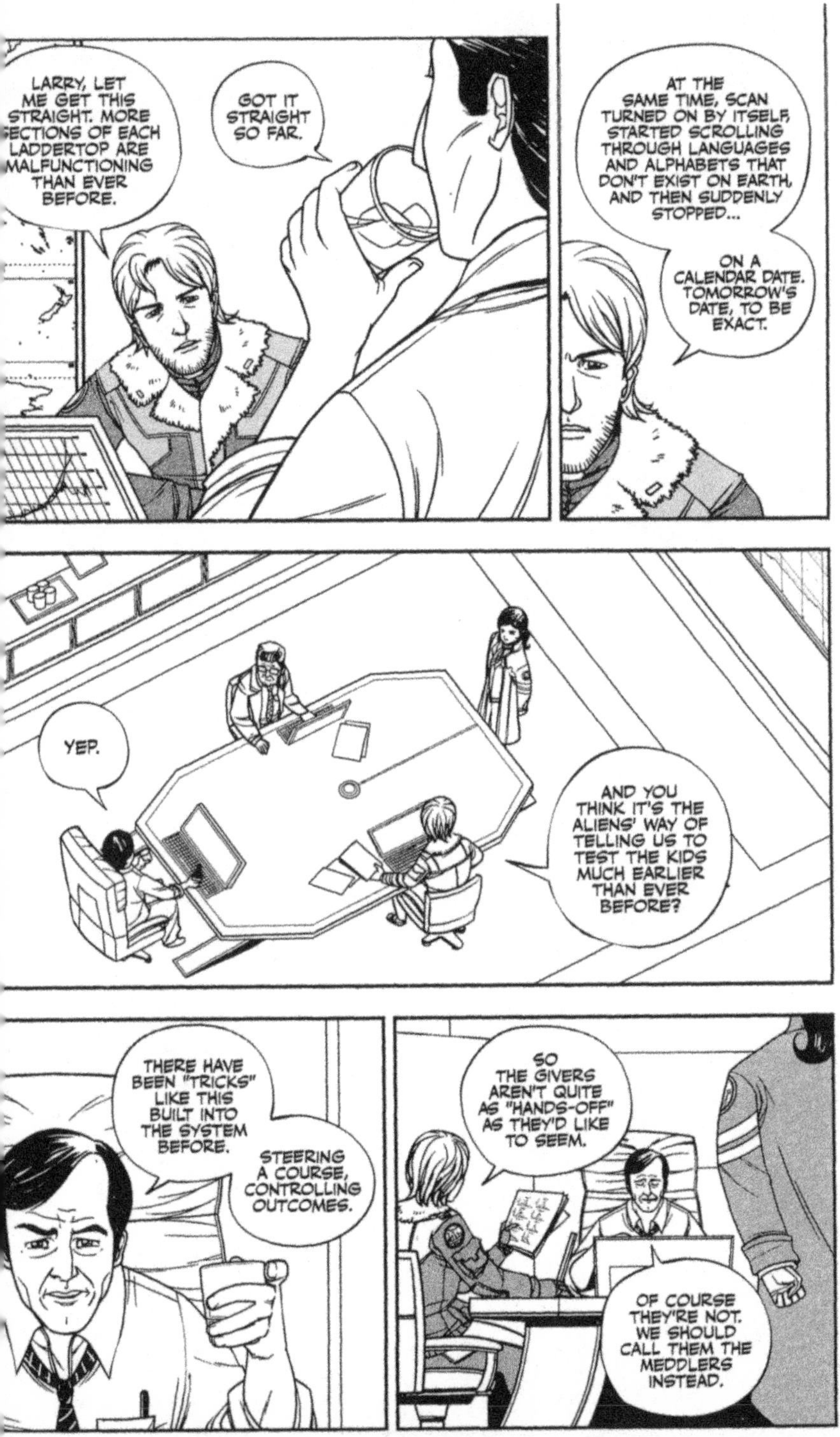
LARRY, LET ME GET THIS STRAIGHT. MORE SECTIONS OF EACH LADDERTOP ARE MALFUNCTIONING THAN EVER BEFORE.
GOT IT STRAIGHT SO FAR.
AT THE SAME TIME, SCAN TURNED ON BY ITSELF, STARTED SCROLLING THROUGH LANGUAGES AND ALPHABETS THAT DON'T EXIST ON EARTH, AND THEN SUDDENLY STOPPED...
ON A CALENDAR DATE. TOMORROW'S DATE, TO BE EXACT.
YEP.
AND YOU THINK IT'S THE ALIENS' WAY OF TELLING US TO TEST THE KIDS MUCH EARLIER THAN EVER BEFORE?
THERE HAVE BEEN "TRICKS" LIKE THIS BUILT INTO THE SYSTEM BEFORE.
STEERING A COURSE, CONTROLLING OUTCOMES.
SO THE GIVERS AREN'T QUITE AS "HANDS-OFF" AS THEY'D LIKE TO SEEM.
OF COURSE THEY'RE NOT. WE SHOULD CALL THEM THE MEDDLERS INSTEAD.

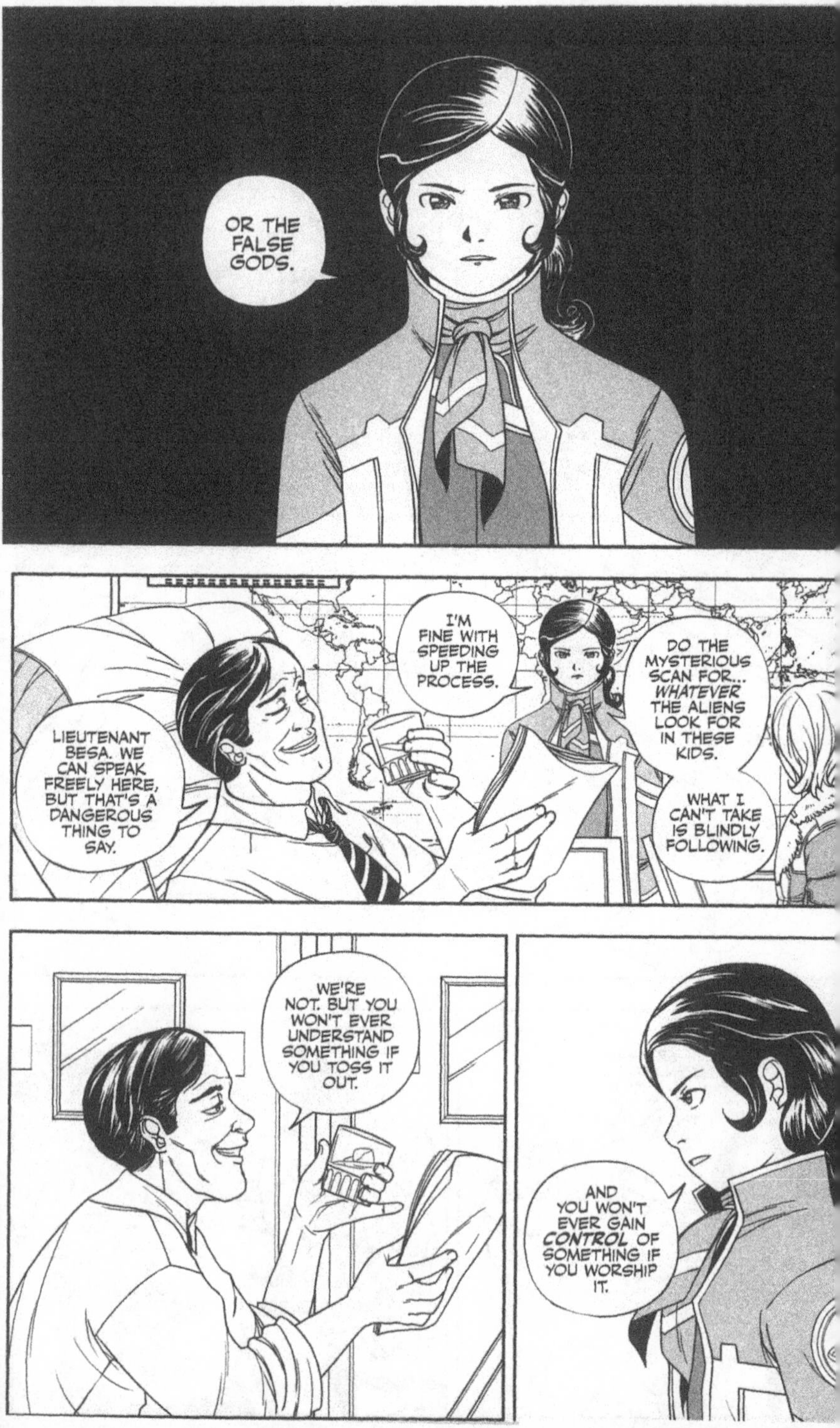
OR THE FALSE GODS.
LIEUTENANT BESA. WE CAN SPEAK FREELY HERE, BUT THAT'S A DANGEROUS THING TO SAY.
I'M FINE WITH SPEEDING UP THE PROCESS.
DO THE MYSTERIOUS SCAN FOR... *WHATEVER* THE ALIENS LOOK FOR IN THESE KIDS.
WHAT I CAN'T TAKE IS BLINDLY FOLLOWING.
WE'RE NOT. BUT YOU WON'T EVER UNDERSTAND SOMETHING IF YOU TOSS IT OUT.
AND YOU WON'T EVER GAIN **CONTROL** OF SOMETHING IF YOU WORSHIP IT.

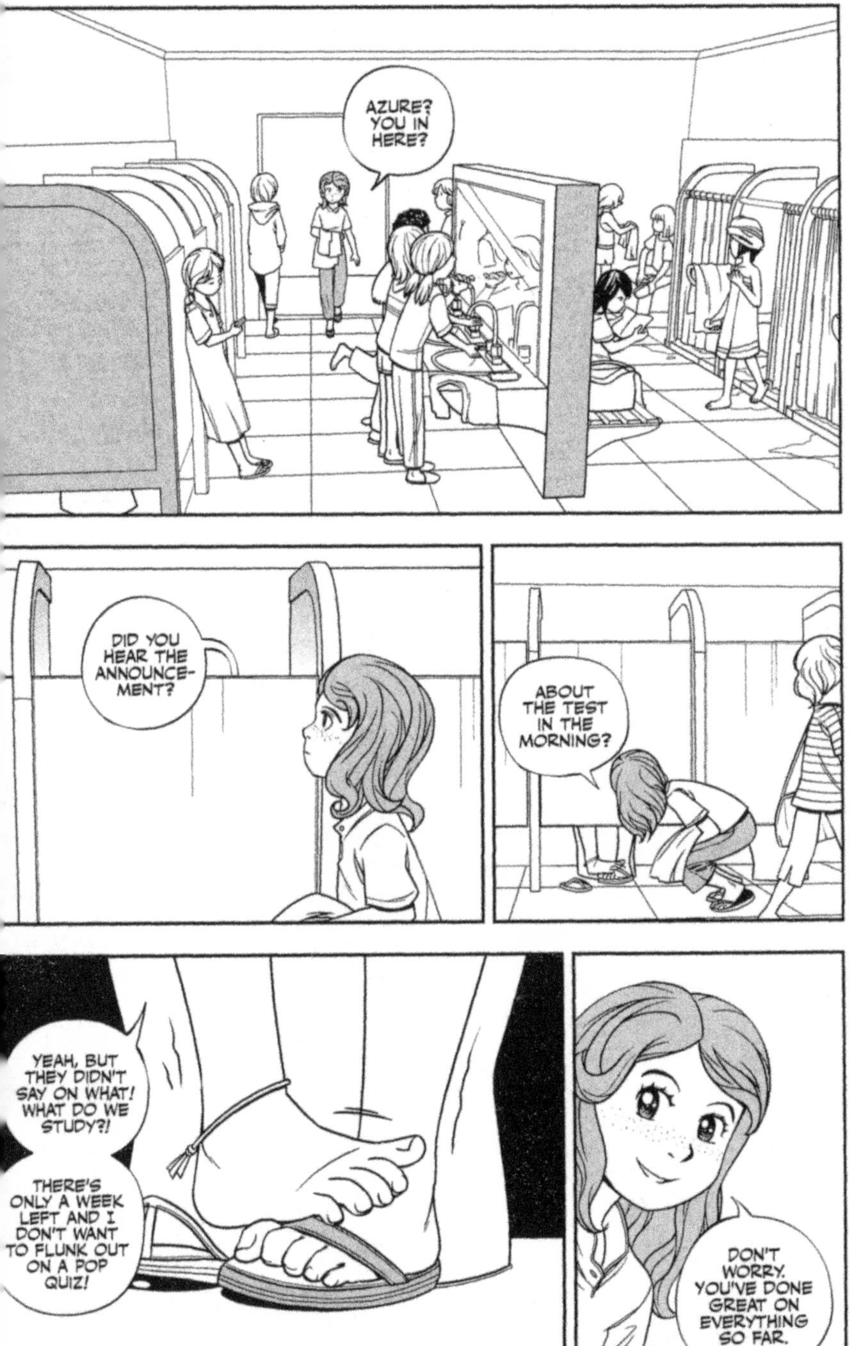
AZURE? YOU IN HERE?
DID YOU HEAR THE ANNOUNCE-MENT?
ABOUT THE TEST IN THE MORNING?
YEAH, BUT THEY DIDN'T SAY ON WHAT! WHAT DO WE STUDY?!
THERE'S ONLY A WEEK LEFT AND I DON'T WANT TO FLUNK OUT ON A POP QUIZ!
DON'T WORRY. YOU'VE DONE GREAT ON EVERYTHING SO FAR.

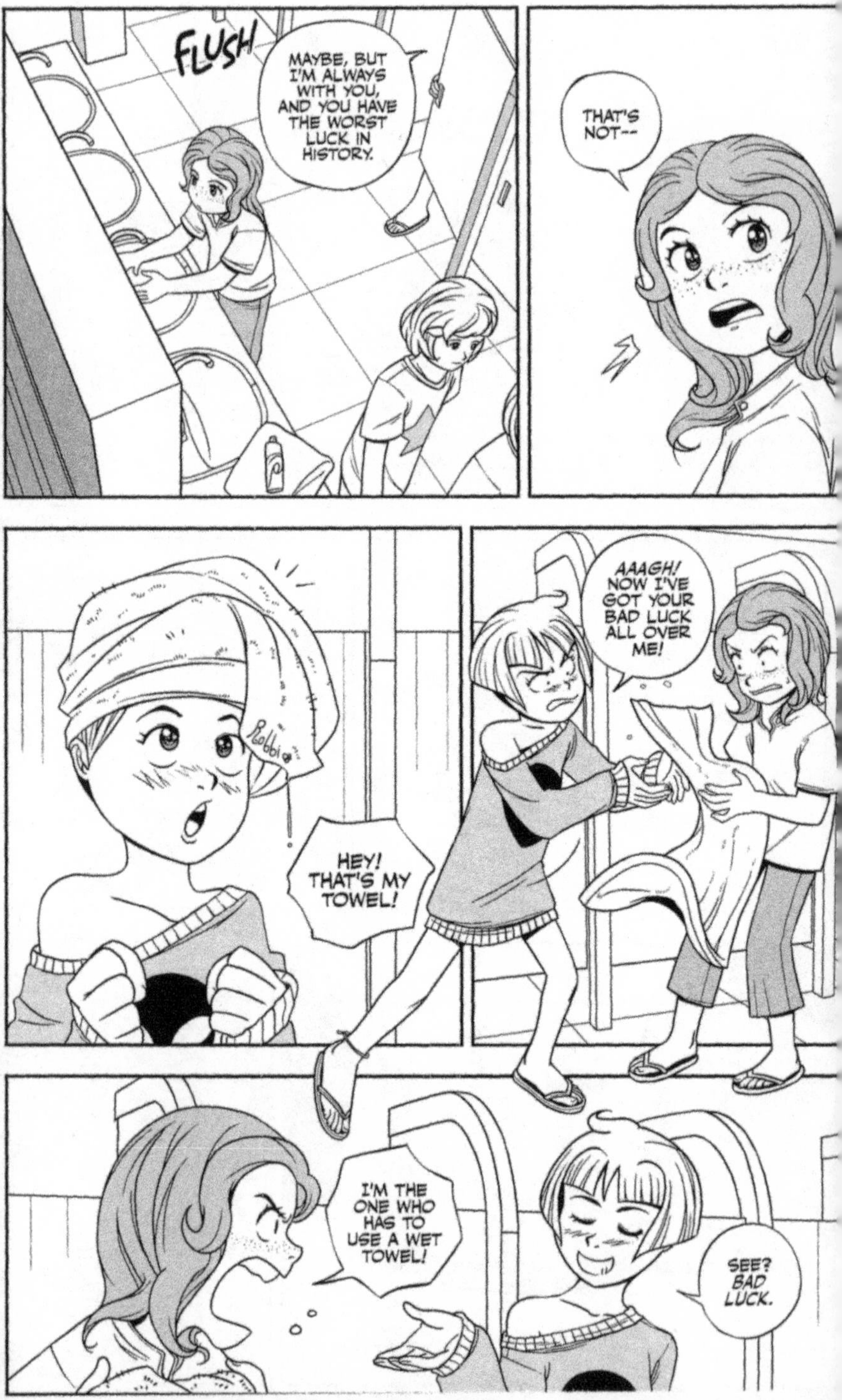
FLUSH
MAYBE, BUT I'M ALWAYS WITH YOU, AND YOU HAVE THE WORST LUCK IN HISTORY.
THAT'S NOT--
HEY! THAT'S MY TOWEL!
AAAGH! NOW I'VE GOT YOUR BAD LUCK ALL OVER ME!
I'M THE ONE WHO HAS TO USE A WET TOWEL!
SEE? BAD LUCK.

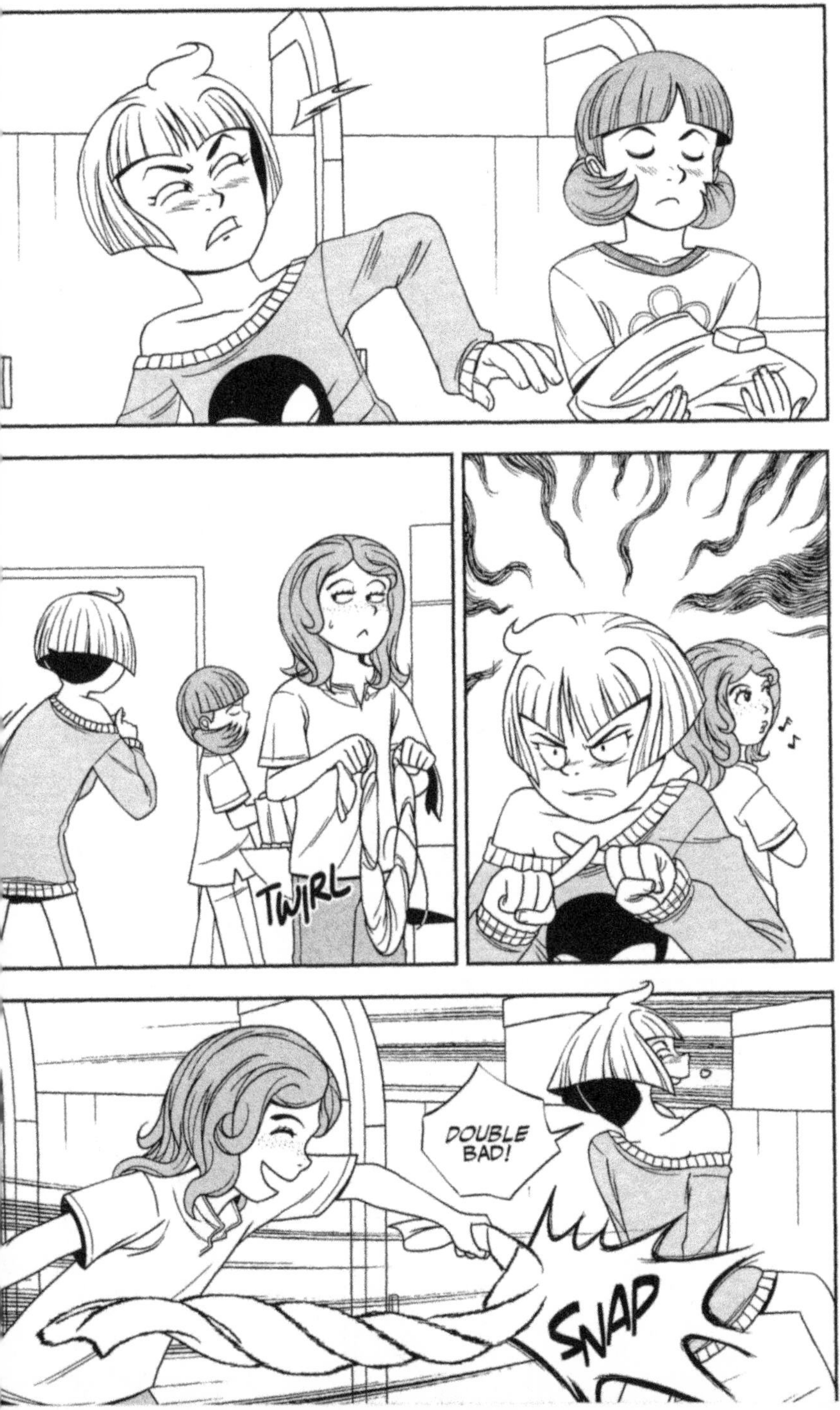
TWIRL
DOUBLE BAD!
SNAP

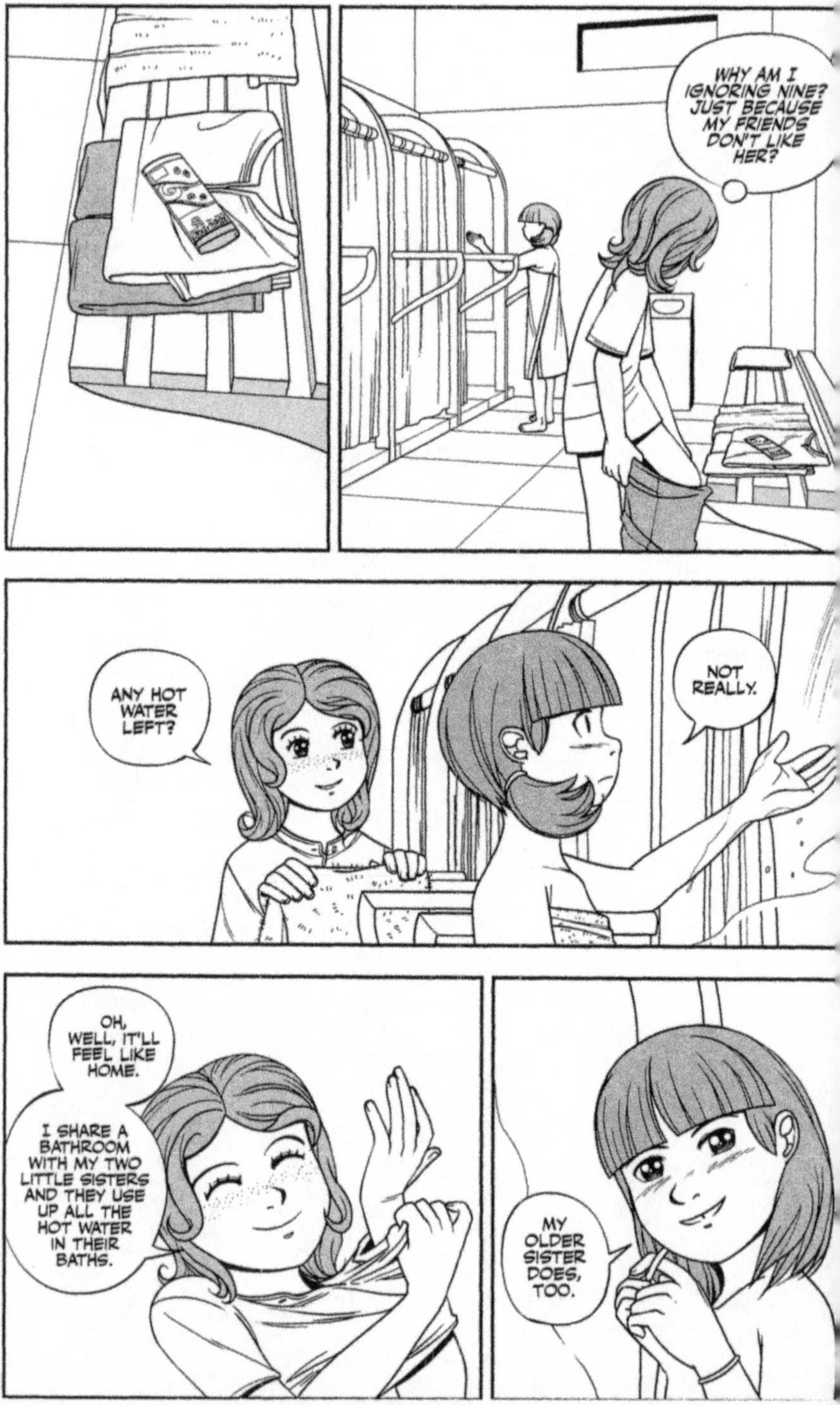
WHY AM I IGNORING NINE? JUST BECAUSE MY FRIENDS DON'T LIKE HER?
ANY HOT WATER LEFT?
NOT REALLY.
OH, WELL, IT'LL FEEL LIKE HOME.
I SHARE A BATHROOM WITH MY TWO LITTLE SISTERS AND THEY USE UP ALL THE HOT WATER IN THEIR BATHS.
MY OLDER SISTER DOES, TOO.

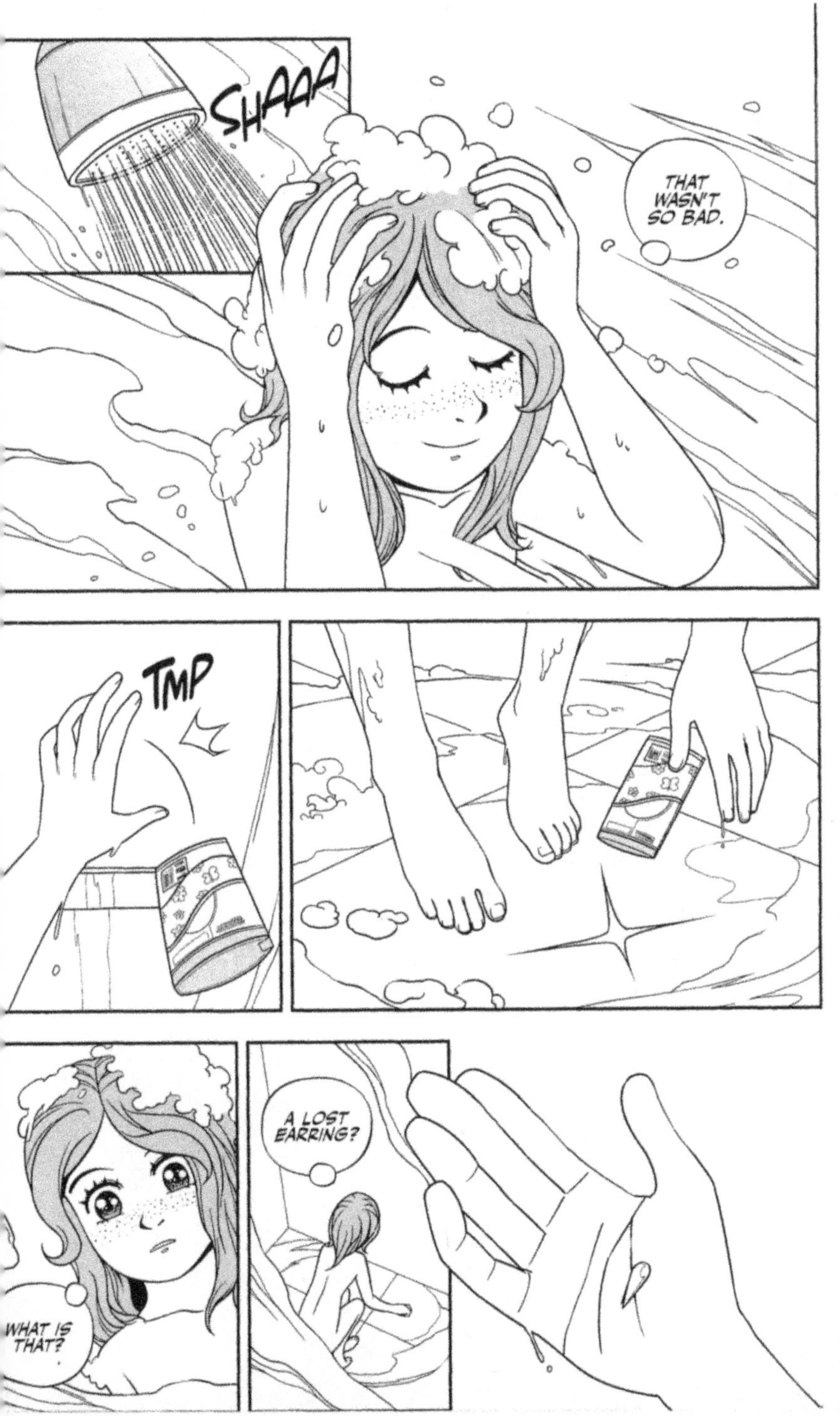
SHAAA
THAT WASN'T SO BAD.
TMP
WHAT IS THAT?
A LOST EARRING?

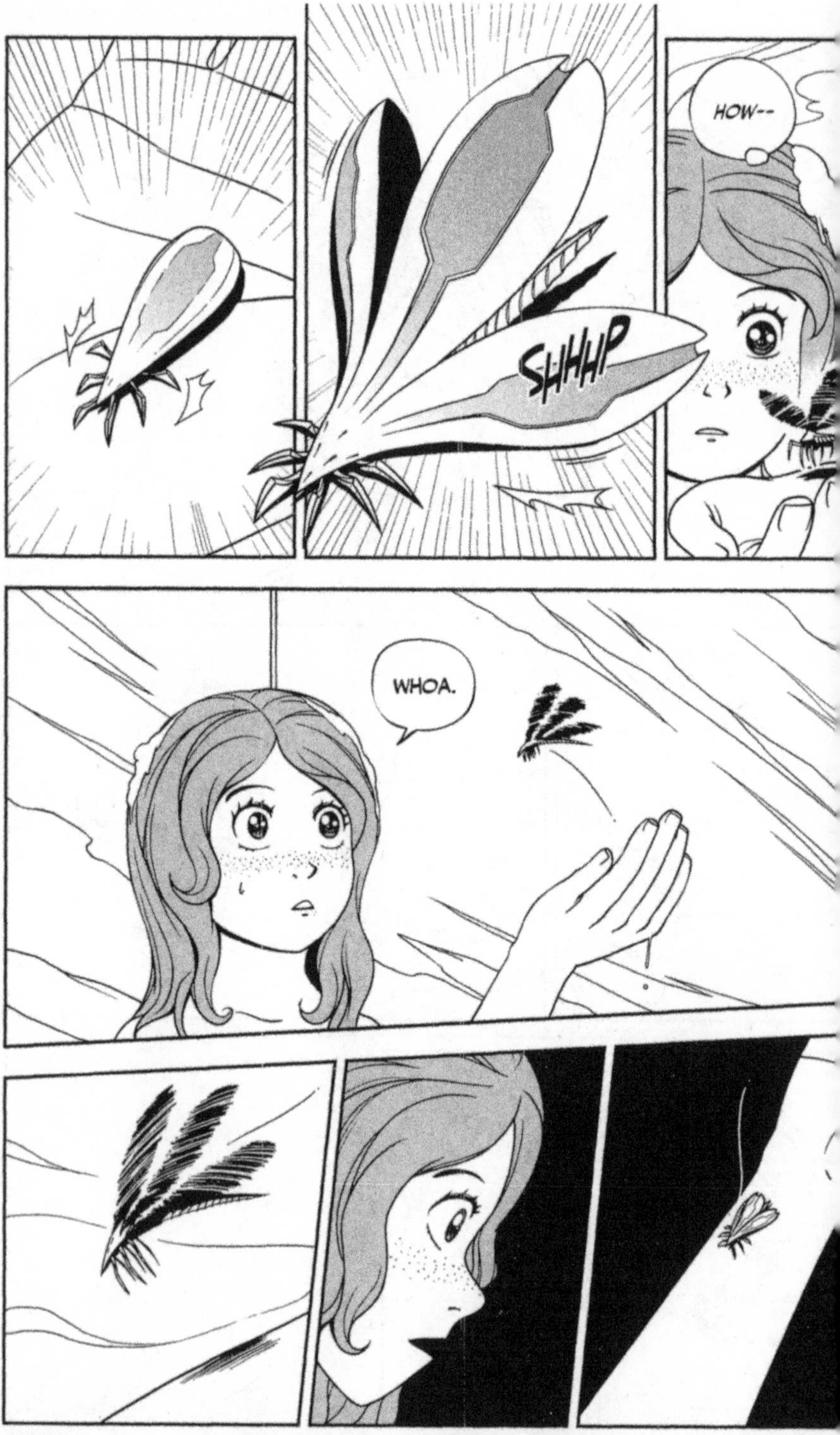
SHHHP
HOW--
WHOA.

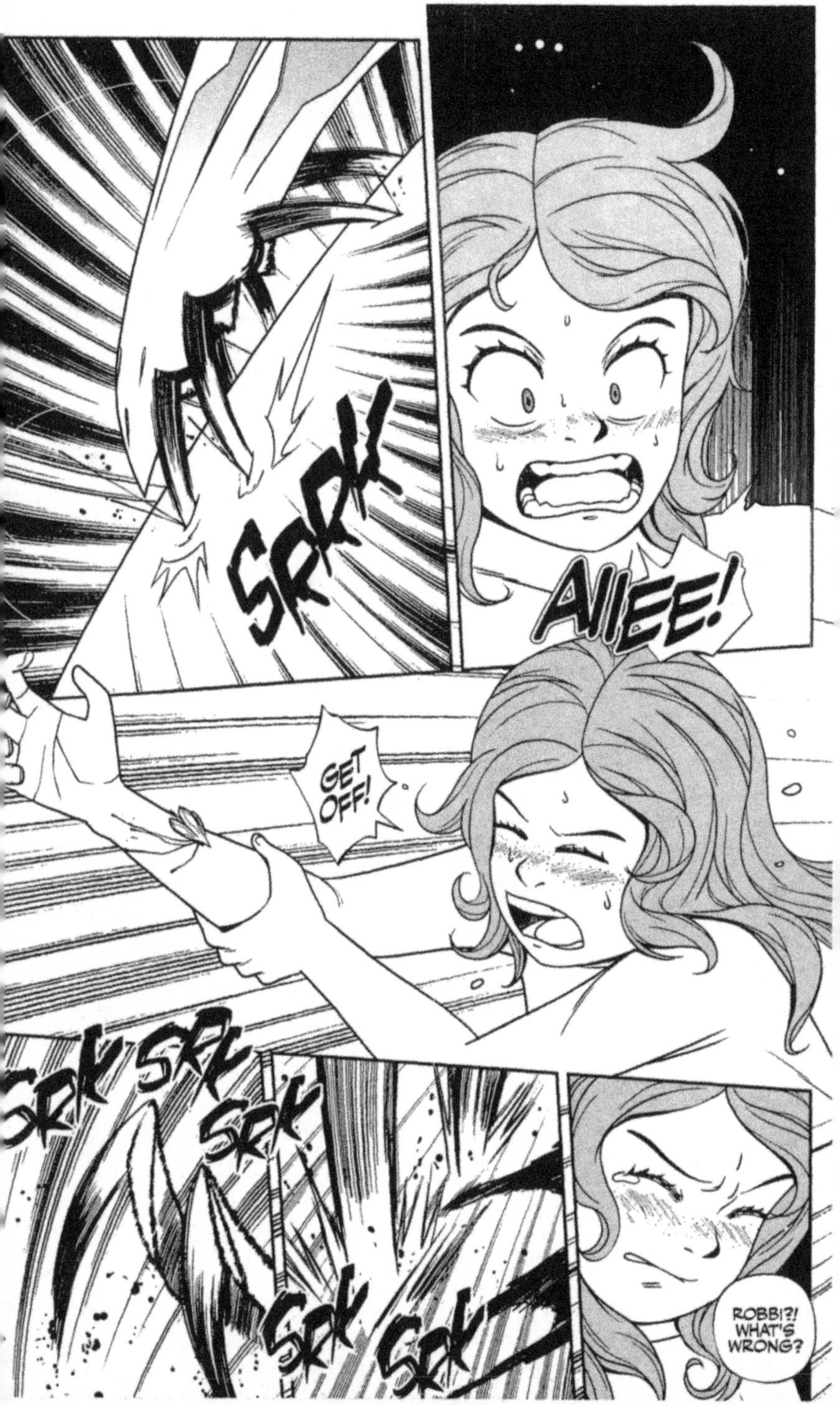
SRRK
AIIEE!
GET OFF!
SRK SRK
SRK
SRK SRK
ROBBI?! WHAT'S WRONG?

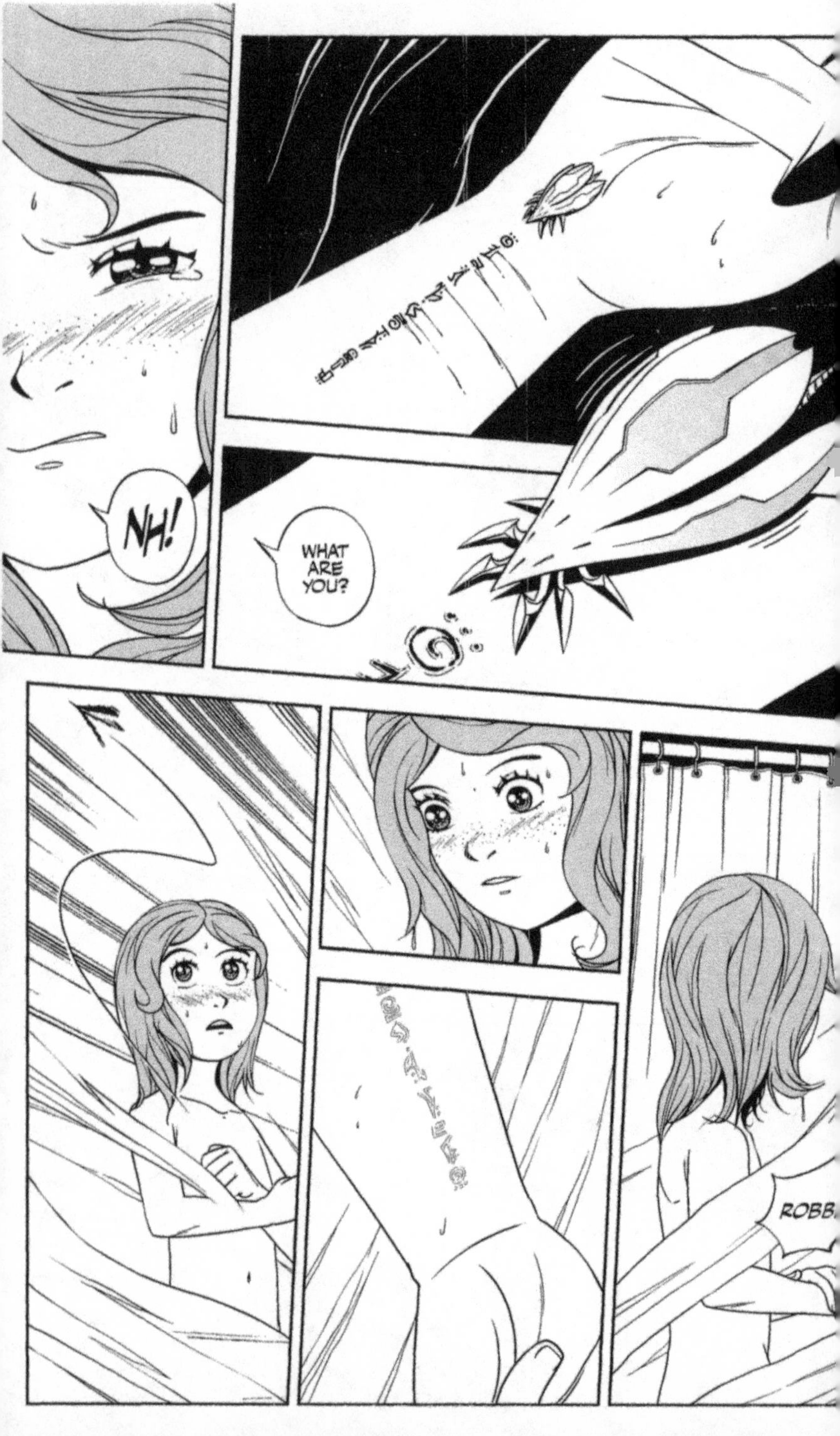
NH!
WHAT ARE YOU?
ROBB

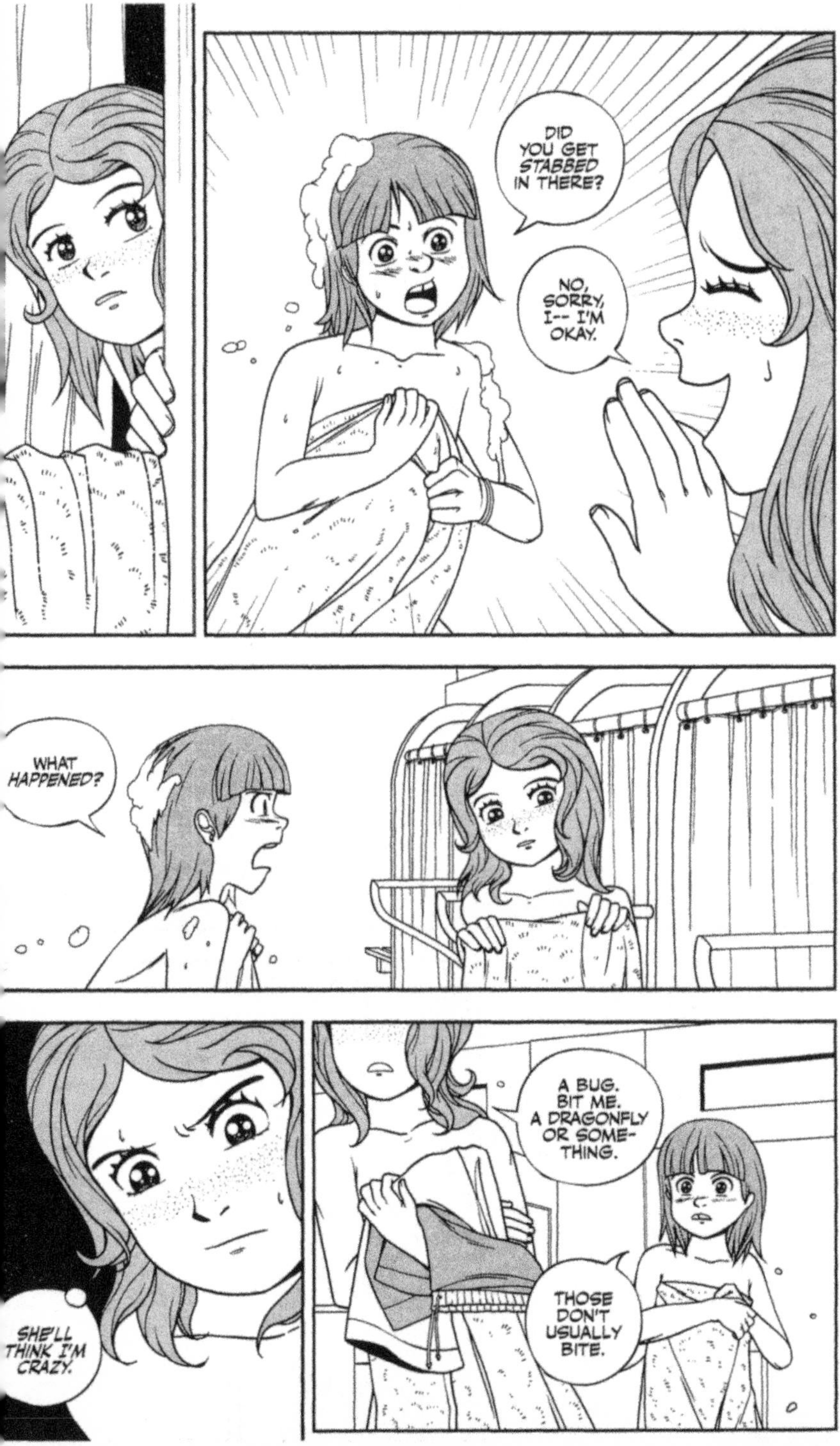
DID YOU GET STABBED IN THERE?
NO, SORRY, I-- I'M OKAY.
WHAT HAPPENED?
SHE'LL THINK I'M CRAZY.
A BUG. BIT ME. A DRAGONFLY OR SOME-THING.
THOSE DON'T USUALLY BITE.

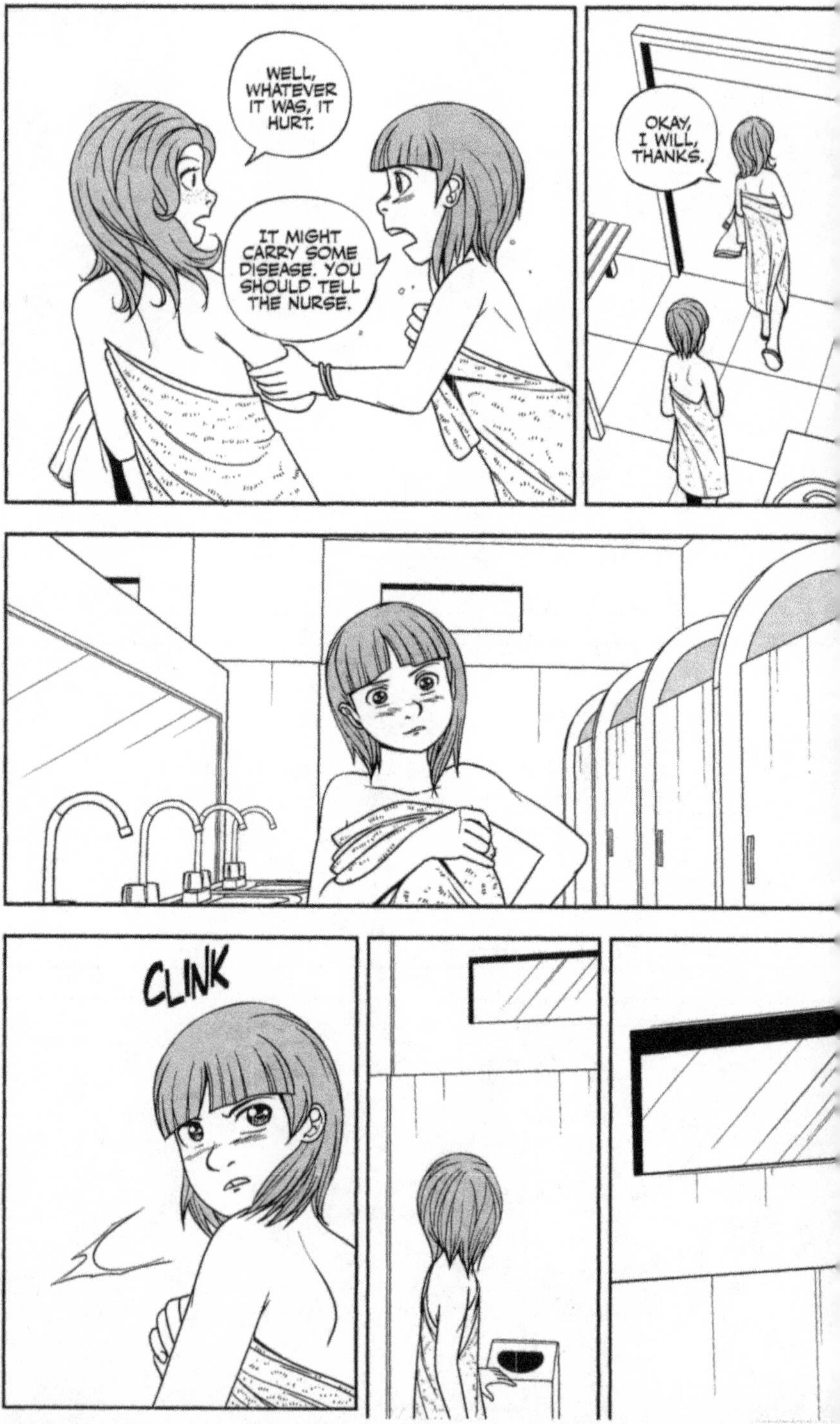
WELL, WHATEVER IT WAS, IT HURT.
IT MIGHT CARRY SOME DISEASE. YOU SHOULD TELL THE NURSE.
OKAY, I WILL, THANKS.
CLINK

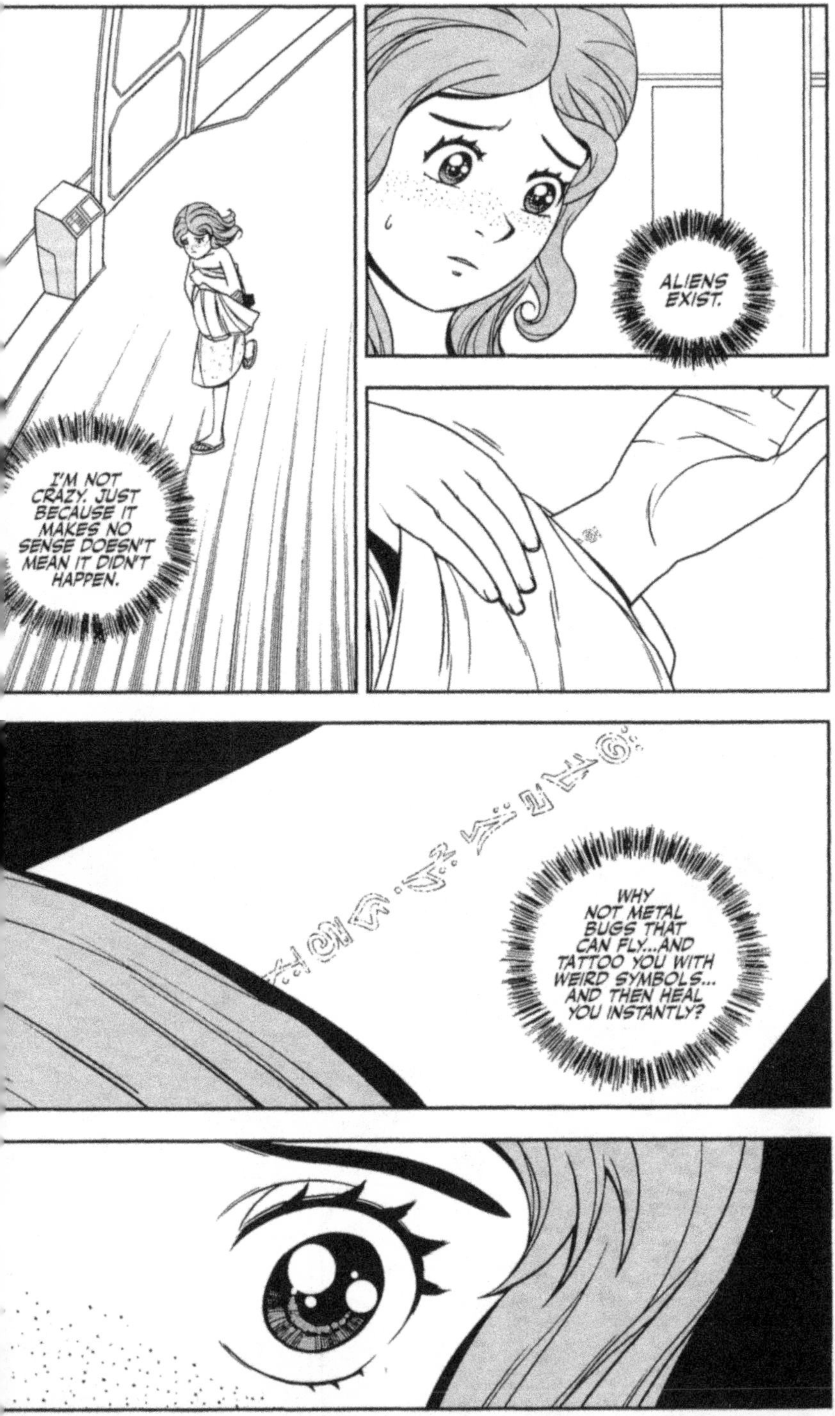
I'M NOT CRAZY. JUST BECAUSE IT MAKES NO SENSE DOESN'T MEAN IT DIDN'T HAPPEN.
ALIENS EXIST.
WHY NOT METAL BUGS THAT CAN FLY...AND TATTOO YOU WITH WEIRD SYMBOLS... AND THEN HEAL YOU INSTANTLY?

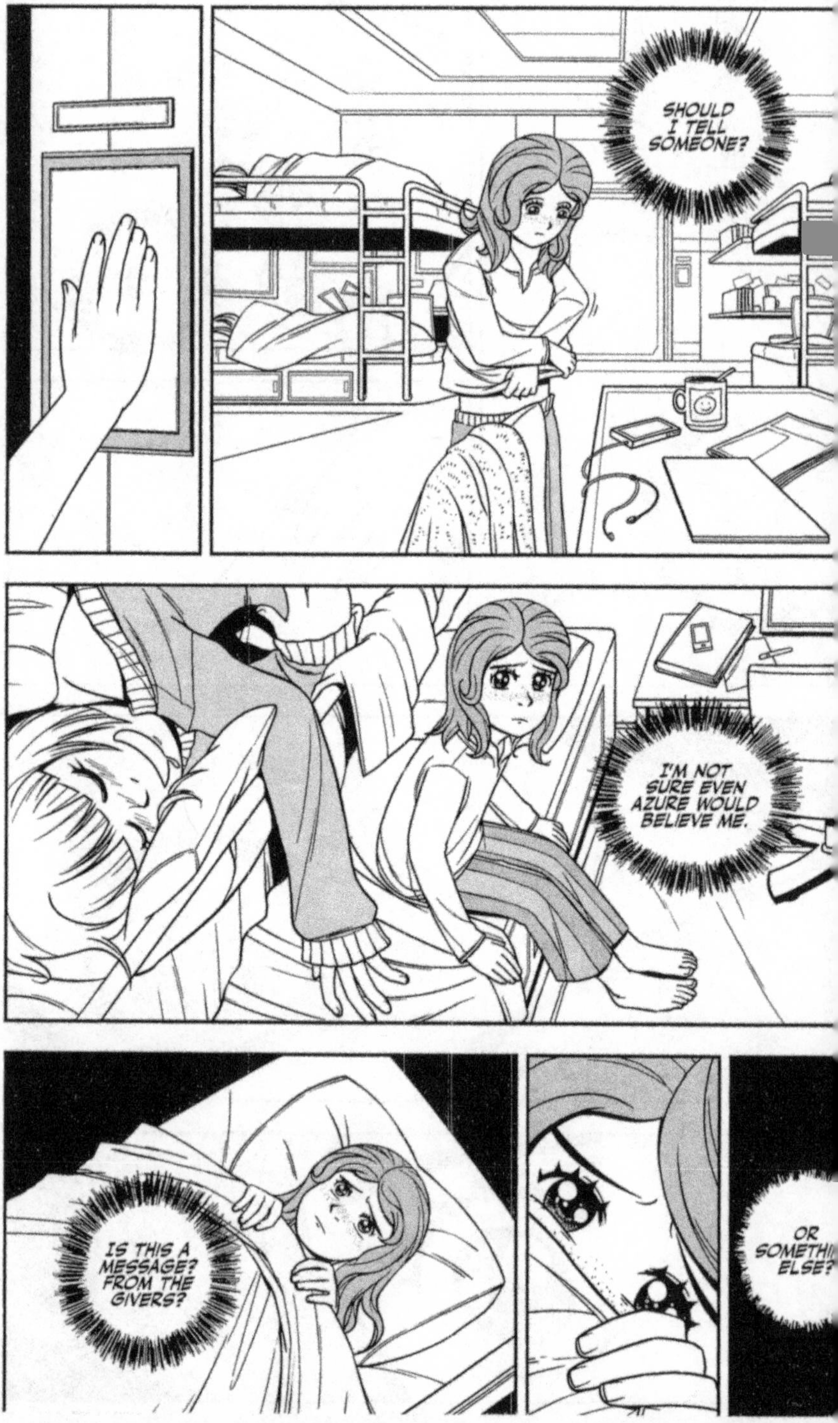
SHOULD I TELL SOMEONE?
I'M NOT SURE EVEN AZURE WOULD BELIEVE ME.
IS THIS A MESSAGE? FROM THE GIVERS?
OR SOMETHI ELSE?

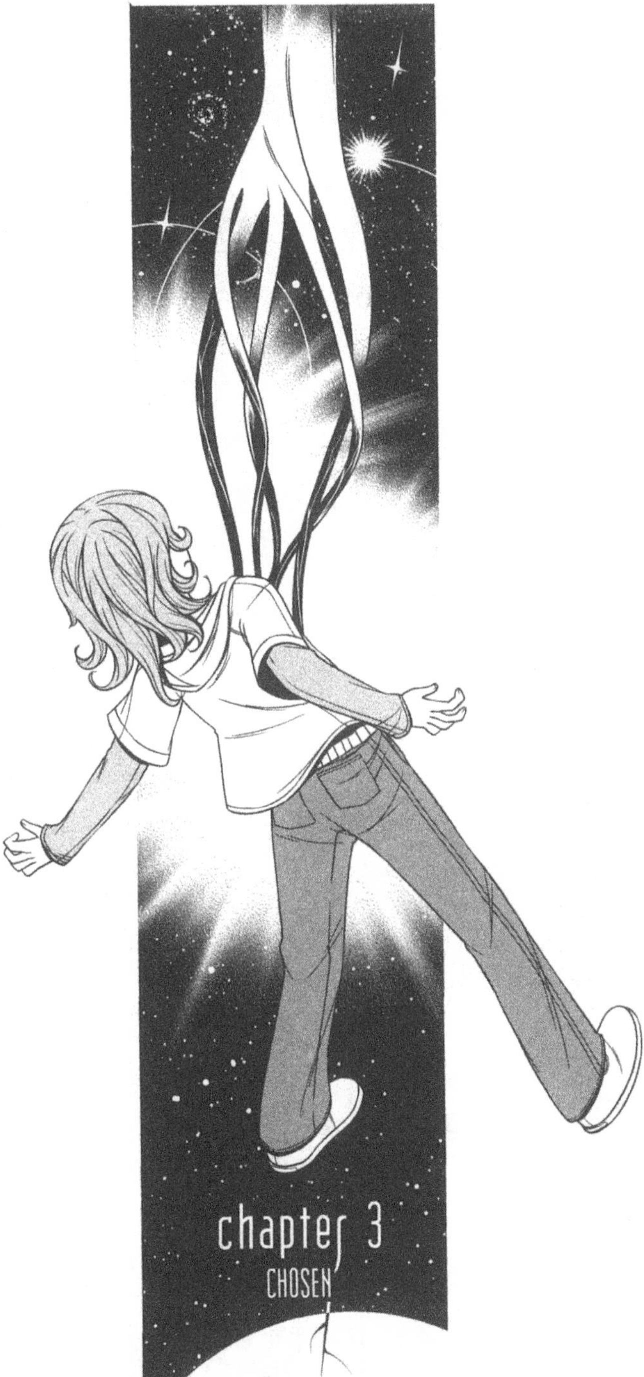
chapter 3
CHOSEN

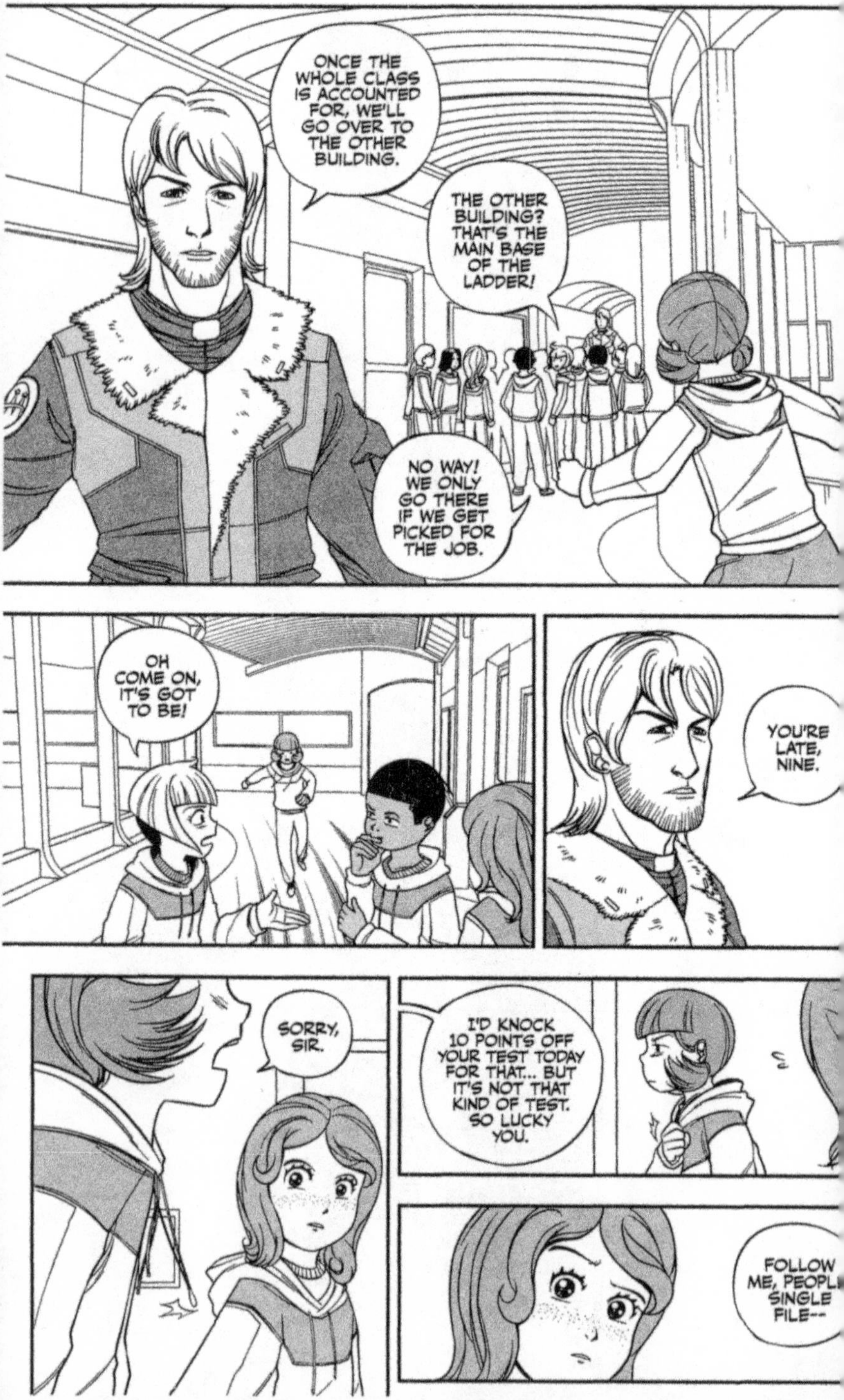
ONCE THE WHOLE CLASS IS ACCOUNTED FOR, WE'LL GO OVER TO THE OTHER BUILDING.
THE OTHER BUILDING? THAT'S THE MAIN BASE OF THE LADDER!
NO WAY! WE ONLY GO THERE IF WE GET PICKED FOR THE JOB.
OH COME ON, IT'S GOT TO BE!
YOU'RE LATE, NINE.
SORRY, SIR.
I'D KNOCK 10 POINTS OFF YOUR TEST TODAY FOR THAT... BUT IT'S NOT THAT KIND OF TEST. SO LUCKY YOU.
FOLLOW ME, PEOPL SINGLE FILE--

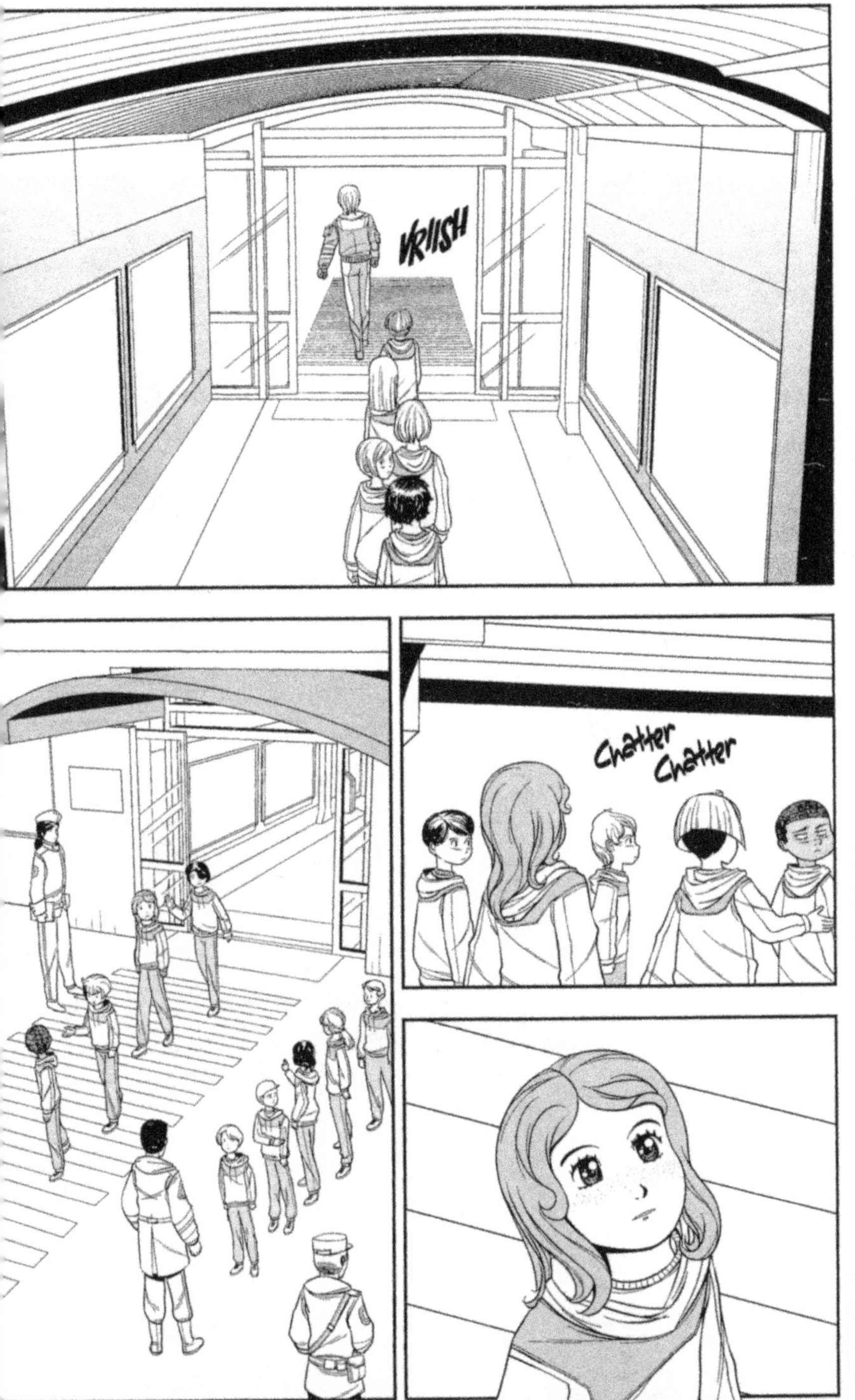
VRIISH
Chatter Chatter

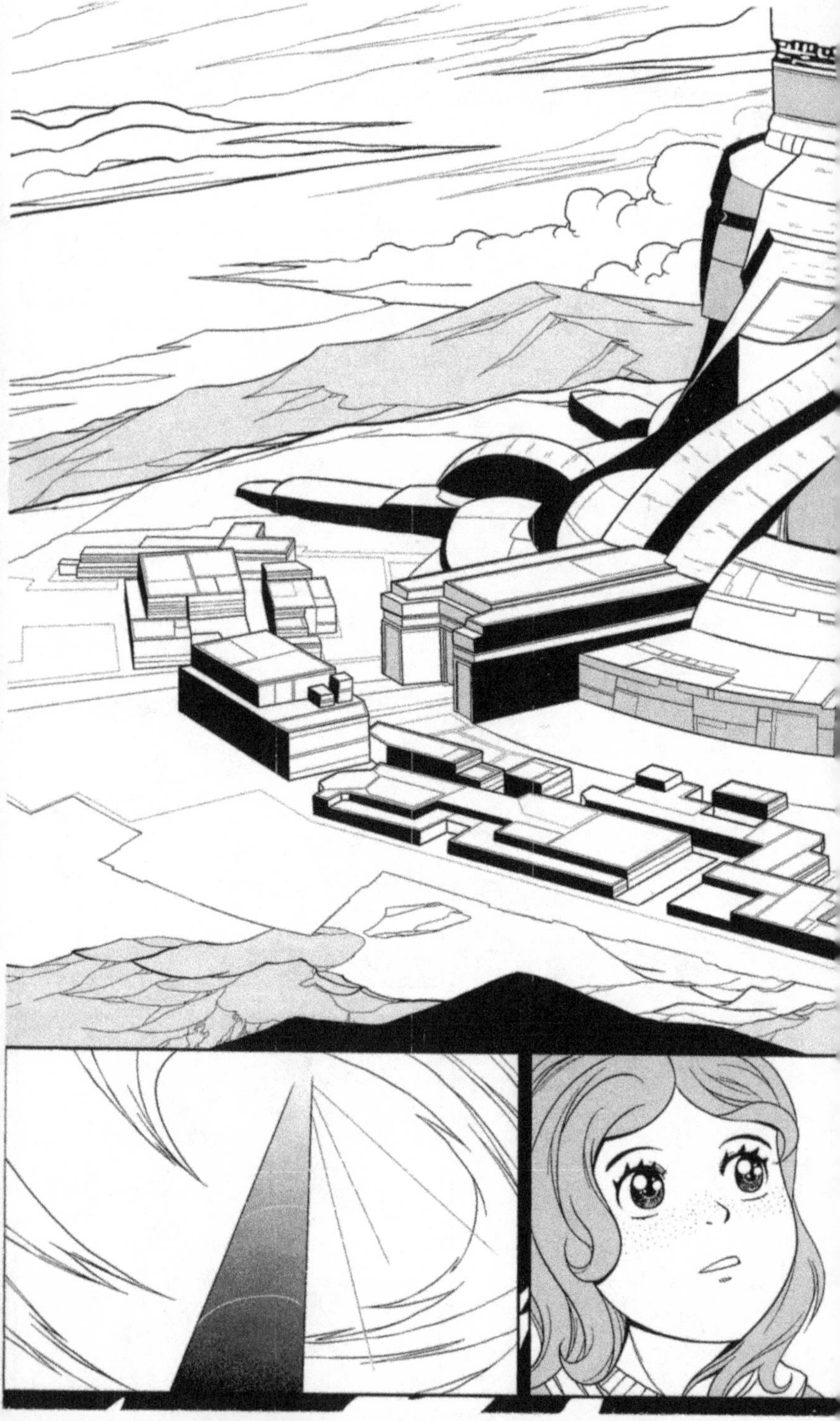

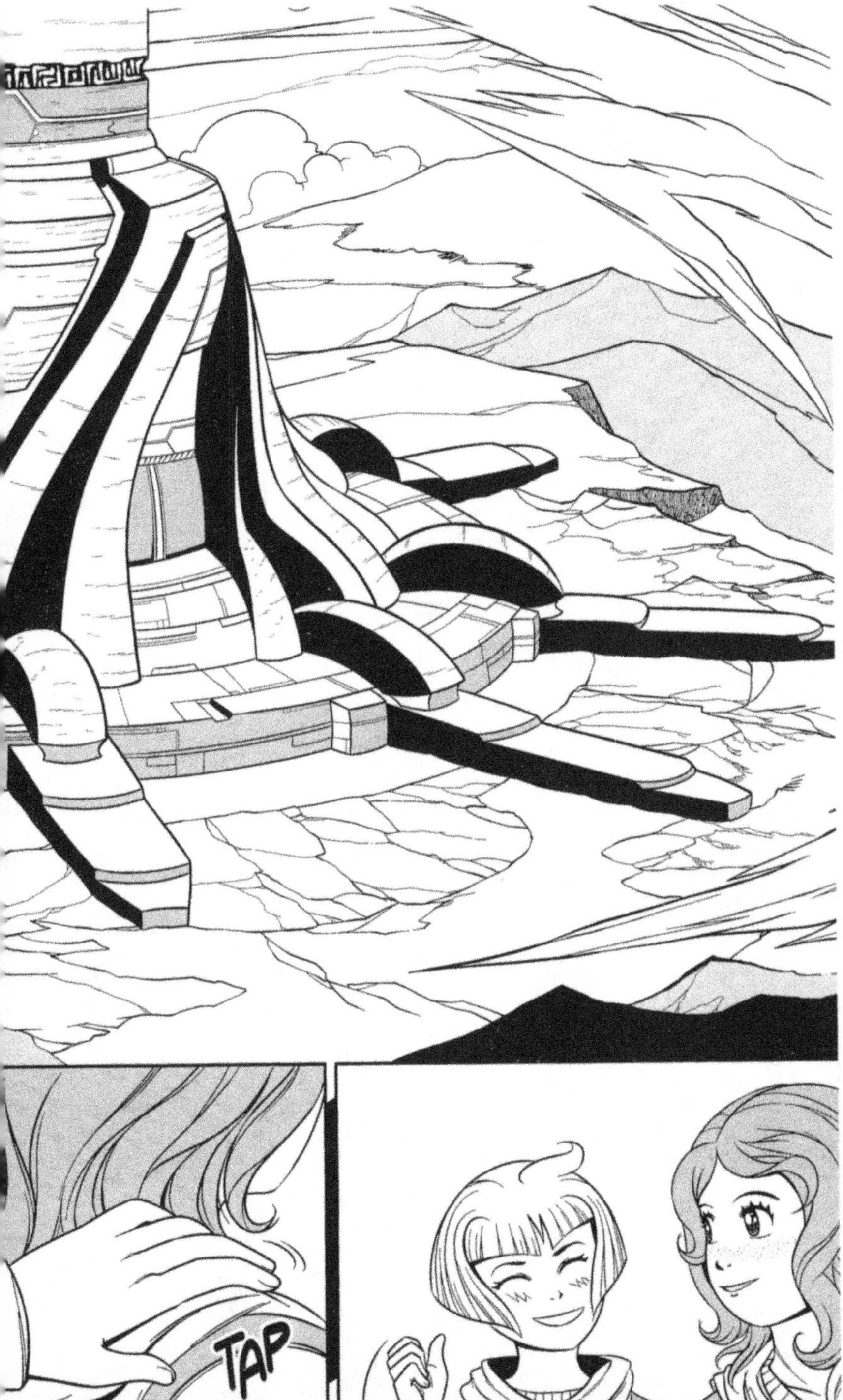
TAP

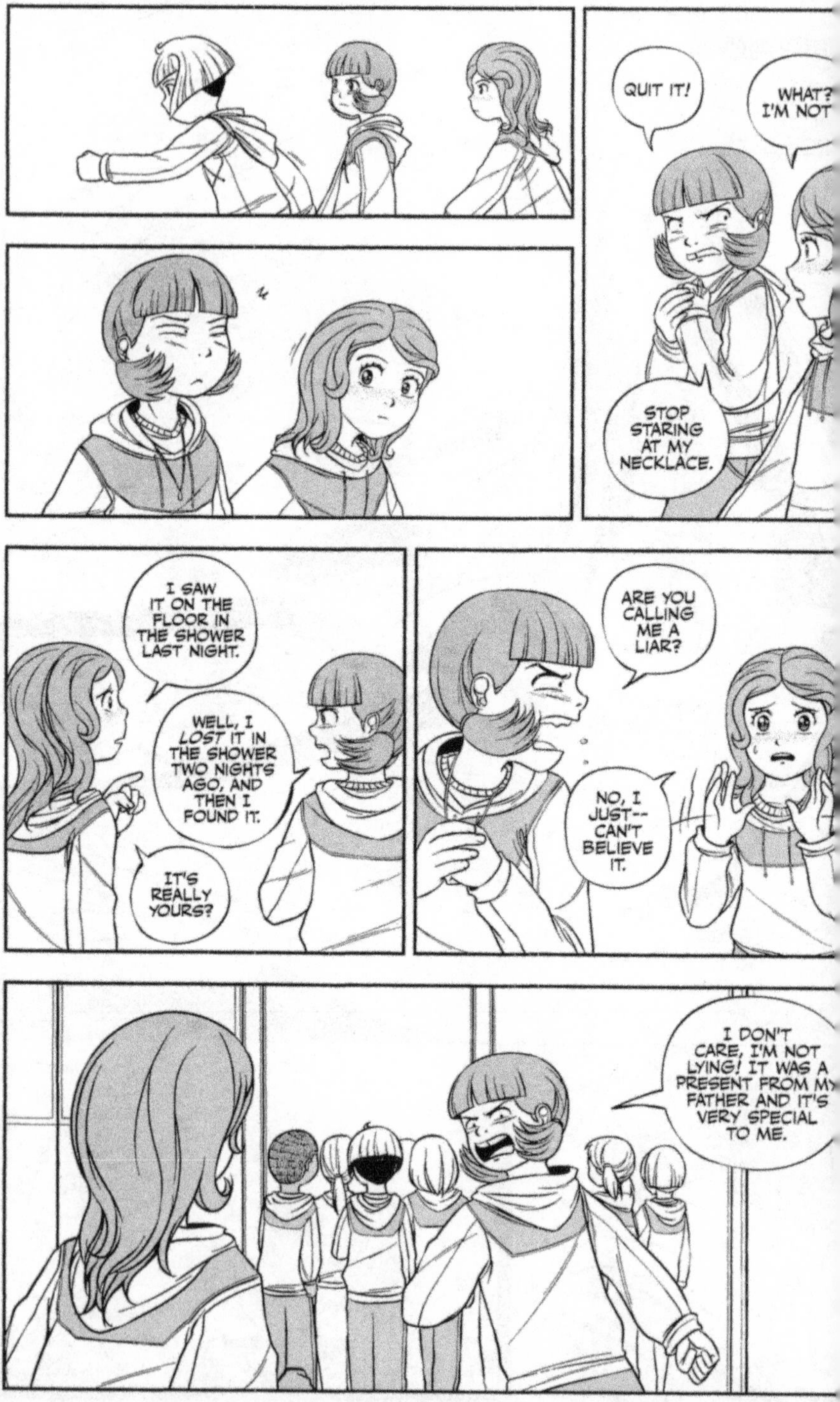

QUIT IT!
WHAT? I'M NOT
STOP STARING AT MY NECKLACE.
I SAW IT ON THE FLOOR IN THE SHOWER LAST NIGHT.
WELL, I *LOST* IT IN THE SHOWER TWO NIGHTS AGO, AND THEN I FOUND IT.
IT'S REALLY YOURS?
ARE YOU CALLING ME A LIAR?
NO, I JUST-- CAN'T BELIEVE IT.
I DON'T CARE, I'M NOT LYING! IT WAS A PRESENT FROM MY FATHER AND IT'S VERY SPECIAL TO ME.

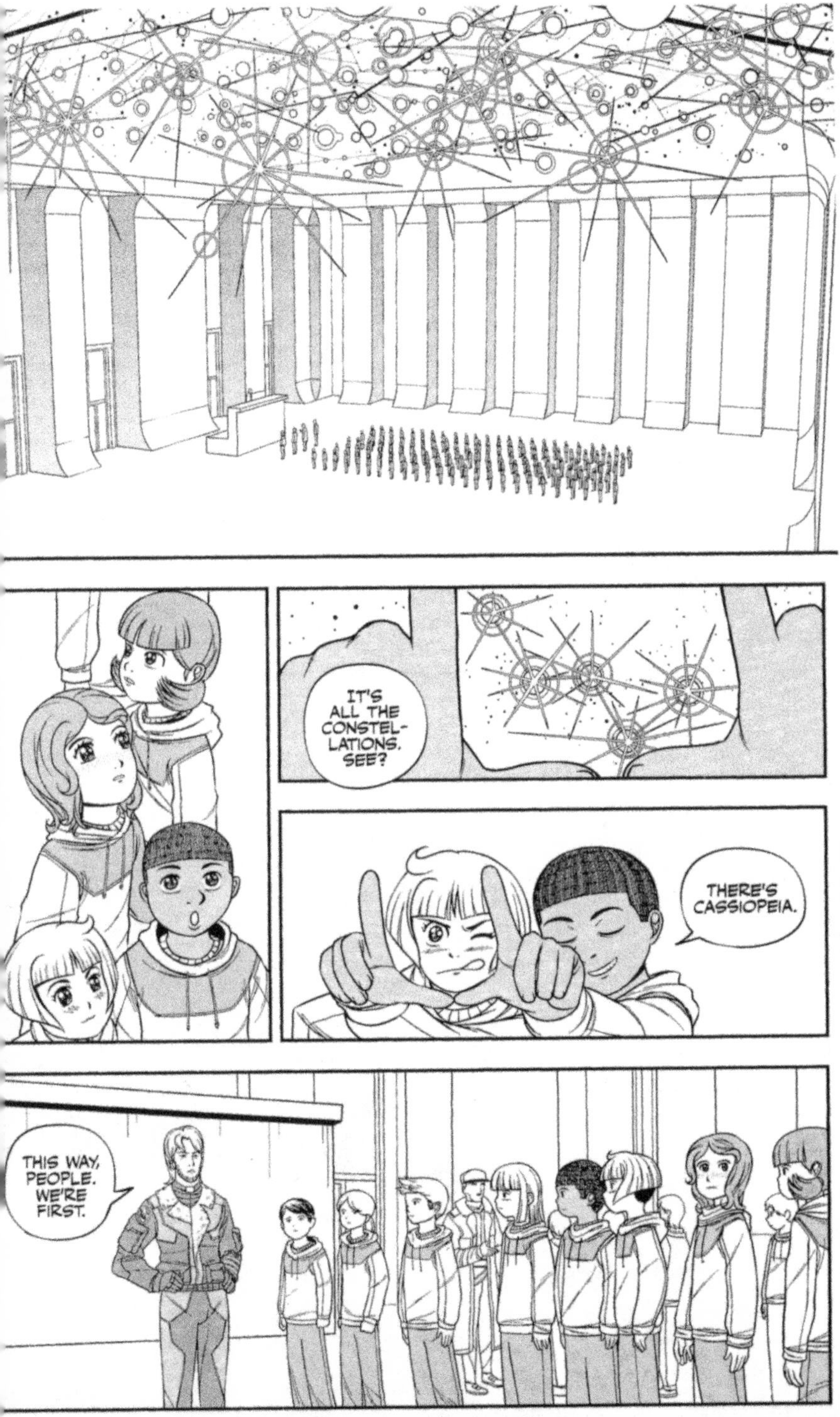
IT'S ALL THE CONSTEL-LATIONS. SEE?
THERE'S CASSIOPEIA.
THIS WAY, PEOPLE. WE'RE FIRST.

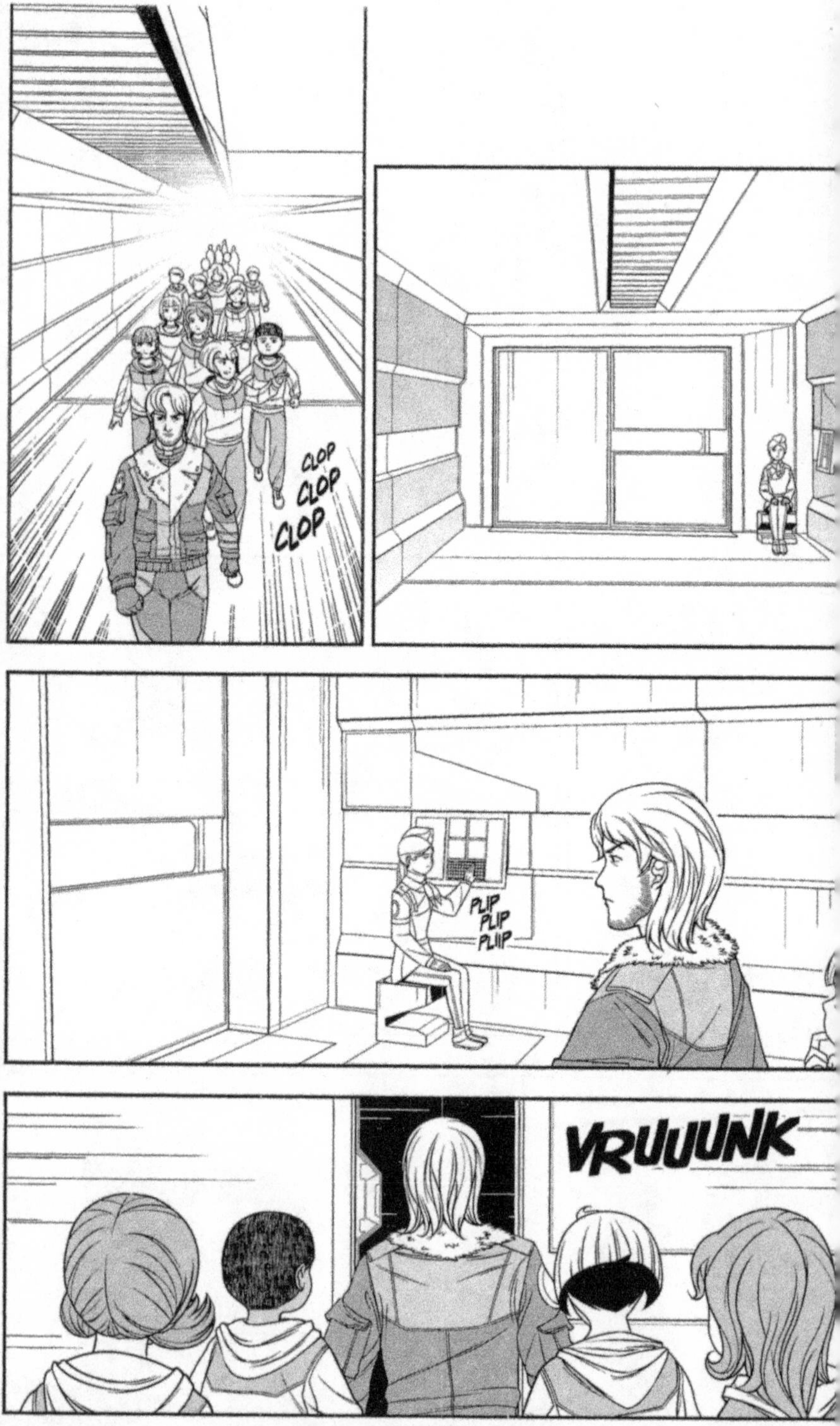
CLOP
CLOP
CLOP
PLIP
PLIP
PLIP
VRUUUNK

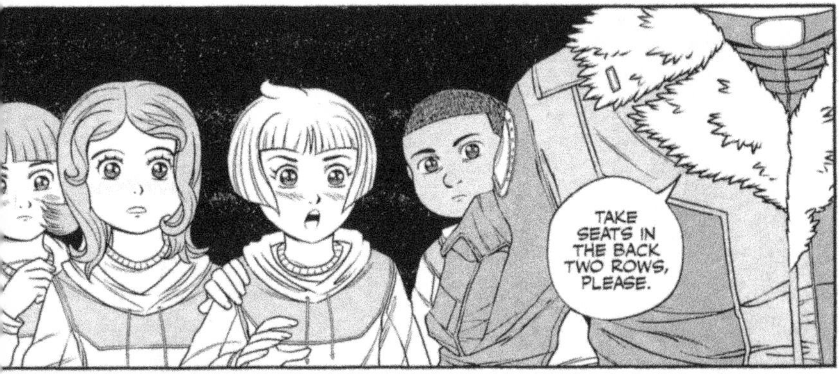
TAKE SEATS IN THE BACK TWO ROWS, PLEASE.
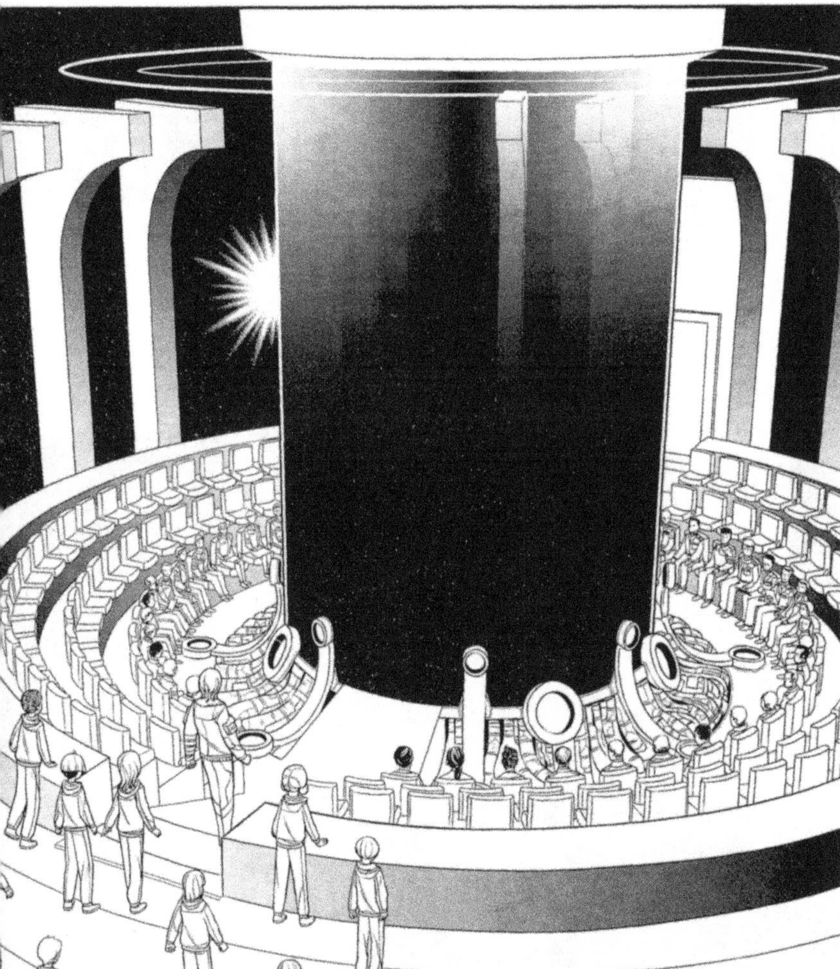

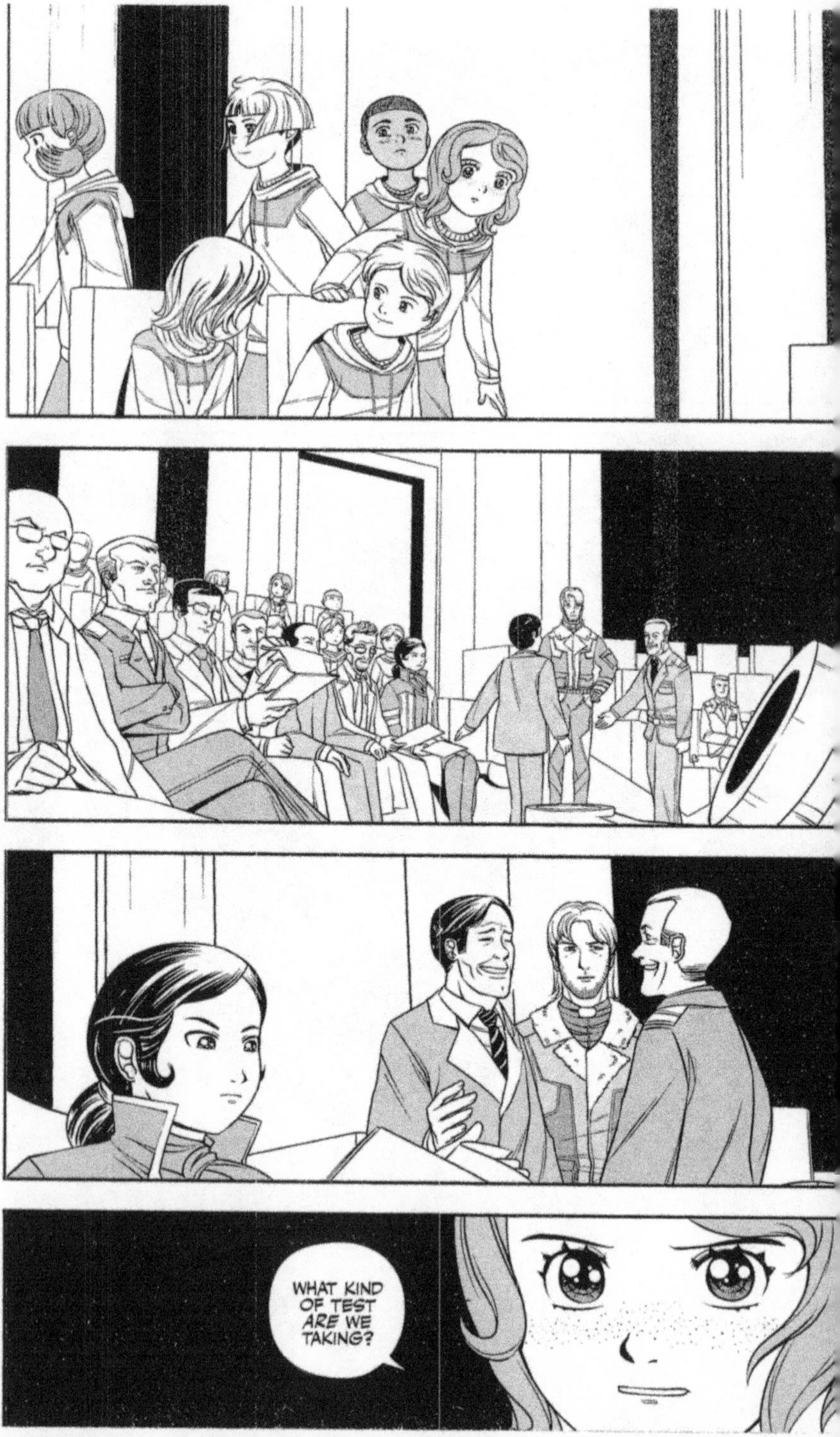
WHAT KIND OF TEST ARE WE TAKING?

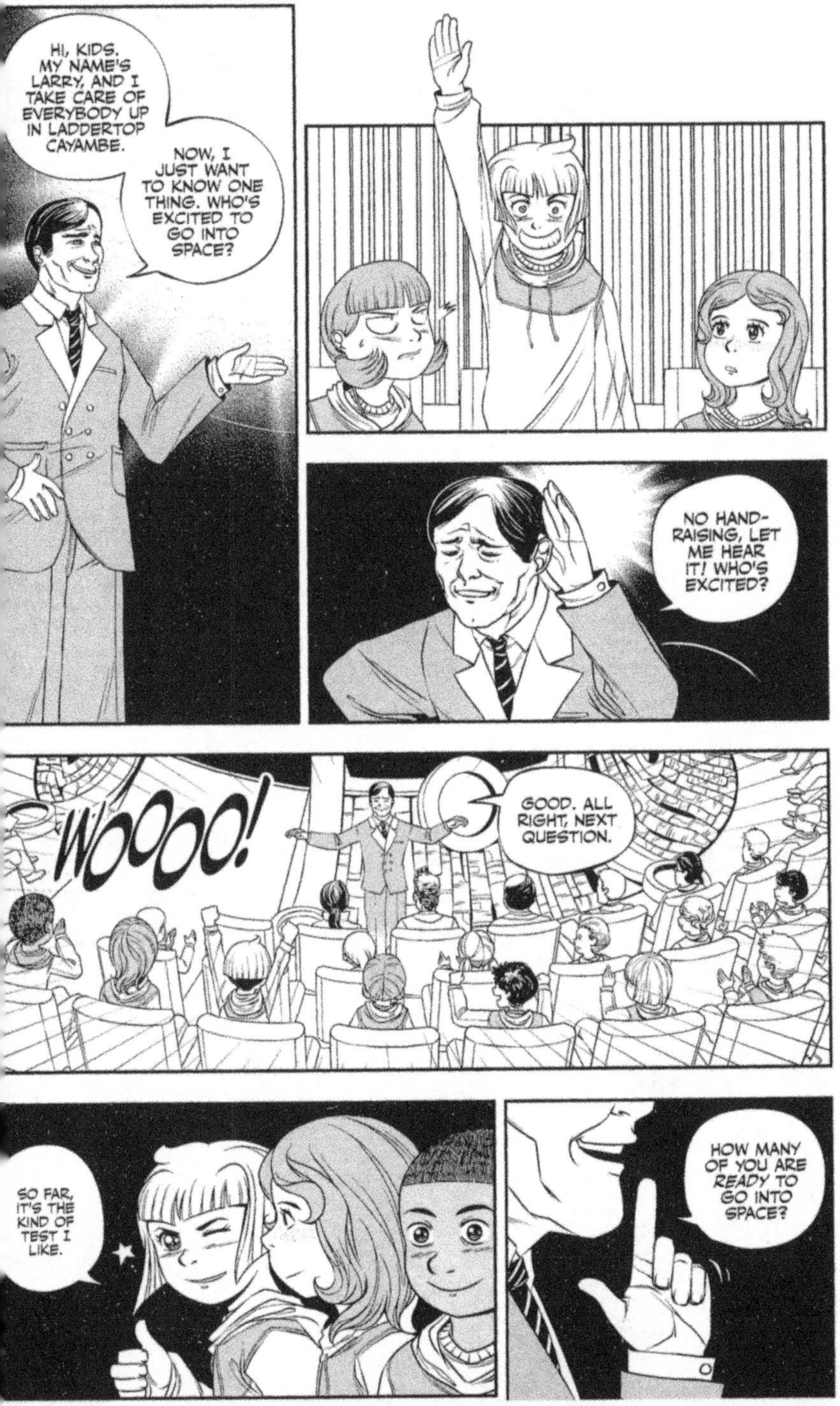
HI, KIDS. MY NAME'S LARRY, AND I TAKE CARE OF EVERYBODY UP IN LADDERTOP CAYAMBE.
NOW, I JUST WANT TO KNOW ONE THING. WHO'S EXCITED TO GO INTO SPACE?
NO HAND-RAISING, LET ME HEAR IT! WHO'S EXCITED?
WOOOO!
GOOD. ALL RIGHT, NEXT QUESTION.
SO FAR, IT'S THE KIND OF TEST I LIKE.
HOW MANY OF YOU ARE *READY* TO GO INTO SPACE?

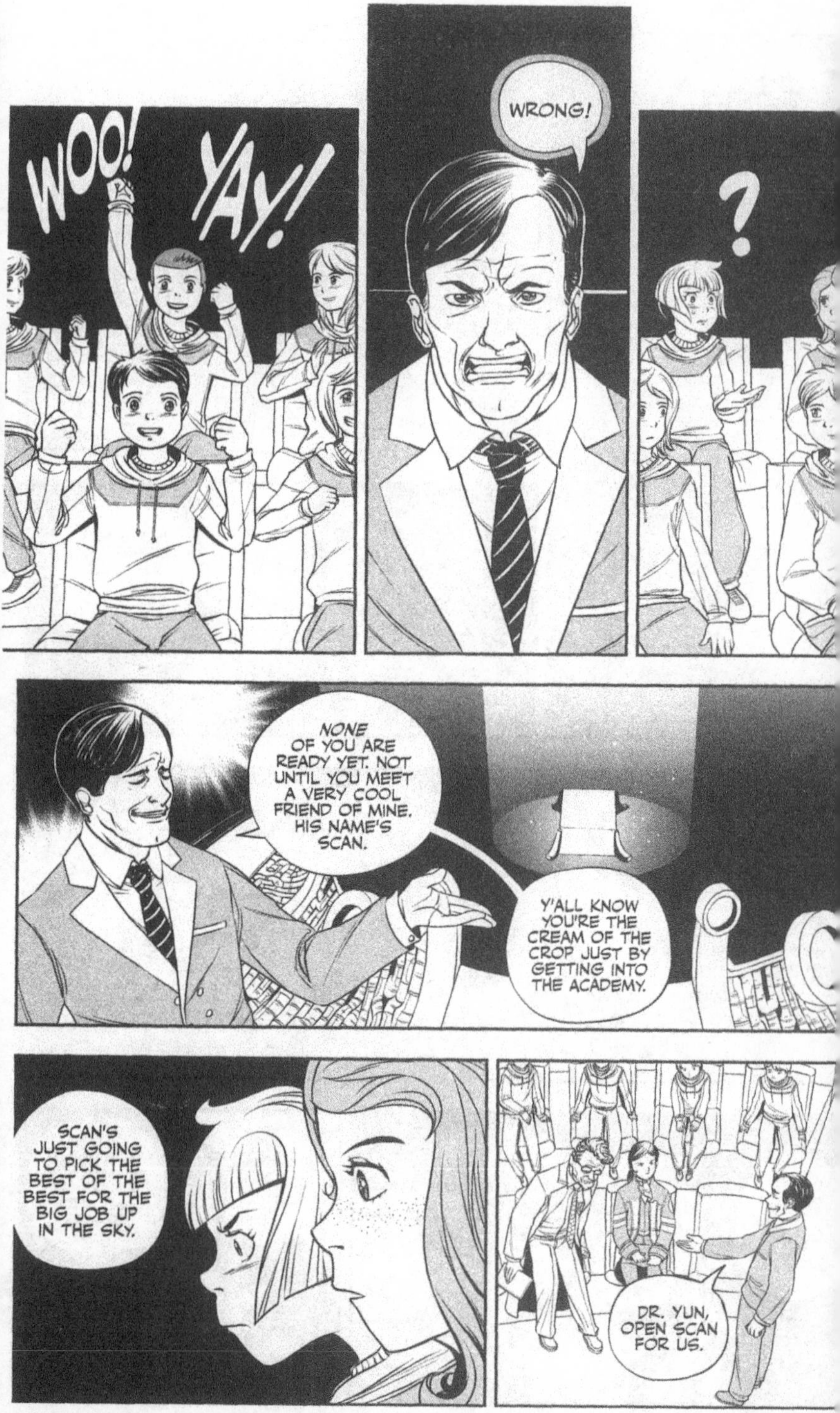
WOO!
YAY!
WRONG!
?
NONE OF YOU ARE READY YET. NOT UNTIL YOU MEET A VERY COOL FRIEND OF MINE. HIS NAME'S SCAN.
Y'ALL KNOW YOU'RE THE CREAM OF THE CROP JUST BY GETTING INTO THE ACADEMY.
SCAN'S JUST GOING TO PICK THE BEST OF THE BEST FOR THE BIG JOB UP IN THE SKY.
DR. YUN, OPEN SCAN FOR US.

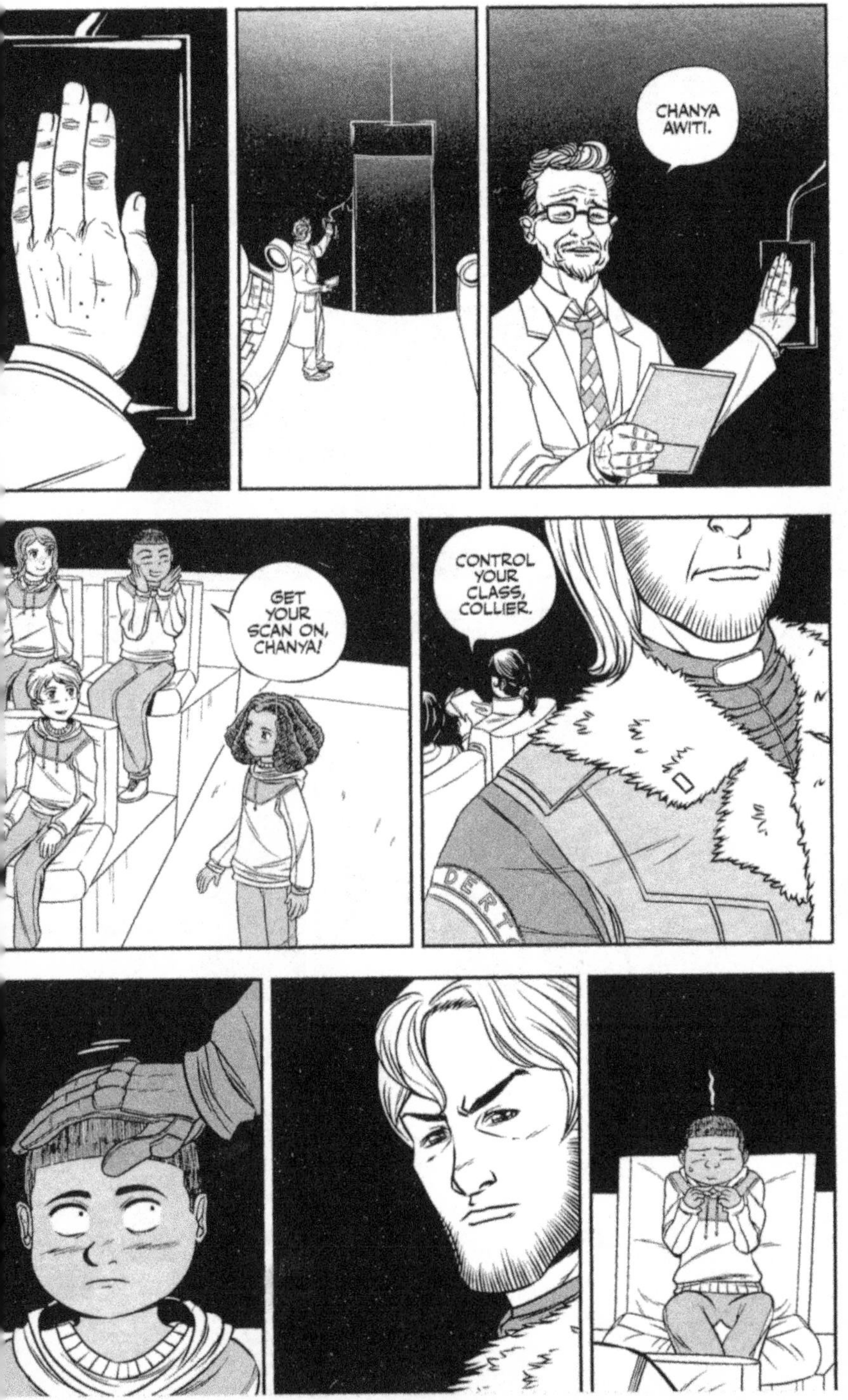
CHANYA AWITI.
GET YOUR SCAN ON, CHANYA!
CONTROL YOUR CLASS, COLLIER.

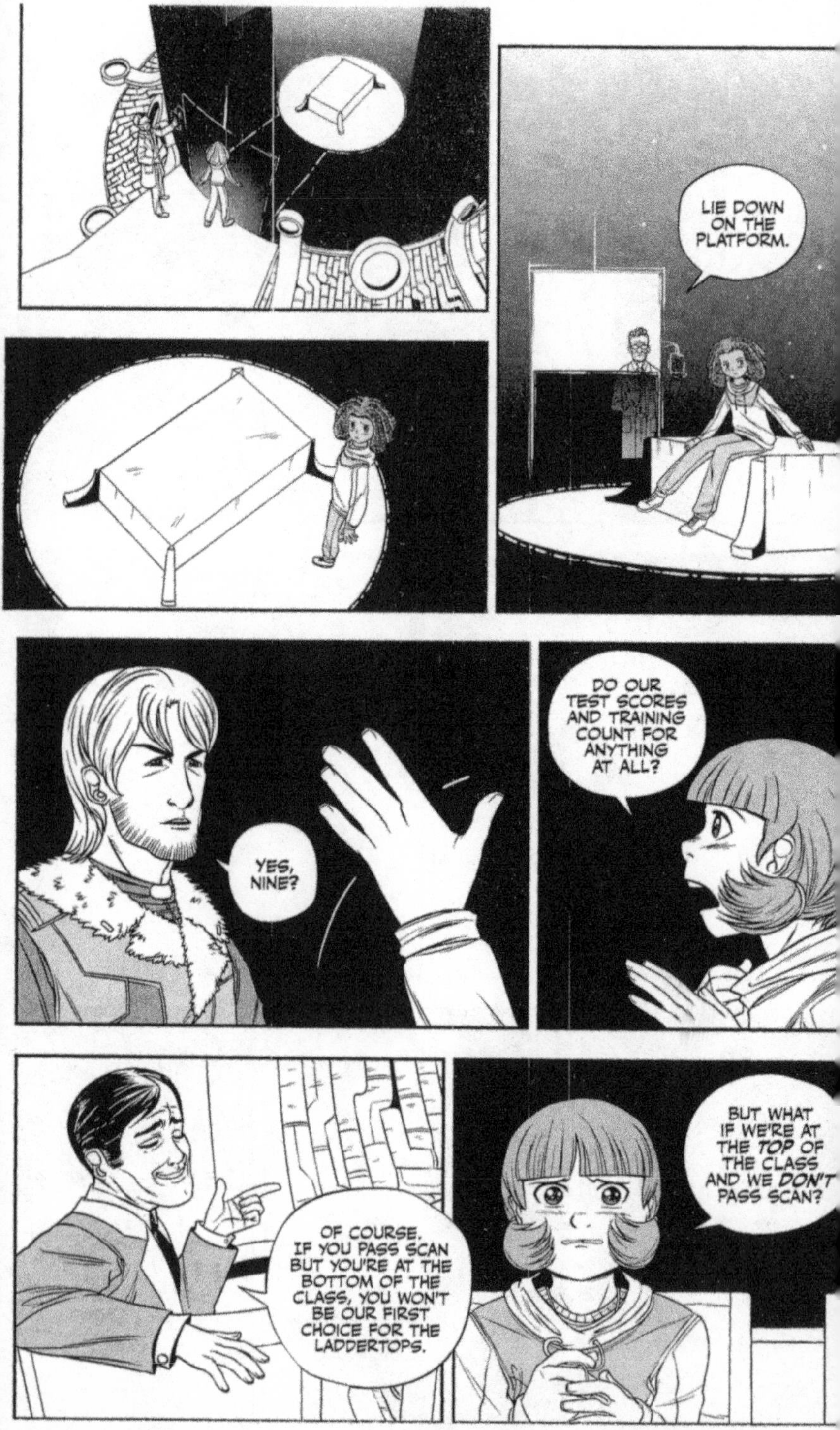
LIE DOWN ON THE PLATFORM.
YES, NINE?
DO OUR TEST SCORES AND TRAINING COUNT FOR ANYTHING AT ALL?
OF COURSE. IF YOU PASS SCAN BUT YOU'RE AT THE BOTTOM OF THE CLASS, YOU WON'T BE OUR FIRST CHOICE FOR THE LADDERTOPS.
BUT WHAT IF WE'RE AT THE *TOP* OF THE CLASS AND WE *DON'T* PASS SCAN?

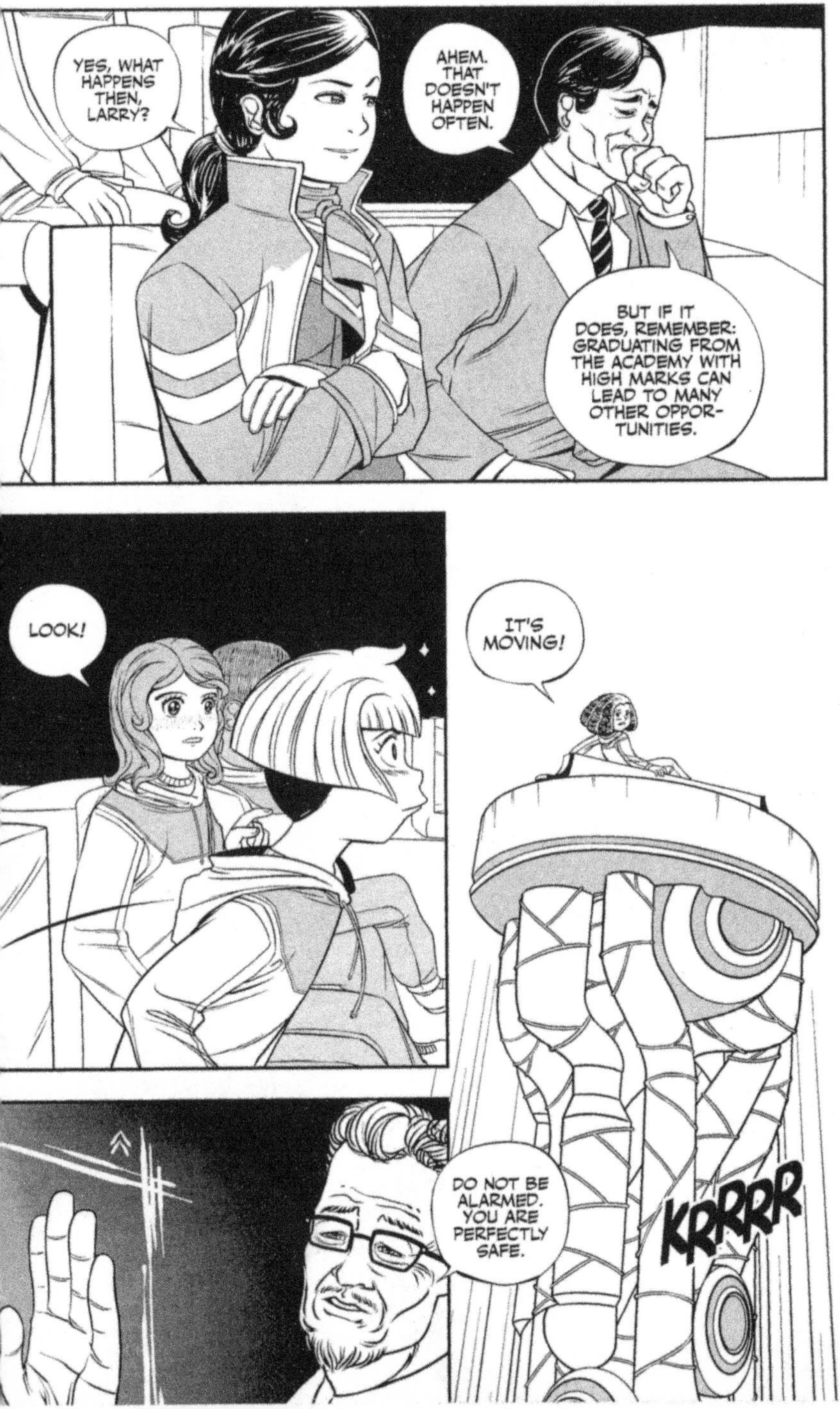

YES, WHAT HAPPENS THEN, LARRY?
AHEM. THAT DOESN'T HAPPEN OFTEN.
BUT IF IT DOES, REMEMBER: GRADUATING FROM THE ACADEMY WITH HIGH MARKS CAN LEAD TO MANY OTHER OPPOR-TUNITIES.
LOOK!
DO NOT BE ALARMED. YOU ARE PERFECTLY SAFE.
IT'S MOVING!
KRRRR

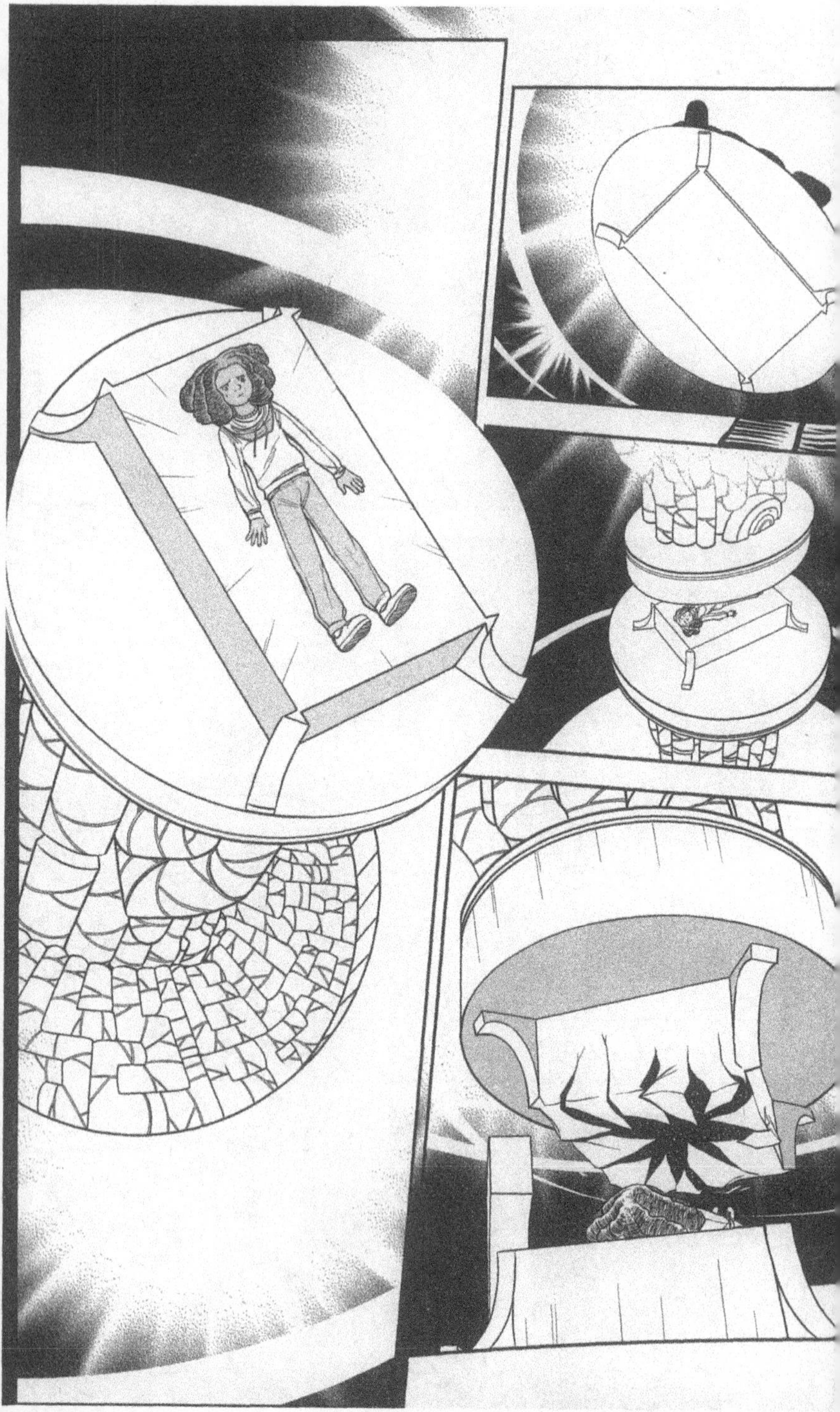

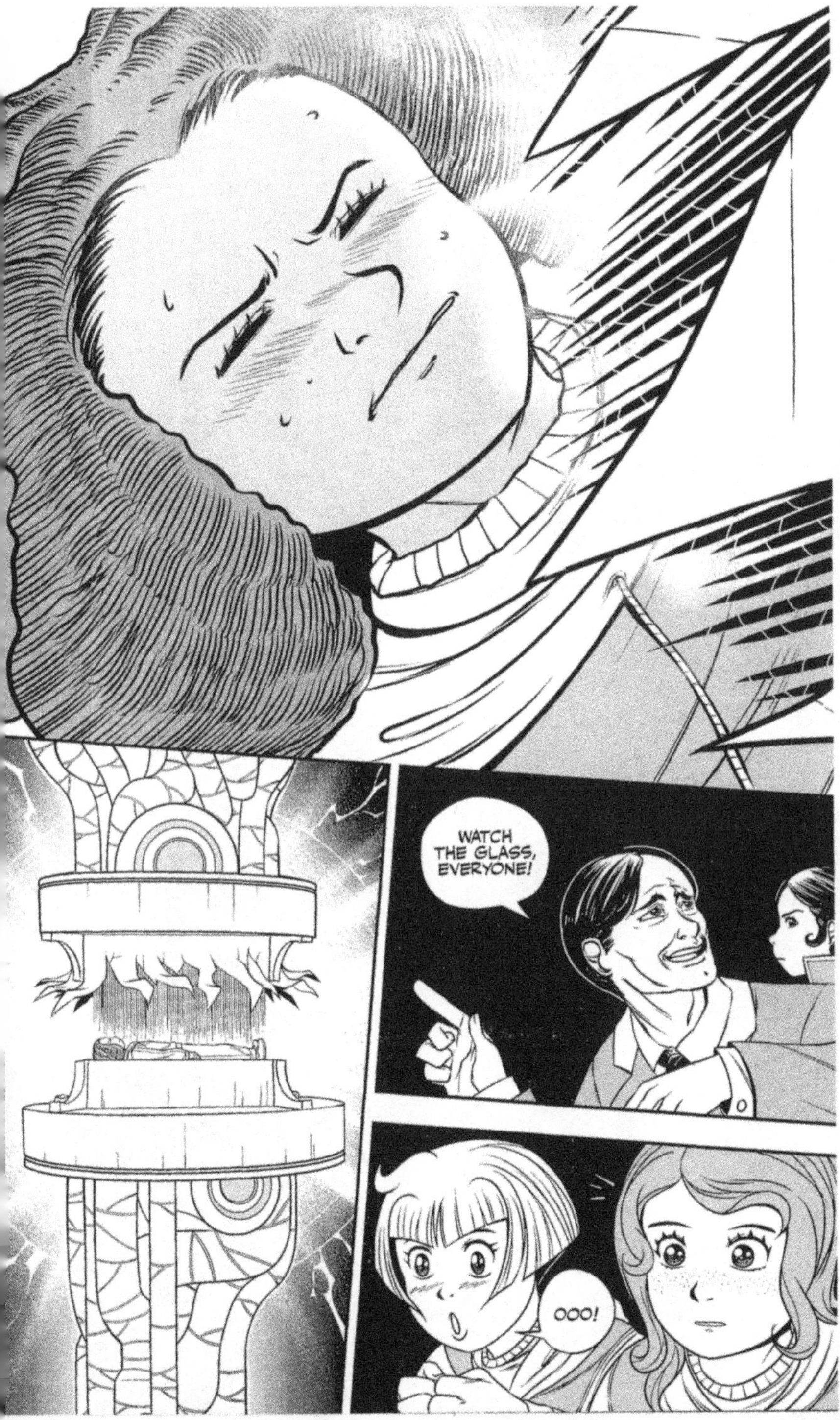
WATCH THE GLASS, EVERYONE!
OOO!

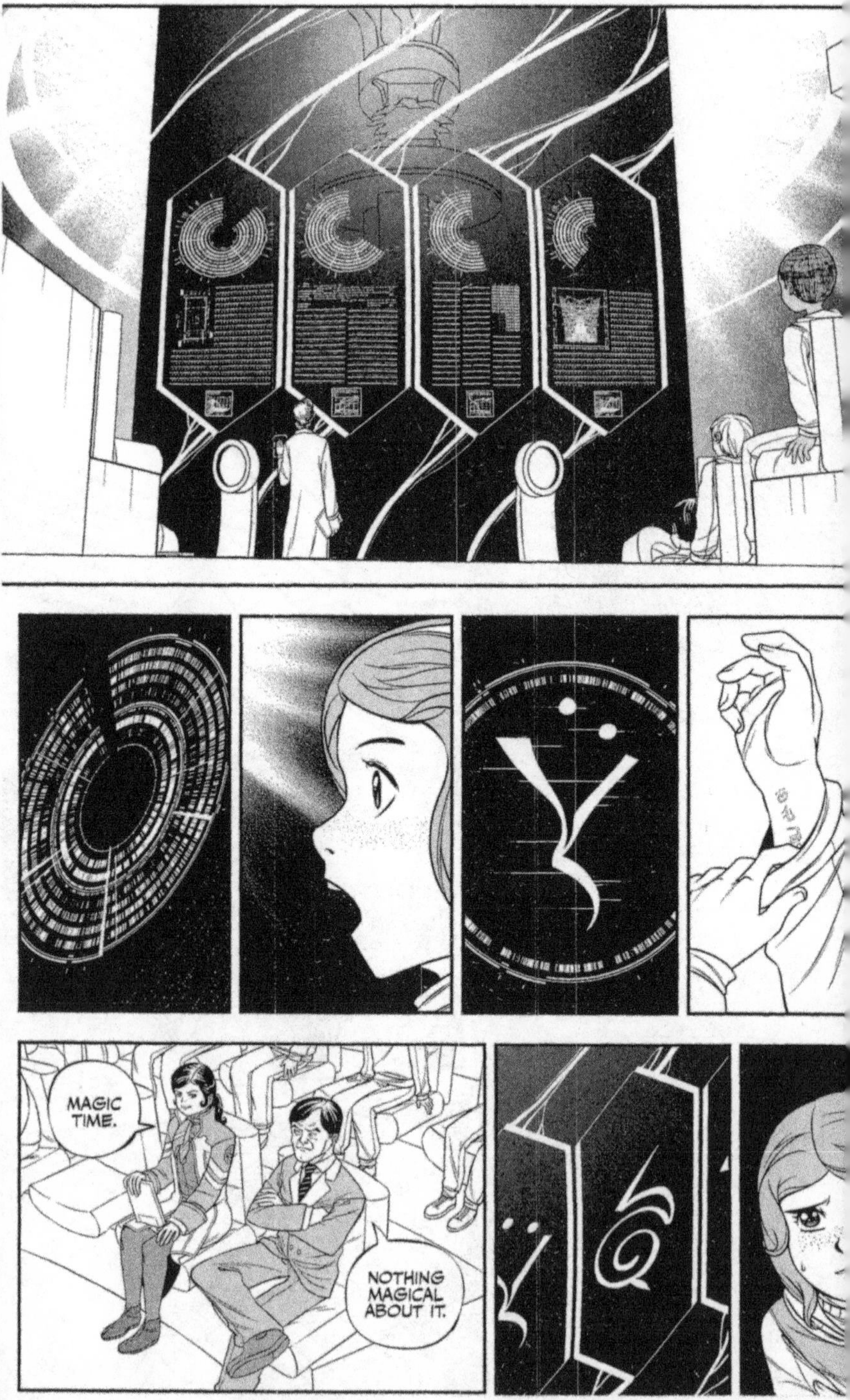
MAGIC TIME.
NOTHING MAGICAL ABOUT IT.

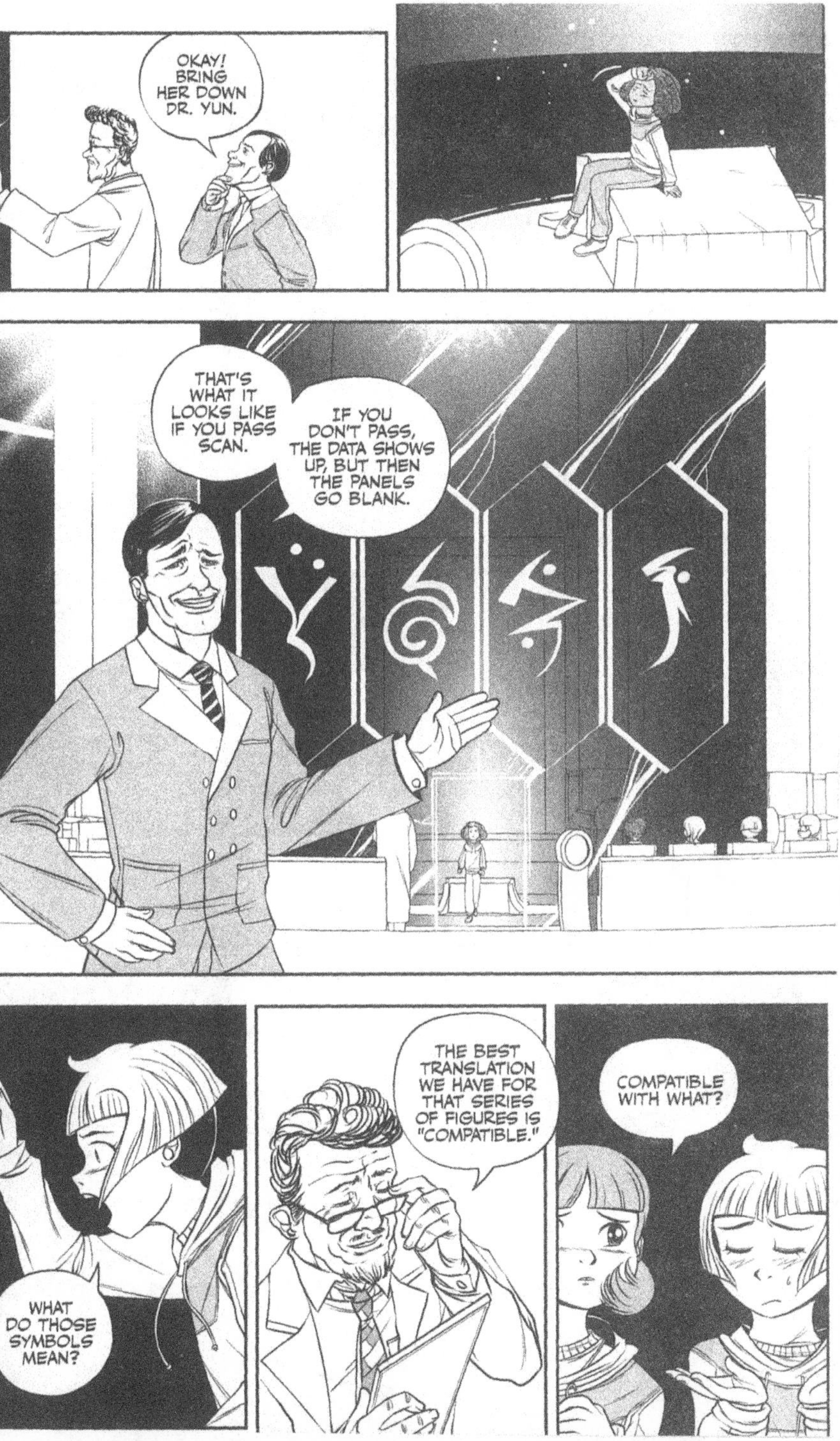
OKAY! BRING HER DOWN DR. YUN.
THAT'S WHAT IT LOOKS LIKE IF YOU PASS SCAN.
IF YOU DON'T PASS, THE DATA SHOWS UP, BUT THEN THE PANELS GO BLANK.
WHAT DO THOSE SYMBOLS MEAN?
THE BEST TRANSLATION WE HAVE FOR THAT SERIES OF FIGURES IS "COMPATIBLE."
COMPATIBLE WITH WHAT?

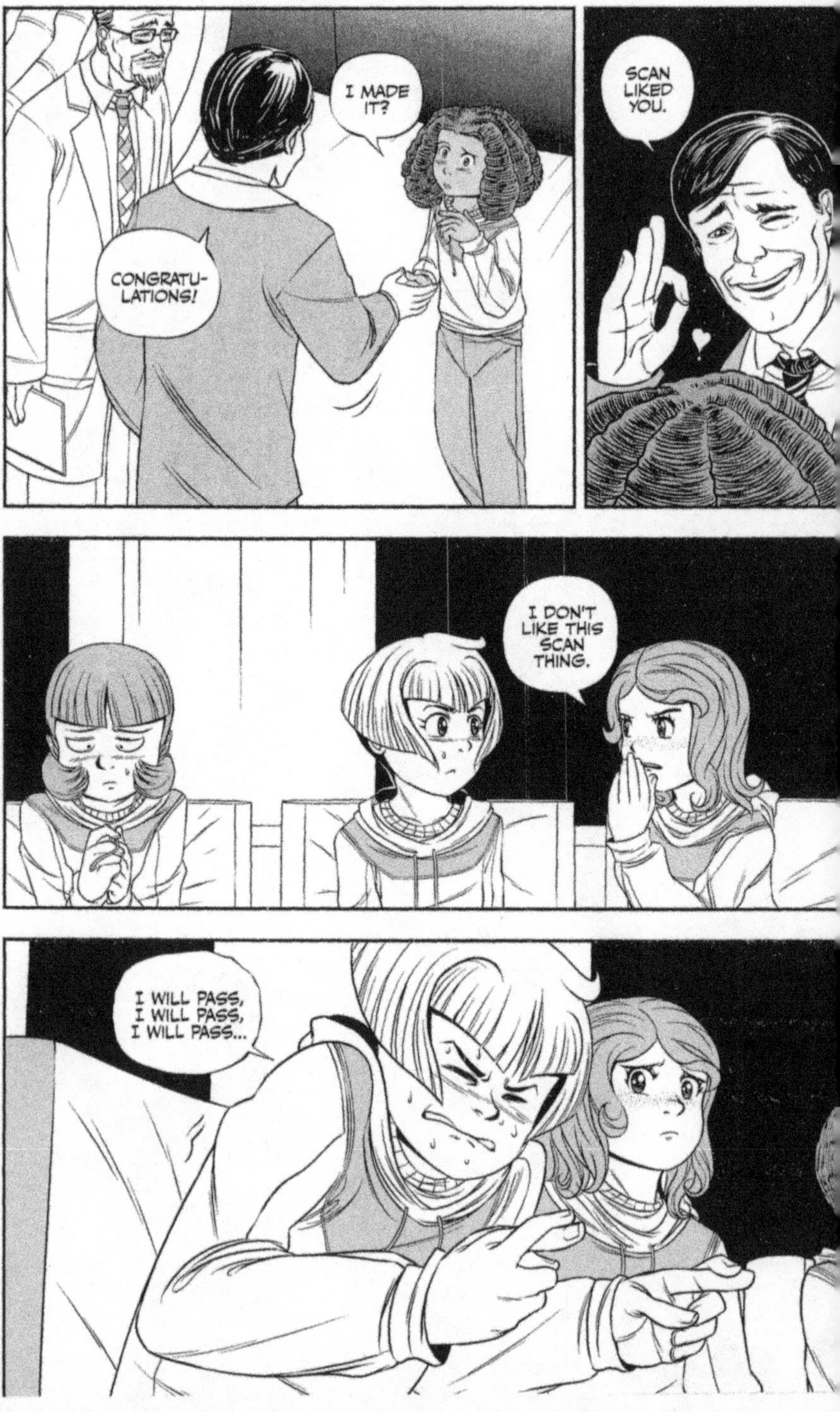
I MADE IT?
CONGRATU-LATIONS!
SCAN LIKED YOU.
I DON'T LIKE THIS SCAN THING.
I WILL PASS, I WILL PASS, I WILL PASS...

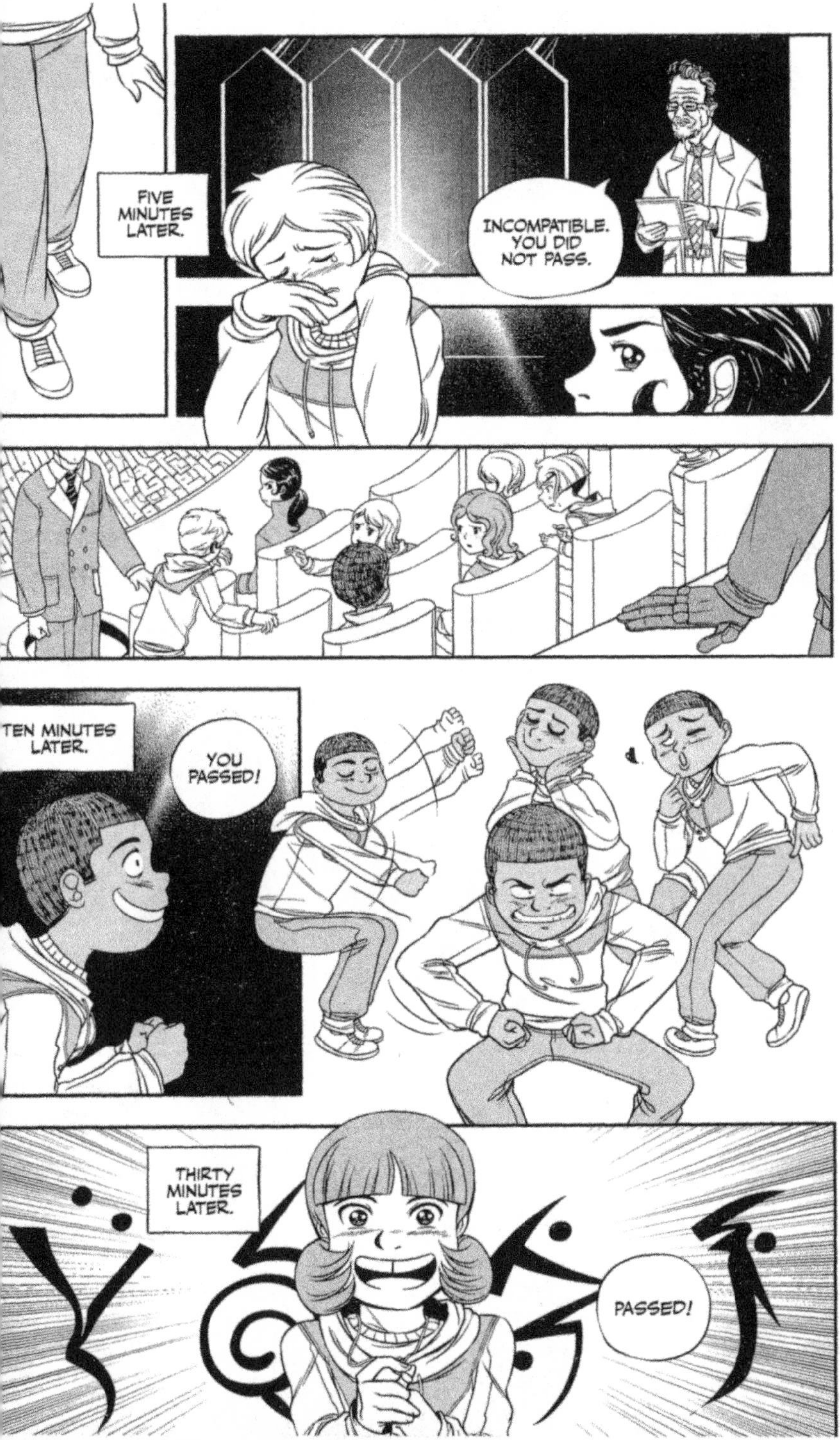
FIVE MINUTES LATER.
INCOMPATIBLE. YOU DID NOT PASS.
TEN MINUTES LATER.
YOU PASSED!
THIRTY MINUTES LATER.
PASSED!

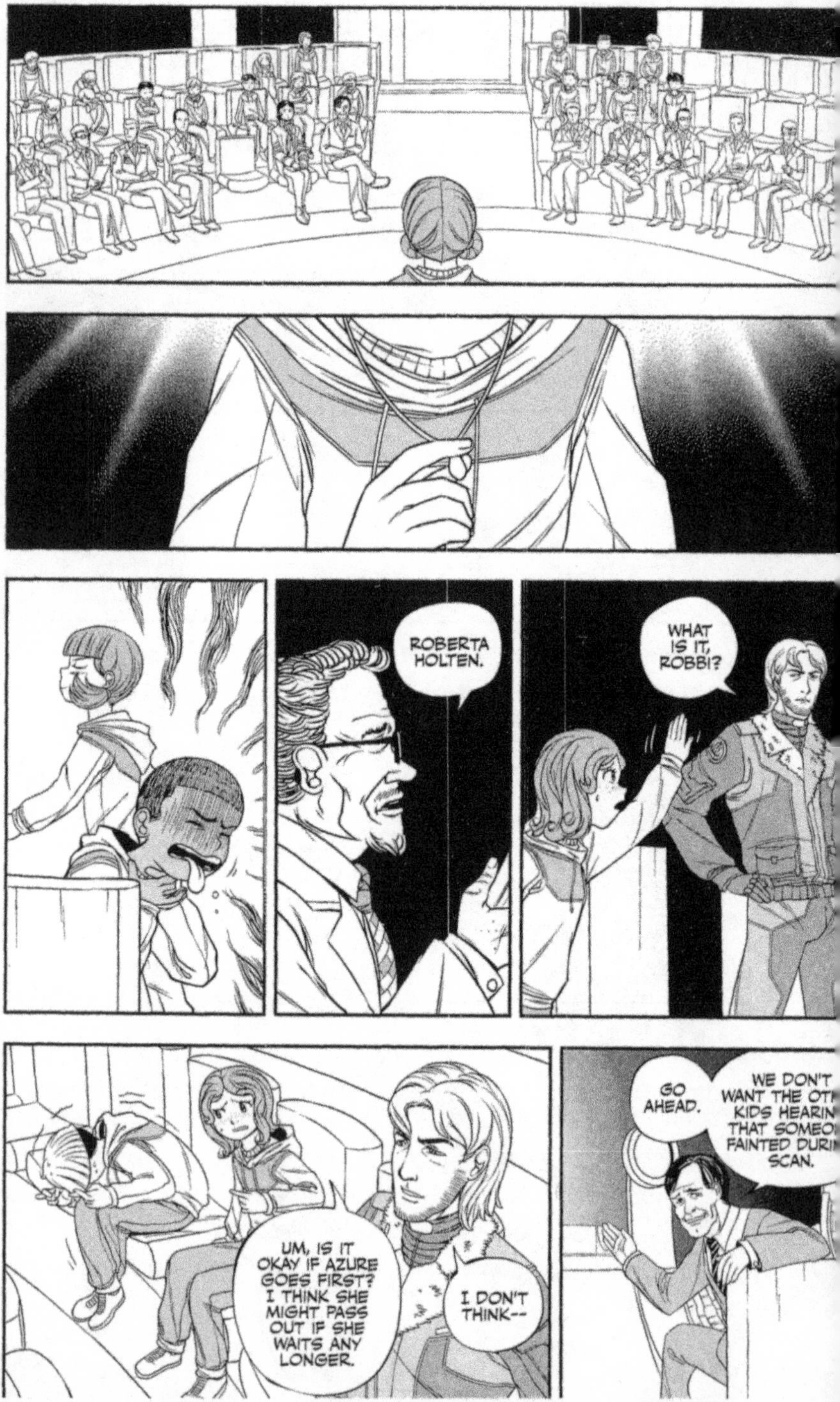
ROBERTA HOLTEN.
WHAT IS IT, ROBBI?
UM, IS IT OKAY IF AZURE GOES FIRST? I THINK SHE MIGHT PASS OUT IF SHE WAITS ANY LONGER.
I DON'T THINK--
GO AHEAD.
WE DON'T WANT THE OT KIDS HEARIN THAT SOMEO FAINTED DURI SCAN.

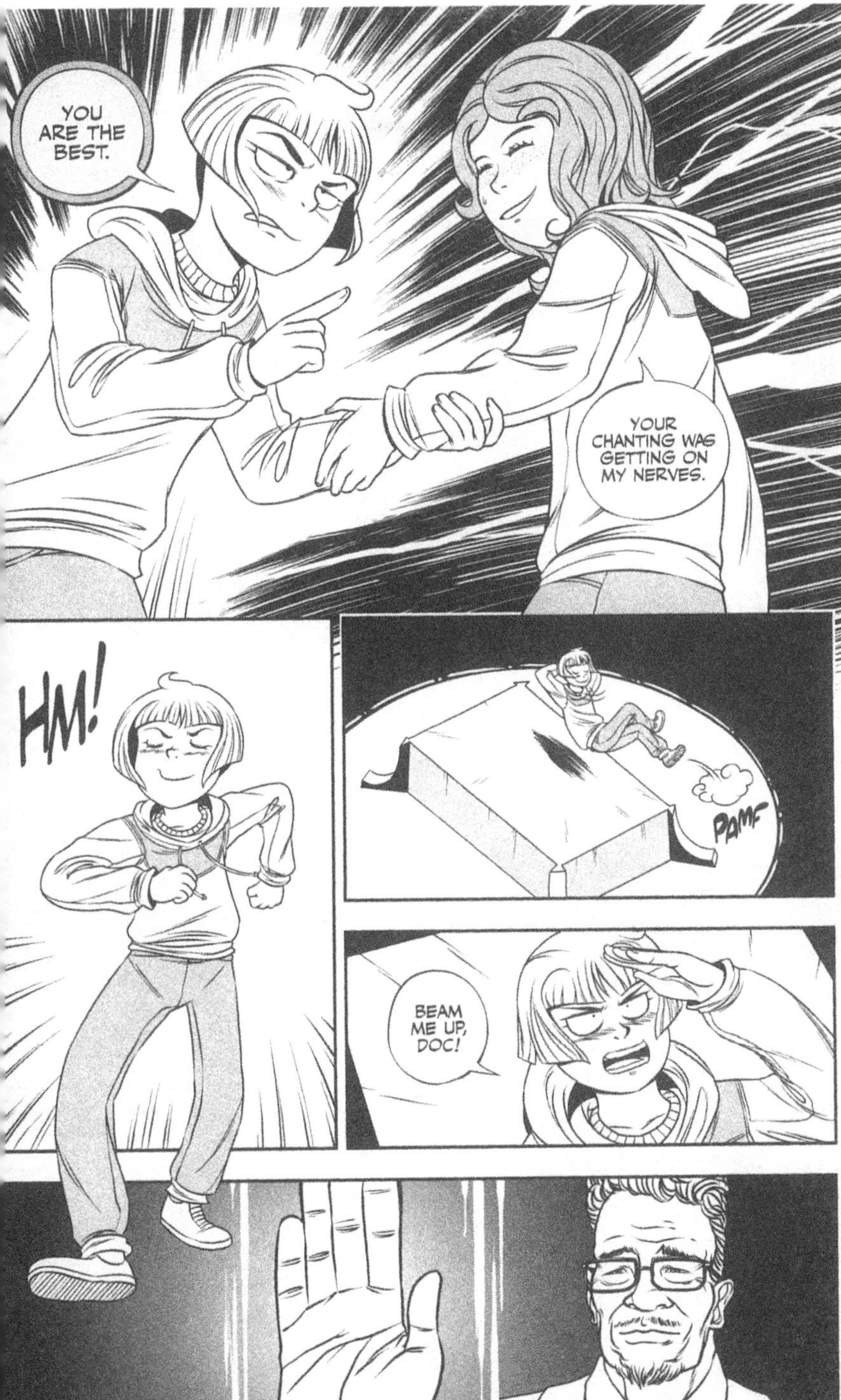
YOU ARE THE BEST.
YOUR CHANTING WAS GETTING ON MY NERVES.
HM!
PAMF
BEAM ME UP, DOC!

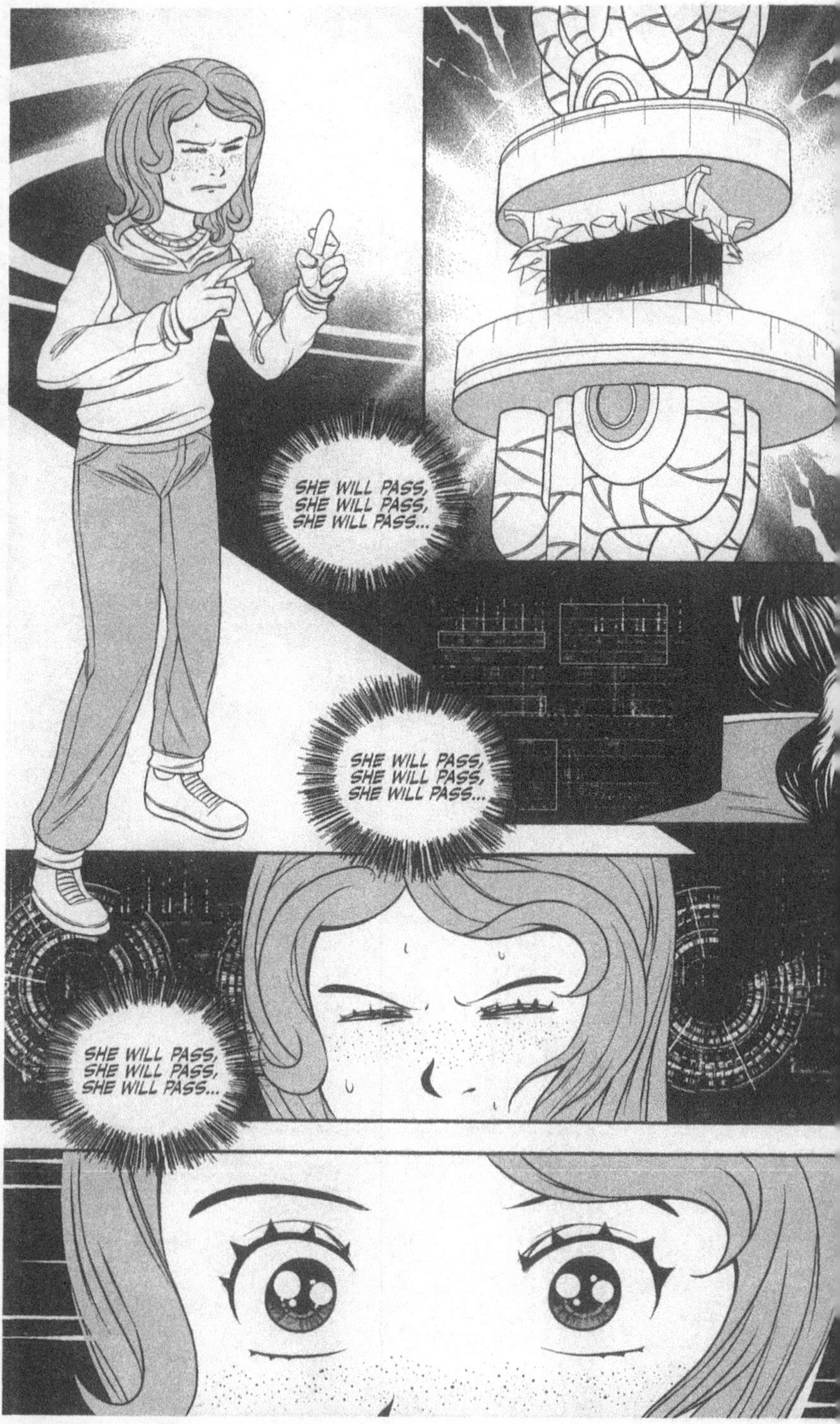
SHE WILL PASS, SHE WILL PASS, SHE WILL PASS...
SHE WILL PASS, SHE WILL PASS, SHE WILL PASS...
SHE WILL PASS, SHE WILL PASS, SHE WILL PASS...

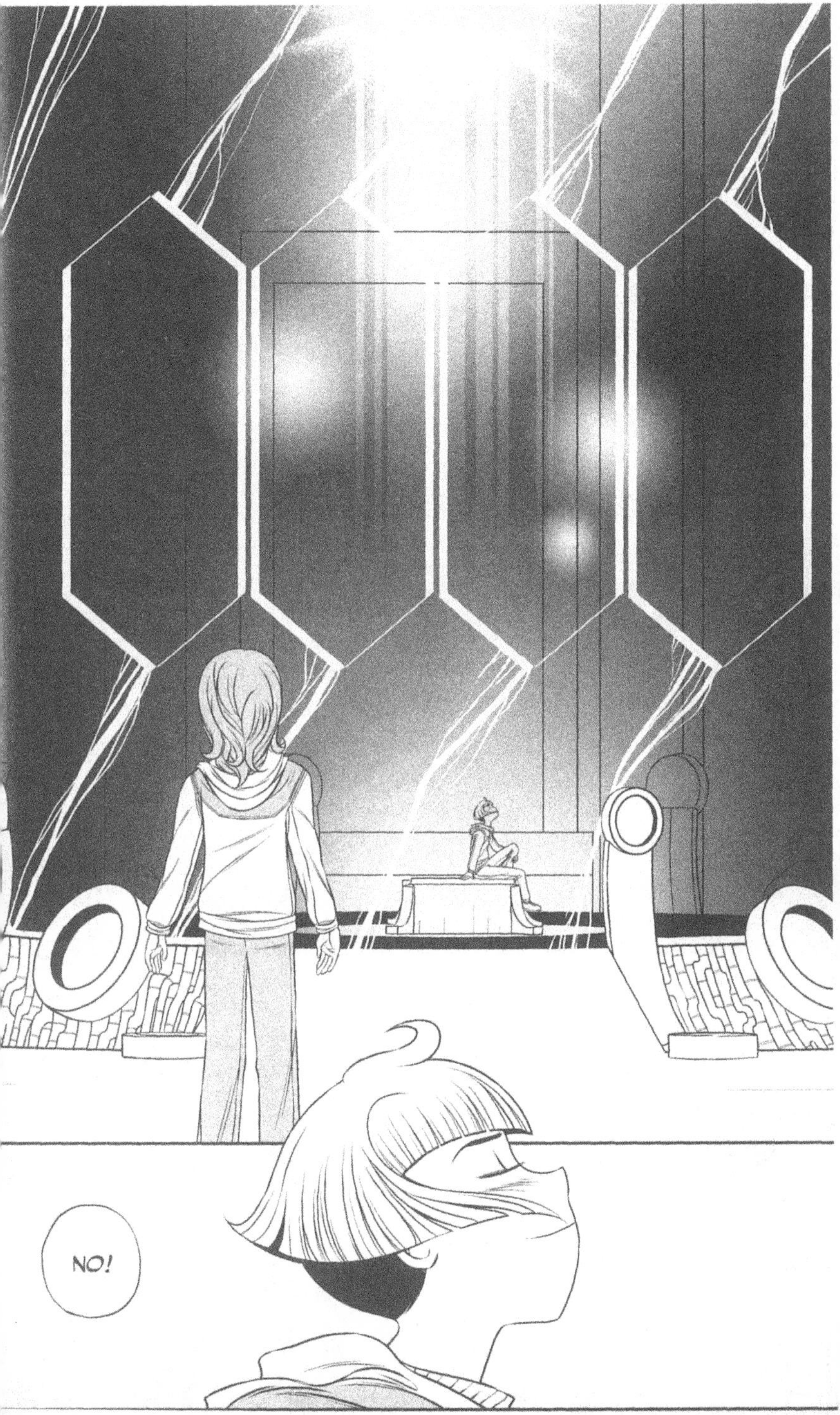
NO!

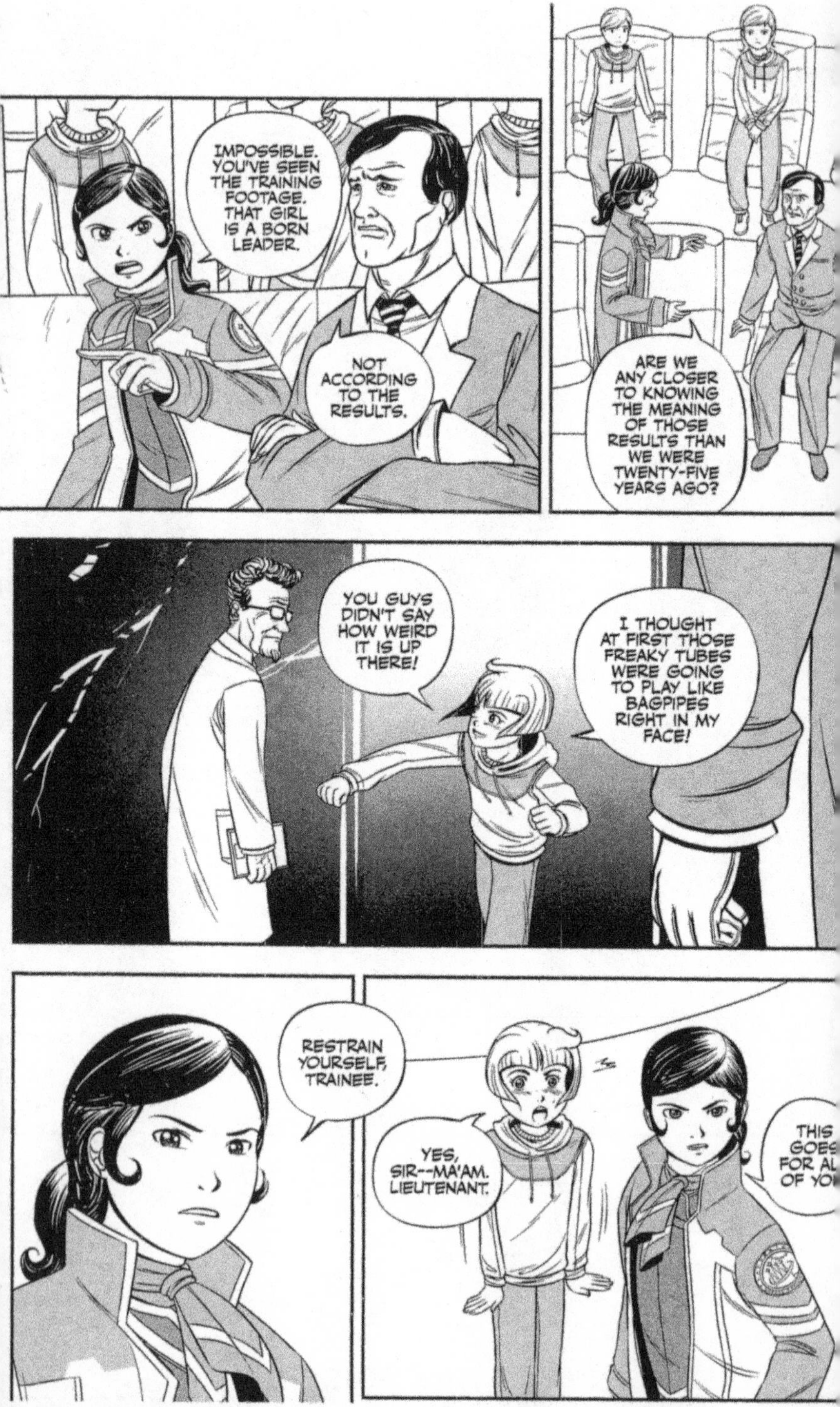
IMPOSSIBLE. YOU'VE SEEN THE TRAINING FOOTAGE. THAT GIRL IS A BORN LEADER.
NOT ACCORDING TO THE RESULTS.
ARE WE ANY CLOSER TO KNOWING THE MEANING OF THOSE RESULTS THAN WE WERE TWENTY-FIVE YEARS AGO?
YOU GUYS DIDN'T SAY HOW WEIRD IT IS UP THERE!
I THOUGHT AT FIRST THOSE FREAKY TUBES WERE GOING TO PLAY LIKE BAGPIPES RIGHT IN MY FACE!
RESTRAIN YOURSELF, TRAINEE.
YES, SIR--MA'AM. LIEUTENANT.

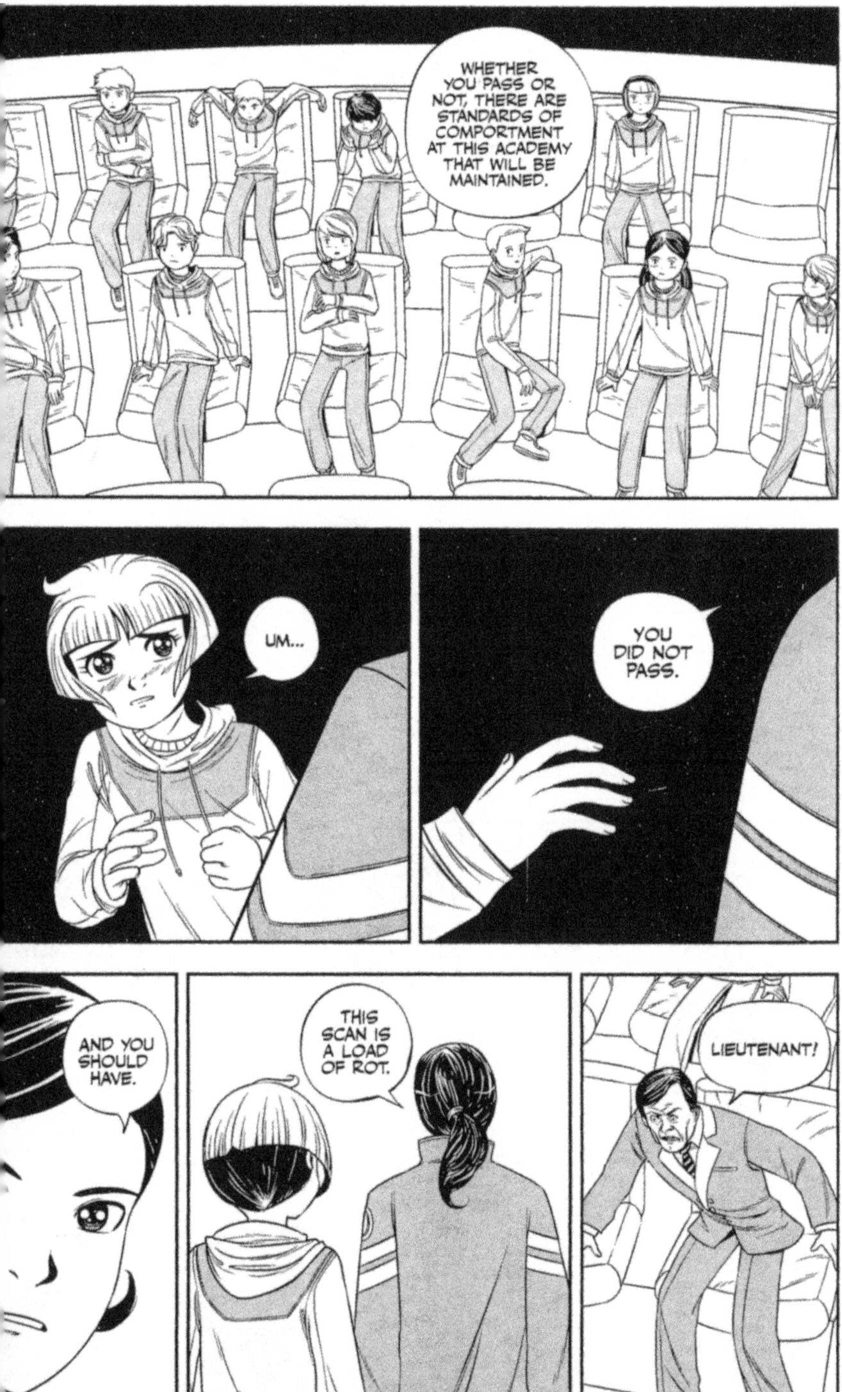
WHETHER YOU PASS OR NOT, THERE ARE STANDARDS OF COMPORTMENT AT THIS ACADEMY THAT WILL BE MAINTAINED.
UM...
YOU DID NOT PASS.
AND YOU SHOULD HAVE.
THIS SCAN IS A LOAD OF ROT.
LIEUTENANT!

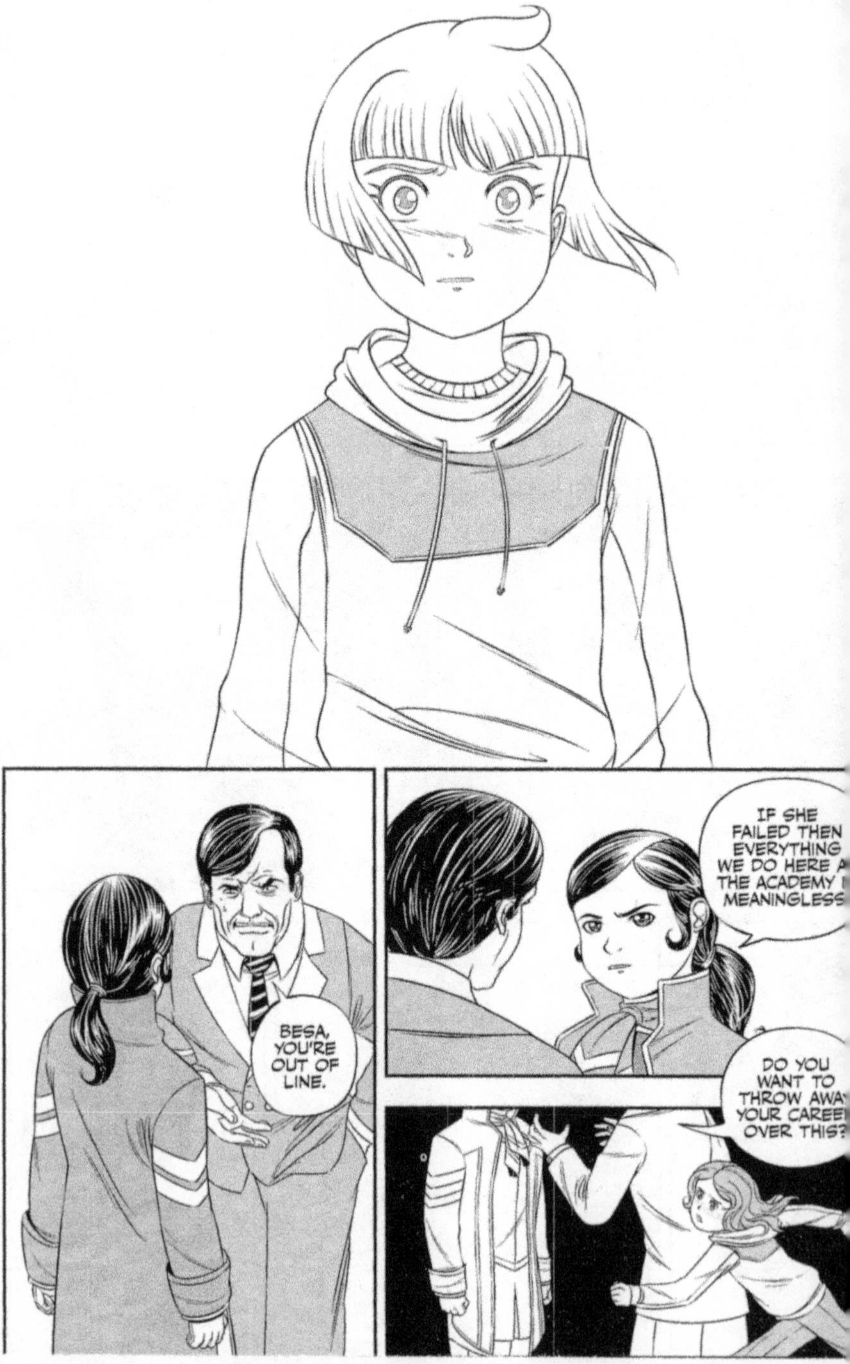
BESA, YOU'RE OUT OF LINE.
IF SHE FAILED THEN EVERYTHING WE DO HERE A THE ACADEMY I MEANINGLESS
DO YOU WANT TO THROW AWA YOUR CAREE OVER THIS?

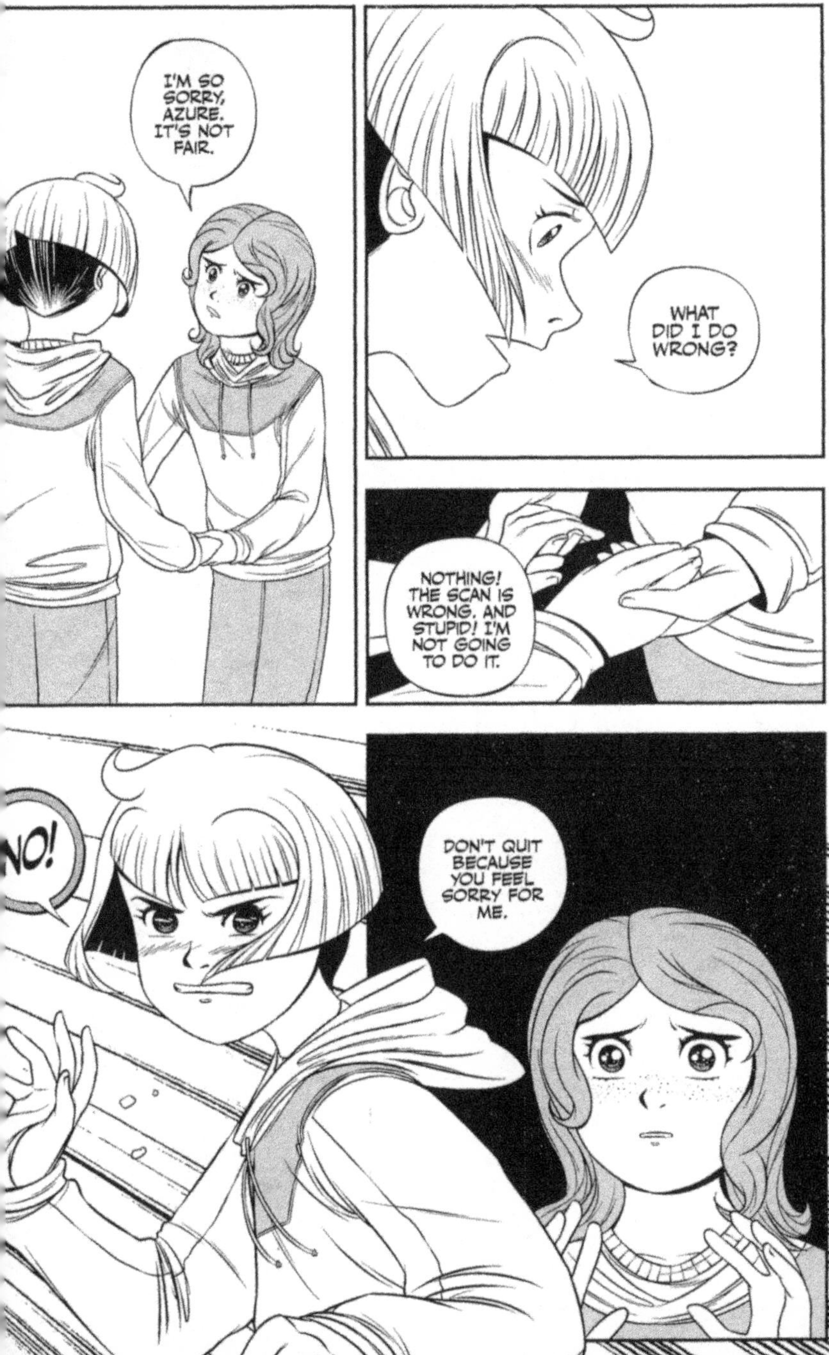
I'M SO SORRY, AZURE. IT'S NOT FAIR.
WHAT DID I DO WRONG?
NOTHING! THE SCAN IS WRONG, AND STUPID! I'M NOT GOING TO DO IT.
NO!
DON'T QUIT BECAUSE YOU FEEL SORRY FOR ME.

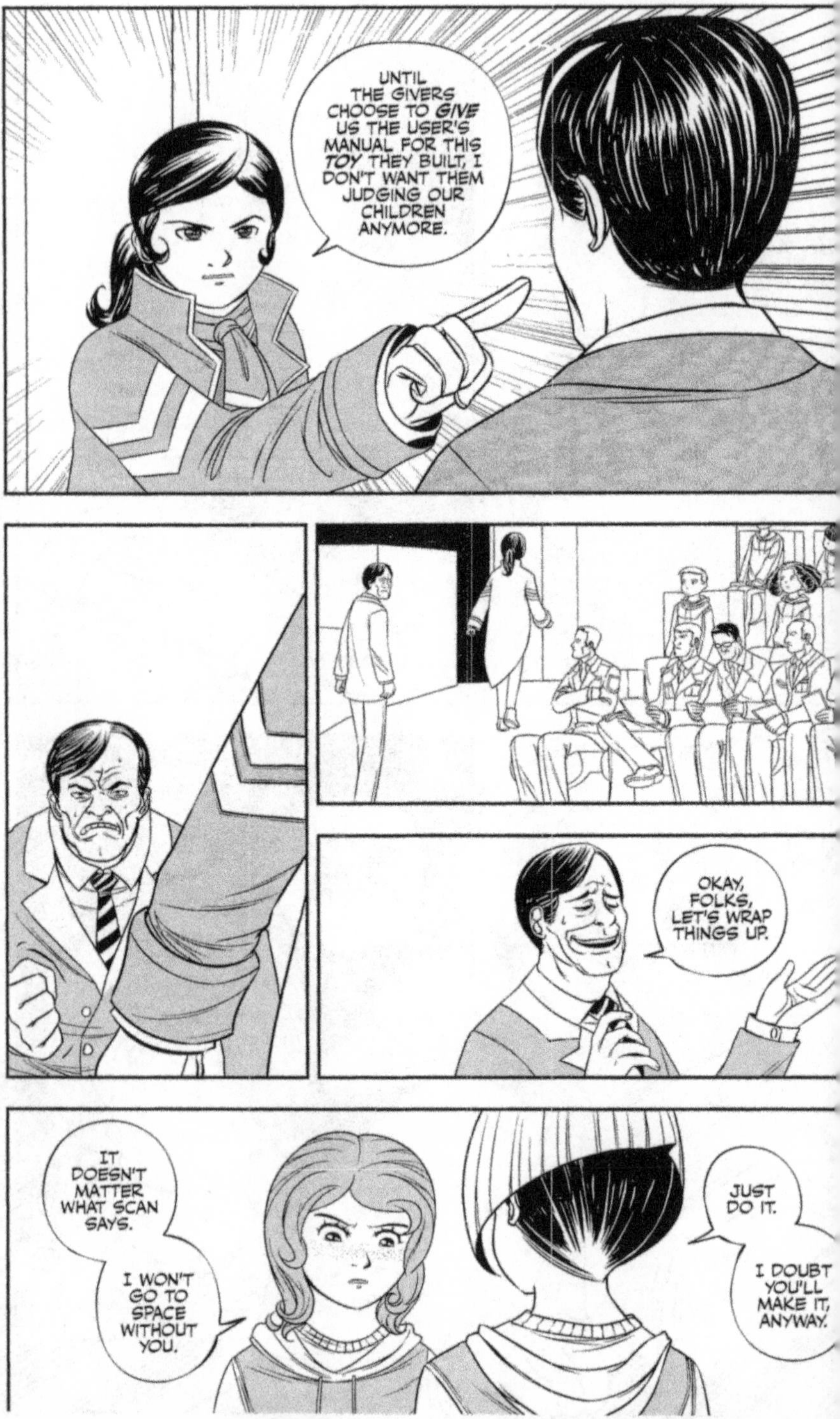
UNTIL THE GIVERS CHOOSE TO *GIVE* US THE USER'S MANUAL FOR THIS *TOY* THEY BUILT, I DON'T WANT THEM JUDGING OUR CHILDREN ANYMORE.
OKAY, FOLKS, LET'S WRAP THINGS UP.
IT DOESN'T MATTER WHAT SCAN SAYS.
I WON'T GO TO SPACE WITHOUT YOU.
JUST DO IT.
I DOUBT YOU'LL MAKE IT, ANYWAY.

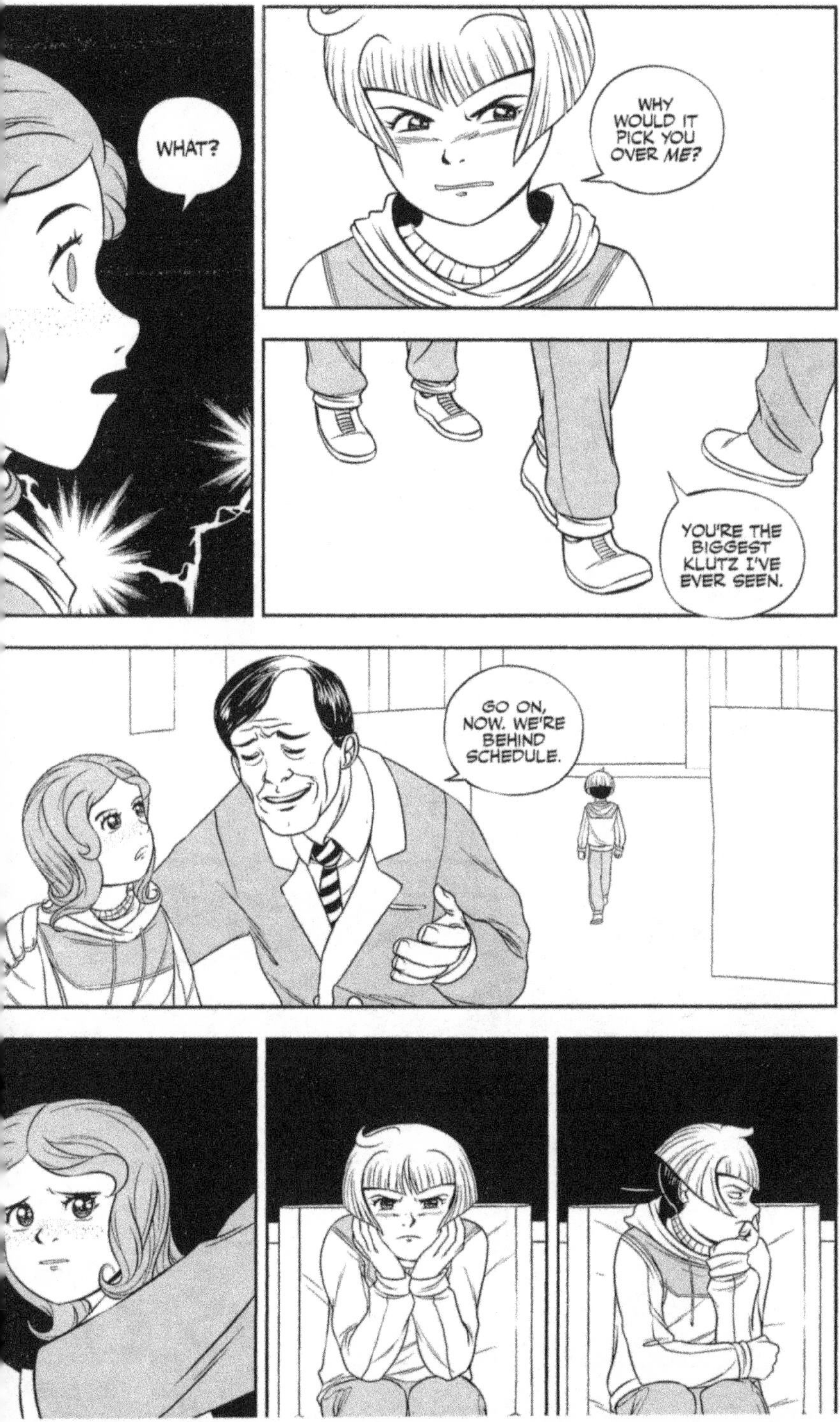
WHAT?
WHY WOULD IT PICK YOU OVER *ME*?
YOU'RE THE BIGGEST KLUTZ I'VE EVER SEEN.
GO ON, NOW. WE'RE BEHIND SCHEDULE.

I THOUGHT NOTHING COULD HURT WORSE THAN MY OWN MOTHER SENDING ME AWAY.

NOW MY BEST FRIEND HATES ME.

THAT HURTS MORE THAN--

HURTS.

MY ARM HURTS.

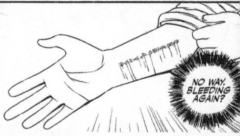

NO WAY. BLEEDING AGAIN?

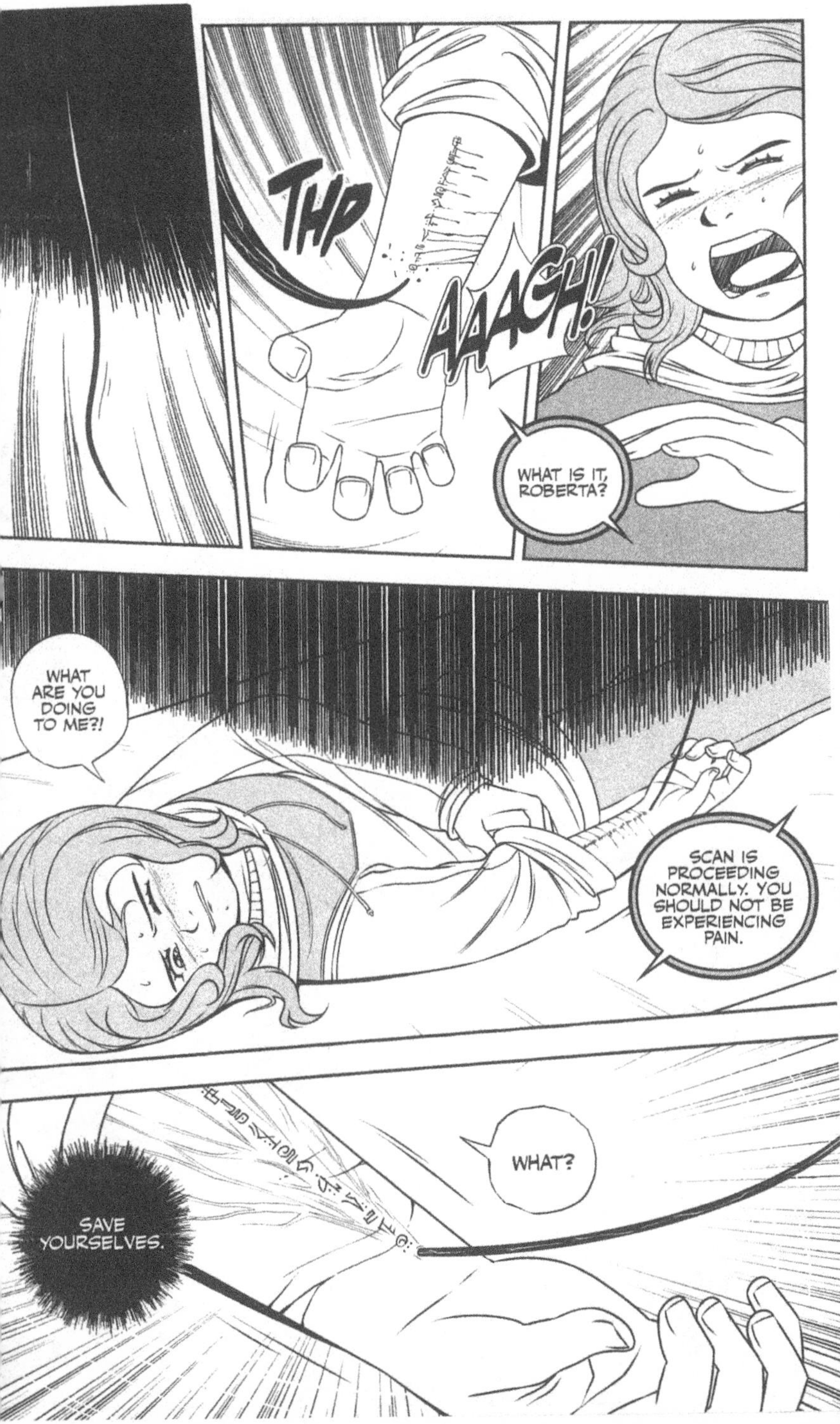
THP
AAAGH!
WHAT IS IT, ROBERTA?
WHAT ARE YOU DOING TO ME?!
SCAN IS PROCEEDING NORMALLY. YOU SHOULD NOT BE EXPERIENCING PAIN.
WHAT?
SAVE YOURSELVES.

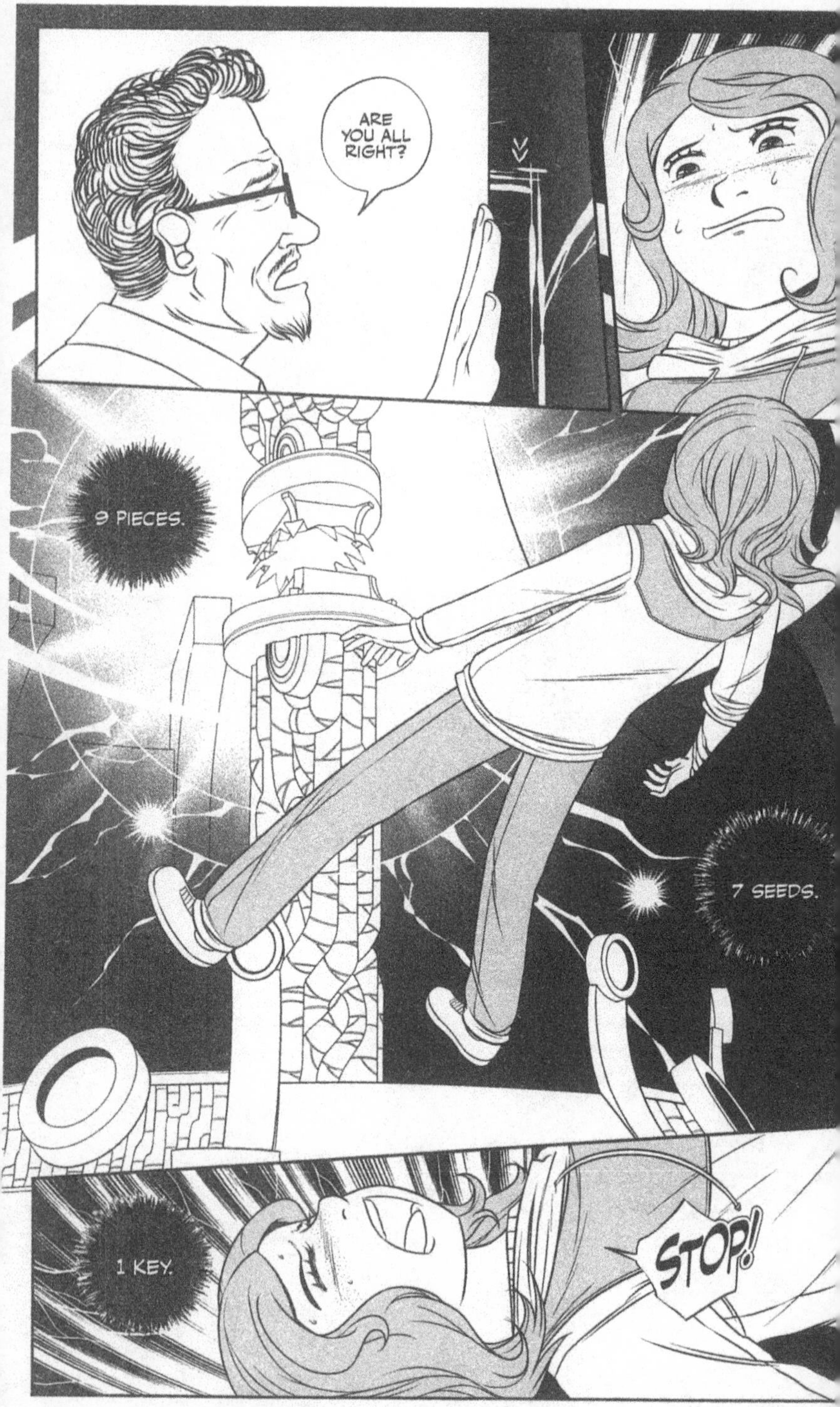
ARE YOU ALL RIGHT?
9 PIECES.
7 SEEDS.
1 KEY.
STOP!

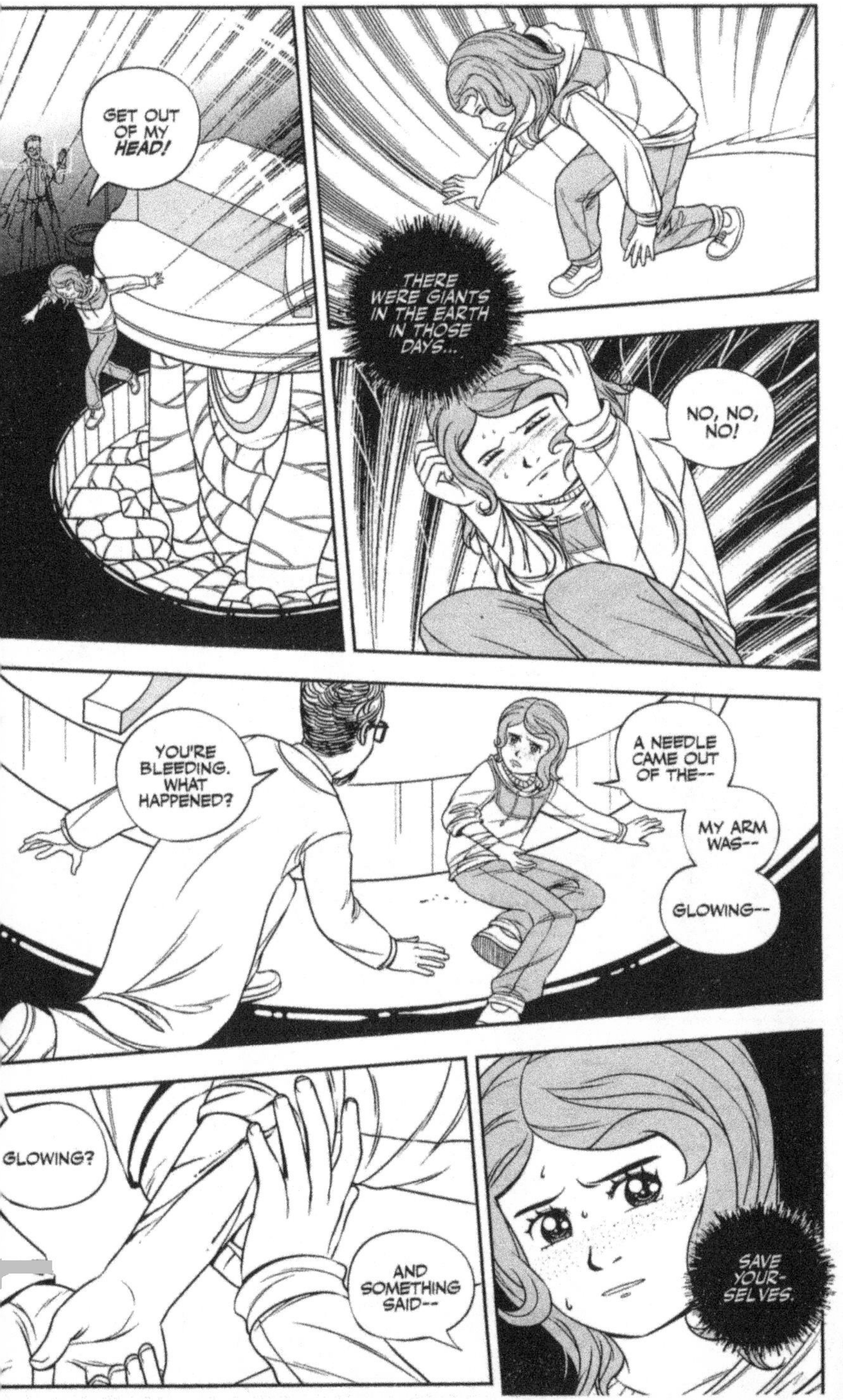
GET OUT OF MY HEAD!
THERE WERE GIANTS IN THE EARTH IN THOSE DAYS...
NO, NO, NO!
YOU'RE BLEEDING. WHAT HAPPENED?
A NEEDLE CAME OUT OF THE--
MY ARM WAS--
GLOWING--
GLOWING?
AND SOMETHING SAID--
SAVE YOUR-SELVES.

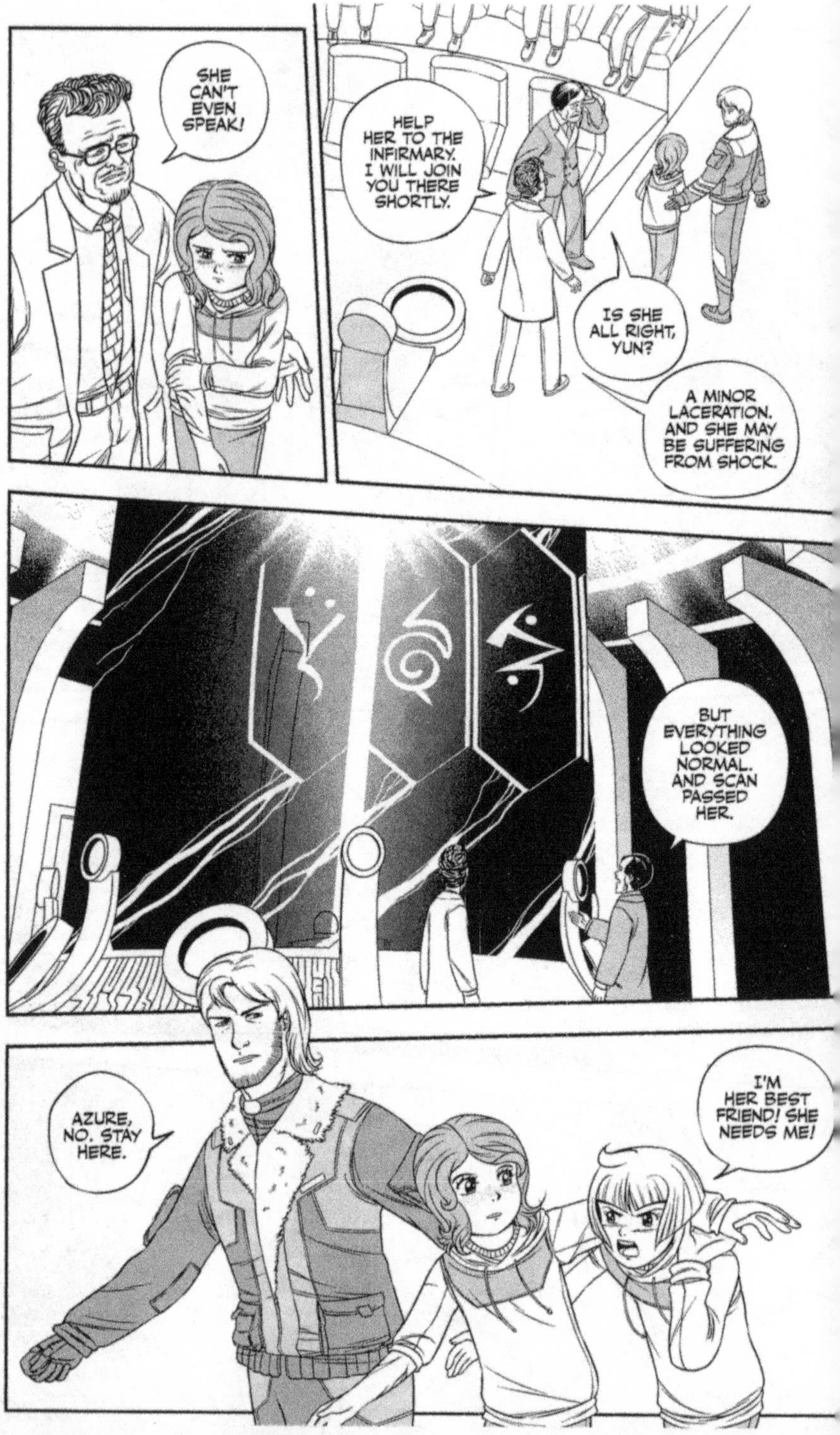
SHE CAN'T EVEN SPEAK!
HELP HER TO THE INFIRMARY. I WILL JOIN YOU THERE SHORTLY.
IS SHE ALL RIGHT, YUN?
A MINOR LACERATION. AND SHE MAY BE SUFFERING FROM SHOCK.
BUT EVERYTHING LOOKED NORMAL. AND SCAN PASSED HER.
AZURE, NO. STAY HERE.
I'M HER BEST FRIEND! SHE NEEDS ME!

DON'T YOU HATE ME?

YOU ALWAYS GIVE UP WHAT YOU WANT FOR THE PEOPLE YOU LOVE.

I SAID THAT STUFF SO YOU WOULDN'T DO THAT FOR ME.

BUT-- THAT'S--

BRILLIANT? I KNOW. HEY, DON'T GET BLOOD ON ME!

SOME PEOPLE DO GET A LITTLE SICK RIDING ON THAT PLATFORM. LIKE IN THE PLEASURE DOME.

YOUR FRIEND WILL BE FINE.

I'LL WALK YOU BACK TO YOUR CLASSROOM TO WAIT FOR YOUR TEACHER. TO MAKE SURE YOU GET THERE, UH, RESPONSIBLY.

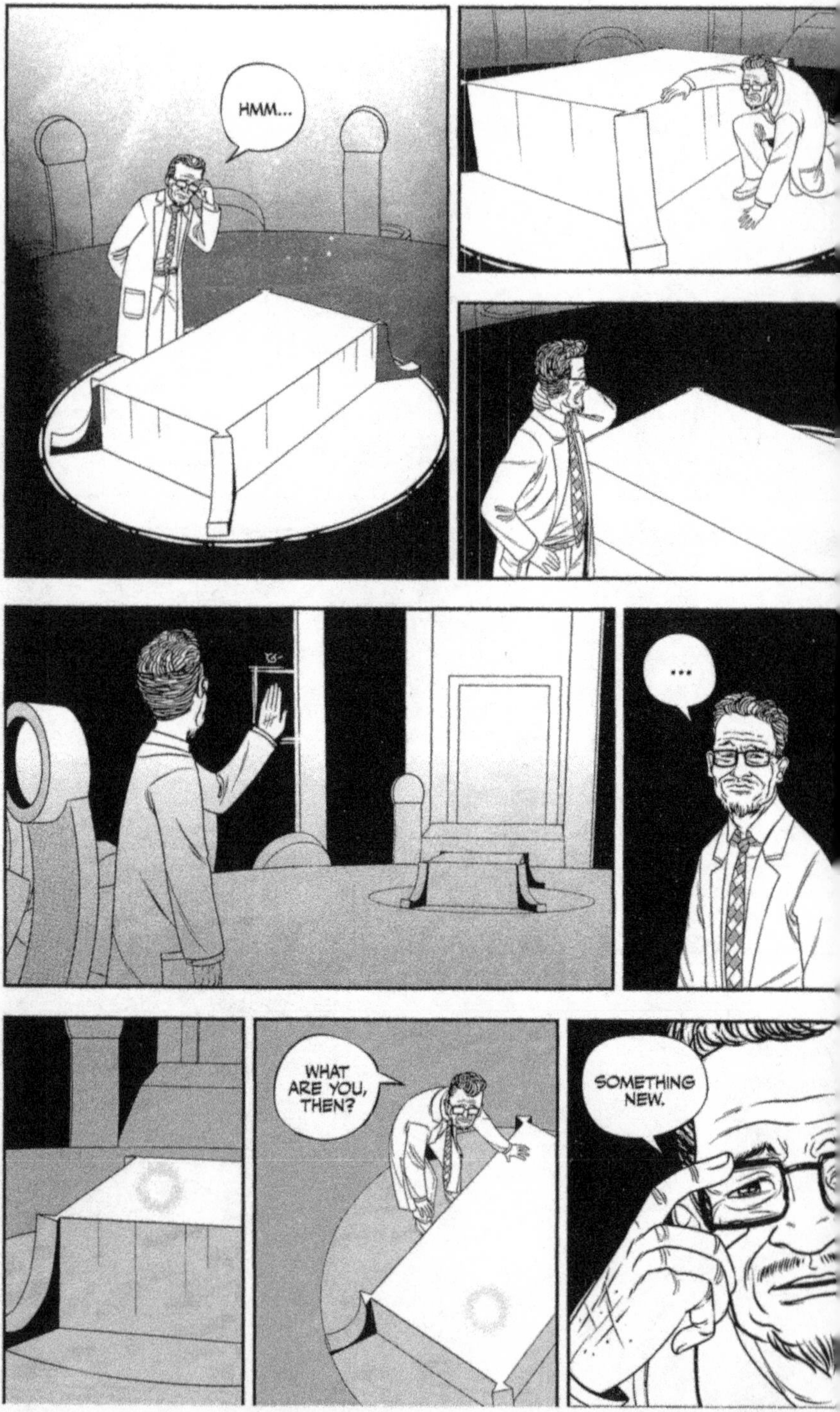
HMM...
...
WHAT ARE YOU, THEN?
SOMETHING NEW.

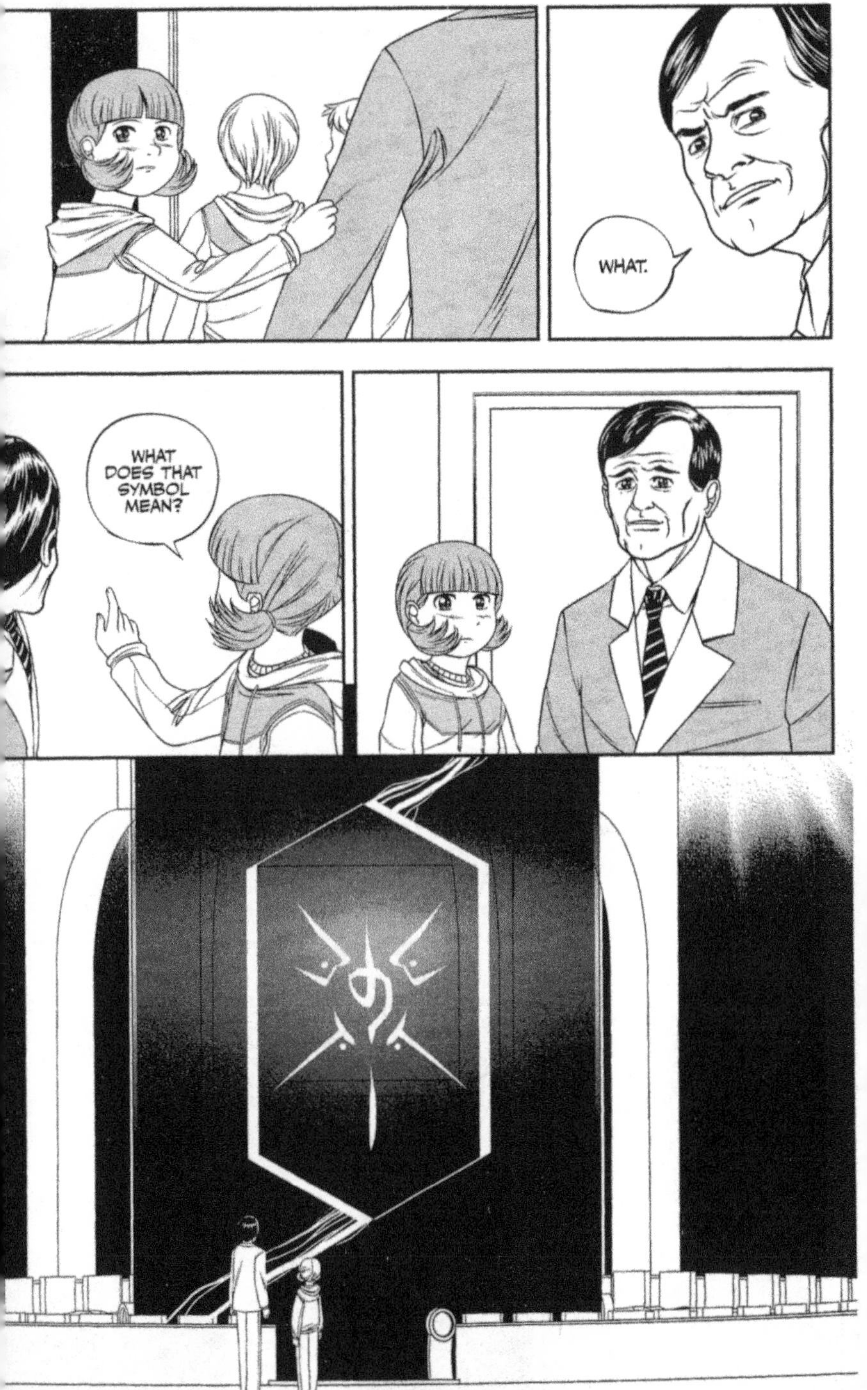
WHAT.
WHAT DOES THAT SYMBOL MEAN?

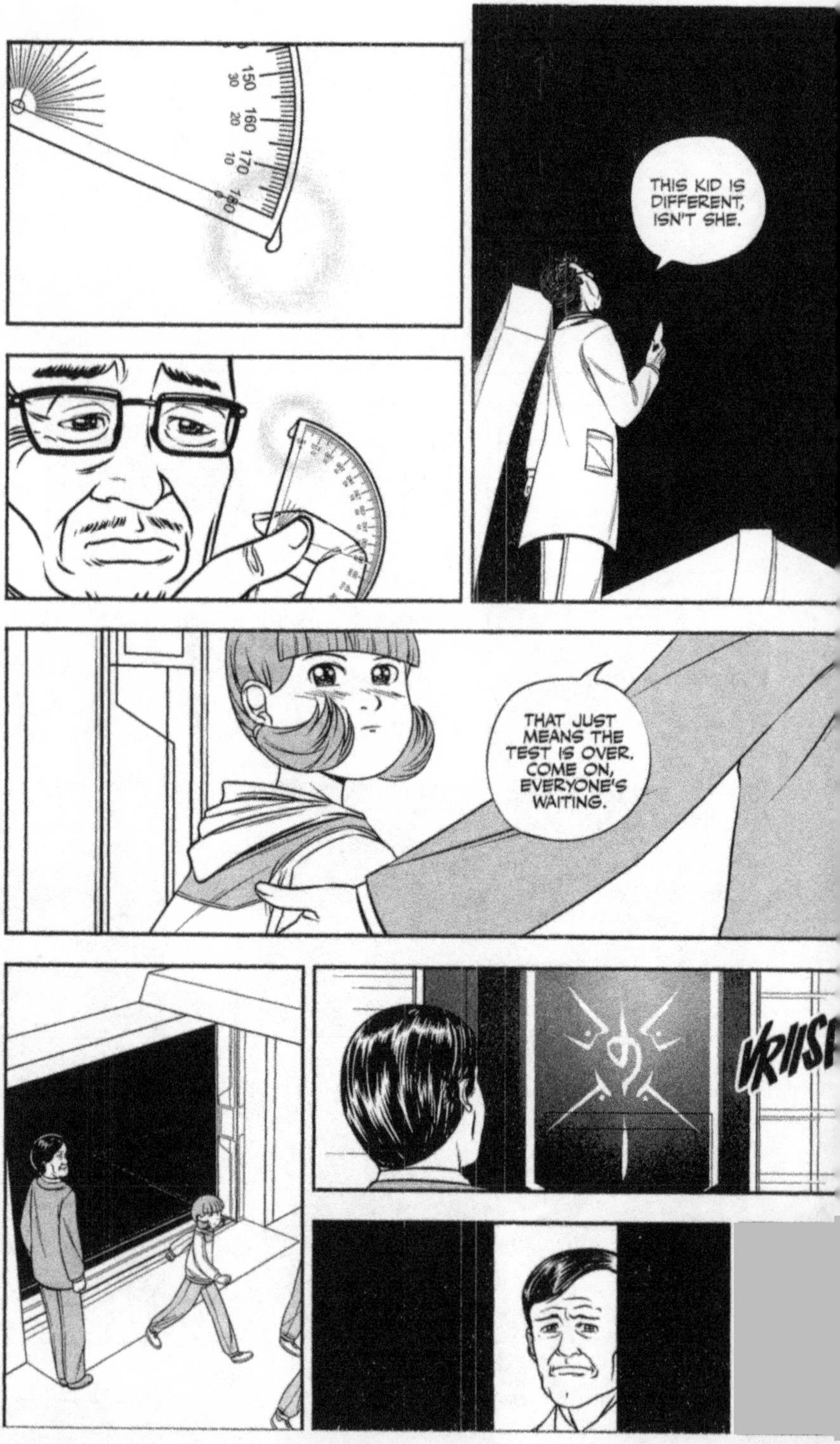
THIS KID IS DIFFERENT, ISN'T SHE.
THAT JUST MEANS THE TEST IS OVER. COME ON, EVERYONE'S WAITING.
VRIIS

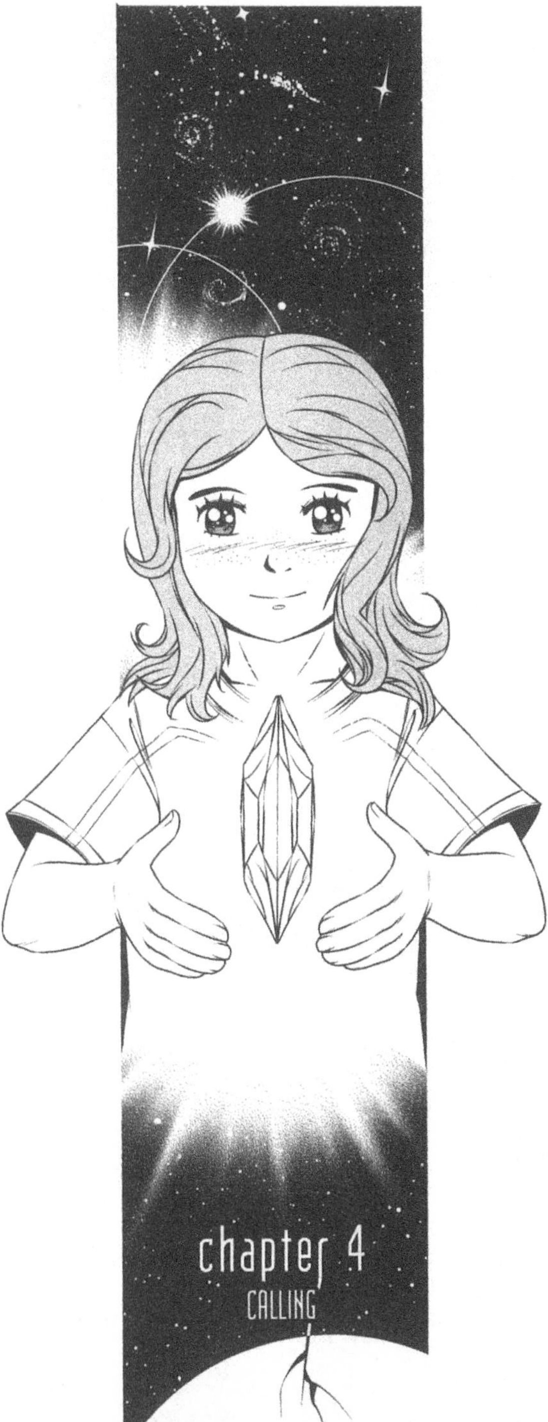
chapter 4
CALLING

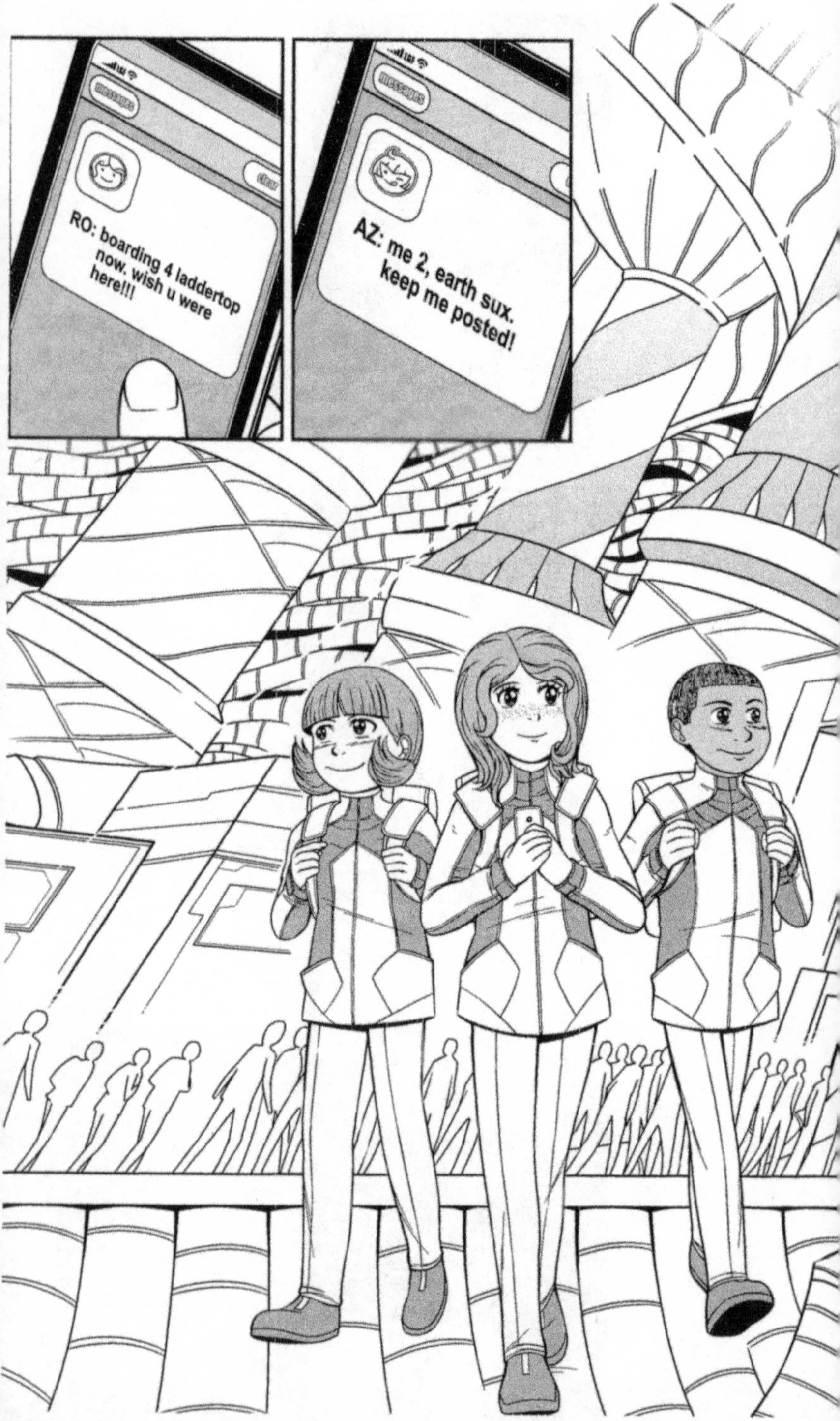
messages
RO: boarding 4 laddertop now. wish u were here!!!
messages
AZ: me 2, earth sux. keep me posted!

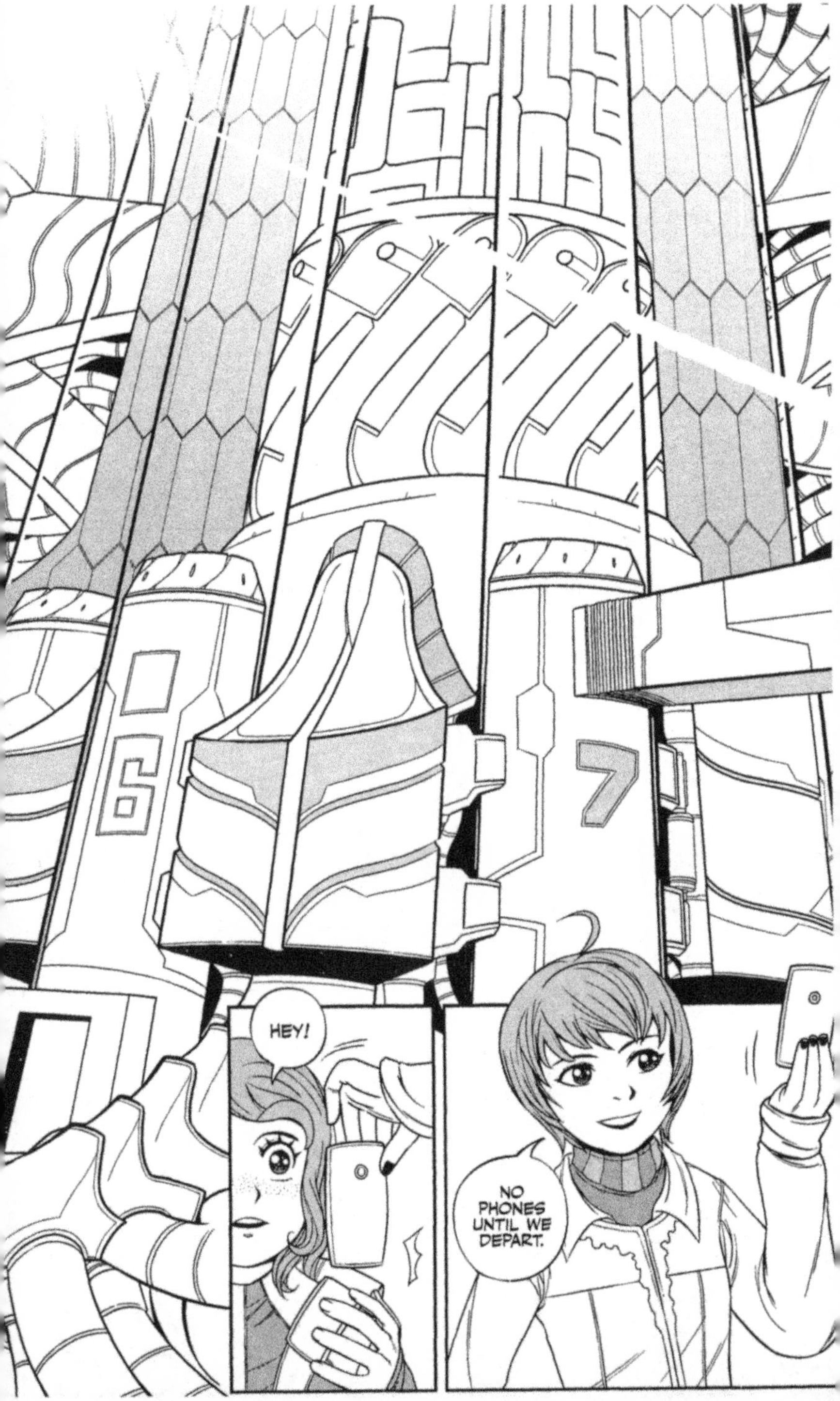
6
7
HEY!
NO PHONES UNTIL WE DEPART.

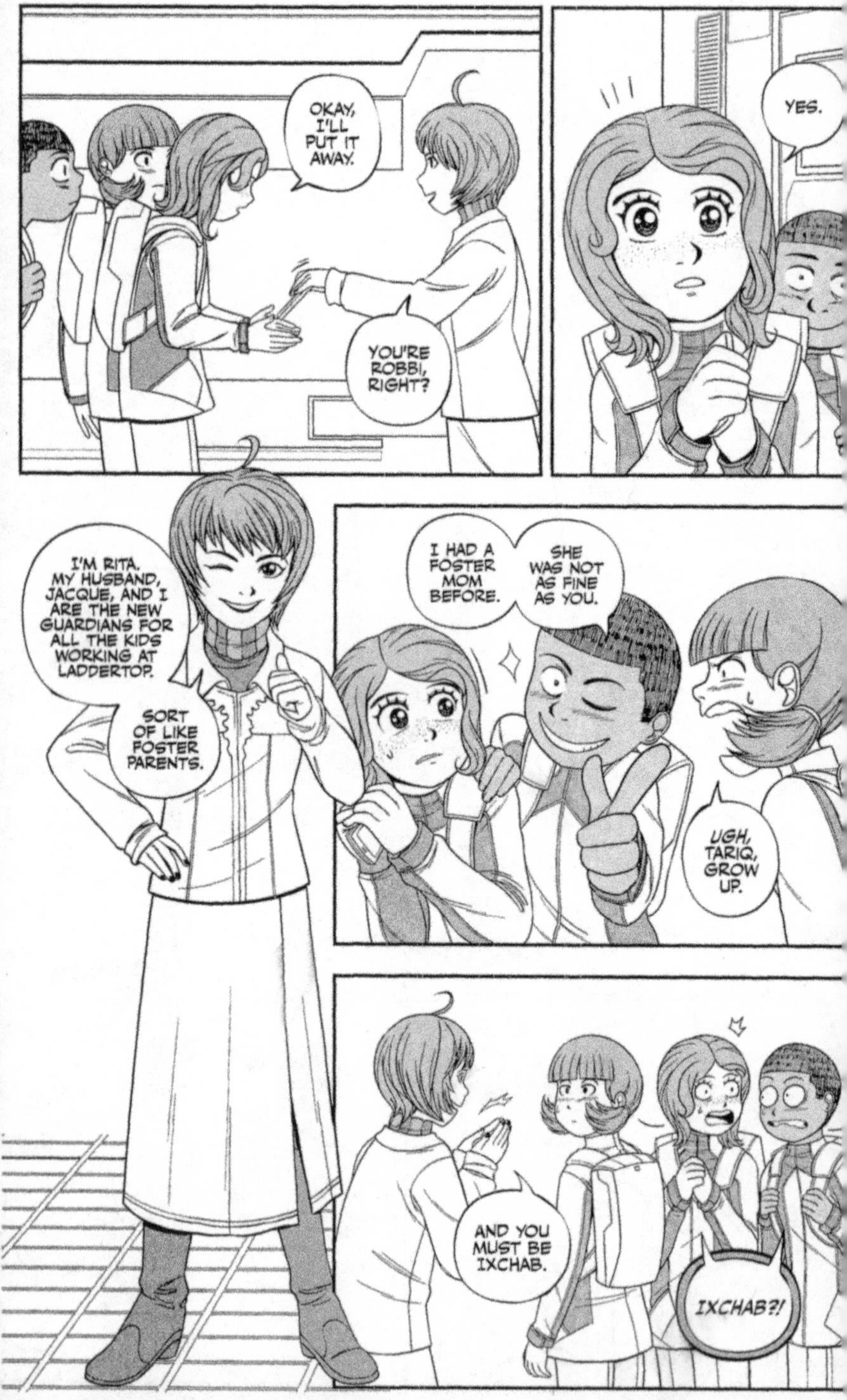
OKAY, I'LL PUT IT AWAY.
YOU'RE ROBBI, RIGHT?
YES.
I'M RITA. MY HUSBAND, JACQUE, AND I ARE THE NEW GUARDIANS FOR ALL THE KIDS WORKING AT LADDERTOP.
SORT OF LIKE FOSTER PARENTS.
I HAD A FOSTER MOM BEFORE.
SHE WAS NOT AS FINE AS YOU.
UGH, TARIQ, GROW UP.
AND YOU MUST BE IXCHAB.
IXCHAB?!

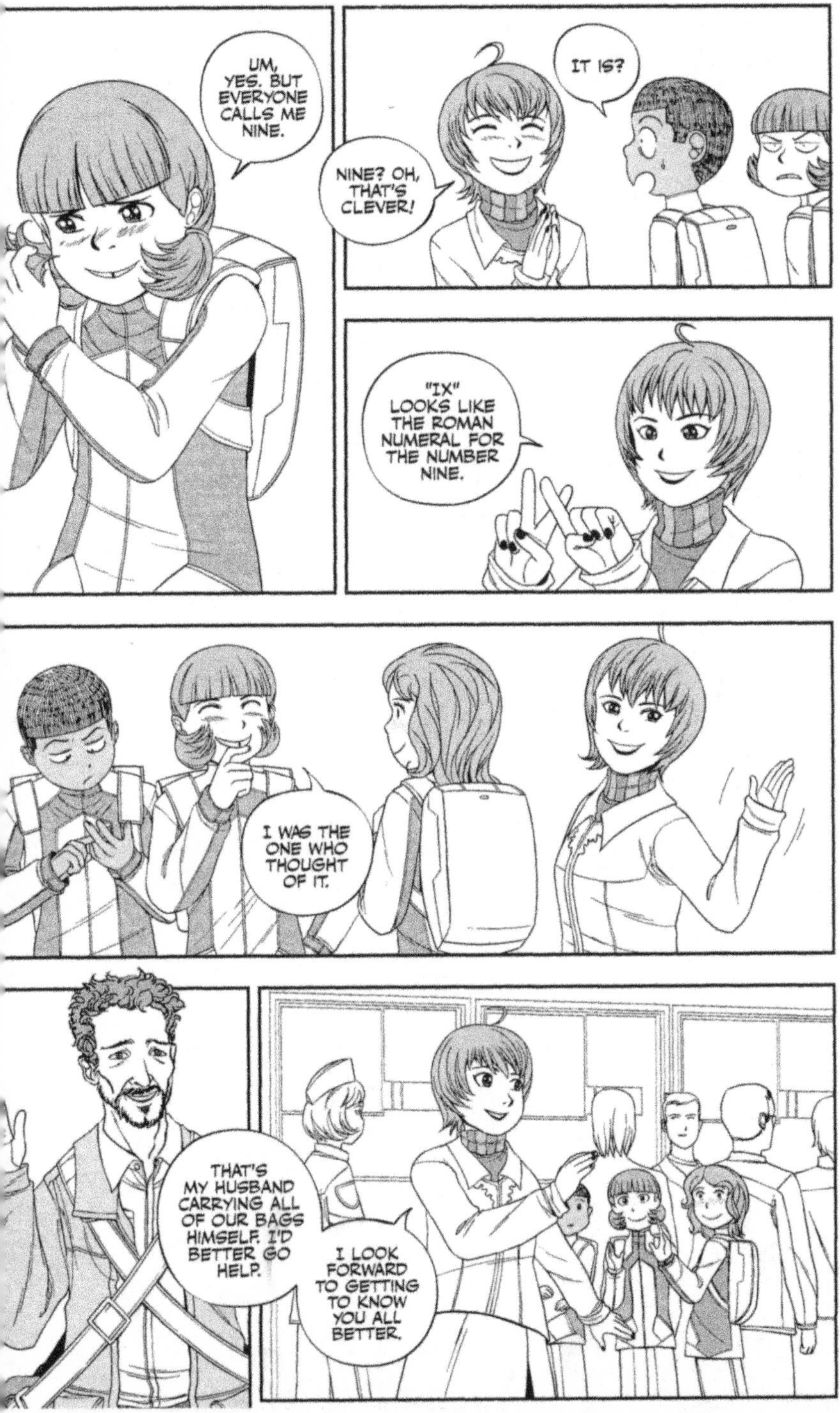
UM, YES. BUT EVERYONE CALLS ME NINE.
NINE? OH, THAT'S CLEVER!
IT IS?
"IX" LOOKS LIKE THE ROMAN NUMERAL FOR THE NUMBER NINE.
I WAS THE ONE WHO THOUGHT OF IT.
THAT'S MY HUSBAND CARRYING ALL OF OUR BAGS HIMSELF. I'D BETTER GO HELP.
I LOOK FORWARD TO GETTING TO KNOW YOU ALL BETTER.

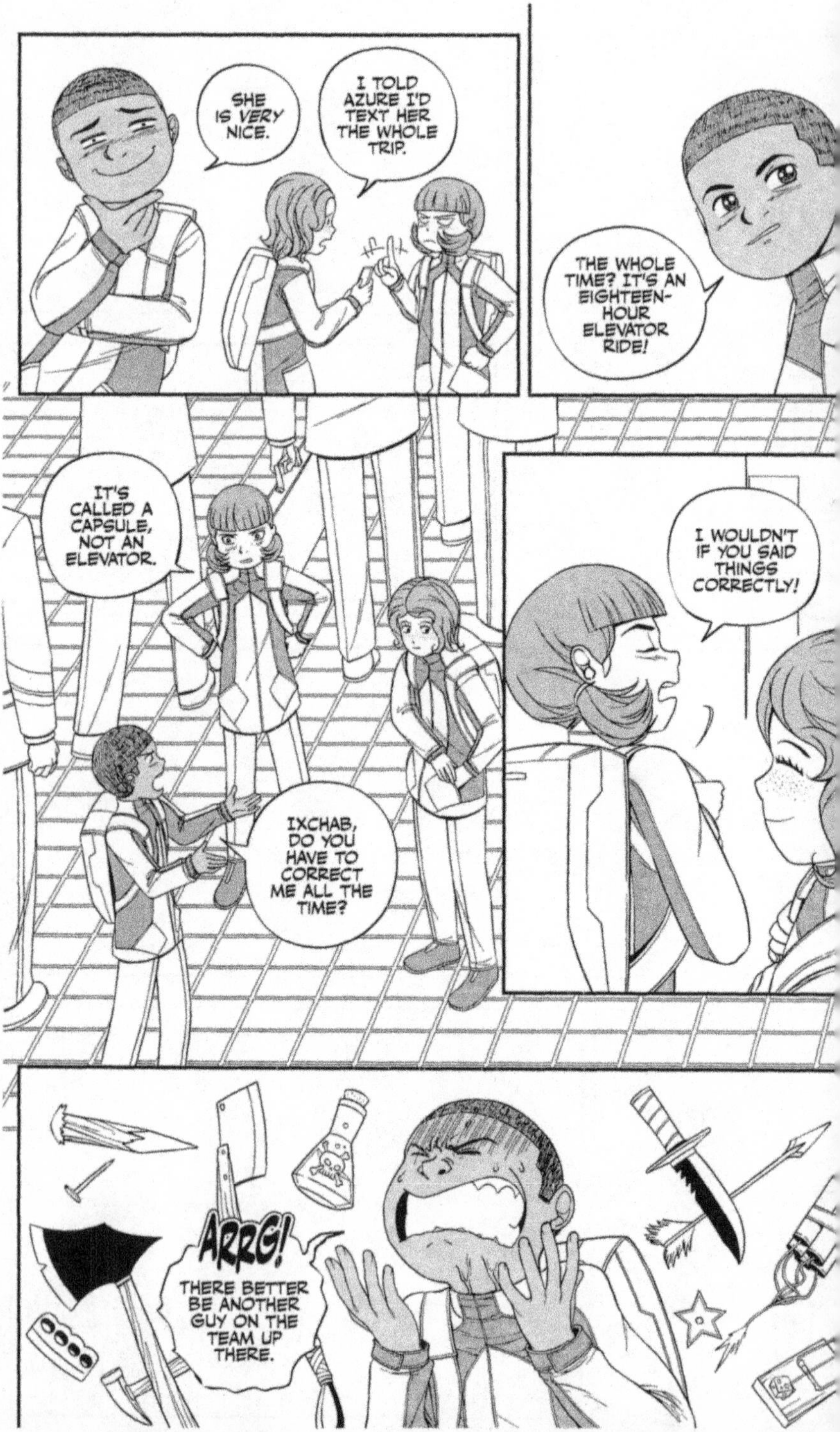
SHE IS *VERY* NICE.
I TOLD AZURE I'D TEXT HER THE WHOLE TRIP.
THE WHOLE TIME? IT'S AN EIGHTEEN-HOUR ELEVATOR RIDE!
IT'S CALLED A CAPSULE, NOT AN ELEVATOR.
IXCHAB, DO YOU HAVE TO CORRECT ME ALL THE TIME?
I WOULDN'T IF YOU SAID THINGS CORRECTLY!
ARRG!
THERE BETTER BE ANOTHER GUY ON THE TEAM UP THERE.

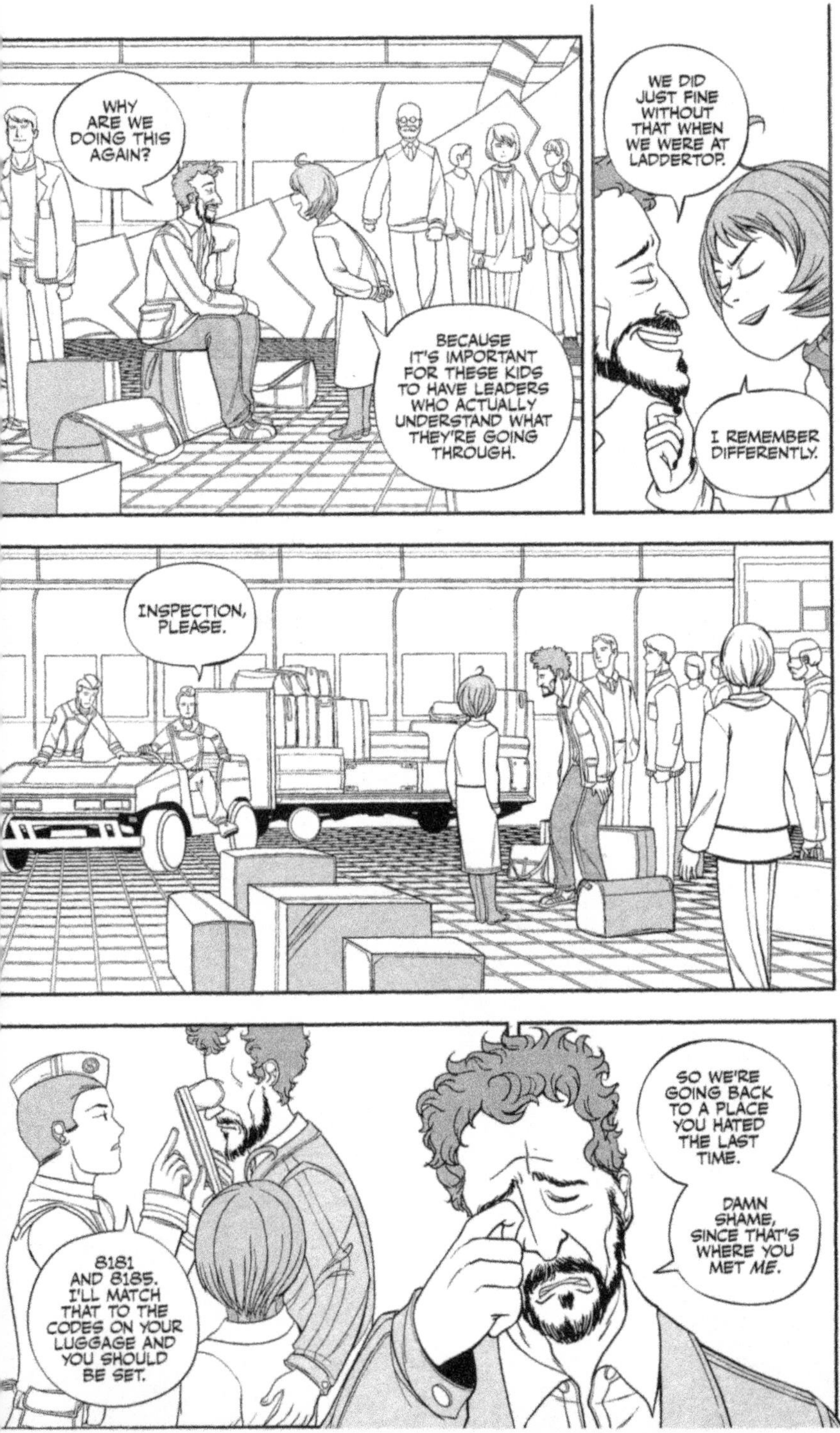
WHY ARE WE DOING THIS AGAIN?
BECAUSE IT'S IMPORTANT FOR THESE KIDS TO HAVE LEADERS WHO ACTUALLY UNDERSTAND WHAT THEY'RE GOING THROUGH.
WE DID JUST FINE WITHOUT THAT WHEN WE WERE AT LADDERTOP.
I REMEMBER DIFFERENTLY.
INSPECTION, PLEASE.
8181 AND 8185. I'LL MATCH THAT TO THE CODES ON YOUR LUGGAGE AND YOU SHOULD BE SET.
SO WE'RE GOING BACK TO A PLACE YOU HATED THE LAST TIME.
DAMN SHAME, SINCE THAT'S WHERE YOU MET *ME*.

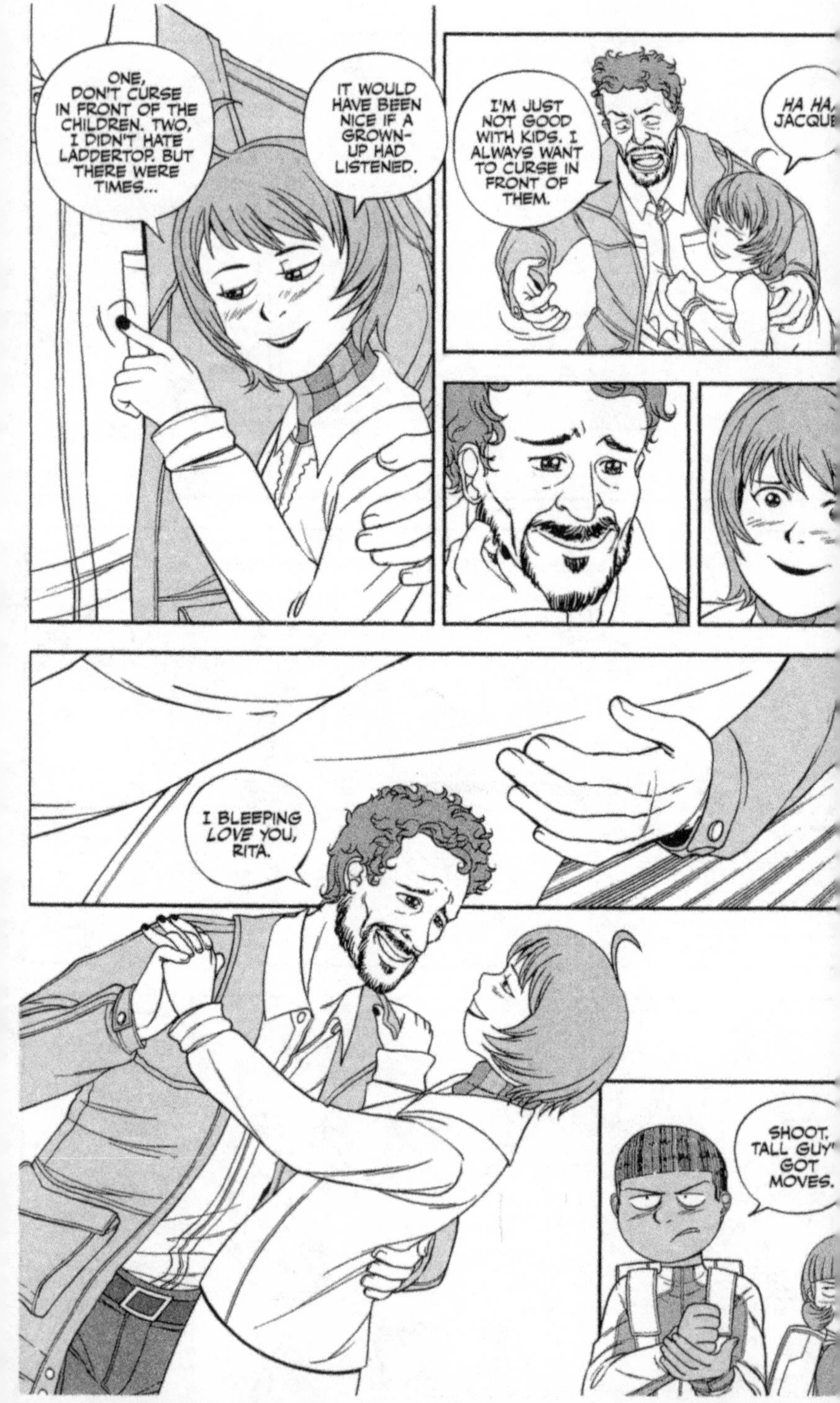
ONE, DON'T CURSE IN FRONT OF THE CHILDREN. TWO, I DIDN'T HATE LADDERTOP. BUT THERE WERE TIMES...
IT WOULD HAVE BEEN NICE IF A GROWN-UP HAD LISTENED.
I'M JUST NOT GOOD WITH KIDS. I ALWAYS WANT TO CURSE IN FRONT OF THEM.
HA HA, JACQU
I BLEEPING *LOVE* YOU, RITA.
SHOOT. TALL GUY' GOT MOVES.

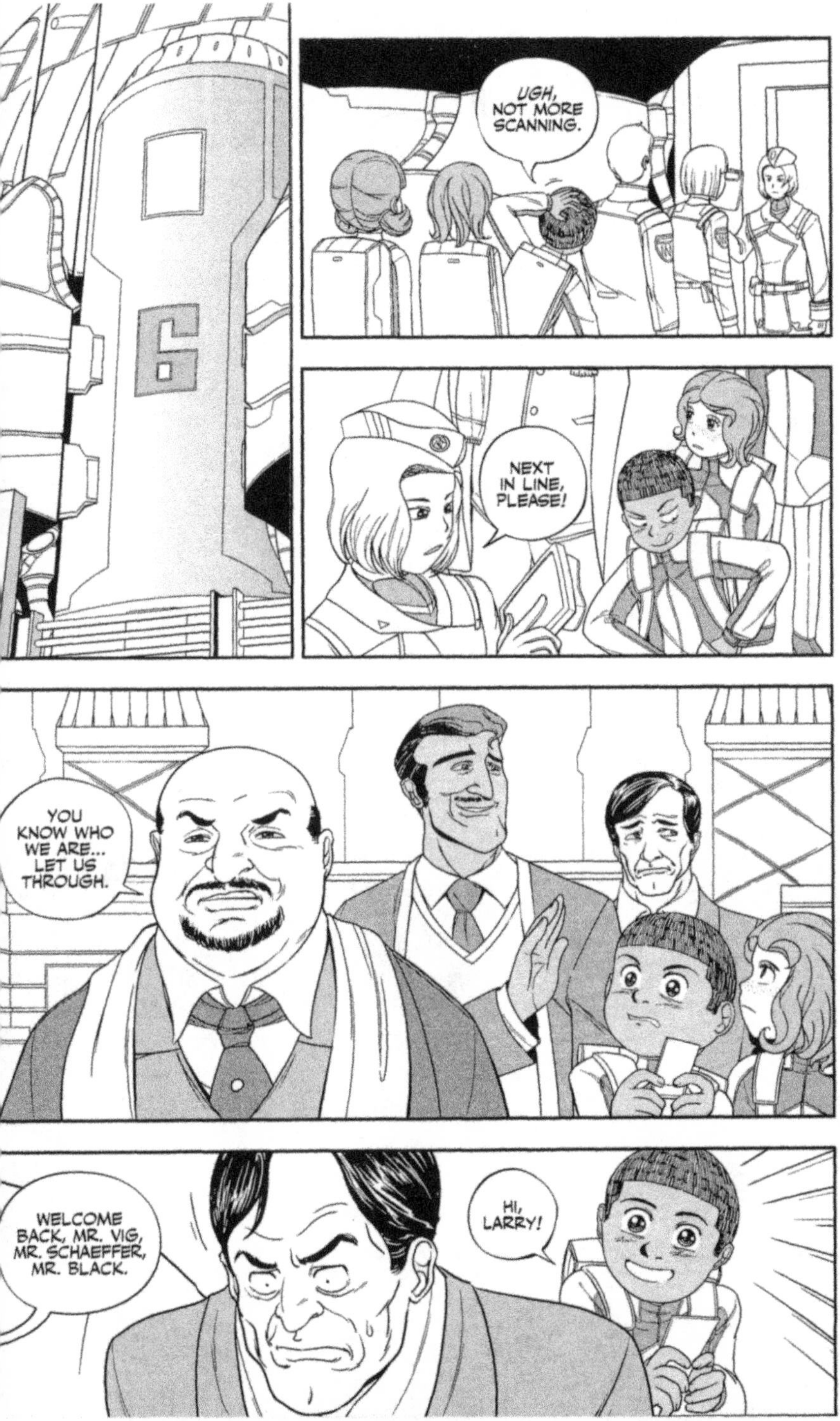
UGH, NOT MORE SCANNING.
NEXT IN LINE, PLEASE!
YOU KNOW WHO WE ARE... LET US THROUGH.
WELCOME BACK, MR. VIG, MR. SCHAEFFER, MR. BLACK.
HI, LARRY!

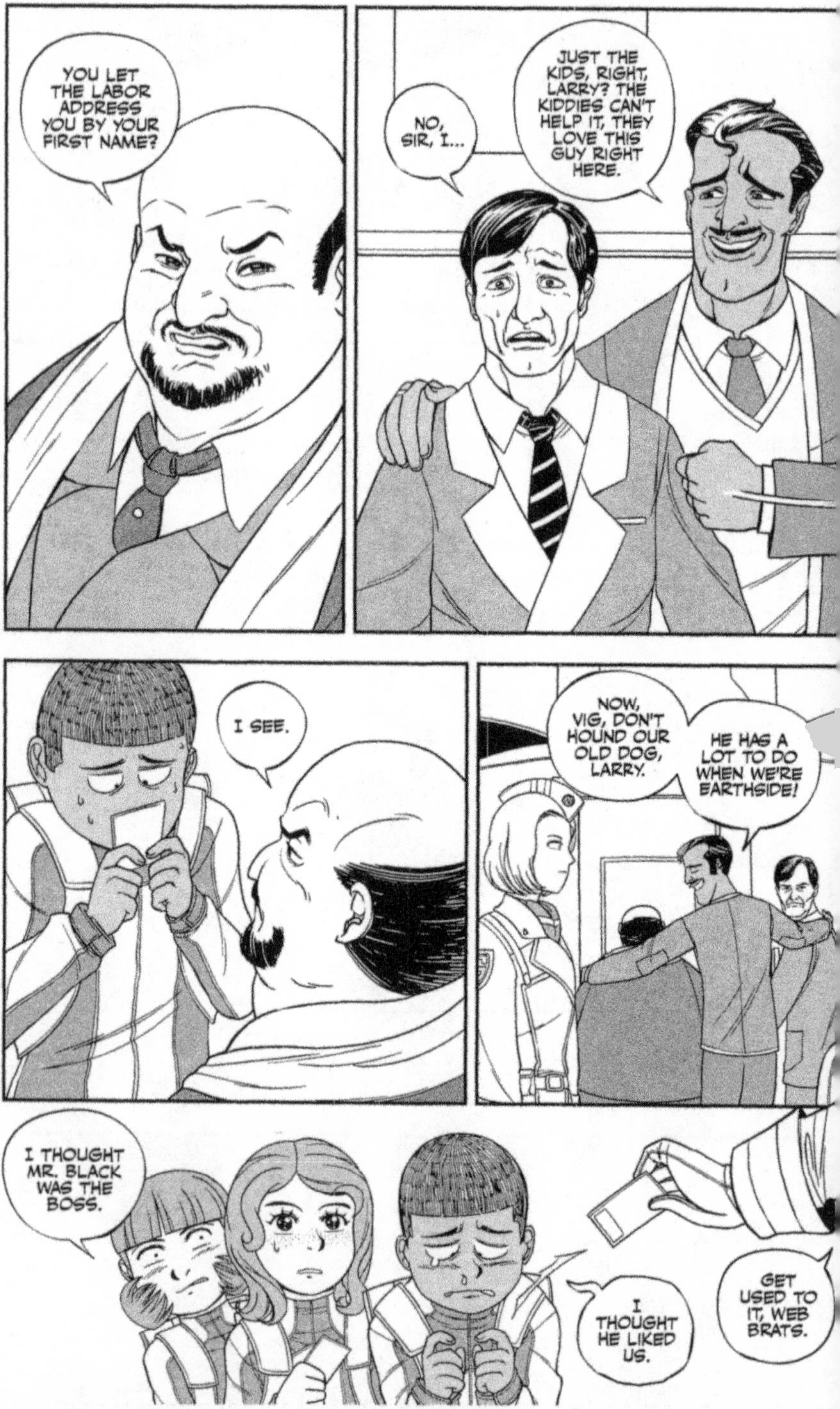
YOU LET THE LABOR ADDRESS YOU BY YOUR FIRST NAME?
NO, SIR, I...
JUST THE KIDS, RIGHT, LARRY? THE KIDDIES CAN'T HELP IT, THEY LOVE THIS GUY RIGHT HERE.
I SEE.
NOW, VIG, DON'T HOUND OUR OLD DOG, LARRY.
HE HAS A LOT TO DO WHEN WE'RE EARTHSIDE!
I THOUGHT MR. BLACK WAS THE BOSS.
I THOUGHT HE LIKED US.
GET USED TO IT, WEB BRATS.

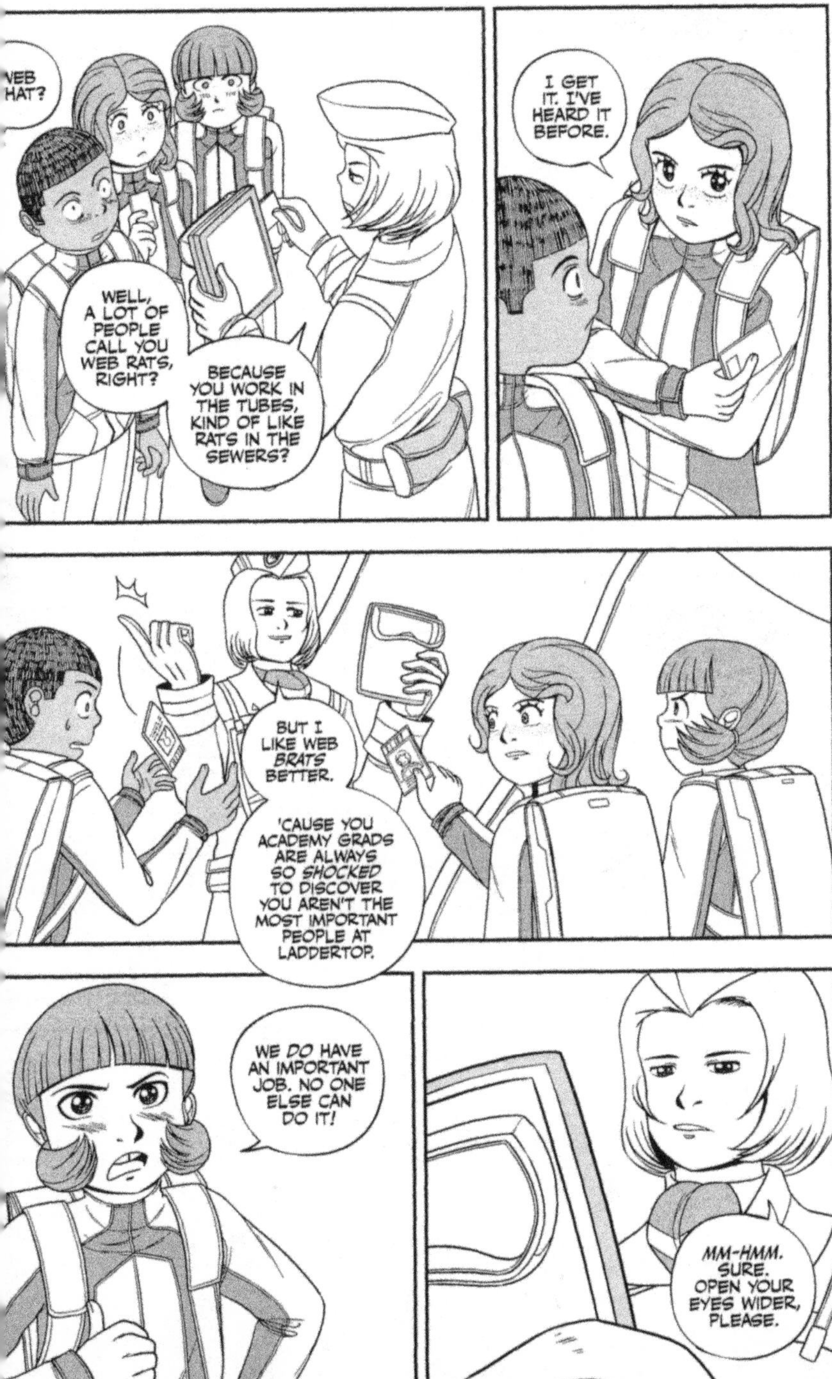
WEB HAT?
WELL, A LOT OF PEOPLE CALL YOU WEB RATS, RIGHT?
BECAUSE YOU WORK IN THE TUBES, KIND OF LIKE RATS IN THE SEWERS?
I GET IT. I'VE HEARD IT BEFORE.
BUT I LIKE WEB *BRATS* BETTER.
'CAUSE YOU ACADEMY GRADS ARE ALWAYS SO *SHOCKED* TO DISCOVER YOU AREN'T THE MOST IMPORTANT PEOPLE AT LADDERTOP.
WE *DO* HAVE AN IMPORTANT JOB. NO ONE ELSE CAN DO IT!
MM-HMM. SURE. OPEN YOUR EYES WIDER, PLEASE.

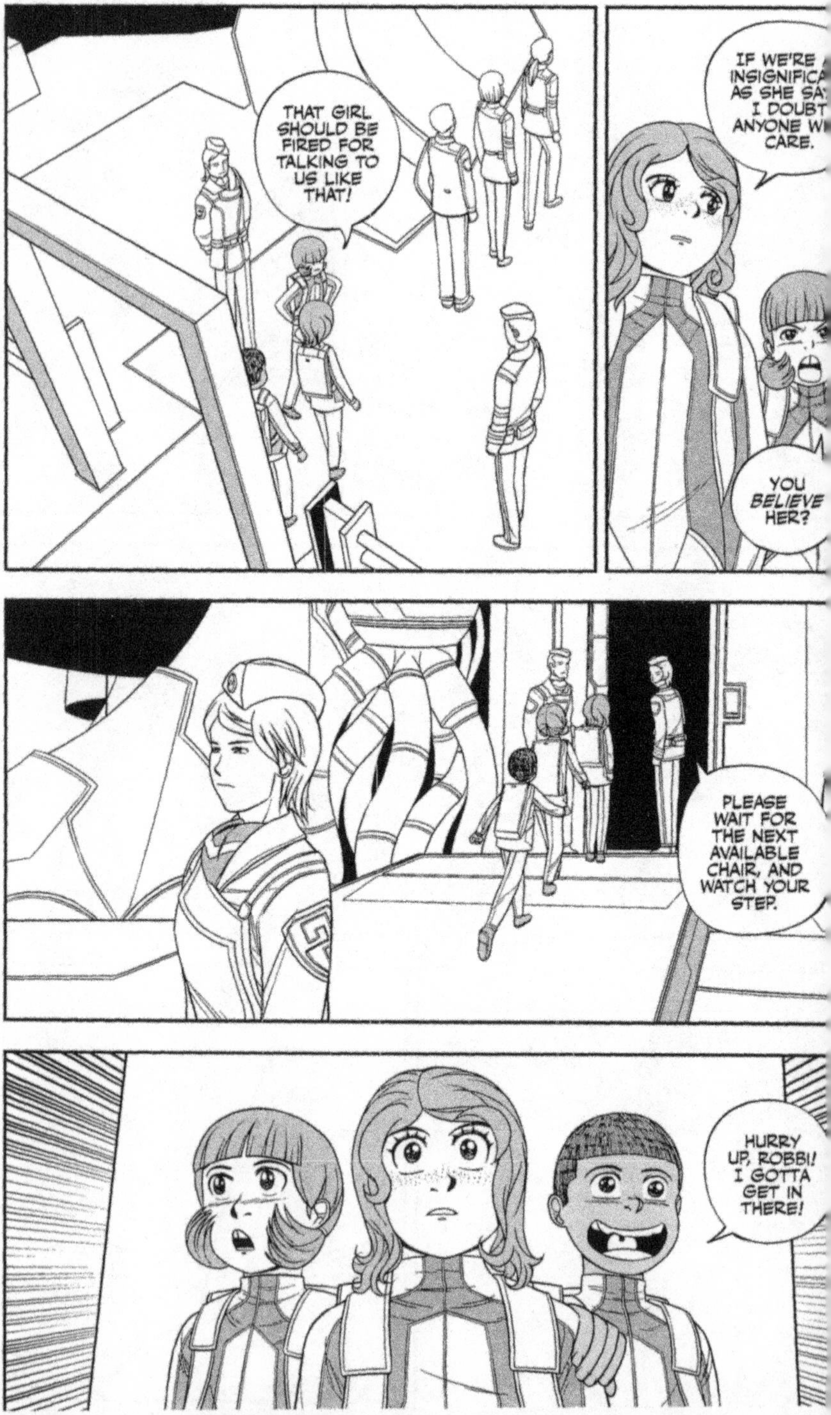
THAT GIRL SHOULD BE FIRED FOR TALKING TO US LIKE THAT!
IF WE'RE INSIGNIFICA AS SHE SA I DOUBT ANYONE W CARE.
YOU *BELIEVE* HER?
PLEASE WAIT FOR THE NEXT AVAILABLE CHAIR, AND WATCH YOUR STEP.
HURRY UP, ROBBI! I GOTTA GET IN THERE!

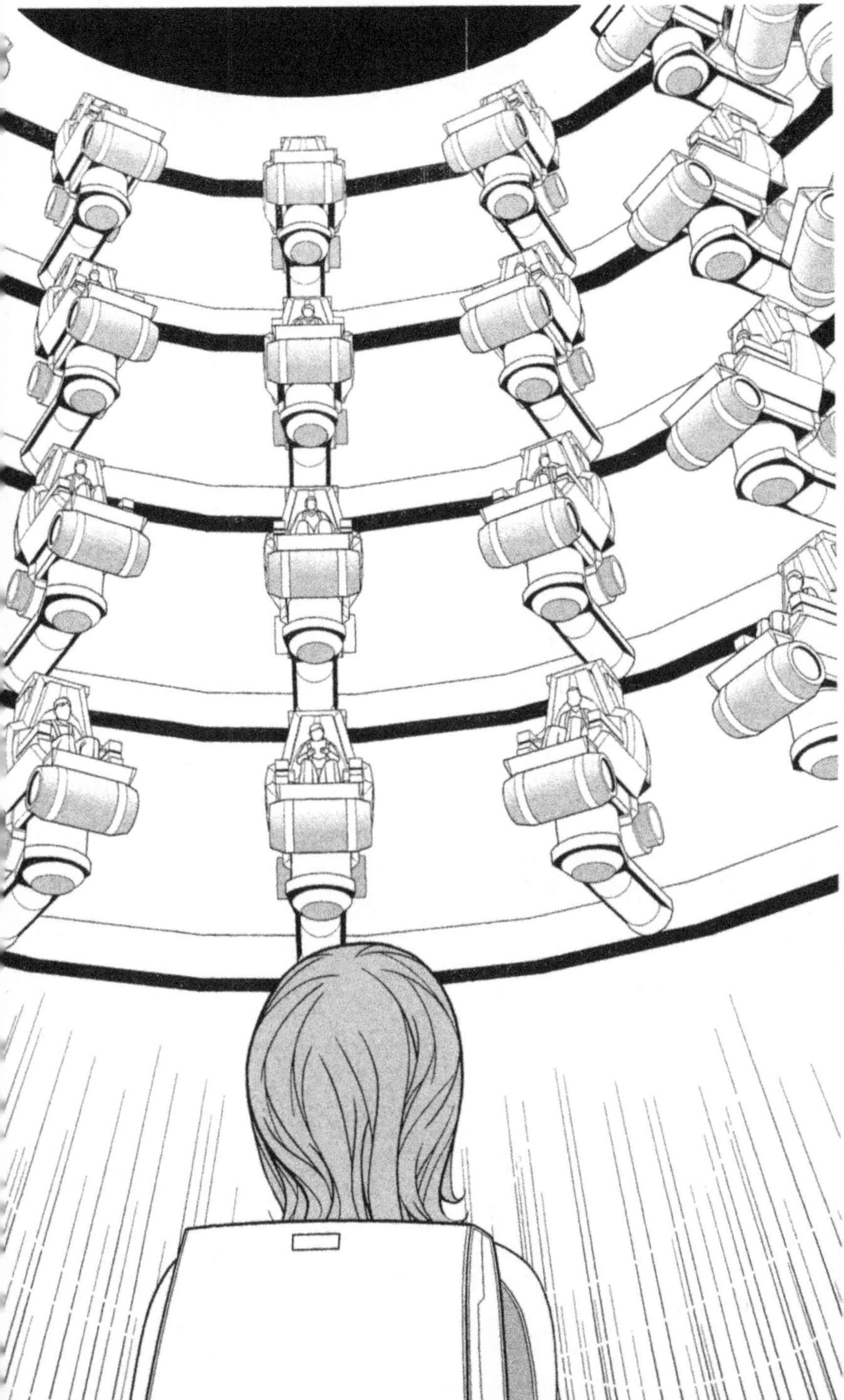

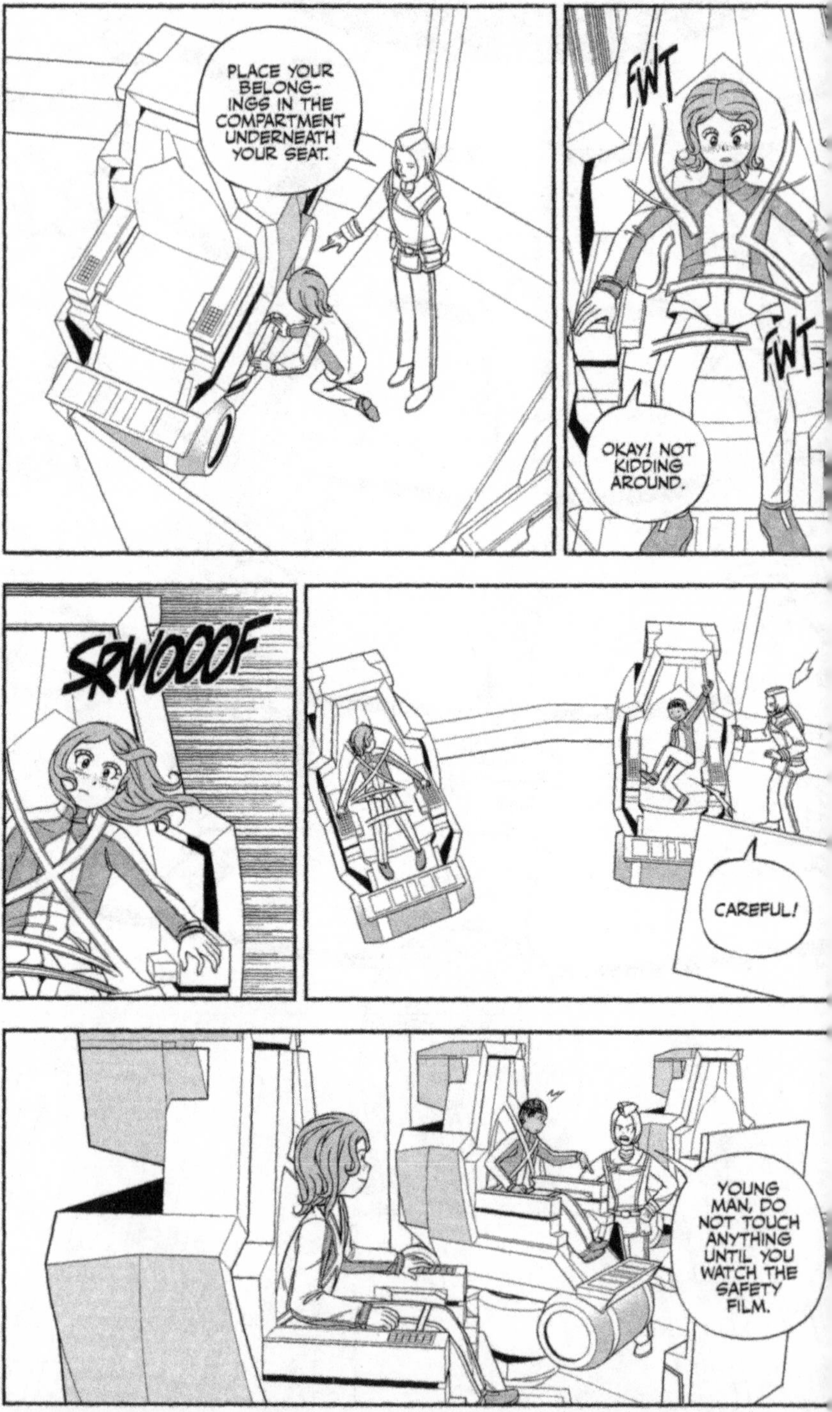
PLACE YOUR BELONGINGS IN THE COMPARTMENT UNDERNEATH YOUR SEAT.
FWT
FWT
OKAY! NOT KIDDING AROUND.
SRWOOOF
CAREFUL!
YOUNG MAN, DO NOT TOUCH ANYTHING UNTIL YOU WATCH THE SAFETY FILM.

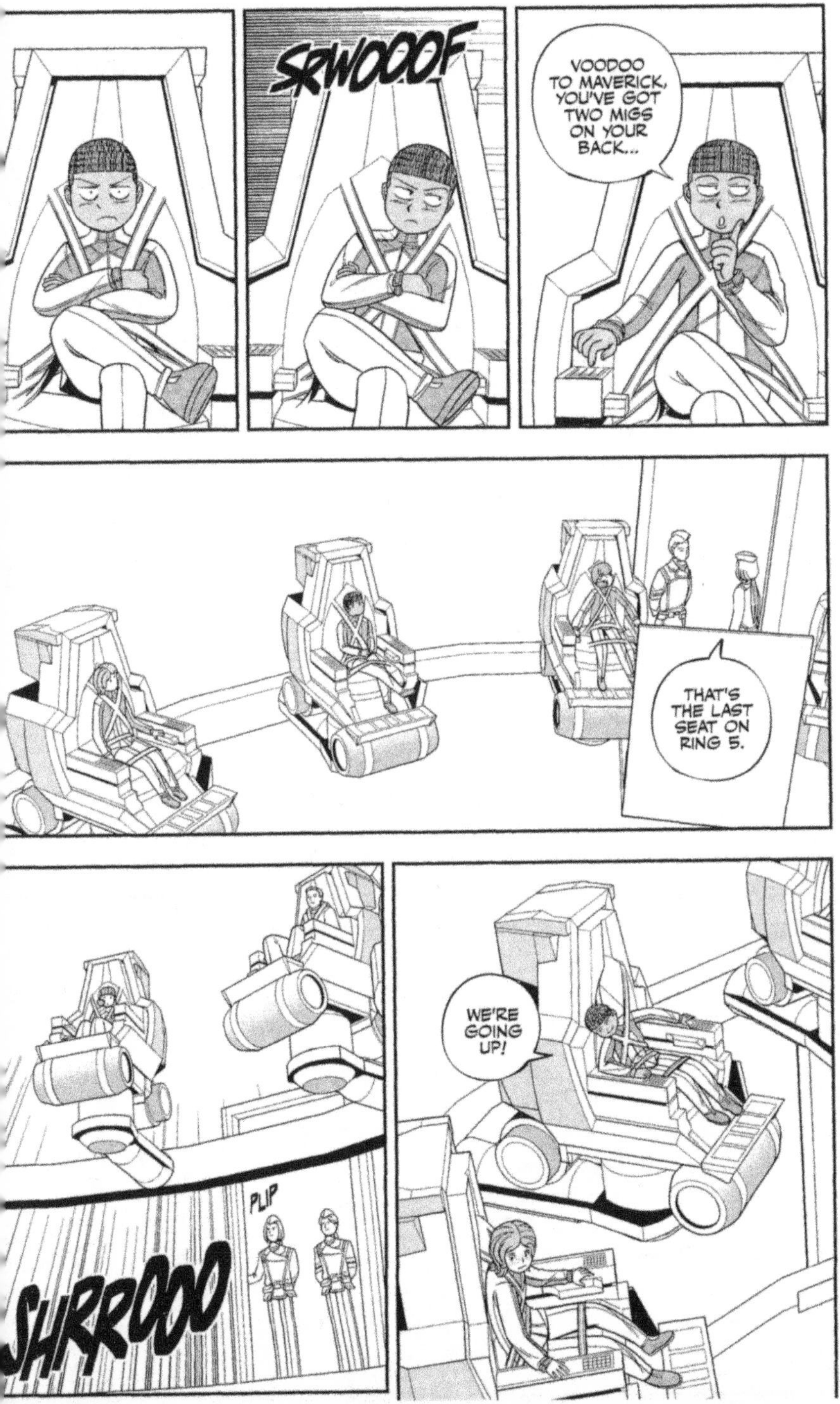
SRWOOOF
VOODOO TO MAVERICK, YOU'VE GOT TWO MIGS ON YOUR BACK...
THAT'S THE LAST SEAT ON RING 5.
PLIP
SHRROOO
WE'RE GOING UP!

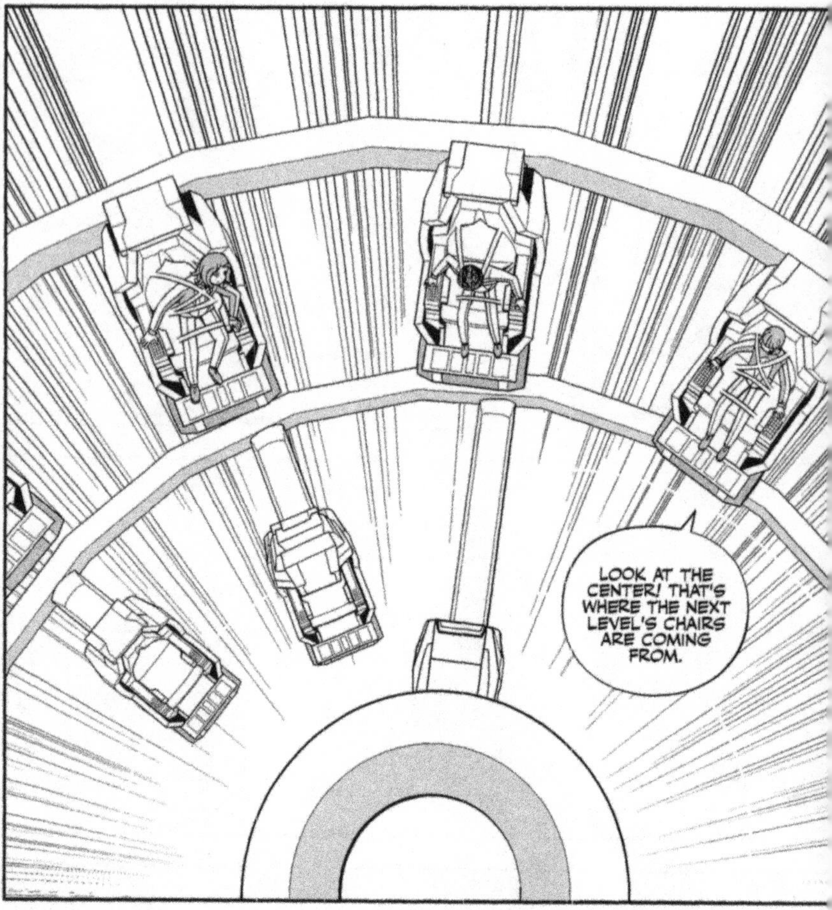
LOOK AT THE CENTER! THAT'S WHERE THE NEXT LEVEL'S CHAIRS ARE COMING FROM.

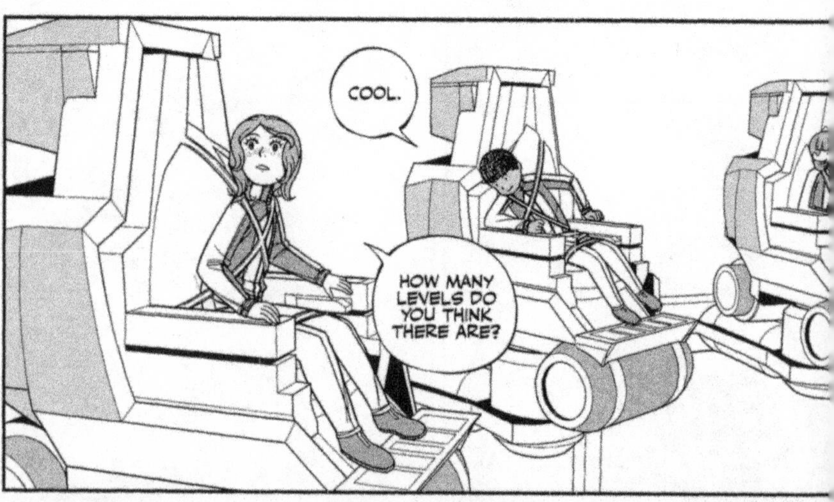
COOL.
HOW MANY LEVELS DO YOU THINK THERE ARE?

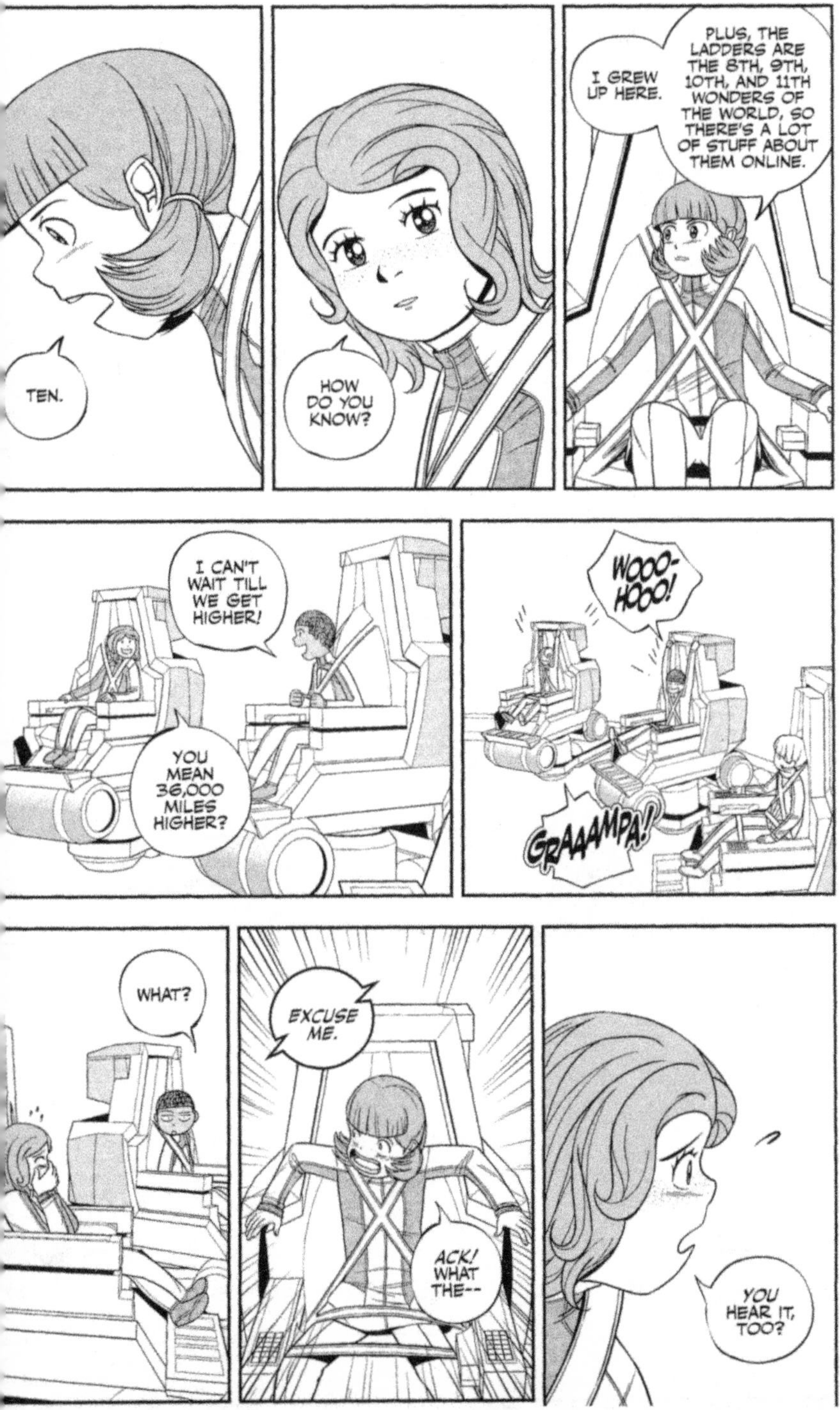
TEN.
HOW DO YOU KNOW?
I GREW UP HERE.
PLUS, THE LADDERS ARE THE 8TH, 9TH, 10TH, AND 11TH WONDERS OF THE WORLD, SO THERE'S A LOT OF STUFF ABOUT THEM ONLINE.
I CAN'T WAIT TILL WE GET HIGHER!
YOU MEAN 36,000 MILES HIGHER?
WOOO-HOOO!
GRAAAMPA!
WHAT?
EXCUSE ME.
ACK! WHAT THE--
YOU HEAR IT, TOO?

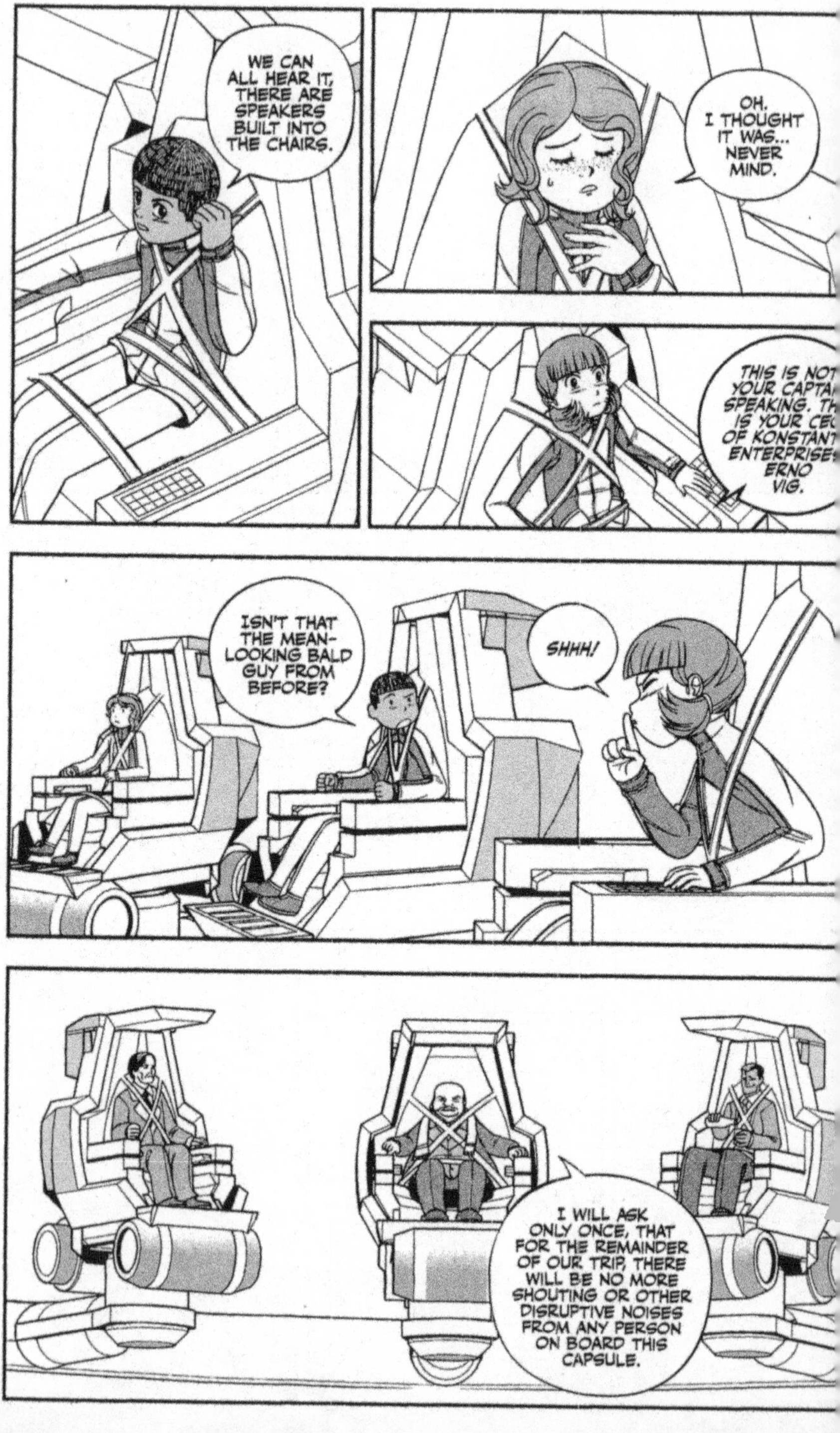
WE CAN ALL HEAR IT, THERE ARE SPEAKERS BUILT INTO THE CHAIRS.
OH. I THOUGHT IT WAS... NEVER MIND.
THIS IS NOT YOUR CAPTA SPEAKING. TH IS YOUR CE OF KONSTANT ENTERPRISE ERNO VIG.
ISN'T THAT THE MEAN-LOOKING BALD GUY FROM BEFORE?
SHHH!
I WILL ASK ONLY ONCE, THAT FOR THE REMAINDER OF OUR TRIP, THERE WILL BE NO MORE SHOUTING OR OTHER DISRUPTIVE NOISES FROM ANY PERSON ON BOARD THIS CAPSULE.

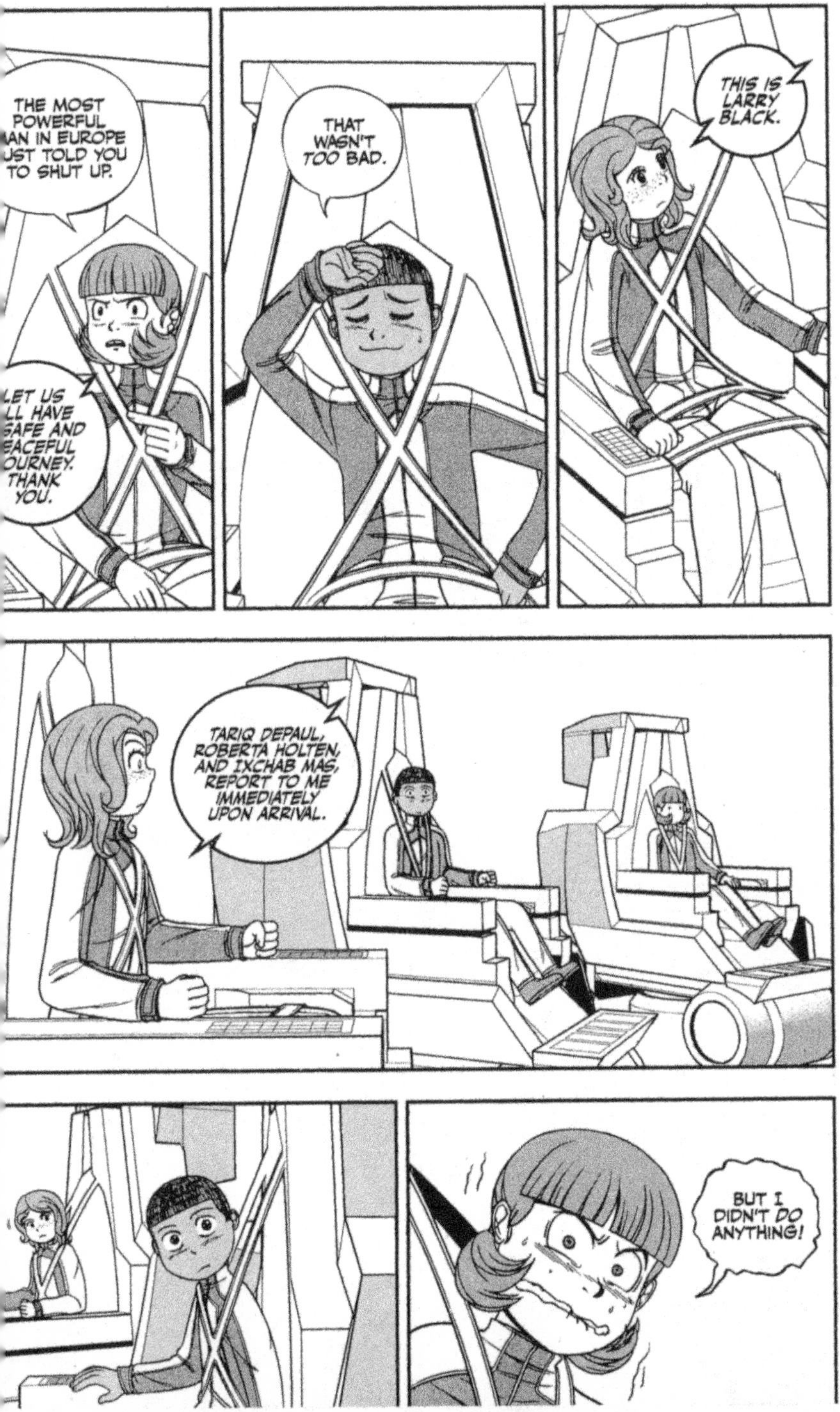
THE MOST POWERFUL AN IN EUROPE UST TOLD YOU TO SHUT UP.
ET US LL HAVE AFE AND EACEFUL OURNEY. THANK YOU.
THAT WASN'T TOO BAD.
THIS IS LARRY BLACK.
TARIQ DEPAUL, ROBERTA HOLTEN, AND IXCHAB MAG, REPORT TO ME IMMEDIATELY UPON ARRIVAL.
BUT I DIDN'T DO ANYTHING!

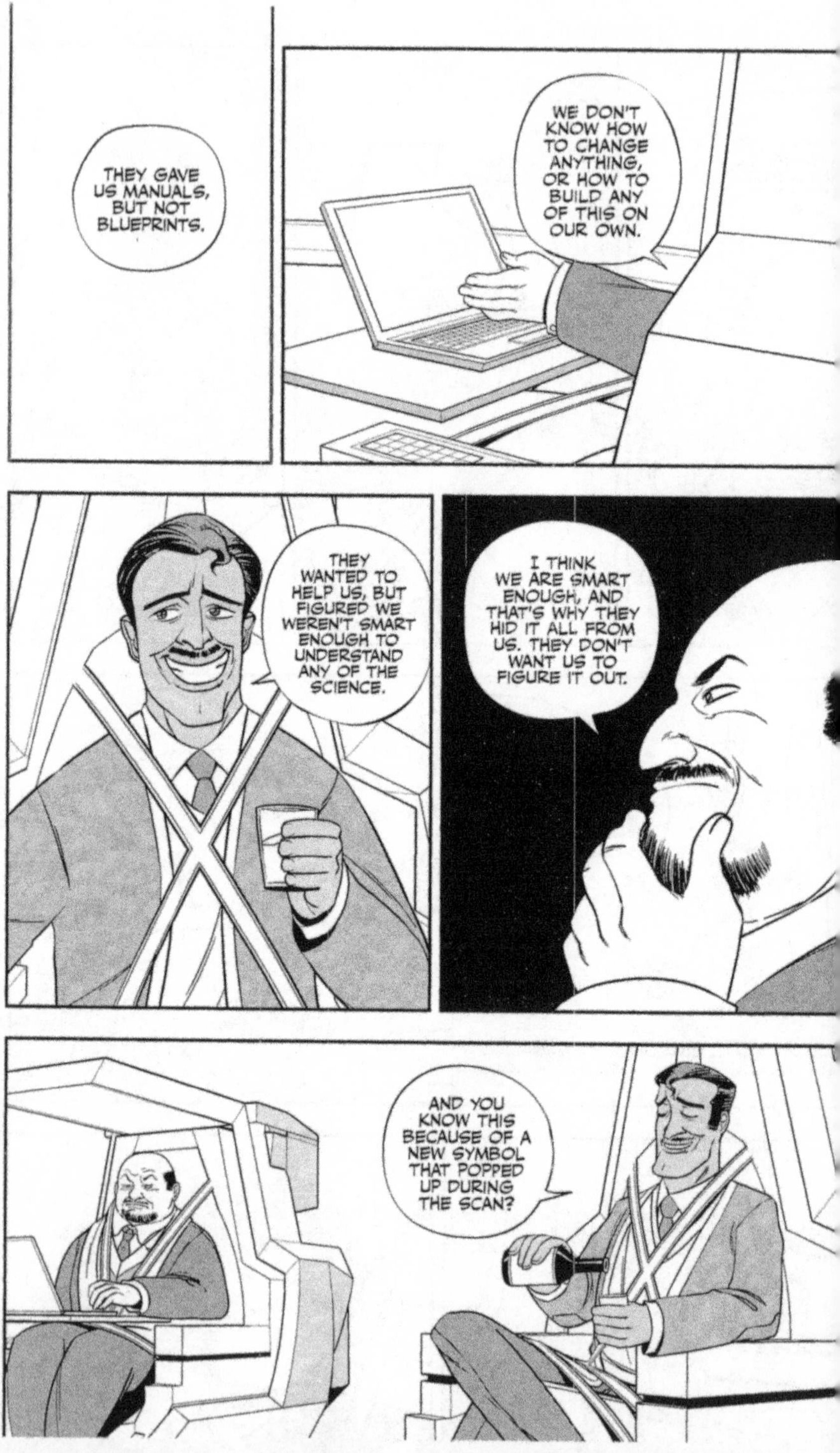
THEY GAVE US MANUALS, BUT NOT BLUEPRINTS.
WE DON'T KNOW HOW TO CHANGE ANYTHING, OR HOW TO BUILD ANY OF THIS ON OUR OWN.
THEY WANTED TO HELP US, BUT FIGURED WE WEREN'T SMART ENOUGH TO UNDERSTAND ANY OF THE SCIENCE.
I THINK WE ARE SMART ENOUGH, AND THAT'S WHY THEY HID IT ALL FROM US. THEY DON'T WANT US TO FIGURE IT OUT.
AND YOU KNOW THIS BECAUSE OF A NEW SYMBOL THAT POPPED UP DURING THE SCAN?

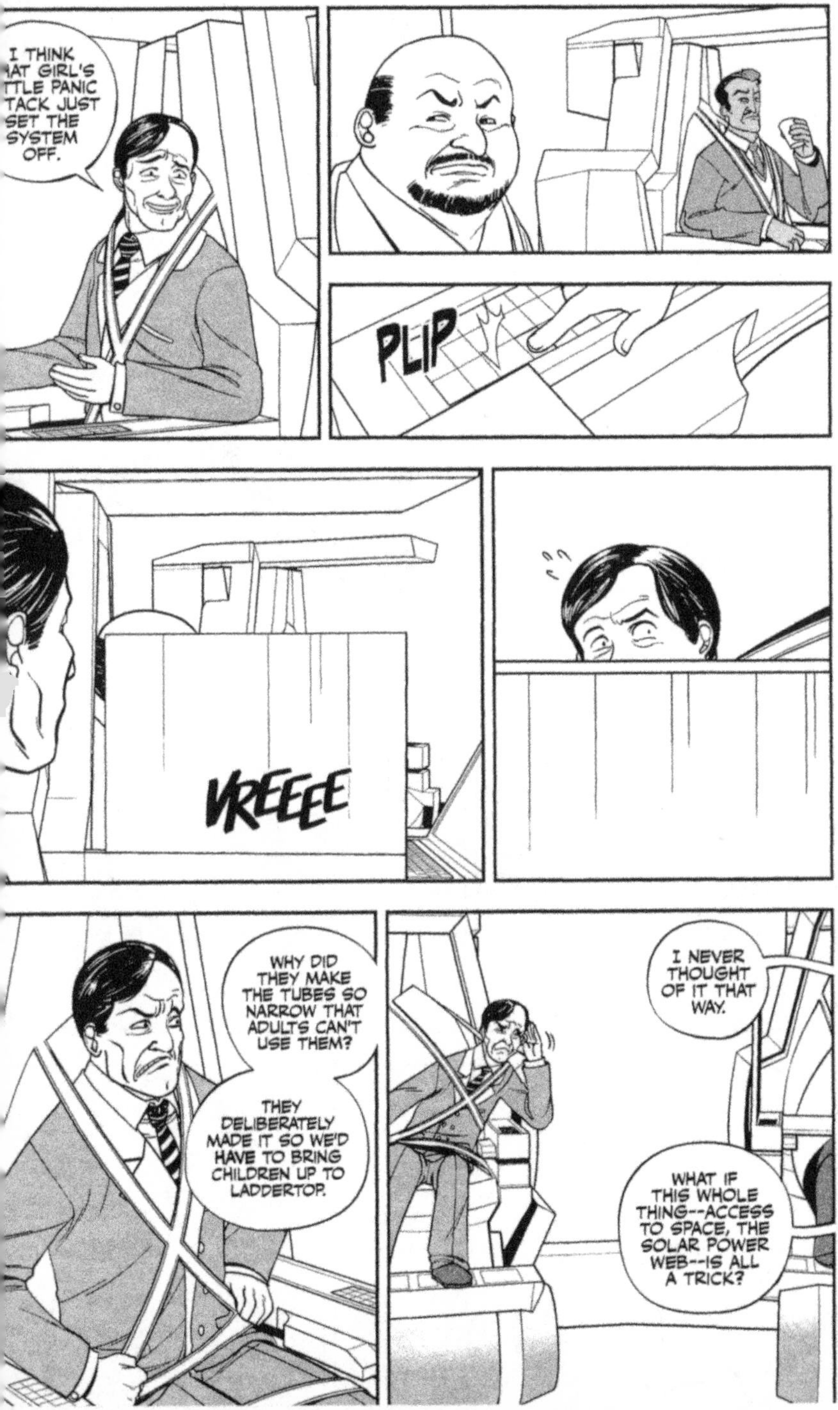
I THINK HAT GIRL'S TTLE PANIC TACK JUST SET THE SYSTEM OFF.
PLIP
VREEEE
WHY DID THEY MAKE THE TUBES SO NARROW THAT ADULTS CAN'T USE THEM?
THEY DELIBERATELY MADE IT SO WE'D HAVE TO BRING CHILDREN UP TO LADDERTOP.
I NEVER THOUGHT OF IT THAT WAY.
WHAT IF THIS WHOLE THING--ACCESS TO SPACE, THE SOLAR POWER WEB--IS ALL A TRICK?

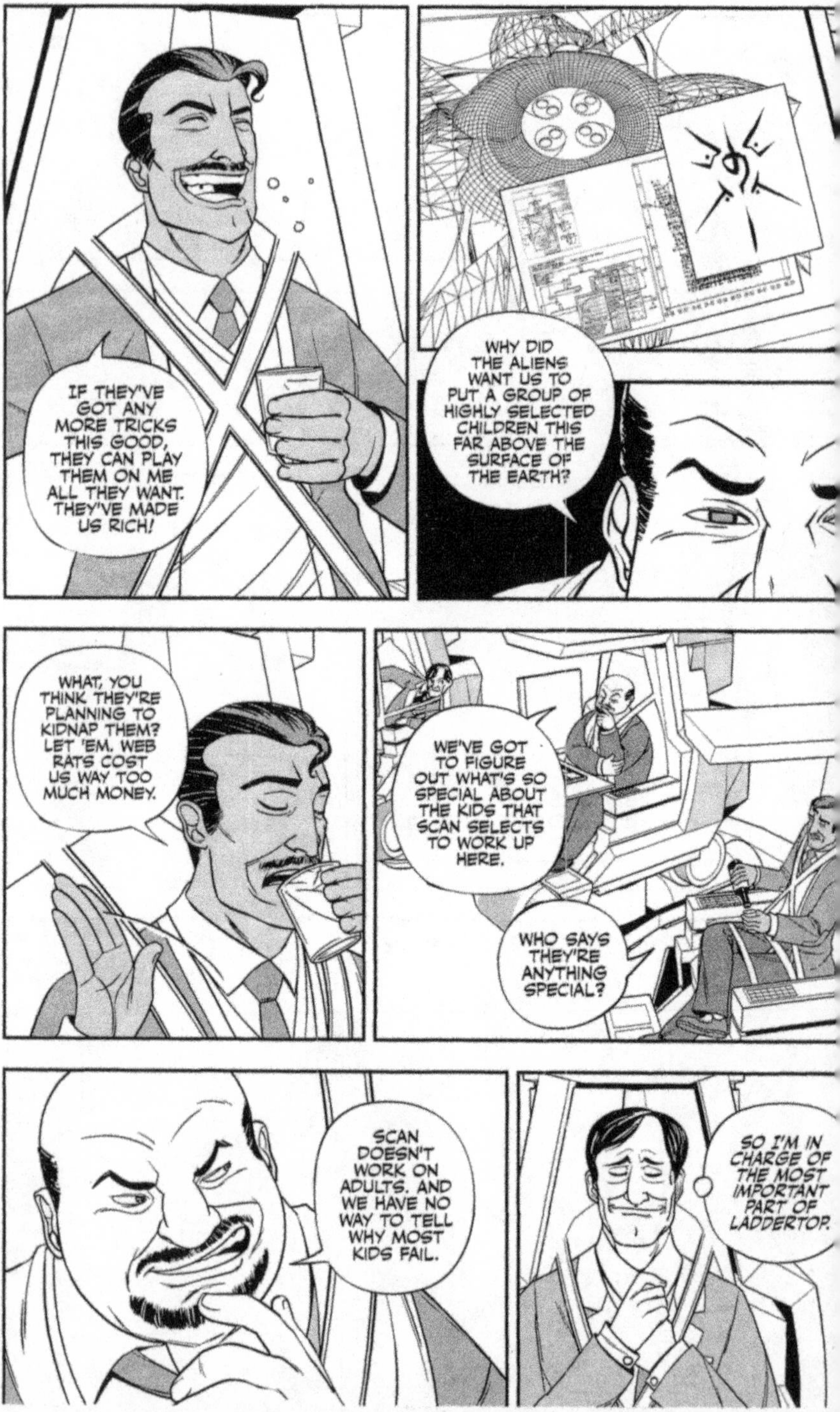
IF THEY'VE GOT ANY MORE TRICKS THIS GOOD, THEY CAN PLAY THEM ON ME ALL THEY WANT. THEY'VE MADE US RICH!
WHY DID THE ALIENS WANT US TO PUT A GROUP OF HIGHLY SELECTED CHILDREN THIS FAR ABOVE THE SURFACE OF THE EARTH?
WHAT, YOU THINK THEY'RE PLANNING TO KIDNAP THEM? LET 'EM. WEB RATS COST US WAY TOO MUCH MONEY.
WE'VE GOT TO FIGURE OUT WHAT'S SO SPECIAL ABOUT THE KIDS THAT SCAN SELECTS TO WORK UP HERE.
WHO SAYS THEY'RE ANYTHING SPECIAL?
SCAN DOESN'T WORK ON ADULTS. AND WE HAVE NO WAY TO TELL WHY MOST KIDS FAIL.
SO I'M IN CHARGE OF THE MOST IMPORTANT PART OF LADDERTOP.

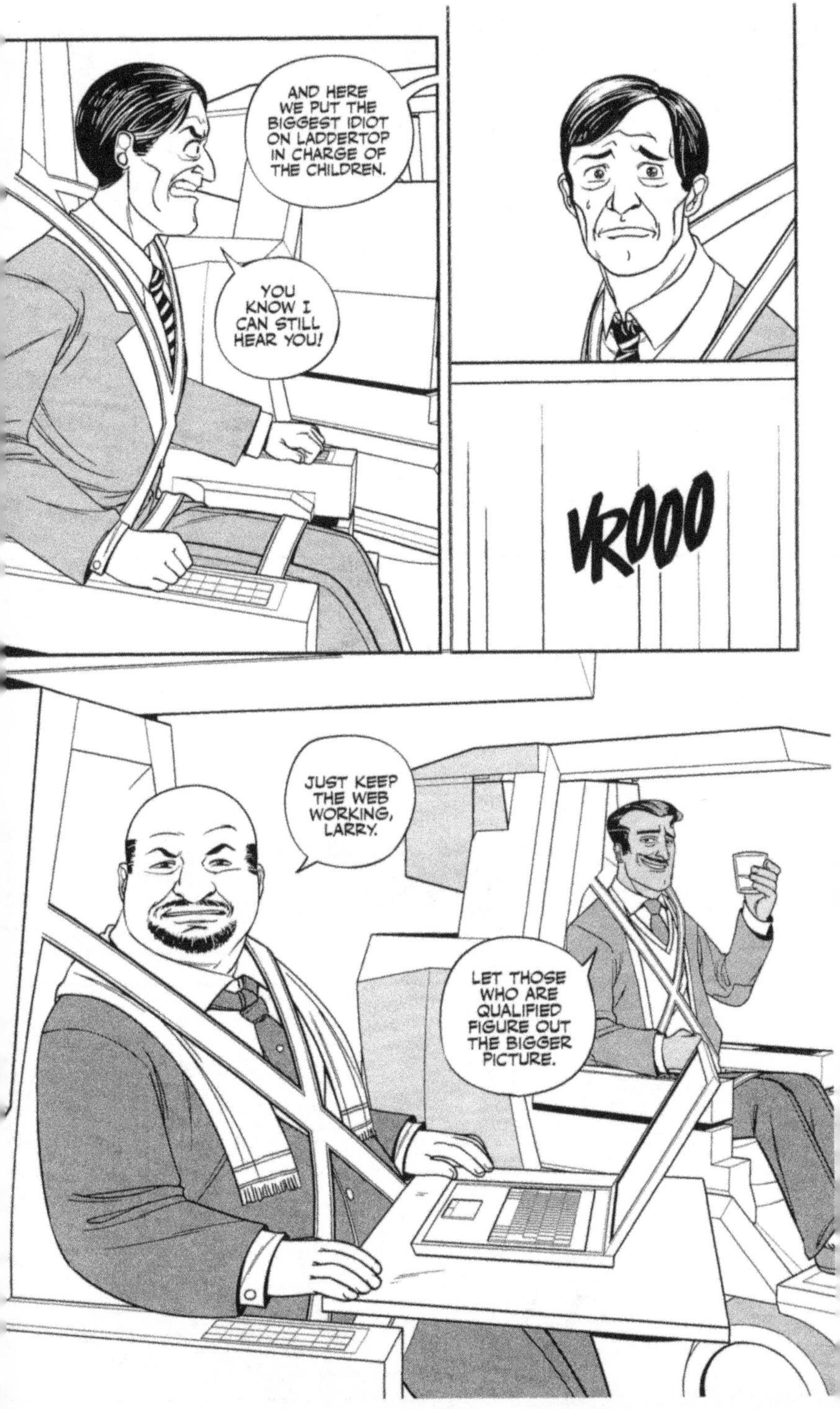
AND HERE WE PUT THE BIGGEST IDIOT ON LADDERTOP IN CHARGE OF THE CHILDREN.
YOU KNOW I CAN STILL HEAR YOU!
VROOO
JUST KEEP THE WEB WORKING, LARRY.
LET THOSE WHO ARE QUALIFIED FIGURE OUT THE BIGGER PICTURE.

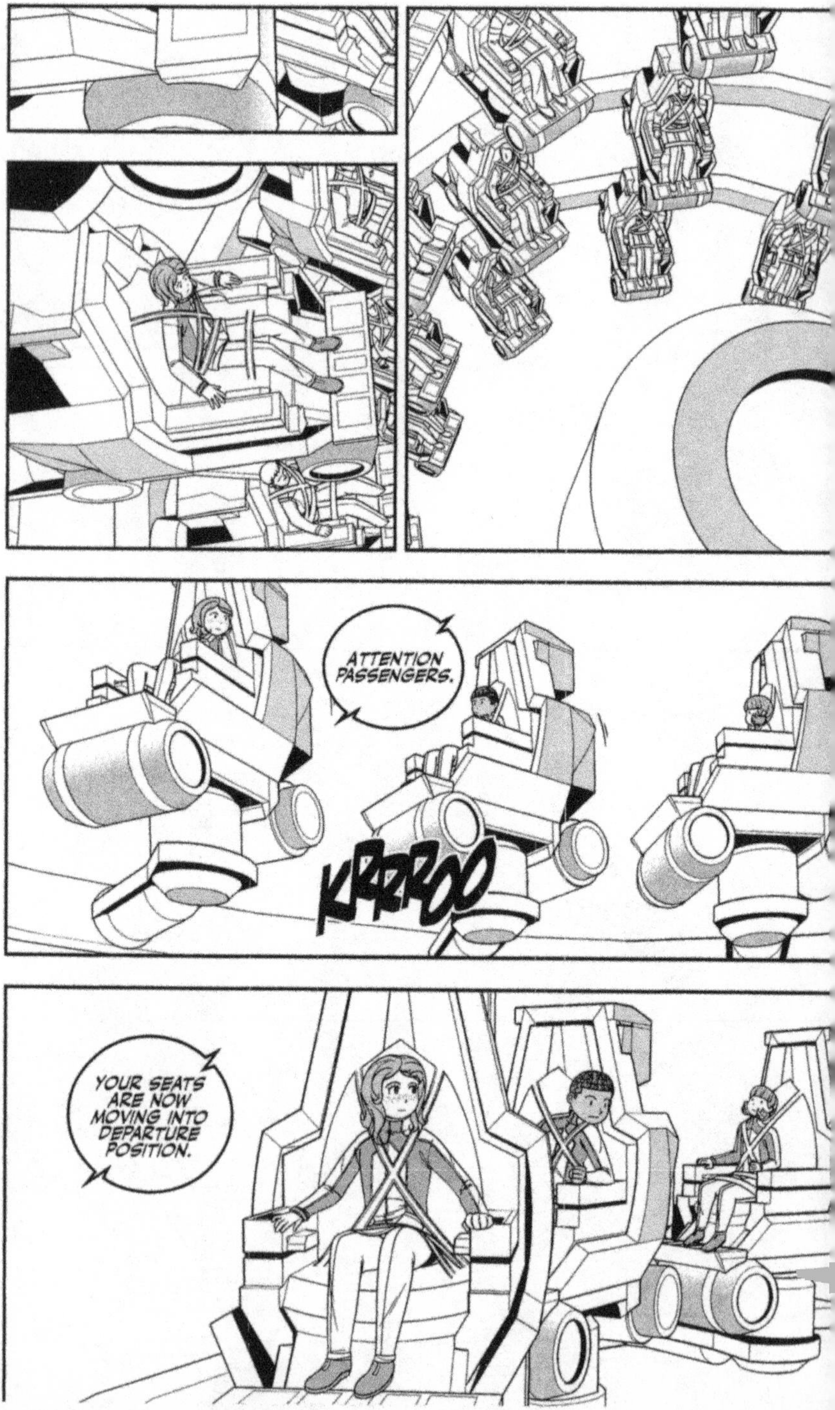
ATTENTION PASSENGERS.
KRRROO
YOUR SEATS ARE NOW MOVING INTO DEPARTURE POSITION.

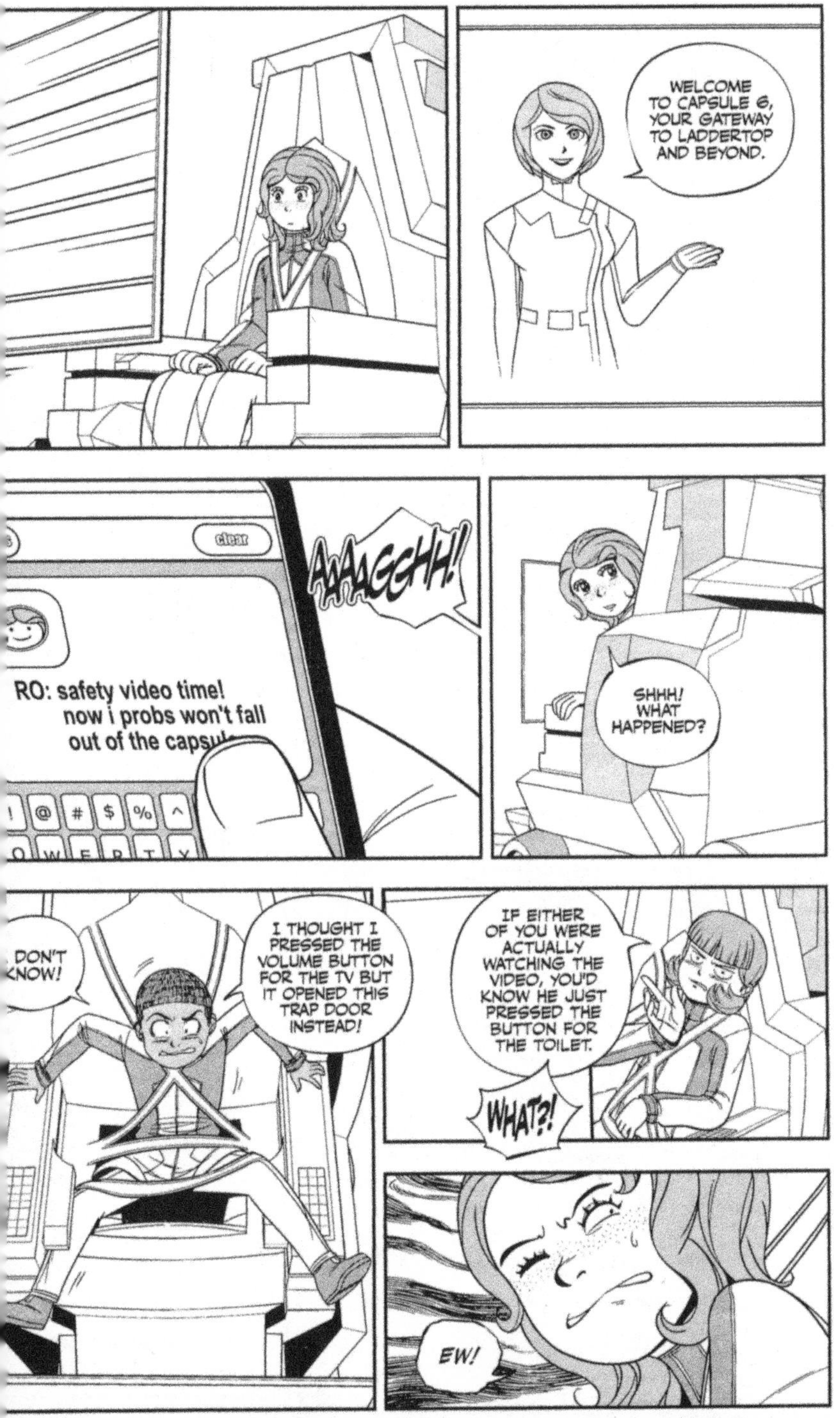
WELCOME TO CAPSULE 6, YOUR GATEWAY TO LADDERTOP AND BEYOND.
clear
RO: safety video time! now i probs won't fall out of the capsul
AAAAGGHH!
SHHH! WHAT HAPPENED?
DON'T KNOW!
I THOUGHT I PRESSED THE VOLUME BUTTON FOR THE TV BUT IT OPENED THIS TRAP DOOR INSTEAD!
IF EITHER OF YOU WERE ACTUALLY WATCHING THE VIDEO, YOU'D KNOW HE JUST PRESSED THE BUTTON FOR THE TOILET.
WHAT?!
EW!

WE'RE STUCK IN THESE CHAIRS FOR EIGHTEEN HOURS, WHAT DID YOU EXPECT?

BUT EVERYONE CAN SEE YOU!

THERE'S A PRIVACY SCREEN YOU CAN PUT UP SO NO ONE CAN SEE YOU DO YOUR BUSINESS.

SO WHERE DO WE GET FOOD AROUND HERE?

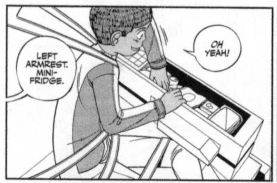

LEFT ARMREST. MINI-FRIDGE.

OH YEAH!

RO: spoke too soon. ari just fell in the toile

AZ: LOL! how did tha happen?

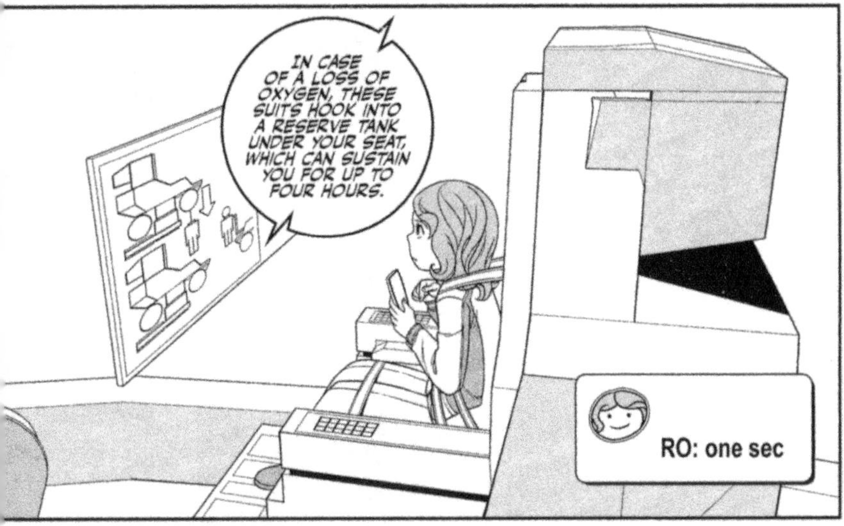
IN CASE OF A LOSS OF OXYGEN, THESE SUITS HOOK INTO A RESERVE TANK UNDER YOUR SEAT, WHICH CAN SUSTAIN YOU FOR UP TO FOUR HOURS.
RO: one sec

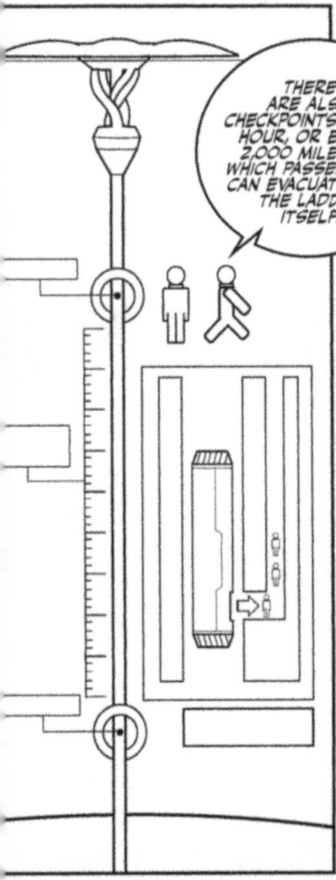
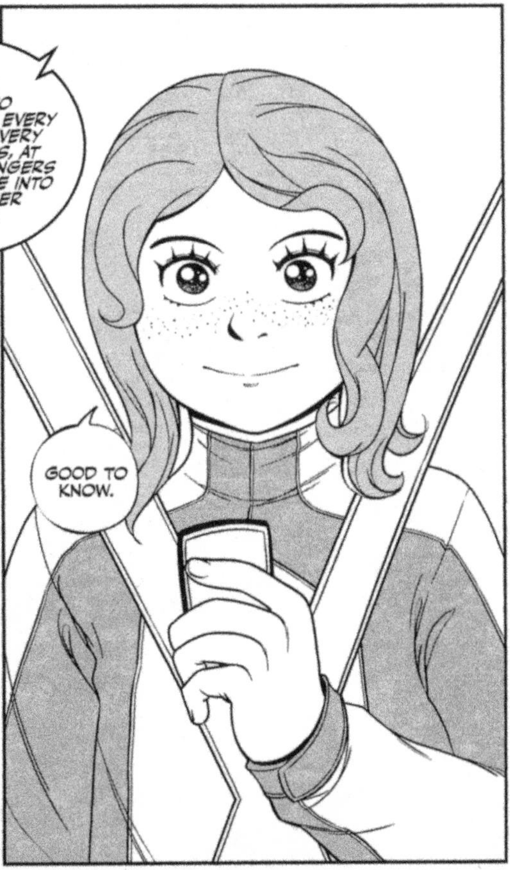
THERE ARE ALSO CHECKPOINTS EVERY HOUR, OR EVERY 2,000 MILES, AT WHICH PASSENGERS CAN EVACUATE INTO THE LADDER ITSELF.
GOOD TO KNOW.

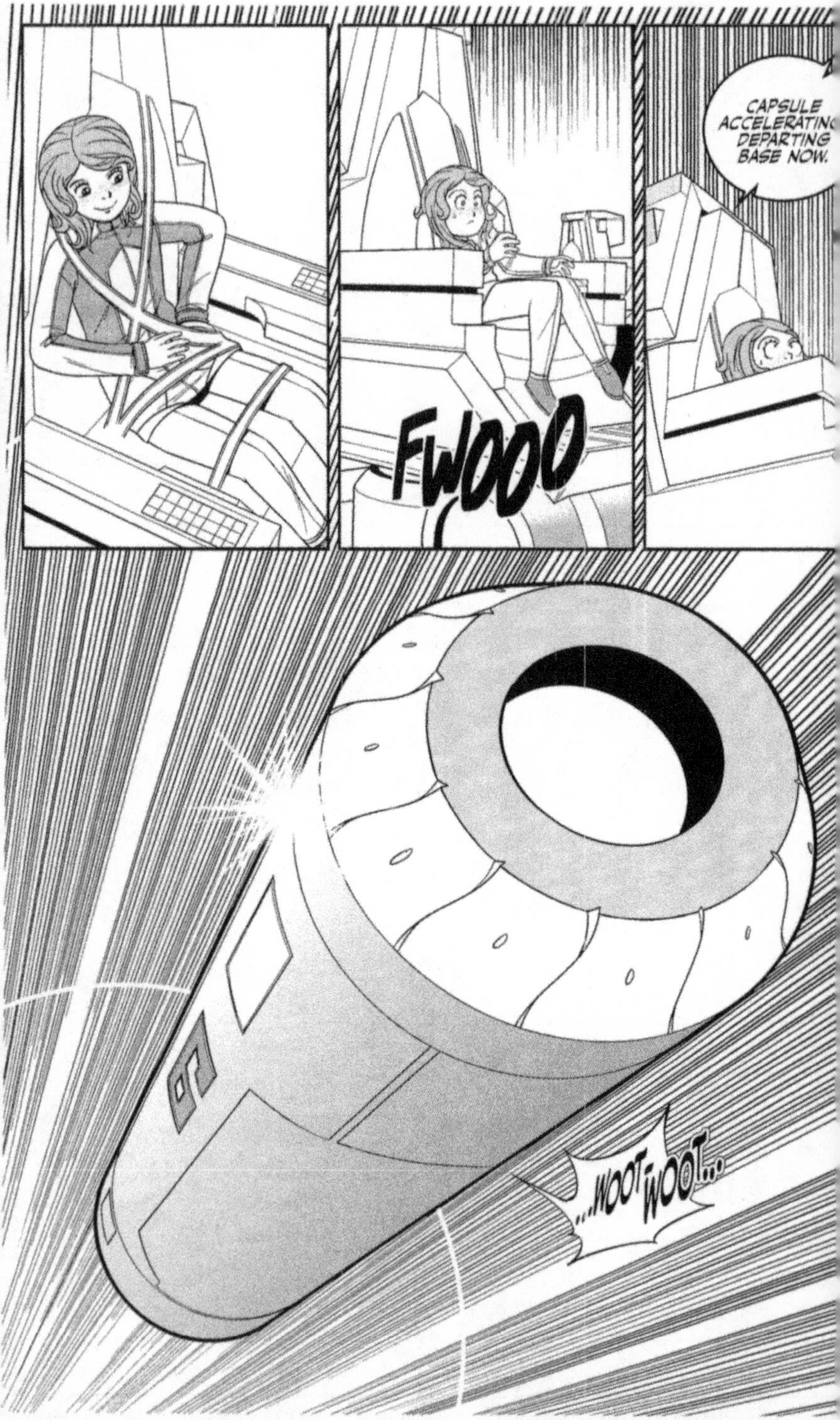
FWOOO
CAPSULE ACCELERATING DEPARTING BASE NOW.
...WOOT WOOT...

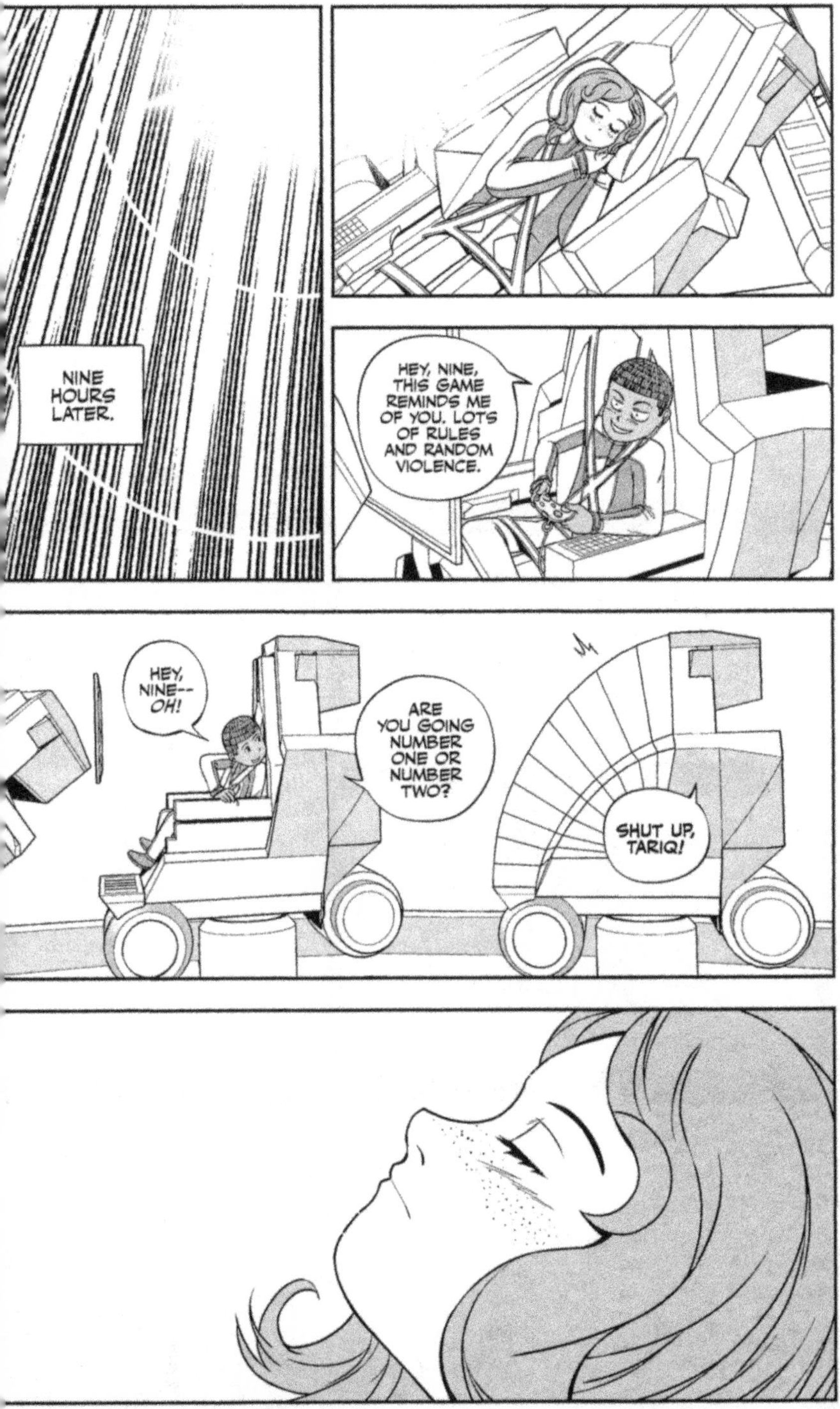
NINE HOURS LATER.
HEY, NINE, THIS GAME REMINDS ME OF YOU. LOTS OF RULES AND RANDOM VIOLENCE.
HEY, NINE-- OH!
ARE YOU GOING NUMBER ONE OR NUMBER TWO?
SHUT UP, TARIQ!

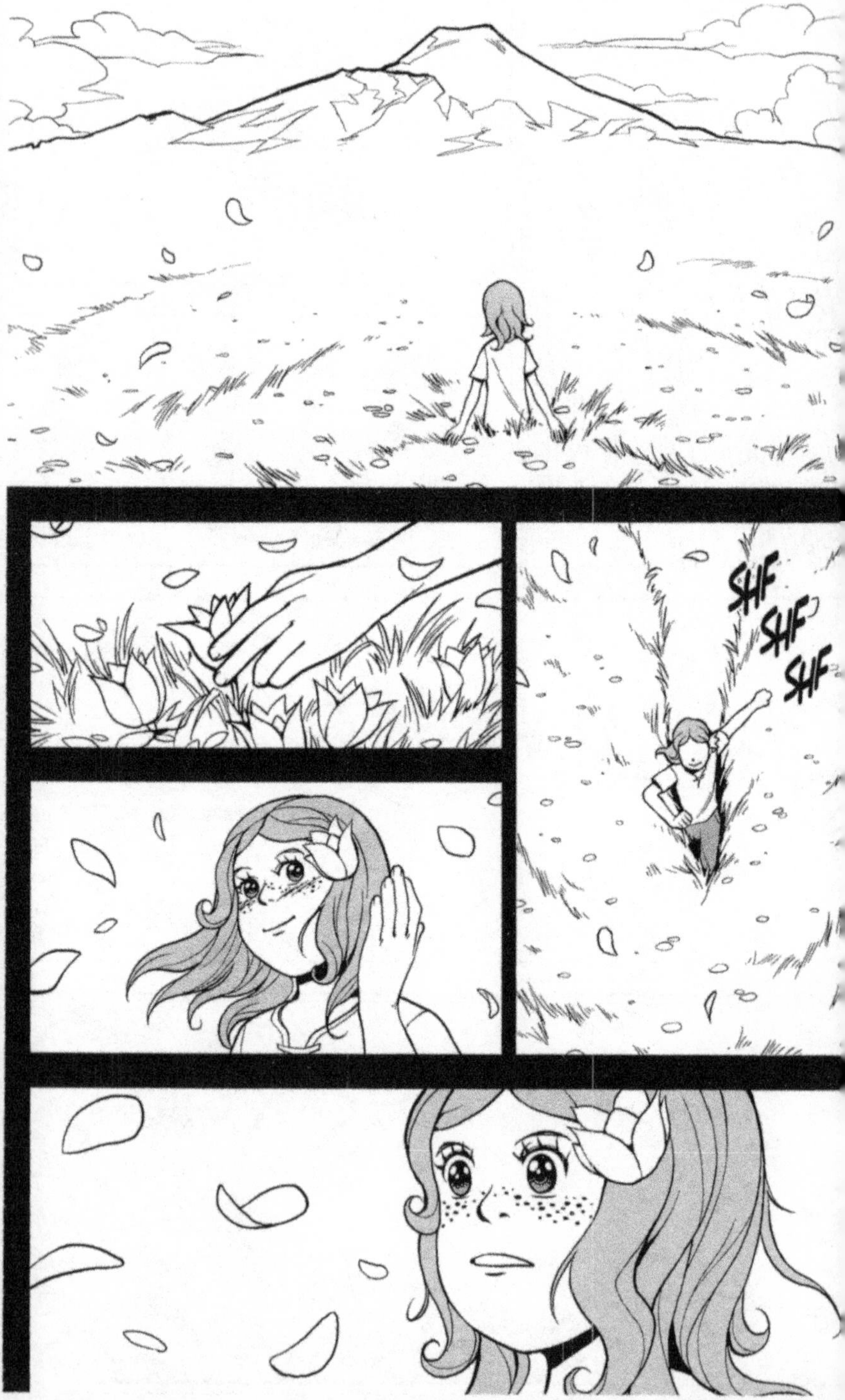
SHF
SHF
SHF

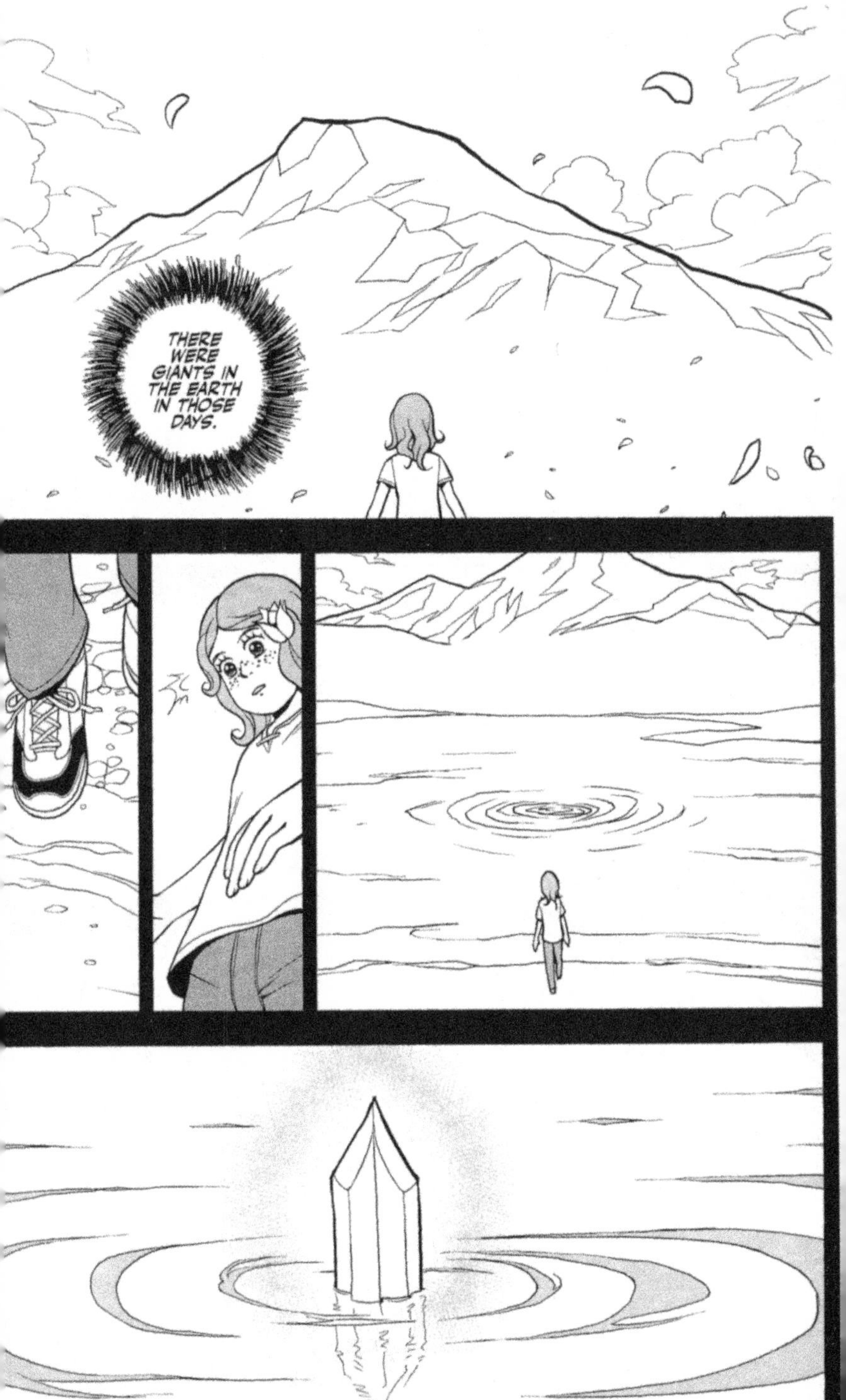
THERE WERE GIANTS IN THE EARTH IN THOSE DAYS.

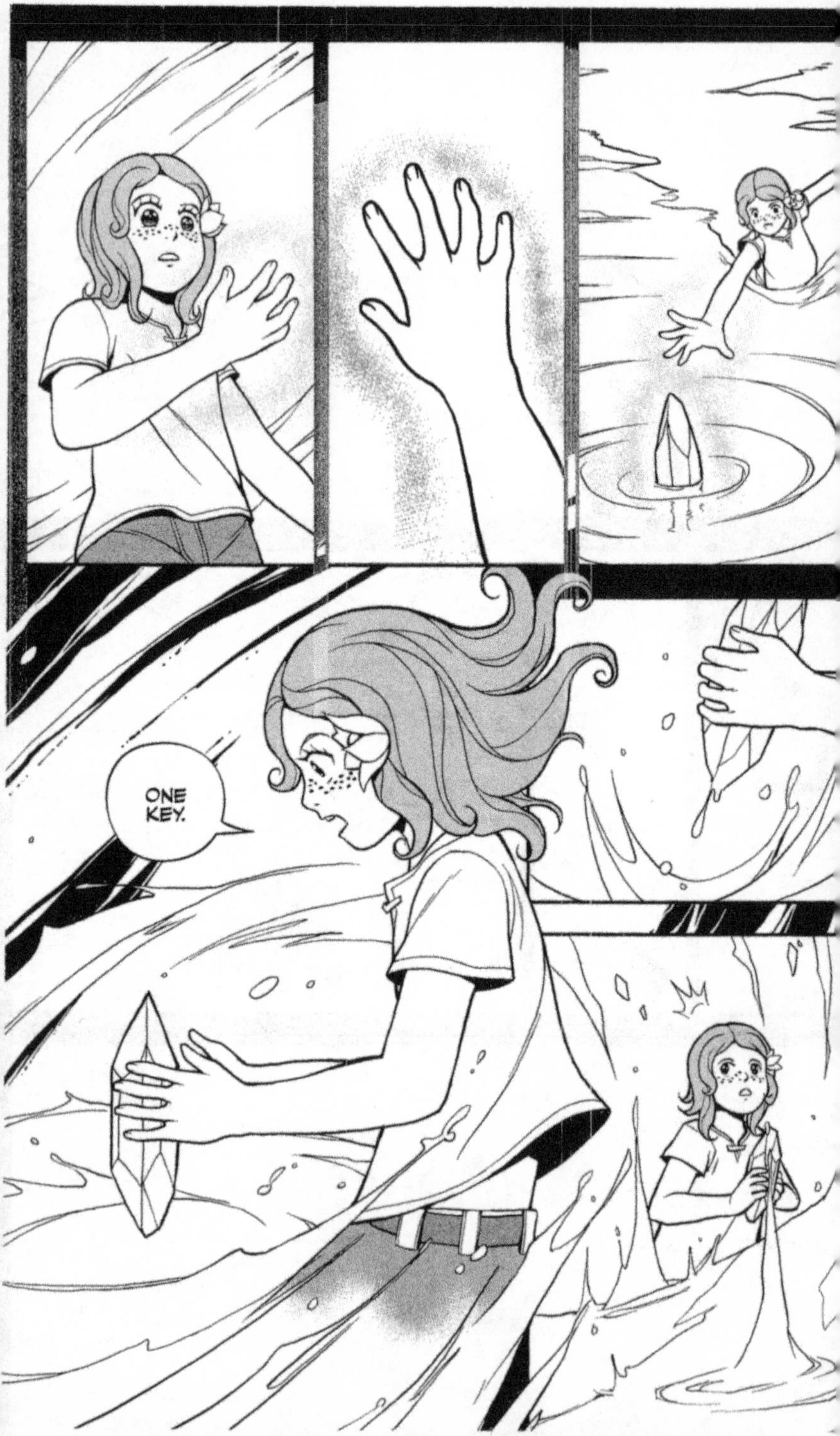
ONE KEY.

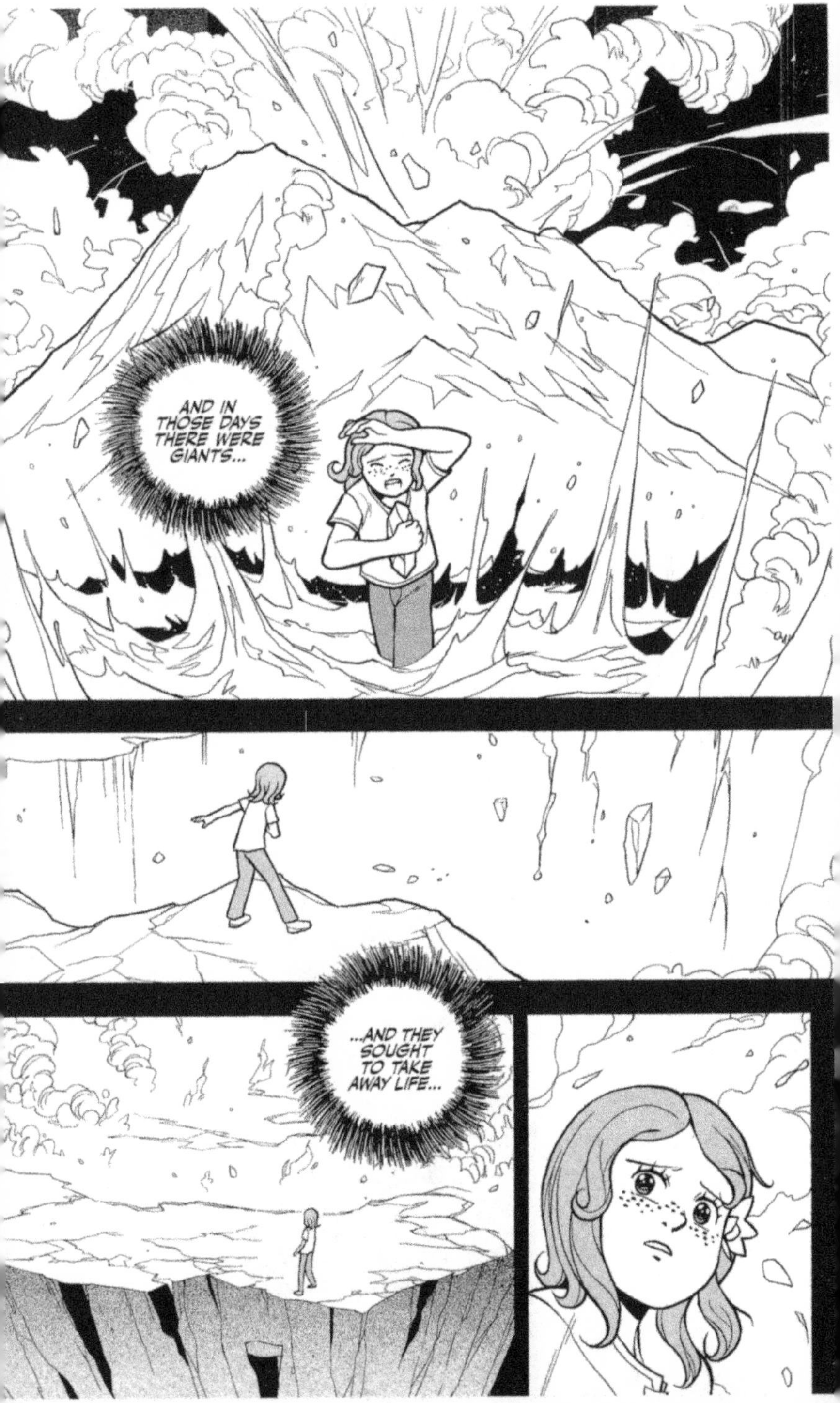
AND IN THOSE DAYS THERE WERE GIANTS...
...AND THEY SOUGHT TO TAKE AWAY LIFE...

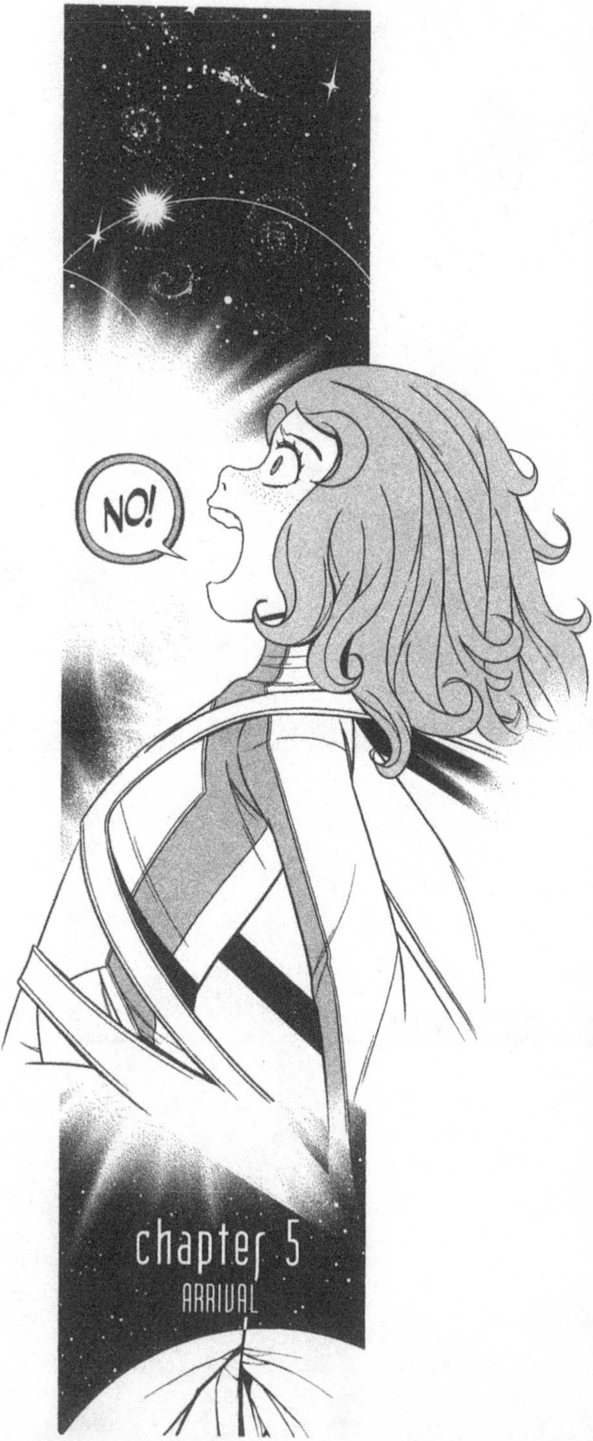
NO!
chapter 5
ARRIVAL

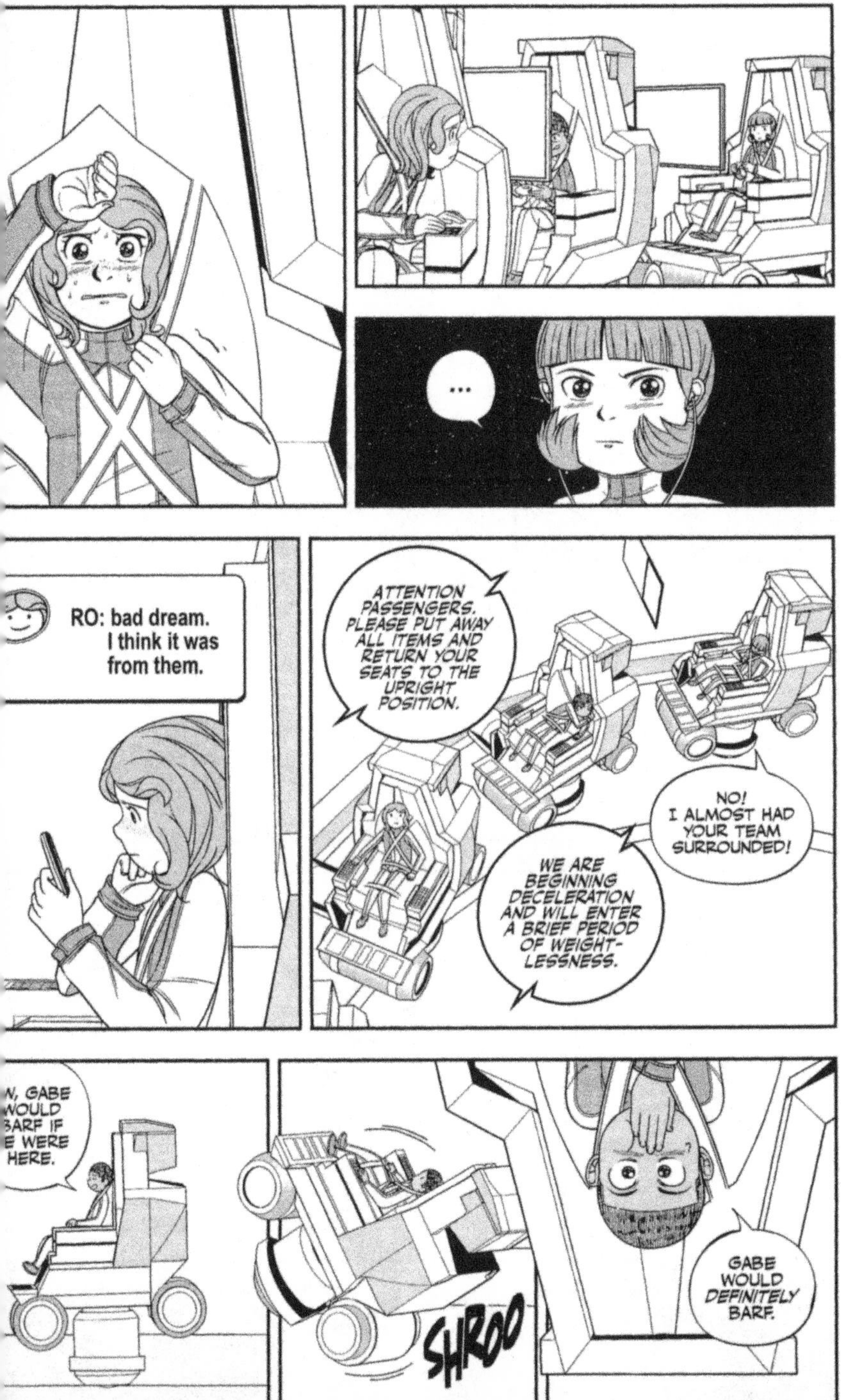
...
RO: bad dream. I think it was from them.
ATTENTION PASSENGERS. PLEASE PUT AWAY ALL ITEMS AND RETURN YOUR SEATS TO THE UPRIGHT POSITION.
NO! I ALMOST HAD YOUR TEAM SURROUNDED!
WE ARE BEGINNING DECELERATION AND WILL ENTER A BRIEF PERIOD OF WEIGHT-LESSNESS.
N, GABE WOULD BARF IF E WERE HERE.
SHROO
GABE WOULD DEFINITELY BARF.

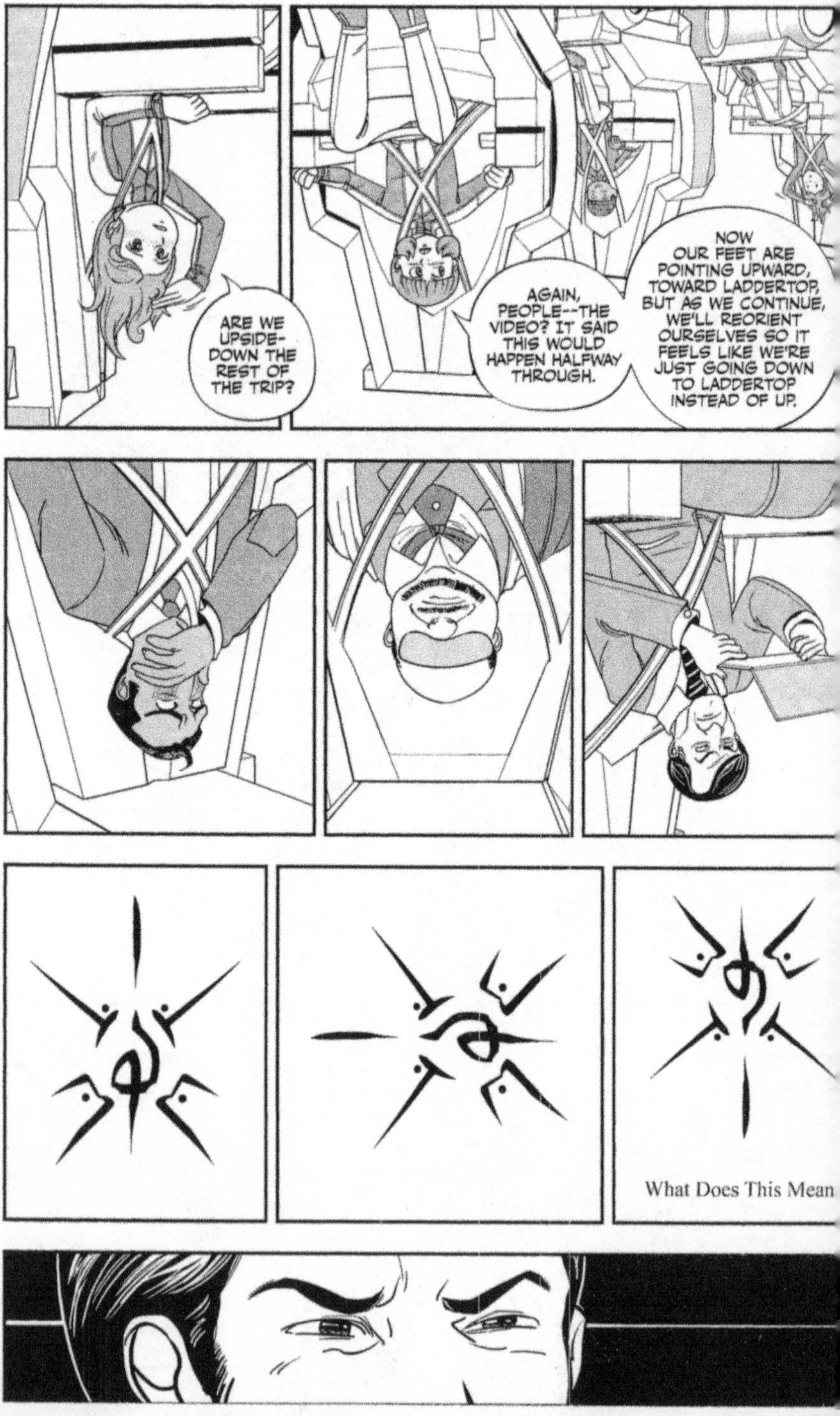
ARE WE UPSIDE-DOWN THE REST OF THE TRIP?
AGAIN, PEOPLE--THE VIDEO? IT SAID THIS WOULD HAPPEN HALFWAY THROUGH.
NOW OUR FEET ARE POINTING UPWARD, TOWARD LADDERTOP, BUT AS WE CONTINUE, WE'LL REORIENT OURSELVES SO IT FEELS LIKE WE'RE JUST GOING DOWN TO LADDERTOP INSTEAD OF UP.
What Does This Mean

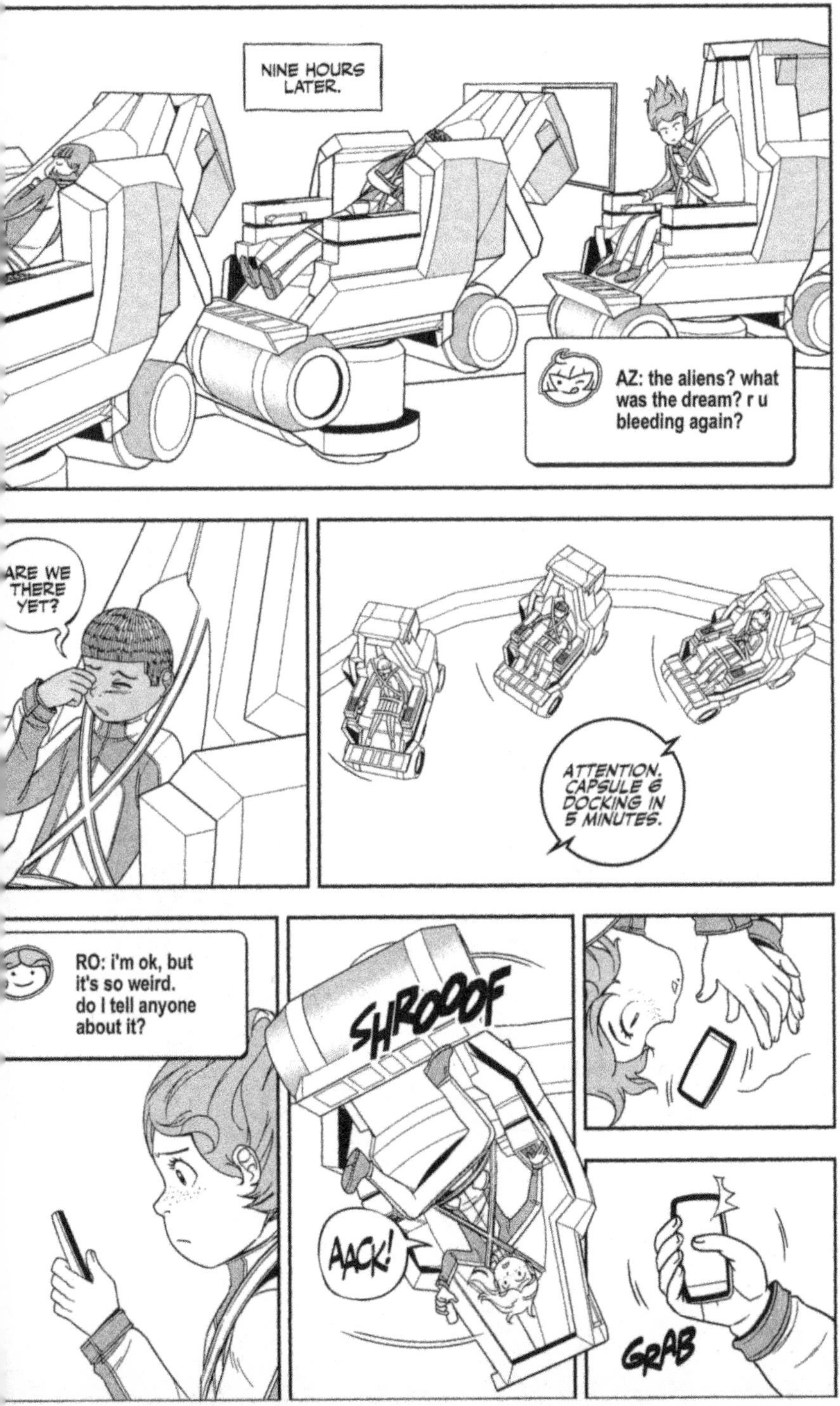
NINE HOURS LATER.
AZ: the aliens? what was the dream? r u bleeding again?
ARE WE THERE YET?
ATTENTION. CAPSULE 6 DOCKING IN 5 MINUTES.
RO: i'm ok, but it's so weird. do I tell anyone about it?
SHROOOF
AACK!
GRAB

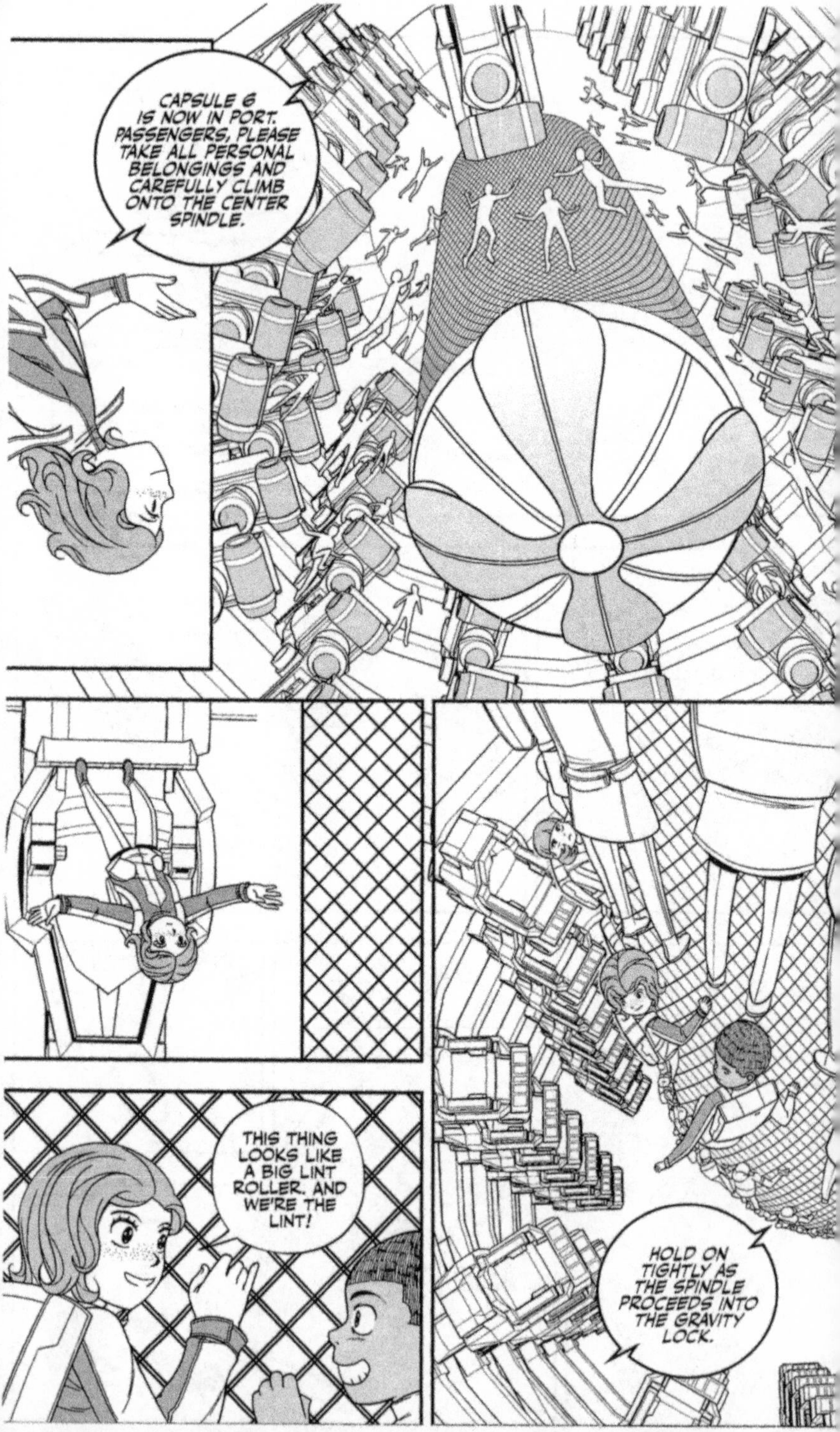
CAPSULE 6 IS NOW IN PORT. PASSENGERS, PLEASE TAKE ALL PERSONAL BELONGINGS AND CAREFULLY CLIMB ONTO THE CENTER SPINDLE.
THIS THING LOOKS LIKE A BIG LINT ROLLER. AND WE'RE THE LINT!
HOLD ON TIGHTLY AS THE SPINDLE PROCEEDS INTO THE GRAVITY LOCK.

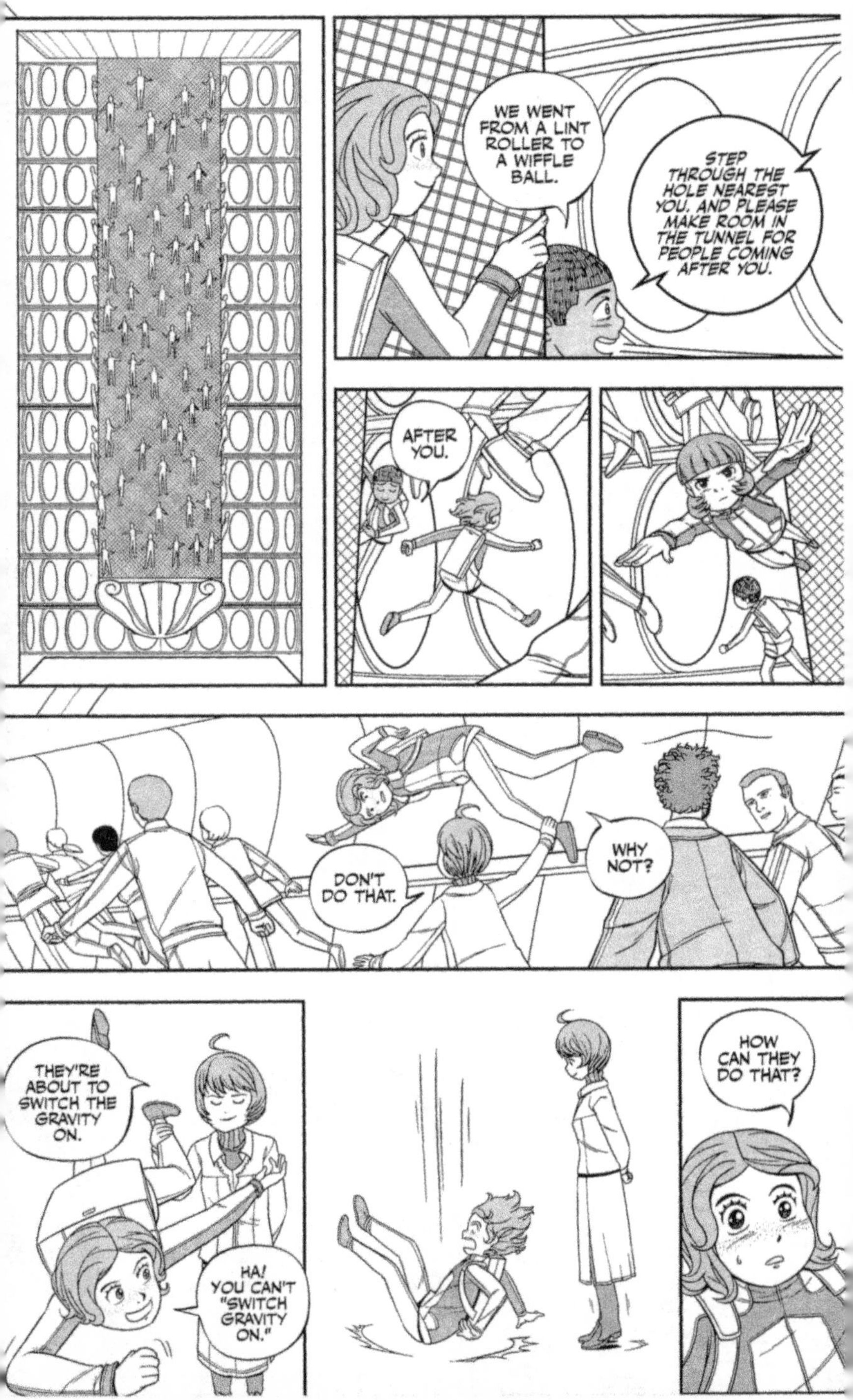
WE WENT FROM A LINT ROLLER TO A WIFFLE BALL.
STEP THROUGH THE HOLE NEAREST YOU. AND PLEASE MAKE ROOM IN THE TUNNEL FOR PEOPLE COMING AFTER YOU.
AFTER YOU.
DON'T DO THAT.
WHY NOT?
THEY'RE ABOUT TO SWITCH THE GRAVITY ON.
HA! YOU CAN'T "SWITCH GRAVITY ON."
HOW CAN THEY DO THAT?

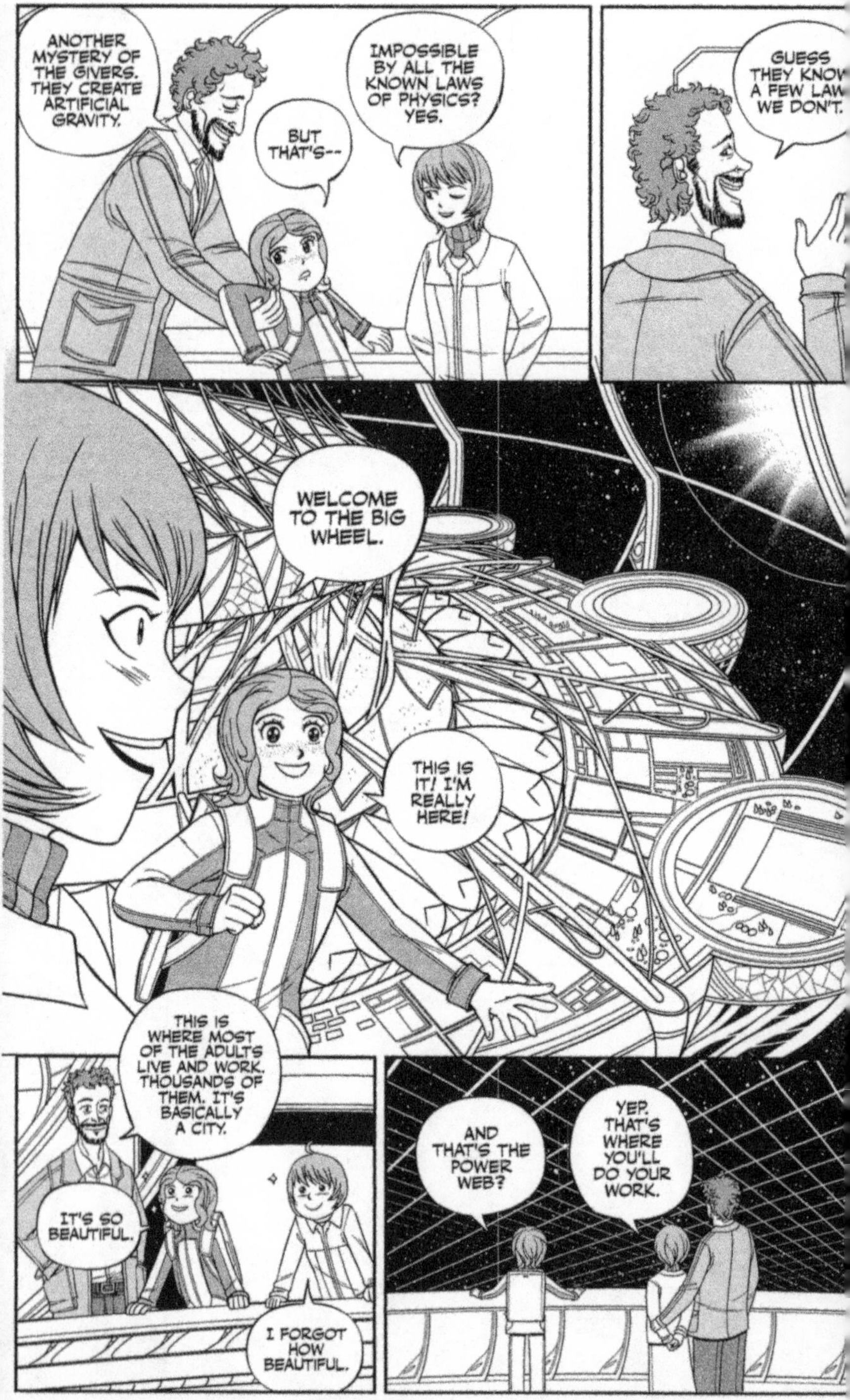
ANOTHER MYSTERY OF THE GIVERS. THEY CREATE ARTIFICIAL GRAVITY.
BUT THAT'S--
IMPOSSIBLE BY ALL THE KNOWN LAWS OF PHYSICS? YES.
GUESS THEY KNOW A FEW LAW WE DON'T.
WELCOME TO THE BIG WHEEL.
THIS IS IT! I'M REALLY HERE!
THIS IS WHERE MOST OF THE ADULTS LIVE AND WORK. THOUSANDS OF THEM. IT'S BASICALLY A CITY.
IT'S SO BEAUTIFUL.
I FORGOT HOW BEAUTIFUL.
AND THAT'S THE POWER WEB?
YEP. THAT'S WHERE YOU'LL DO YOUR WORK.

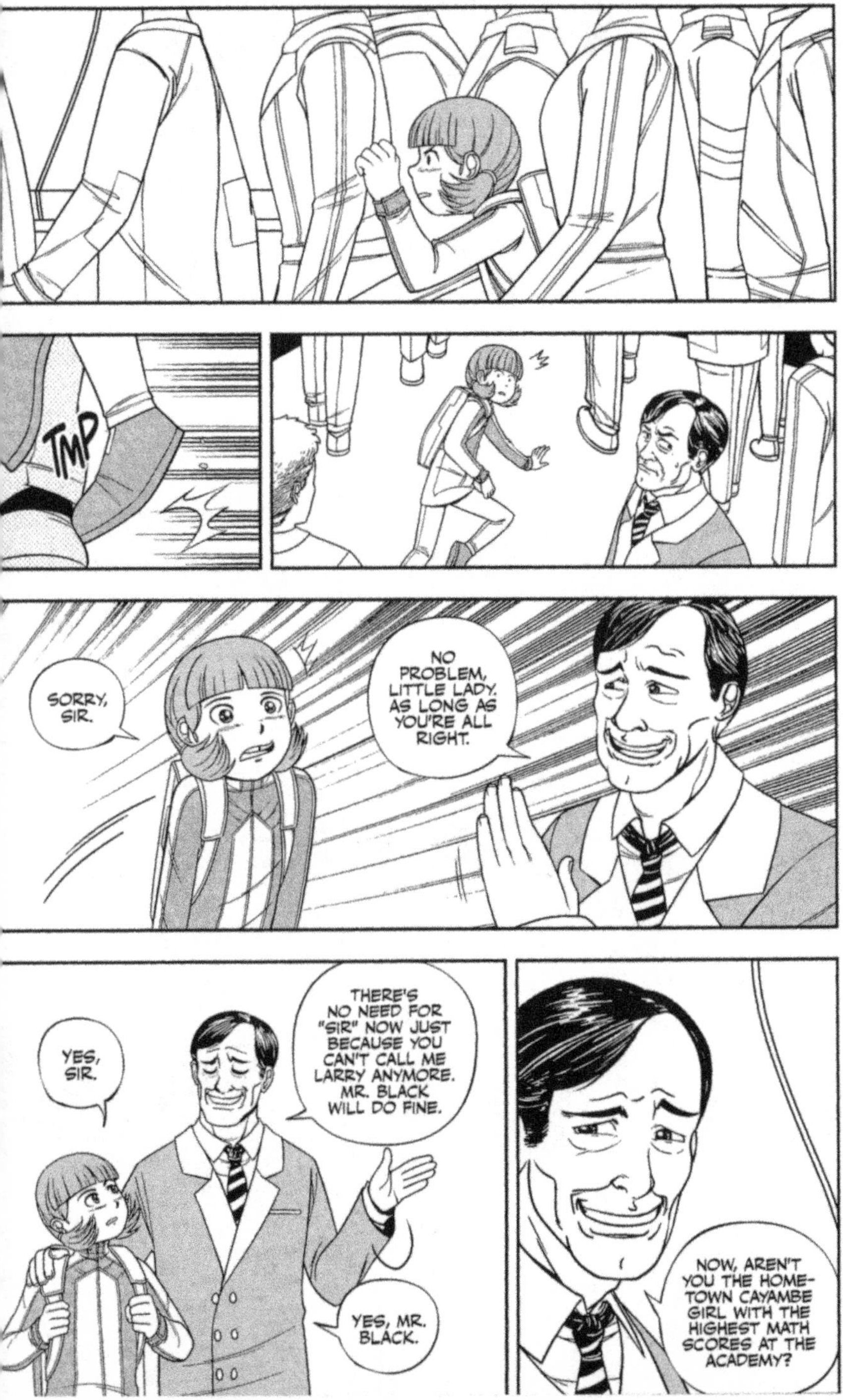
TMP
SORRY, SIR.
NO PROBLEM, LITTLE LADY. AS LONG AS YOU'RE ALL RIGHT.
YES, SIR.
THERE'S NO NEED FOR "SIR" NOW JUST BECAUSE YOU CAN'T CALL ME LARRY ANYMORE. MR. BLACK WILL DO FINE.
YES, MR. BLACK.
NOW, AREN'T YOU THE HOME-TOWN CAYAMBE GIRL WITH THE HIGHEST MATH SCORES AT THE ACADEMY?

INCREDIBLE, ISN'T IT?

NOW, LOOK, I KNOW I TOLD YOU AND YOUR FRIENDS TO COME SEE ME--

THEY'RE NOT MY FRIENDS, SIR. I TOOK NO PART IN THEIR RUDENESS AND ROUGH-HOUSING.

THAT ROBERTA GIRL AND HER HISTRIONICS! I WAS AGAINST BRINGING HER HERE AT ALL.

SHE IS STRANGE. SHE SHOUTS WEIRD STUFF IN HER SLEEP...

AND ONE TIM SHE YELLED IN SHOWERS AND T SAID A DRAGON BIT HER, WHIC DRAGONFLIES HARDLY EVER DO--

REALLY?

THANK YOU FOR TELLING ME. I'LL KEEP A CLOSE EYE ON HER. WHY DON'T YOU DO THE SAME?

NOW, RUN ALONG TO YOUR LEADERS.

AND TELL YOUR *TEAMMATES* THEY DON'T HAVE TO MEET WITH ME AFTER ALL.

I'VE DROPPED ALL CHARGES.

YES, SIR. MR. BLACK.

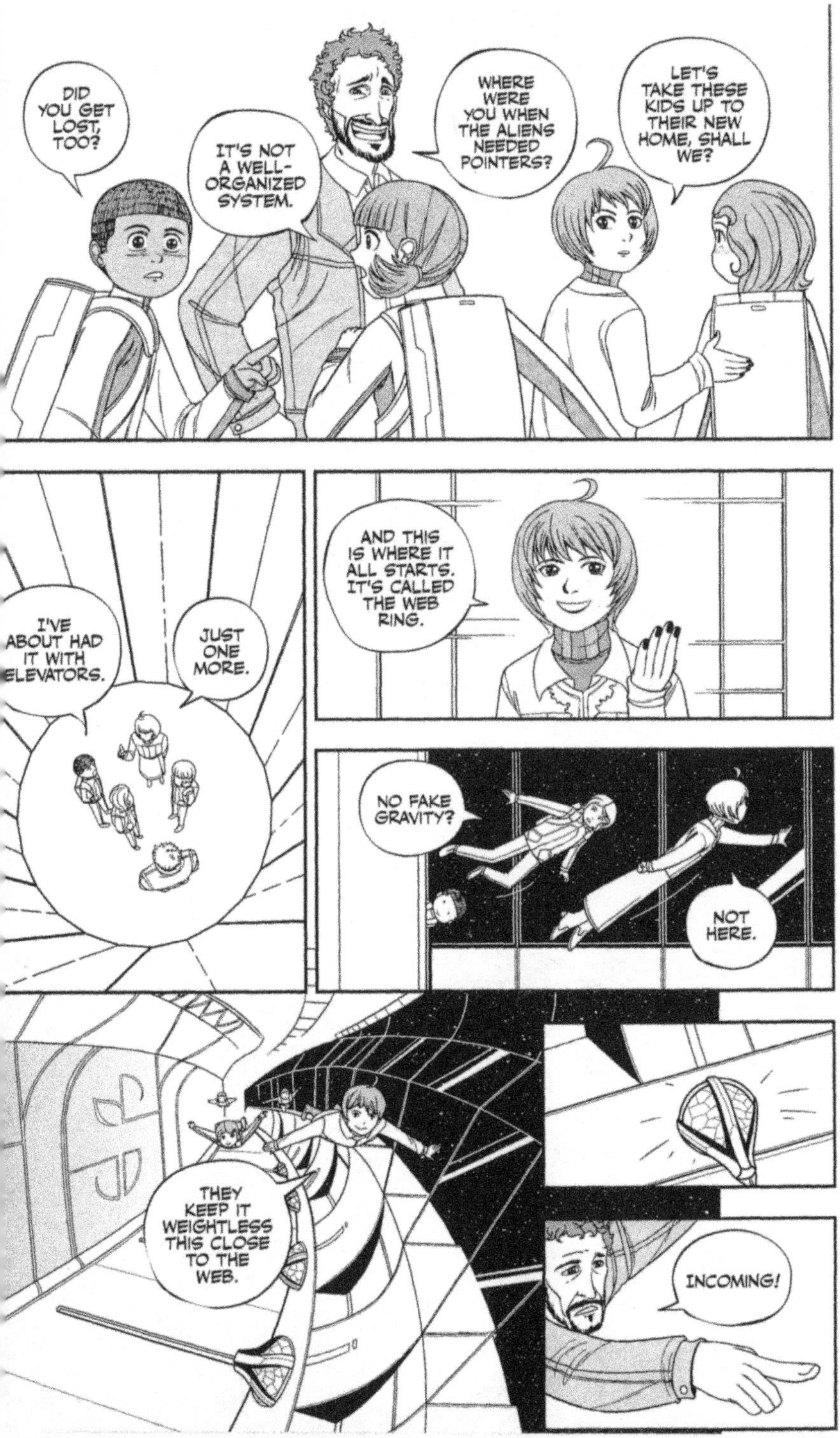
DID YOU GET LOST, TOO?
IT'S NOT A WELL-ORGANIZED SYSTEM.
WHERE WERE YOU WHEN THE ALIENS NEEDED POINTERS?
LET'S TAKE THESE KIDS UP TO THEIR NEW HOME, SHALL WE?
I'VE ABOUT HAD IT WITH ELEVATORS.
JUST ONE MORE.
AND THIS IS WHERE IT ALL STARTS. IT'S CALLED THE WEB RING.
NO FAKE GRAVITY?
NOT HERE.
THEY KEEP IT WEIGHTLESS THIS CLOSE TO THE WEB.
INCOMING!

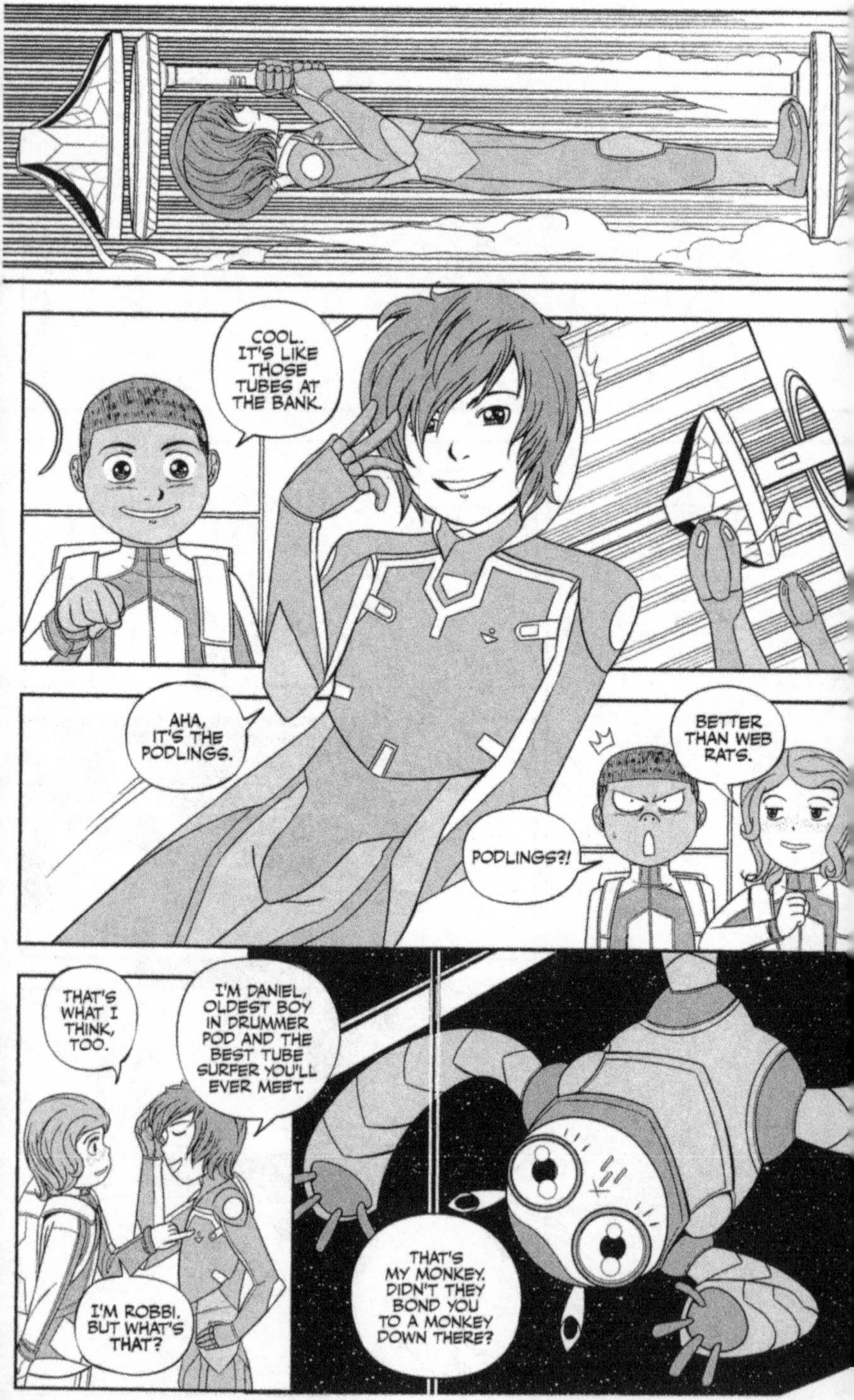

COOL. IT'S LIKE THOSE TUBES AT THE BANK.
AHA, IT'S THE PODLINGS.
BETTER THAN WEB RATS.
PODLINGS?!
THAT'S WHAT I THINK, TOO.
I'M DANIEL, OLDEST BOY IN DRUMMER POD AND THE BEST TUBE SURFER YOU'LL EVER MEET.
I'M ROBBI. BUT WHAT'S THAT?
THAT'S MY MONKEY. DIDN'T THEY BOND YOU TO A MONKEY DOWN THERE?

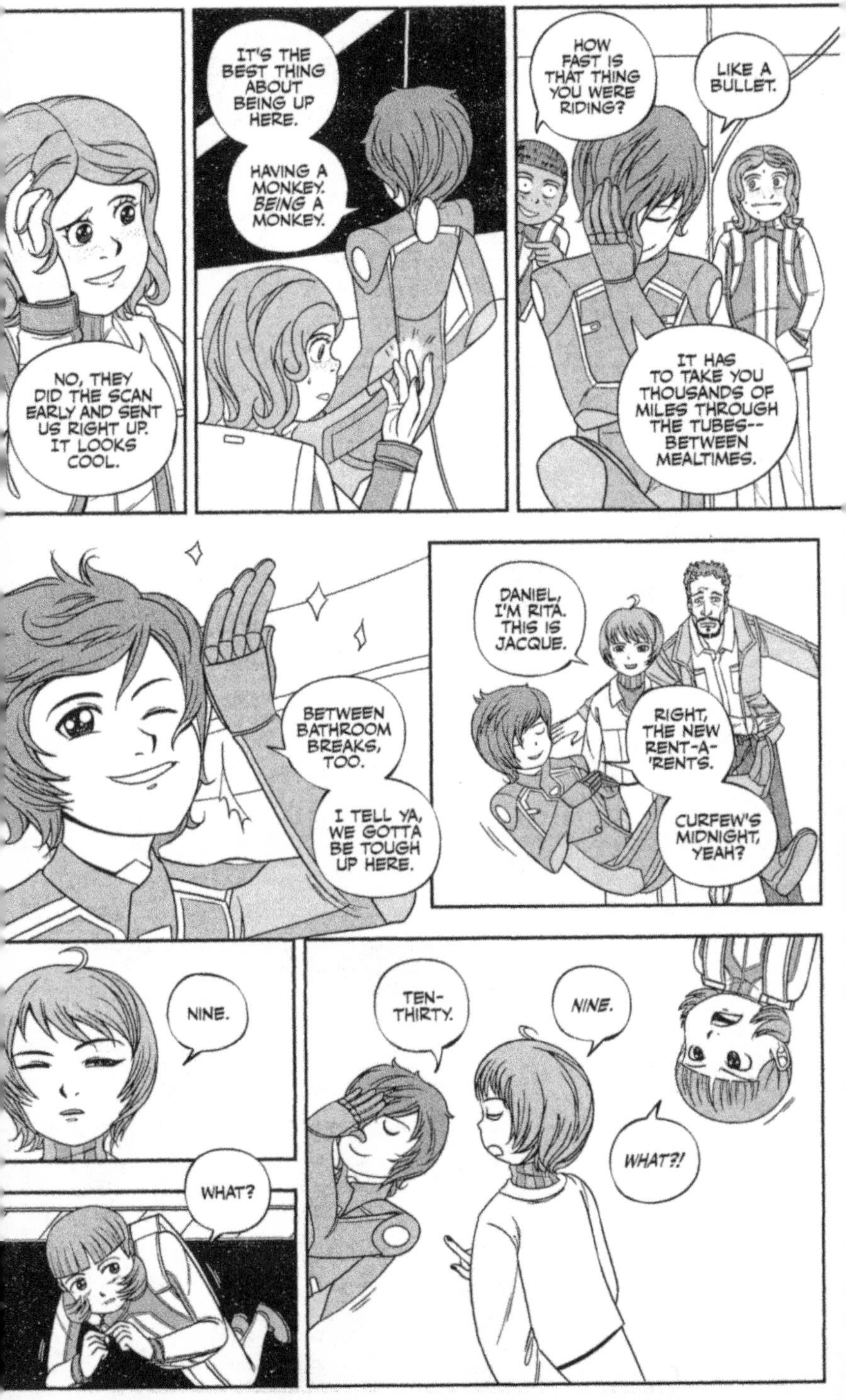
NO, THEY DID THE SCAN EARLY AND SENT US RIGHT UP. IT LOOKS COOL.
IT'S THE BEST THING ABOUT BEING UP HERE.
HAVING A MONKEY. *BEING* A MONKEY.
HOW FAST IS THAT THING YOU WERE RIDING?
LIKE A BULLET.
IT HAS TO TAKE YOU THOUSANDS OF MILES THROUGH THE TUBES-- BETWEEN MEALTIMES.
BETWEEN BATHROOM BREAKS, TOO.
I TELL YA, WE GOTTA BE TOUGH UP HERE.
DANIEL, I'M RITA. THIS IS JACQUE.
RIGHT, THE NEW RENT-A-'RENTS.
CURFEW'S MIDNIGHT, YEAH?
NINE.
WHAT?
TEN-THIRTY.
NINE.
WHAT?!

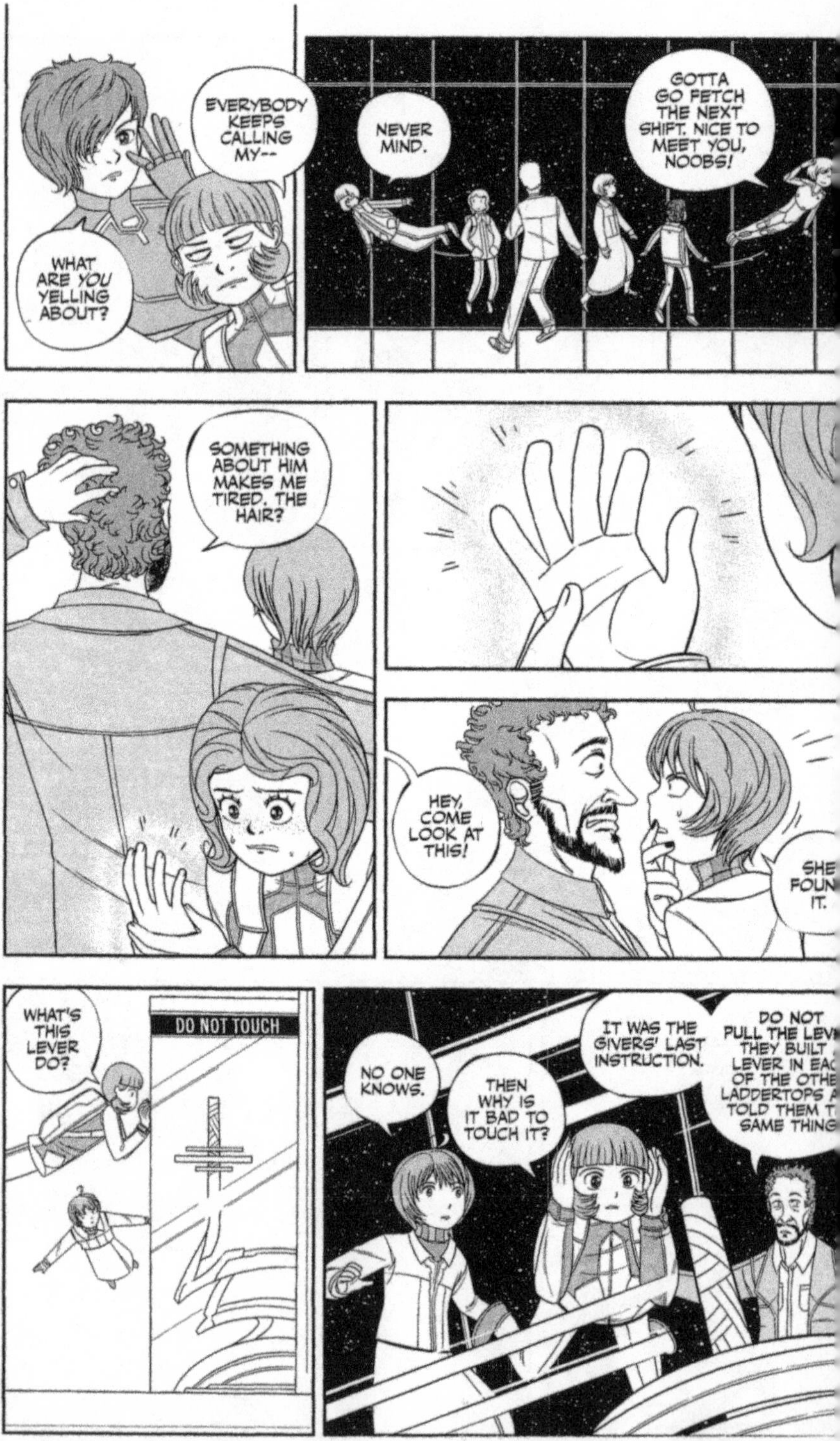
EVERYBODY KEEPS CALLING MY--
WHAT ARE *YOU* YELLING ABOUT?
NEVER MIND.
GOTTA GO FETCH THE NEXT SHIFT. NICE TO MEET YOU, NOOBS!
SOMETHING ABOUT HIM MAKES ME TIRED. THE HAIR?
HEY, COME LOOK AT THIS!
SHE FOUN IT.
WHAT'S THIS LEVER DO?
DO NOT TOUCH
NO ONE KNOWS.
THEN WHY IS IT BAD TO TOUCH IT?
IT WAS THE GIVERS' LAST INSTRUCTION.
DO NOT PULL THE LEV THEY BUILT LEVER IN EAC OF THE OTHE LADDERTOPS A TOLD THEM T SAME THING

SO THEY JUST LEFT THAT HERE TO DRIVE US CRAZY.

AND NO ONE'S *EVER* TRIED TO PULL THE LEVER?

WHAT DO YOU THINK THE GLASS IS FOR?

NINE, COME DOWN FROM THERE. LET'S GO FIND OUR ROOMS AND UNPACK, OKAY?

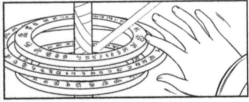

IT'S LIKE MY DREAM.

ROBBI?

RIGHT BEHIND YOU!

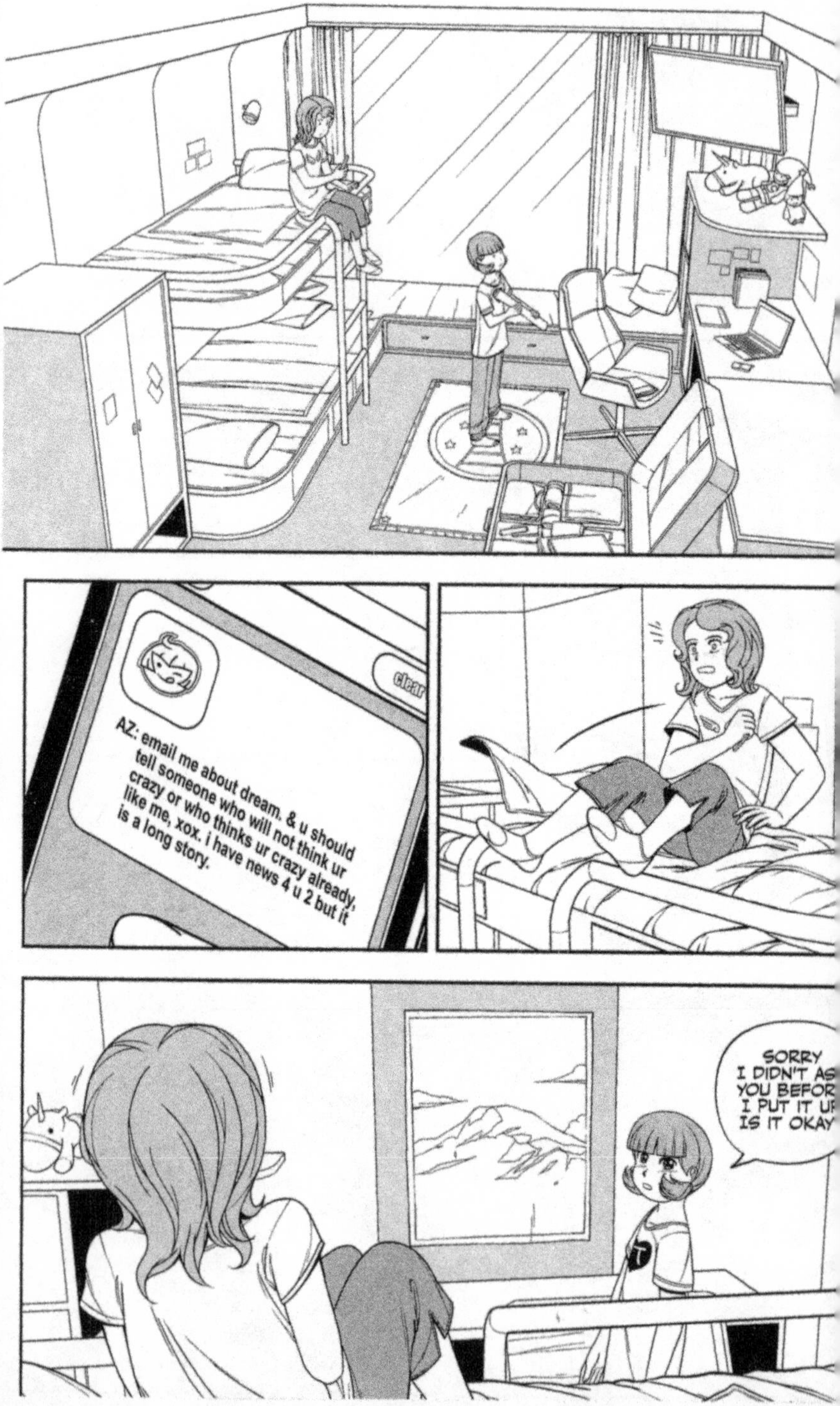
clear
AZ: email me about dream. & u should tell someone who will not think ur crazy or who thinks ur crazy already, like me, xox. i have news 4 u 2 but it is a long story.
SORRY I DIDN'T AS YOU BEFOR I PUT IT U IS IT OKAY

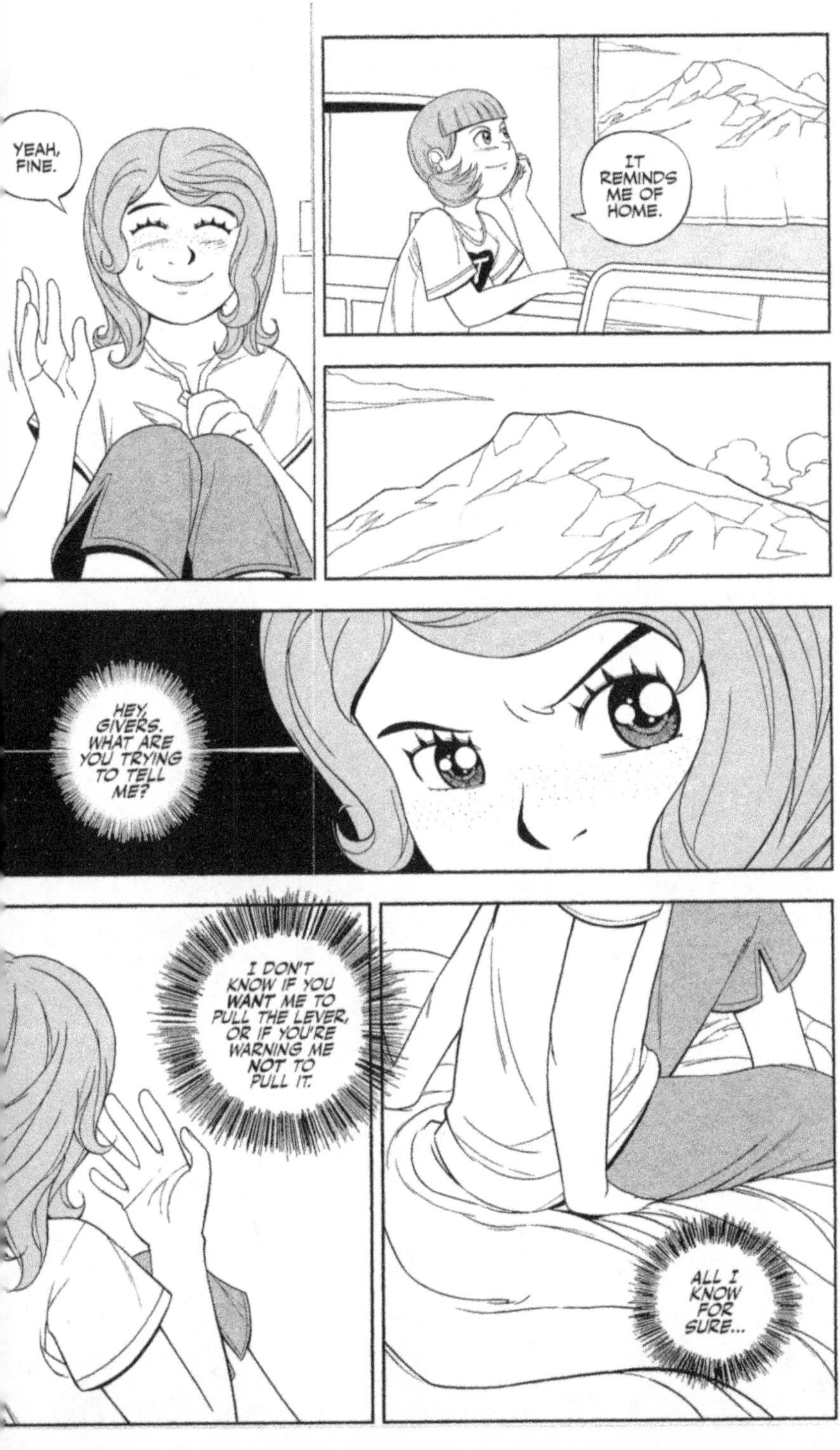
YEAH, FINE.
IT REMINDS ME OF HOME.
HEY, GIVERS. WHAT ARE YOU TRYING TO TELL ME?
I DON'T KNOW IF YOU WANT ME TO PULL THE LEVER, OR IF YOU'RE WARNING ME NOT TO PULL IT.
ALL I KNOW FOR SURE...

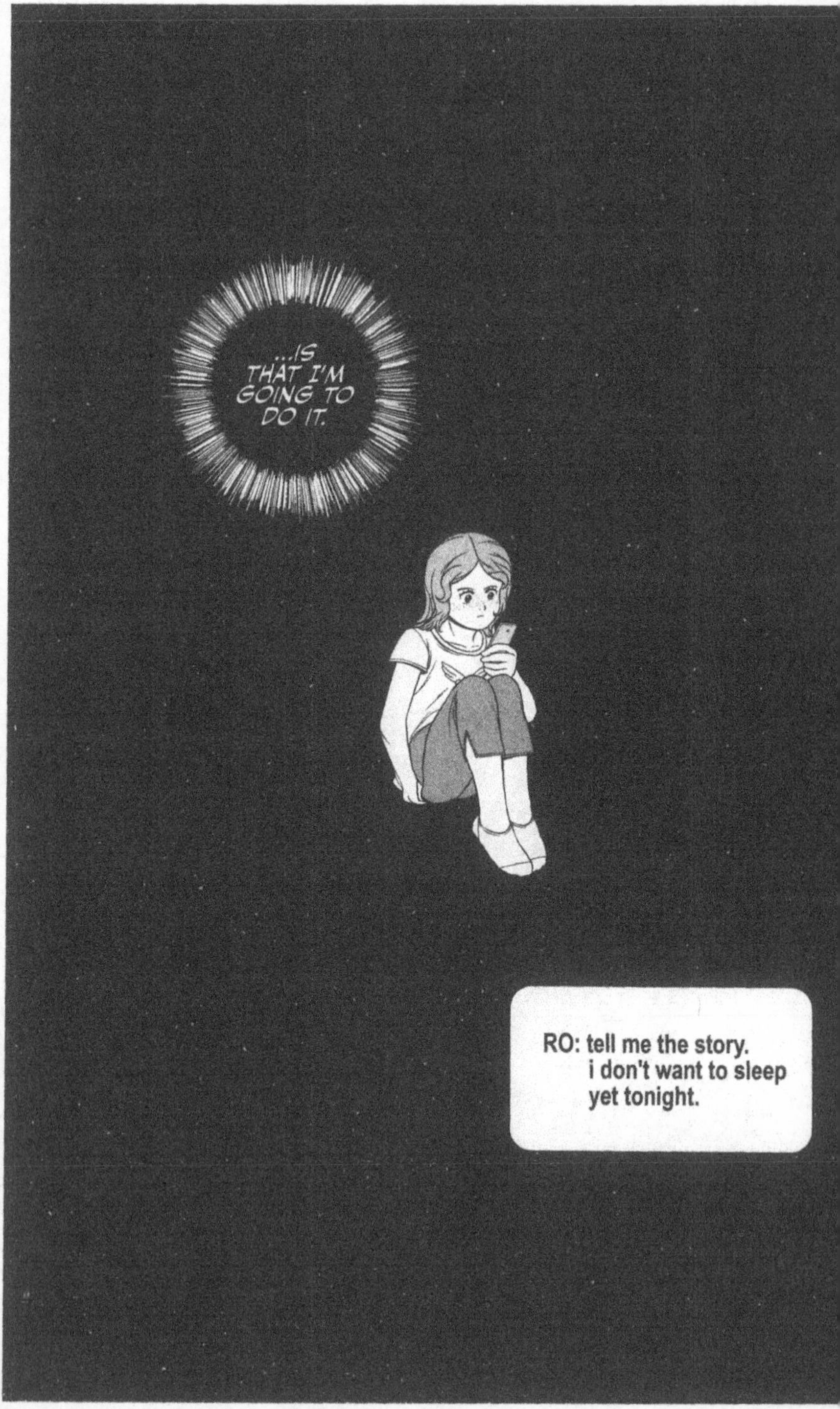
...IS THAT I'M GOING TO DO IT.
RO: tell me the story. i don't want to sleep yet tonight.

Laddertop

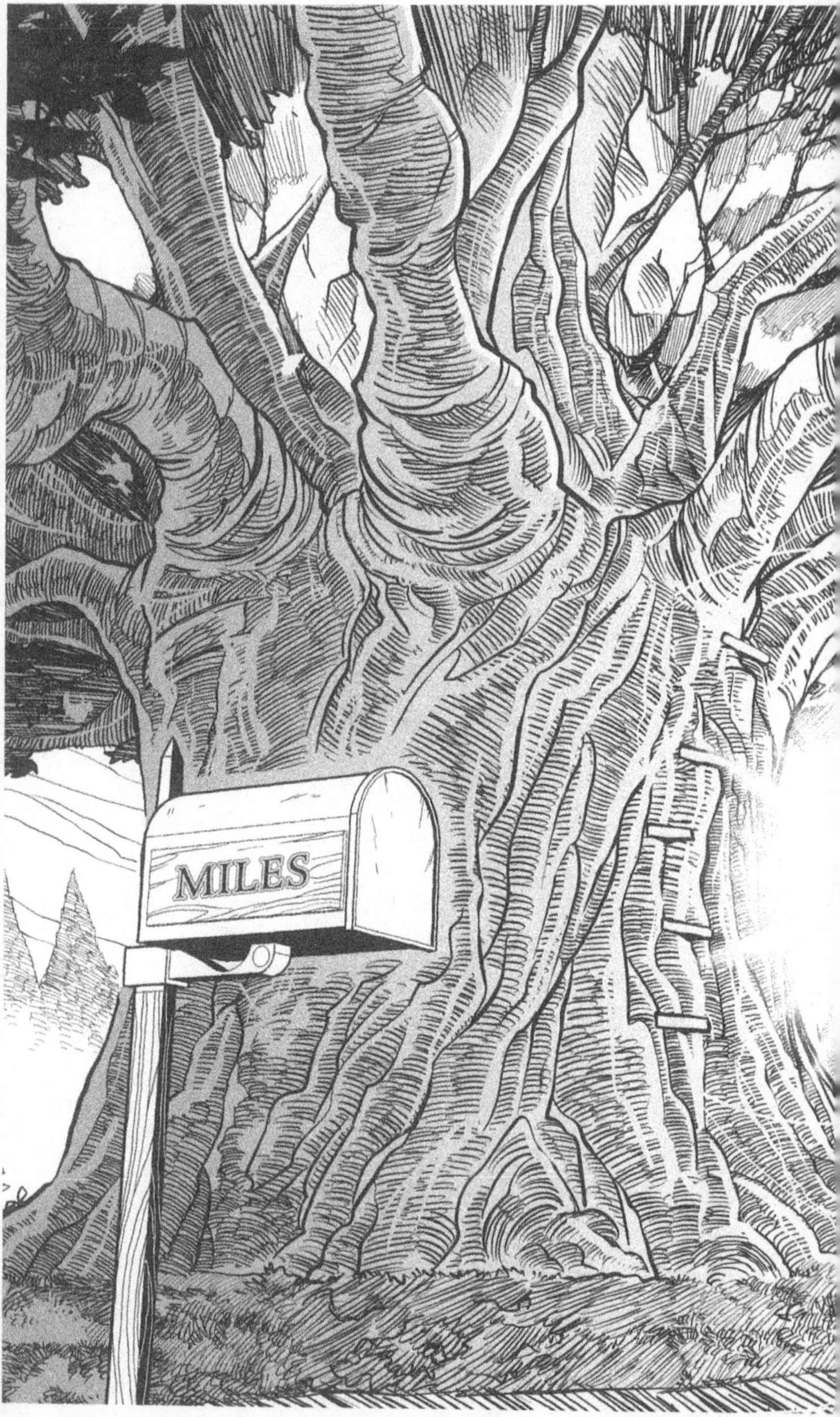
MILES

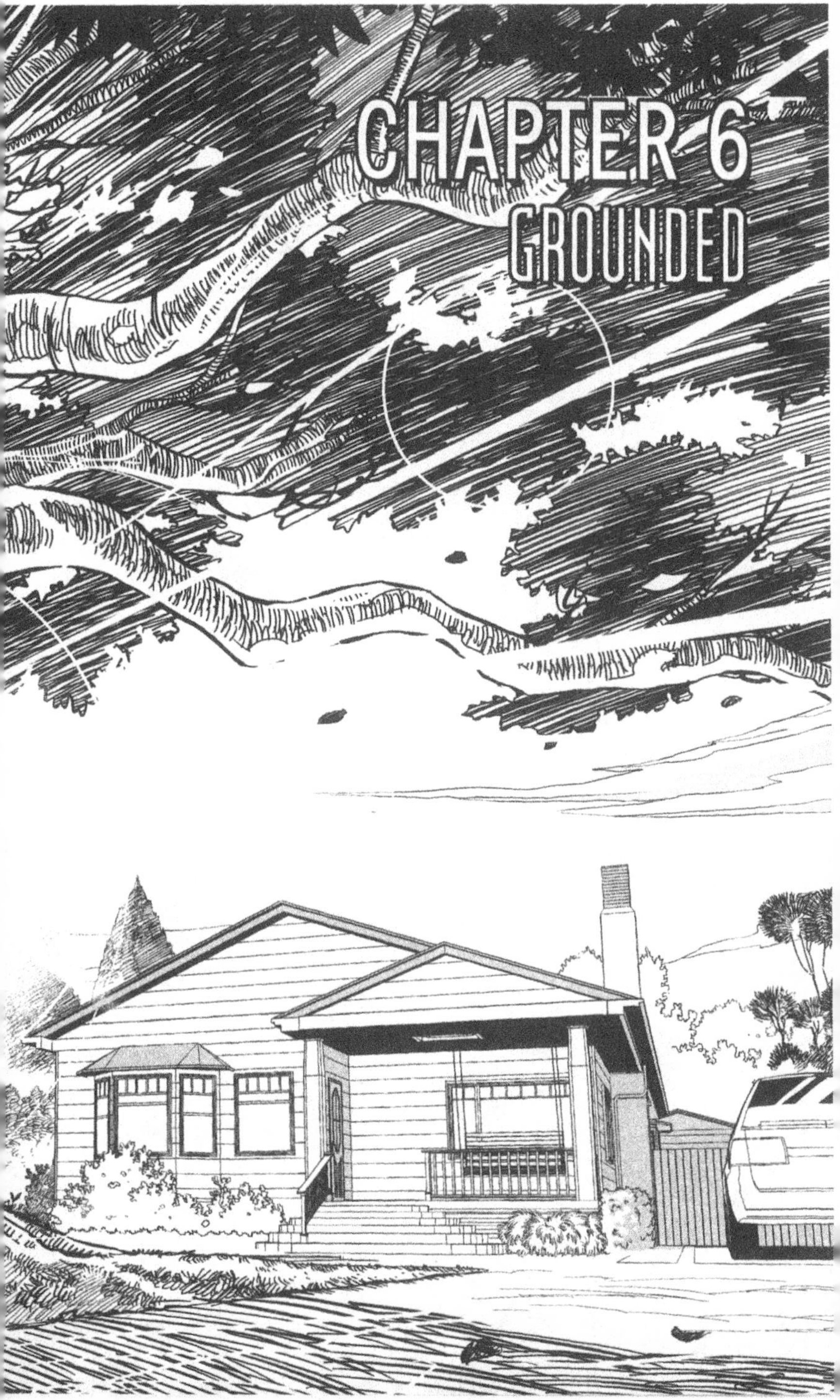
CHAPTER 6
GROUNDED

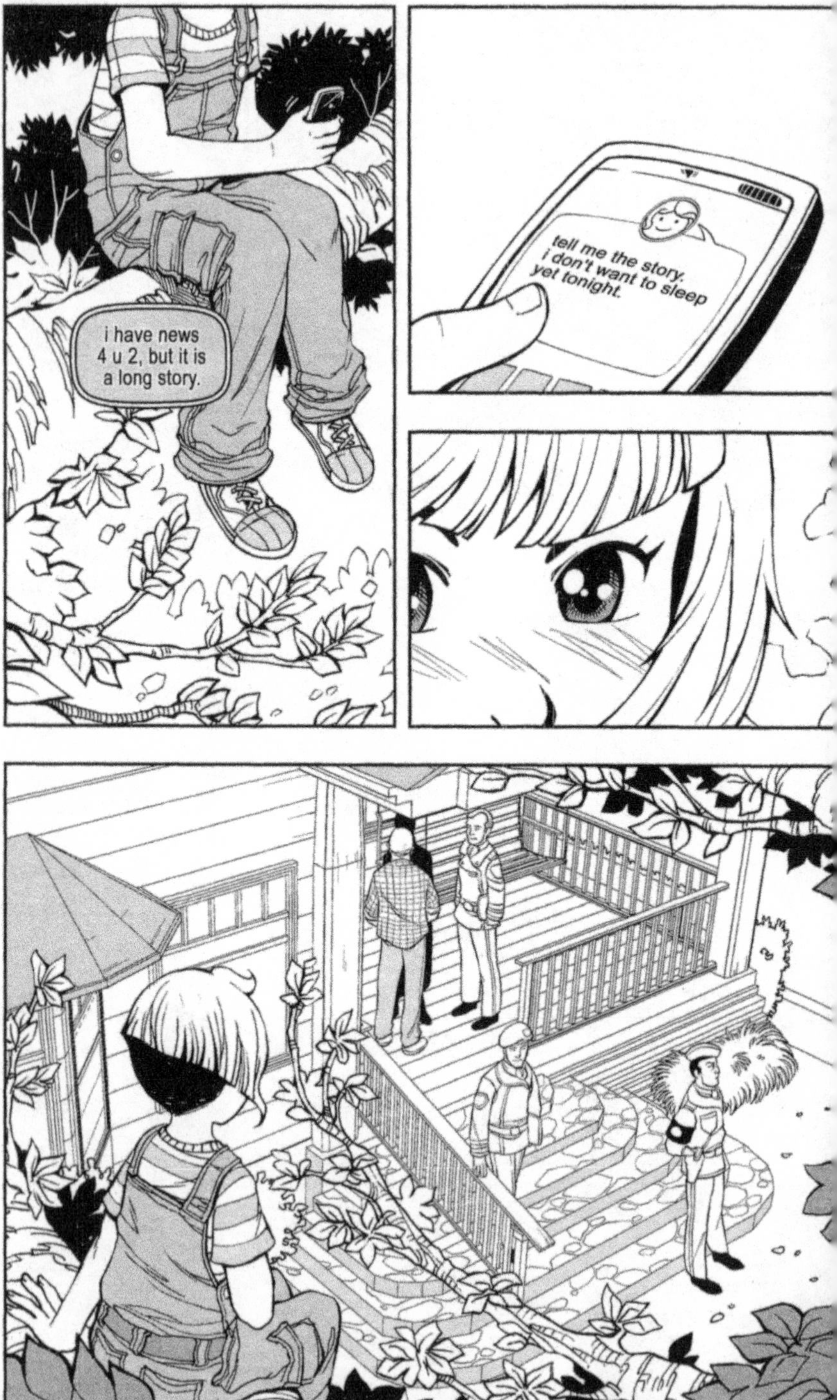
i have news
4 u 2, but it is
a long story.
tell me the story.
i don't want to sleep
yet tonight.

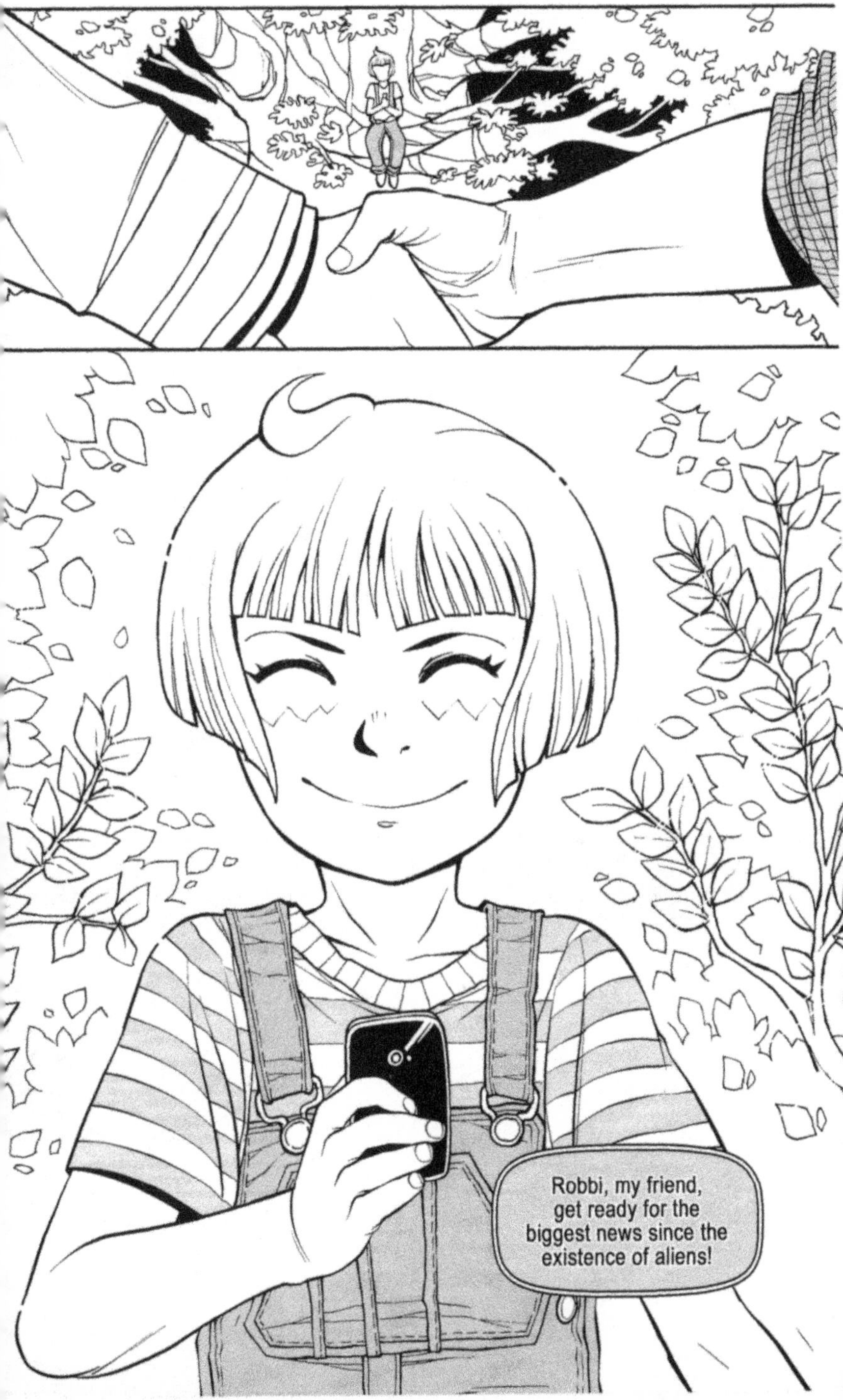
Robbi, my friend, get ready for the biggest news since the existence of aliens!

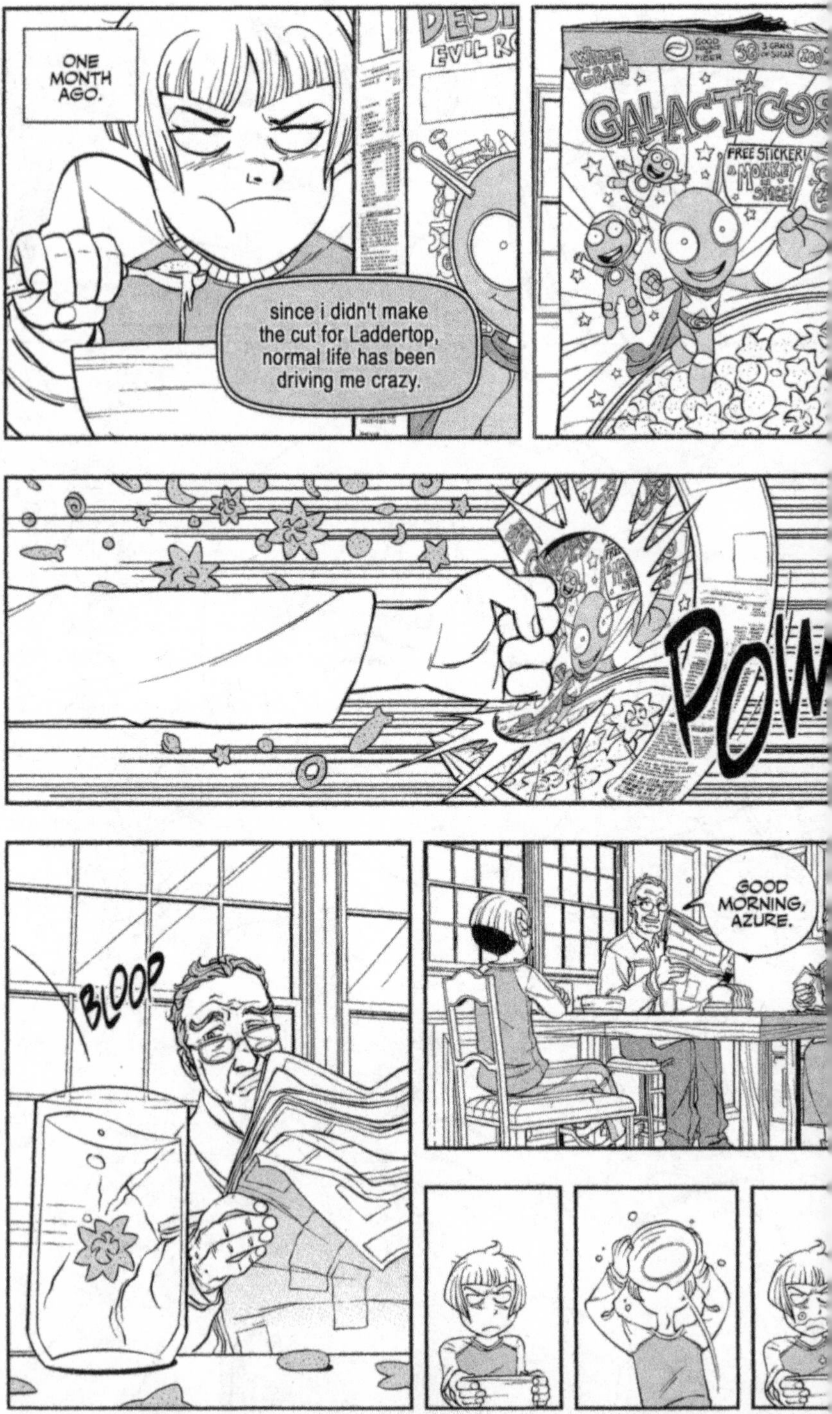
ONE MONTH AGO.
since i didn't make the cut for Laddertop, normal life has been driving me crazy.
EVIL R
WHOLE GRAIN
GOOD
FIBER
3 GRAMS OF SUGAR
GALACTICOS
FREE STICKER!
POW
BLOOP
GOOD MORNING, AZURE.

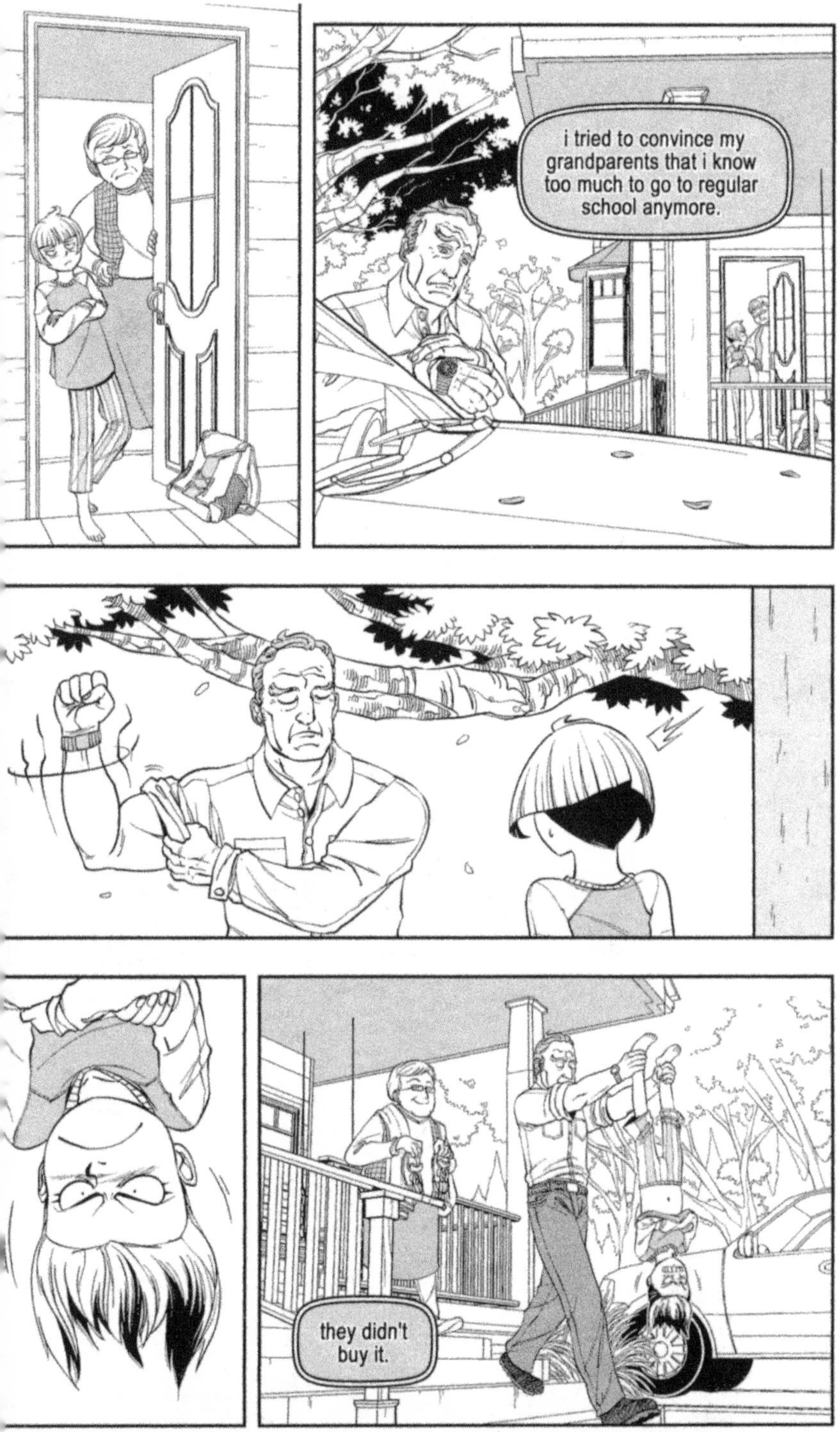
i tried to convince my grandparents that i know too much to go to regular school anymore.
they didn't buy it.

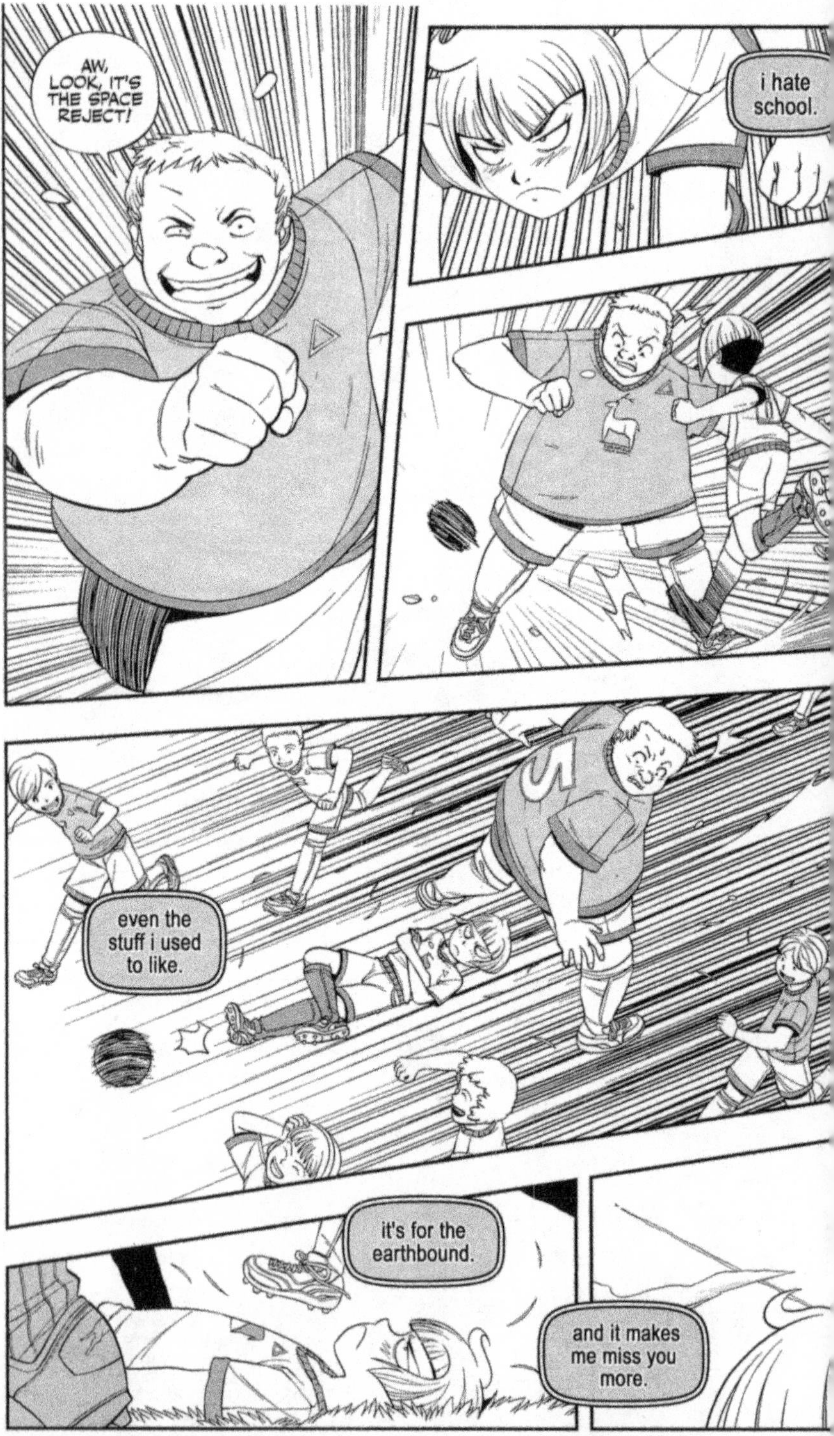
AW, LOOK, IT'S THE SPACE REJECT!
i hate school.
even the stuff i used to like.
it's for the earthbound.
and it makes me miss you more.

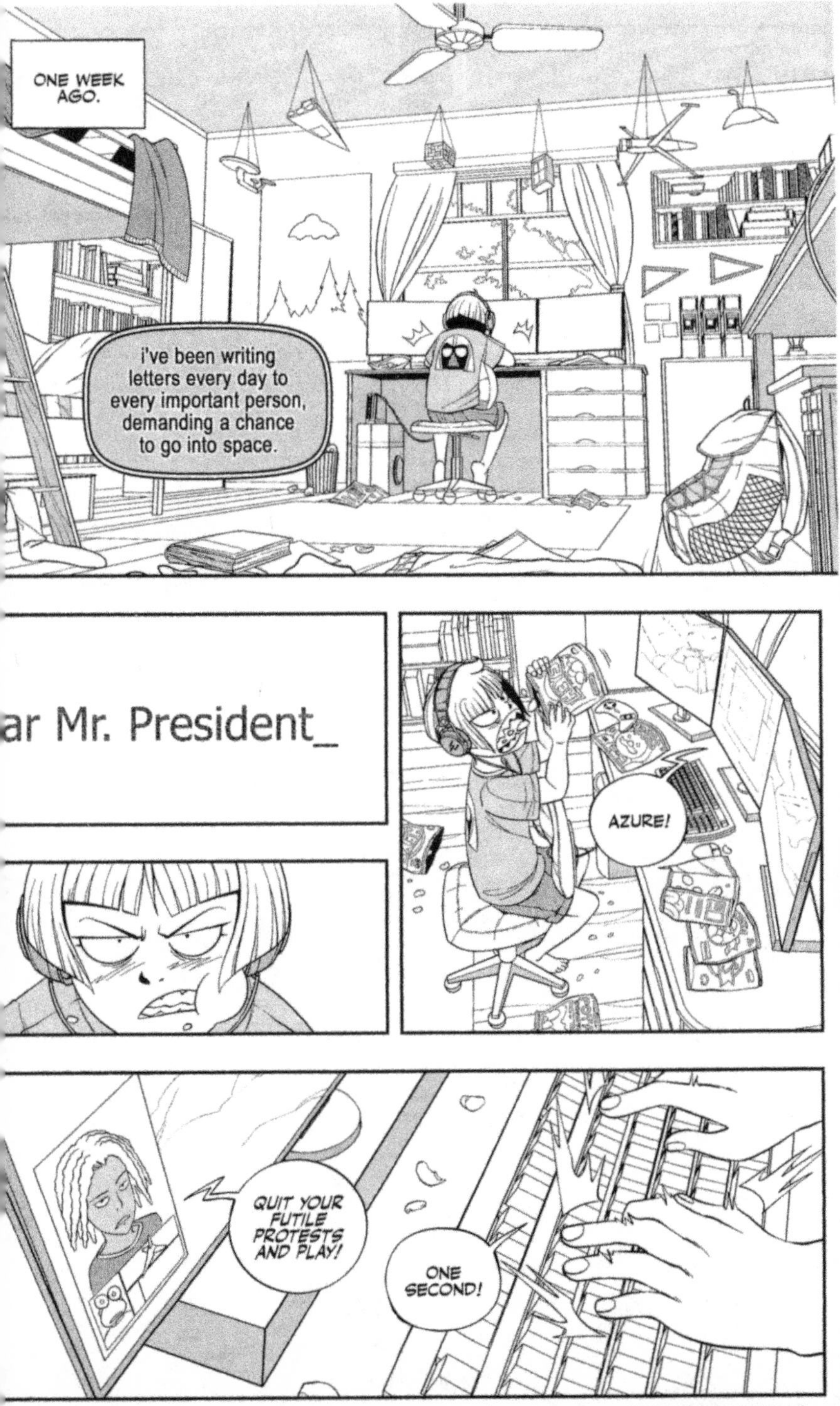
ONE WEEK AGO.
i've been writing letters every day to every important person, demanding a chance to go into space.
ar Mr. President_
AZURE!
QUIT YOUR FUTILE PROTESTS AND PLAY!
ONE SECOND!

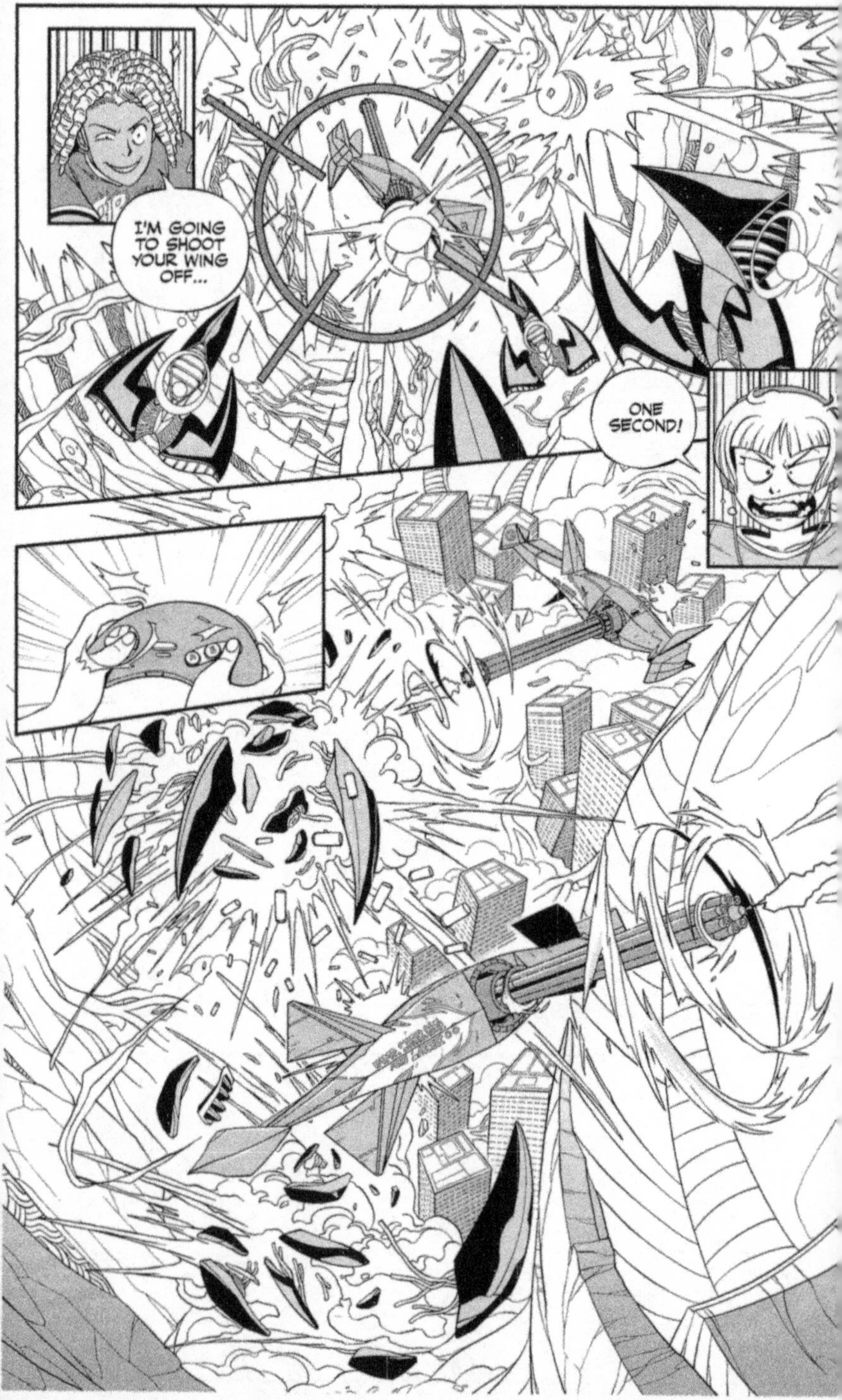
I'M GOING TO SHOOT YOUR WING OFF...
ONE SECOND!

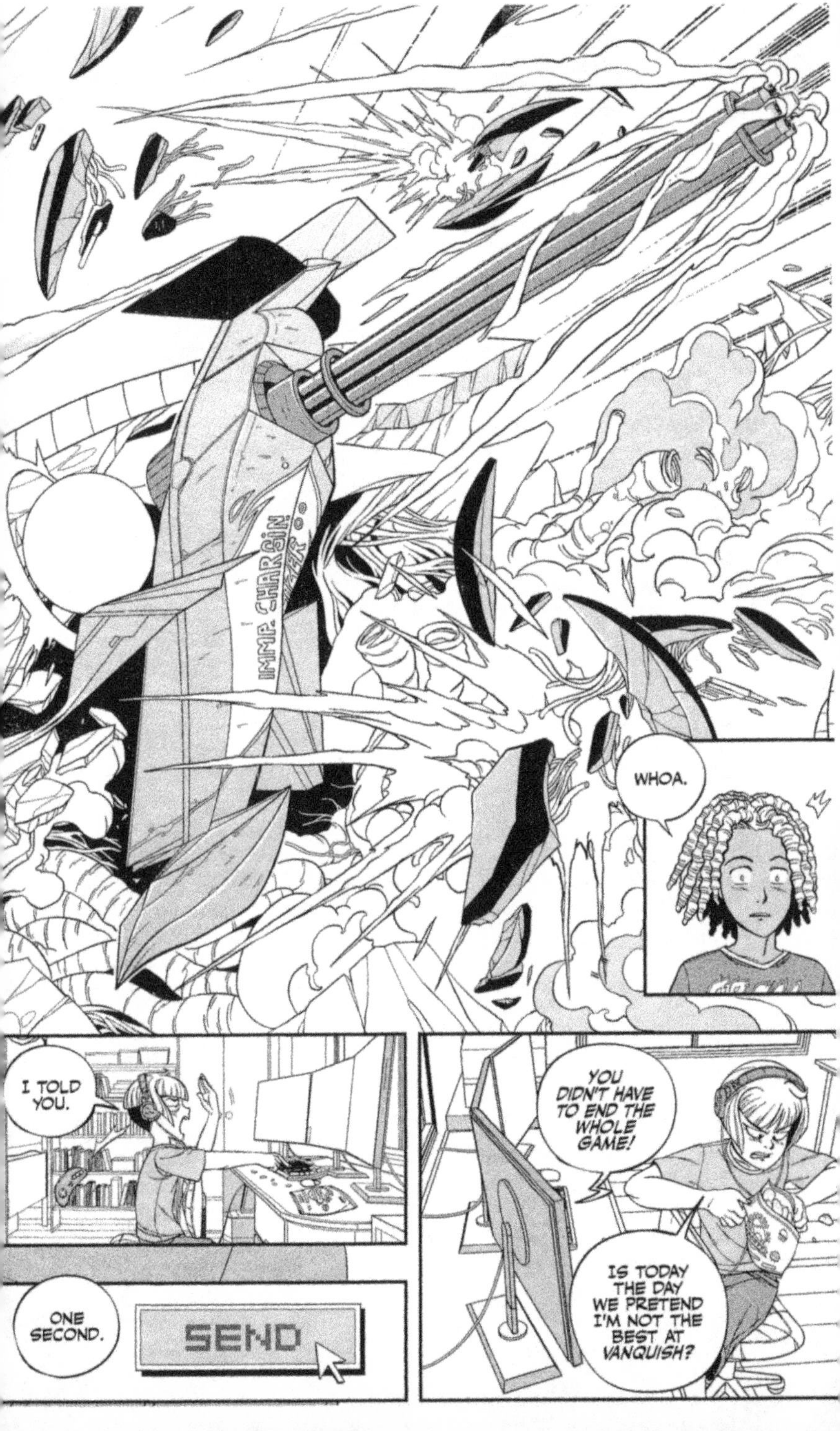
WHOA.
I TOLD YOU.
ONE SECOND.
SEND
YOU DIDN'T HAVE TO END THE WHOLE GAME!
IS TODAY THE DAY WE PRETEND I'M NOT THE BEST AT *VANQUISH?*

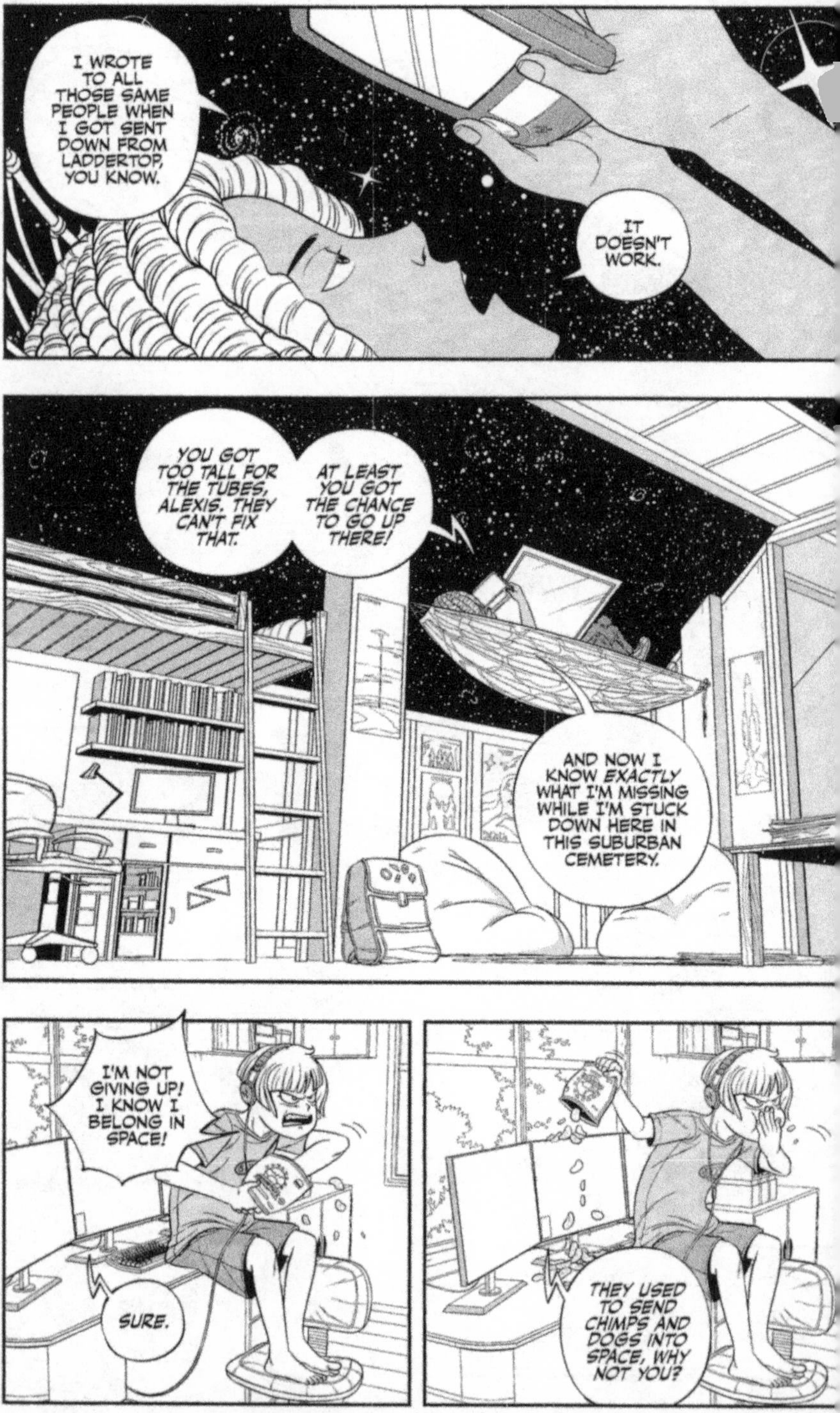
I WROTE TO ALL THOSE SAME PEOPLE WHEN I GOT SENT DOWN FROM LADDERTOP, YOU KNOW.
IT DOESN'T WORK.
YOU GOT TOO TALL FOR THE TUBES, ALEXIS. THEY CAN'T FIX THAT.
AT LEAST YOU GOT THE CHANCE TO GO UP THERE!
AND NOW I KNOW *EXACTLY* WHAT I'M MISSING WHILE I'M STUCK DOWN HERE IN THIS SUBURBAN CEMETERY.
I'M NOT GIVING UP! I KNOW I BELONG IN SPACE!
SURE.
THEY USED TO SEND CHIMPS AND DOGS INTO SPACE, WHY NOT YOU?

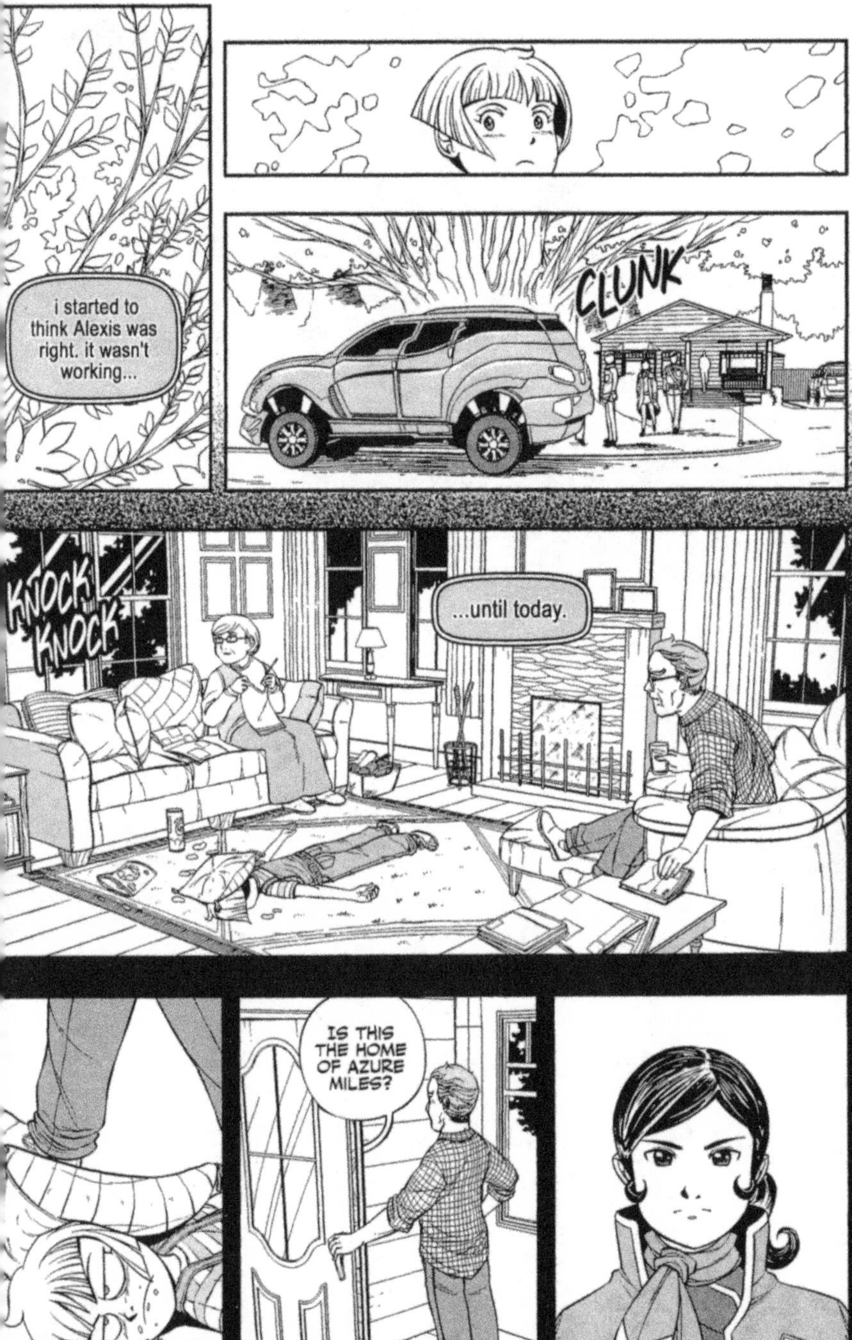
i started to think Alexis was right. it wasn't working...
CLUNK
KNOCK KNOCK
...until today.
IS THIS THE HOME OF AZURE MILES?

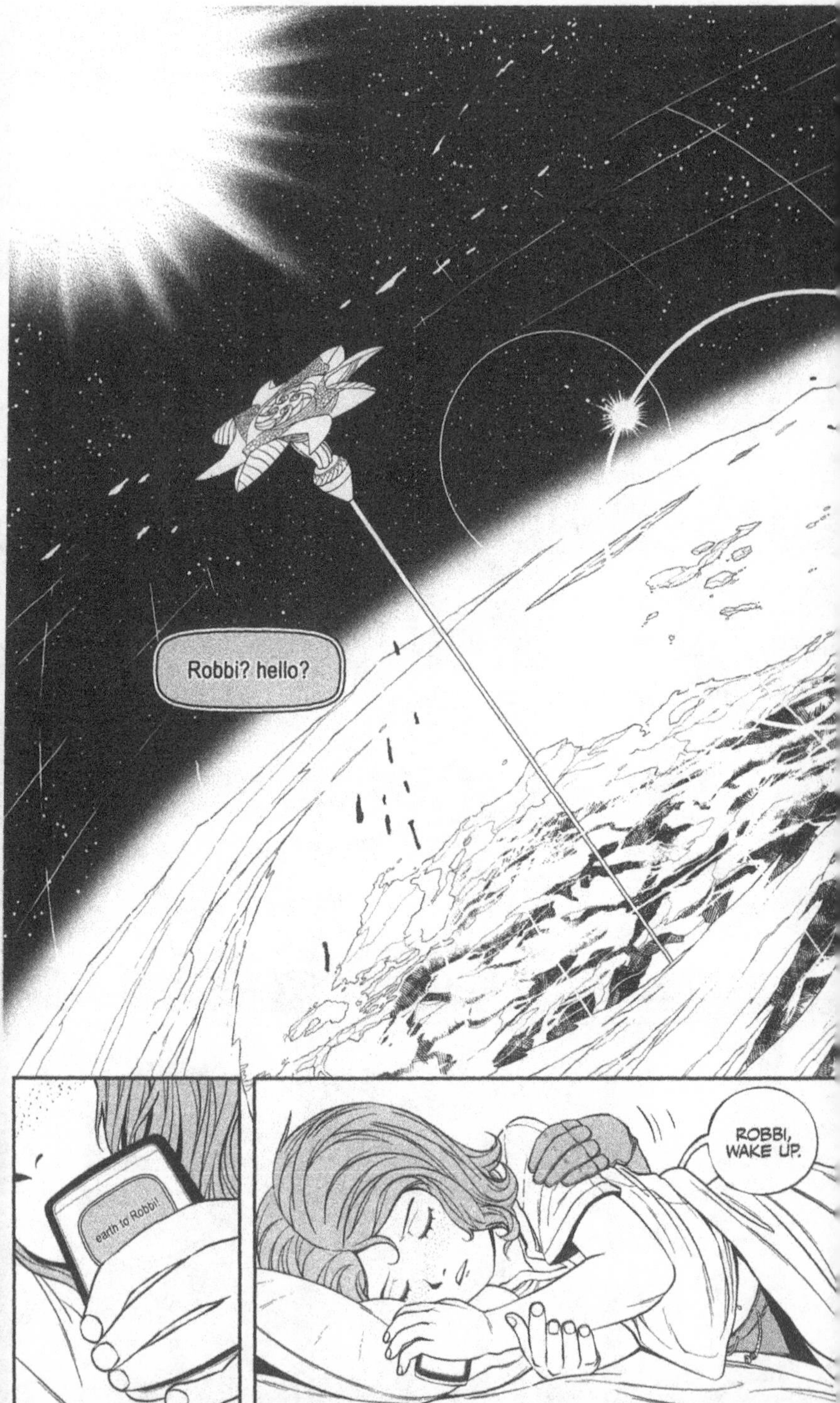
Robbi? hello?
earth to Robbi!
ROBBI, WAKE UP.

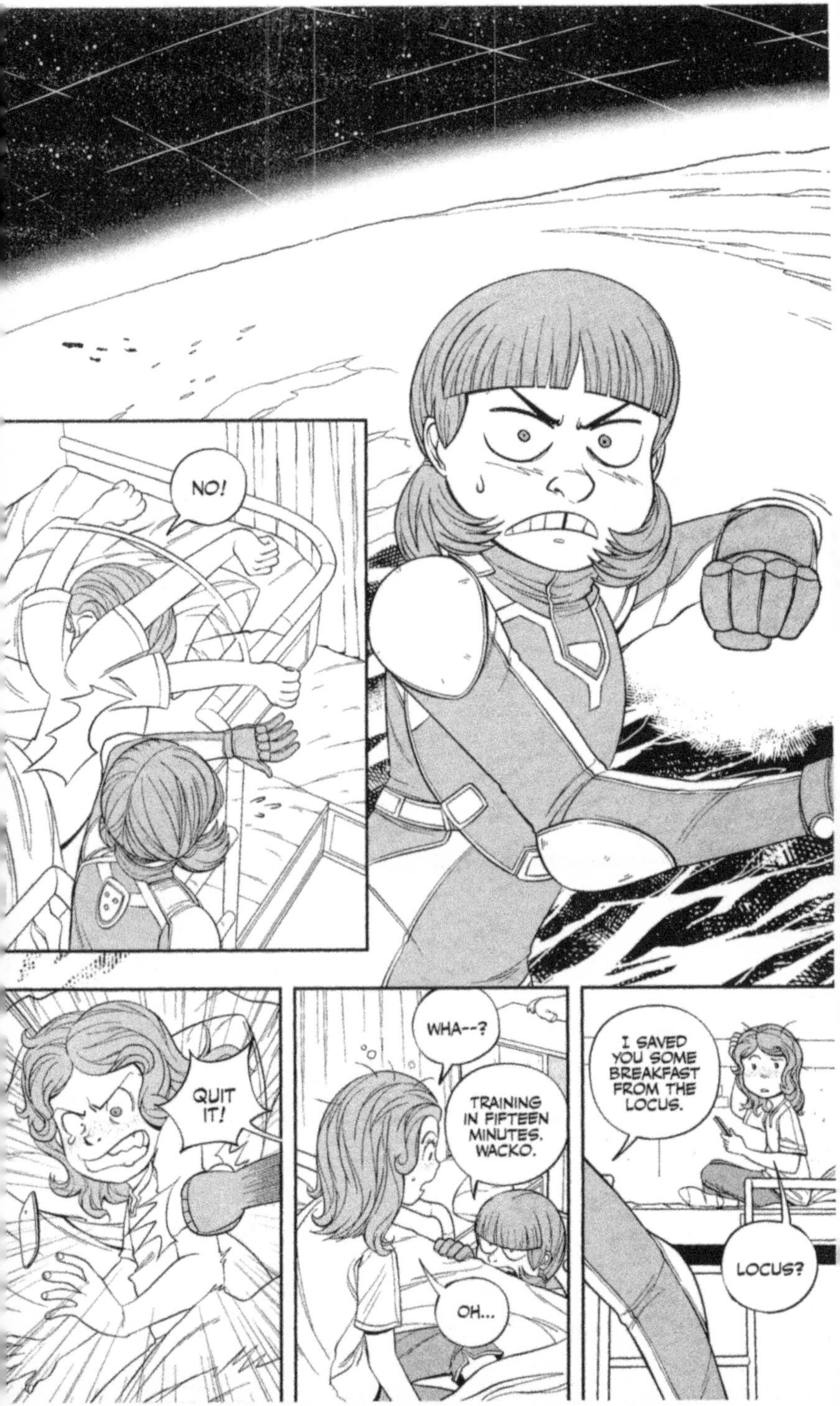
NO!
QUIT IT!
WHA--?
TRAINING IN FIFTEEN MINUTES, WACKO.
OH...
I SAVED YOU SOME BREAKFAST FROM THE LOCUS.
LOCUS?

THAT'S WHAT THEY CALL THE COMMON AREA. CAFETERIA AND LOUNGE AND STUFF.

THANKS, NINE. I DIDN'T MEAN TO SLEEP SO LATE.

ALL YOUR TALKING IN YOUR SLEEP WOKE ME UP.

SOR

YOU SNORE, TOO.

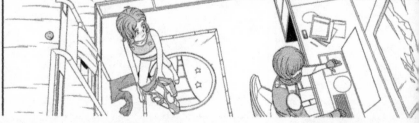

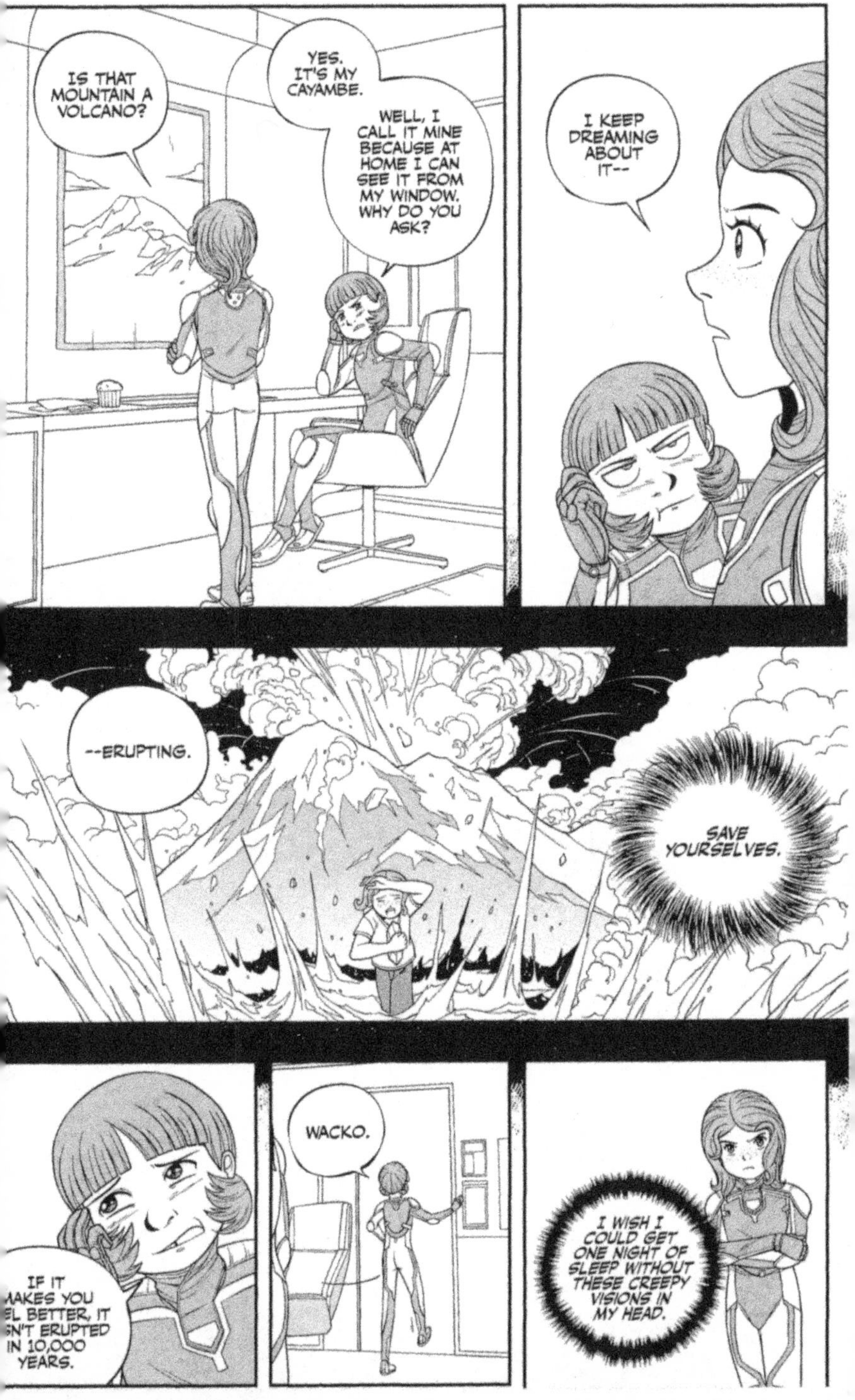
IS THAT MOUNTAIN A VOLCANO?
YES. IT'S MY CAYAMBE.
WELL, I CALL IT MINE BECAUSE AT HOME I CAN SEE IT FROM MY WINDOW. WHY DO YOU ASK?
I KEEP DREAMING ABOUT IT--
--ERUPTING.
SAVE YOURSELVES.
IF IT AKES YOU L BETTER, IT N'T ERUPTED IN 10,000 YEARS.
WACKO.
I WISH I COULD GET ONE NIGHT OF SLEEP WITHOUT THESE CREEPY VISIONS IN MY HEAD.

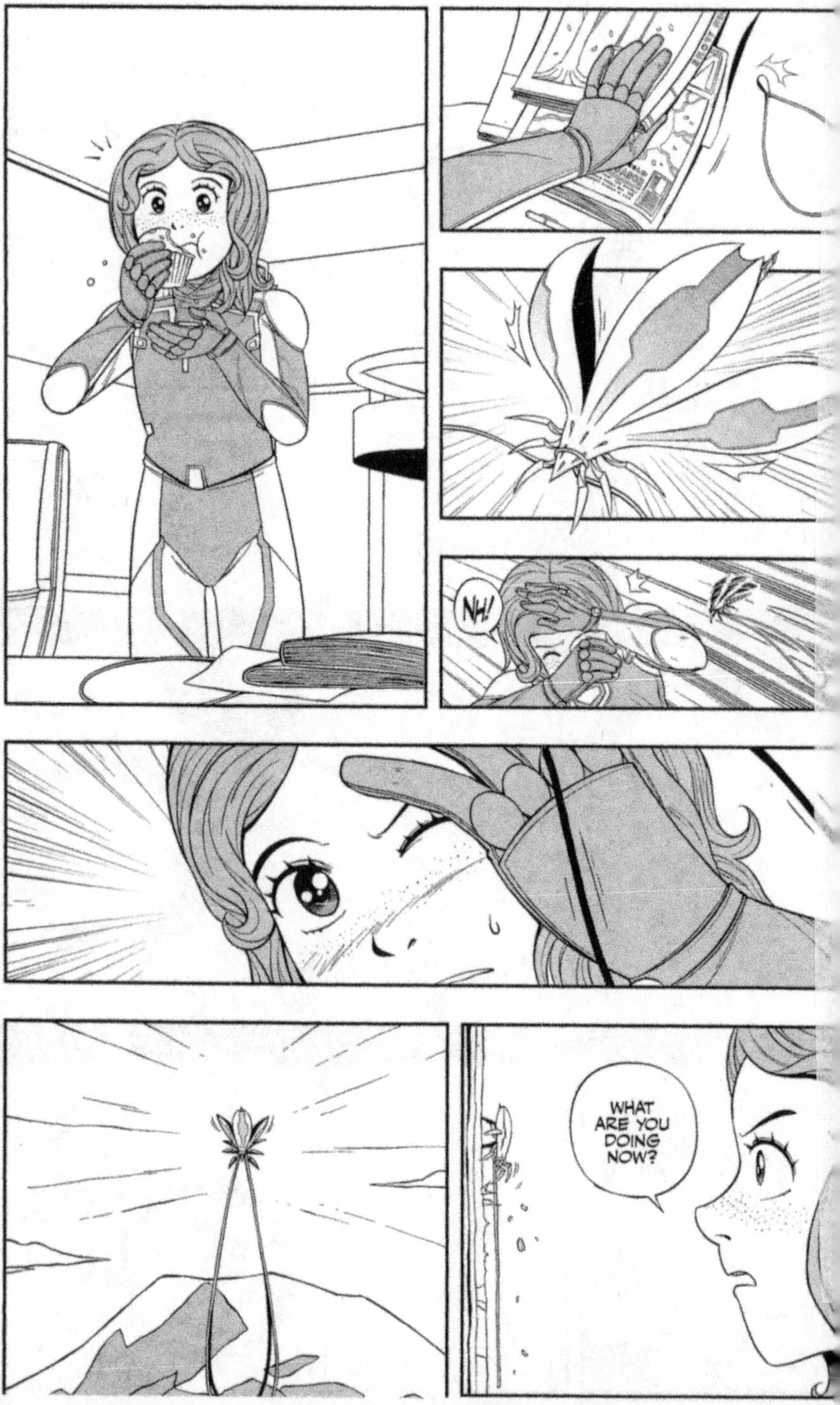
NH!
WHAT ARE YOU DOING NOW?

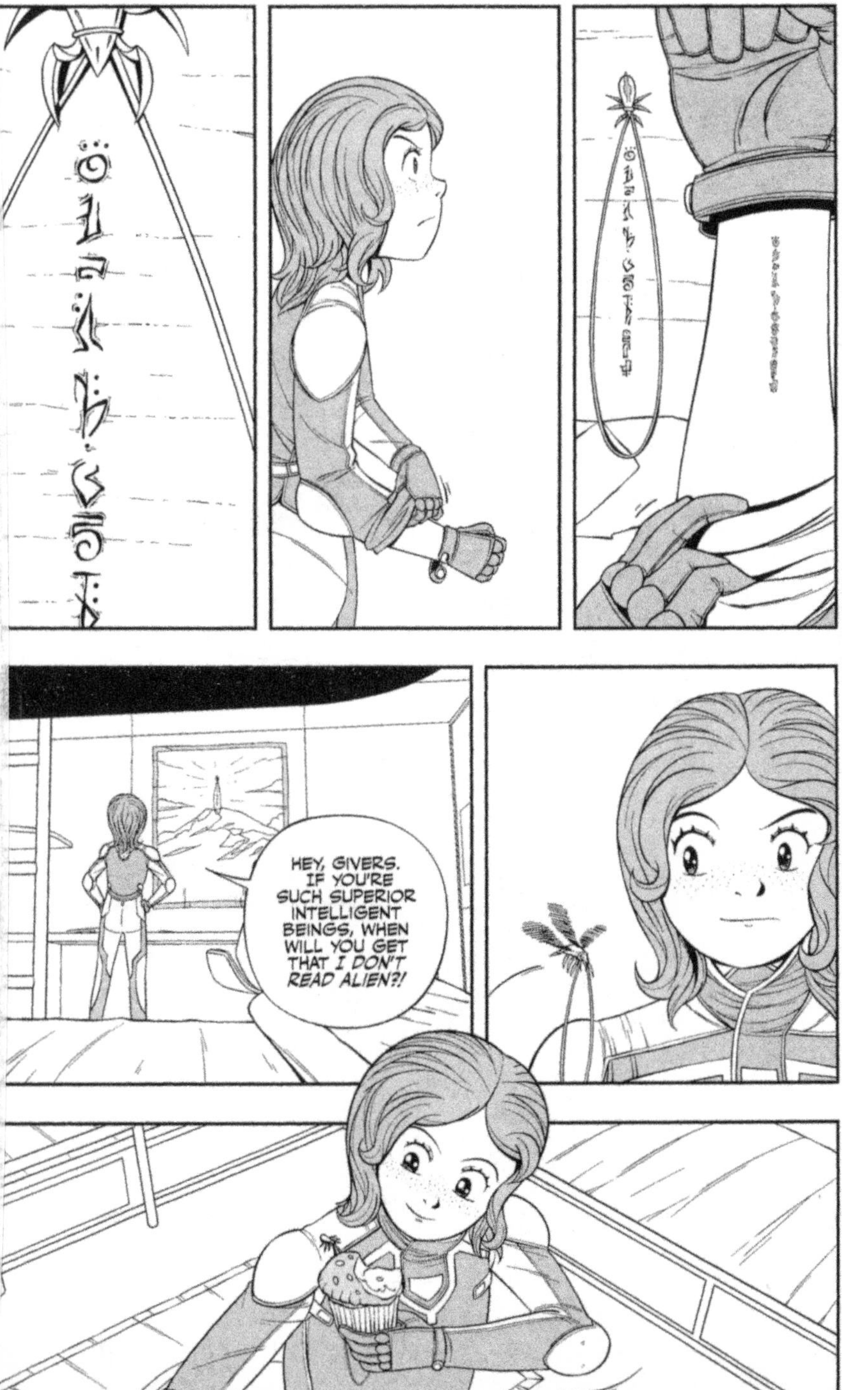
HEY, GIVERS. IF YOU'RE SUCH SUPERIOR INTELLIGENT BEINGS, WHEN WILL YOU GET THAT *I DON'T READ ALIEN?!*

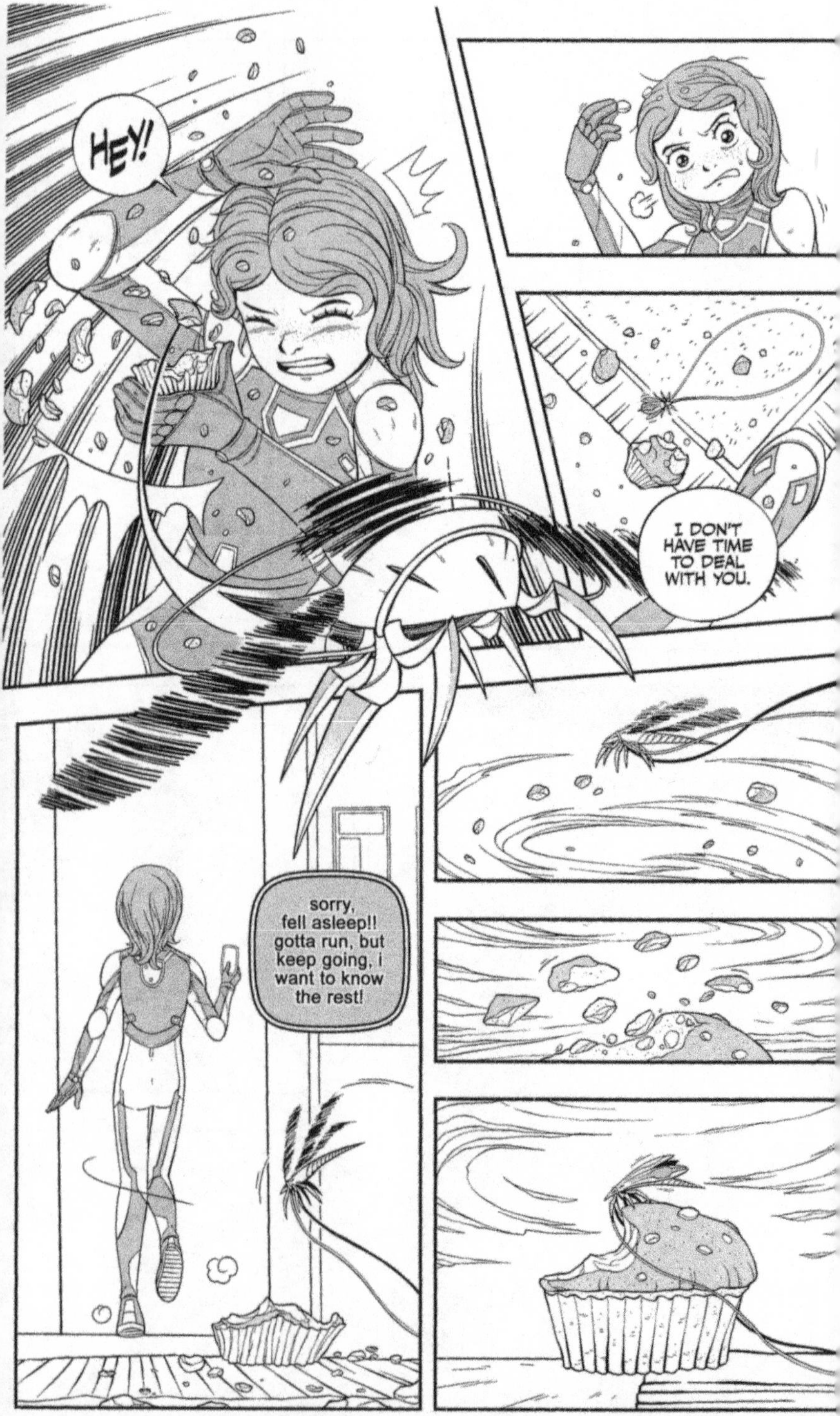
HEY!
I DON'T HAVE TIME TO DEAL WITH YOU.
sorry, fell asleep!! gotta run, but keep going, i want to know the rest!

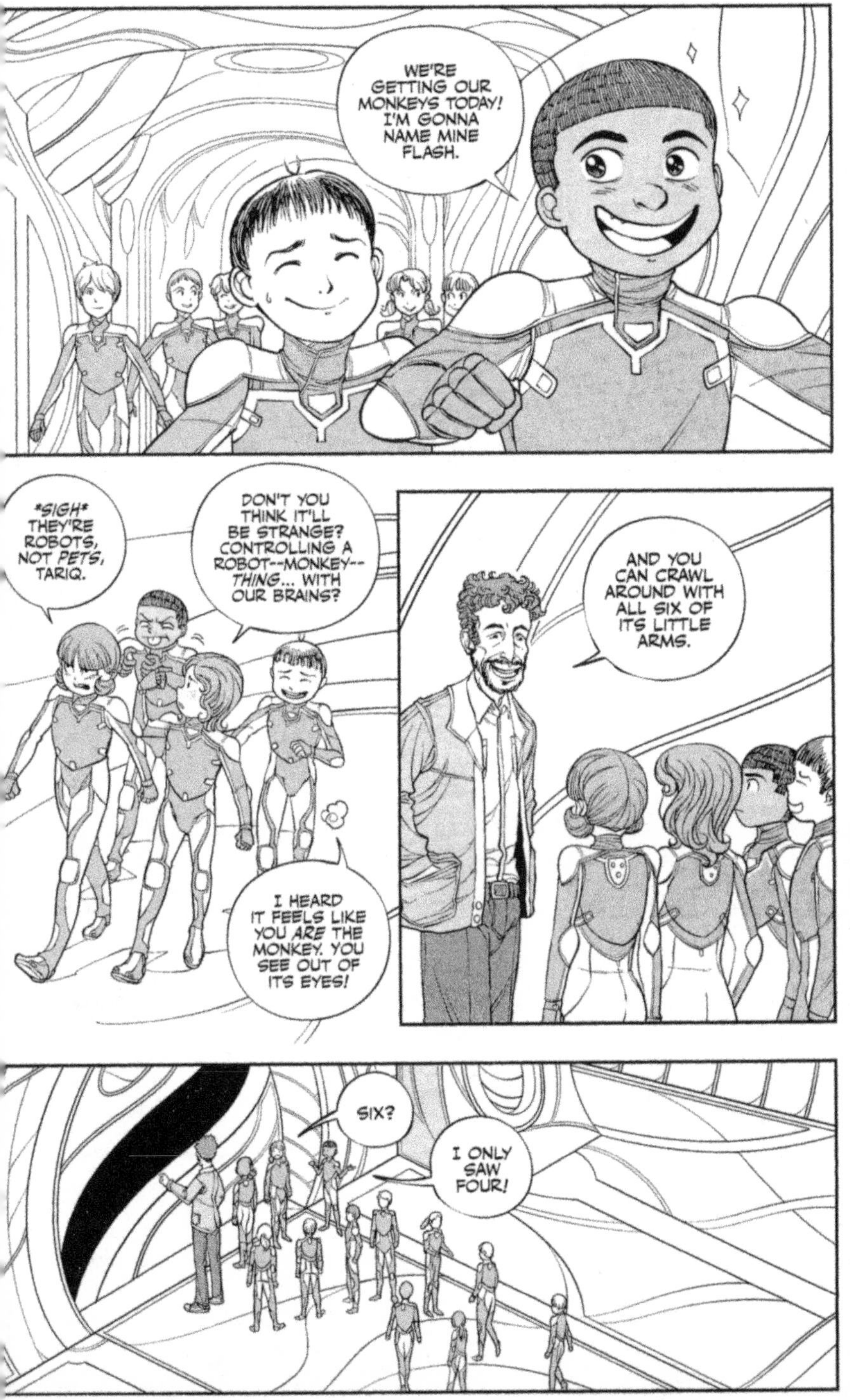
WE'RE GETTING OUR MONKEYS TODAY! I'M GONNA NAME MINE FLASH.
SIGH THEY'RE ROBOTS, NOT *PETS*, TARIQ.
DON'T YOU THINK IT'LL BE STRANGE? CONTROLLING A ROBOT--MONKEY--*THING*... WITH OUR BRAINS?
I HEARD IT FEELS LIKE YOU *ARE* THE MONKEY. YOU SEE OUT OF ITS EYES!
AND YOU CAN CRAWL AROUND WITH ALL SIX OF ITS LITTLE ARMS.
SIX?
I ONLY SAW FOUR!

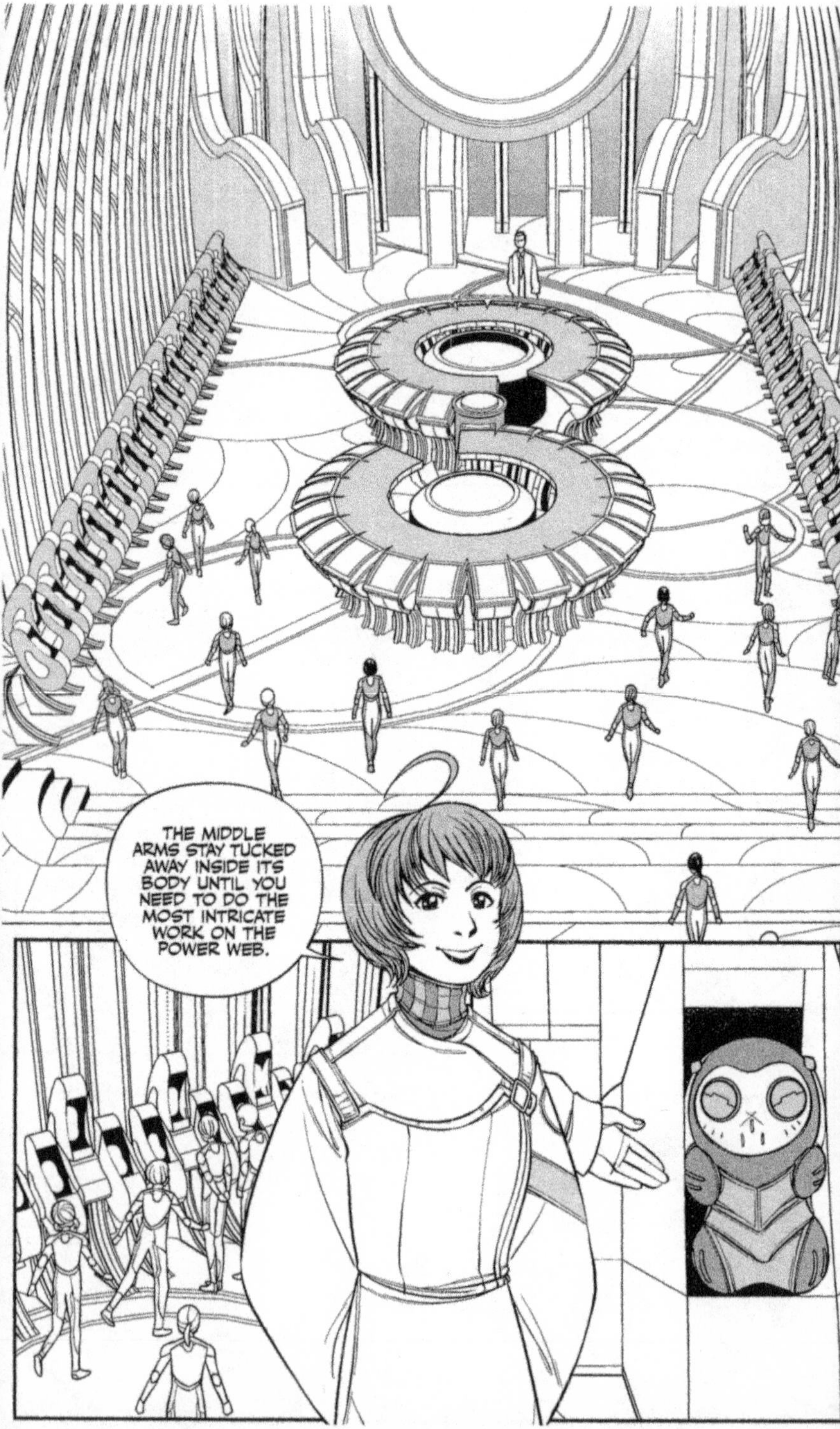
THE MIDDLE ARMS STAY TUCKED AWAY INSIDE ITS BODY UNTIL YOU NEED TO DO THE MOST INTRICATE WORK ON THE POWER WEB.

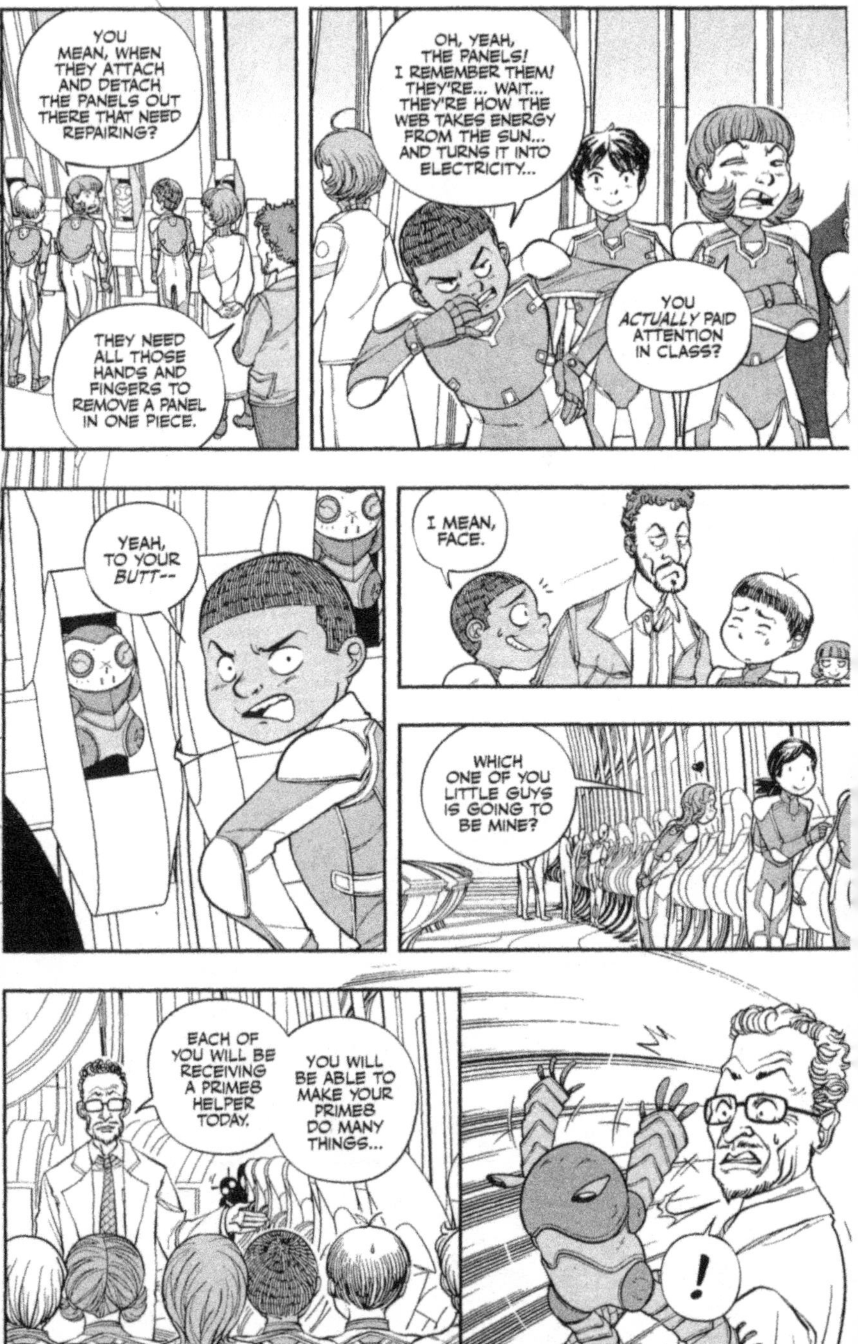
YOU MEAN, WHEN THEY ATTACH AND DETACH THE PANELS OUT THERE THAT NEED REPAIRING?
THEY NEED ALL THOSE HANDS AND FINGERS TO REMOVE A PANEL IN ONE PIECE.
OH, YEAH, THE PANELS! I REMEMBER THEM! THEY'RE... WAIT... THEY'RE HOW THE WEB TAKES ENERGY FROM THE SUN... AND TURNS IT INTO ELECTRICITY...
YOU *ACTUALLY* PAID ATTENTION IN CLASS?
YEAH, TO YOUR *BUTT--*
I MEAN, FACE.
WHICH ONE OF YOU LITTLE GUYS IS GOING TO BE MINE?
EACH OF YOU WILL BE RECEIVING A PRIMES HELPER TODAY.
YOU WILL BE ABLE TO MAKE YOUR PRIMES DO MANY THINGS...
!

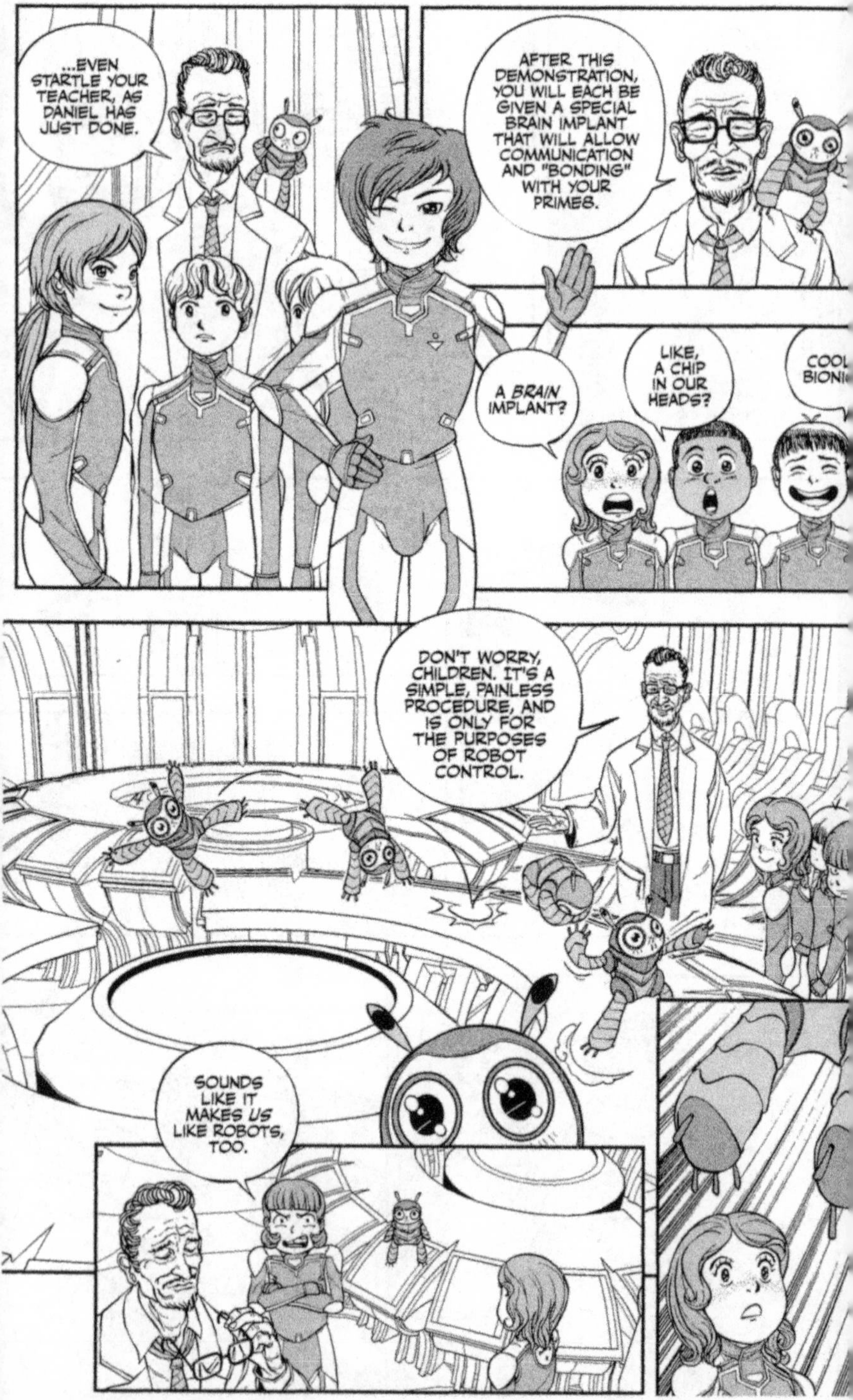
...EVEN STARTLE YOUR TEACHER, AS DANIEL HAS JUST DONE.
AFTER THIS DEMONSTRATION, YOU WILL EACH BE GIVEN A SPECIAL BRAIN IMPLANT THAT WILL ALLOW COMMUNICATION AND "BONDING" WITH YOUR PRIMES.
A *BRAIN* IMPLANT?
LIKE, A CHIP IN OUR HEADS?
COOL BIONI
DON'T WORRY, CHILDREN. IT'S A SIMPLE, PAINLESS PROCEDURE, AND IS ONLY FOR THE PURPOSES OF ROBOT CONTROL.
SOUNDS LIKE IT MAKES *US* LIKE ROBOTS, TOO.

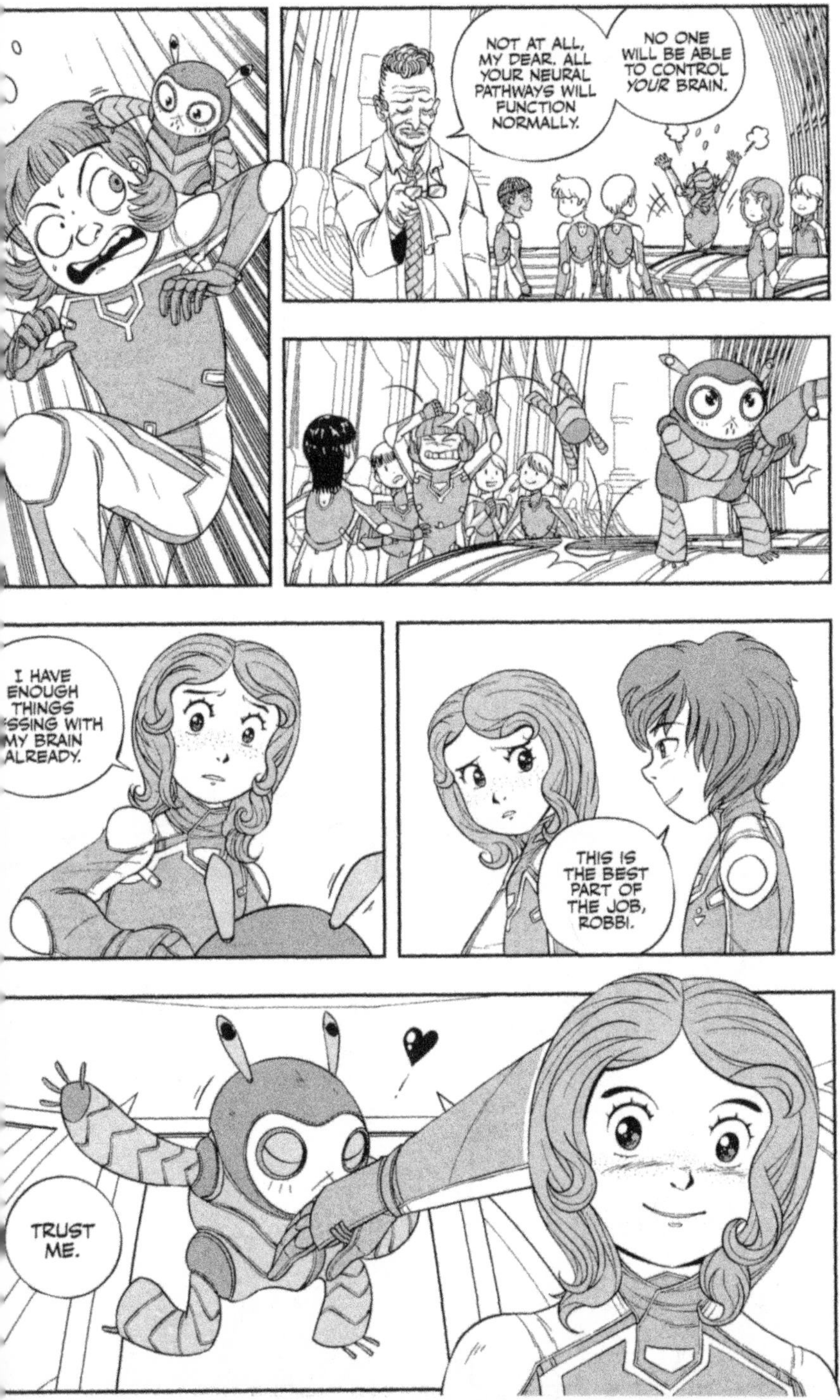
NOT AT ALL, MY DEAR. ALL YOUR NEURAL PATHWAYS WILL FUNCTION NORMALLY.
NO ONE WILL BE ABLE TO CONTROL *YOUR* BRAIN.
I HAVE ENOUGH THINGS SSING WITH MY BRAIN ALREADY.
THIS IS THE BEST PART OF THE JOB, ROBBI.
TRUST ME.

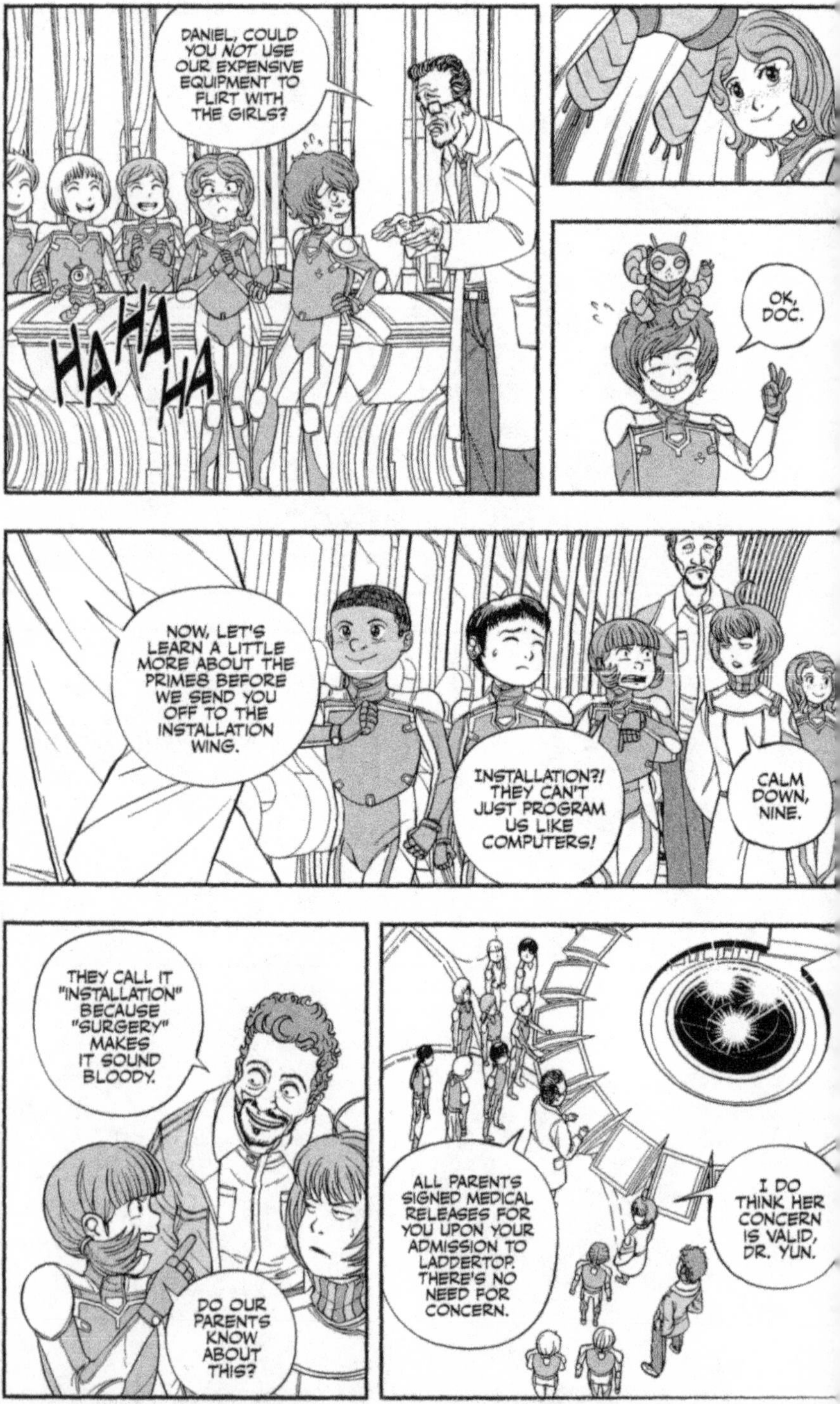
DANIEL, COULD YOU *NOT* USE OUR EXPENSIVE EQUIPMENT TO FLIRT WITH THE GIRLS?
HAHAHA
OK, DOC.
NOW, LET'S LEARN A LITTLE MORE ABOUT THE PRIMES BEFORE WE SEND YOU OFF TO THE INSTALLATION WING.
INSTALLATION?! THEY CAN'T JUST PROGRAM US LIKE COMPUTERS!
CALM DOWN, NINE.
THEY CALL IT "INSTALLATION" BECAUSE "SURGERY" MAKES IT SOUND BLOODY.
DO OUR PARENTS KNOW ABOUT THIS?
ALL PARENTS SIGNED MEDICAL RELEASES FOR YOU UPON YOUR ADMISSION TO LADDERTOP. THERE'S NO NEED FOR CONCERN.
I DO THINK HER CONCERN IS VALID, DR. YUN.

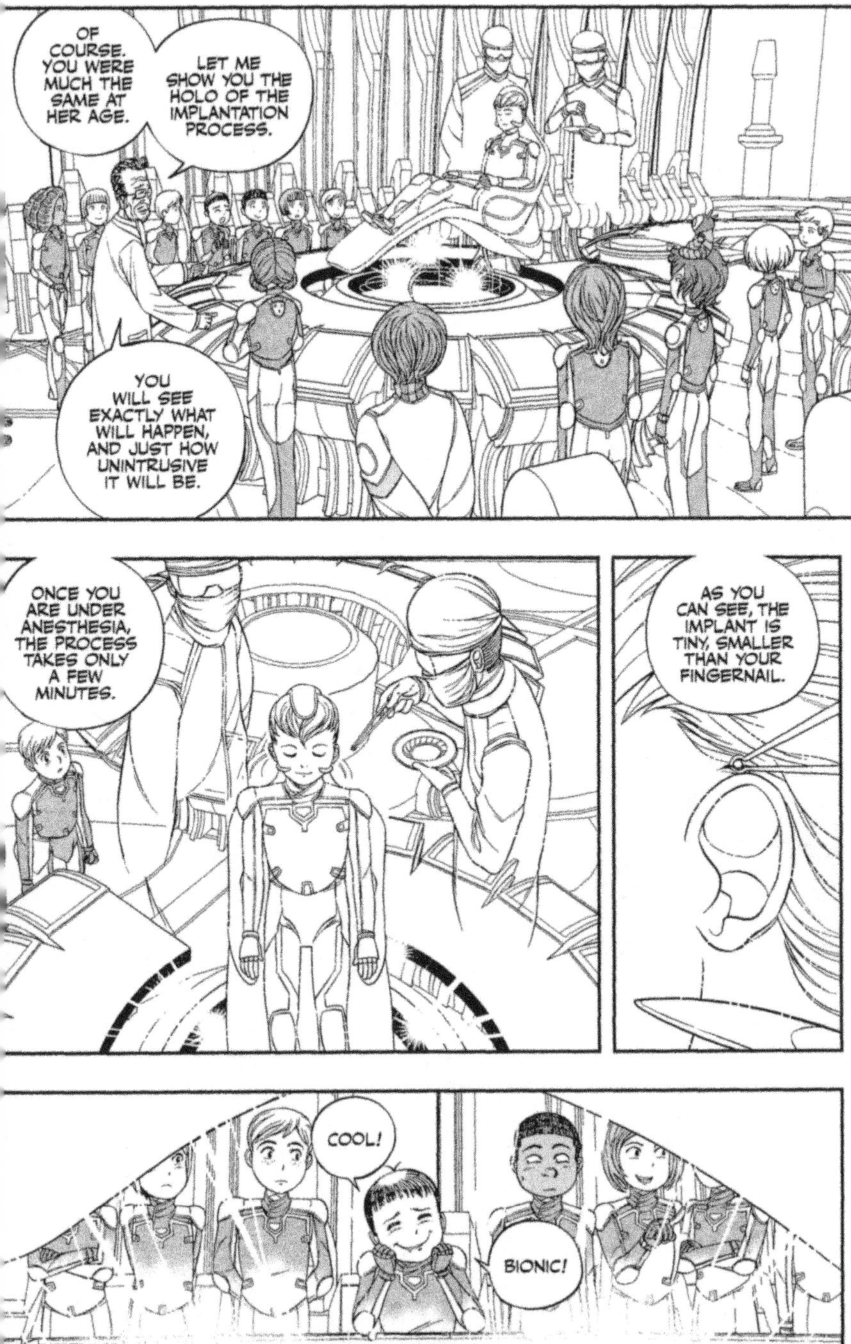
OF COURSE. YOU WERE MUCH THE SAME AT HER AGE.
LET ME SHOW YOU THE HOLO OF THE IMPLANTATION PROCESS.
YOU WILL SEE EXACTLY WHAT WILL HAPPEN, AND JUST HOW UNINTRUSIVE IT WILL BE.
ONCE YOU ARE UNDER ANESTHESIA, THE PROCESS TAKES ONLY A FEW MINUTES.
AS YOU CAN SEE, THE IMPLANT IS TINY, SMALLER THAN YOUR FINGERNAIL.
COOL!
BIONIC!

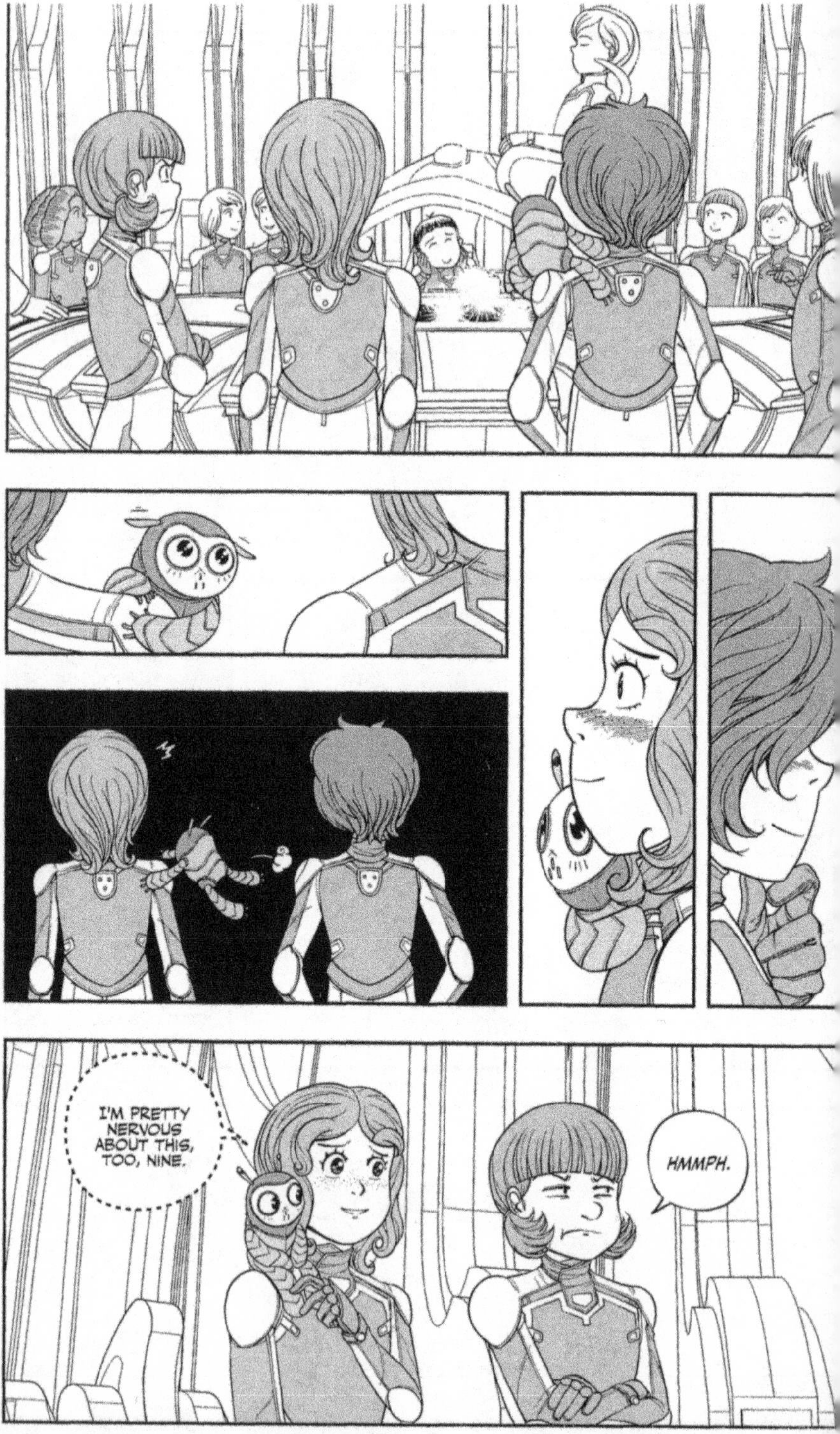
I'M PRETTY NERVOUS ABOUT THIS, TOO, NINE.
HMMPH.

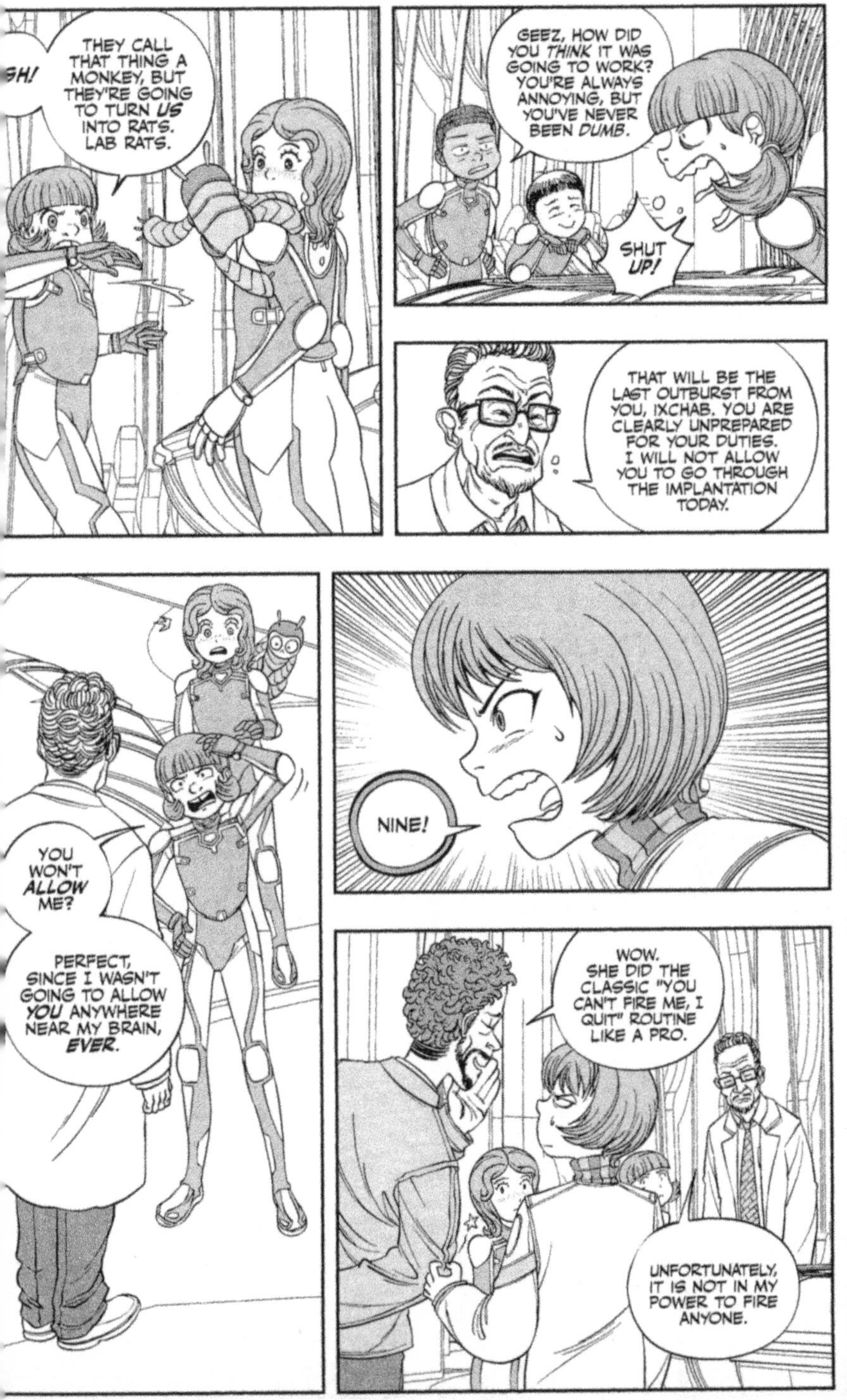
GH!
THEY CALL THAT THING A MONKEY, BUT THEY'RE GOING TO TURN *US* INTO RATS. LAB RATS.
GEEZ, HOW DID YOU *THINK* IT WAS GOING TO WORK? YOU'RE ALWAYS ANNOYING, BUT YOU'VE NEVER BEEN *DUMB*.
SHUT *UP!*
THAT WILL BE THE LAST OUTBURST FROM YOU, IXCHAB. YOU ARE CLEARLY UNPREPARED FOR YOUR DUTIES. I WILL NOT ALLOW YOU TO GO THROUGH THE IMPLANTATION TODAY.
YOU WON'T *ALLOW* ME?
PERFECT, SINCE I WASN'T GOING TO ALLOW *YOU* ANYWHERE NEAR MY BRAIN, ***EVER***.
NINE!
WOW. SHE DID THE CLASSIC "YOU CAN'T FIRE ME, I QUIT" ROUTINE LIKE A PRO.
UNFORTUNATELY, IT IS NOT IN MY POWER TO FIRE ANYONE.

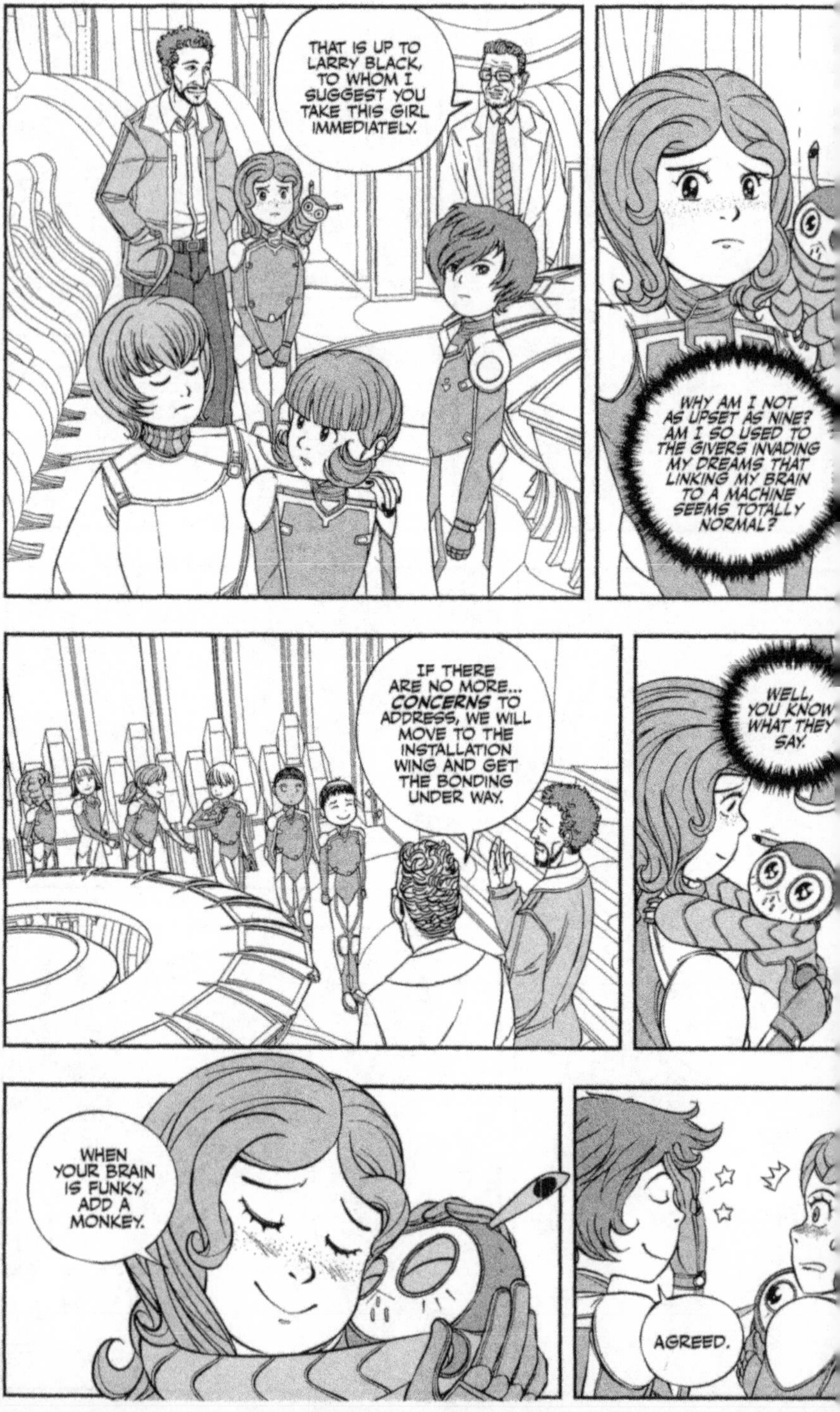
THAT IS UP TO LARRY BLACK, TO WHOM I SUGGEST YOU TAKE THIS GIRL IMMEDIATELY.
WHY AM I NOT AS UPSET AS NINE? AM I SO USED TO THE GIVERS INVADING MY DREAMS THAT LINKING MY BRAIN TO A MACHINE SEEMS TOTALLY NORMAL?
IF THERE ARE NO MORE... CONCERNS TO ADDRESS, WE WILL MOVE TO THE INSTALLATION WING AND GET THE BONDING UNDER WAY.
WELL, YOU KNOW WHAT THEY SAY.
WHEN YOUR BRAIN IS FUNKY, ADD A MONKEY.
AGREED.

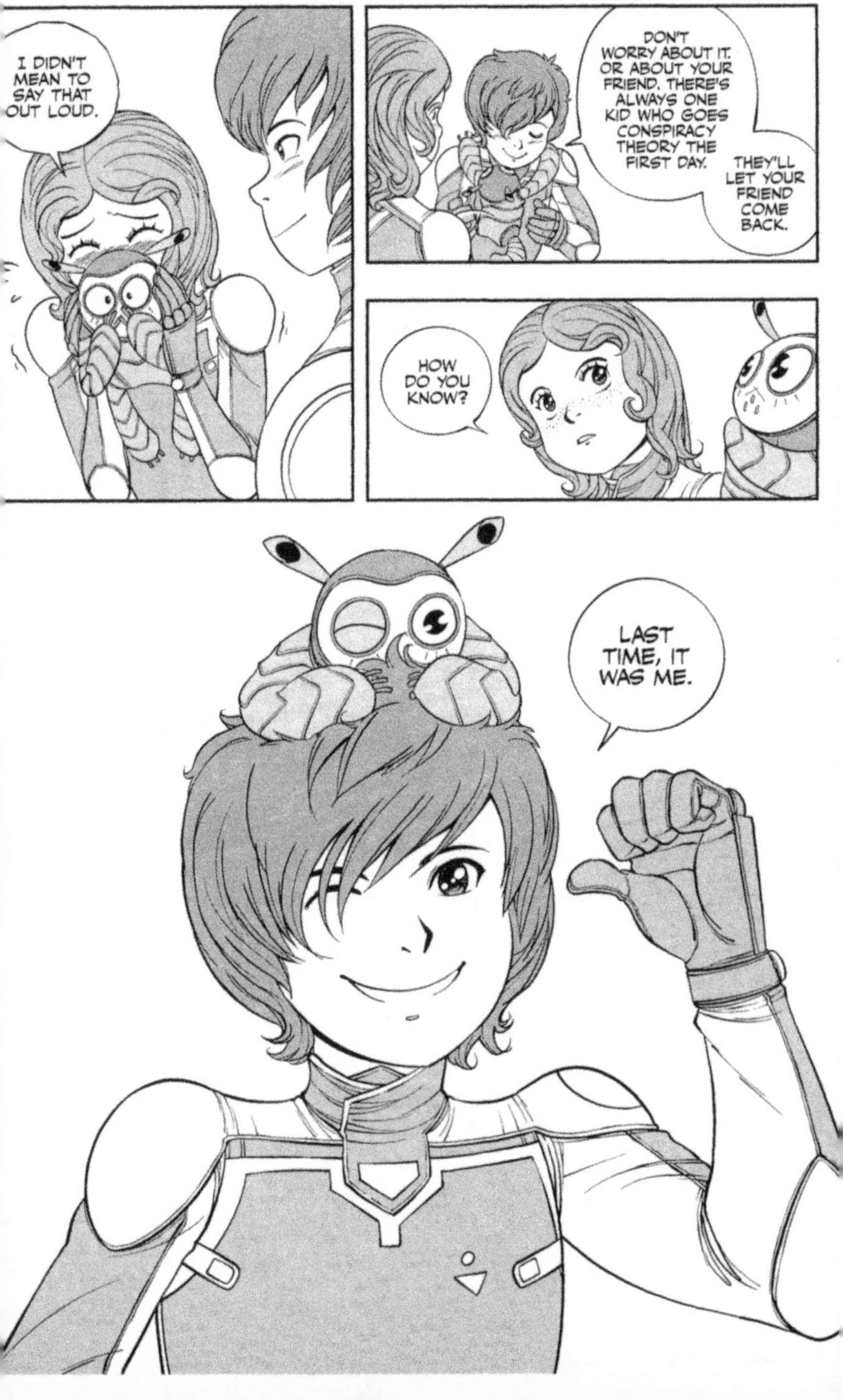
I DIDN'T MEAN TO SAY THAT OUT LOUD.
DON'T WORRY ABOUT IT. OR ABOUT YOUR FRIEND. THERE'S ALWAYS ONE KID WHO GOES CONSPIRACY THEORY THE FIRST DAY.
THEY'LL LET YOUR FRIEND COME BACK.
HOW DO YOU KNOW?
LAST TIME, IT WAS ME.

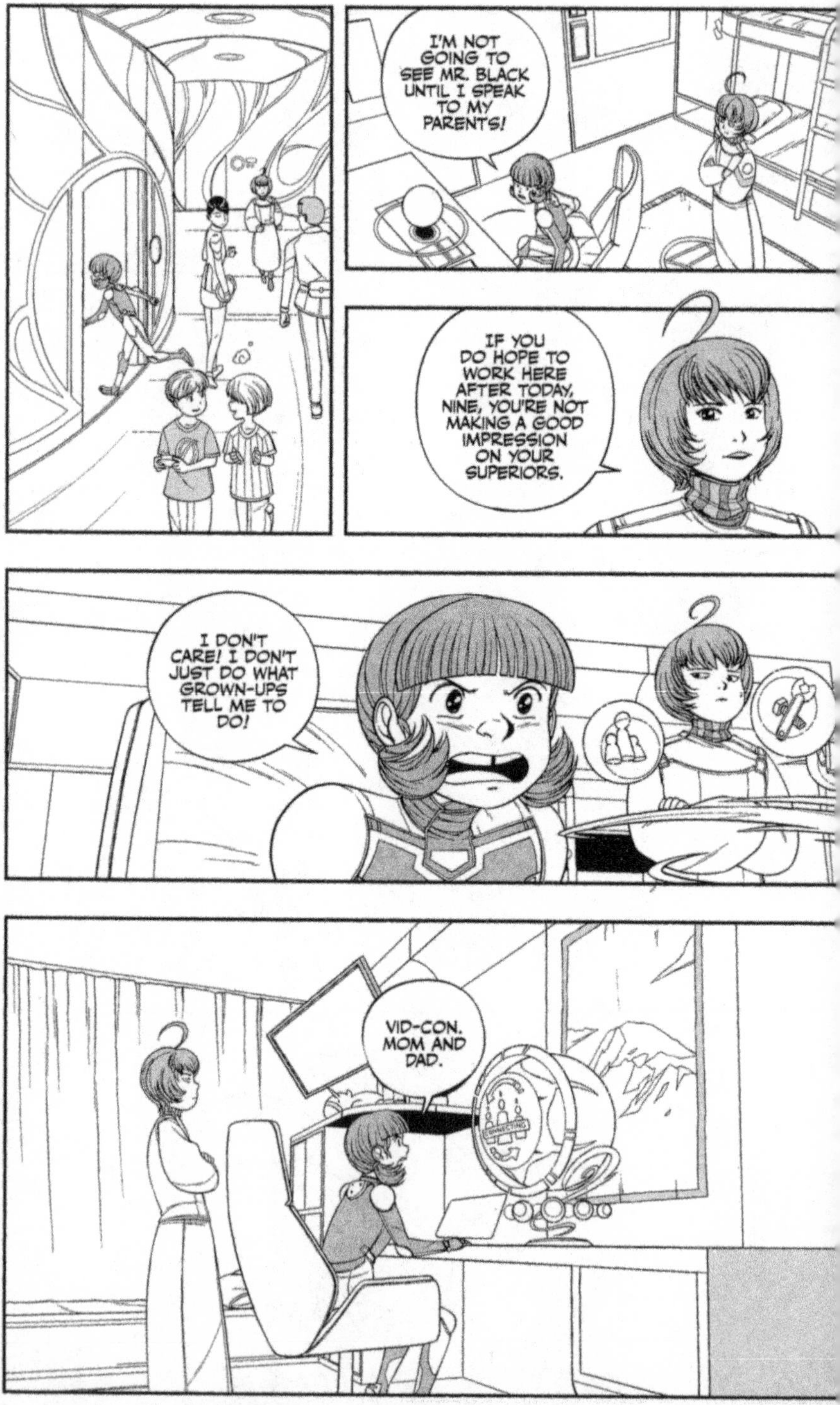
I'M NOT GOING TO SEE MR. BLACK UNTIL I SPEAK TO MY PARENTS!
IF YOU DO HOPE TO WORK HERE AFTER TODAY, NINE, YOU'RE NOT MAKING A GOOD IMPRESSION ON YOUR SUPERIORS.
I DON'T CARE! I DON'T JUST DO WHAT GROWN-UPS TELL ME TO DO!
VID-CON. MOM AND DAD.

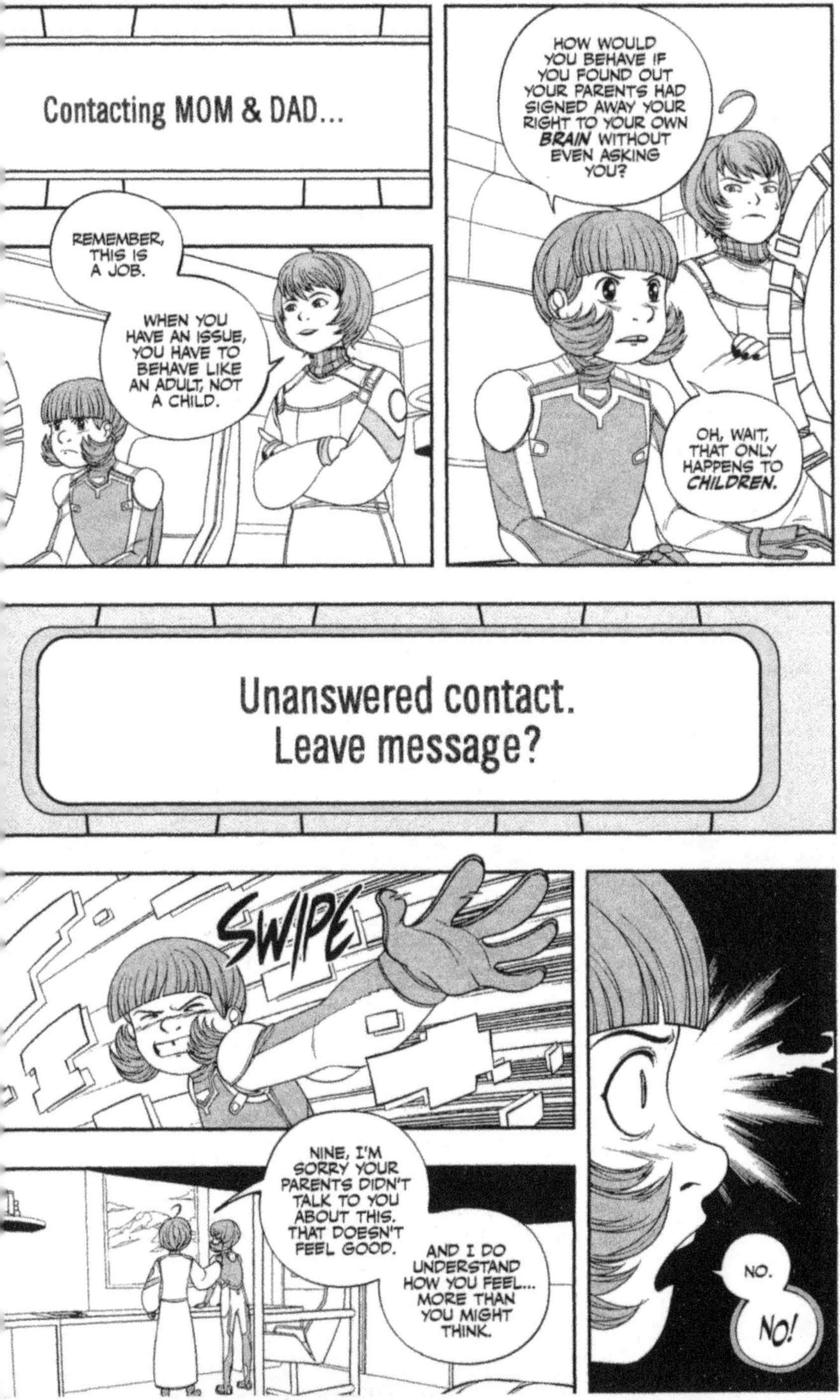
Contacting MOM & DAD...
REMEMBER, THIS IS A JOB.
WHEN YOU HAVE AN ISSUE, YOU HAVE TO BEHAVE LIKE AN ADULT, NOT A CHILD.
HOW WOULD YOU BEHAVE IF YOU FOUND OUT YOUR PARENTS HAD SIGNED AWAY YOUR RIGHT TO YOUR OWN BRAIN WITHOUT EVEN ASKING YOU?
OH, WAIT, THAT ONLY HAPPENS TO CHILDREN.
Unanswered contact. Leave message?
SWIPE
NINE, I'M SORRY YOUR PARENTS DIDN'T TALK TO YOU ABOUT THIS. THAT DOESN'T FEEL GOOD.
AND I DO UNDERSTAND HOW YOU FEEL... MORE THAN YOU MIGHT THINK.
NO.
NO!

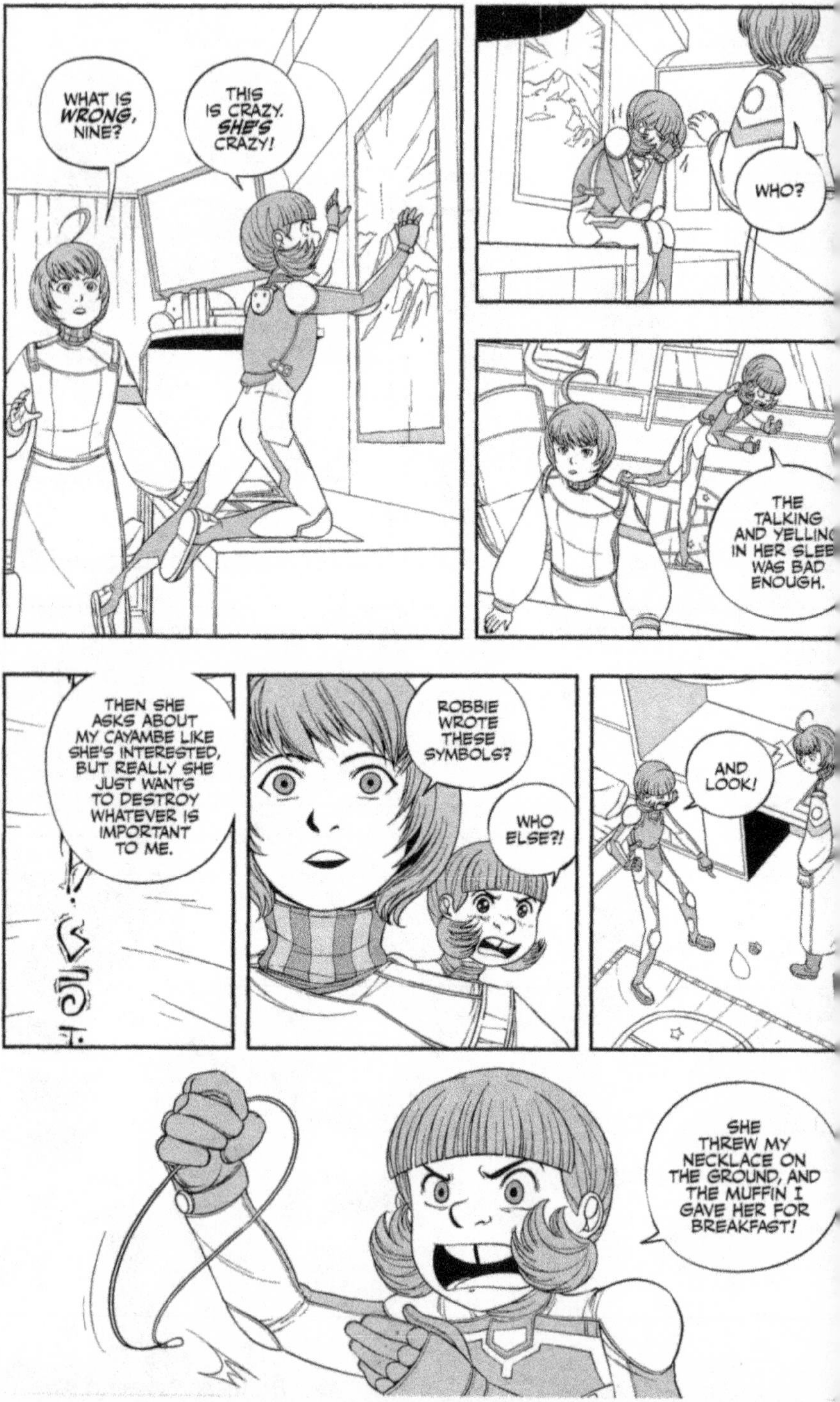
WHAT IS *WRONG*, NINE?
THIS IS CRAZY. *SHE'S* CRAZY!
WHO?
THE TALKING AND YELLIN IN HER SLEE WAS BAD ENOUGH.
THEN SHE ASKS ABOUT MY CAYAMBE LIKE SHE'S INTERESTED, BUT REALLY SHE JUST WANTS TO DESTROY WHATEVER IS IMPORTANT TO ME.
ROBBIE WROTE THESE SYMBOLS?
WHO ELSE?!
AND LOOK!
SHE THREW MY NECKLACE ON THE GROUND, AND THE MUFFIN I GAVE HER FOR BREAKFAST!

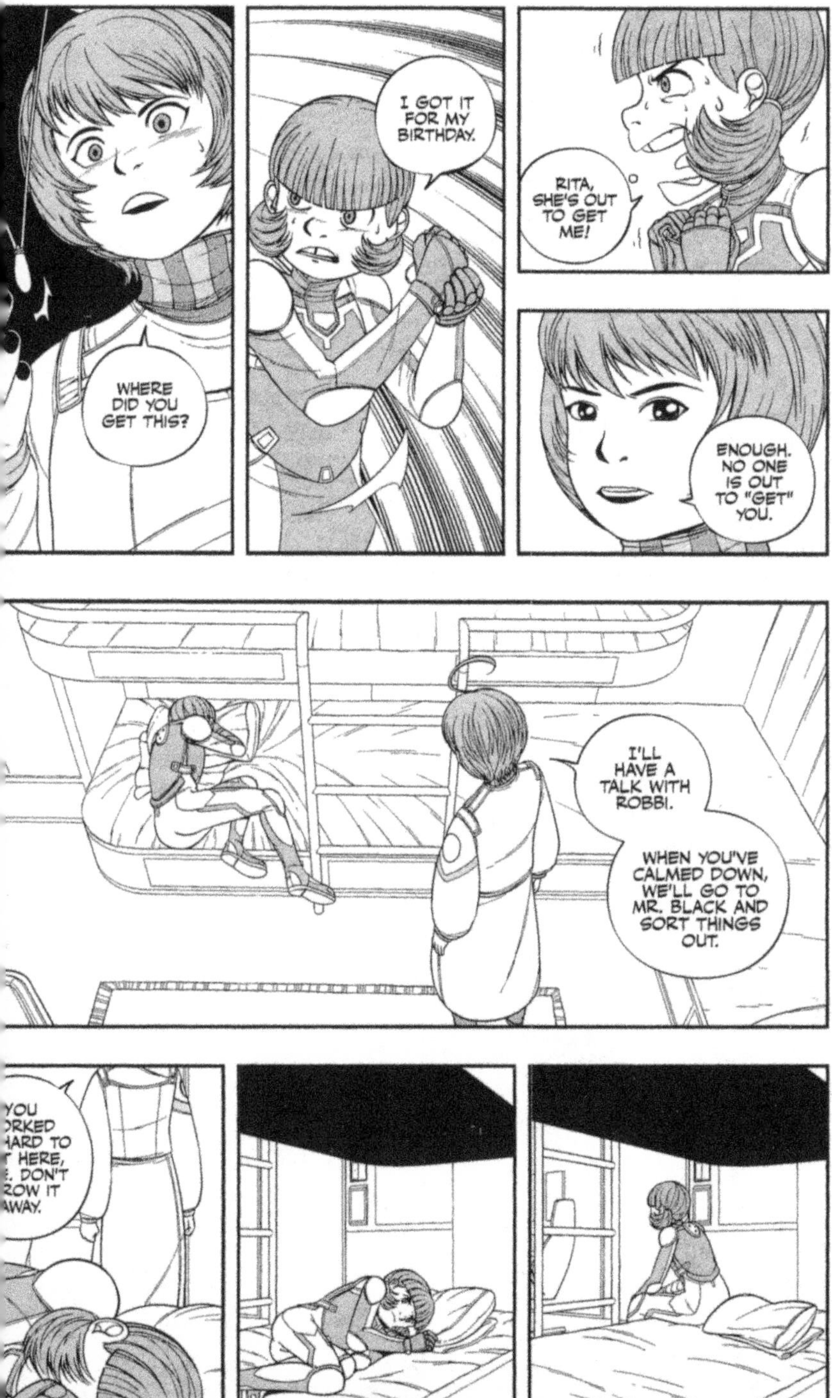
WHERE DID YOU GET THIS?
I GOT IT FOR MY BIRTHDAY.
RITA, SHE'S OUT TO GET ME!
ENOUGH. NO ONE IS OUT TO "GET" YOU.
I'LL HAVE A TALK WITH ROBBI.
WHEN YOU'VE CALMED DOWN, WE'LL GO TO MR. BLACK AND SORT THINGS OUT.
YOU ORKED HARD TO T HERE, E. DON'T ROW IT AWAY.

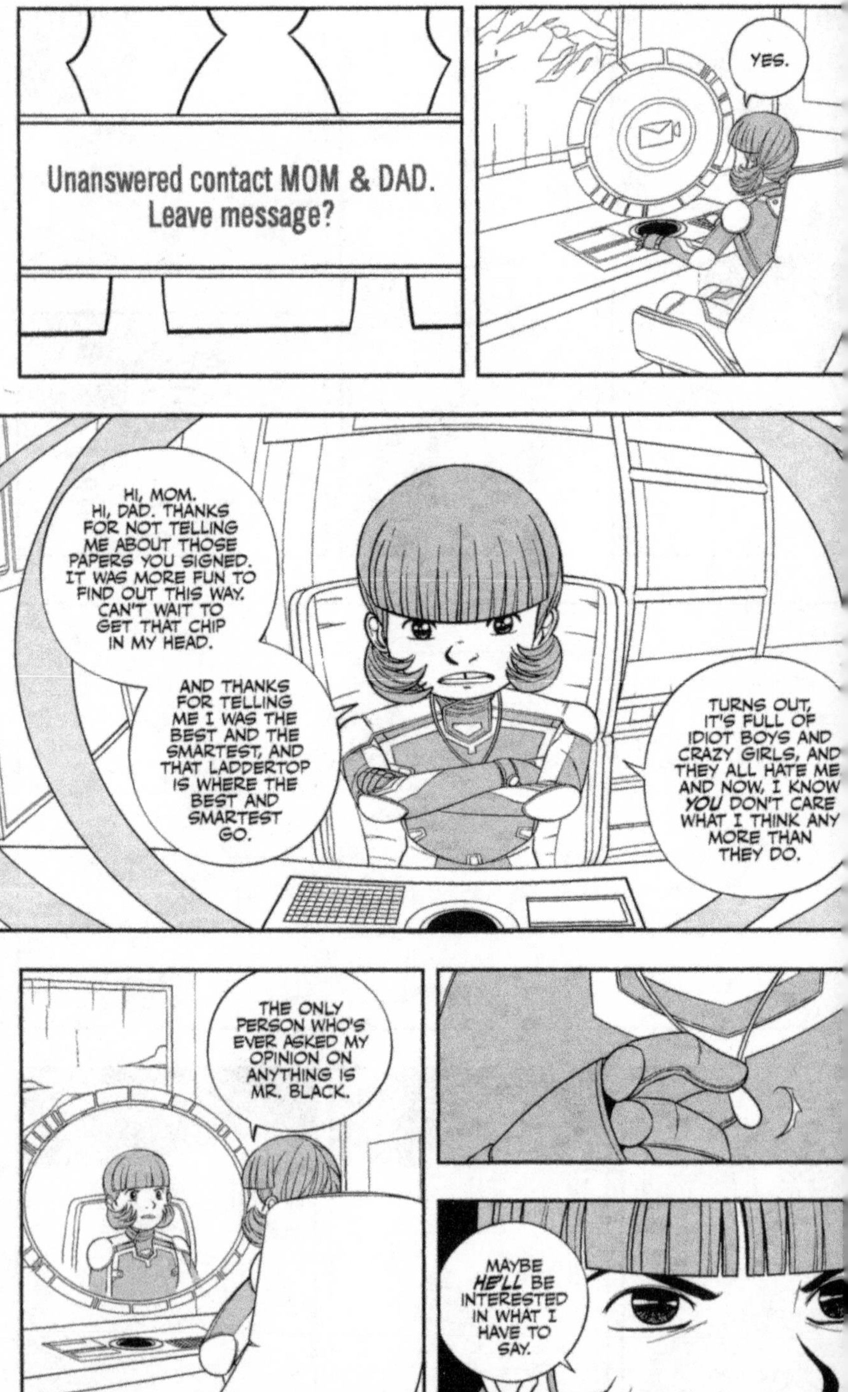
Unanswered contact MOM & DAD. Leave message?
YES.
HI, MOM. HI, DAD. THANKS FOR NOT TELLING ME ABOUT THOSE PAPERS YOU SIGNED. IT WAS MORE FUN TO FIND OUT THIS WAY. CAN'T WAIT TO GET THAT CHIP IN MY HEAD.
AND THANKS FOR TELLING ME I WAS THE BEST AND THE SMARTEST, AND THAT LADDERTOP IS WHERE THE BEST AND SMARTEST GO.
TURNS OUT, IT'S FULL OF IDIOT BOYS AND CRAZY GIRLS, AND THEY ALL HATE ME AND NOW, I KNOW *YOU* DON'T CARE WHAT I THINK ANY MORE THAN THEY DO.
THE ONLY PERSON WHO'S EVER ASKED MY OPINION ON ANYTHING IS MR. BLACK.
MAYBE *HE'LL* BE INTERESTED IN WHAT I HAVE TO SAY.

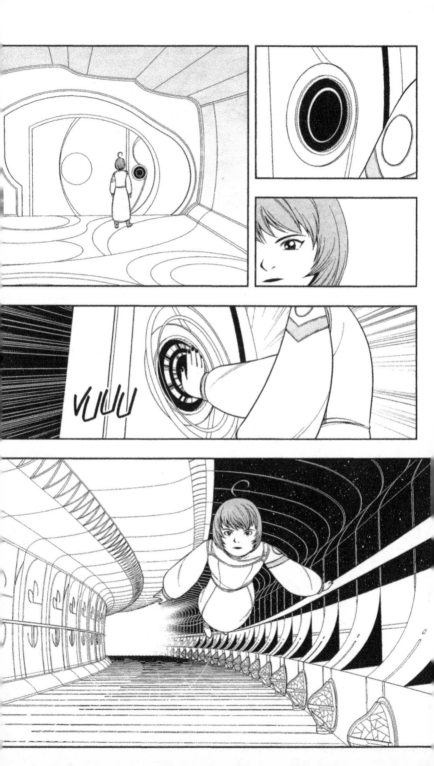

VUUU

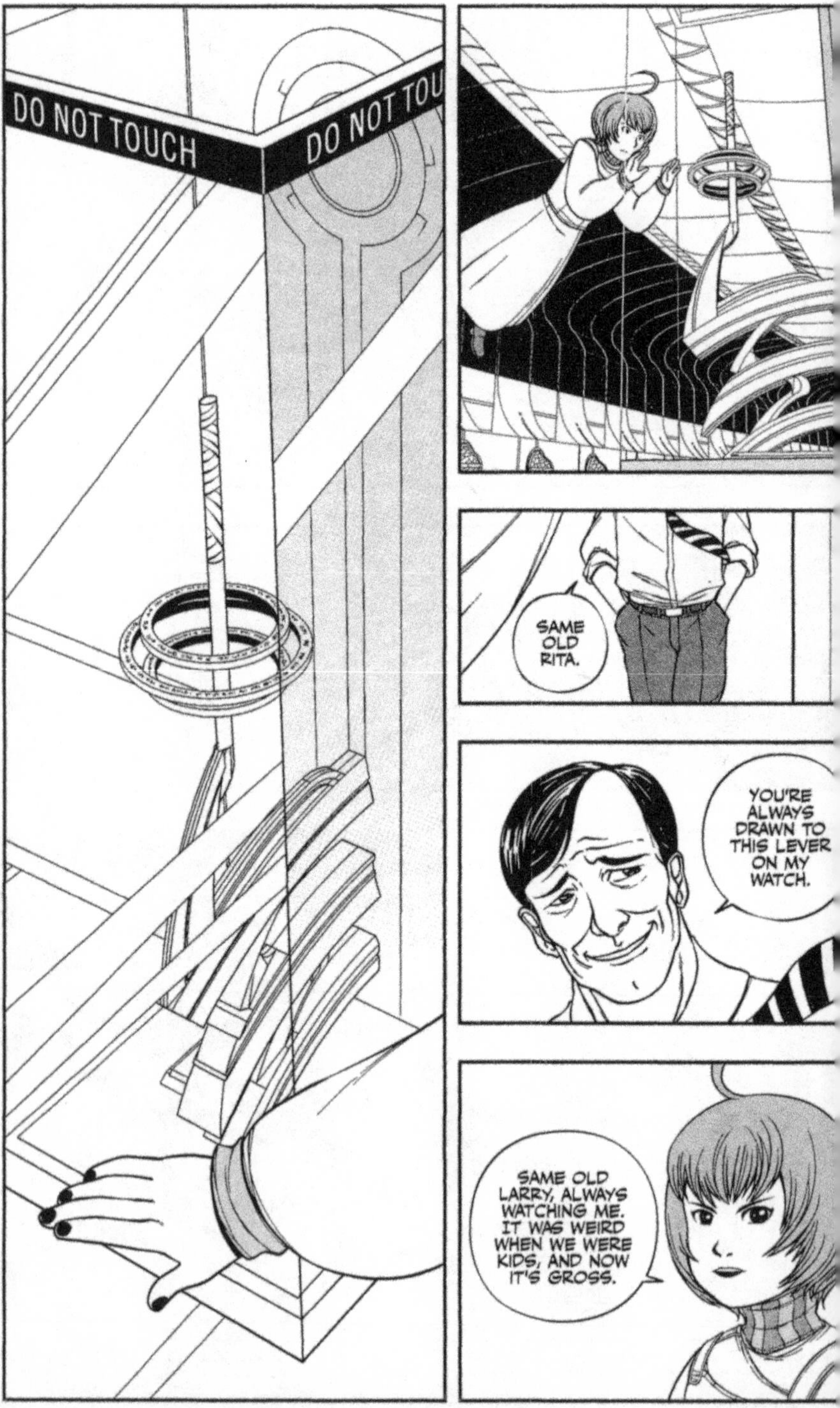
DO NOT TOUCH
DO NOT TOU
SAME OLD RITA.
YOU'RE ALWAYS DRAWN TO THIS LEVER ON MY WATCH.
SAME OLD LARRY, ALWAYS WATCHING ME. IT WAS WEIRD WHEN WE WERE KIDS, AND NOW IT'S GROSS.

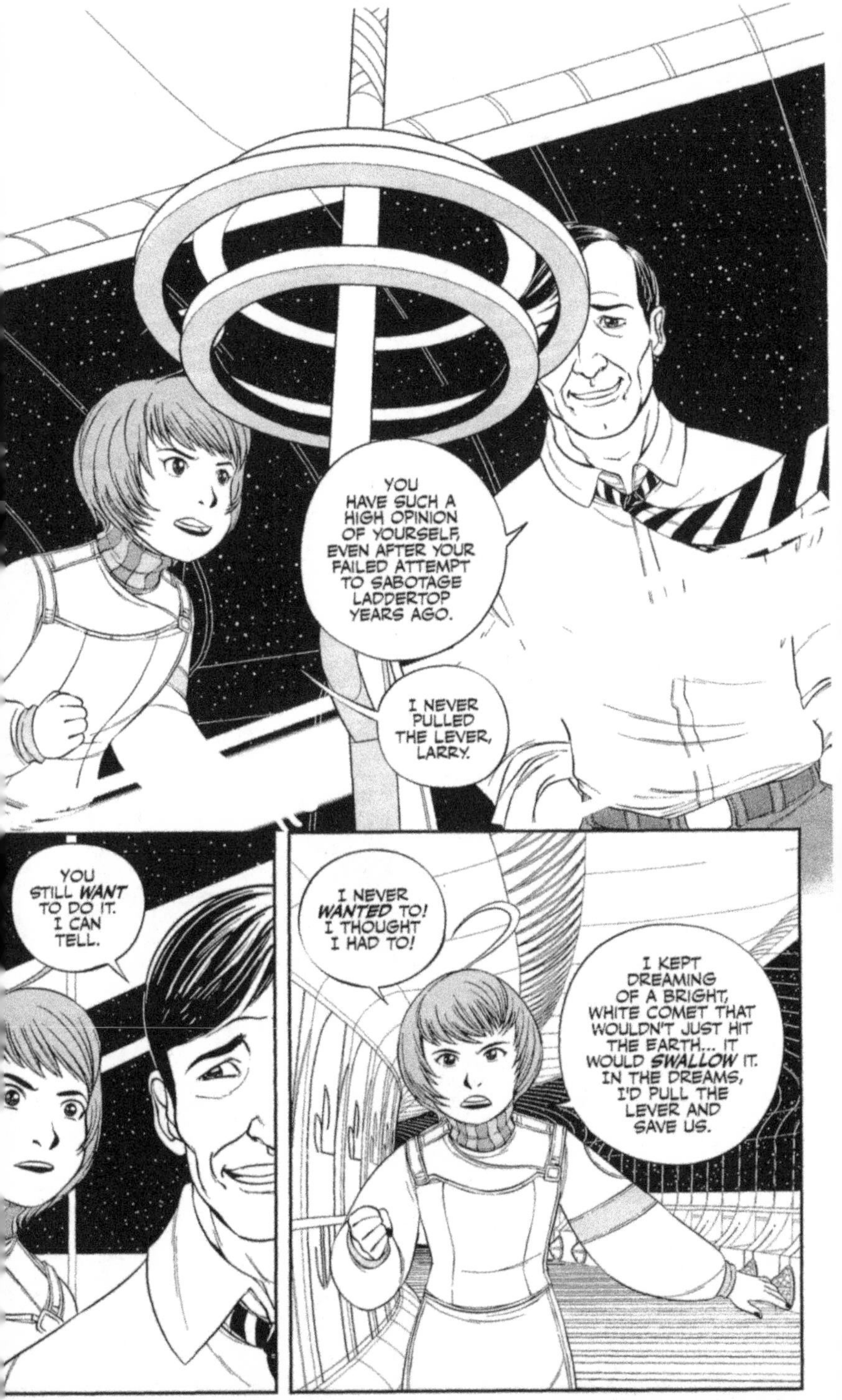
YOU HAVE SUCH A HIGH OPINION OF YOURSELF, EVEN AFTER YOUR FAILED ATTEMPT TO SABOTAGE LADDERTOP YEARS AGO.
I NEVER PULLED THE LEVER, LARRY.
YOU STILL WANT TO DO IT. I CAN TELL.
I NEVER WANTED TO! I THOUGHT I HAD TO!
I KEPT DREAMING OF A BRIGHT, WHITE COMET THAT WOULDN'T JUST HIT THE EARTH... IT WOULD SWALLOW IT. IN THE DREAMS, I'D PULL THE LEVER AND SAVE US.

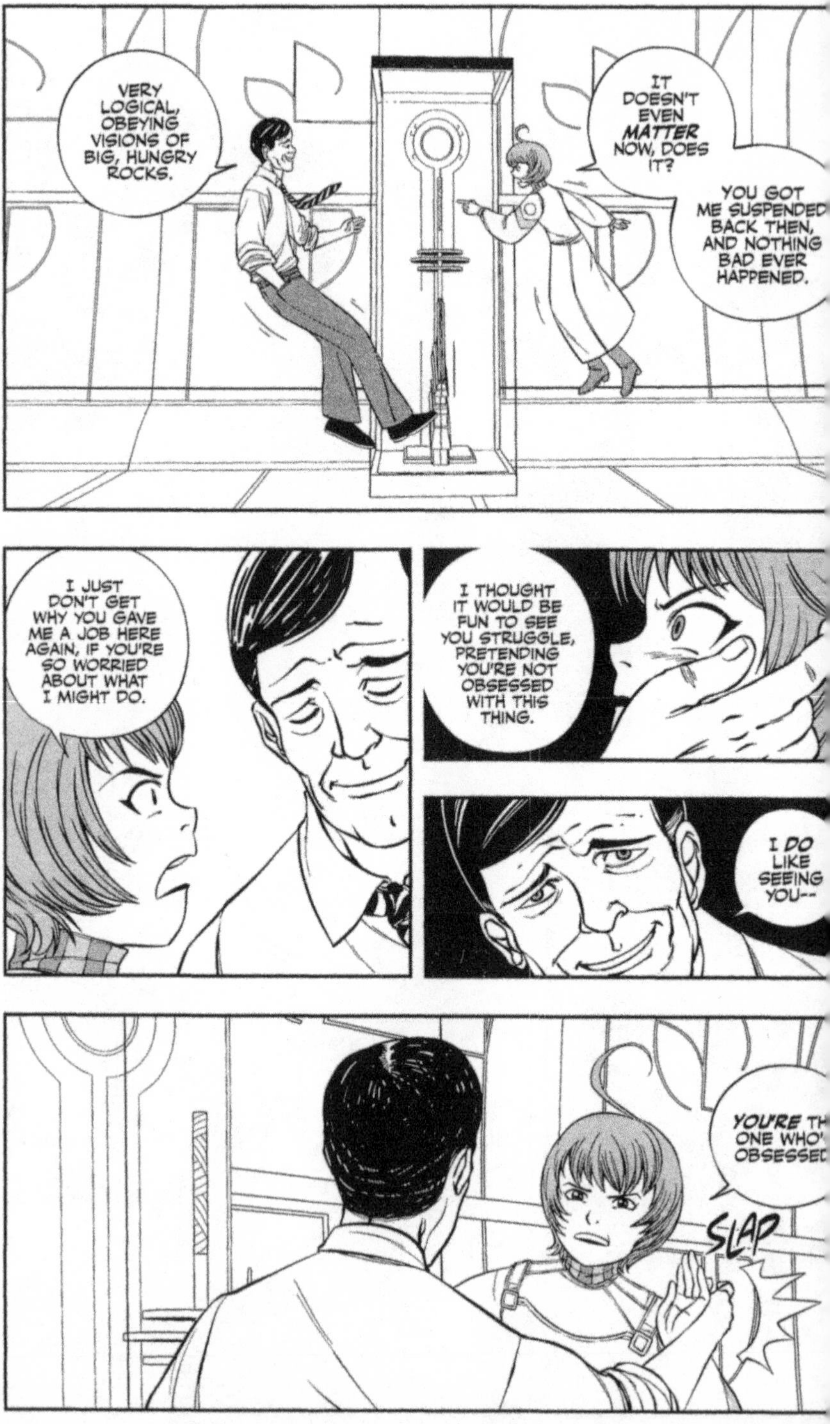
VERY LOGICAL, OBEYING VISIONS OF BIG, HUNGRY ROCKS.
IT DOESN'T EVEN *MATTER* NOW, DOES IT?
YOU GOT ME SUSPENDED BACK THEN, AND NOTHING BAD EVER HAPPENED.
I JUST DON'T GET WHY YOU GAVE ME A JOB HERE AGAIN, IF YOU'RE SO WORRIED ABOUT WHAT I MIGHT DO.
I THOUGHT IT WOULD BE FUN TO SEE YOU STRUGGLE, PRETENDING YOU'RE NOT OBSESSED WITH THIS THING.
I *DO* LIKE SEEING YOU--
SLAP

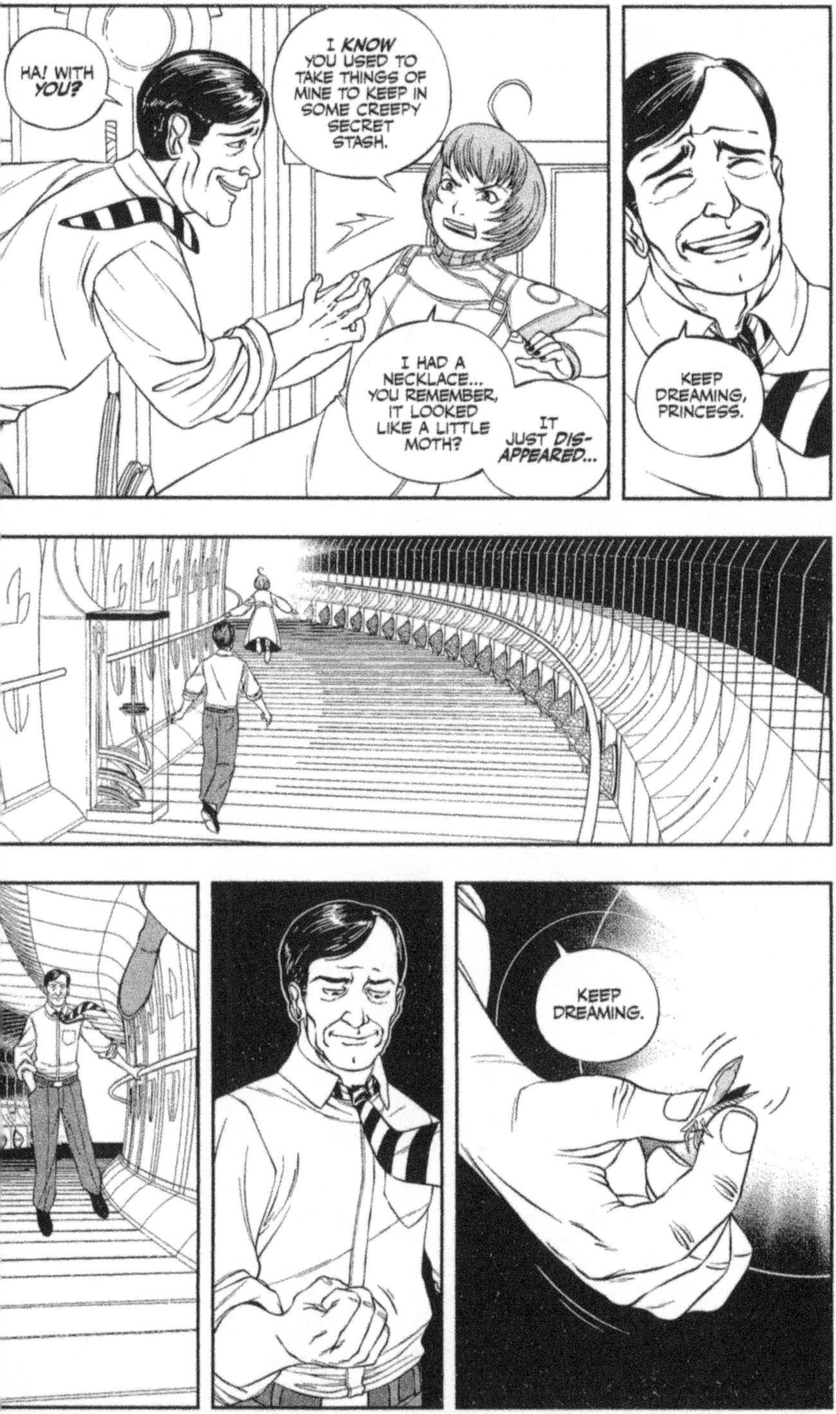
HA! WITH *YOU?*
I *KNOW* YOU USED TO TAKE THINGS OF MINE TO KEEP IN SOME CREEPY SECRET STASH.
I HAD A NECKLACE... YOU REMEMBER, IT LOOKED LIKE A LITTLE MOTH?
IT JUST *DIS-APPEARED...*
KEEP DREAMING, PRINCESS.
KEEP DREAMING.

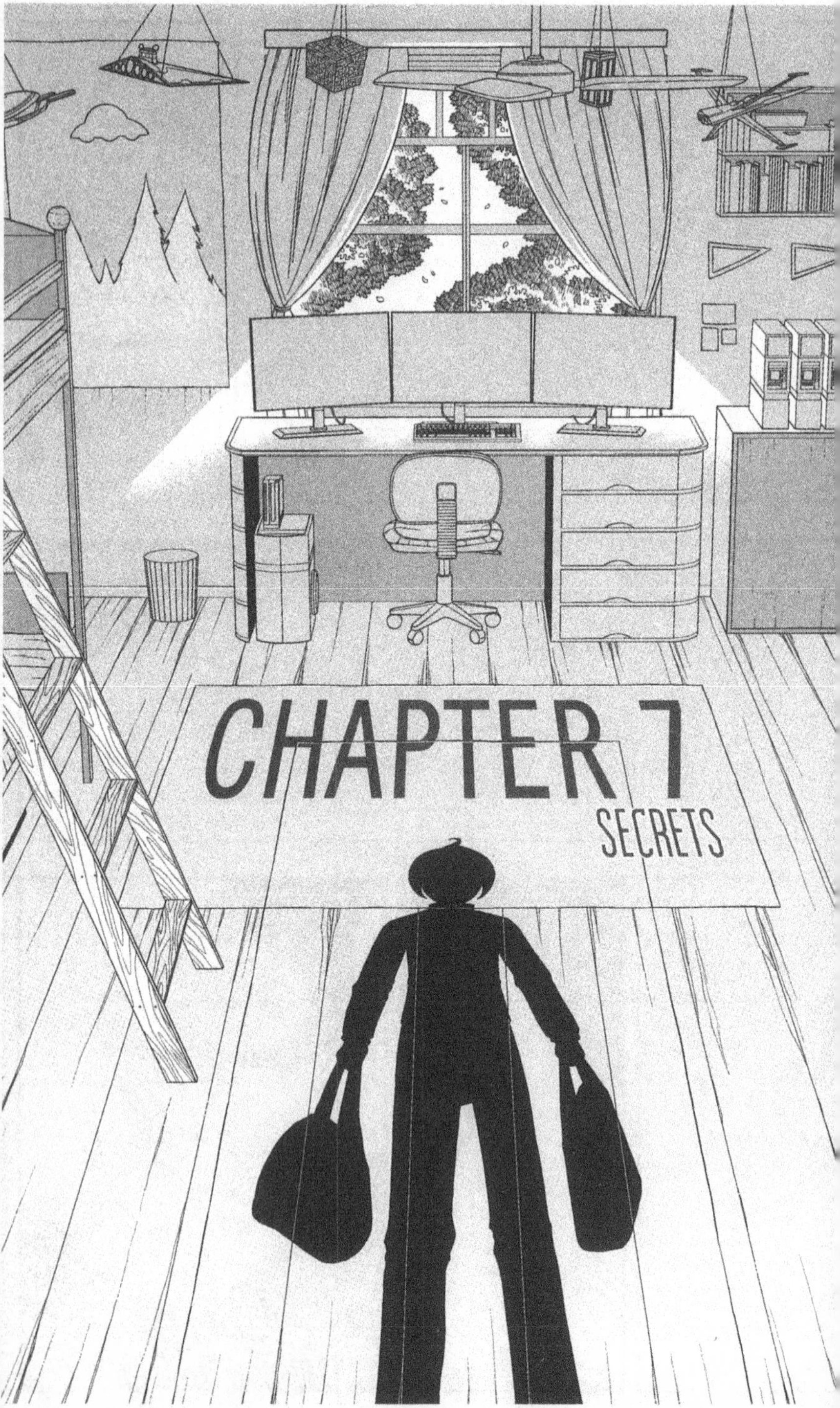
CHAPTER 7
SECRETS

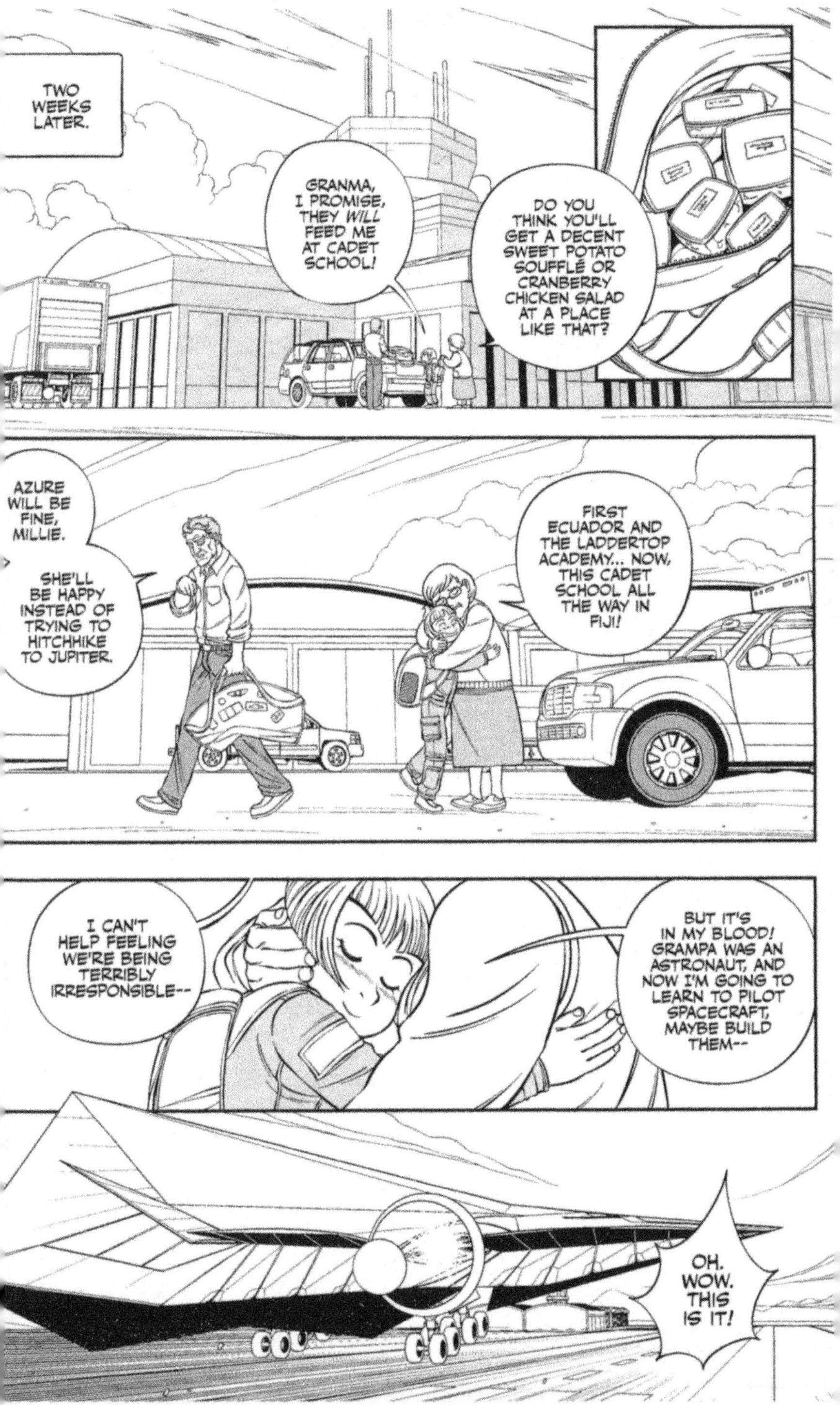
TWO WEEKS LATER.
GRANMA, I PROMISE, THEY *WILL* FEED ME AT CADET SCHOOL!
DO YOU THINK YOU'LL GET A DECENT SWEET POTATO SOUFFLÉ OR CRANBERRY CHICKEN SALAD AT A PLACE LIKE THAT?
AZURE WILL BE FINE, MILLIE.
SHE'LL BE HAPPY INSTEAD OF TRYING TO HITCHHIKE TO JUPITER.
FIRST ECUADOR AND THE LADDERTOP ACADEMY... NOW, THIS CADET SCHOOL ALL THE WAY IN FIJI!
I CAN'T HELP FEELING WE'RE BEING TERRIBLY IRRESPONSIBLE--
BUT IT'S IN MY BLOOD! GRAMPA WAS AN ASTRONAUT, AND NOW I'M GOING TO LEARN TO PILOT SPACECRAFT, MAYBE BUILD THEM--
OH. WOW. THIS IS IT!

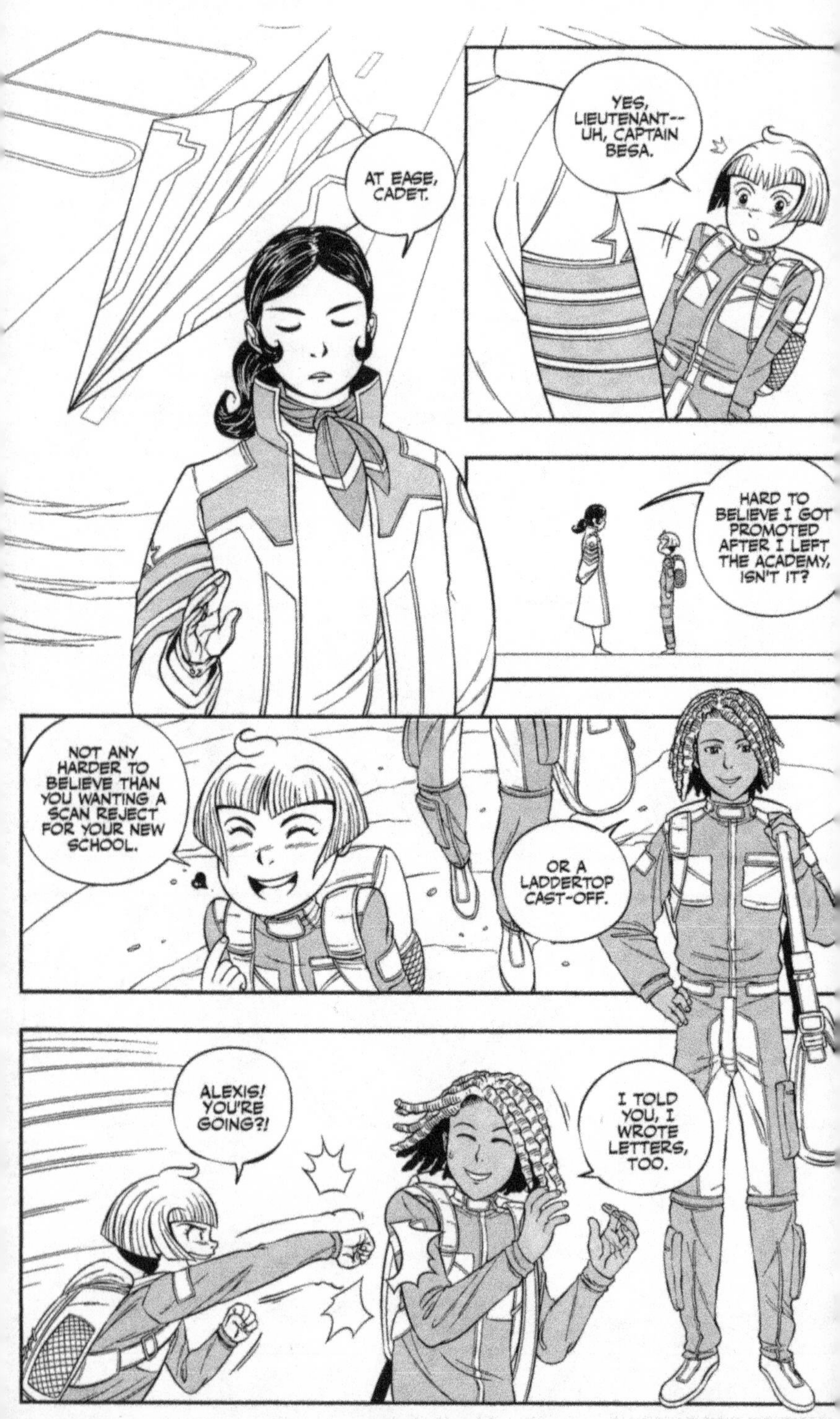
AT EASE, CADET.
YES, LIEUTENANT-- UH, CAPTAIN BESA.
HARD TO BELIEVE I GOT PROMOTED AFTER I LEFT THE ACADEMY, ISN'T IT?
NOT ANY HARDER TO BELIEVE THAN YOU WANTING A SCAN REJECT FOR YOUR NEW SCHOOL.
OR A LADDERTOP CAST-OFF.
ALEXIS! YOU'RE GOING?!
I TOLD YOU, I WROTE LETTERS, TOO.

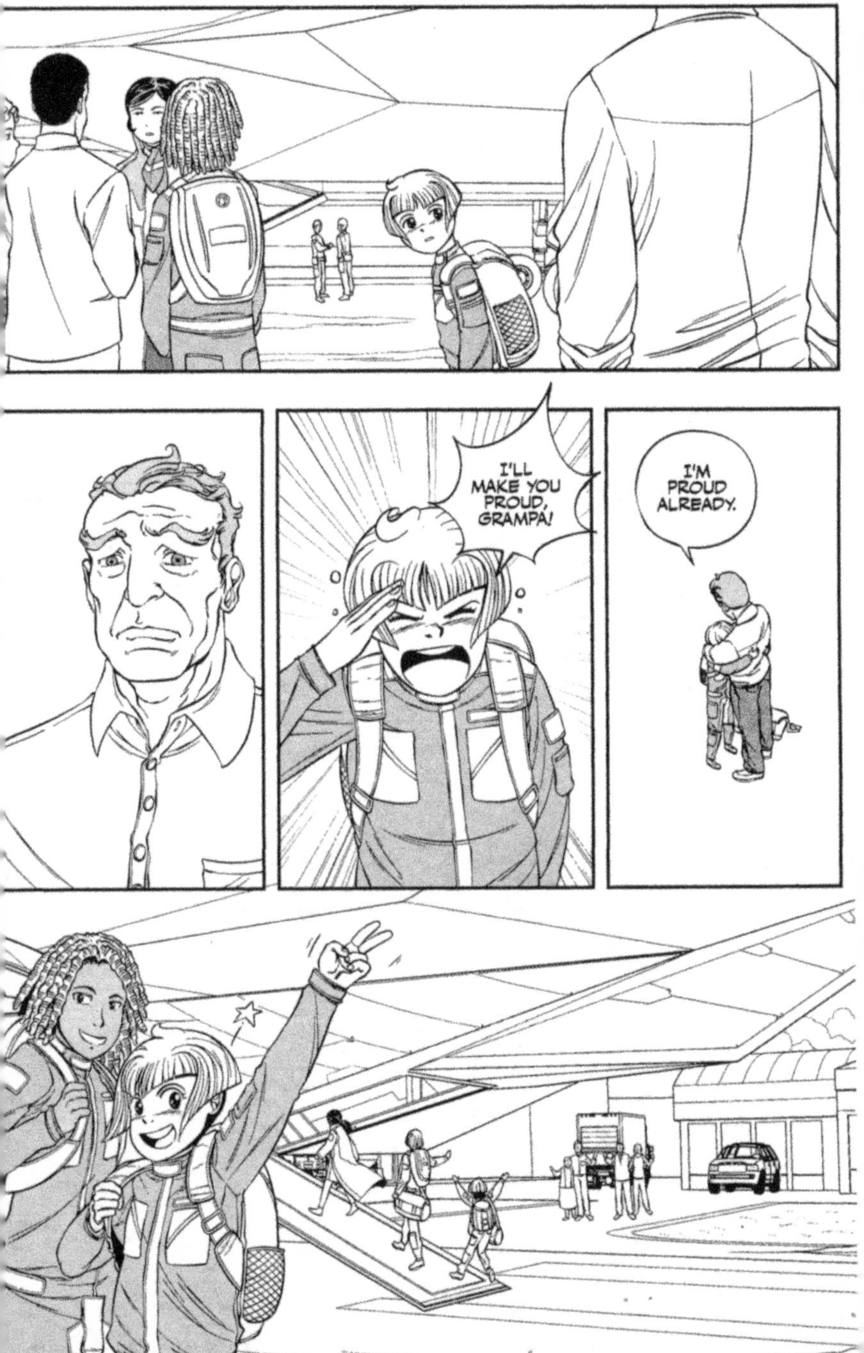
I'LL MAKE YOU PROUD, GRAMPA!
I'M PROUD ALREADY.

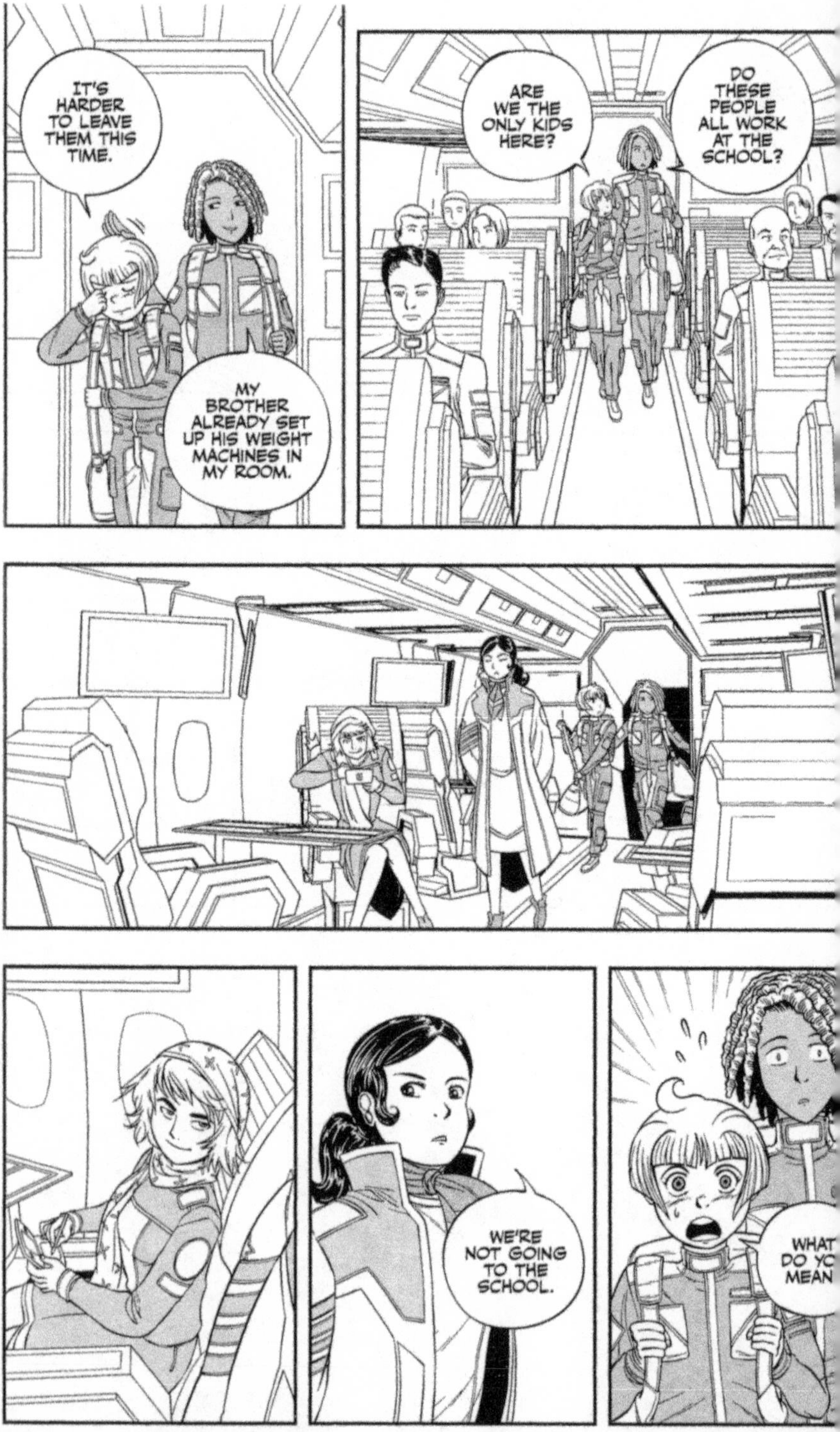
IT'S HARDER TO LEAVE THEM THIS TIME.
MY BROTHER ALREADY SET UP HIS WEIGHT MACHINES IN MY ROOM.
ARE WE THE ONLY KIDS HERE?
DO THESE PEOPLE ALL WORK AT THE SCHOOL?
WE'RE NOT GOING TO THE SCHOOL.

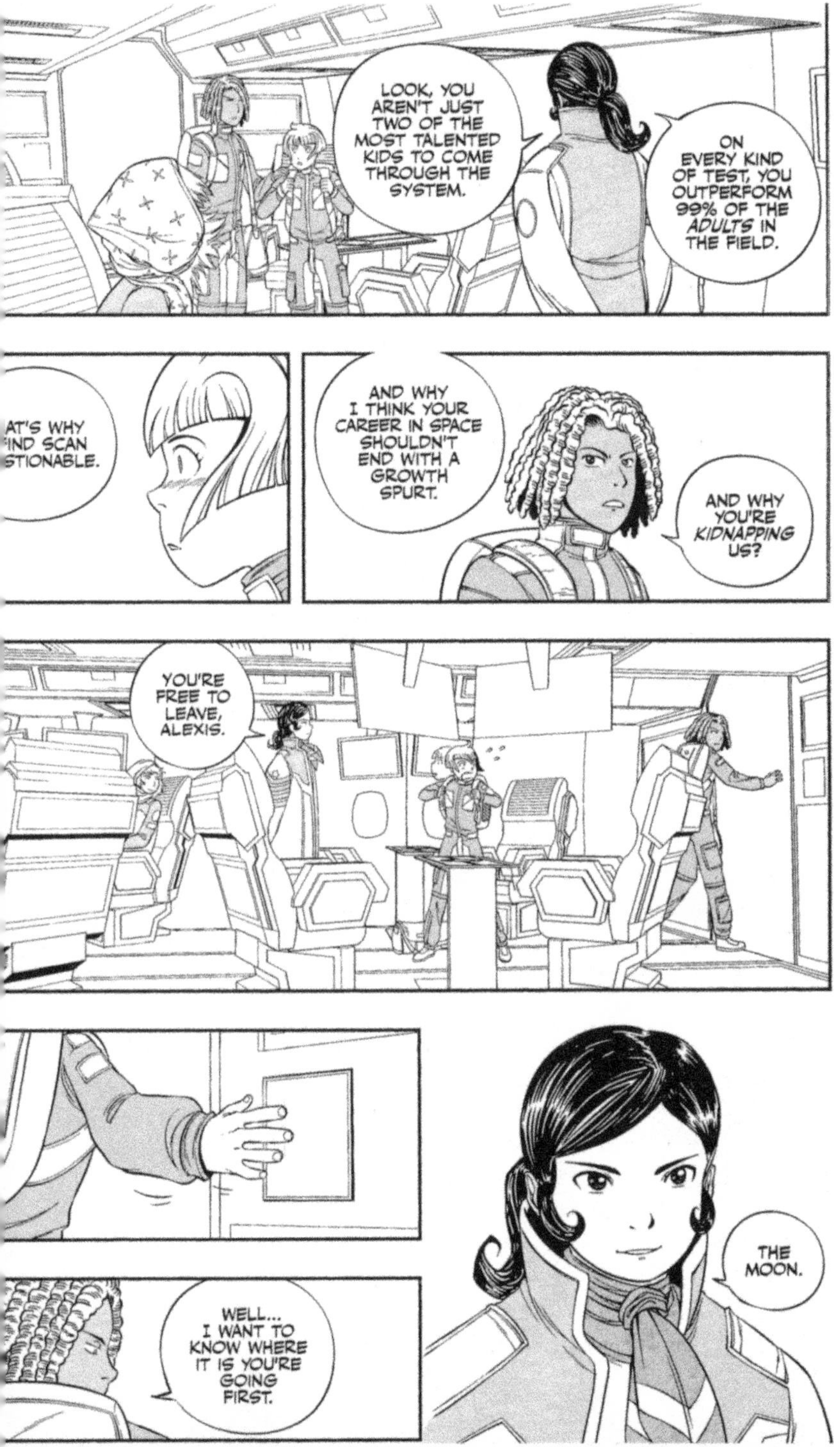
LOOK, YOU AREN'T JUST TWO OF THE MOST TALENTED KIDS TO COME THROUGH THE SYSTEM.
ON EVERY KIND OF TEST, YOU OUTPERFORM 99% OF THE *ADULTS* IN THE FIELD.
AT'S WHY FIND SCAN STIONABLE.
AND WHY I THINK YOUR CAREER IN SPACE SHOULDN'T END WITH A GROWTH SPURT.
AND WHY YOU'RE *KIDNAPPING* US?
YOU'RE FREE TO LEAVE, ALEXIS.
WELL... I WANT TO KNOW WHERE IT IS YOU'RE GOING FIRST.
THE MOON.

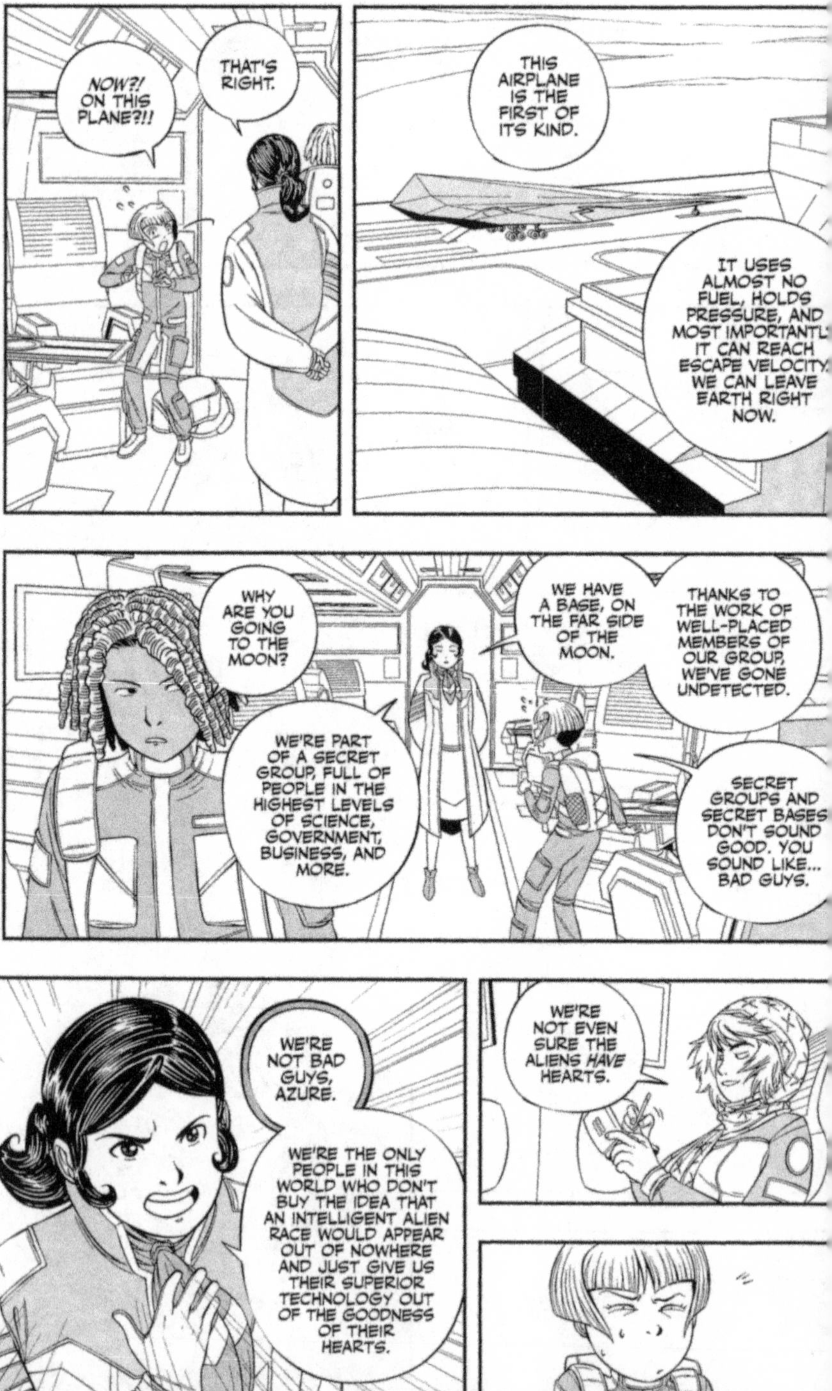
NOW?! ON THIS PLANE?!!
THAT'S RIGHT.
THIS AIRPLANE IS THE FIRST OF ITS KIND.
IT USES ALMOST NO FUEL, HOLDS PRESSURE, AND MOST IMPORTANTLY IT CAN REACH ESCAPE VELOCITY. WE CAN LEAVE EARTH RIGHT NOW.
WHY ARE YOU GOING TO THE MOON?
WE'RE PART OF A SECRET GROUP, FULL OF PEOPLE IN THE HIGHEST LEVELS OF SCIENCE, GOVERNMENT, BUSINESS, AND MORE.
WE HAVE A BASE, ON THE FAR SIDE OF THE MOON.
THANKS TO THE WORK OF WELL-PLACED MEMBERS OF OUR GROUP, WE'VE GONE UNDETECTED.
SECRET GROUPS AND SECRET BASES DON'T SOUND GOOD. YOU SOUND LIKE... BAD GUYS.
WE'RE NOT BAD GUYS, AZURE.
WE'RE THE ONLY PEOPLE IN THIS WORLD WHO DON'T BUY THE IDEA THAT AN INTELLIGENT ALIEN RACE WOULD APPEAR OUT OF NOWHERE AND JUST GIVE US THEIR SUPERIOR TECHNOLOGY OUT OF THE GOODNESS OF THEIR HEARTS.
WE'RE NOT EVEN SURE THE ALIENS *HAVE* HEARTS.

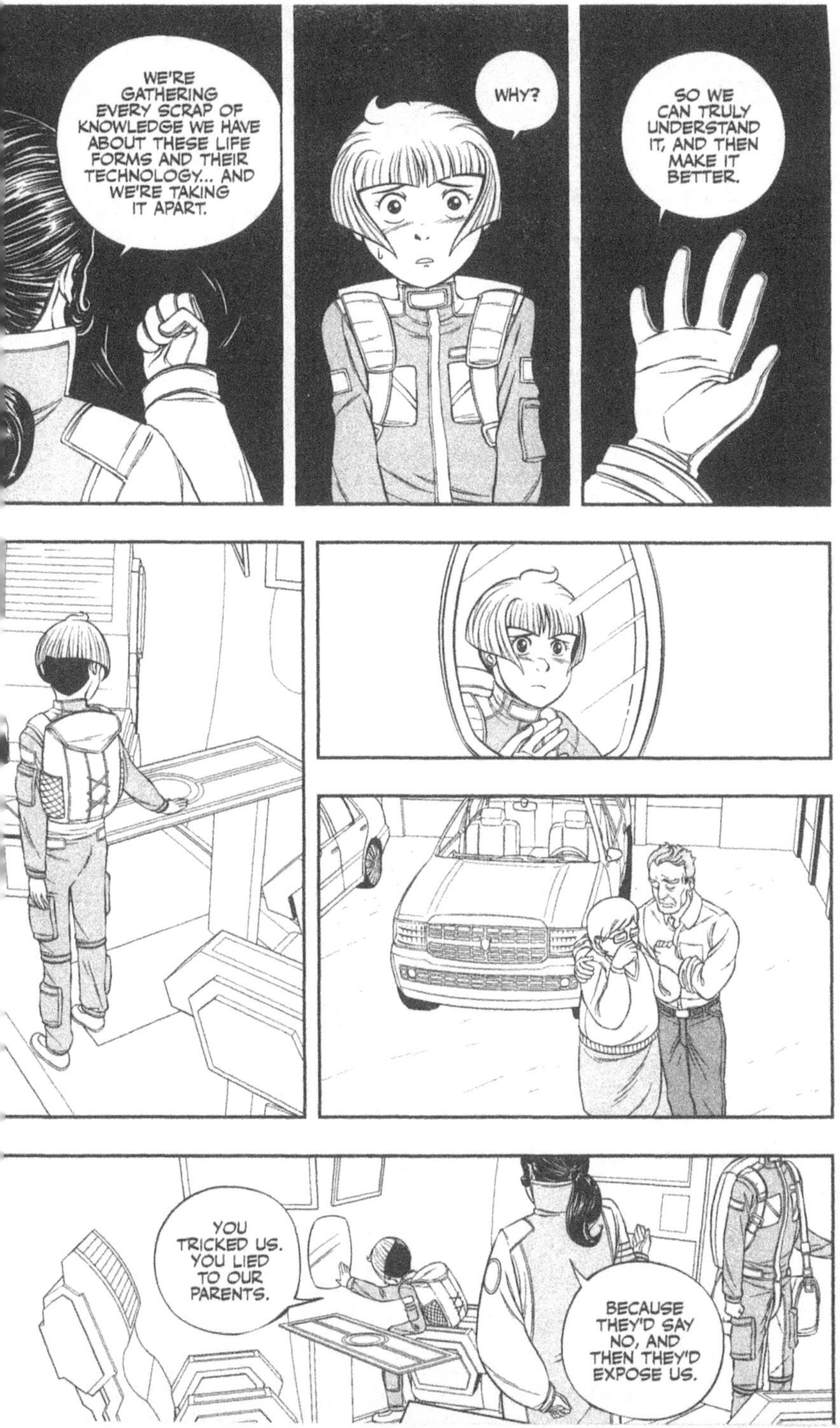
WE'RE GATHERING EVERY SCRAP OF KNOWLEDGE WE HAVE ABOUT THESE LIFE FORMS AND THEIR TECHNOLOGY... AND WE'RE TAKING IT APART.
WHY?
SO WE CAN TRULY UNDERSTAND IT, AND THEN MAKE IT BETTER.
YOU TRICKED US. YOU LIED TO OUR PARENTS.
BECAUSE THEY'D SAY NO, AND THEN THEY'D EXPOSE US.

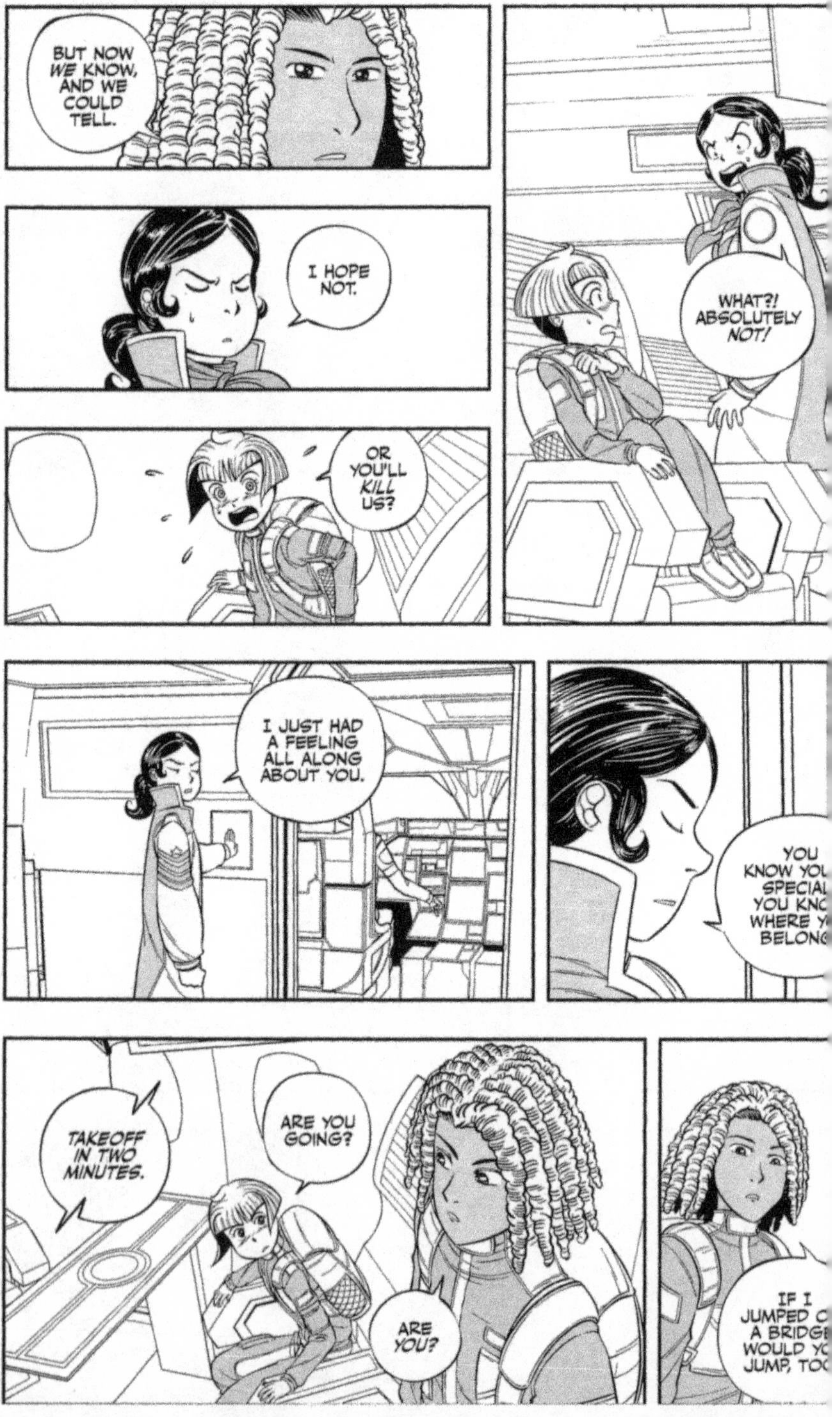
BUT NOW WE KNOW, AND WE COULD TELL.
I HOPE NOT.
OR YOU'LL KILL US?
WHAT?! ABSOLUTELY NOT!
I JUST HAD A FEELING ALL ALONG ABOUT YOU.
YOU KNOW YO SPECIAL YOU KNO WHERE Y BELONG
TAKEOFF IN TWO MINUTES.
ARE YOU GOING?
ARE YOU?
IF I JUMPED C A BRIDGE WOULD Y JUMP, TO

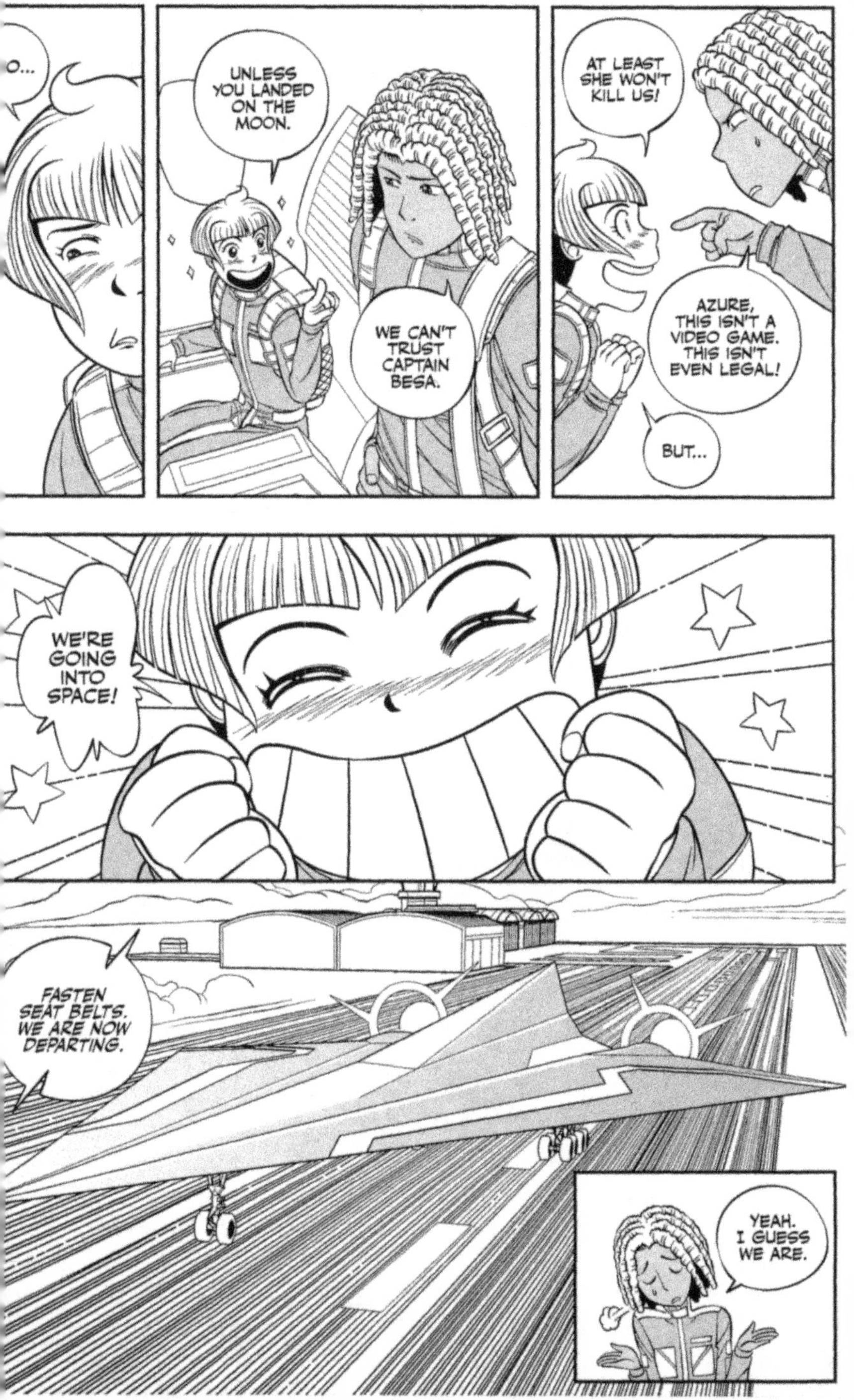
O...
UNLESS YOU LANDED ON THE MOON.
WE CAN'T TRUST CAPTAIN BESA.
AT LEAST SHE WON'T KILL US!
AZURE, THIS ISN'T A VIDEO GAME. THIS ISN'T EVEN LEGAL!
BUT...
WE'RE GOING INTO SPACE!
FASTEN SEAT BELTS. WE ARE NOW DEPARTING.
YEAH. I GUESS WE ARE.

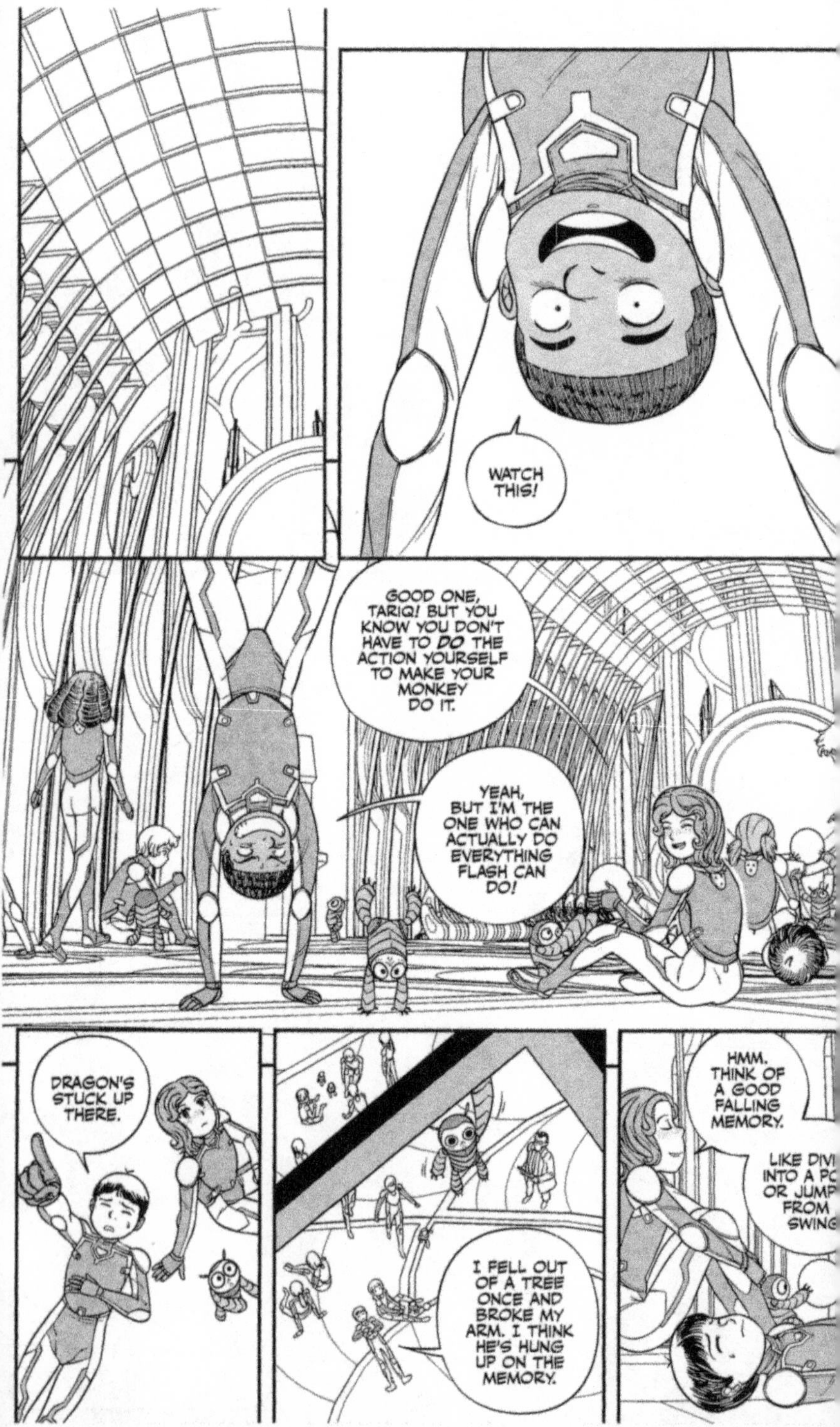
WATCH THIS!
GOOD ONE, TARIQ! BUT YOU KNOW YOU DON'T HAVE TO *DO* THE ACTION YOURSELF TO MAKE YOUR MONKEY DO IT.
YEAH, BUT I'M THE ONE WHO CAN ACTUALLY DO EVERYTHING FLASH CAN DO!
DRAGON'S STUCK UP THERE.
I FELL OUT OF A TREE ONCE AND BROKE MY ARM. I THINK HE'S HUNG UP ON THE MEMORY.
HMM. THINK OF A GOOD FALLING MEMORY.
LIKE DIVI INTO A PO OR JUMP FROM SWING

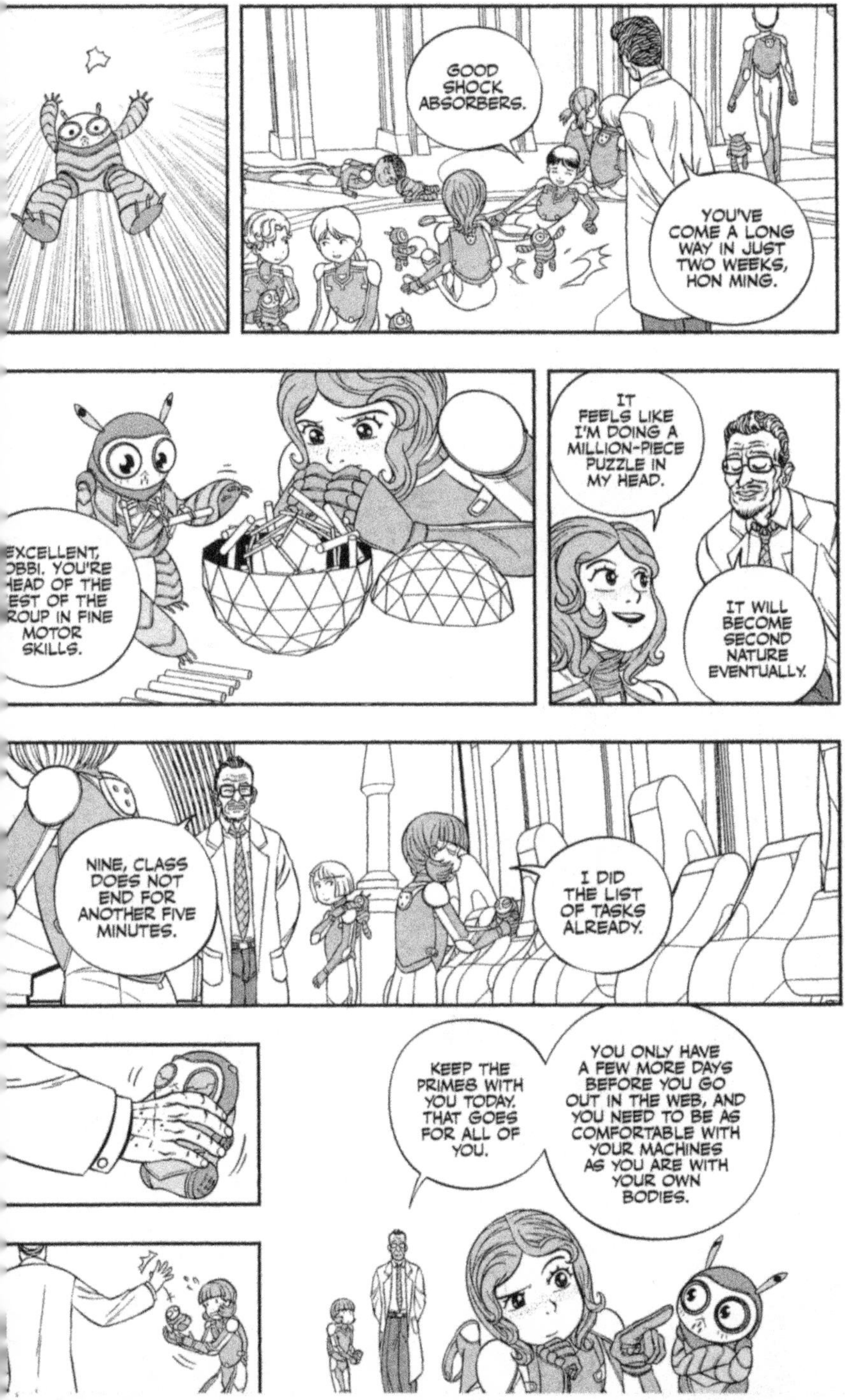
GOOD SHOCK ABSORBERS.
YOU'VE COME A LONG WAY IN JUST TWO WEEKS, HON MING.
EXCELLENT, OBBI. YOU'RE HEAD OF THE EST OF THE ROUP IN FINE MOTOR SKILLS.
IT FEELS LIKE I'M DOING A MILLION-PIECE PUZZLE IN MY HEAD.
IT WILL BECOME SECOND NATURE EVENTUALLY.
NINE, CLASS DOES NOT END FOR ANOTHER FIVE MINUTES.
I DID THE LIST OF TASKS ALREADY.
KEEP THE PRIMES WITH YOU TODAY. THAT GOES FOR ALL OF YOU.
YOU ONLY HAVE A FEW MORE DAYS BEFORE YOU GO OUT IN THE WEB, AND YOU NEED TO BE AS COMFORTABLE WITH YOUR MACHINES AS YOU ARE WITH YOUR OWN BODIES.

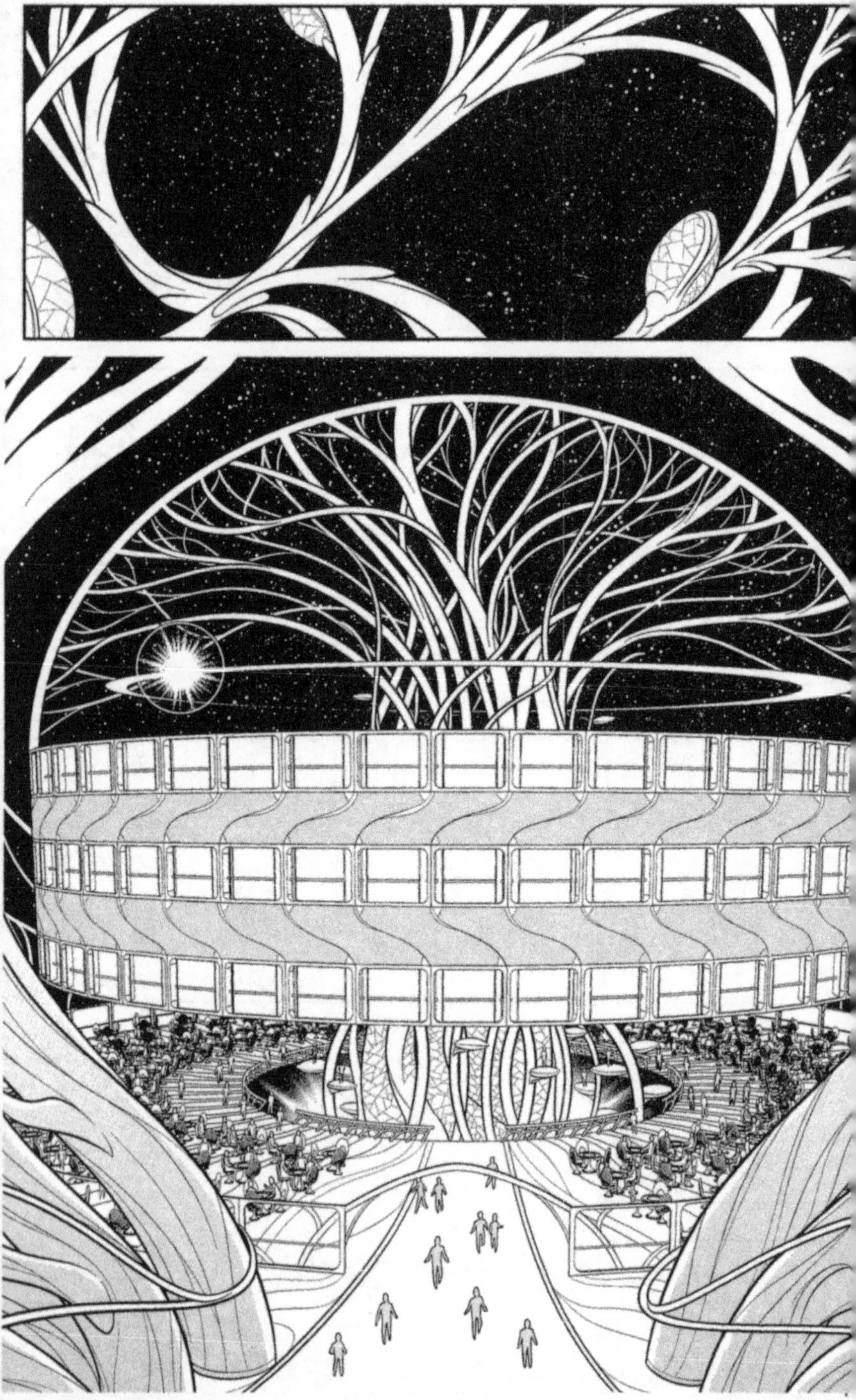

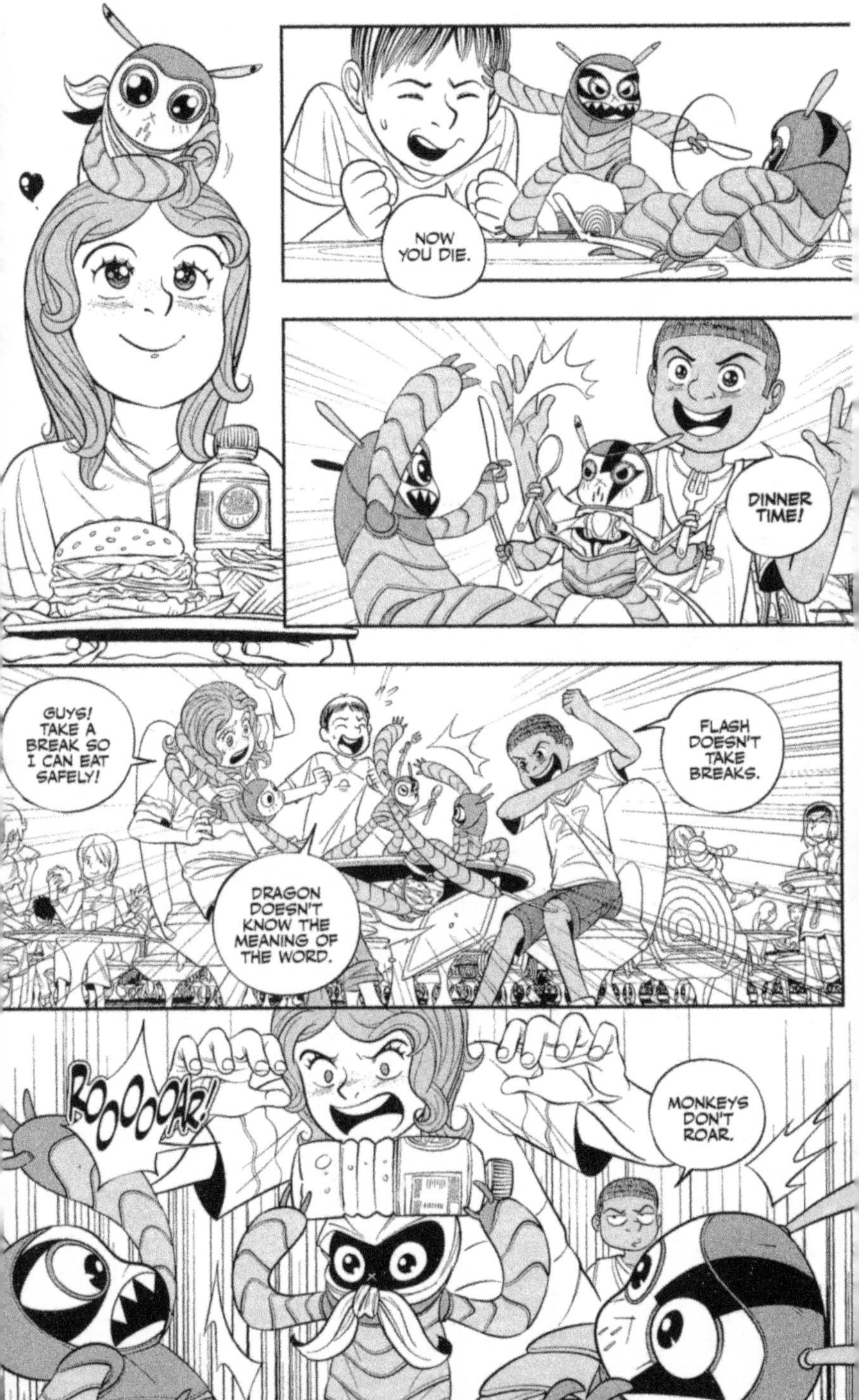
NOW YOU DIE.
DINNER TIME!
GUYS! TAKE A BREAK SO I CAN EAT SAFELY!
FLASH DOESN'T TAKE BREAKS.
DRAGON DOESN'T KNOW THE MEANING OF THE WORD.
ROOOOOAR!
MONKEYS DON'T ROAR.

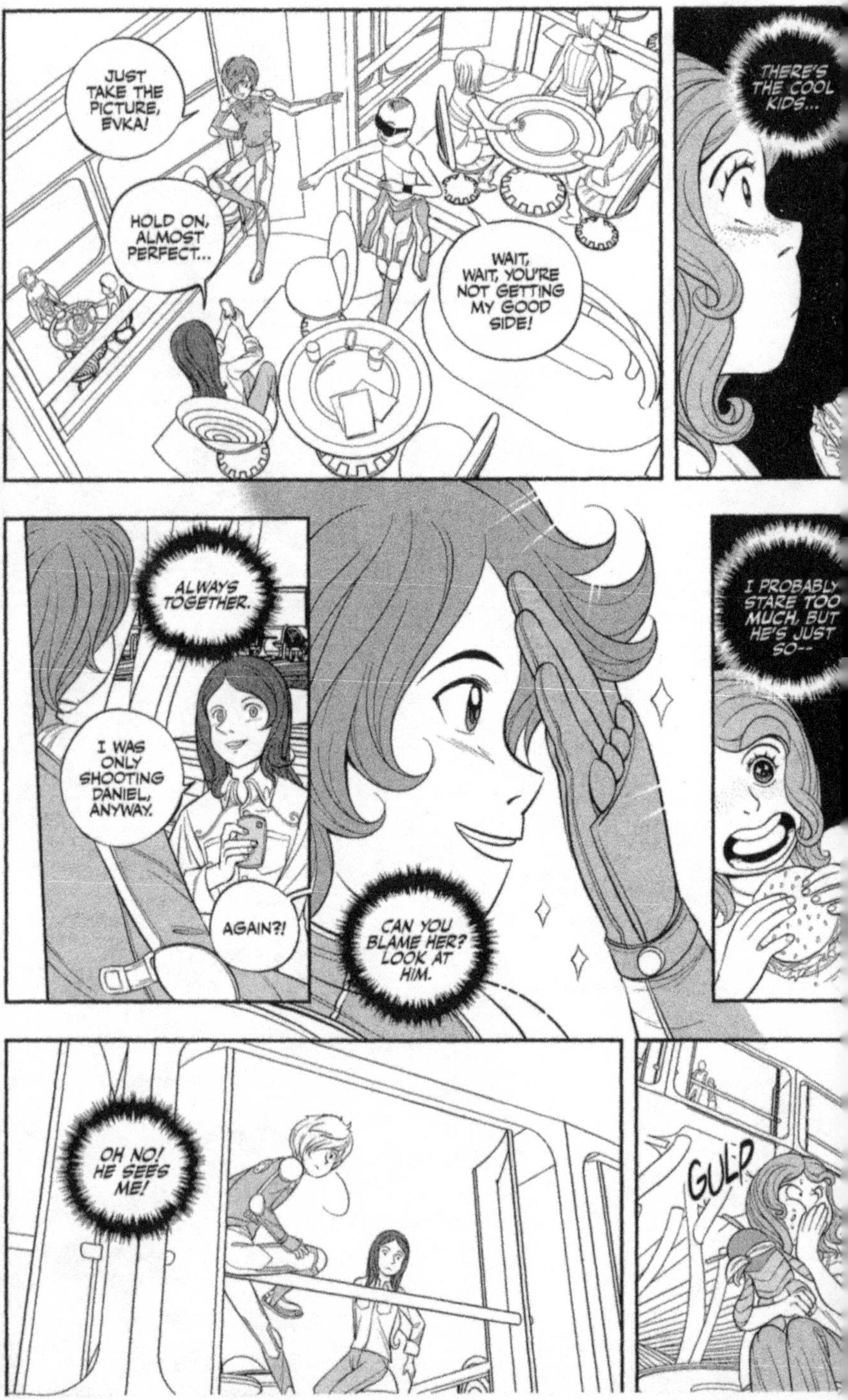
JUST TAKE THE PICTURE, EVKA!
HOLD ON, ALMOST PERFECT...
WAIT, WAIT, YOU'RE NOT GETTING MY GOOD SIDE!
THERE'S THE COOL KIDS...
ALWAYS TOGETHER.
I WAS ONLY SHOOTING DANIEL, ANYWAY.
AGAIN?!
CAN YOU BLAME HER? LOOK AT HIM.
I PROBABLY STARE TOO MUCH, BUT HE'S JUST SO--
OH NO! HE SEES ME!
GULP

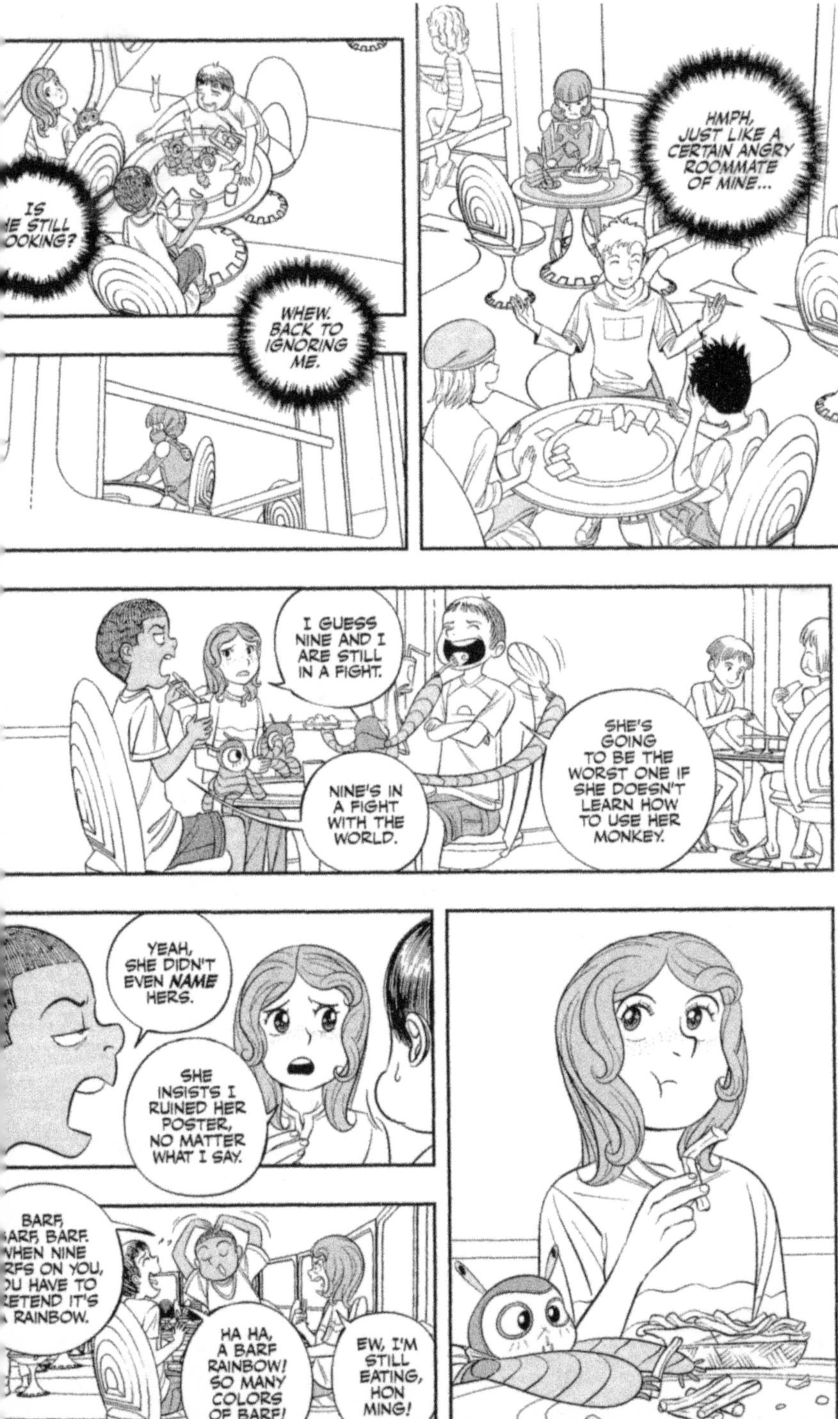
IS
HE STILL
LOOKING?
WHEW. BACK TO IGNORING ME.
HMPH, JUST LIKE A CERTAIN ANGRY ROOMMATE OF MINE...
I GUESS NINE AND I ARE STILL IN A FIGHT.
NINE'S IN A FIGHT WITH THE WORLD.
SHE'S GOING TO BE THE WORST ONE IF SHE DOESN'T LEARN HOW TO USE HER MONKEY.
YEAH, SHE DIDN'T EVEN ***NAME*** HERS.
SHE INSISTS I RUINED HER POSTER, NO MATTER WHAT I SAY.
BARF, BARF, BARF. WHEN NINE BARFS ON YOU, YOU HAVE TO PRETEND IT'S A RAINBOW.
HA HA, A BARF RAINBOW! SO MANY COLORS OF BARF!
EW, I'M STILL EATING, HON MING!

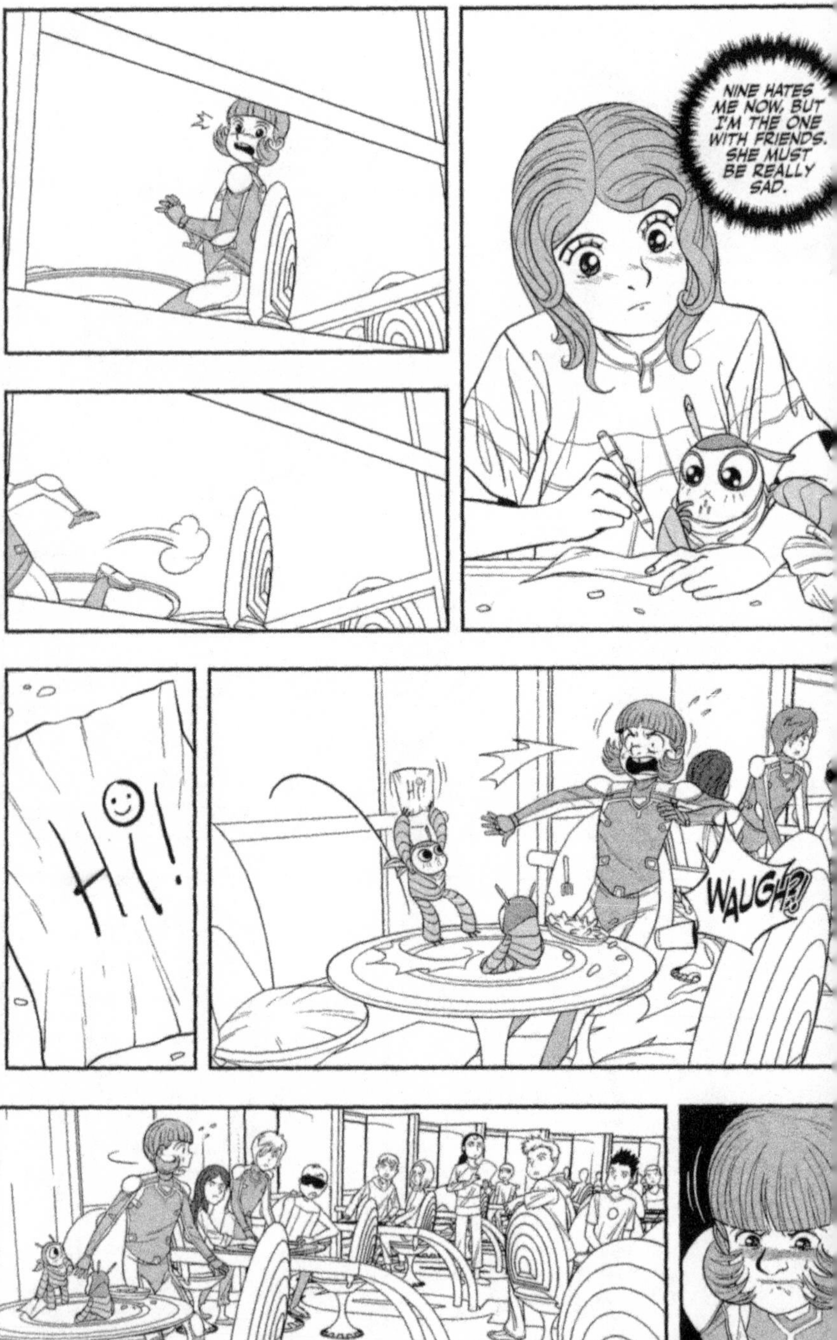
NINE HATES ME NOW, BUT I'M THE ONE WITH FRIENDS. SHE MUST BE REALLY SAD.
HI!
HI!
WAUGH?!

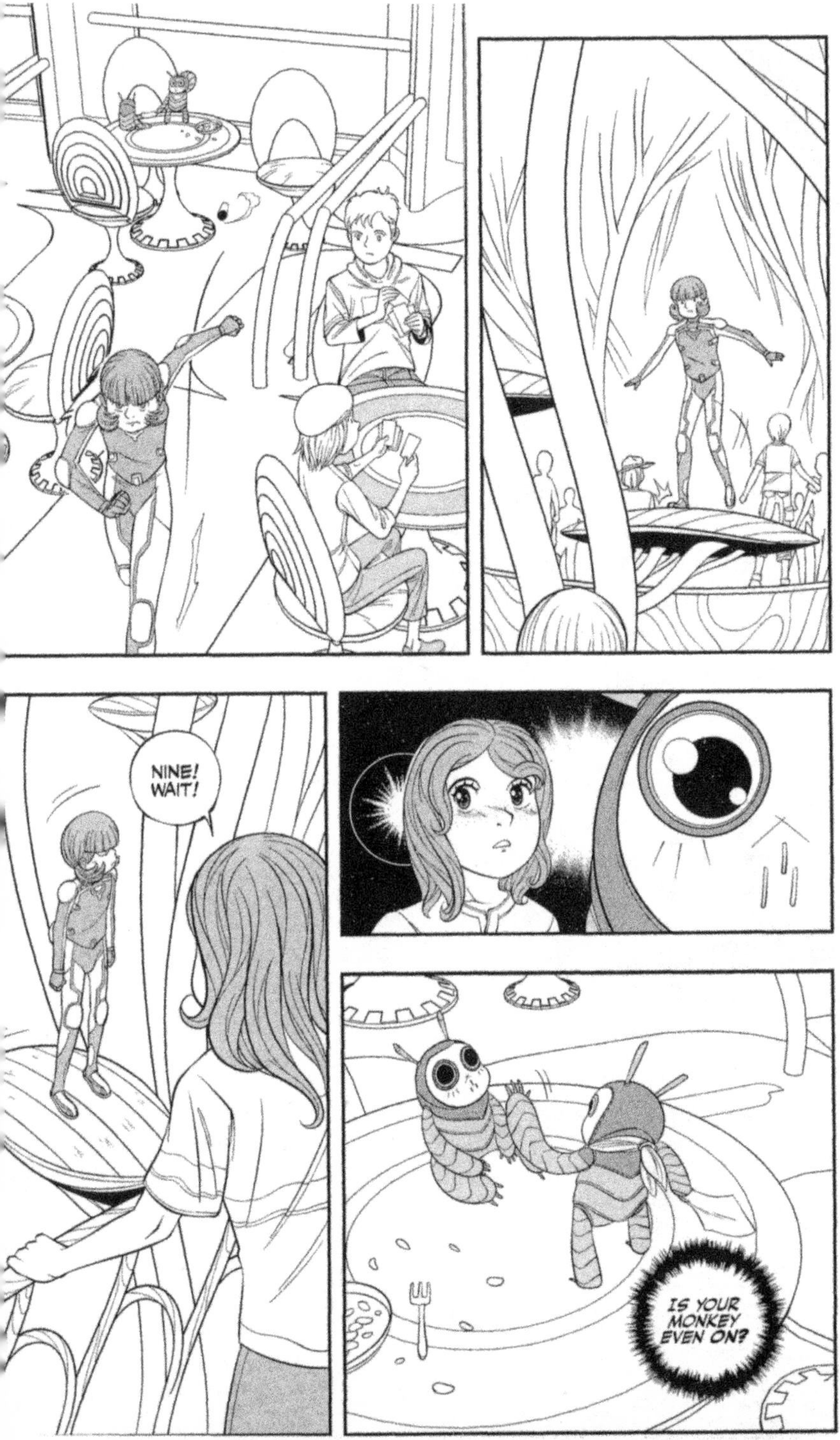
NINE! WAIT!
IS YOUR MONKEY EVEN ON?

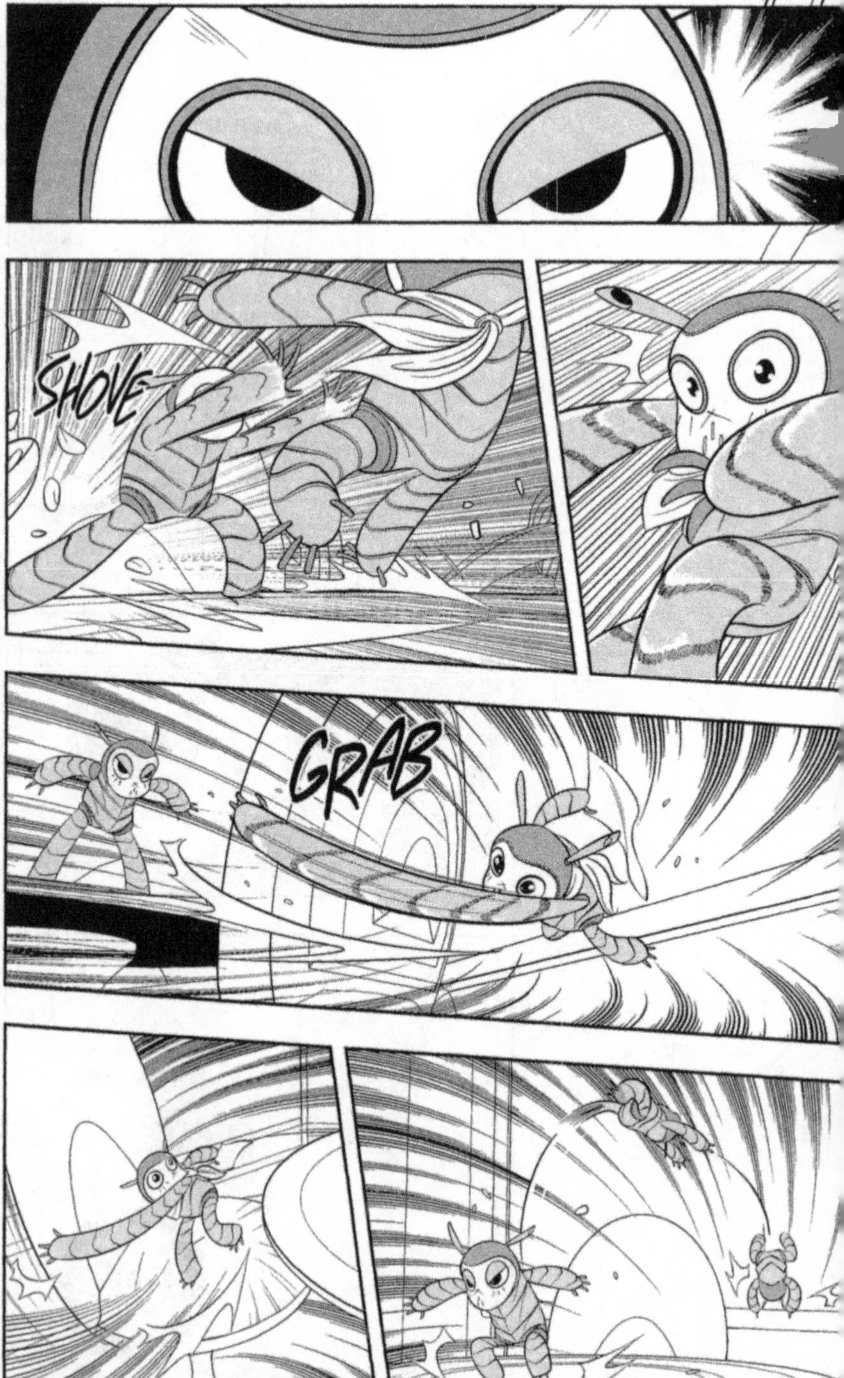
SHOVE
GRAB

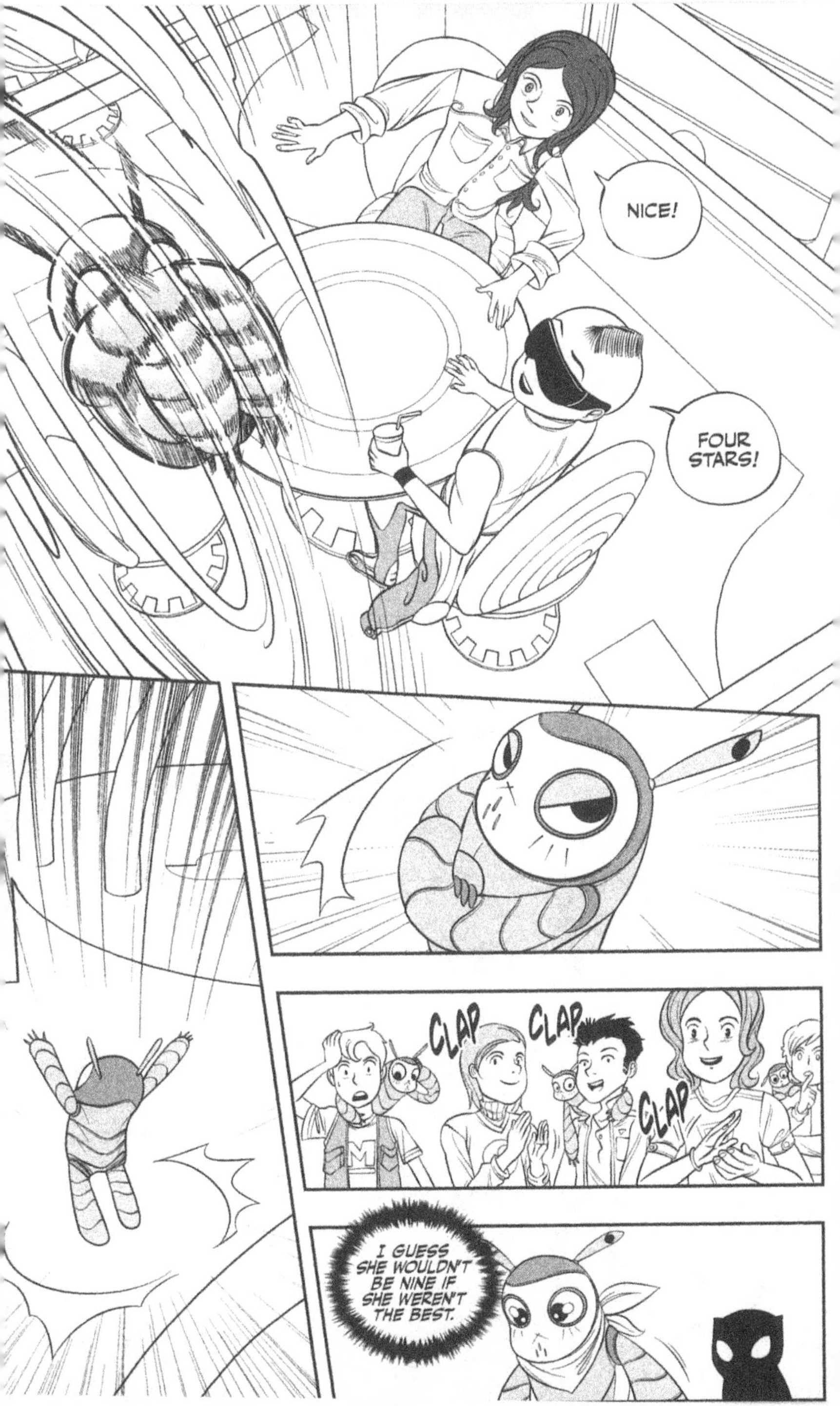
NICE!
FOUR STARS!
CLAP
CLAP
CLAP
I GUESS SHE WOULDN'T BE NINE IF SHE WEREN'T THE BEST.

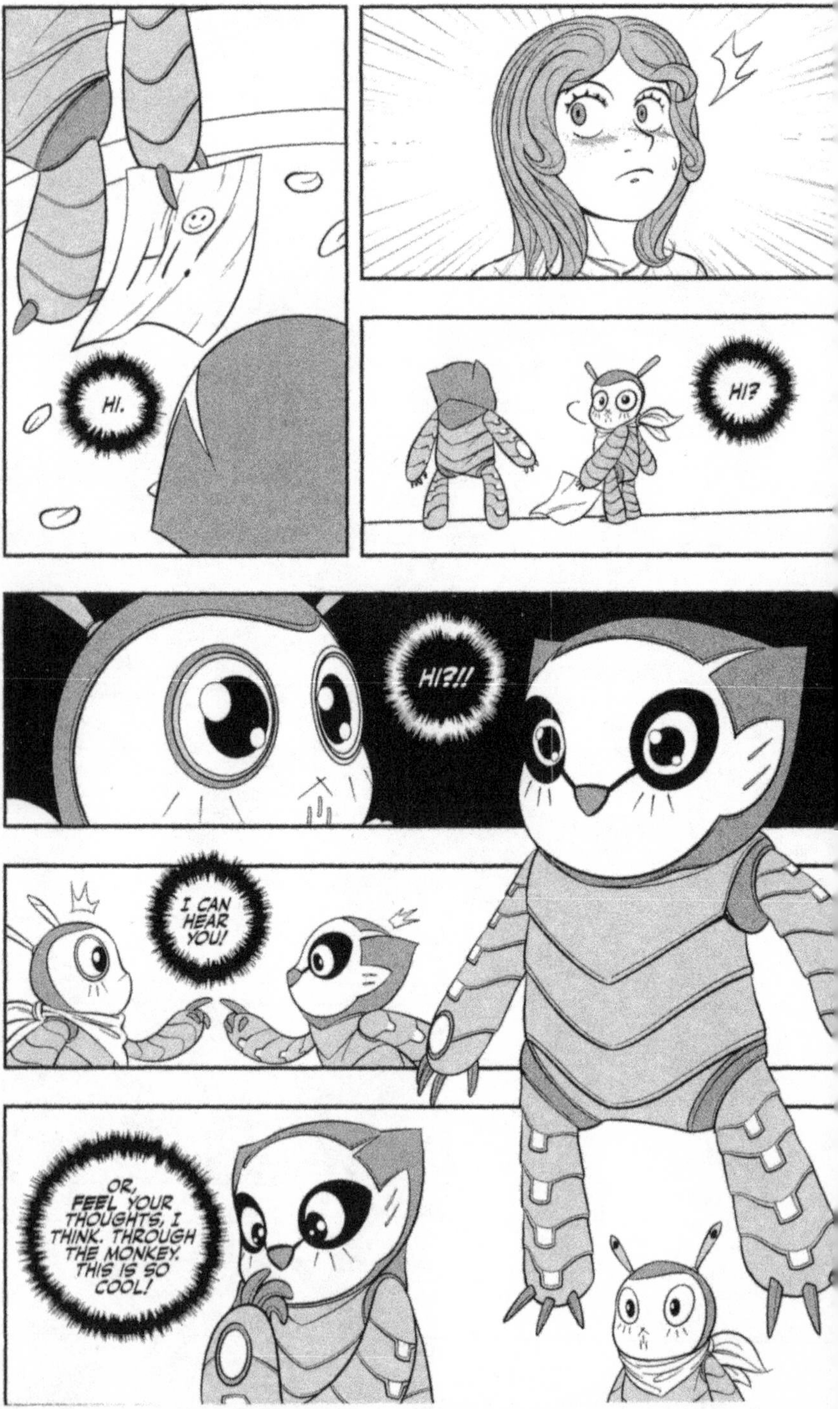
HI.
HI?
HI?!!
I CAN HEAR YOU!
OR, FEEL YOUR THOUGHTS, I THINK. THROUGH THE MONKEY. THIS IS SO COOL!

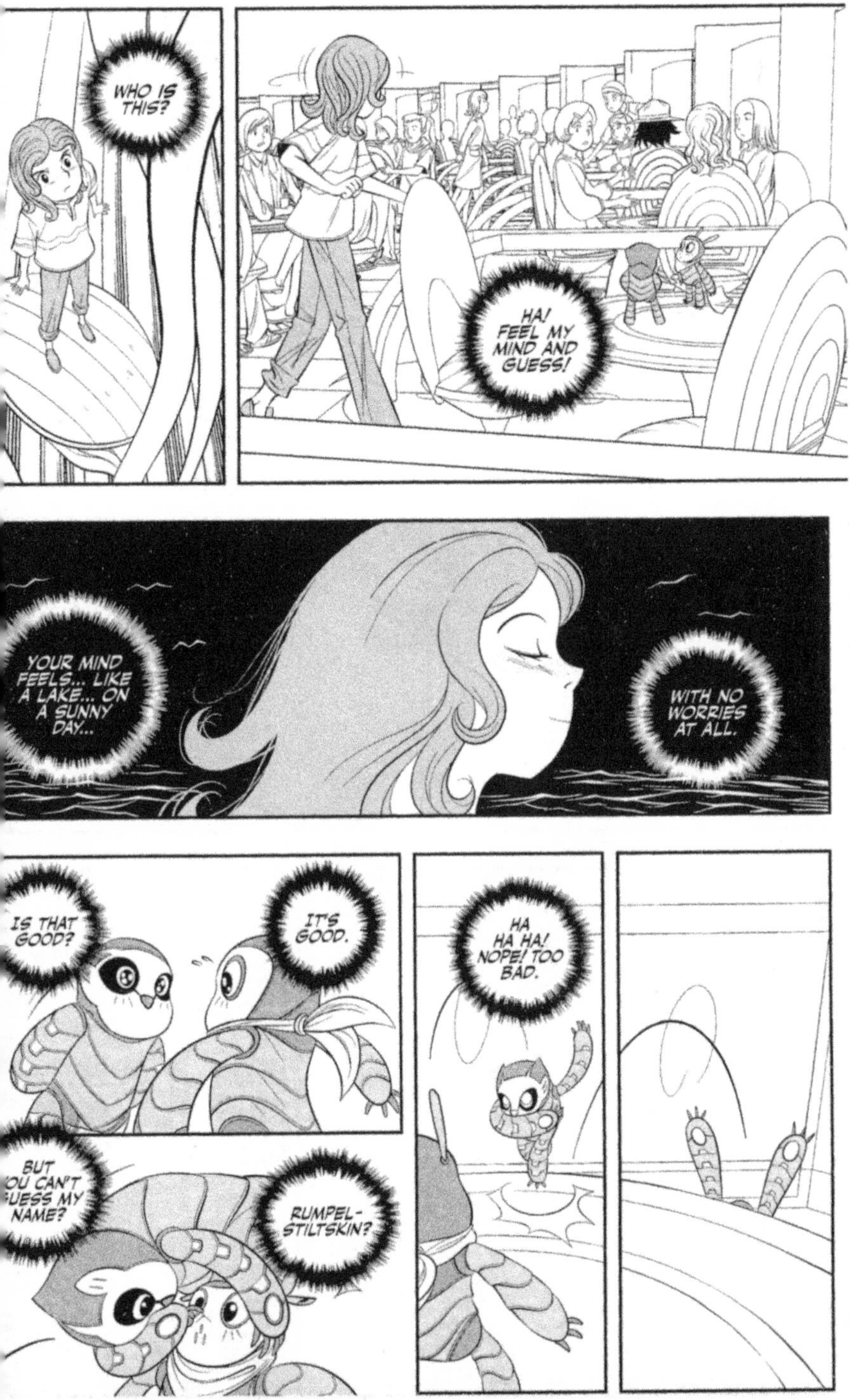
WHO IS THIS?
HA! FEEL MY MIND AND GUESS!
YOUR MIND FEELS... LIKE A LAKE... ON A SUNNY DAY...
WITH NO WORRIES AT ALL.
IS THAT GOOD?
IT'S GOOD.
BUT YOU CAN'T GUESS MY NAME?
RUMPEL-STILTSKIN?
HA HA HA! NOPE! TOO BAD.

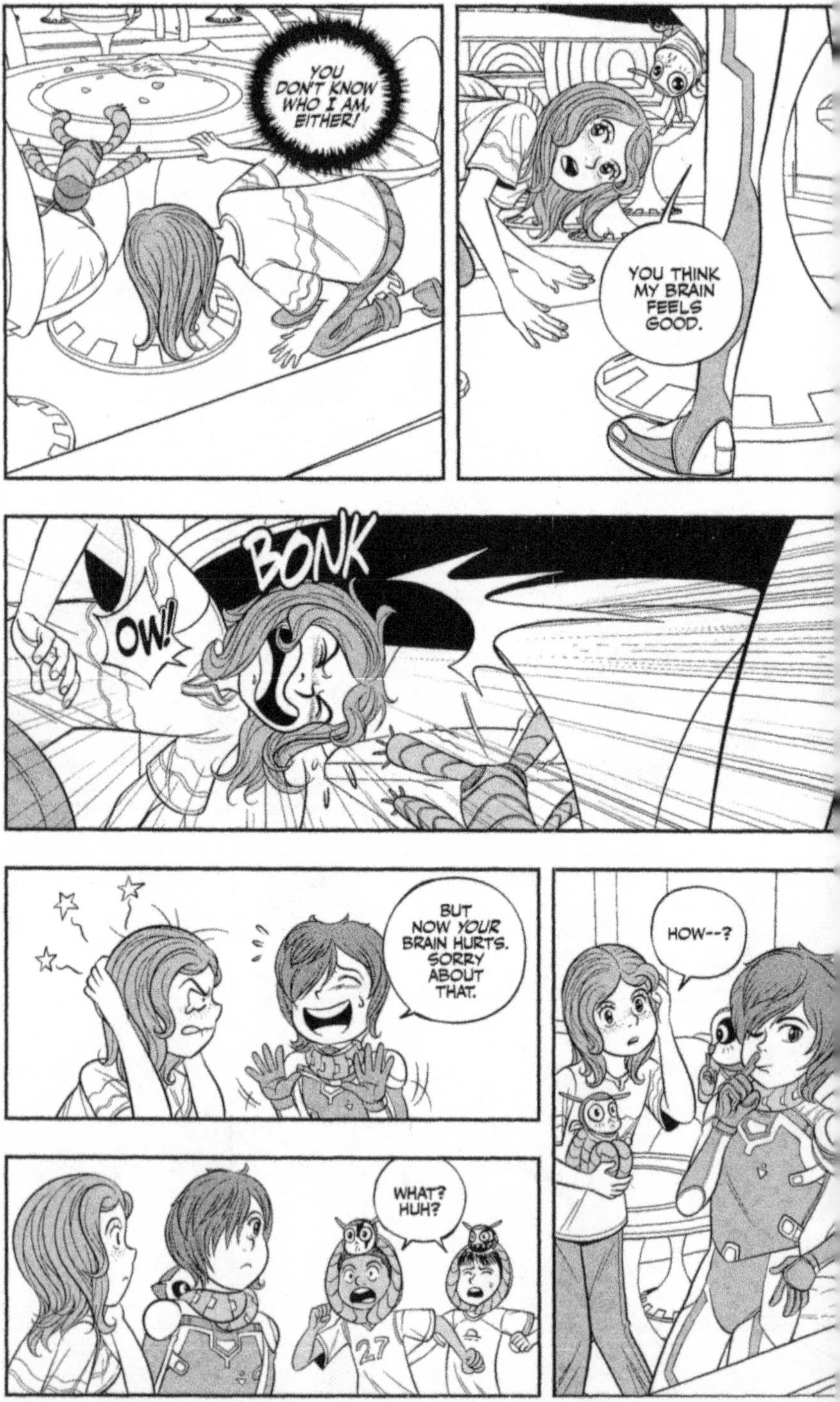
YOU DON'T KNOW WHO I AM, EITHER!
YOU THINK MY BRAIN FEELS GOOD.
BONK
OW!
BUT NOW *YOUR* BRAIN HURTS. SORRY ABOUT THAT.
WHAT? HUH?
27
HOW--?

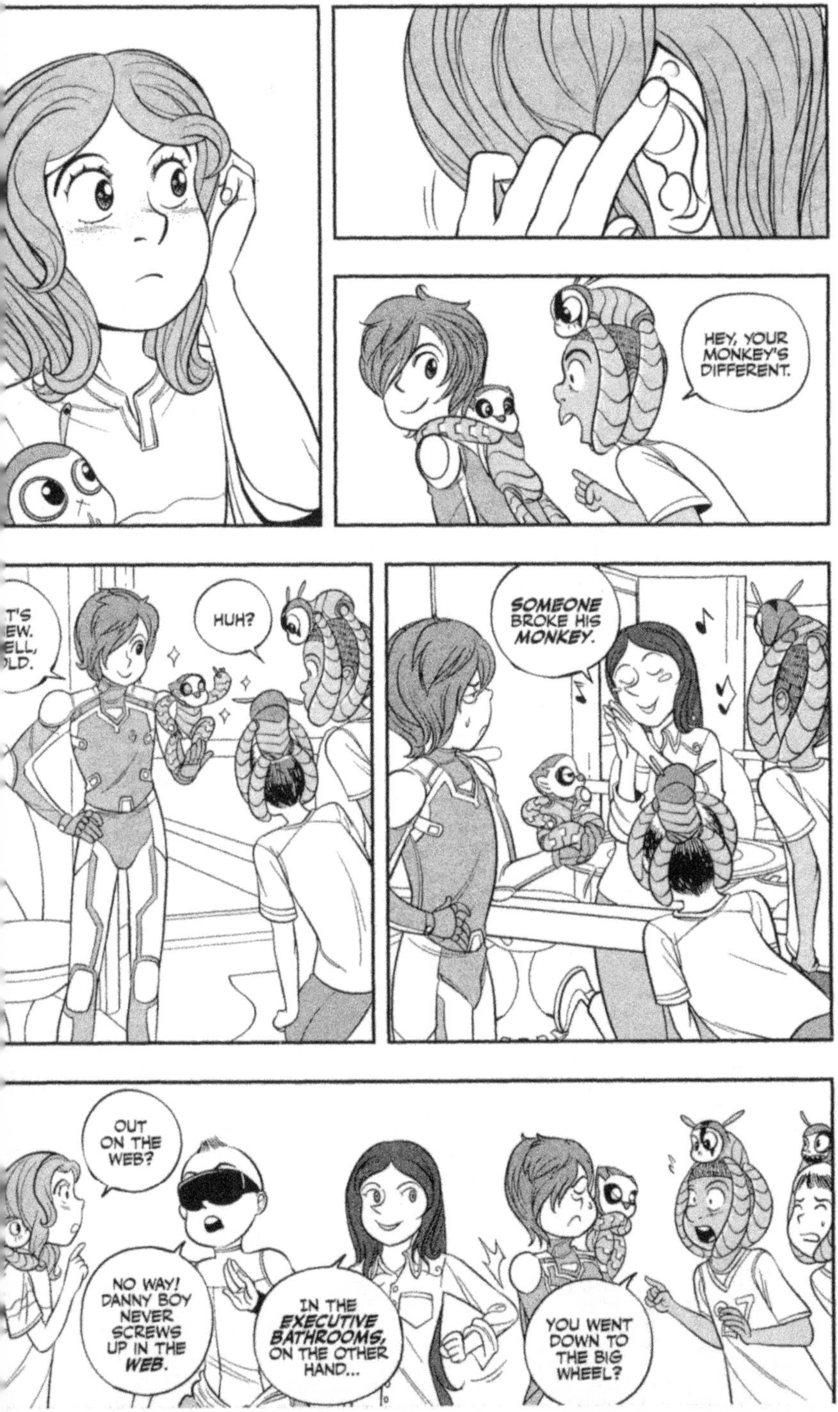
HEY, YOUR MONKEY'S DIFFERENT.
HUH?
SOMEONE BROKE HIS *MONKEY*.
OUT ON THE WEB?
NO WAY! DANNY BOY NEVER SCREWS UP IN THE *WEB*.
IN THE *EXECUTIVE BATHROOMS,* ON THE OTHER HAND...
YOU WENT DOWN TO THE BIG WHEEL?

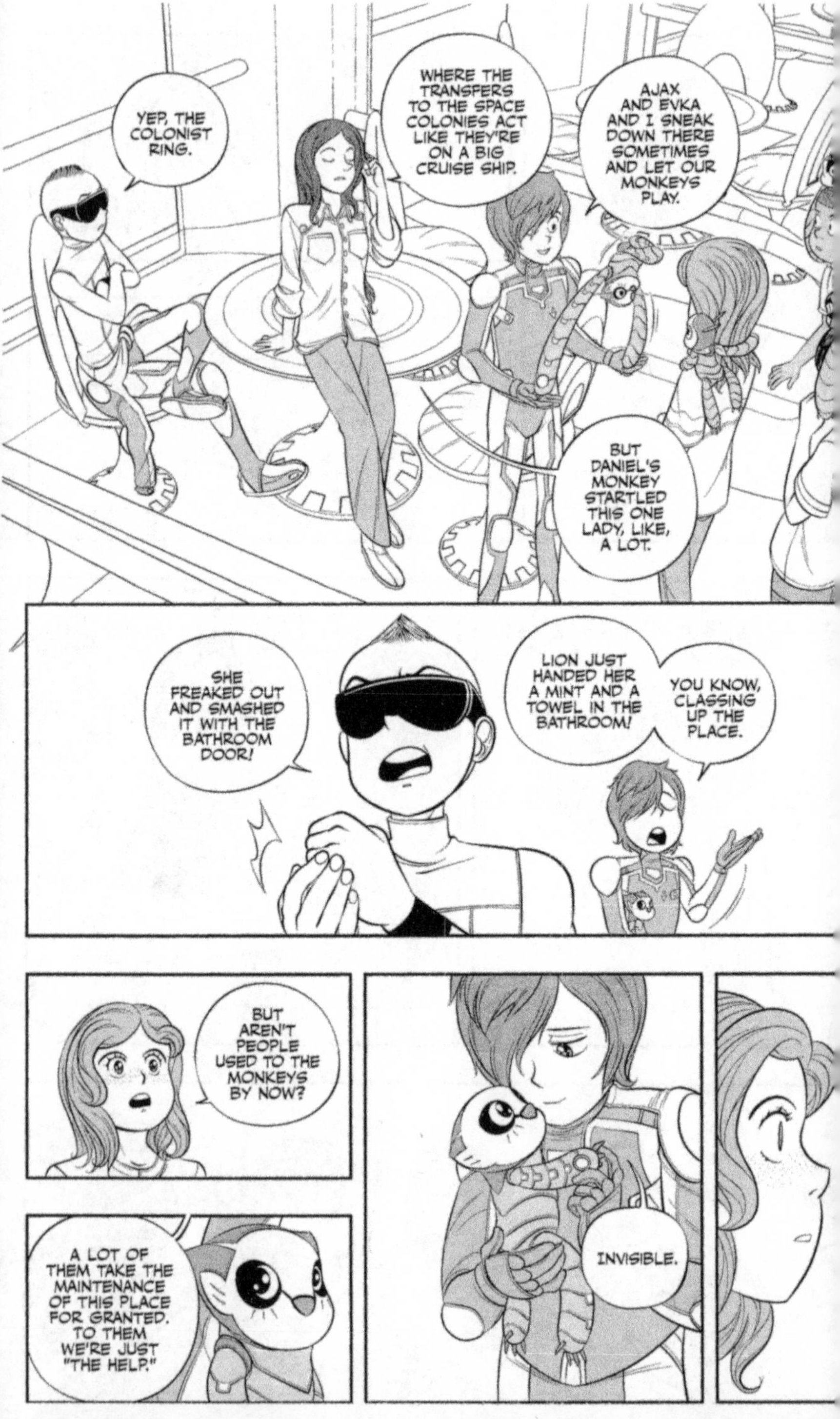
YEP, THE COLONIST RING.
WHERE THE TRANSFERS TO THE SPACE COLONIES ACT LIKE THEY'RE ON A BIG CRUISE SHIP.
AJAX AND EVKA AND I SNEAK DOWN THERE SOMETIMES AND LET OUR MONKEYS PLAY.
BUT DANIEL'S MONKEY STARTLED THIS ONE LADY, LIKE, A LOT.
SHE FREAKED OUT AND SMASHED IT WITH THE BATHROOM DOOR!
LION JUST HANDED HER A MINT AND A TOWEL IN THE BATHROOM!
YOU KNOW, CLASSING UP THE PLACE.
BUT AREN'T PEOPLE USED TO THE MONKEYS BY NOW?
A LOT OF THEM TAKE THE MAINTENANCE OF THIS PLACE FOR GRANTED. TO THEM WE'RE JUST "THE HELP."
INVISIBLE.

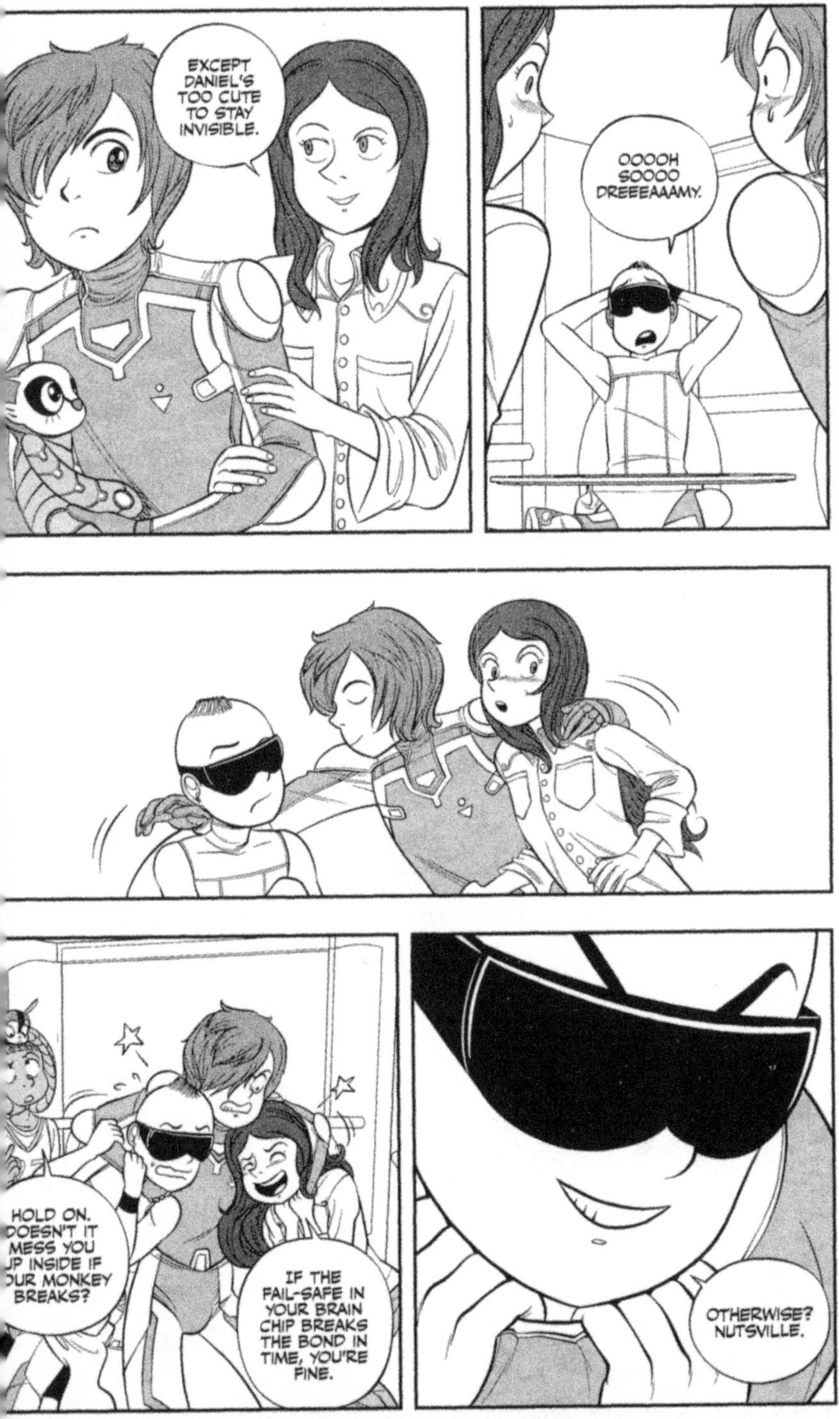
EXCEPT DANIEL'S TOO CUTE TO STAY INVISIBLE.
OOOOH SOOOO DREEEAAAMY.
HOLD ON. DOESN'T IT MESS YOU UP INSIDE IF OUR MONKEY BREAKS?
IF THE FAIL-SAFE IN YOUR BRAIN CHIP BREAKS THE BOND IN TIME, YOU'RE FINE.
OTHERWISE? NUTSVILLE.

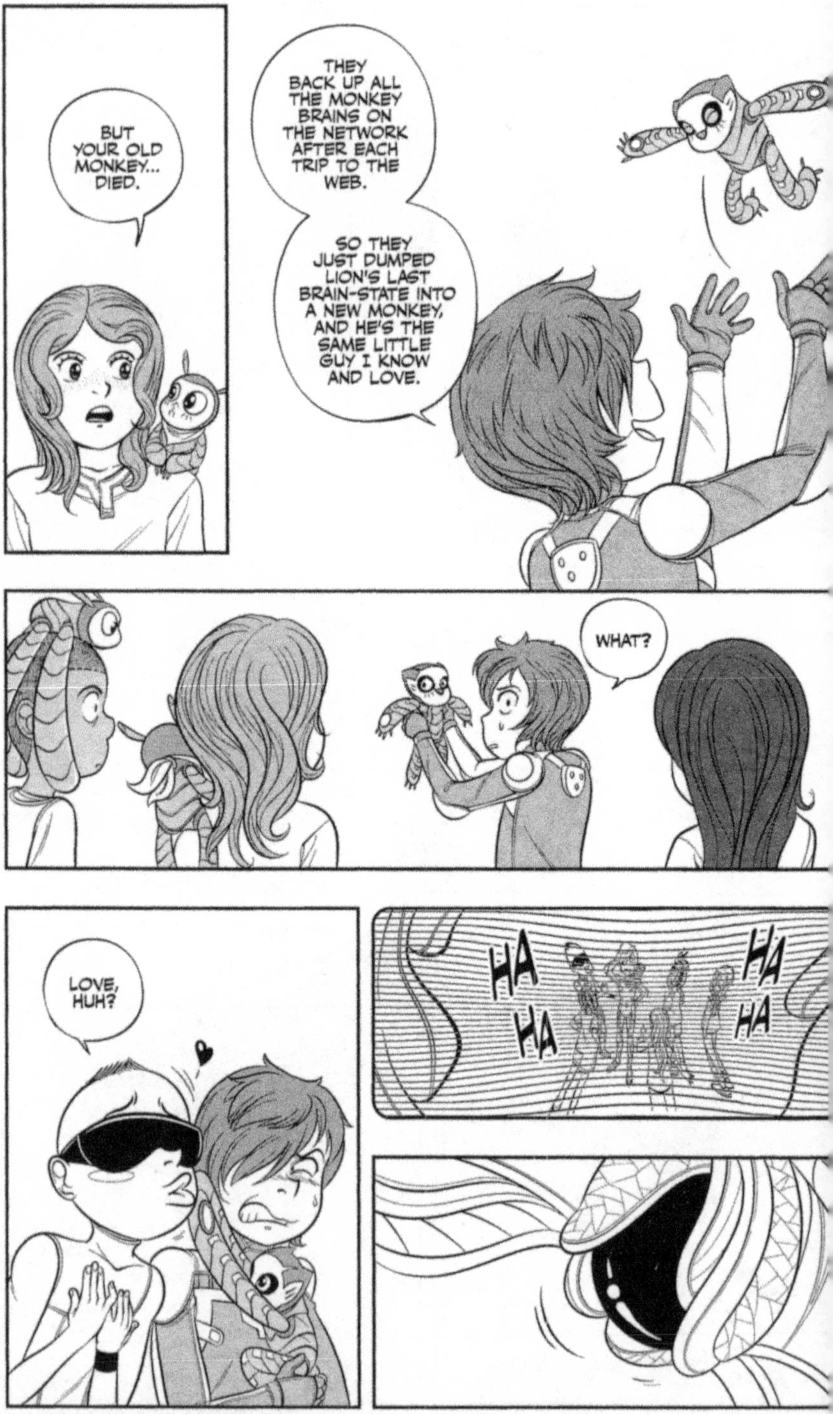
BUT YOUR OLD MONKEY... DIED.
THEY BACK UP ALL THE MONKEY BRAINS ON THE NETWORK AFTER EACH TRIP TO THE WEB.
SO THEY JUST DUMPED LION'S LAST BRAIN-STATE INTO A NEW MONKEY, AND HE'S THE SAME LITTLE GUY I KNOW AND LOVE.
WHAT?
LOVE, HUH?
HA HA
HA HA

I MIGHT AS WELL RUN A SUMMER CAMP.

I OFTEN WONDER WHY THE GIVERS DESIGNED THE WEB TUBES SO THAT ONLY CHILDREN COULD USE THEM.

...SIR--

I *AM* GLAD YOU DECIDED TO ACCEPT THE IMPLANT AND REMAIN HERE.

I STILL THINK THERE SHOULD BE A BETTER PLAN THAN THIS KID/ROBOT MIND-MELD THE GIVERS DUMPED ON US.

AH, FORGIVE ME, NINE. YOU'RE A MATURE EXCEPTION AMONG YOUR PEERS.

I AGREE. BUT LIKE I TOLD YOU BEFORE, IF YOU CRITICIZE THE GIVERS, IT UPSETS PEOPLE. YOU GET SHUT OUT OF THE SYSTEM.

SO YOU'RE GOING TO CHANGE THINGS?

...WORKING ...N IT. THERE ...E ALREADY ...NGES FROM ...OTHER SIDE. ...ROM THE ...GIVERS.

THEY'RE BACK?

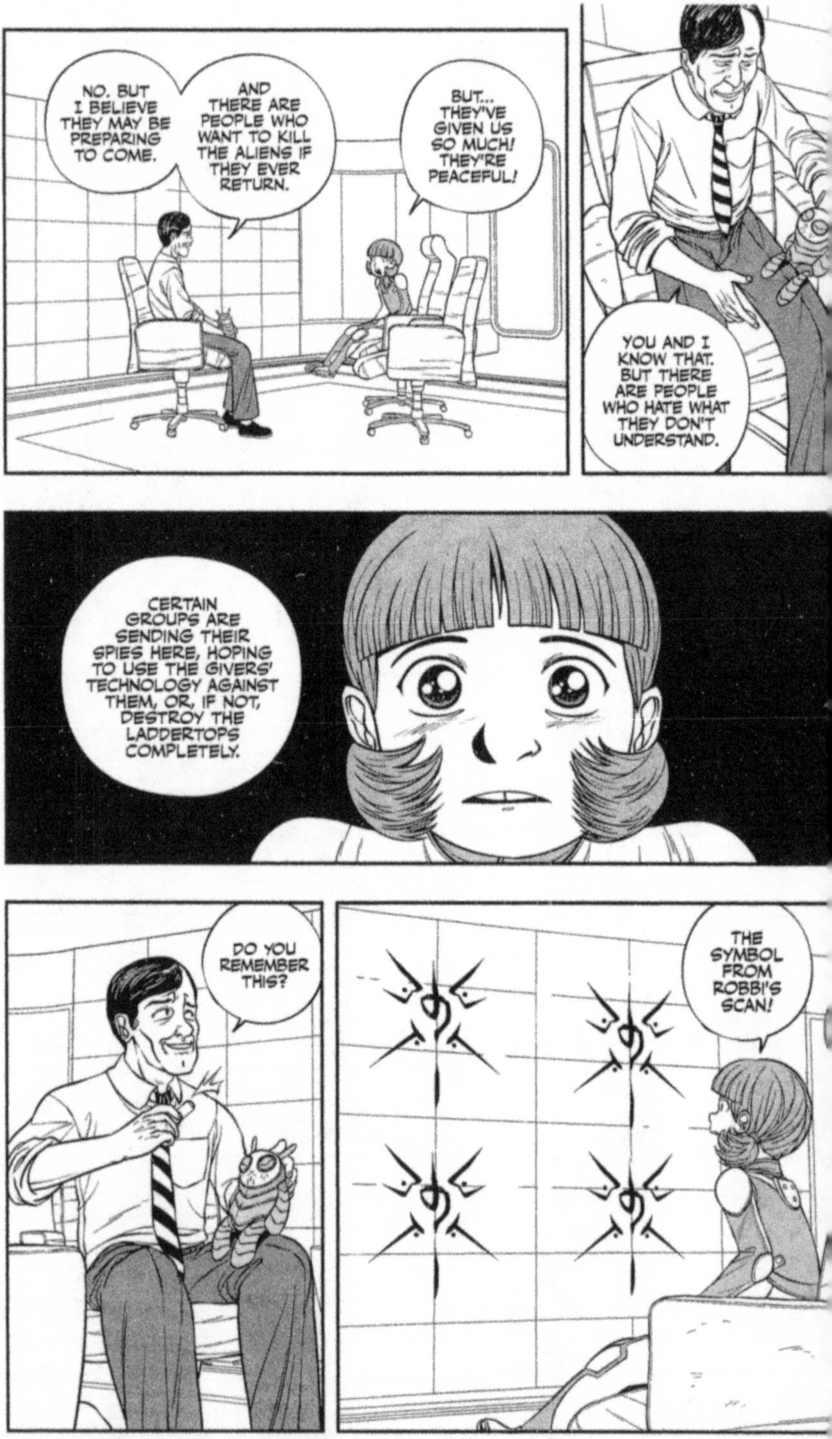
NO. BUT I BELIEVE THEY MAY BE PREPARING TO COME.
AND THERE ARE PEOPLE WHO WANT TO KILL THE ALIENS IF THEY EVER RETURN.
BUT... THEY'VE GIVEN US SO MUCH! THEY'RE PEACEFUL!
YOU AND I KNOW THAT. BUT THERE ARE PEOPLE WHO HATE WHAT THEY DON'T UNDERSTAND.
CERTAIN GROUPS ARE SENDING THEIR SPIES HERE, HOPING TO USE THE GIVERS' TECHNOLOGY AGAINST THEM, OR, IF NOT, DESTROY THE LADDERTOPS COMPLETELY.
DO YOU REMEMBER THIS?
THE SYMBOL FROM ROBBI'S SCAN!

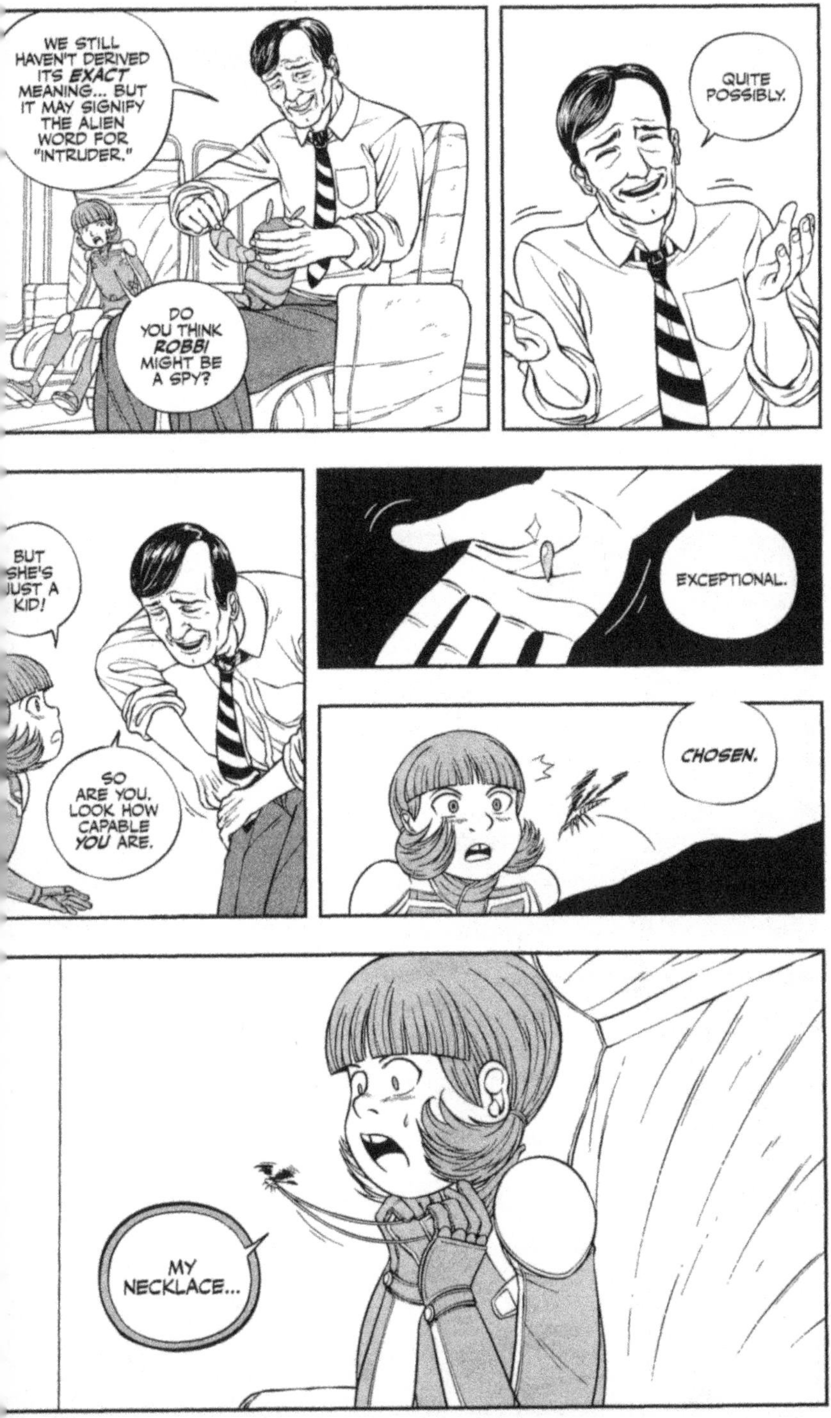
WE STILL HAVEN'T DERIVED ITS *EXACT* MEANING... BUT IT MAY SIGNIFY THE ALIEN WORD FOR "INTRUDER."
DO YOU THINK *ROBBI* MIGHT BE A SPY?
QUITE POSSIBLY.
BUT SHE'S JUST A KID!
SO ARE YOU. LOOK HOW CAPABLE *YOU* ARE.
EXCEPTIONAL.
CHOSEN.
MY NECKLACE...

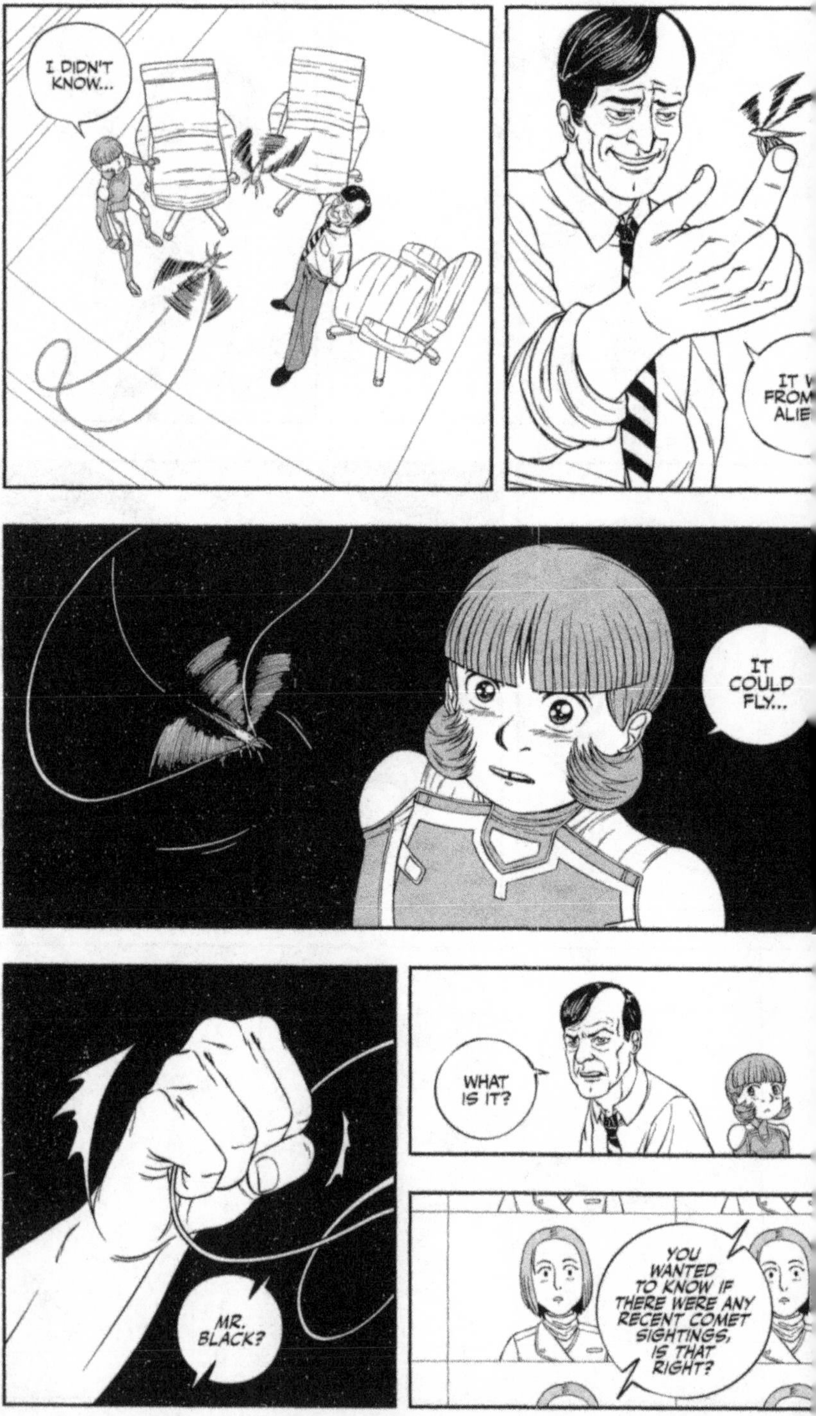
I DIDN'T KNOW...
IT W FROM ALIE
IT COULD FLY...
MR. BLACK?
WHAT IS IT?
YOU WANTED TO KNOW IF THERE WERE ANY RECENT COMET SIGHTINGS, IS THAT RIGHT?

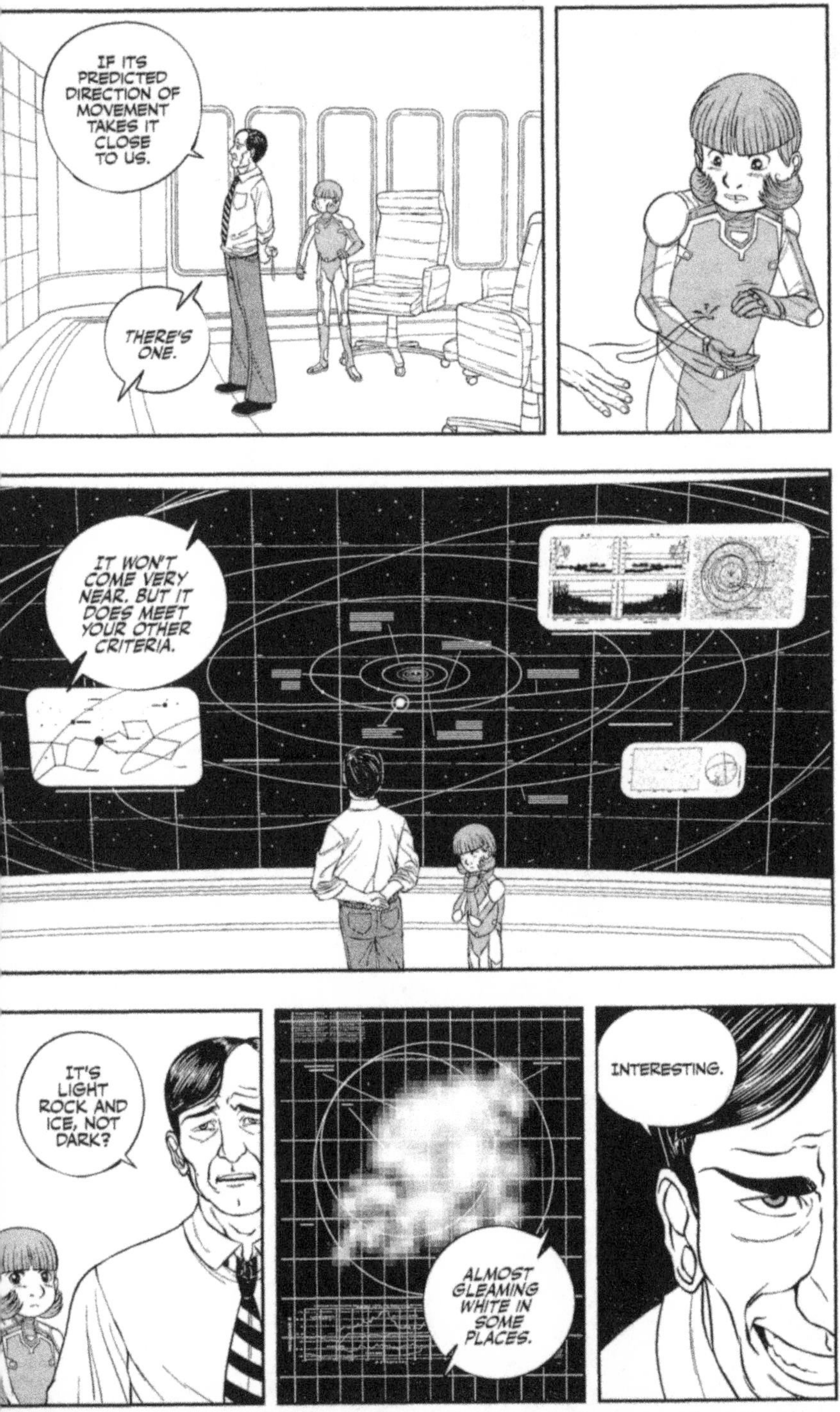
IF ITS PREDICTED DIRECTION OF MOVEMENT TAKES IT CLOSE TO US.
THERE'S ONE.
IT WON'T COME VERY NEAR. BUT IT DOES MEET YOUR OTHER CRITERIA.
IT'S LIGHT ROCK AND ICE, NOT DARK?
ALMOST GLEAMING WHITE IN SOME PLACES.
INTERESTING.

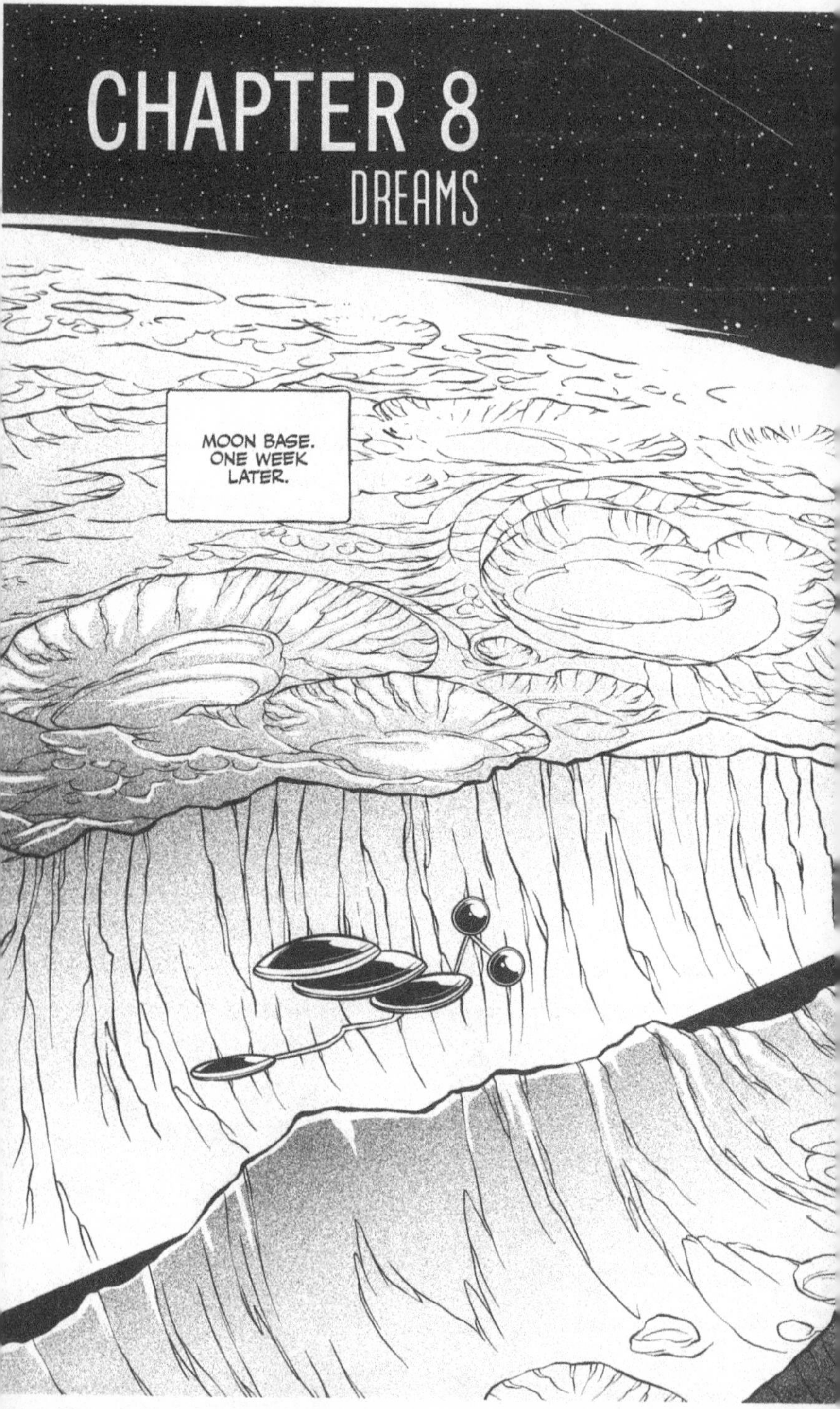
CHAPTER 8
DREAMS
MOON BASE. ONE WEEK LATER.

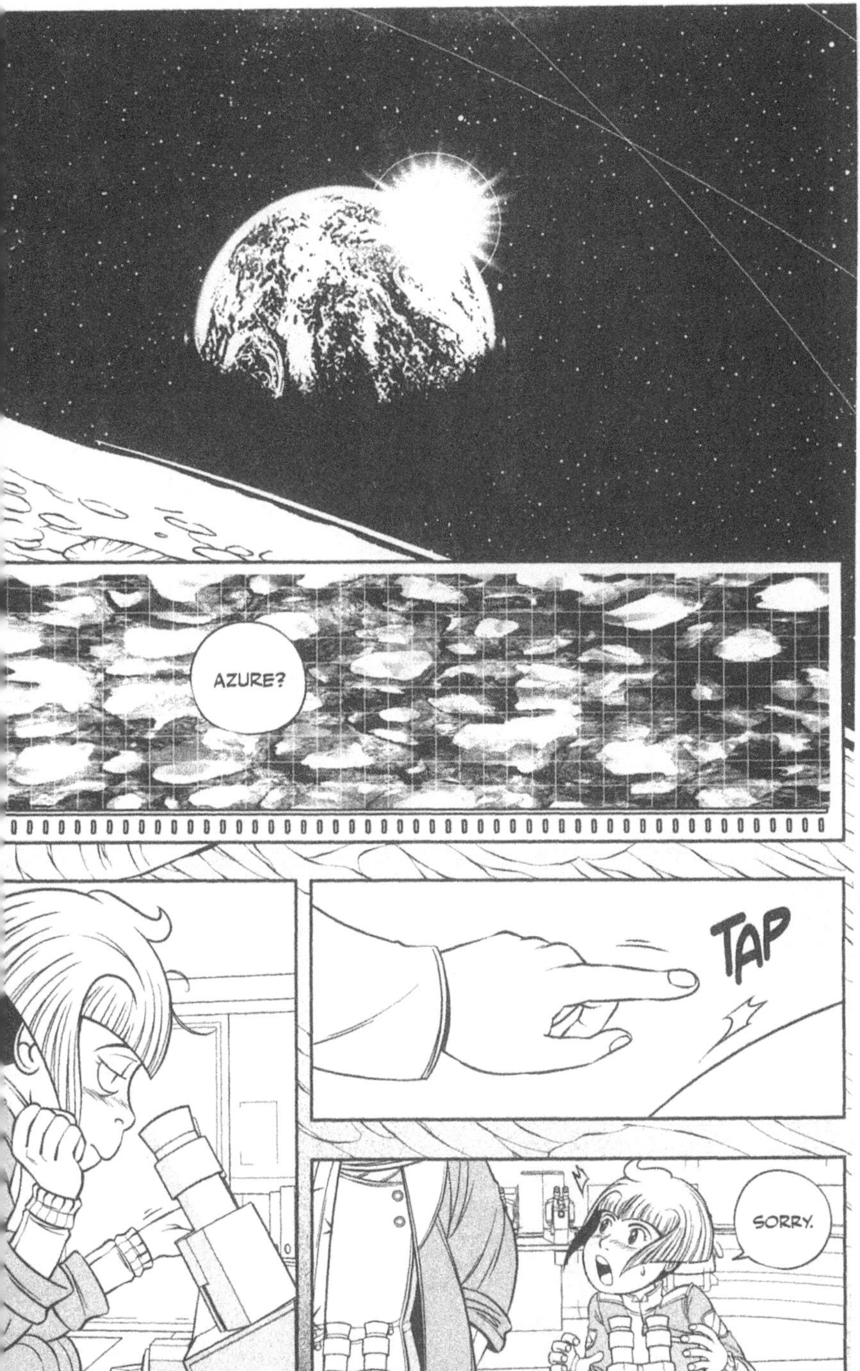
AZURE?
TAP
SORRY.

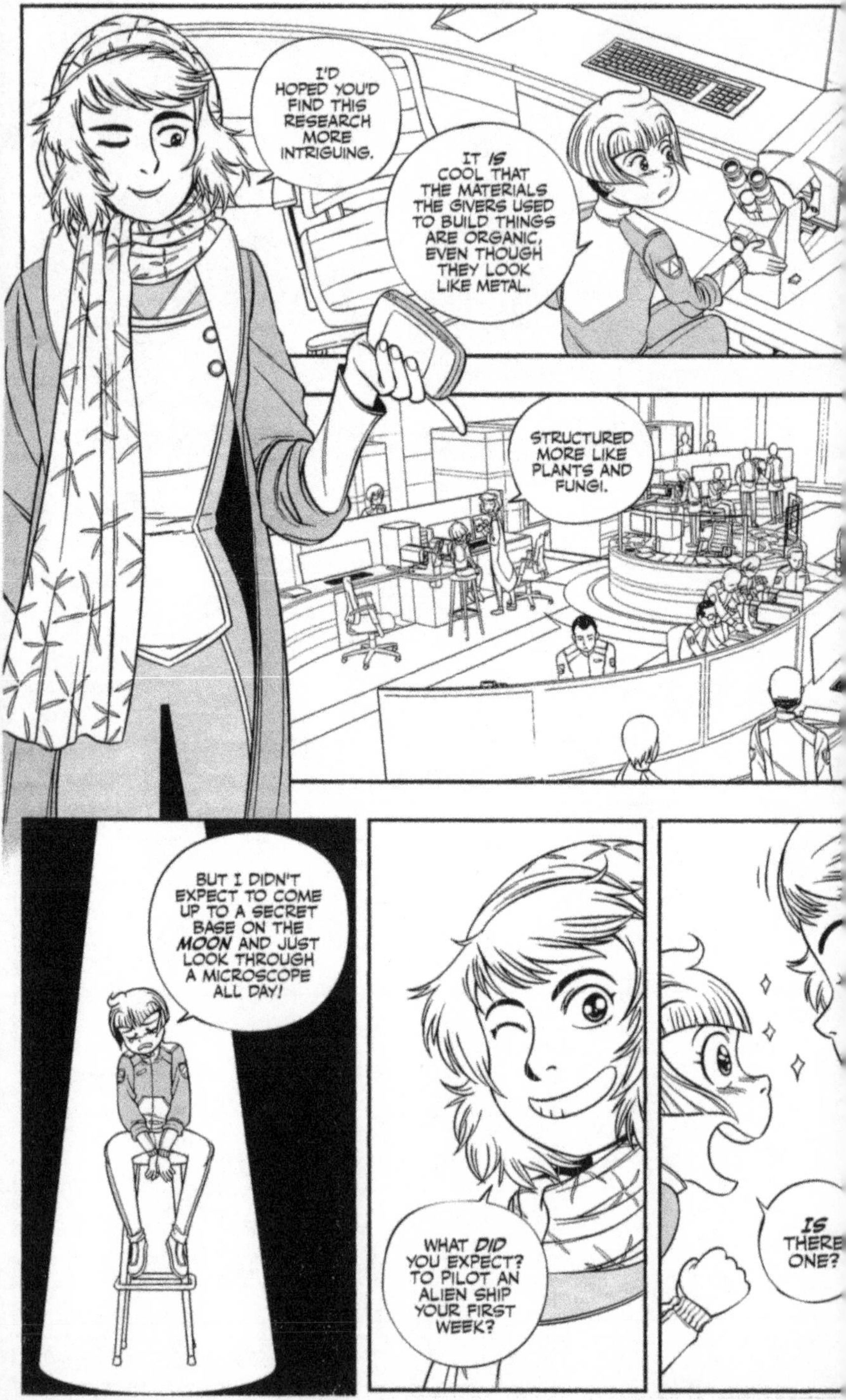
I'D HOPED YOU'D FIND THIS RESEARCH MORE INTRIGUING.
IT *IS* COOL THAT THE MATERIALS THE GIVERS USED TO BUILD THINGS ARE ORGANIC, EVEN THOUGH THEY LOOK LIKE METAL.
STRUCTURED MORE LIKE PLANTS AND FUNGI.
BUT I DIDN'T EXPECT TO COME UP TO A SECRET BASE ON THE *MOON* AND JUST LOOK THROUGH A MICROSCOPE ALL DAY!
WHAT *DID* YOU EXPECT? TO PILOT AN ALIEN SHIP YOUR FIRST WEEK?
IS THERE ONE?

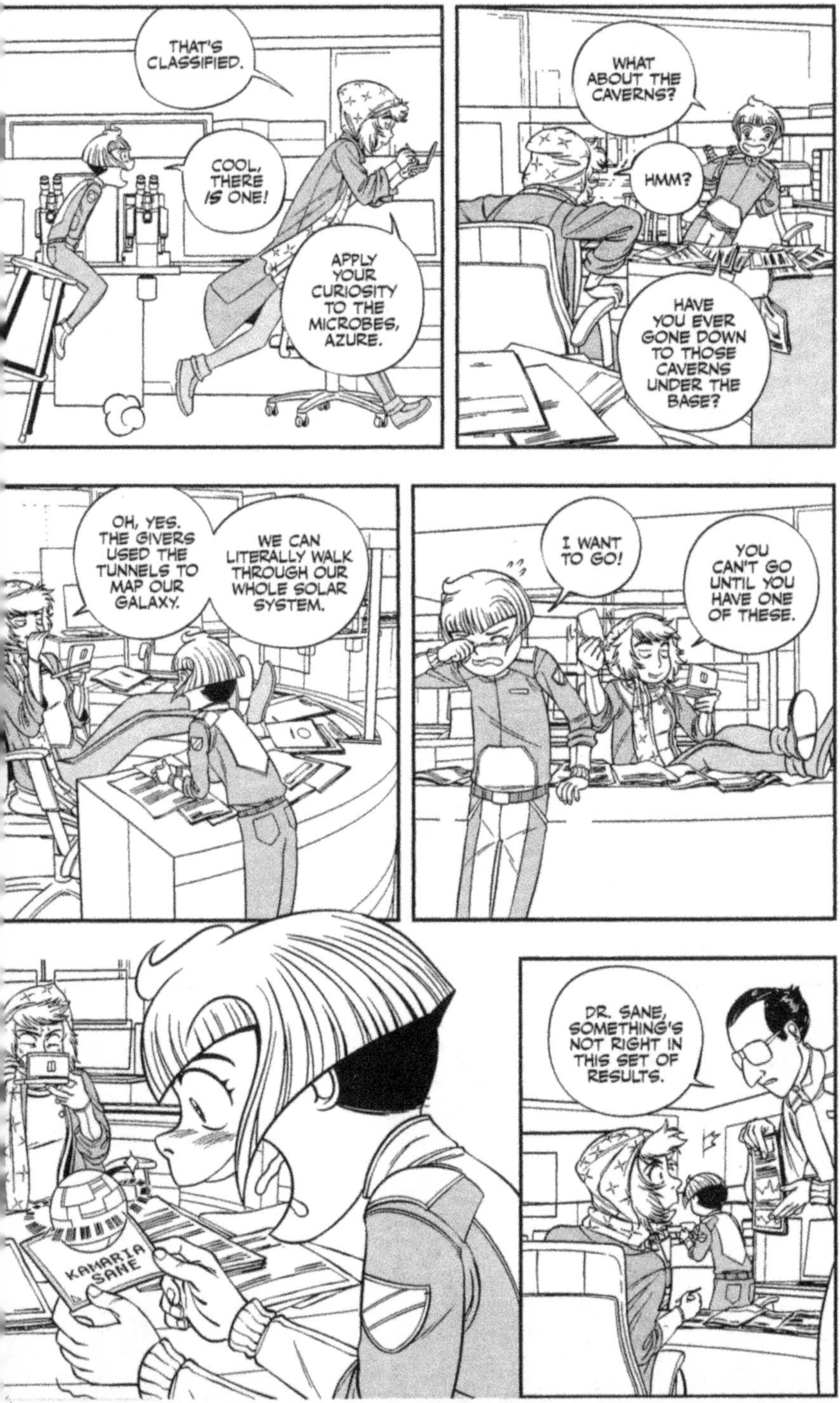
THAT'S CLASSIFIED.
COOL, THERE *IS* ONE!
APPLY YOUR CURIOSITY TO THE MICROBES, AZURE.
WHAT ABOUT THE CAVERNS?
HMM?
HAVE YOU EVER GONE DOWN TO THOSE CAVERNS UNDER THE BASE?
OH, YES. THE GIVERS USED THE TUNNELS TO MAP OUR GALAXY.
WE CAN LITERALLY WALK THROUGH OUR WHOLE SOLAR SYSTEM.
10
I WANT TO GO!
YOU CAN'T GO UNTIL YOU HAVE ONE OF THESE.
KAMARIA SANE
DR. SANE, SOMETHING'S NOT RIGHT IN THIS SET OF RESULTS.

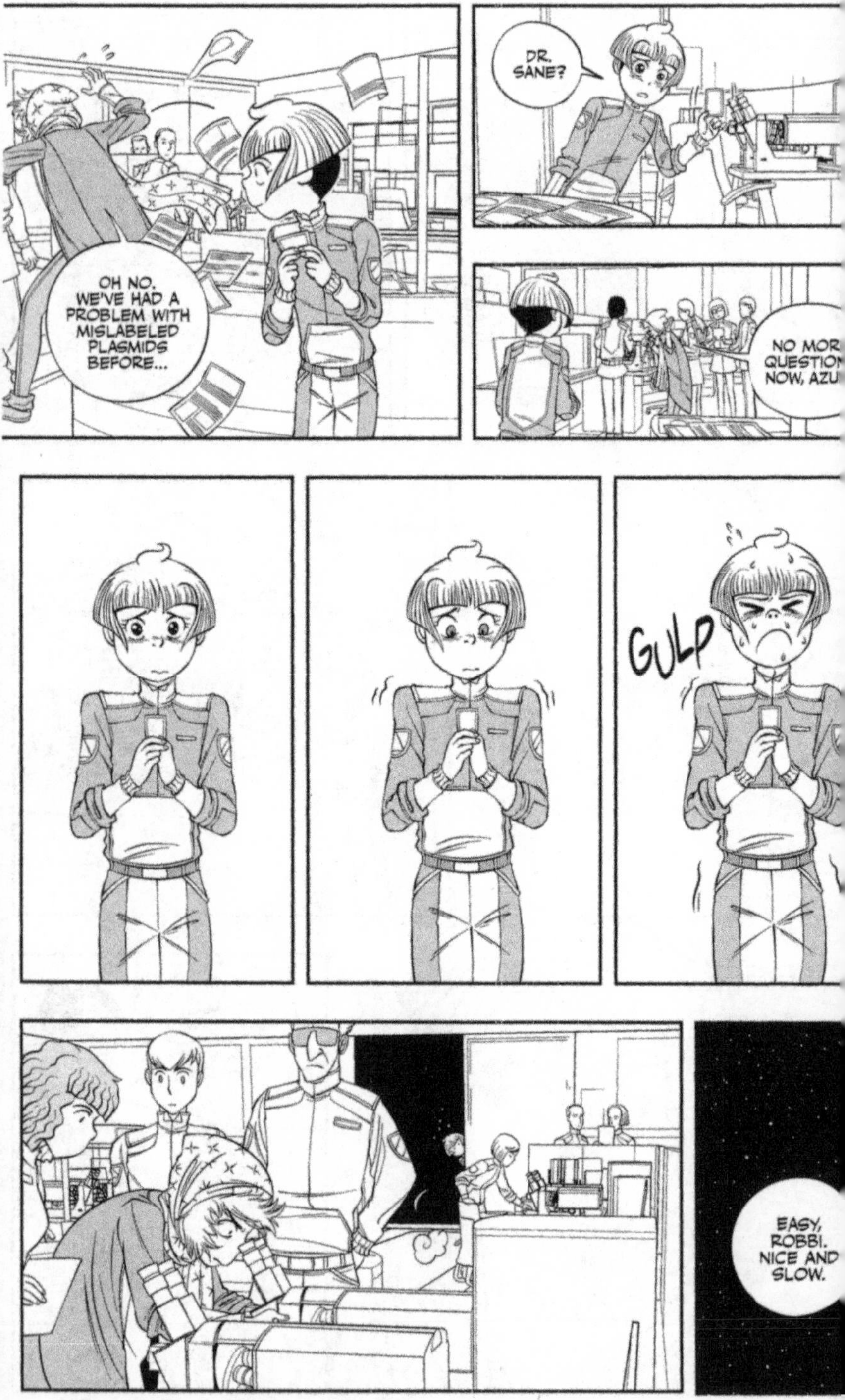
OH NO. WE'VE HAD A PROBLEM WITH MISLABELED PLASMIDS BEFORE...
DR. SANE?
NO MOR QUESTION NOW, AZU
GULP
EASY, ROBBI. NICE AND SLOW.

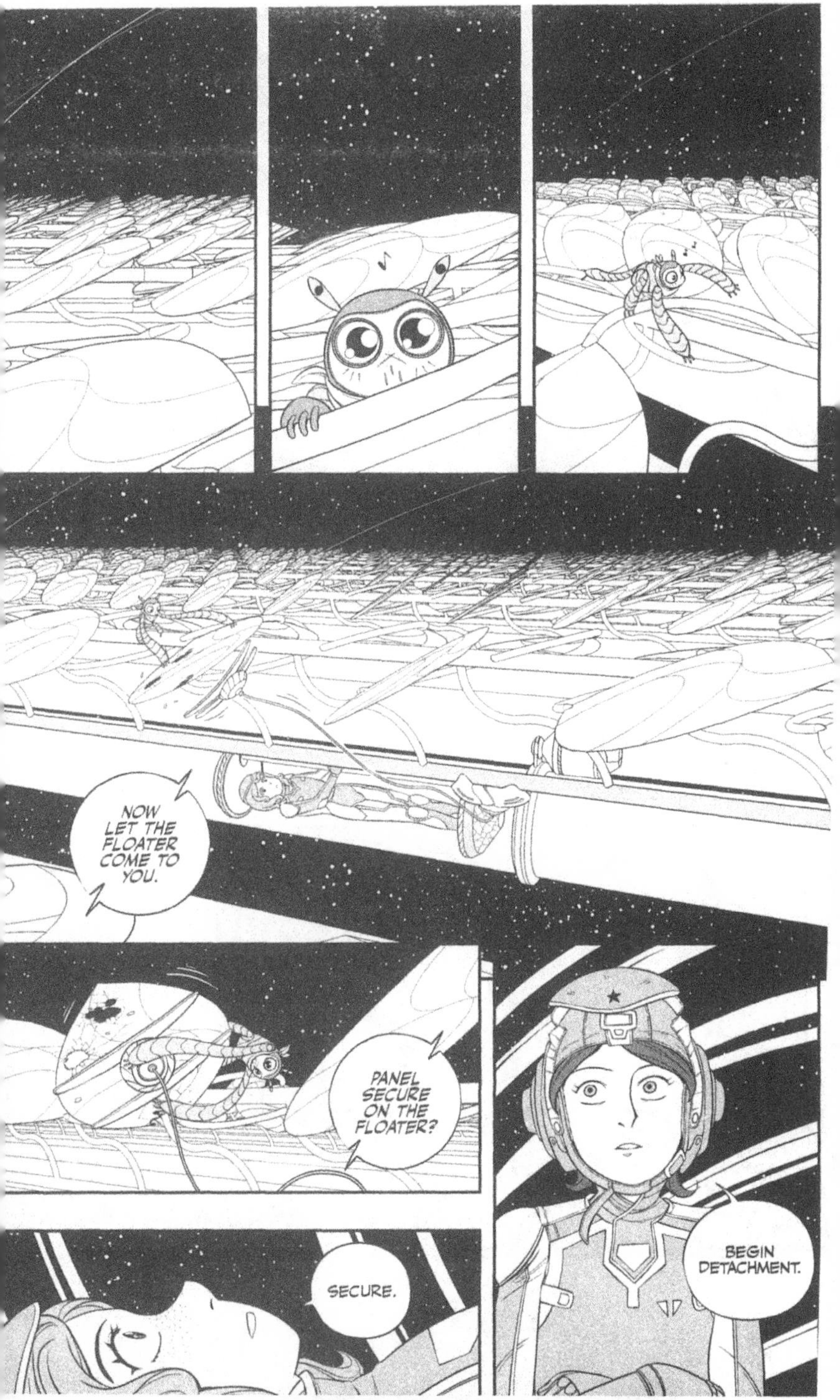
NOW LET THE FLOATER COME TO YOU.
PANEL SECURE ON THE FLOATER?
SECURE.
BEGIN DETACHMENT.

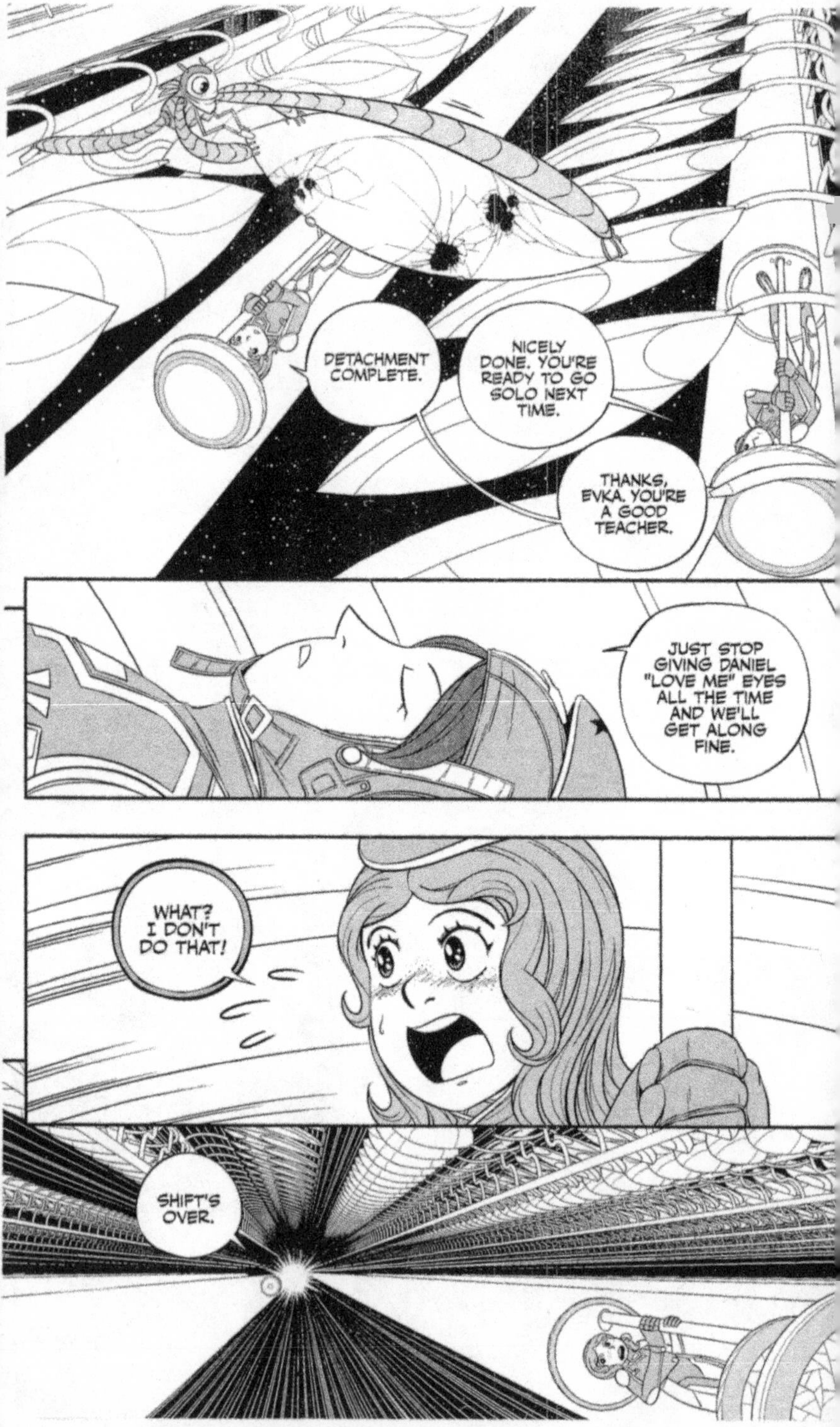
DETACHMENT COMPLETE.
NICELY DONE. YOU'RE READY TO GO SOLO NEXT TIME.
THANKS, EVKA. YOU'RE A GOOD TEACHER.
JUST STOP GIVING DANIEL "LOVE ME" EYES ALL THE TIME AND WE'LL GET ALONG FINE.
WHAT? I DON'T DO THAT!
SHIFT'S OVER.

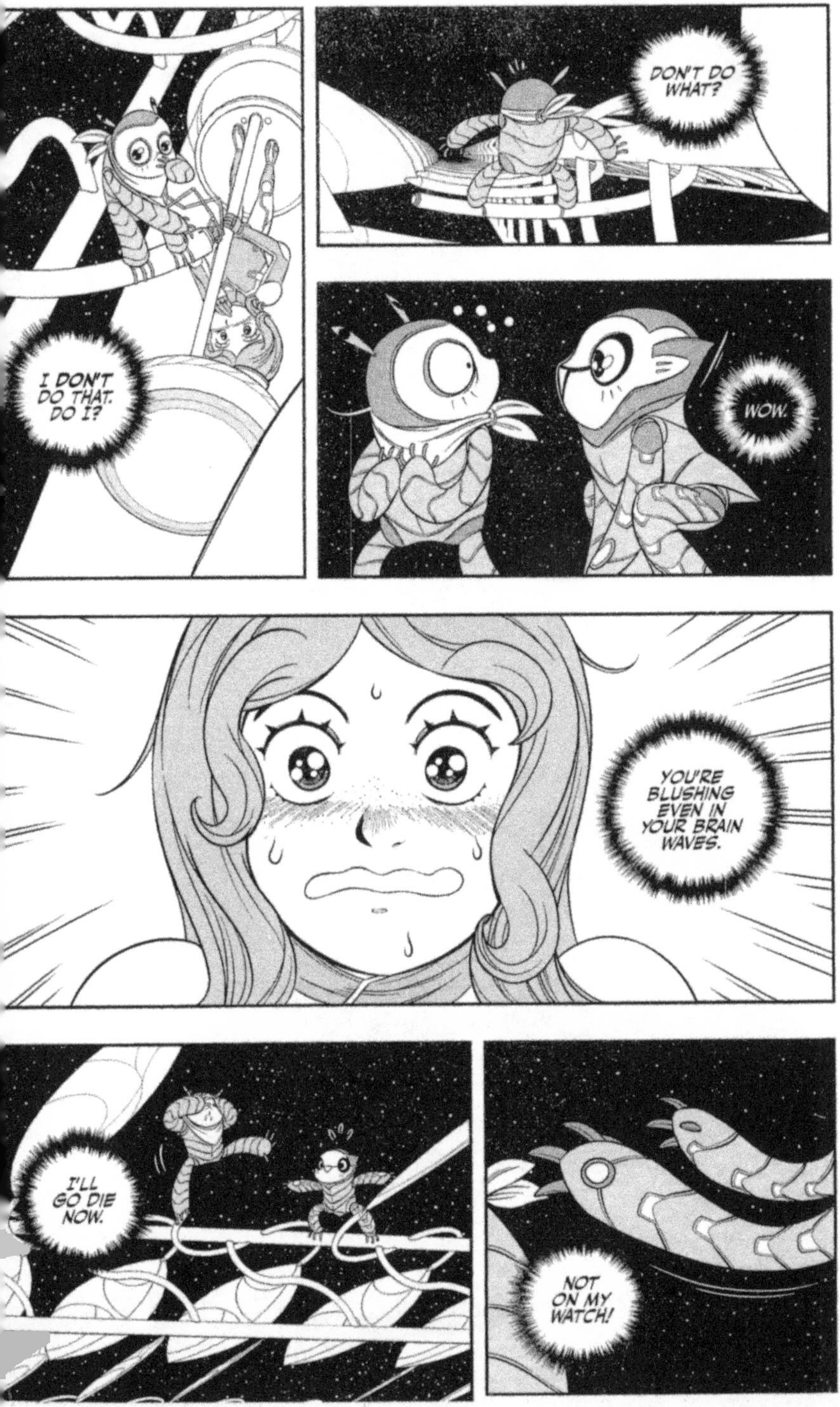
I DON'T DO THAT. DO I?
DON'T DO WHAT?
WOW.
YOU'RE BLUSHING EVEN IN YOUR BRAIN WAVES.
I'LL GO DIE NOW.
NOT ON MY WATCH!

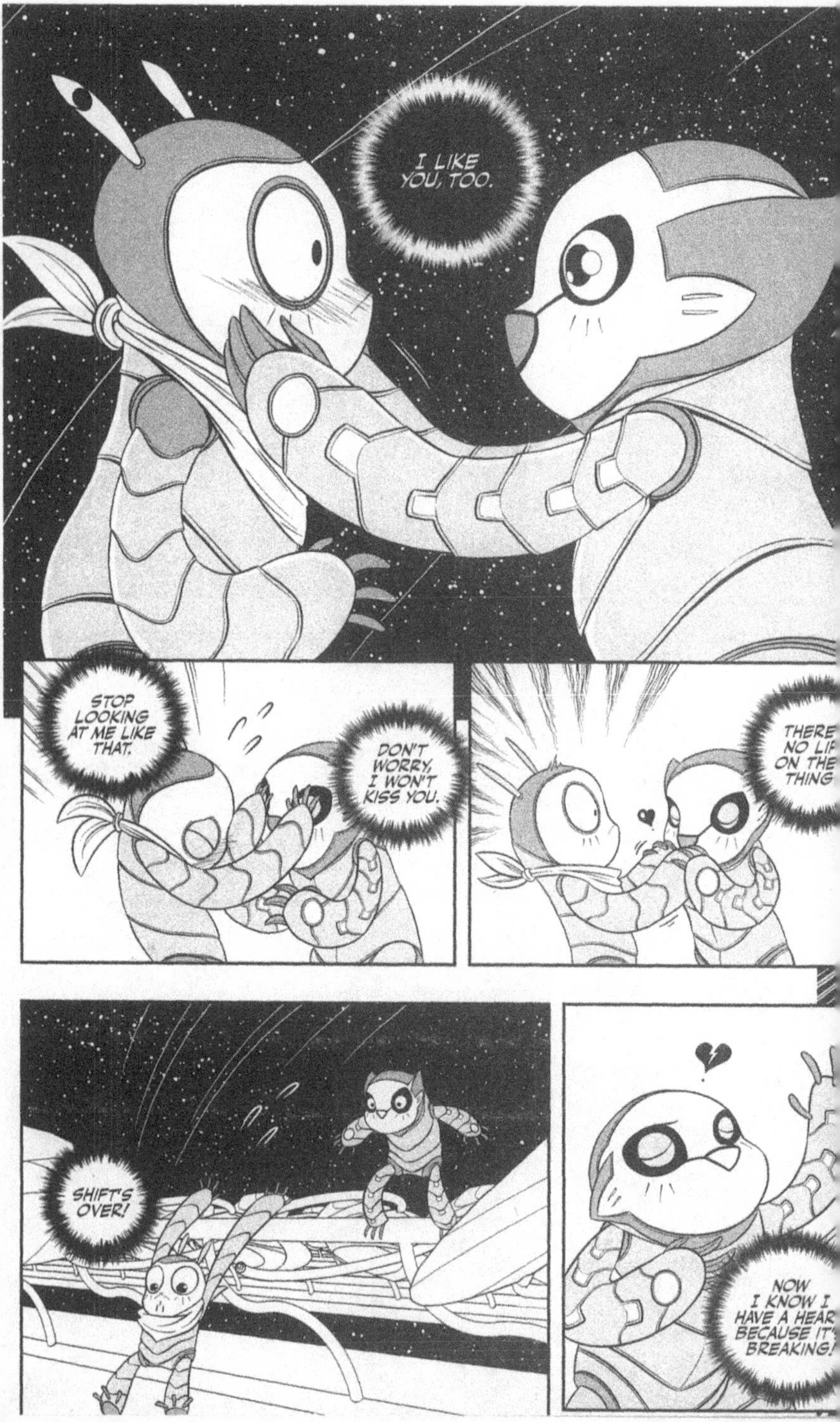
I LIKE YOU, TOO.
STOP LOOKING AT ME LIKE THAT.
DON'T WORRY, I WON'T KISS YOU.
THERE NO LI ON THE THING
SHIFT'S OVER!
NOW I KNOW I HAVE A HEAR BECAUSE IT' BREAKING!

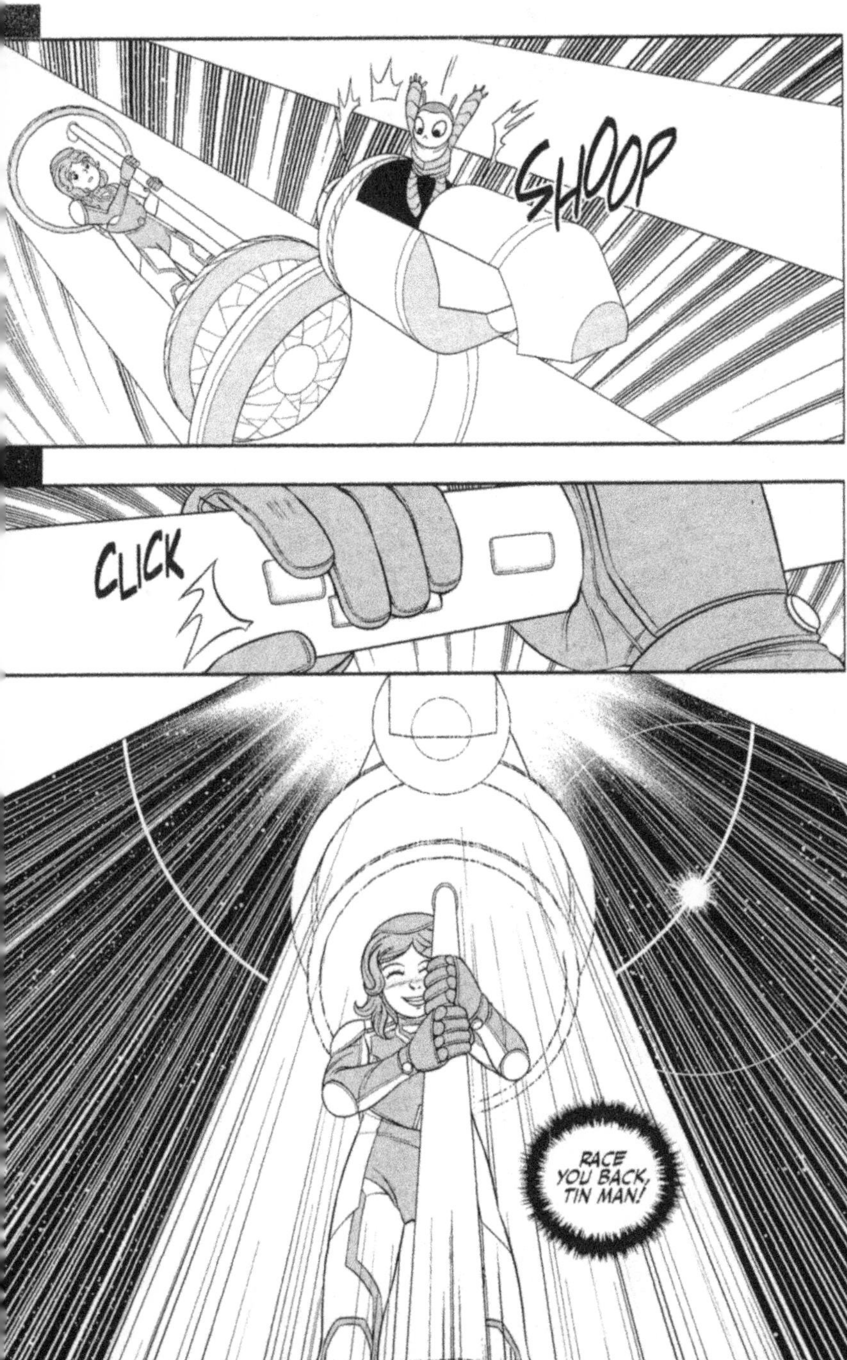
SHOOP
CLICK
RACE YOU BACK, TIN MAN!

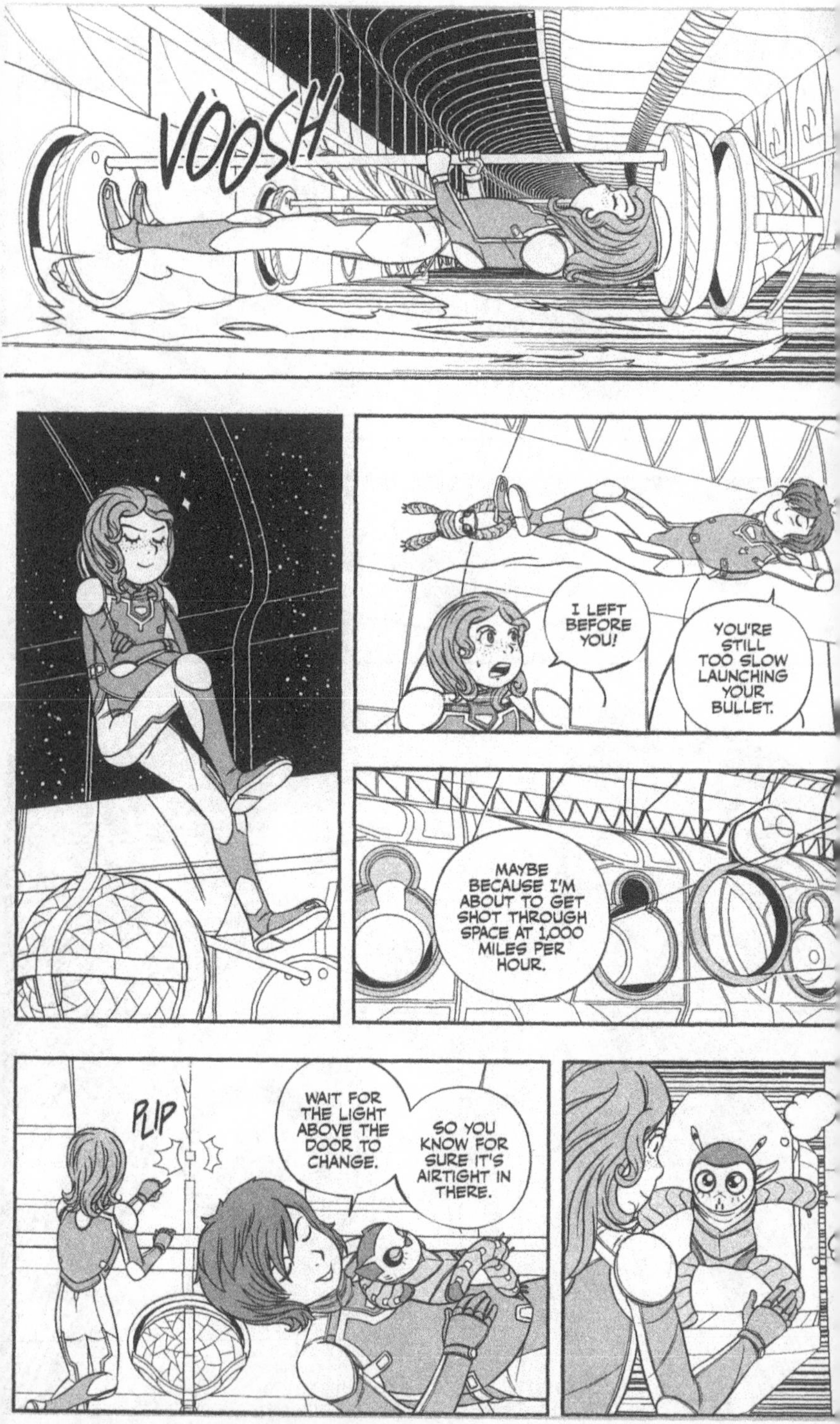
VOOSH
I LEFT BEFORE YOU!
YOU'RE STILL TOO SLOW LAUNCHING YOUR BULLET.
MAYBE BECAUSE I'M ABOUT TO GET SHOT THROUGH SPACE AT 1,000 MILES PER HOUR.
PLIP
WAIT FOR THE LIGHT ABOVE THE DOOR TO CHANGE.
SO YOU KNOW FOR SURE IT'S AIRTIGHT IN THERE.

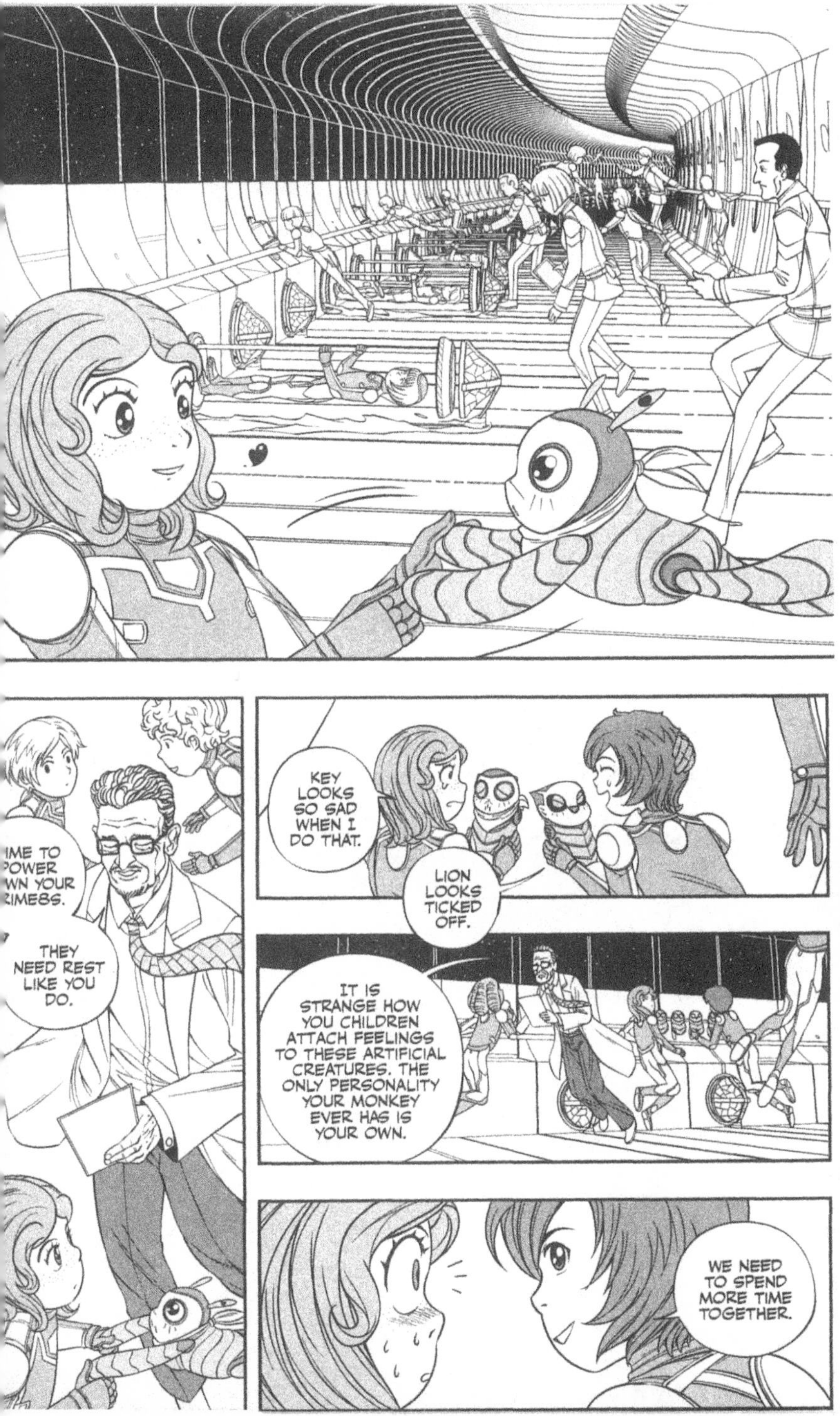
IME TO POWER WN YOUR ZIMEBS.
THEY NEED REST LIKE YOU DO.
KEY LOOKS SO SAD WHEN I DO THAT.
LION LOOKS TICKED OFF.
IT IS STRANGE HOW YOU CHILDREN ATTACH FEELINGS TO THESE ARTIFICIAL CREATURES. THE ONLY PERSONALITY YOUR MONKEY EVER HAS IS YOUR OWN.
WE NEED TO SPEND MORE TIME TOGETHER.

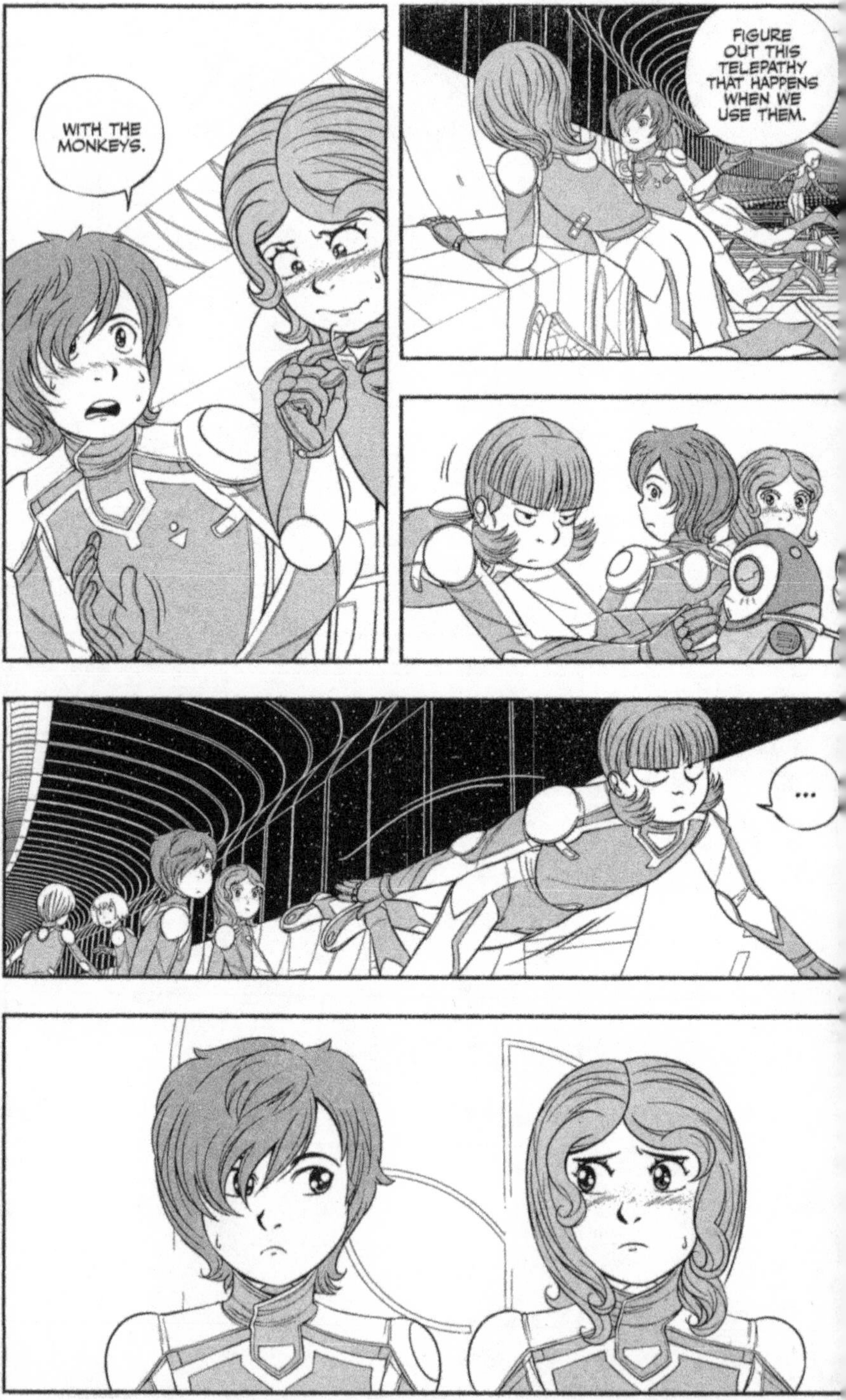
WITH THE MONKEYS.
FIGURE OUT THIS TELEPATHY THAT HAPPENS WHEN WE USE THEM.
...

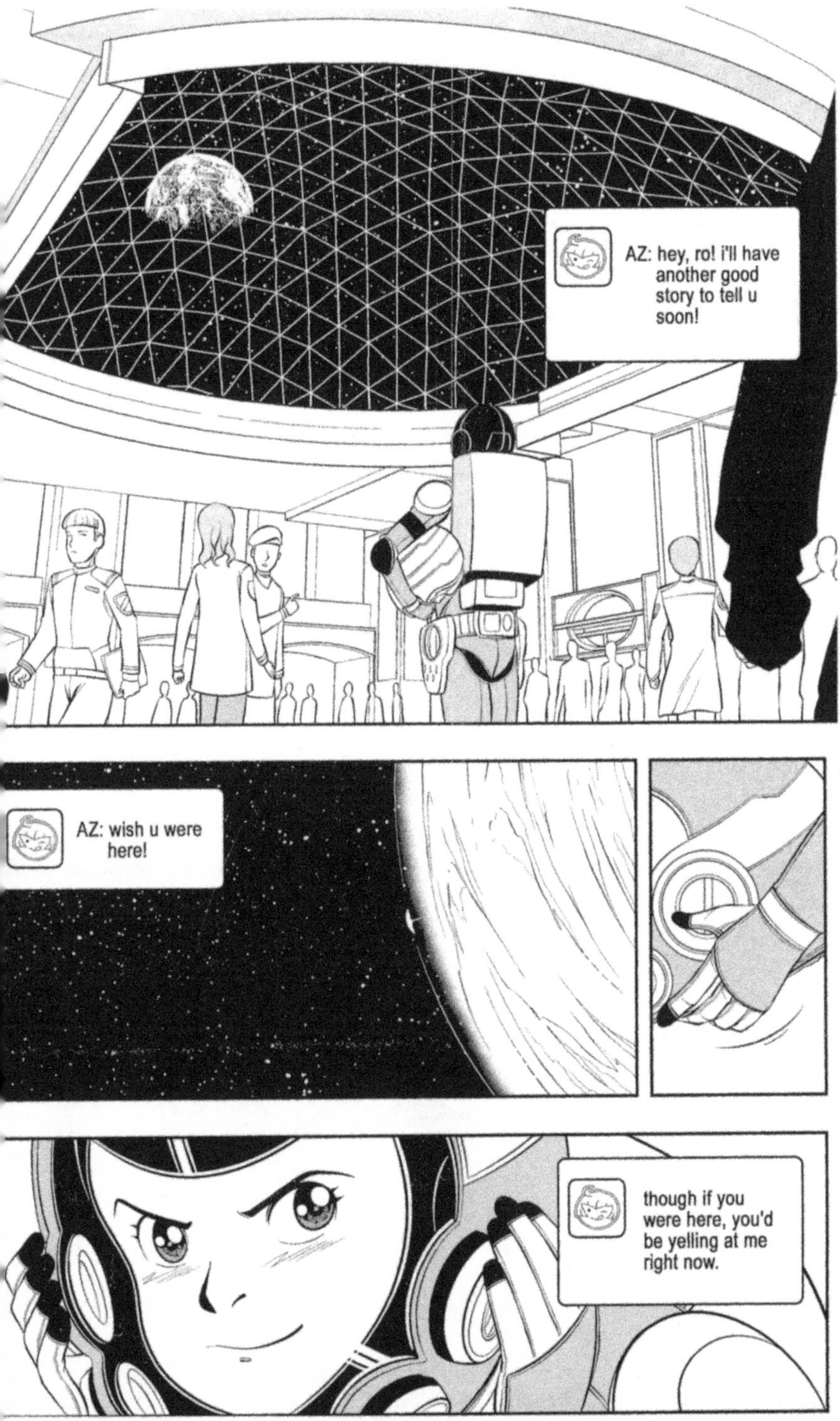
AZ: hey, ro! i'll have another good story to tell u soon!
AZ: wish u were here!
though if you were here, you'd be yelling at me right now.

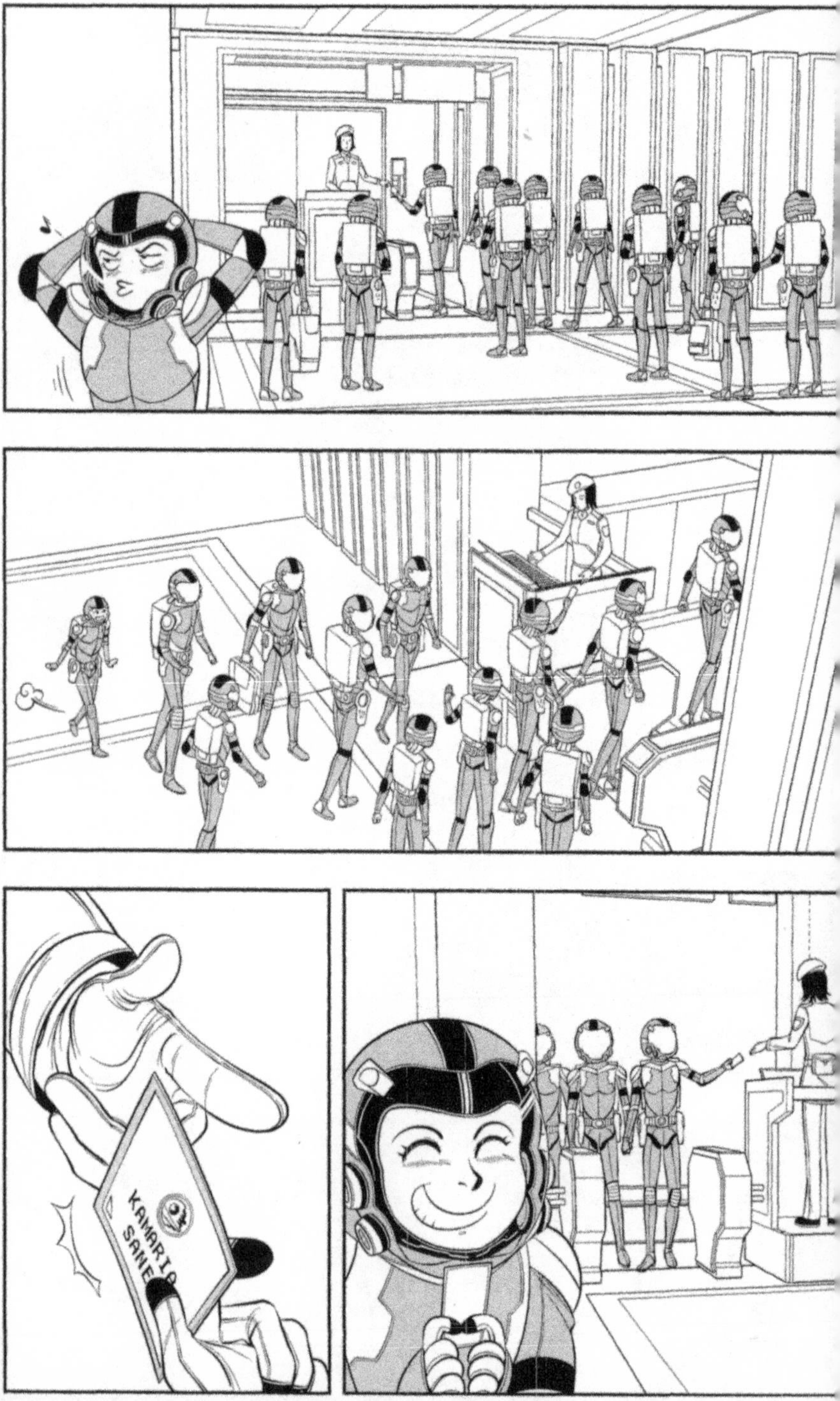
KAMARIA
SANE

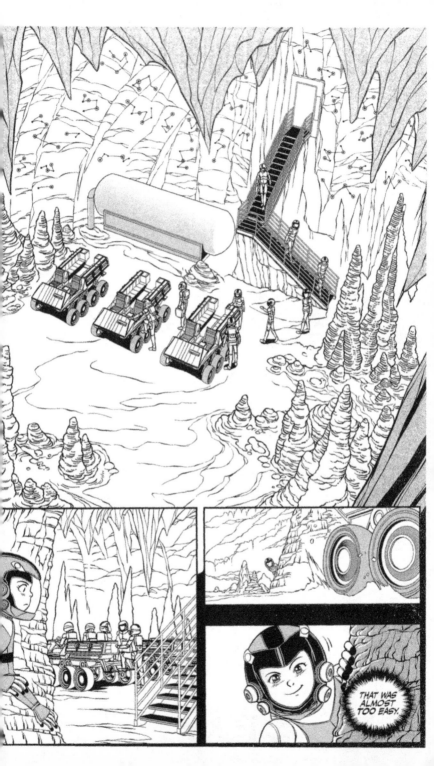

THAT WAS
ALMOST
TOO EASY.

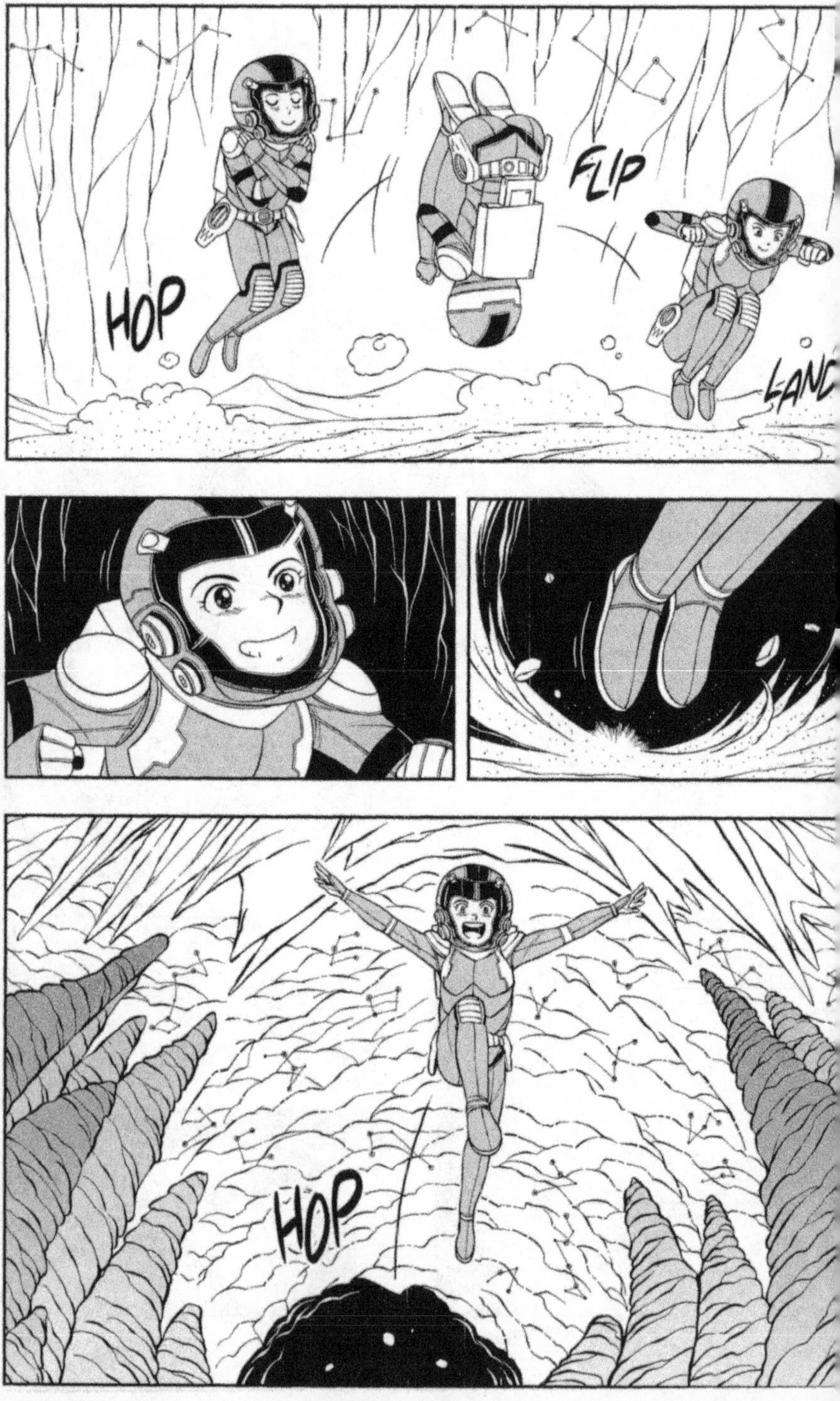
HOP
FLIP
LAND
HOP

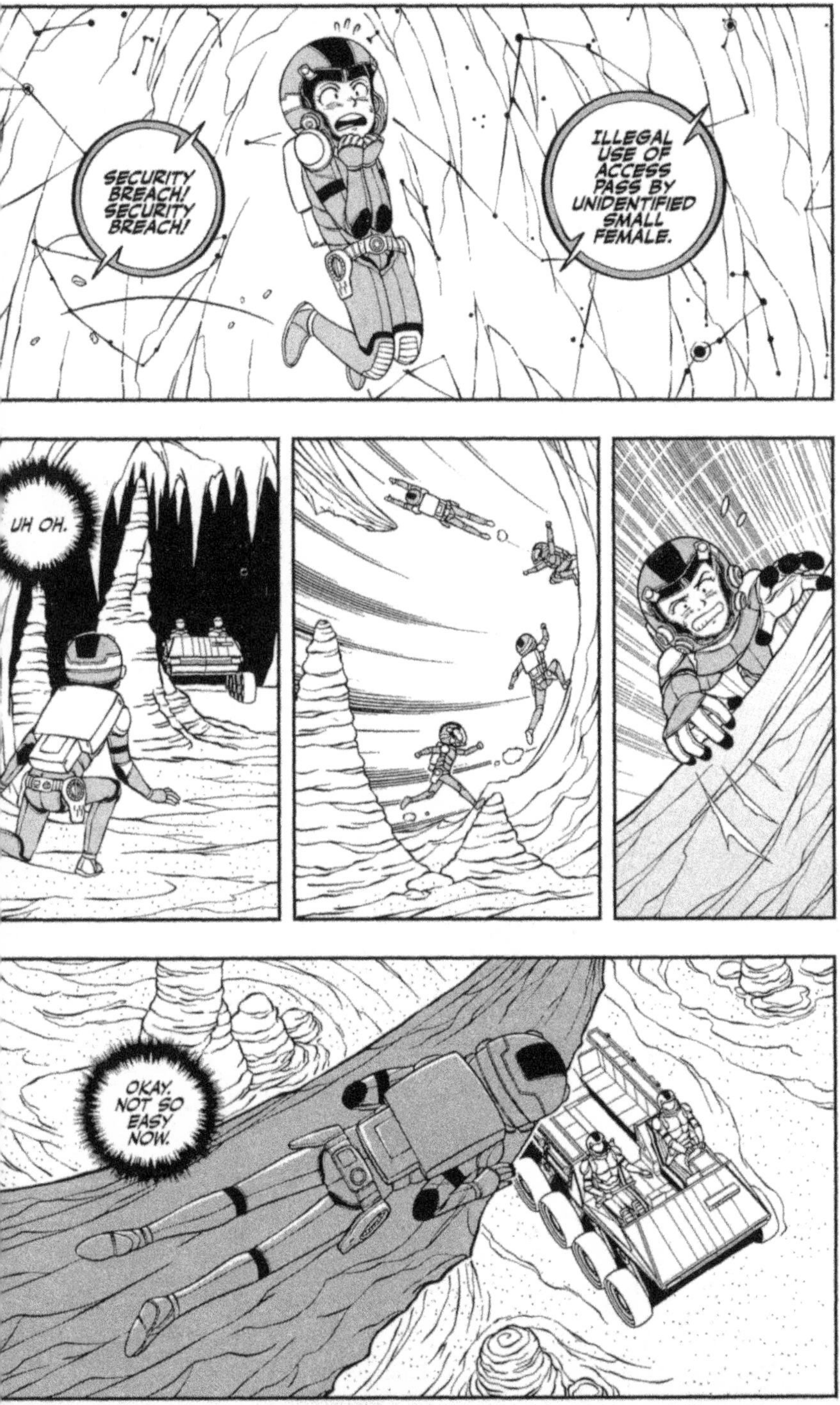
SECURITY BREACH! SECURITY BREACH!
ILLEGAL USE OF ACCESS PASS BY UNIDENTIFIED SMALL FEMALE.
UH OH.
OKAY. NOT SO EASY NOW.

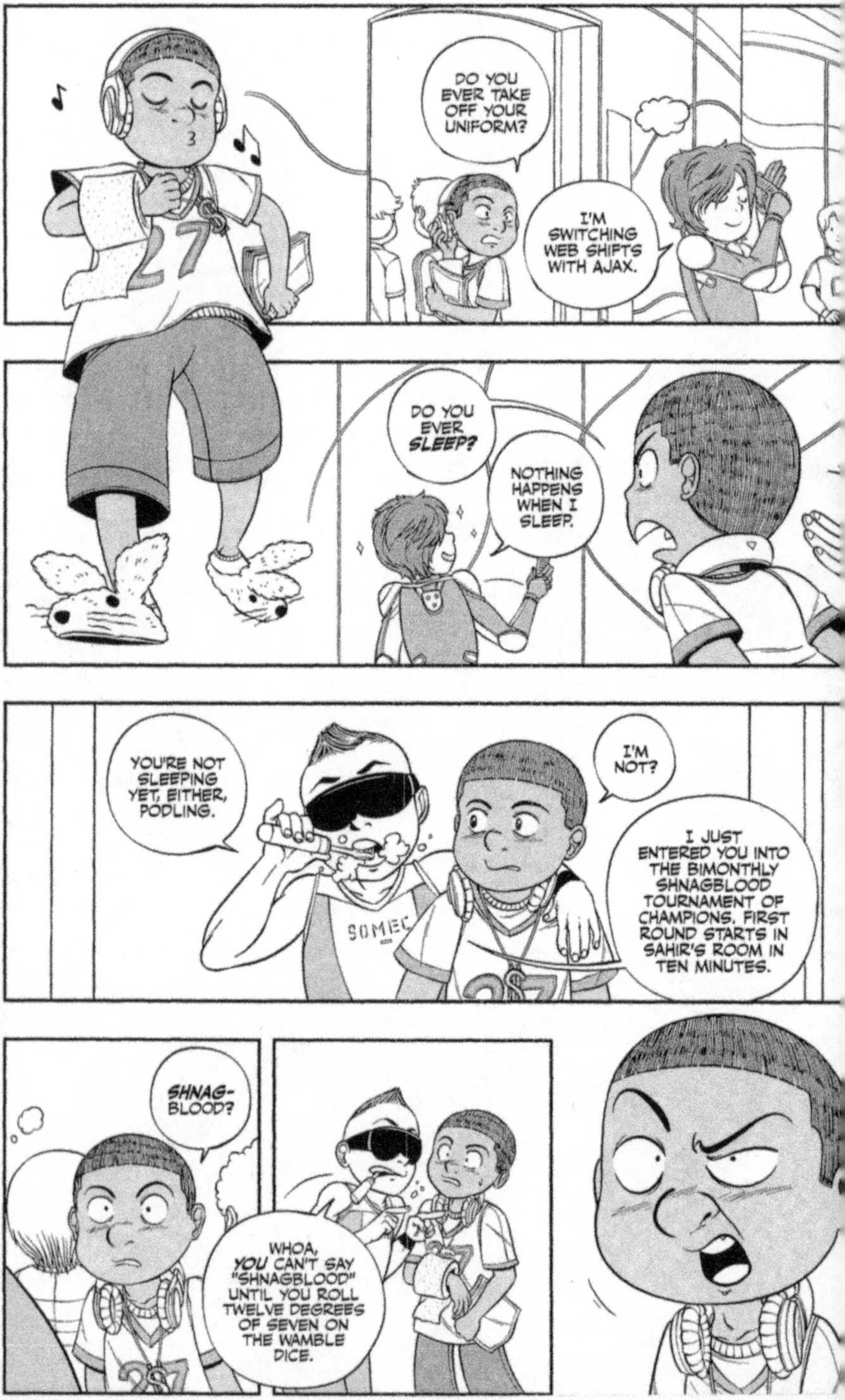
DO YOU EVER TAKE OFF YOUR UNIFORM?
I'M SWITCHING WEB SHIFTS WITH AJAX.
DO YOU EVER SLEEP?
NOTHING HAPPENS WHEN I SLEEP.
YOU'RE NOT SLEEPING YET, EITHER, PODLING.
I'M NOT?
I JUST ENTERED YOU INTO THE BIMONTHLY SHNAGBLOOD TOURNAMENT OF CHAMPIONS. FIRST ROUND STARTS IN SAHIR'S ROOM IN TEN MINUTES.
SHNAG-BLOOD?
WHOA, YOU CAN'T SAY "SHNAGBLOOD" UNTIL YOU ROLL TWELVE DEGREES OF SEVEN ON THE WAMBLE DICE.

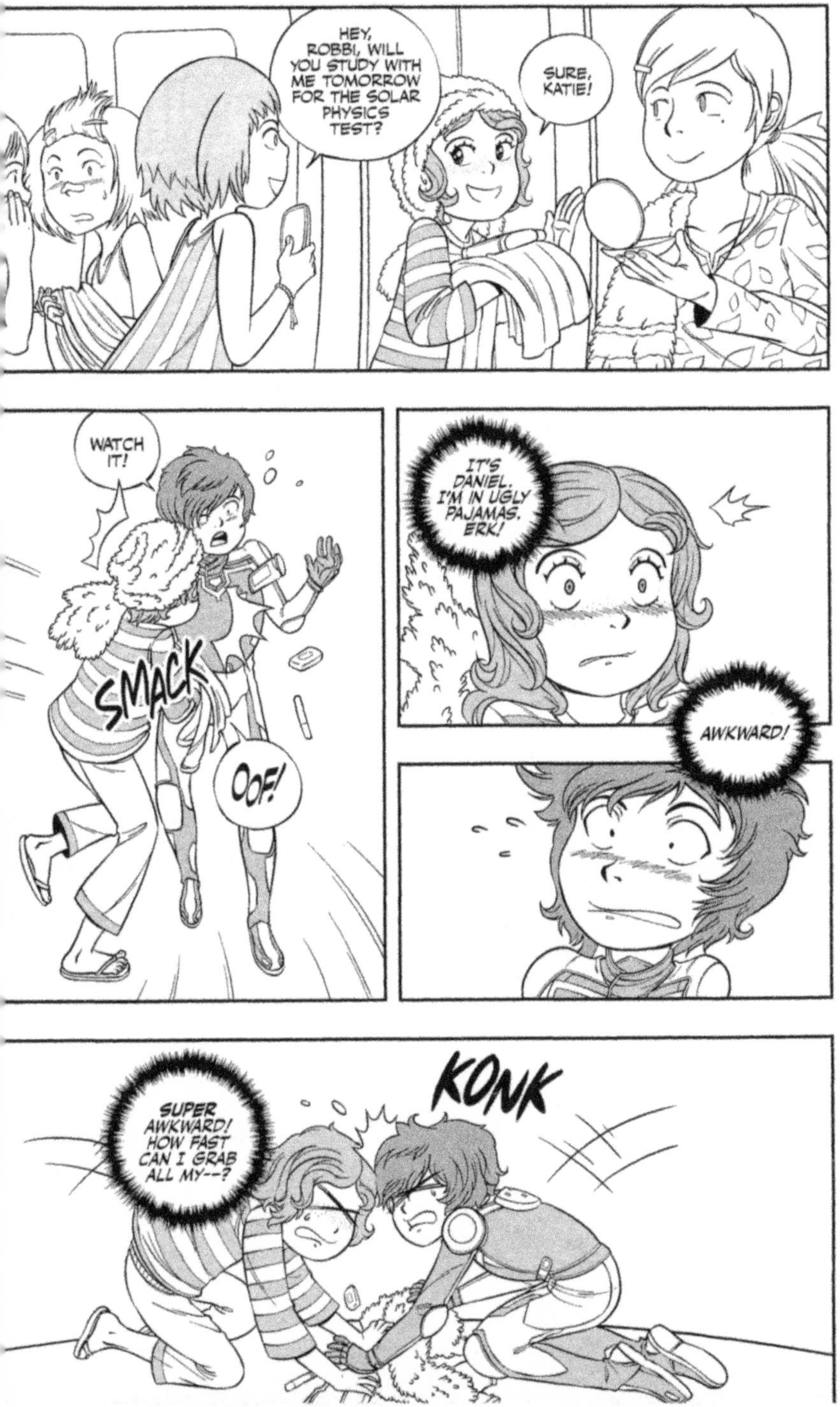
HEY, ROBBI, WILL YOU STUDY WITH ME TOMORROW FOR THE SOLAR PHYSICS TEST?
SURE, KATIE!
WATCH IT!
SMACK
OOF!
IT'S DANIEL. I'M IN UGLY PAJAMAS. ERK!
AWKWARD!
SUPER AWKWARD! HOW FAST CAN I GRAB ALL MY--?
KONK

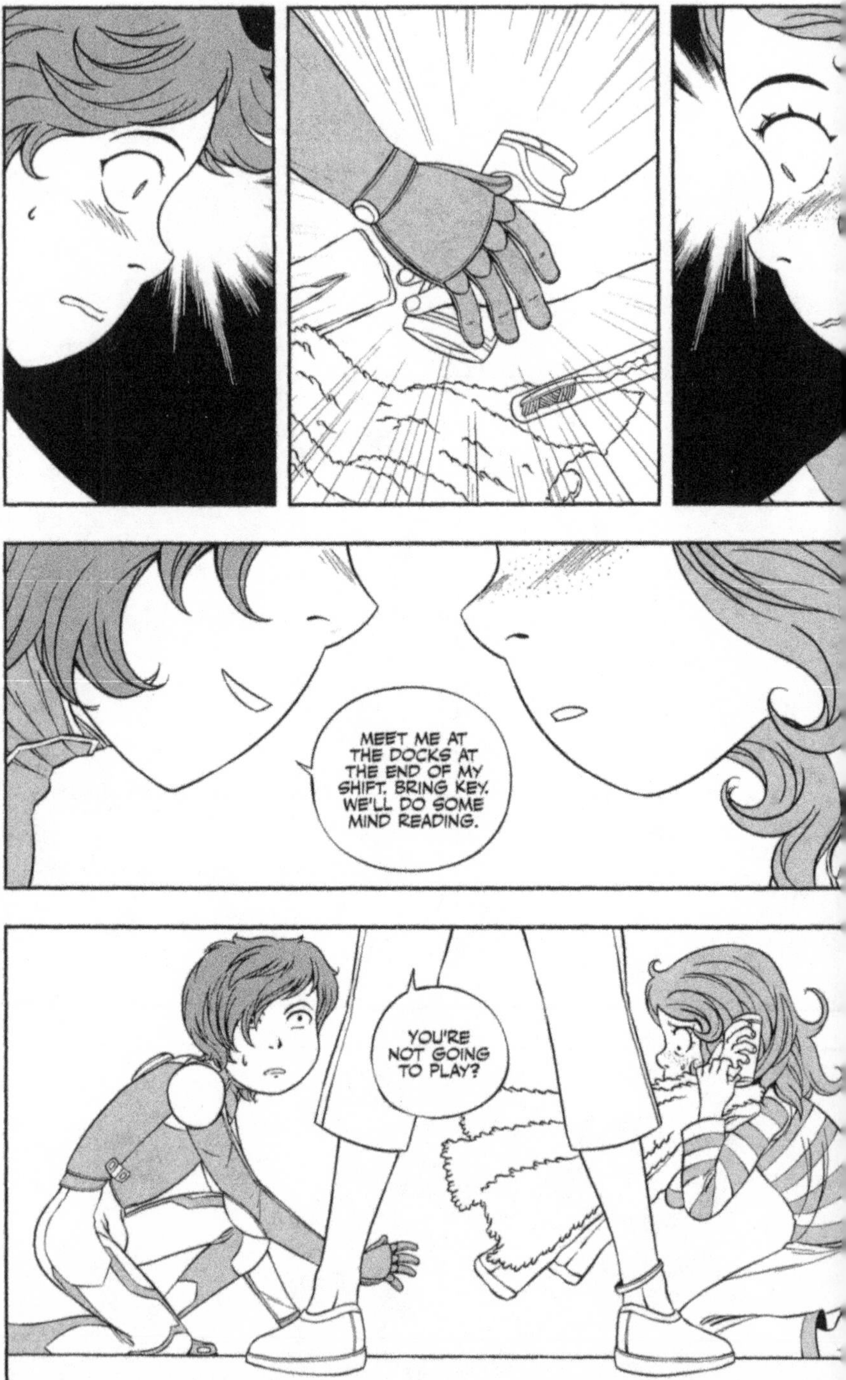
MEET ME AT THE DOCKS AT THE END OF MY SHIFT. BRING KEY. WE'LL DO SOME MIND READING.
YOU'RE NOT GOING TO PLAY?

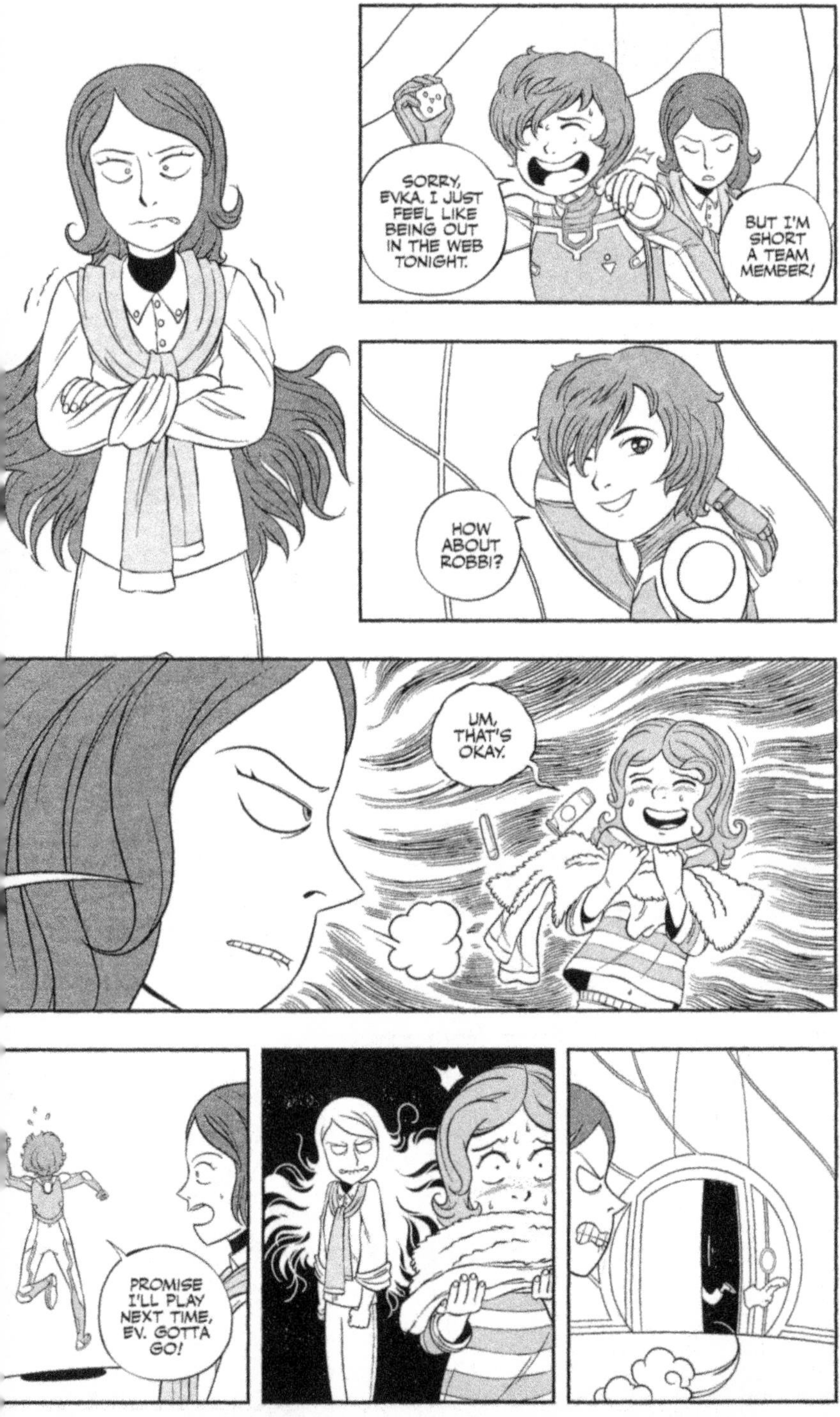
SORRY, EVKA. I JUST FEEL LIKE BEING OUT IN THE WEB TONIGHT.
BUT I'M SHORT A TEAM MEMBER!
HOW ABOUT ROBBI?
UM, THAT'S OKAY.
PROMISE I'LL PLAY NEXT TIME, EV. GOTTA GO!

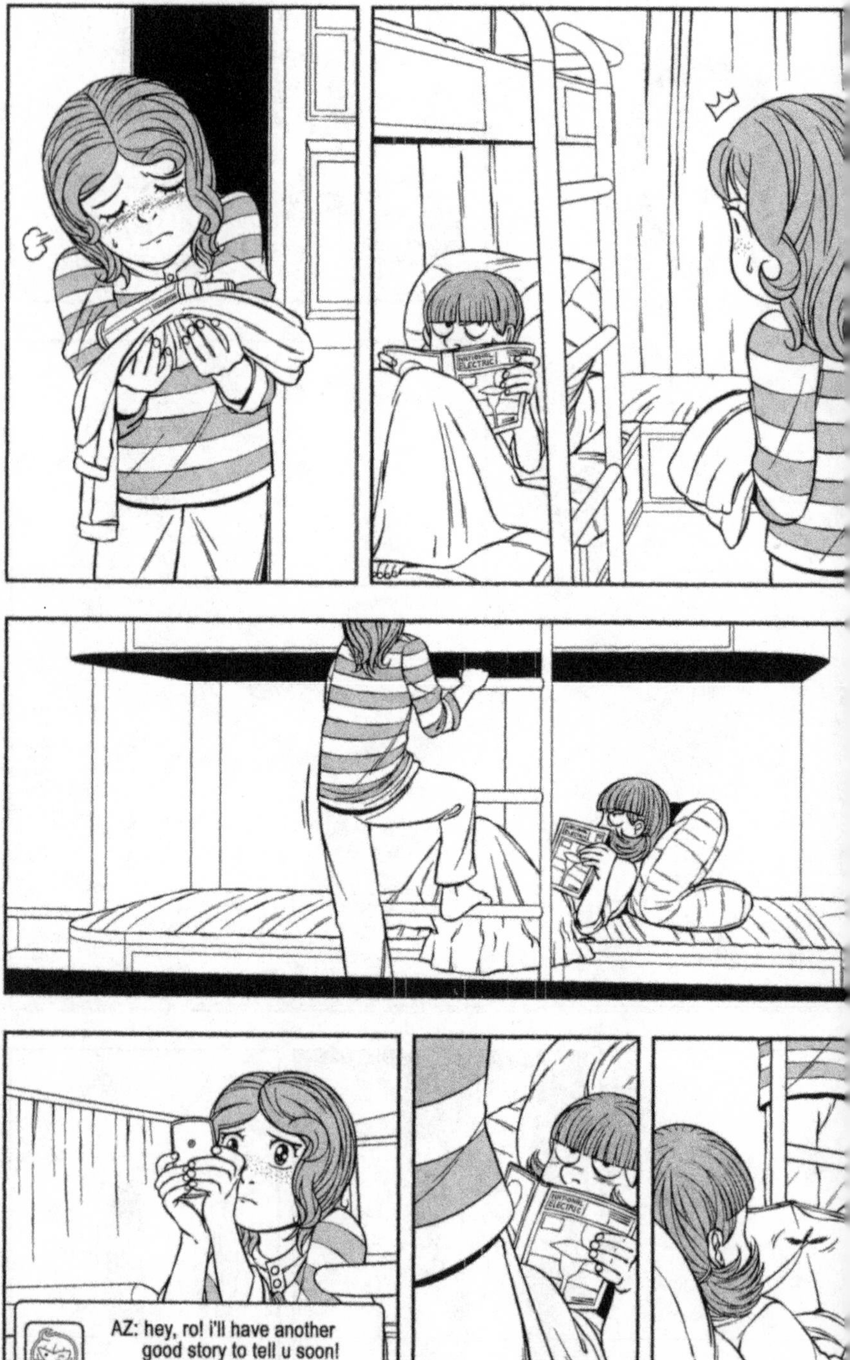
NATIONAL ELECTRIC
AZ: hey, ro! i'll have another good story to tell u soon! wish u were here!

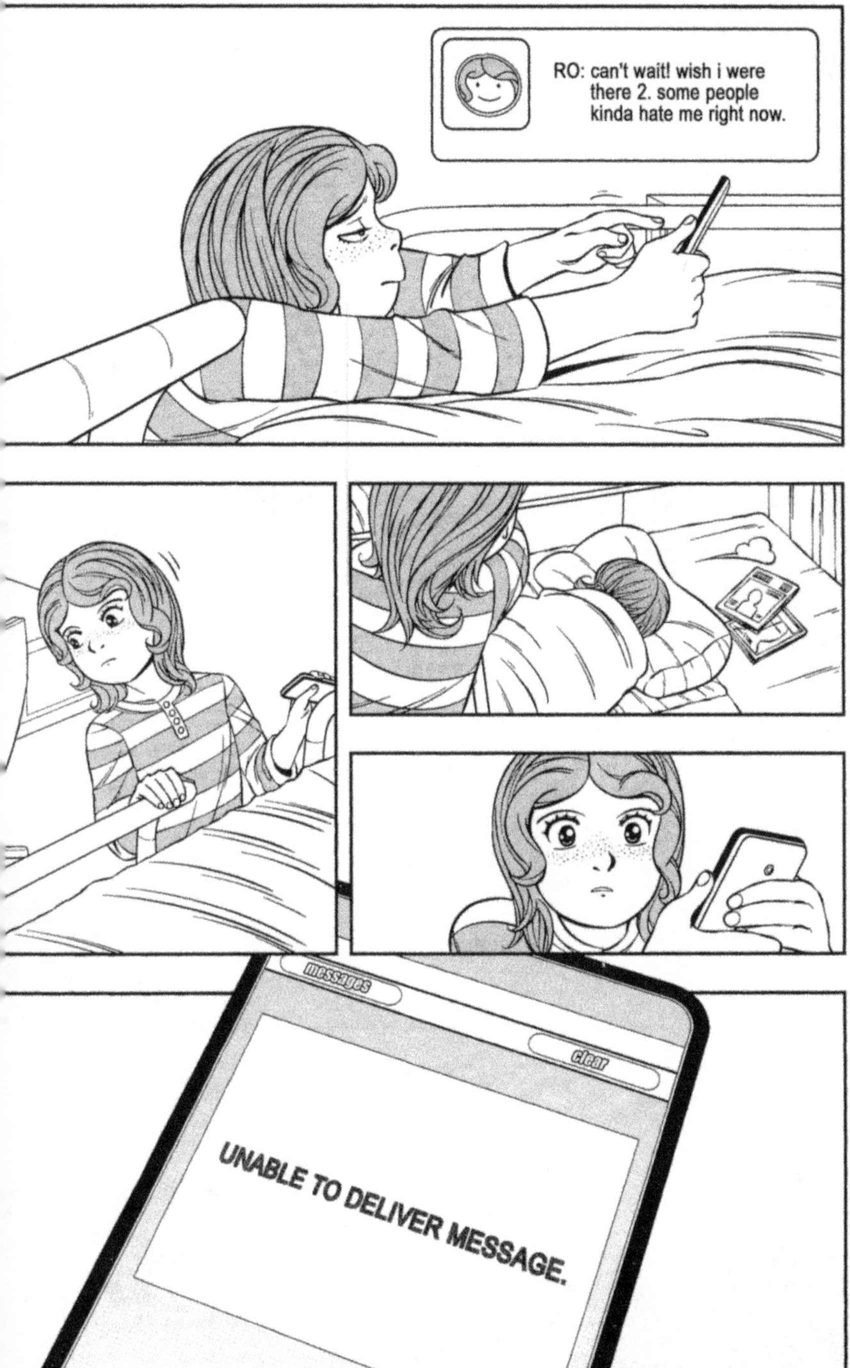
RO: can't wait! wish i were there 2. some people kinda hate me right now.
messages
clear
UNABLE TO DELIVER MESSAGE.

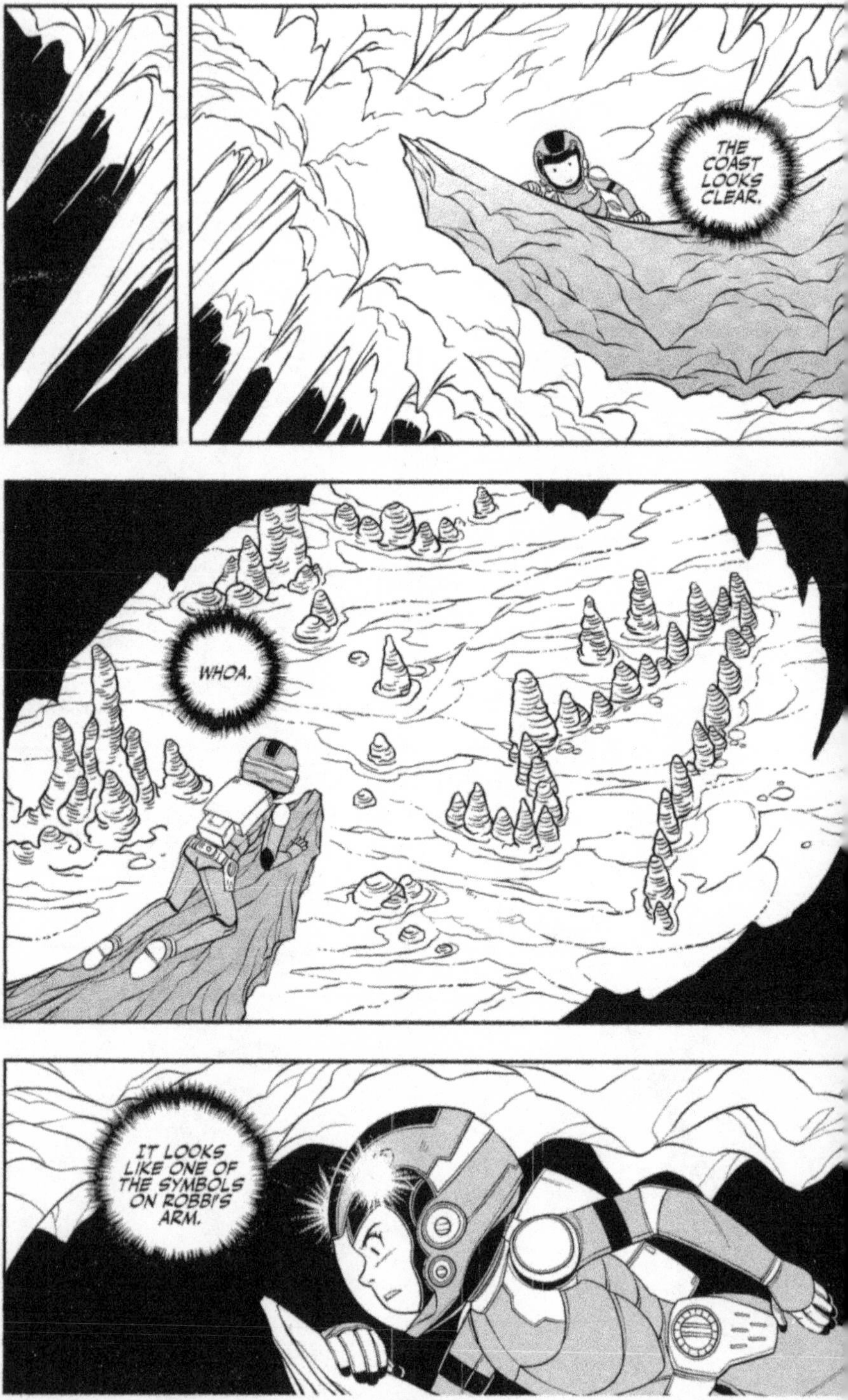
THE COAST LOOKS CLEAR.
WHOA.
IT LOOKS LIKE ONE OF THE SYMBOLS ON ROBBI'S ARM.

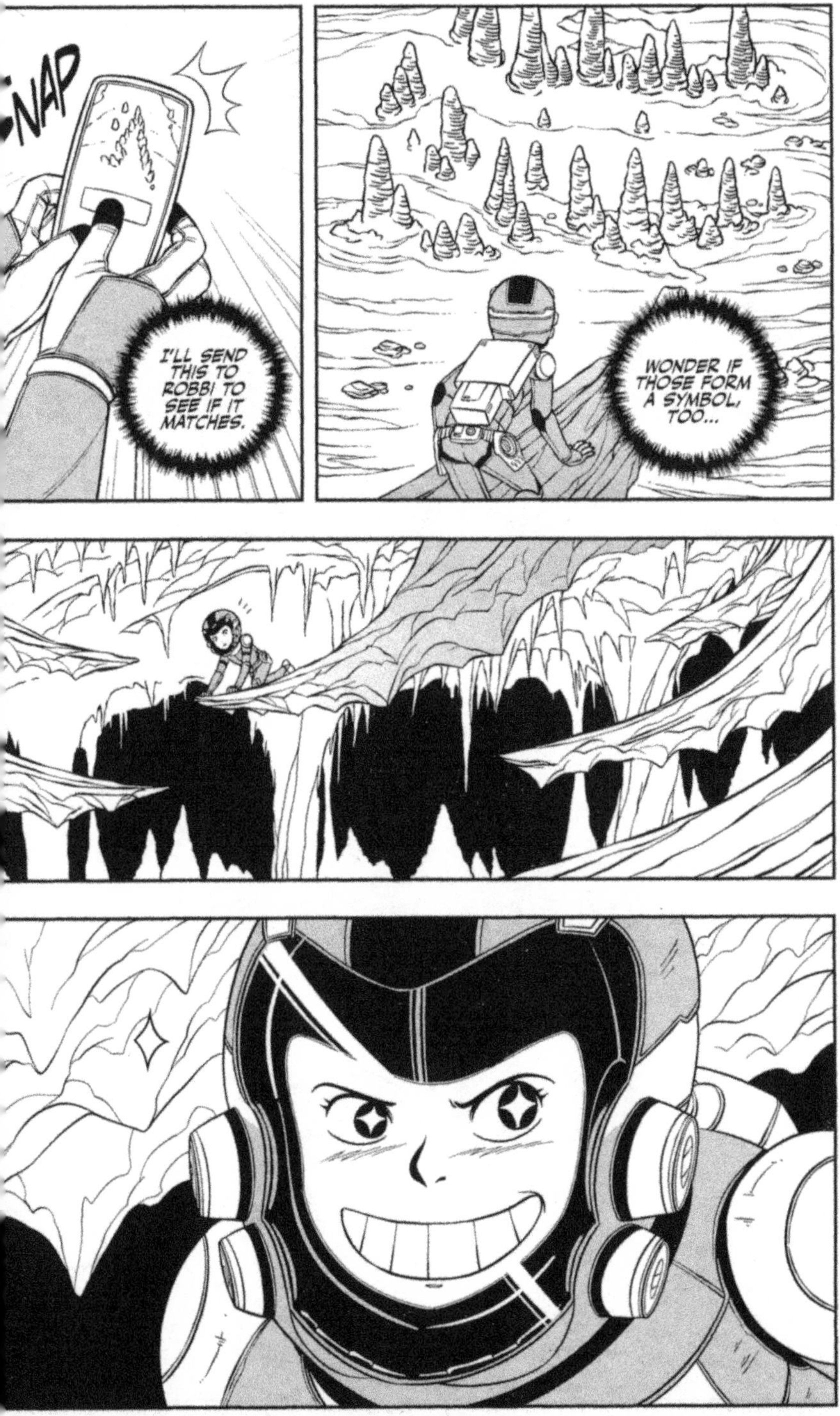
SNAP
I'LL SEND THIS TO ROBBI TO SEE IF IT MATCHES.
WONDER IF THOSE FORM A SYMBOL, TOO...

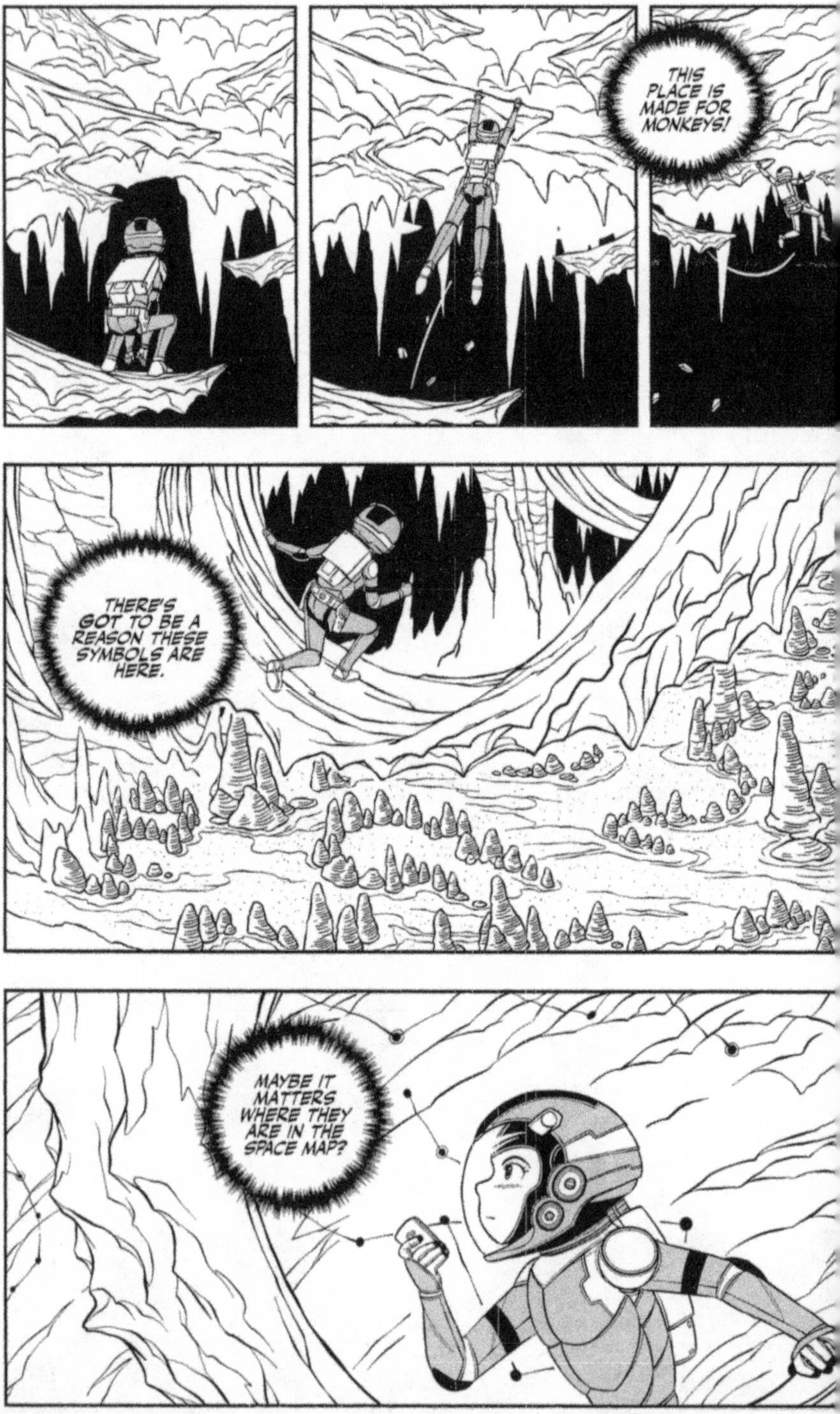
THIS PLACE IS MADE FOR MONKEYS!
THERE'S GOT TO BE A REASON THESE SYMBOLS ARE HERE.
MAYBE IT MATTERS WHERE THEY ARE IN THE SPACE MAP?

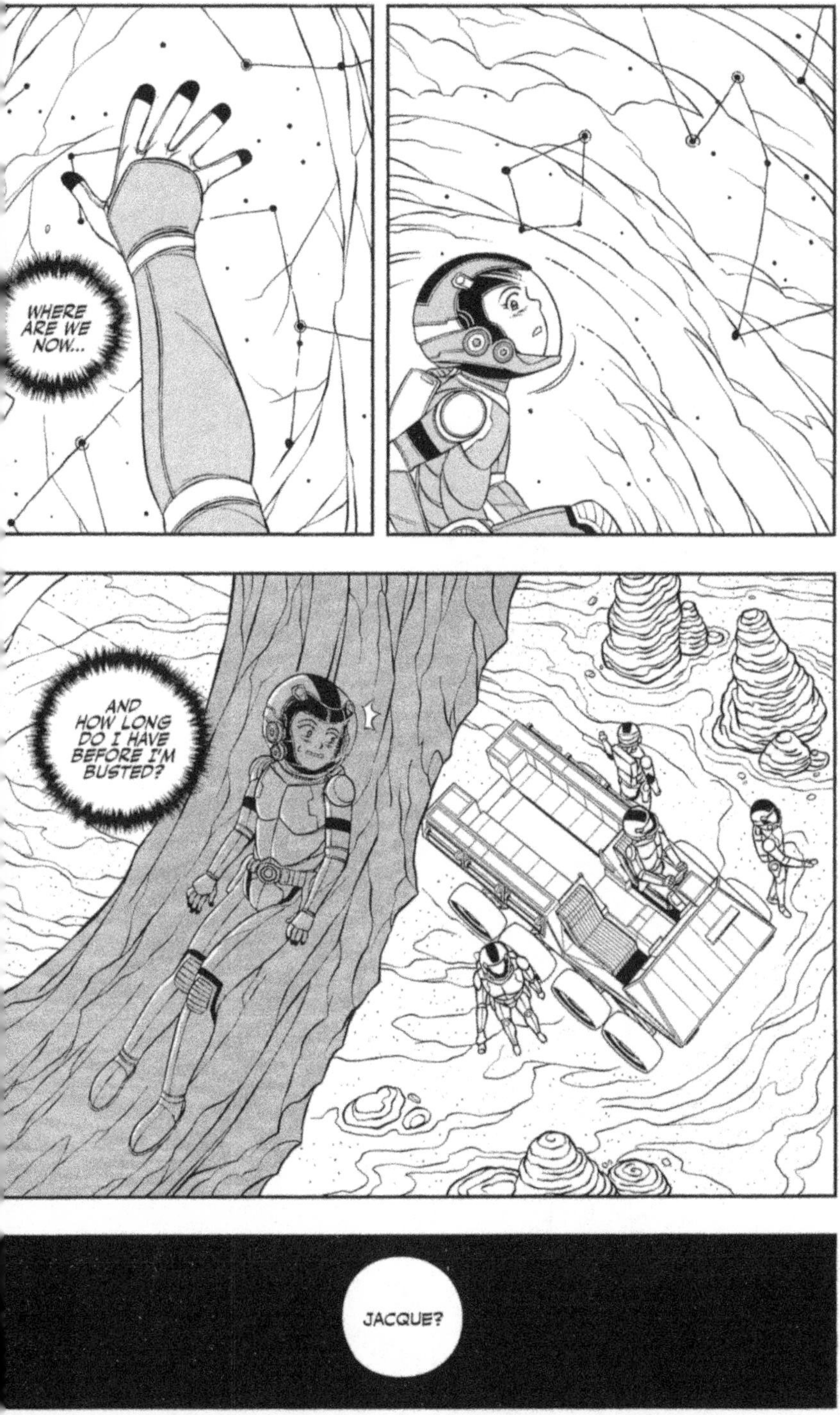
WHERE ARE WE NOW...
AND HOW LONG DO I HAVE BEFORE I'M BUSTED?
JACQUE?

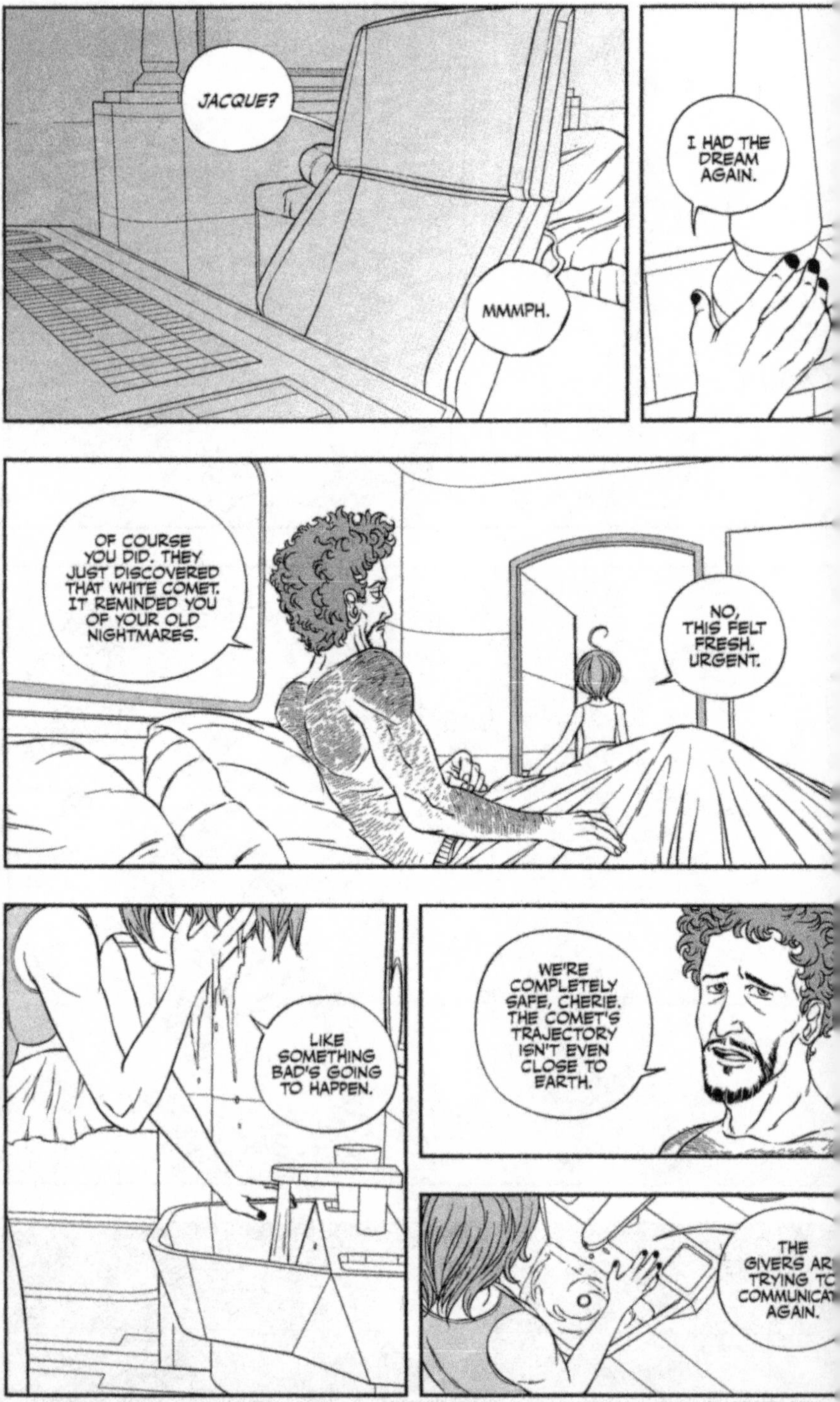
JACQUE?
MMMPH.
I HAD THE DREAM AGAIN.
OF COURSE YOU DID. THEY JUST DISCOVERED THAT WHITE COMET. IT REMINDED YOU OF YOUR OLD NIGHTMARES.
NO, THIS FELT FRESH. URGENT.
LIKE SOMETHING BAD'S GOING TO HAPPEN.
WE'RE COMPLETELY SAFE, CHERIE. THE COMET'S TRAJECTORY ISN'T EVEN CLOSE TO EARTH.

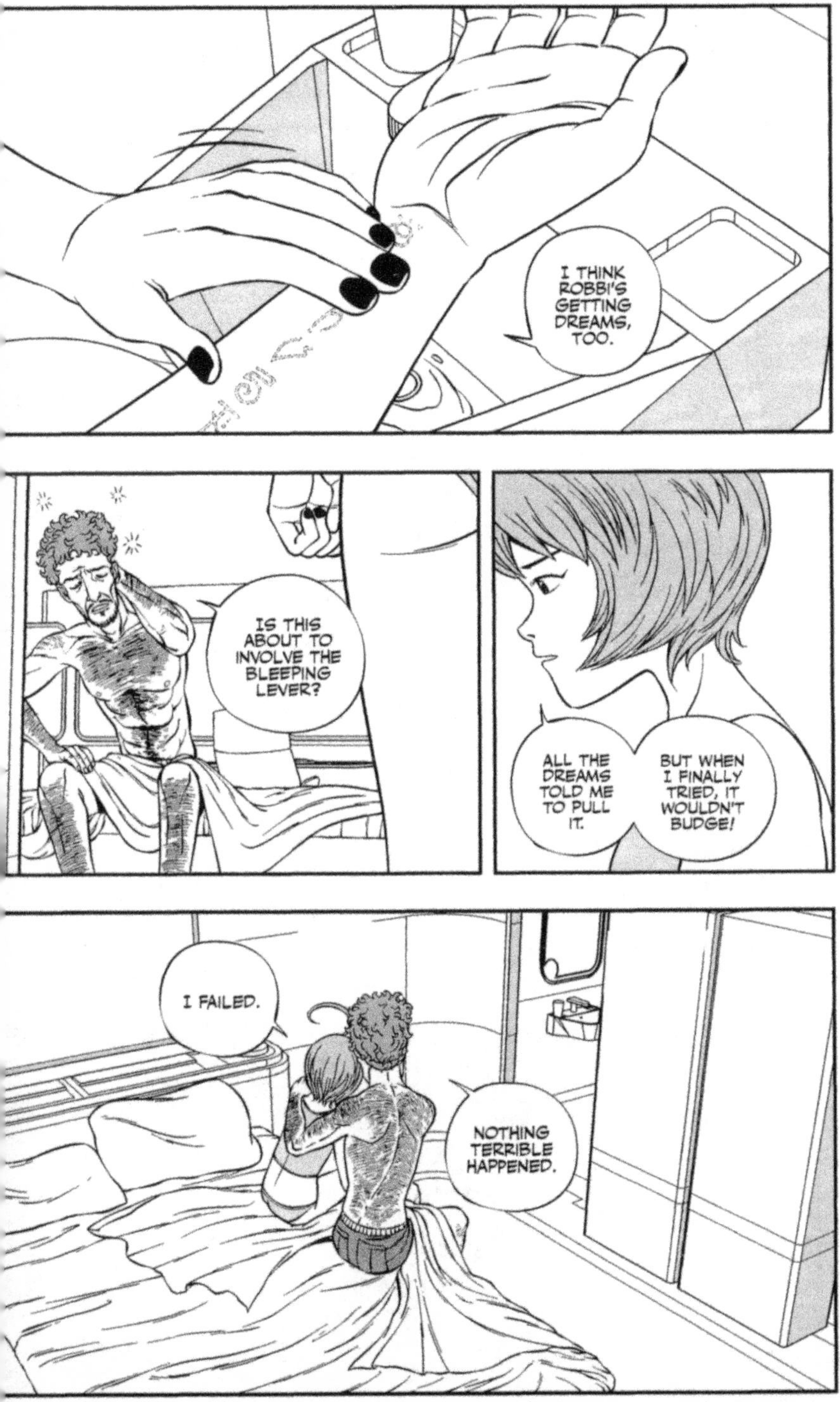
I THINK ROBBI'S GETTING DREAMS, TOO.
IS THIS ABOUT TO INVOLVE THE BLEEPING LEVER?
ALL THE DREAMS TOLD ME TO PULL IT.
BUT WHEN I FINALLY TRIED, IT WOULDN'T BUDGE!
I FAILED.
NOTHING TERRIBLE HAPPENED.

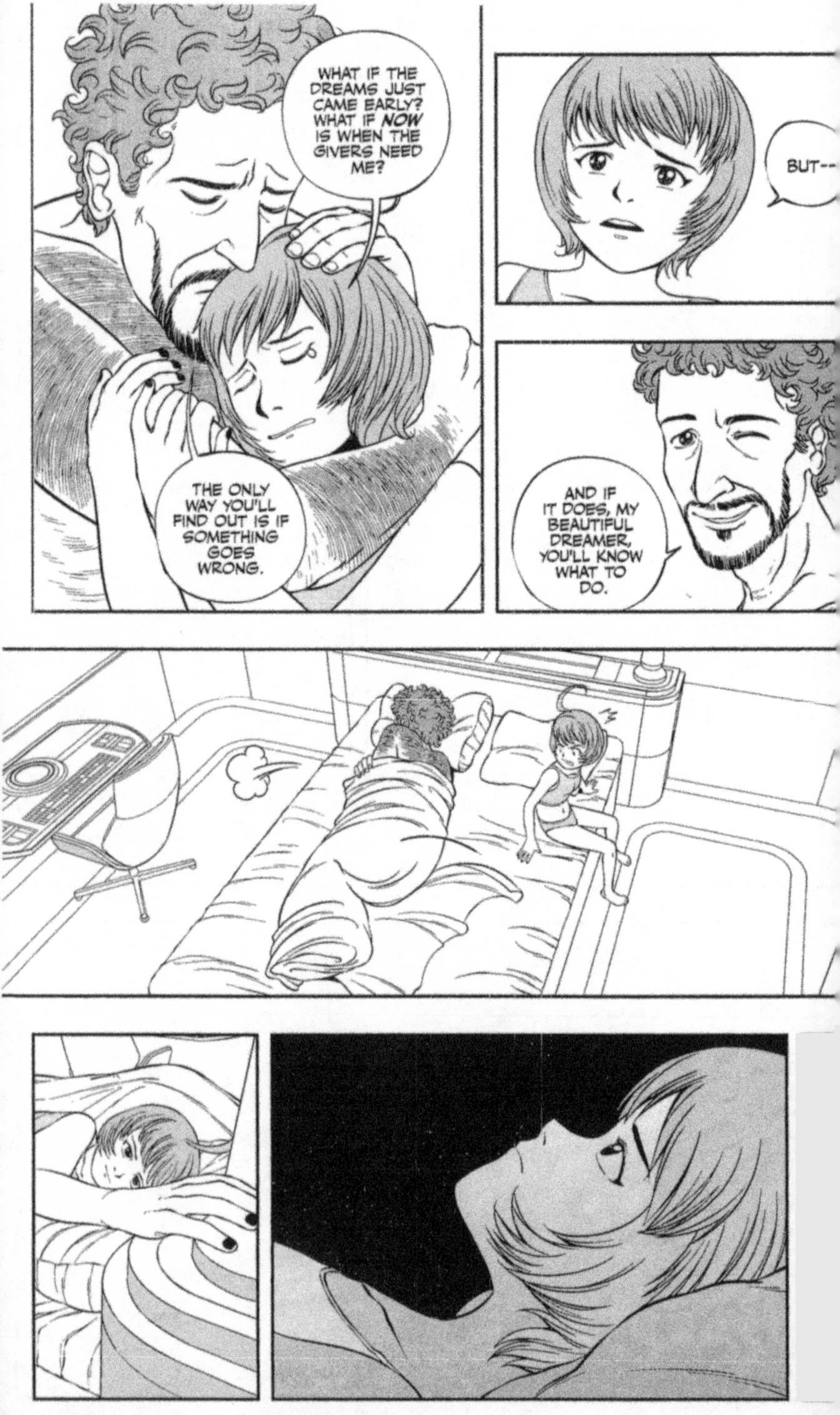
WHAT IF THE DREAMS JUST CAME EARLY? WHAT IF *NOW* IS WHEN THE GIVERS NEED ME?
THE ONLY WAY YOU'LL FIND OUT IS IF SOMETHING GOES WRONG.
BUT--
AND IF IT DOES, MY BEAUTIFUL DREAMER, YOU'LL KNOW WHAT TO DO.

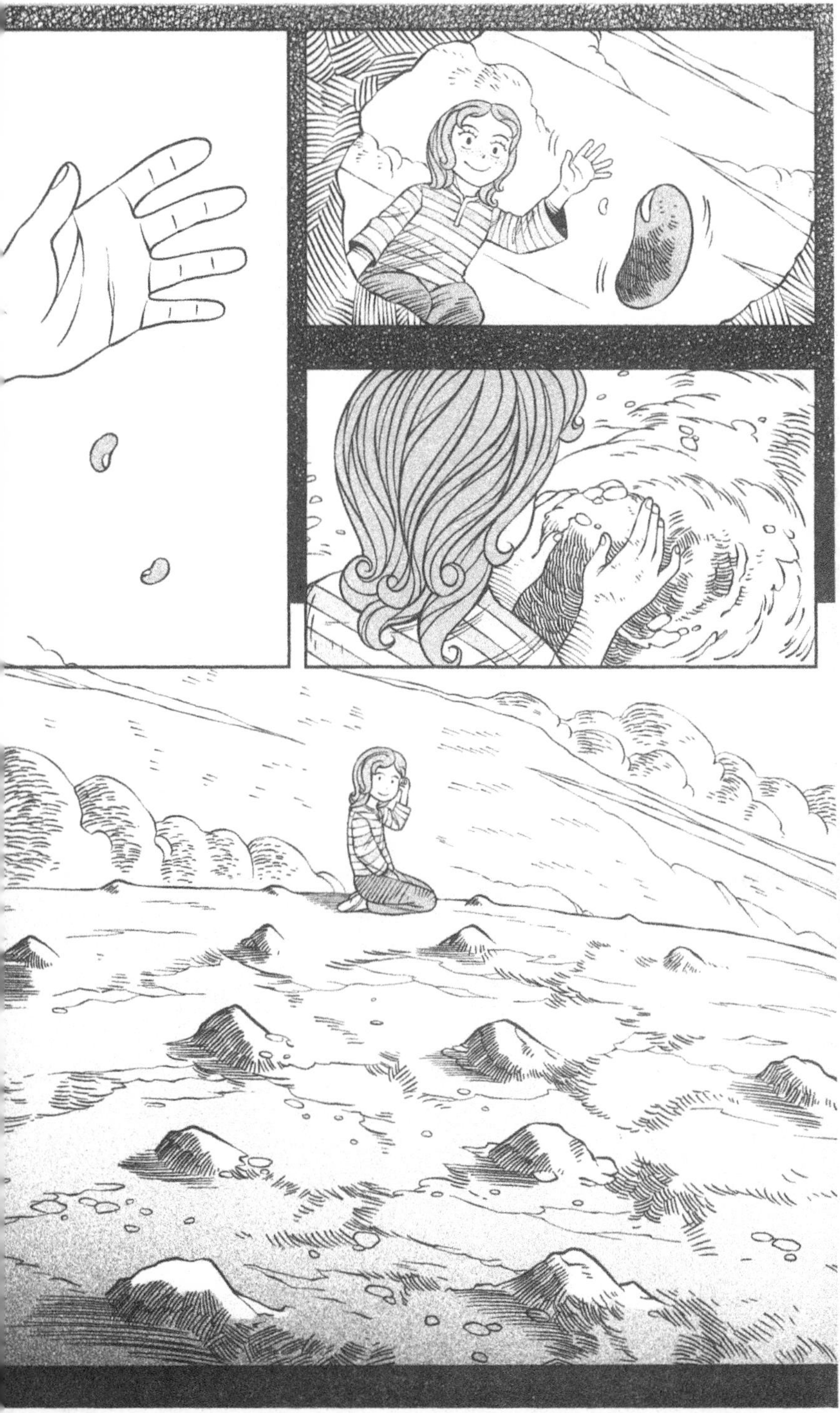

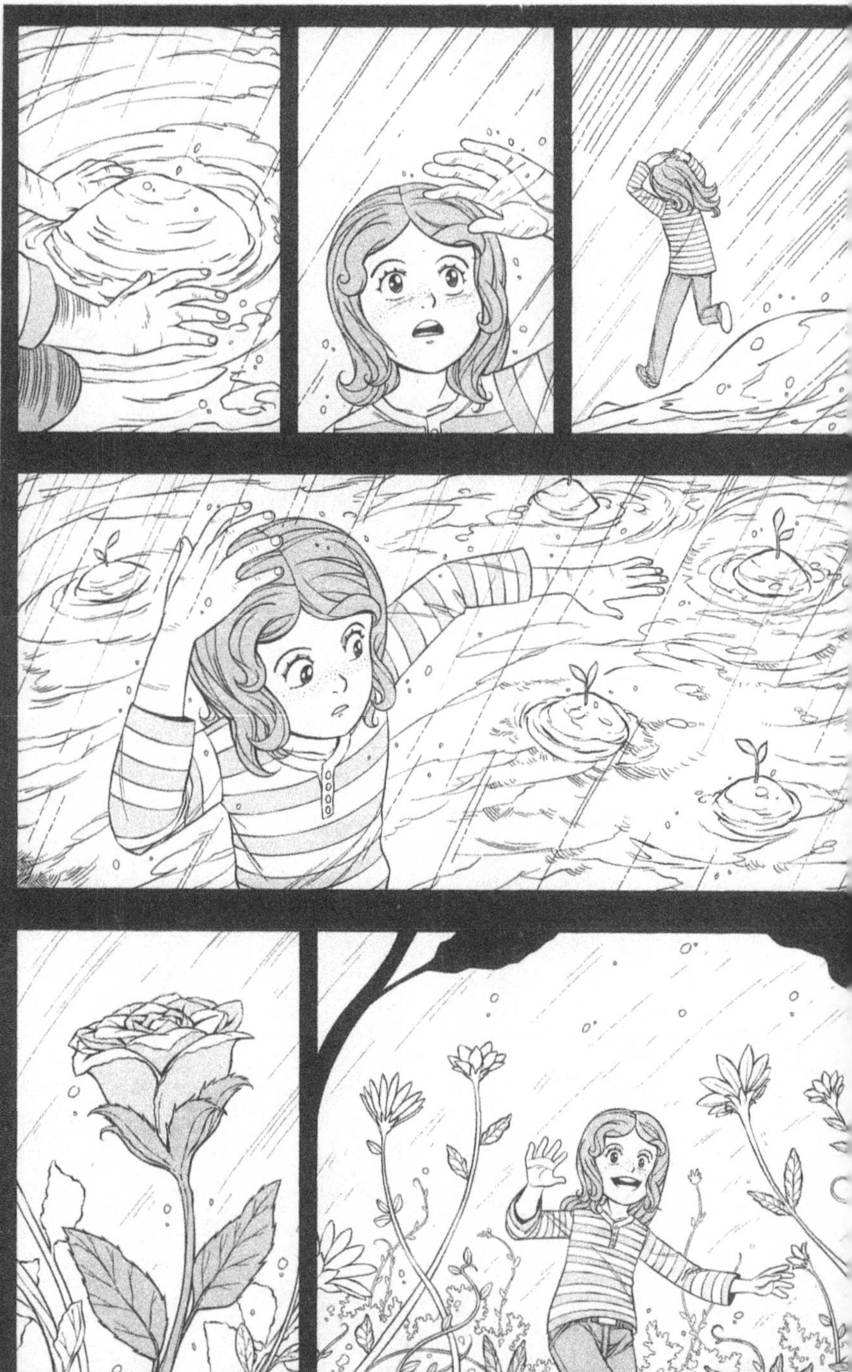

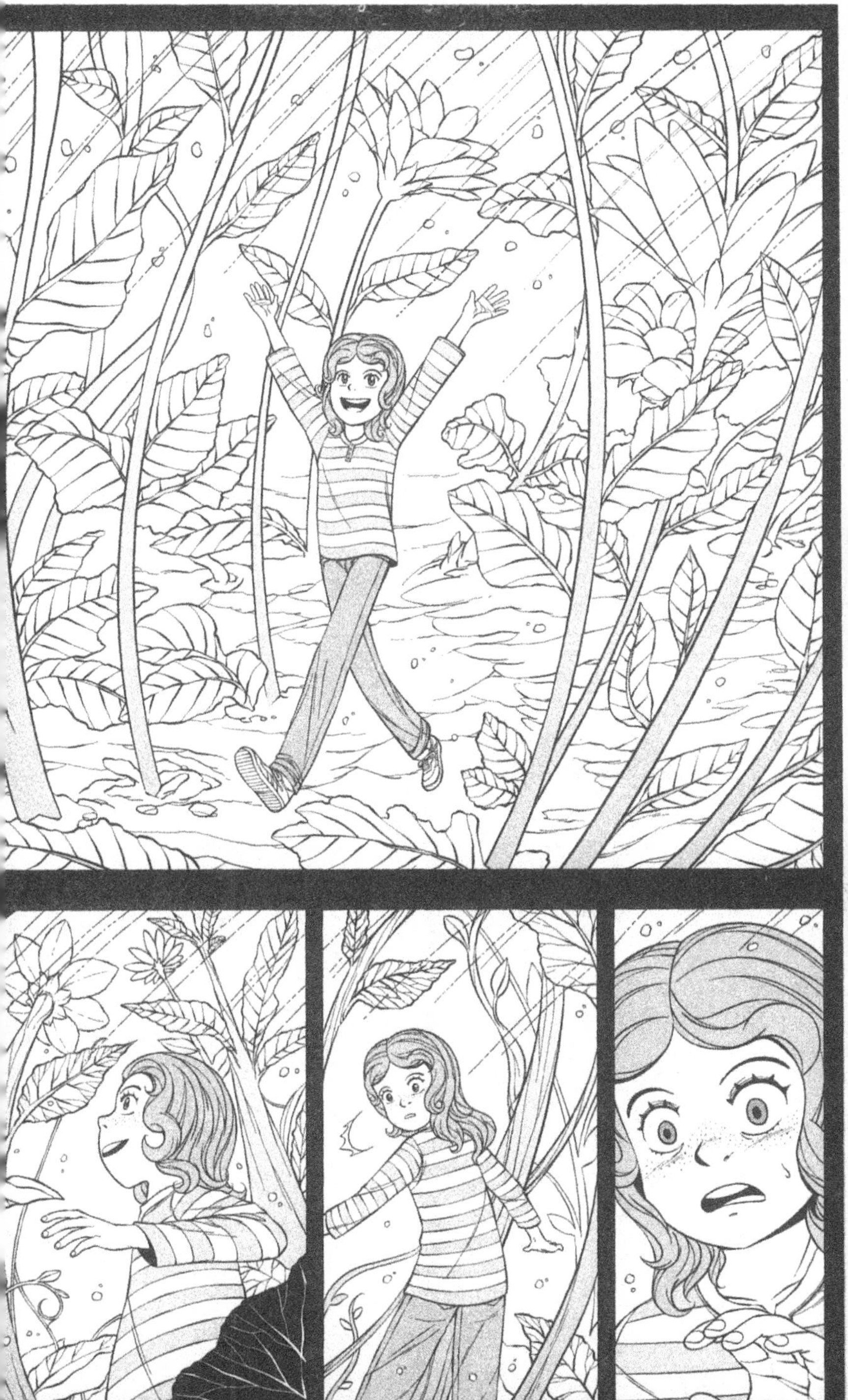

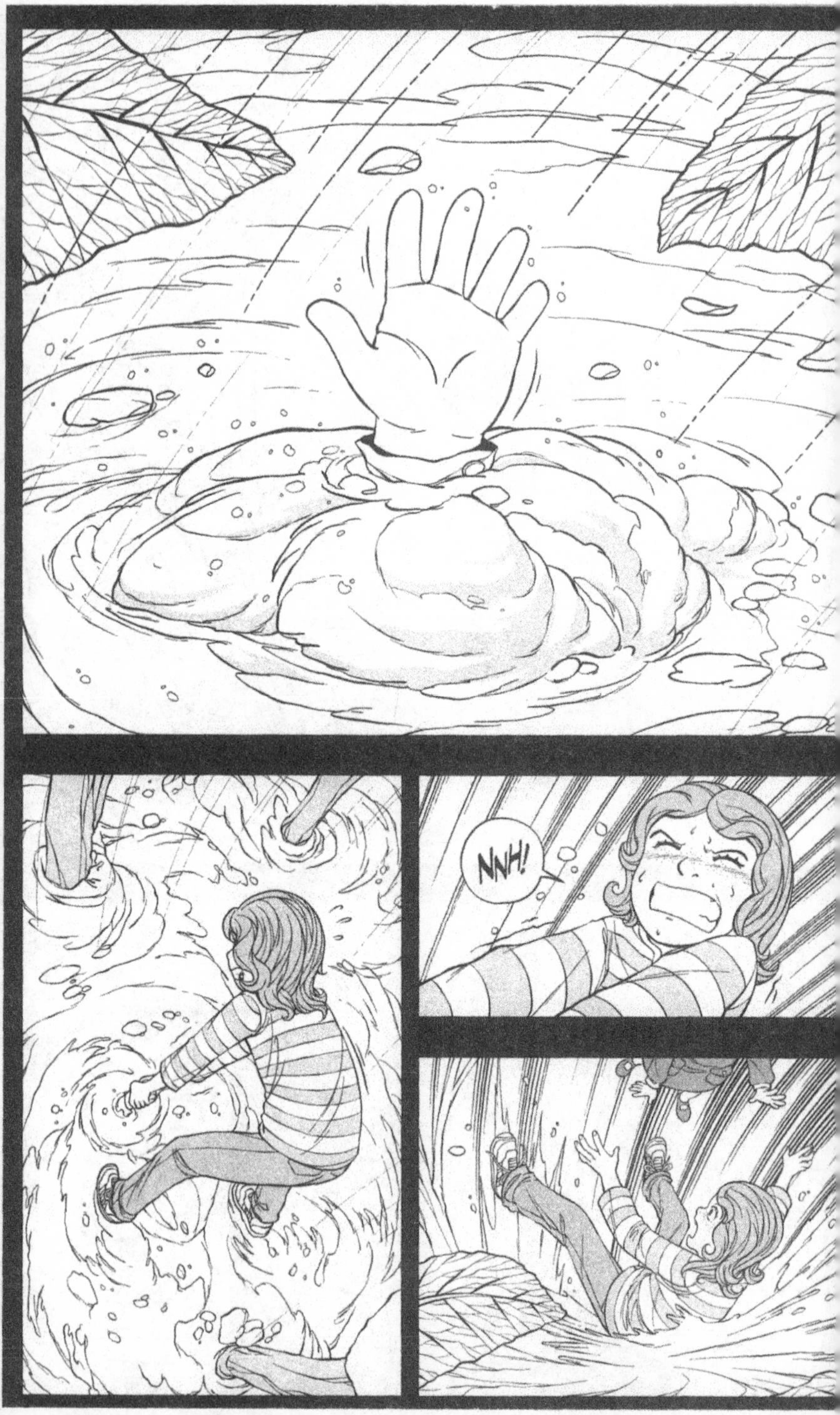
NNH!

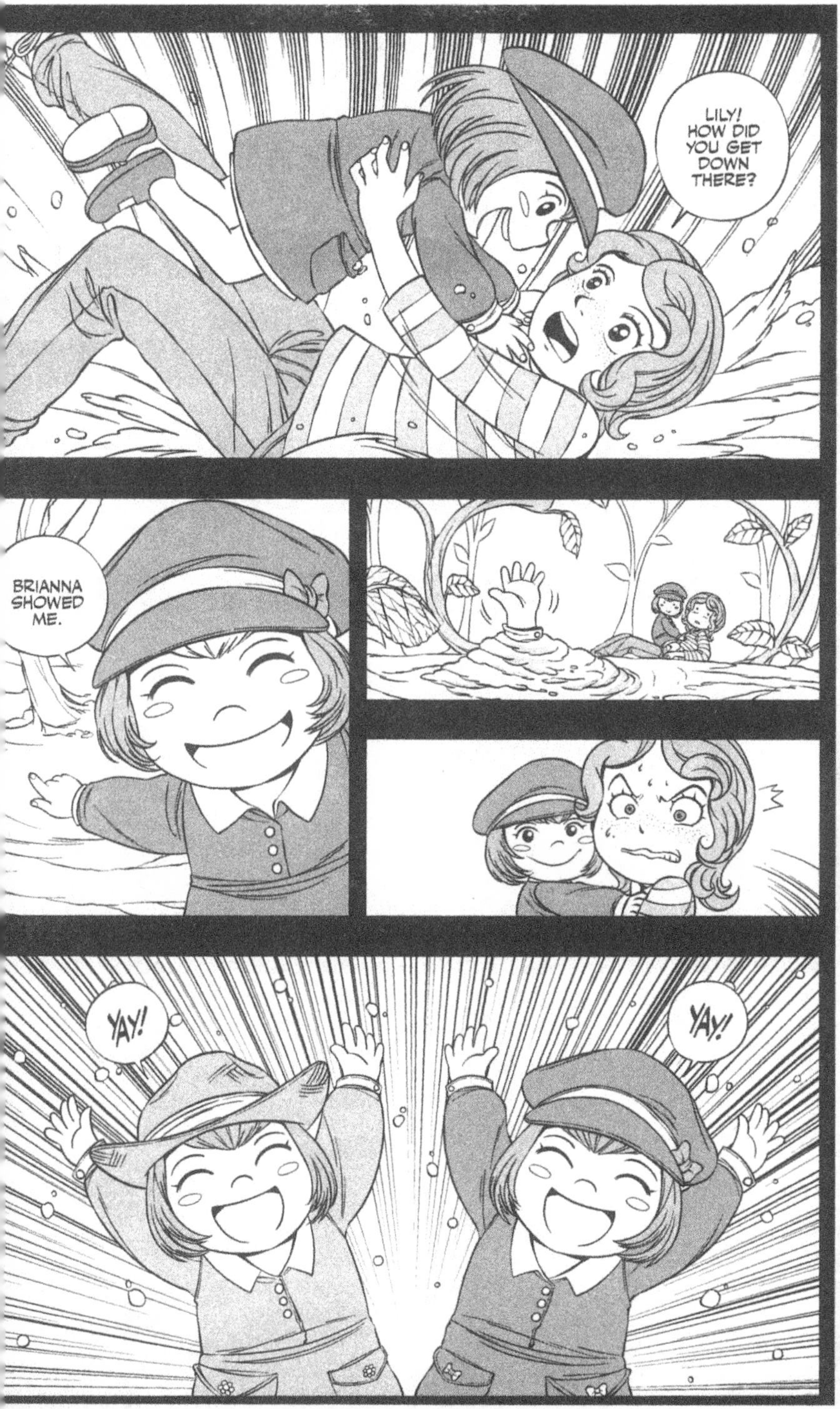
LILY! HOW DID YOU GET DOWN THERE?
BRIANNA SHOWED ME.
YAY!
YAY!

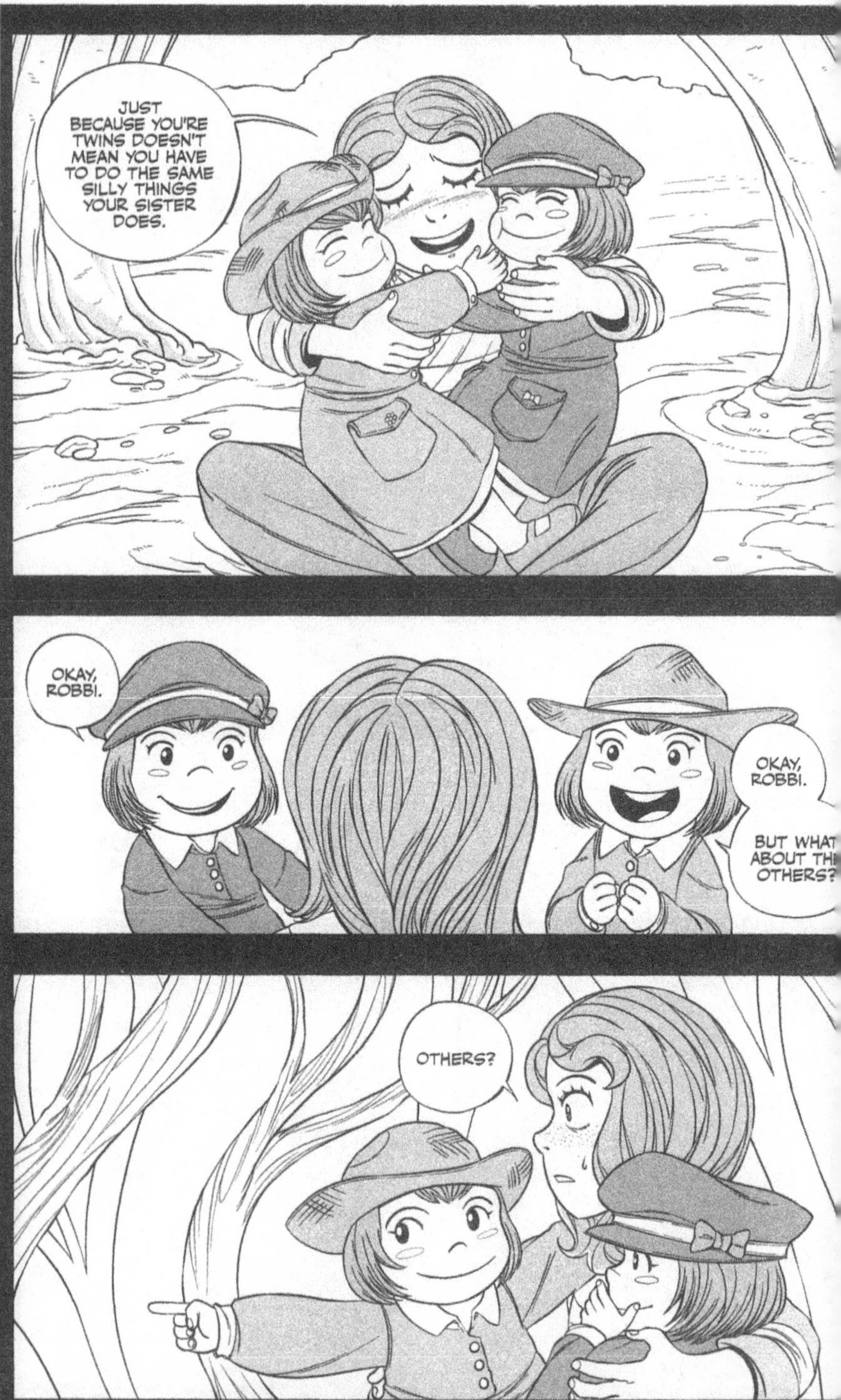
JUST BECAUSE YOU'RE TWINS DOESN'T MEAN YOU HAVE TO DO THE SAME SILLY THINGS YOUR SISTER DOES.
OKAY, ROBBI.
OKAY, ROBBI.
BUT WHAT ABOUT THE OTHERS?
OTHERS?

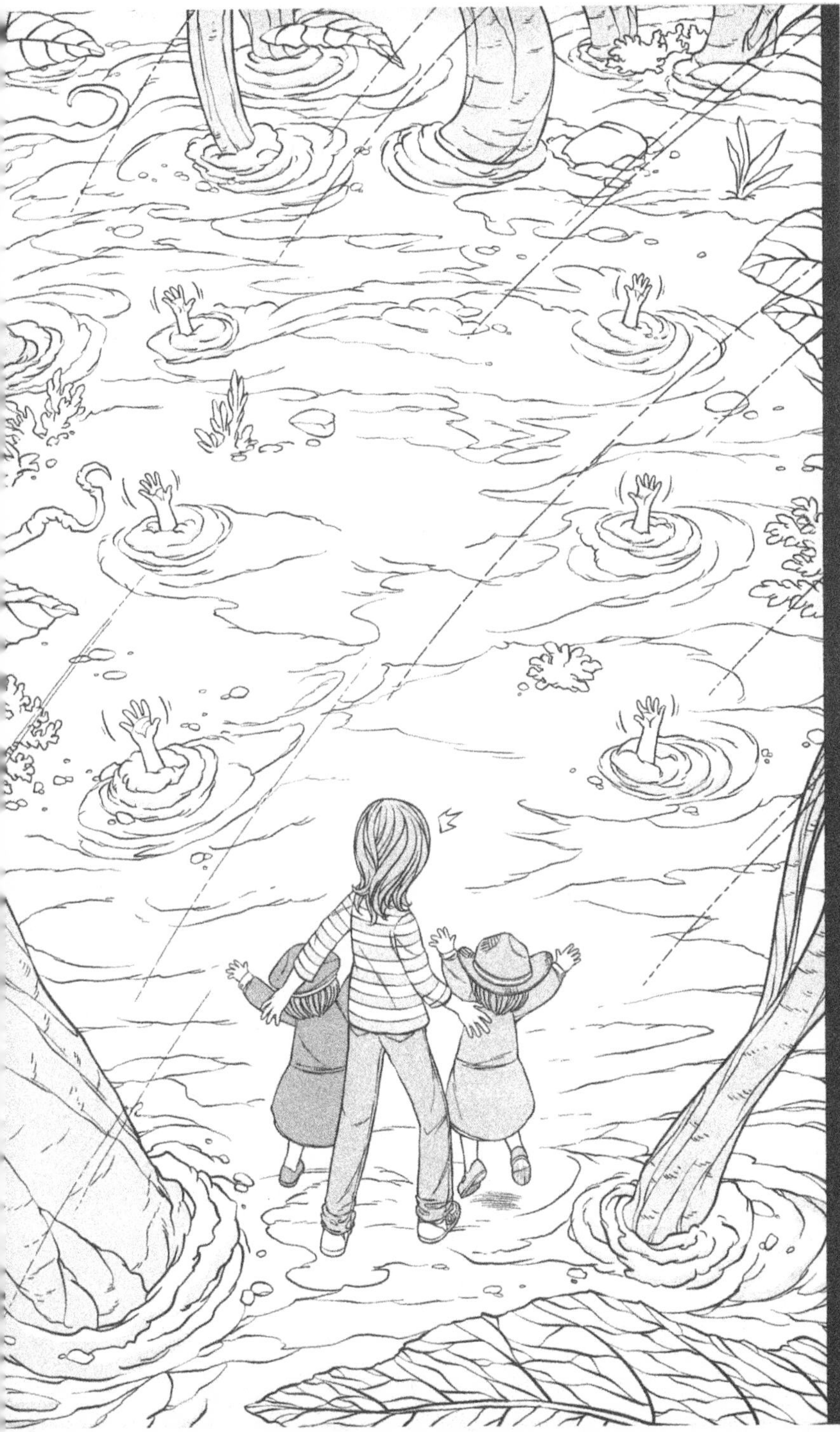

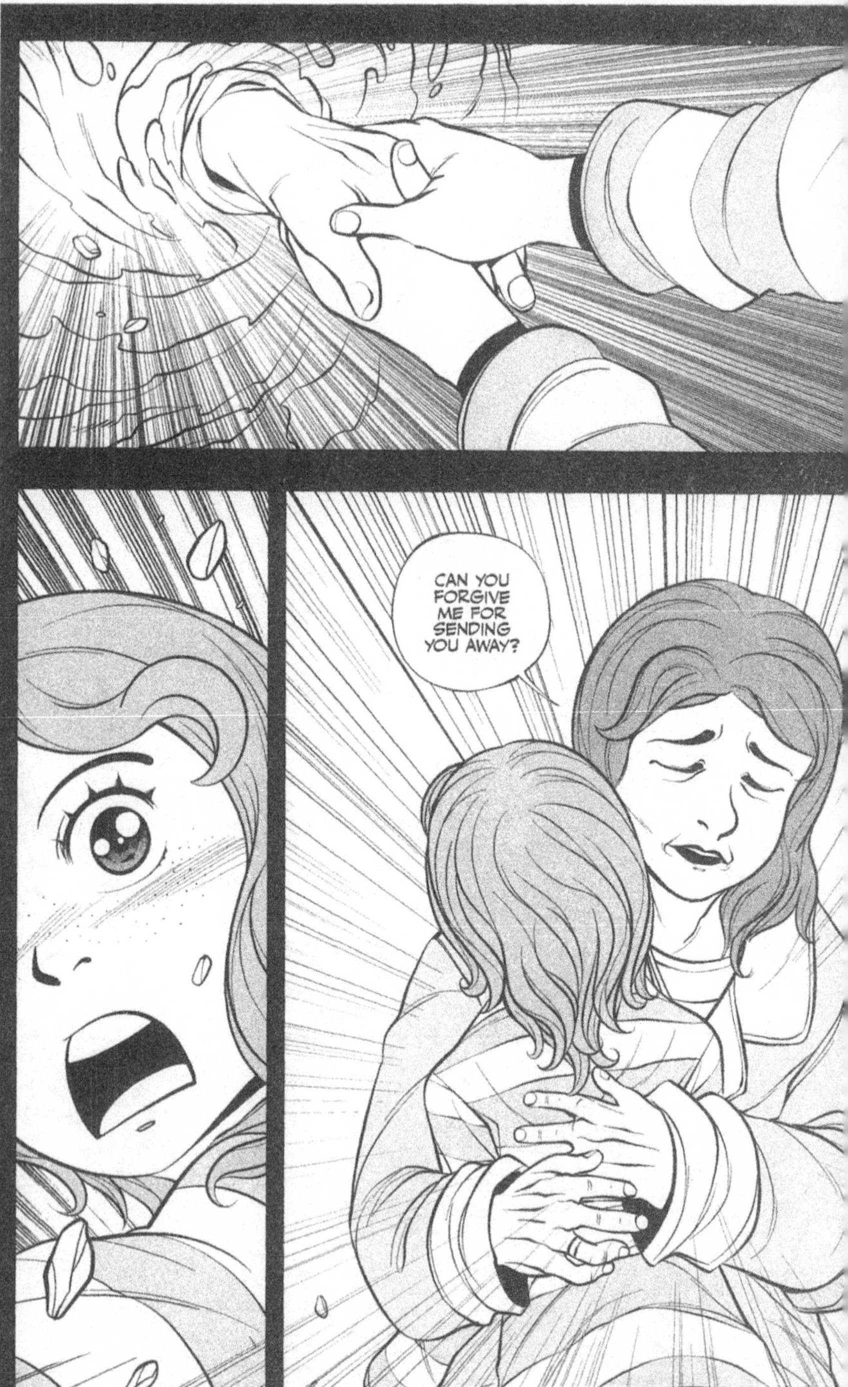
CAN YOU FORGIVE ME FOR SENDING YOU AWAY?

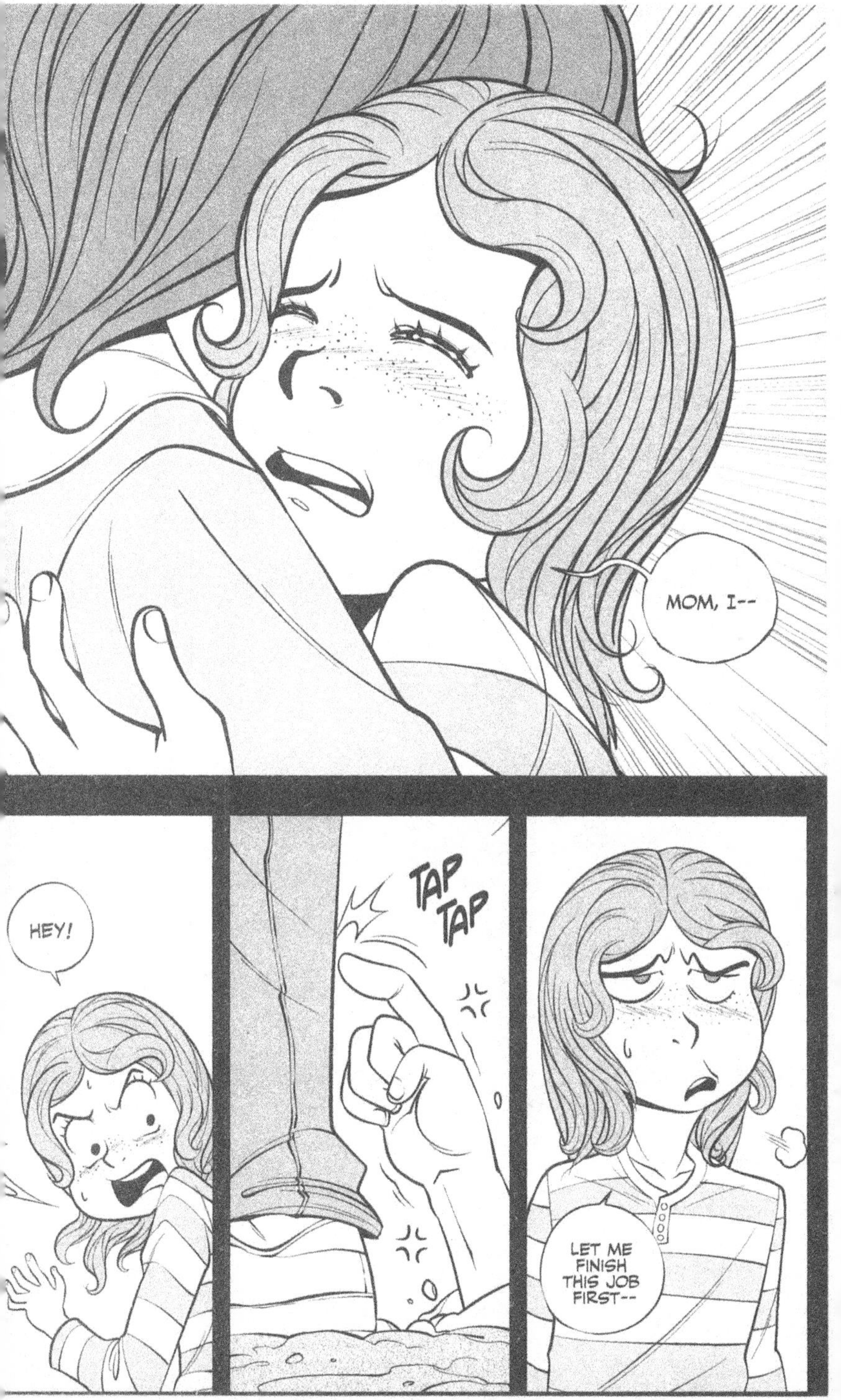
MOM, I--
HEY!
TAP TAP
LET ME FINISH THIS JOB FIRST--

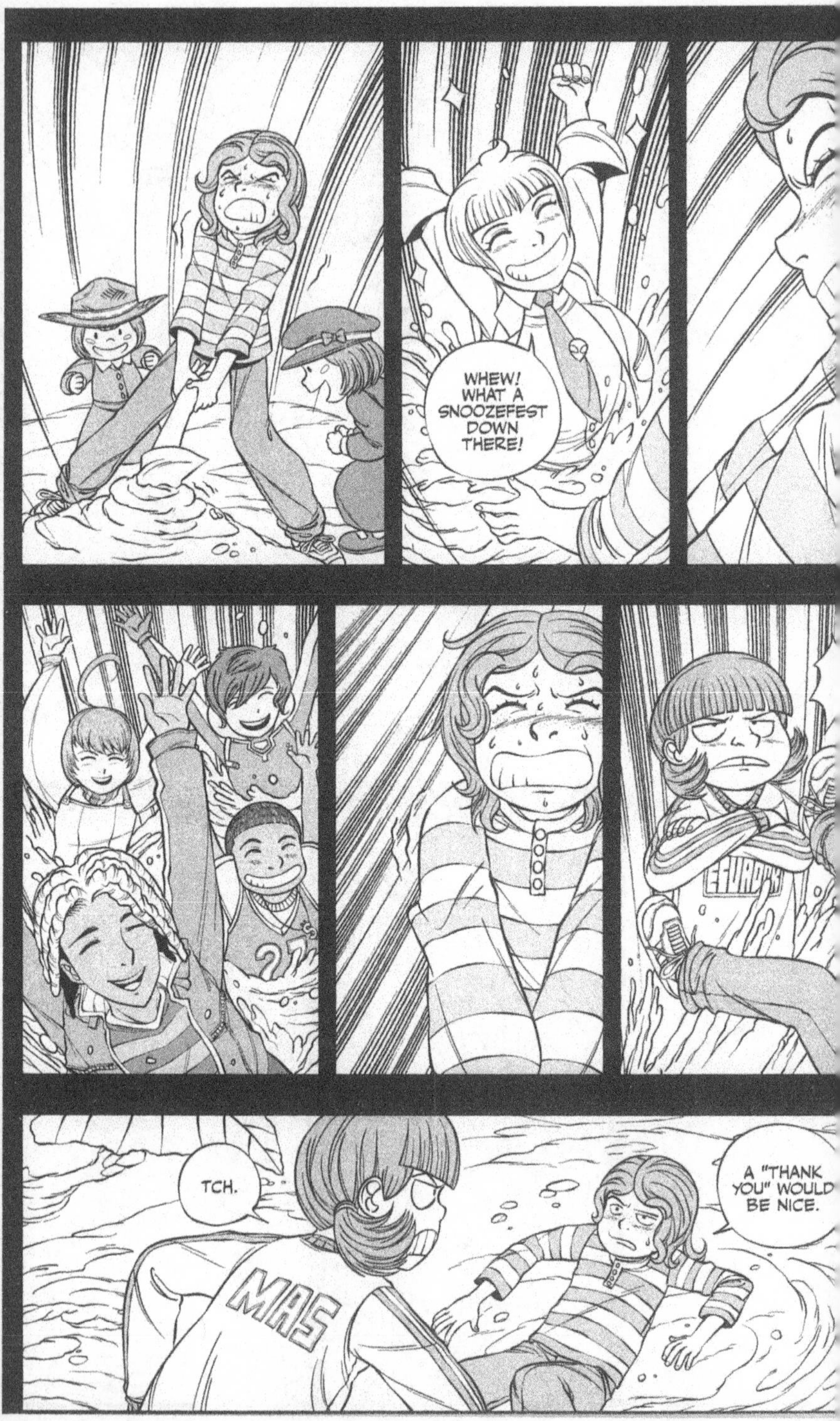
WHEW! WHAT A SNOOZEFEST DOWN THERE!
TCH.
A "THANK YOU" WOULD BE NICE.

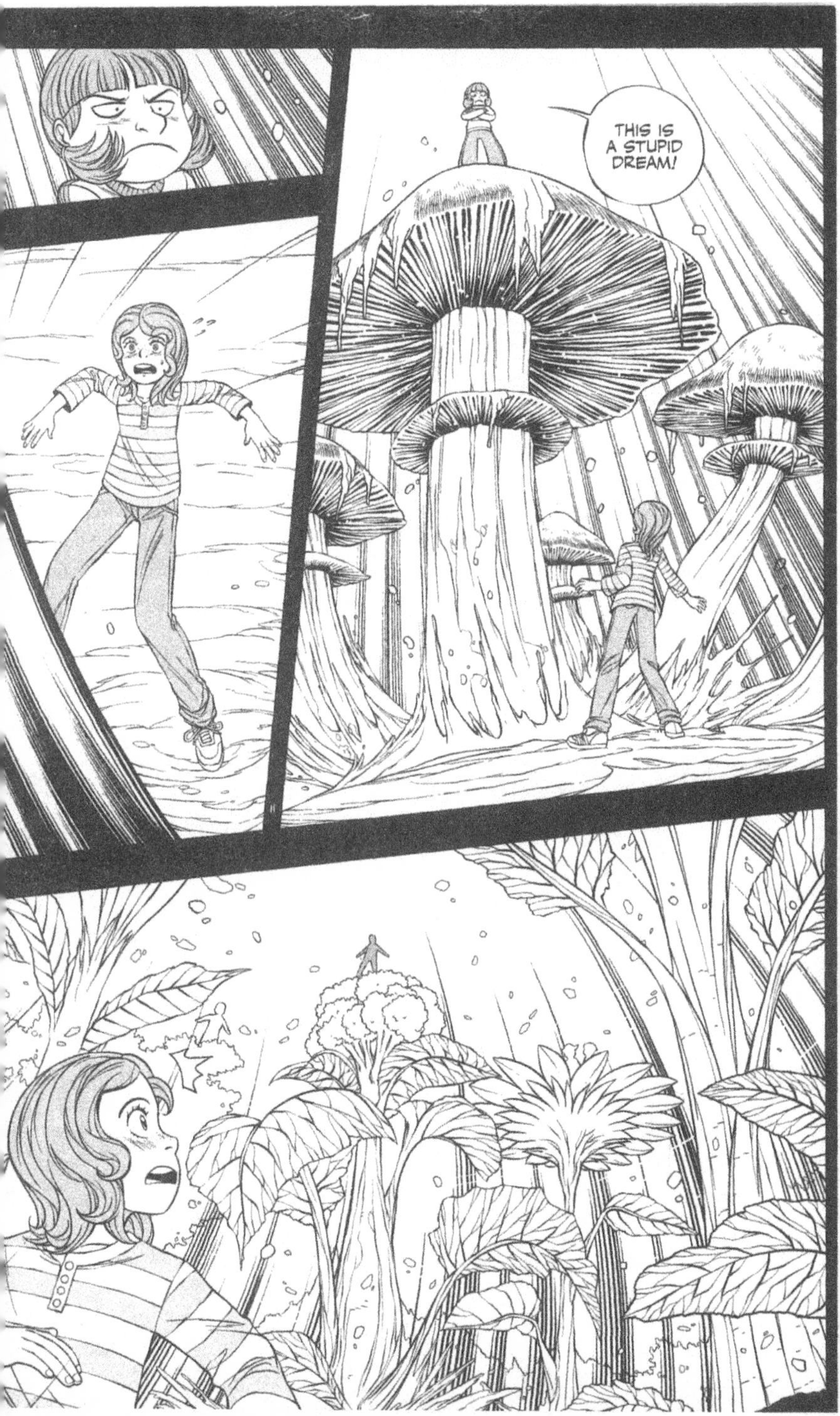
THIS IS A STUPID DREAM!

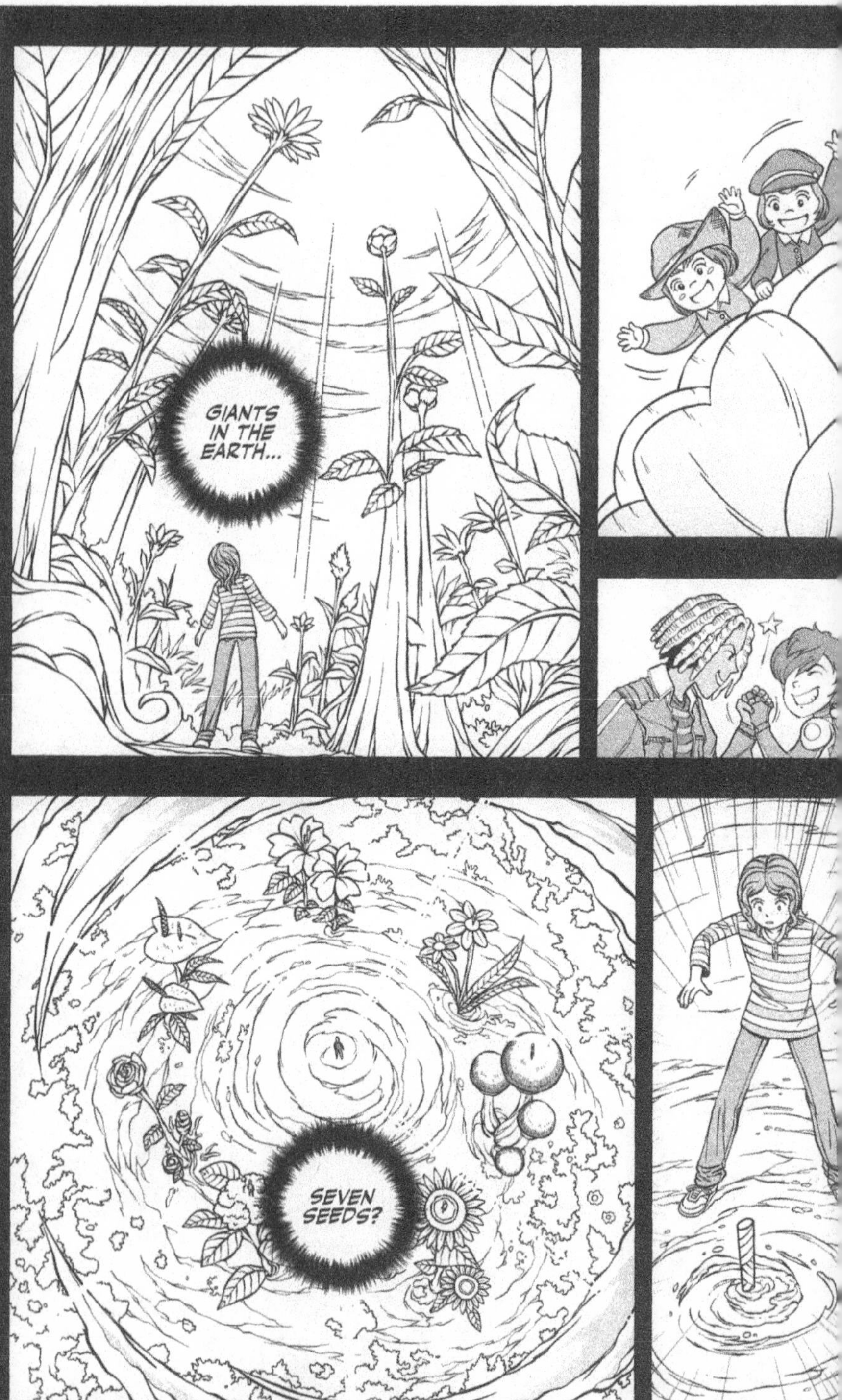
GIANTS IN THE EARTH...
SEVEN SEEDS?

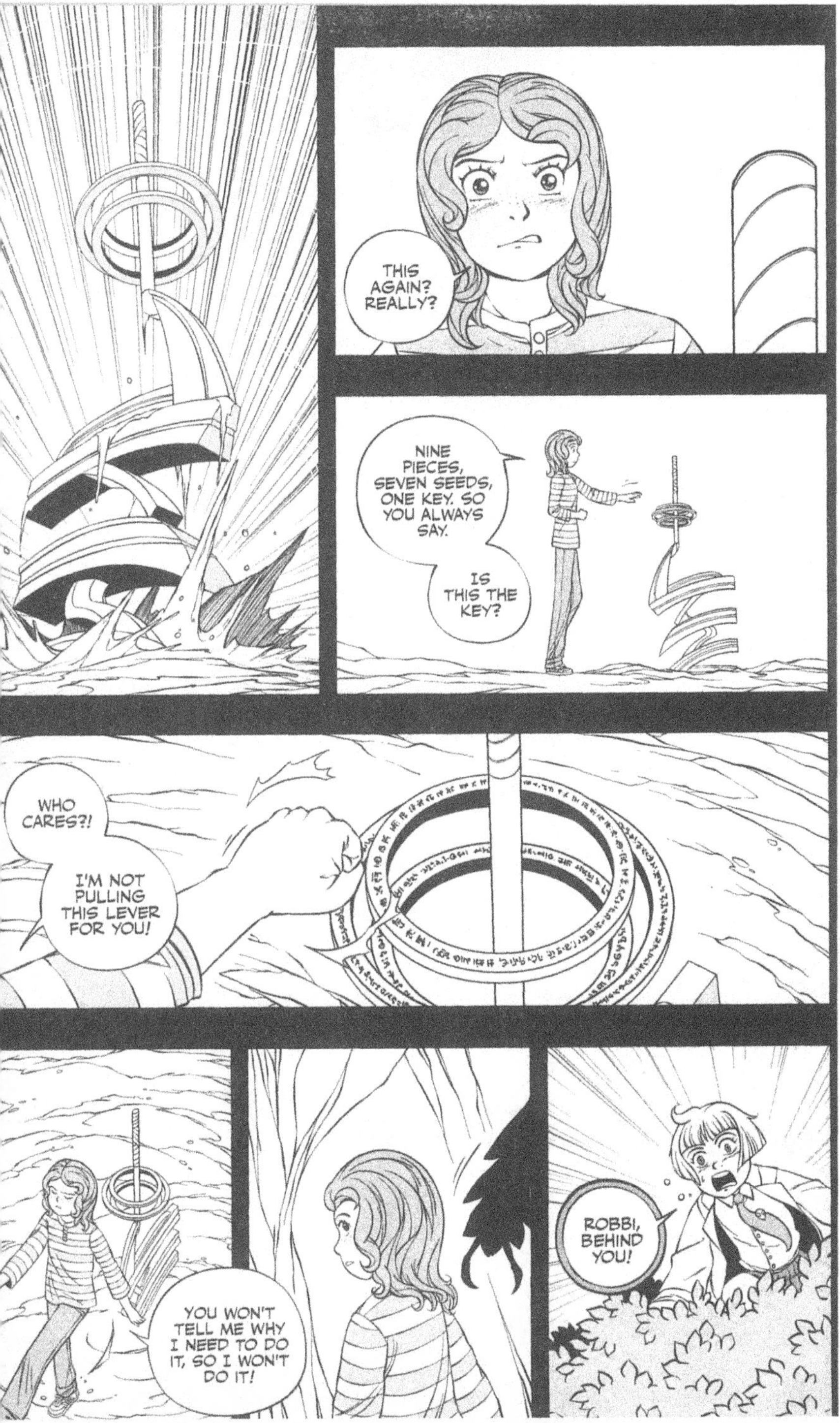
THIS AGAIN? REALLY?
NINE PIECES, SEVEN SEEDS, ONE KEY. SO YOU ALWAYS SAY.
IS THIS THE KEY?
WHO CARES?!
I'M NOT PULLING THIS LEVER FOR YOU!
YOU WON'T TELL ME WHY I NEED TO DO IT, SO I WON'T DO IT!
ROBBI, BEHIND YOU!

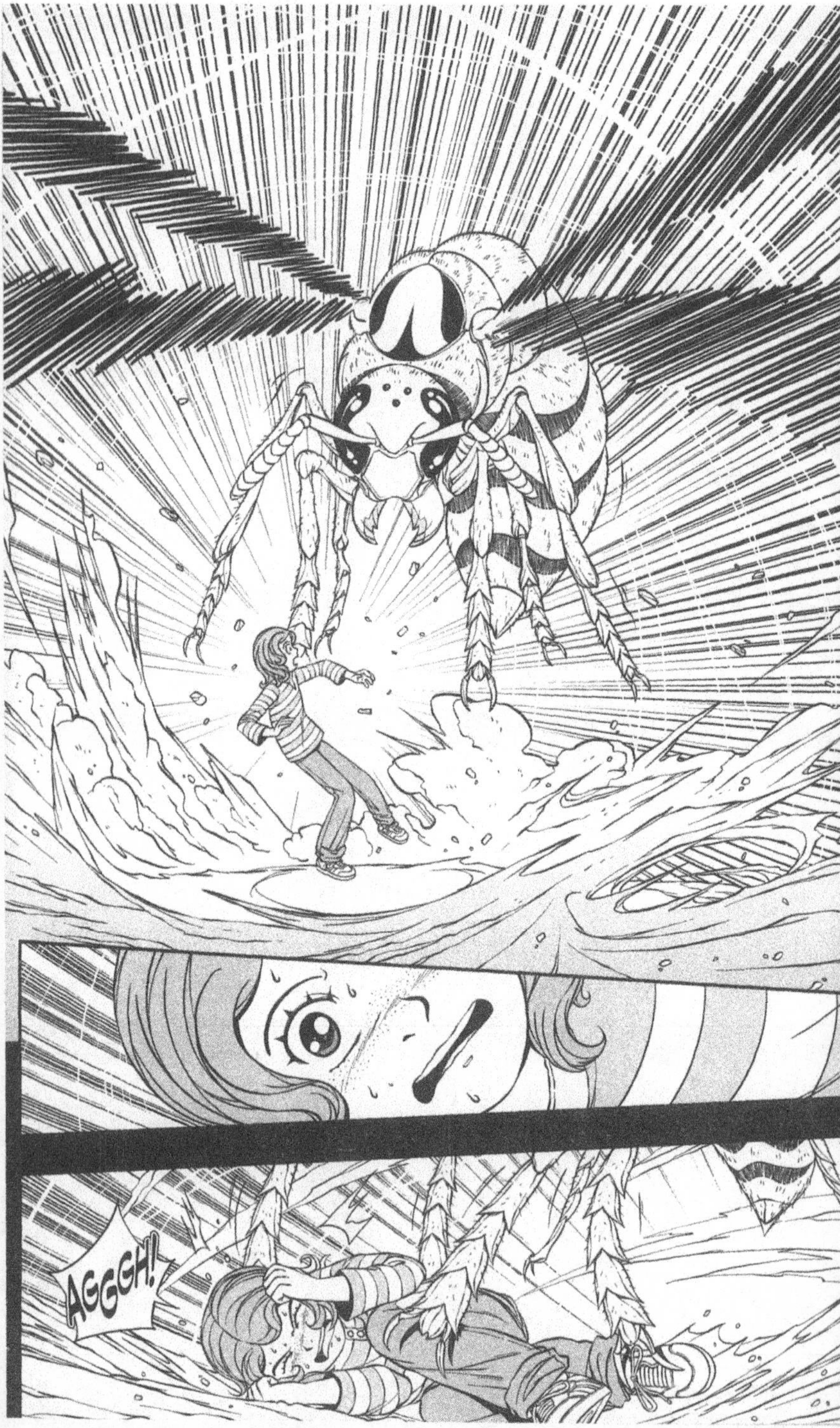
AGGGH!

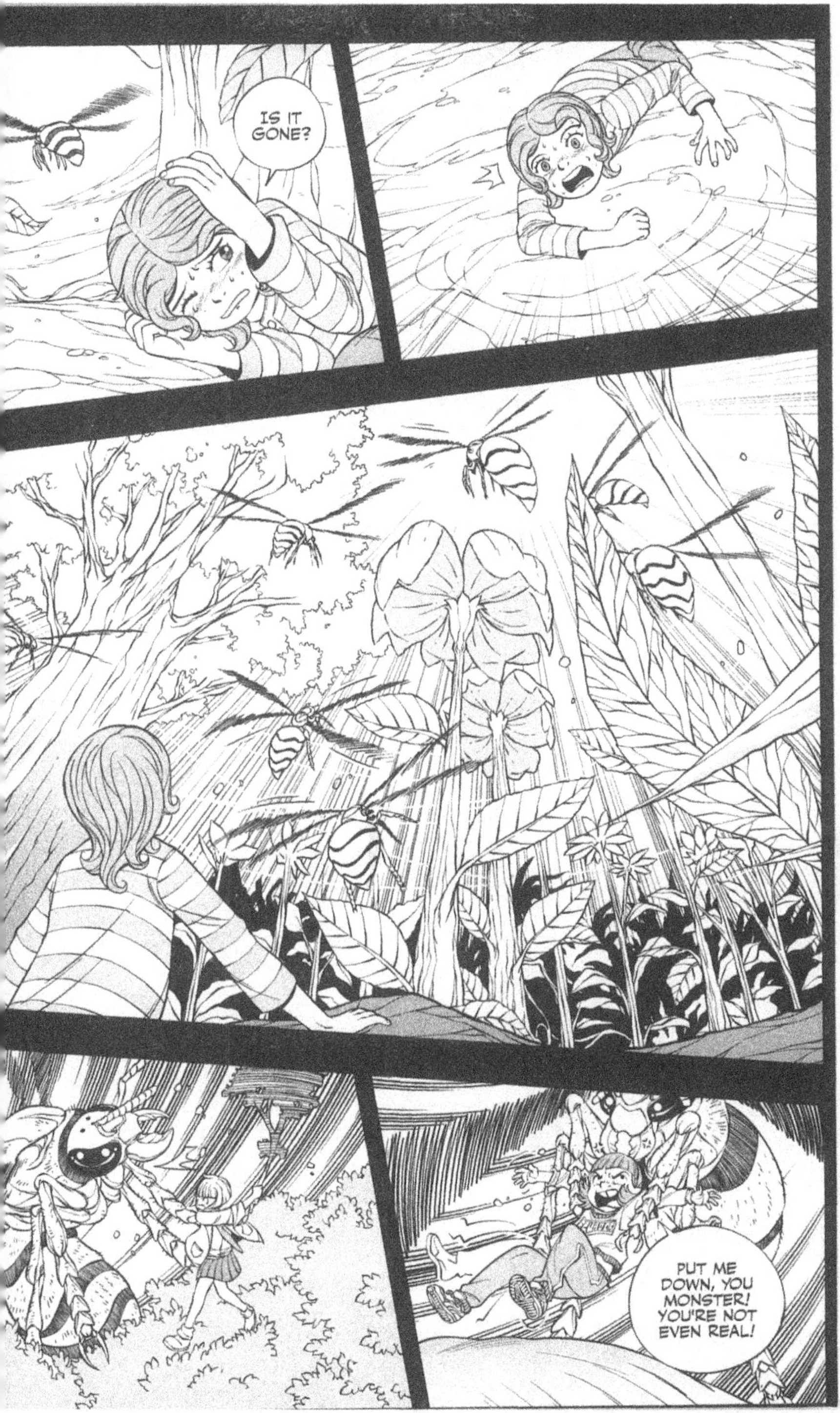
IS IT GONE?
PUT ME DOWN, YOU MONSTER! YOU'RE NOT EVEN REAL!

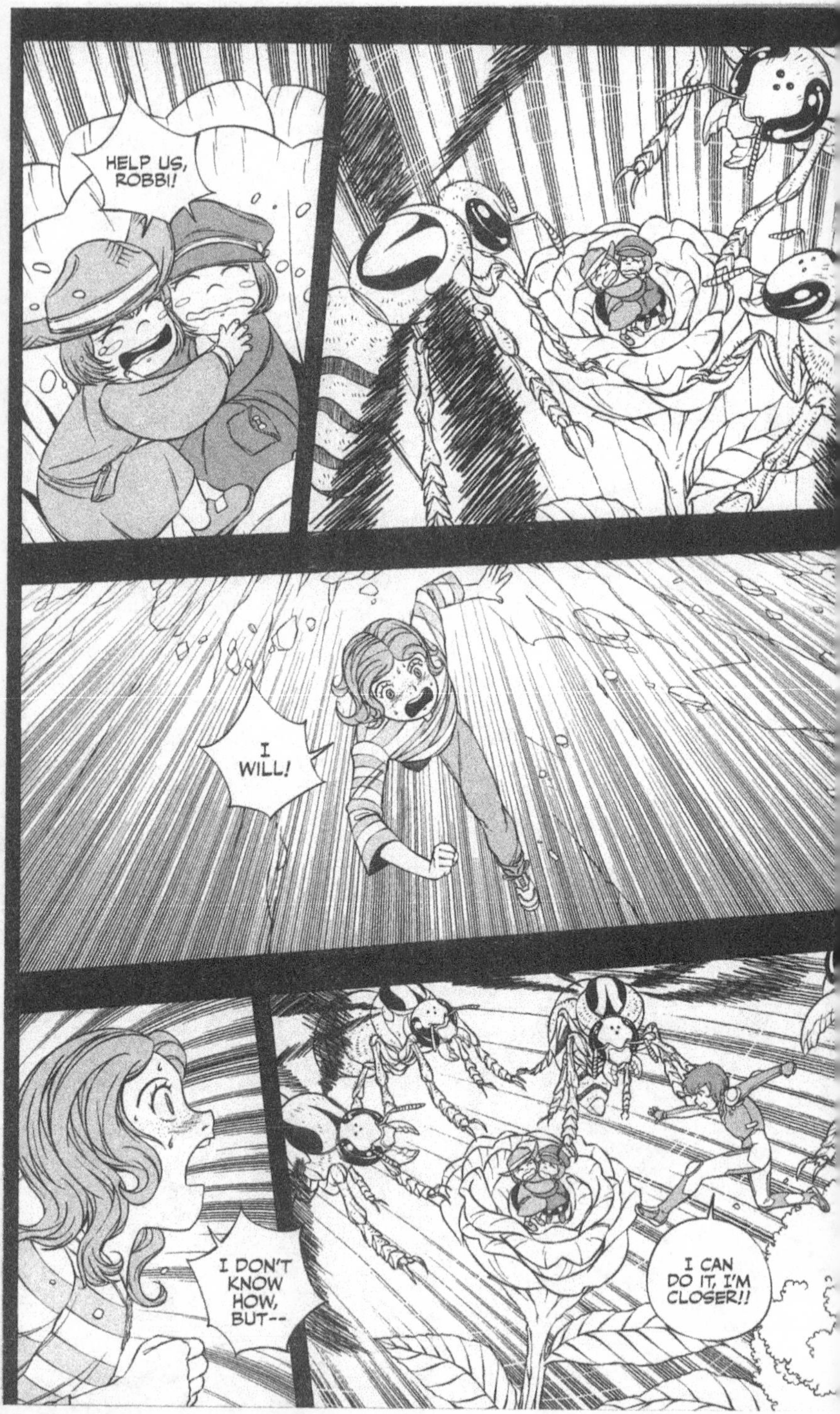
HELP US, ROBBI!
I WILL!
I DON'T KNOW HOW, BUT--
I CAN DO IT, I'M CLOSER!!

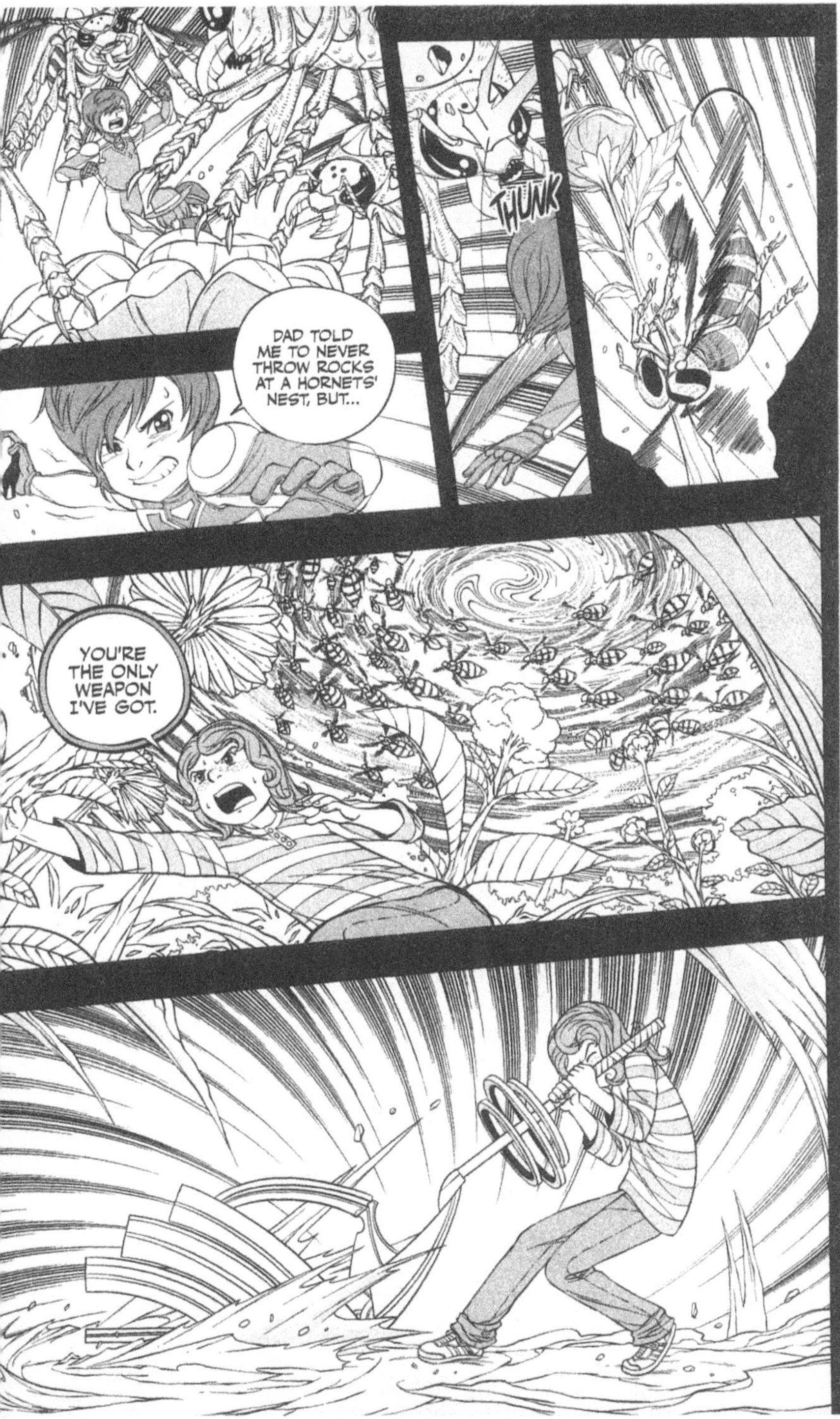
THUNK
DAD TOLD ME TO NEVER THROW ROCKS AT A HORNETS' NEST, BUT...
YOU'RE THE ONLY WEAPON I'VE GOT.

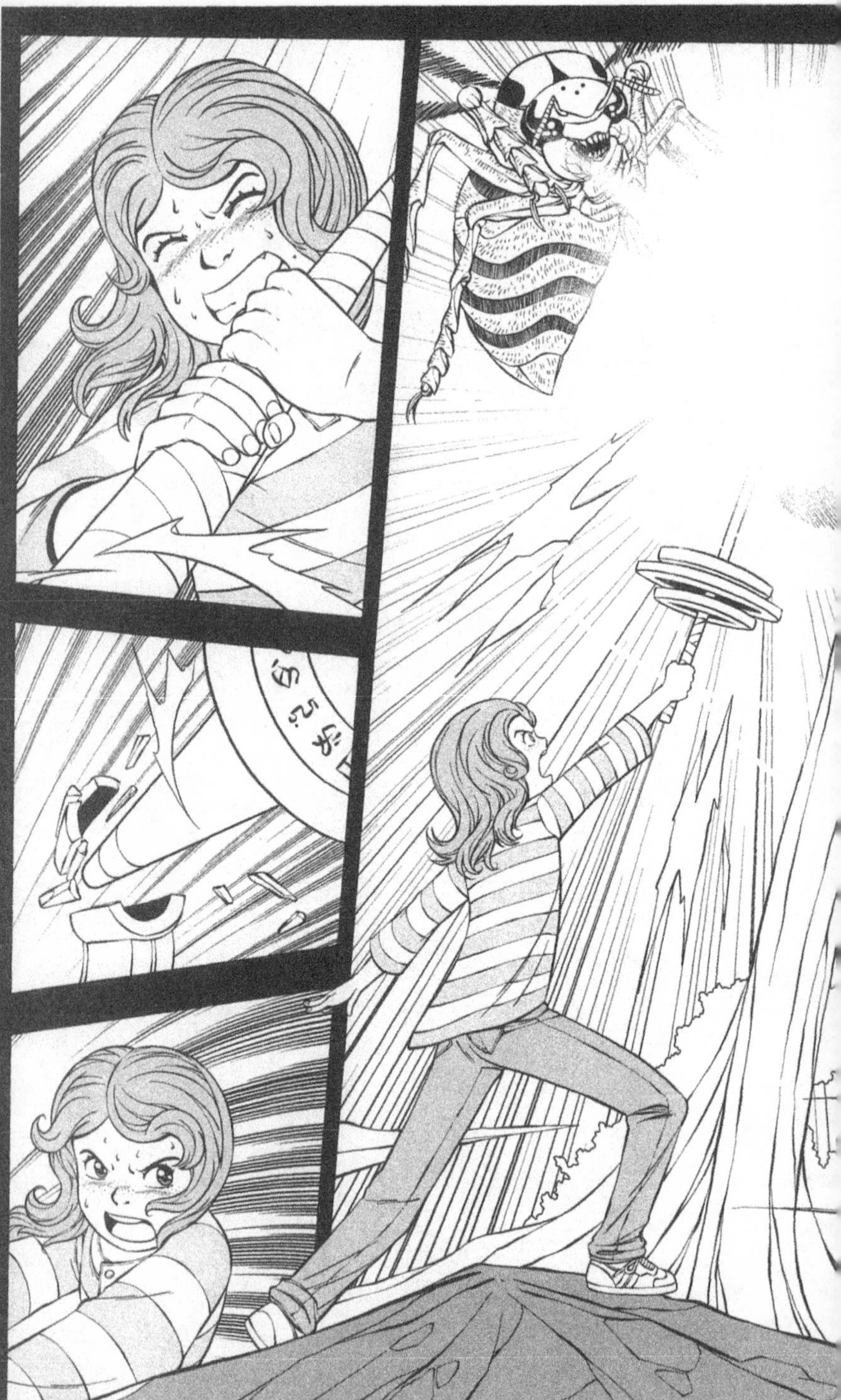

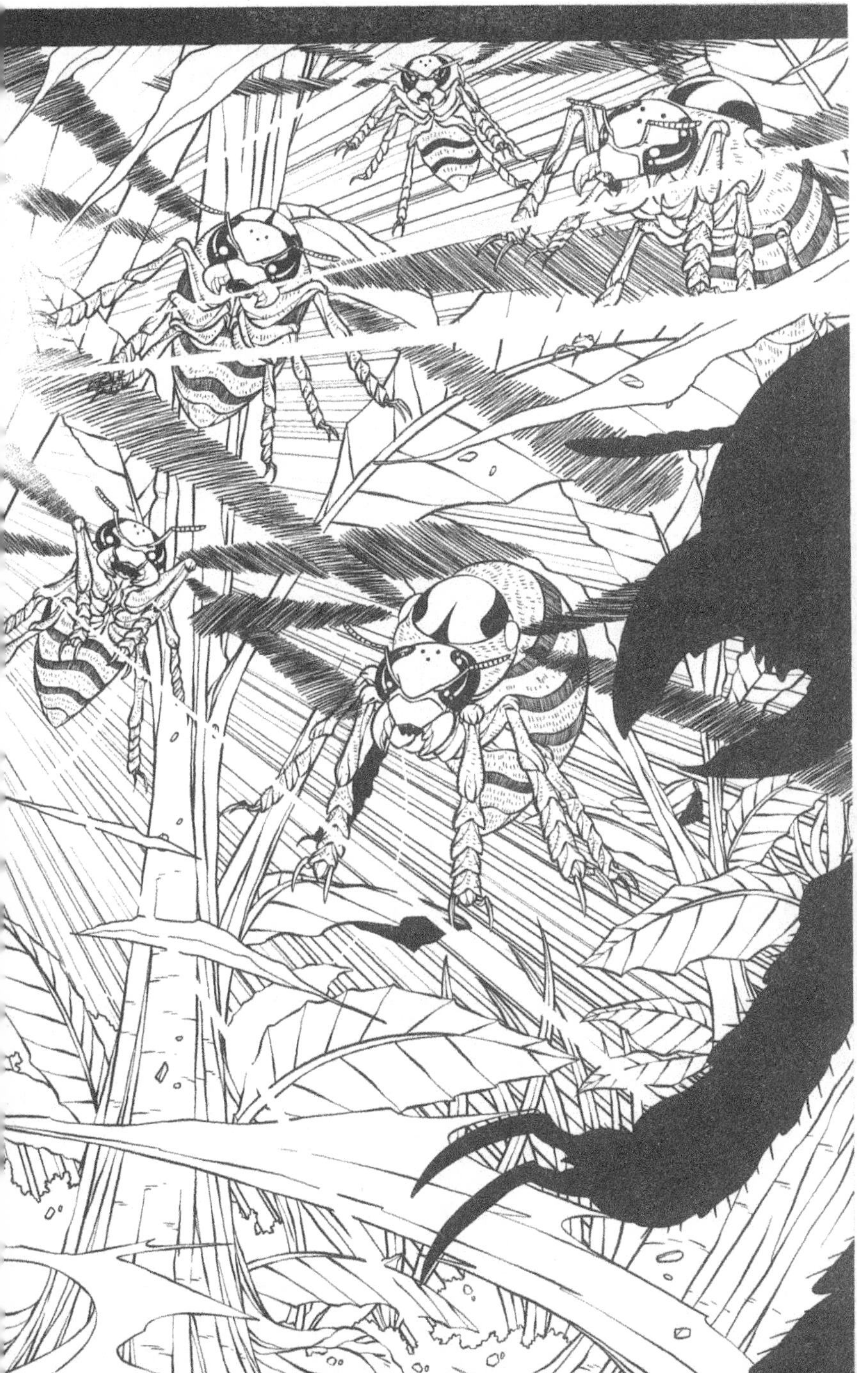

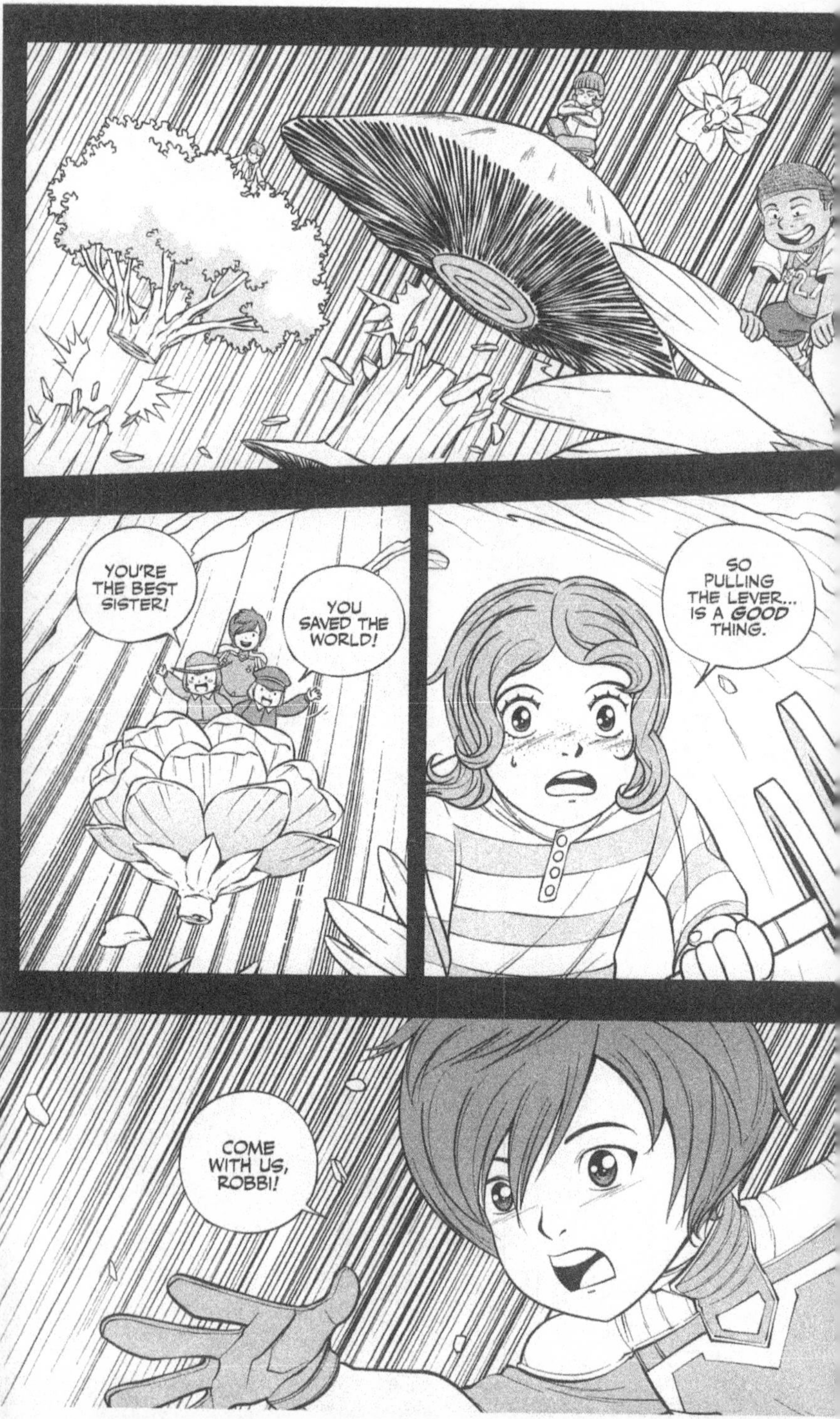
YOU'RE THE BEST SISTER!
YOU SAVED THE WORLD!
SO PULLING THE LEVER... IS A *GOOD* THING.
COME WITH US, ROBBI!

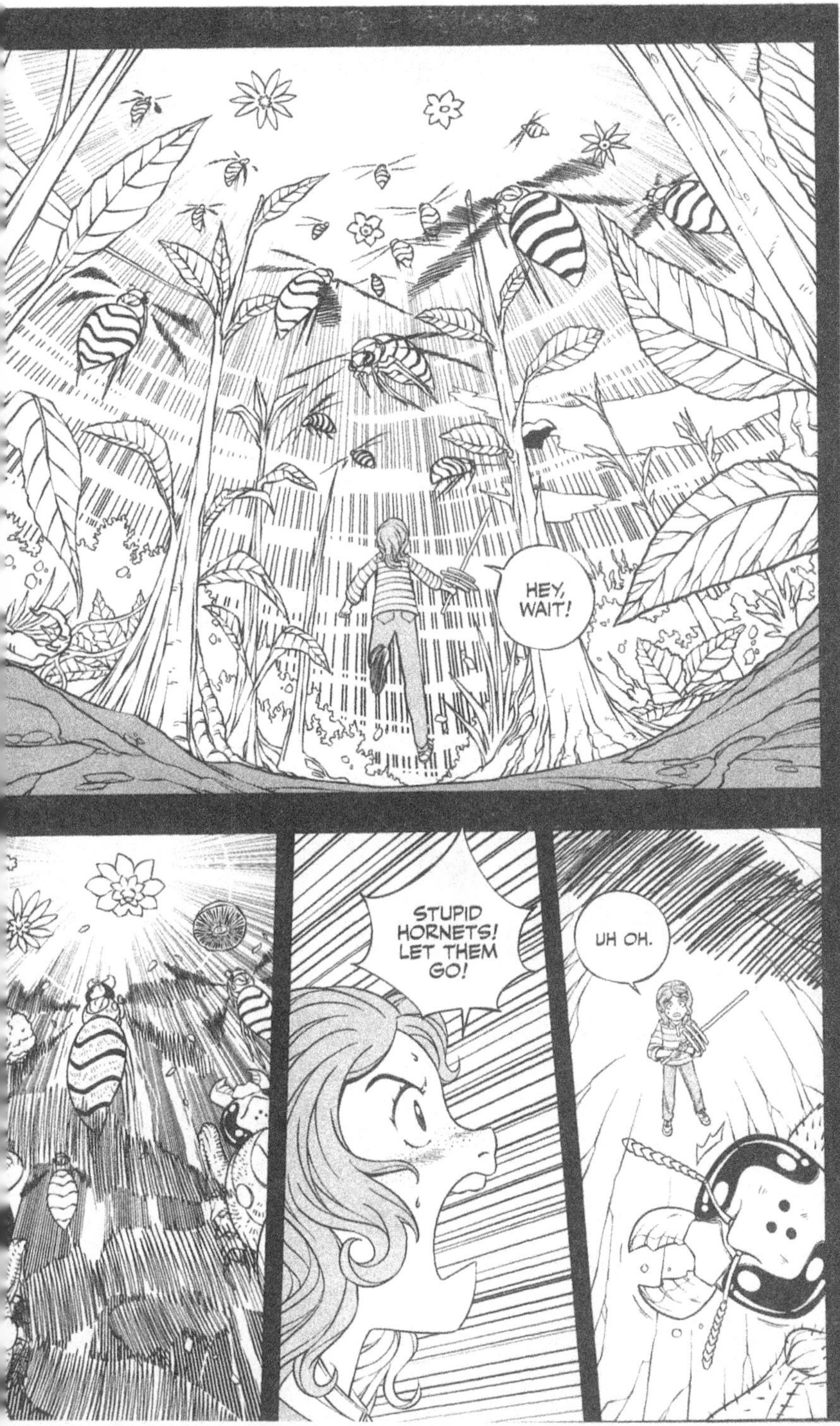
HEY, WAIT!
STUPID HORNETS! LET THEM GO!
UH OH.

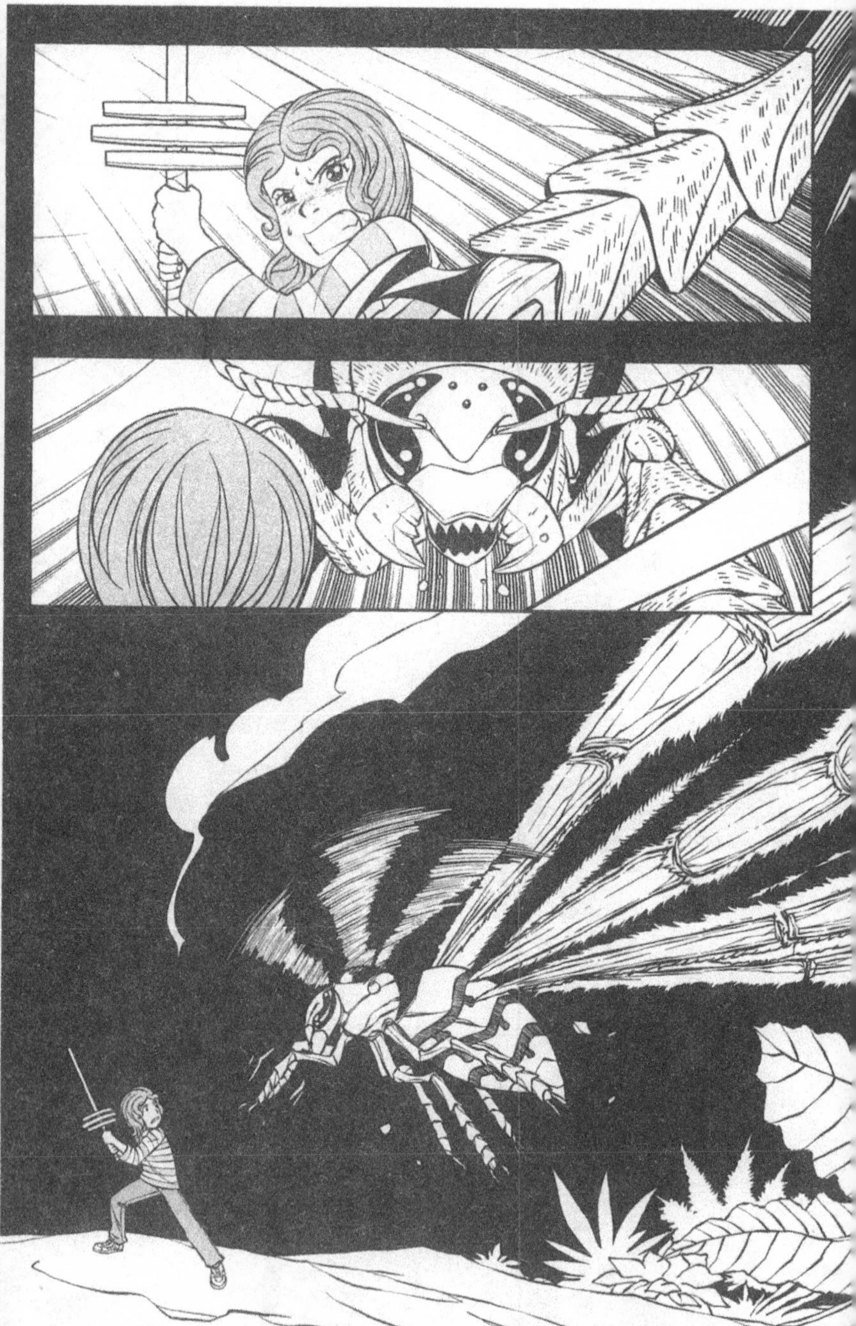

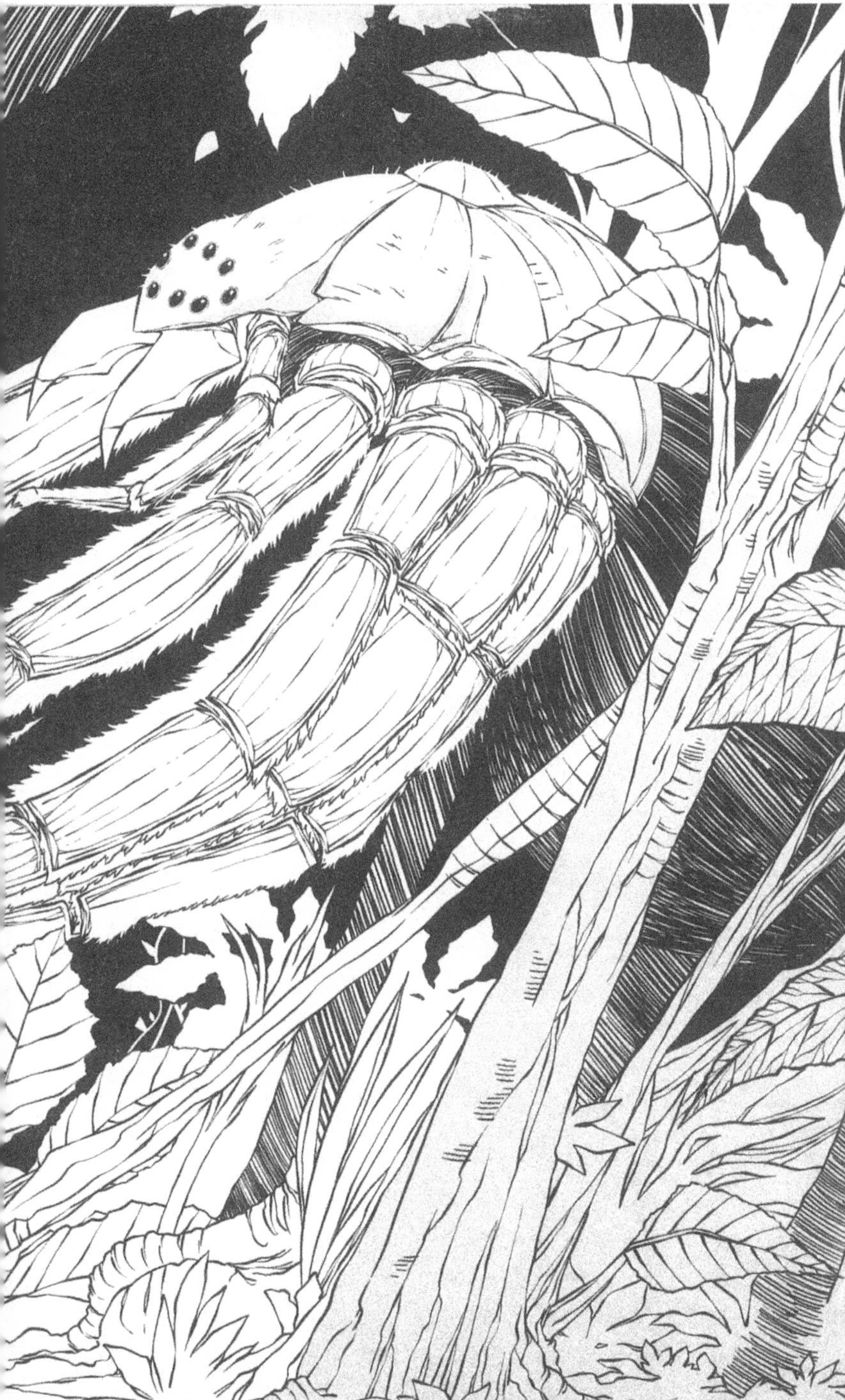

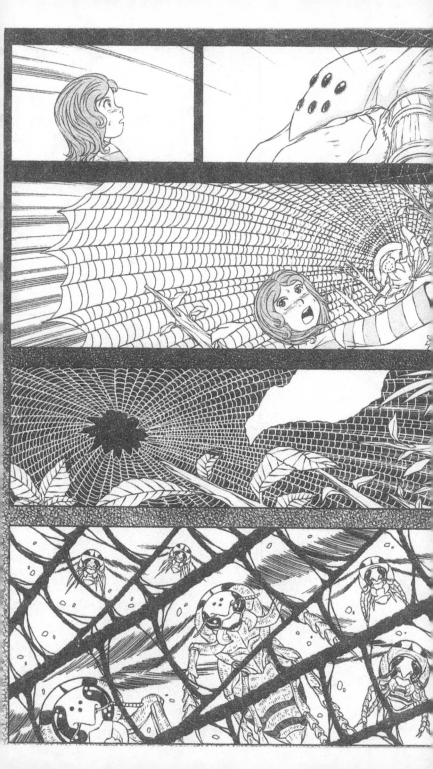

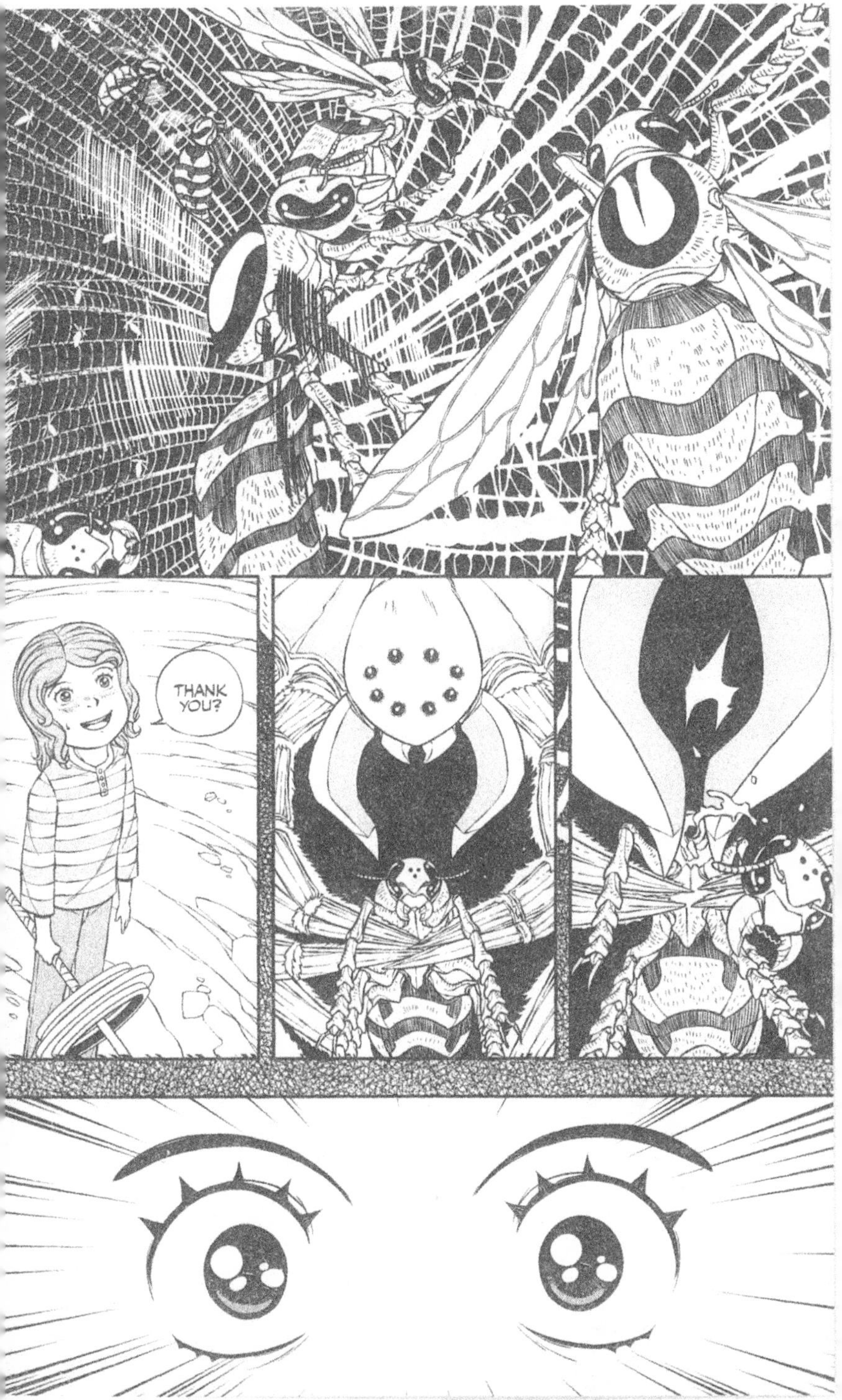
THANK YOU?

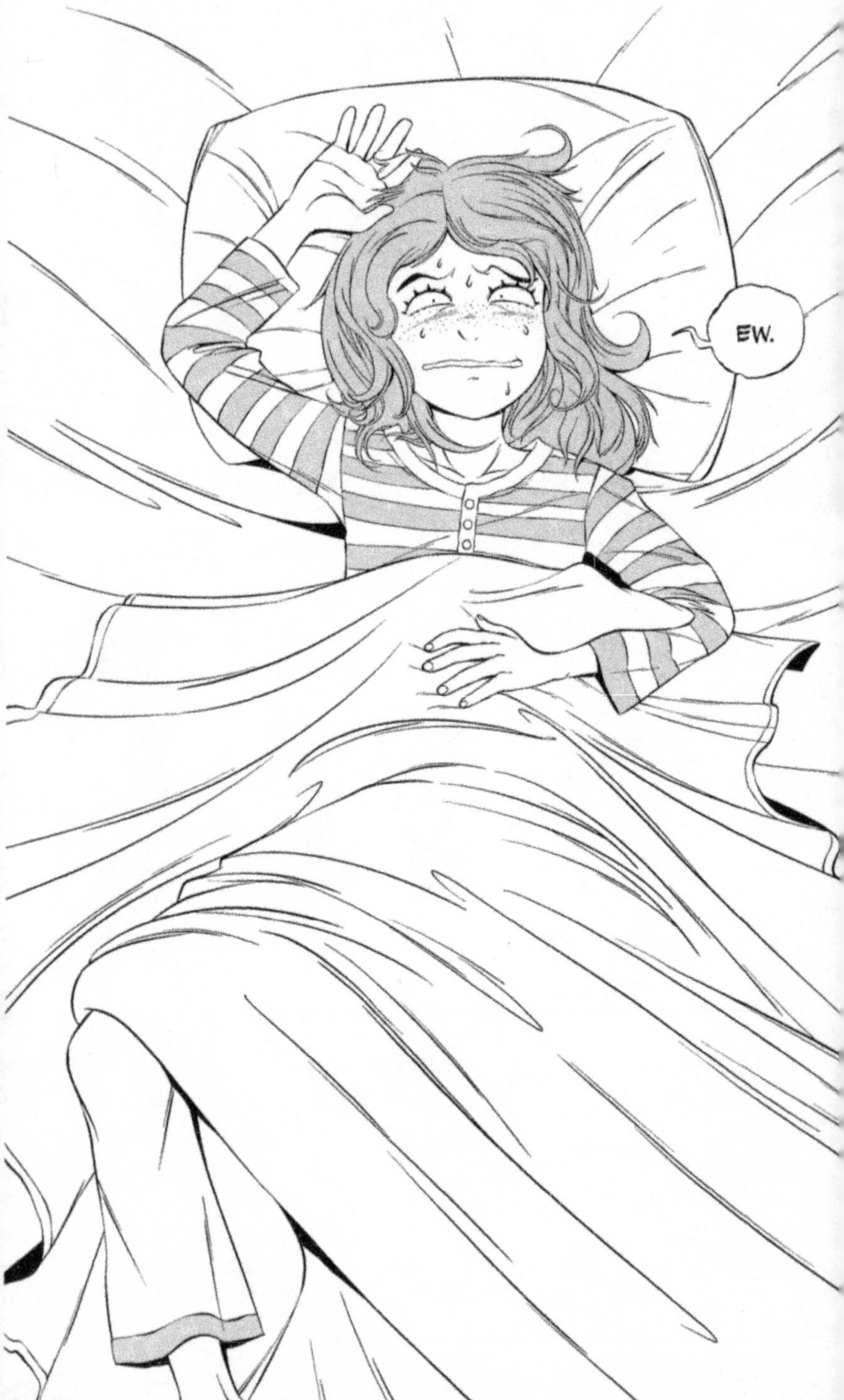
EW.

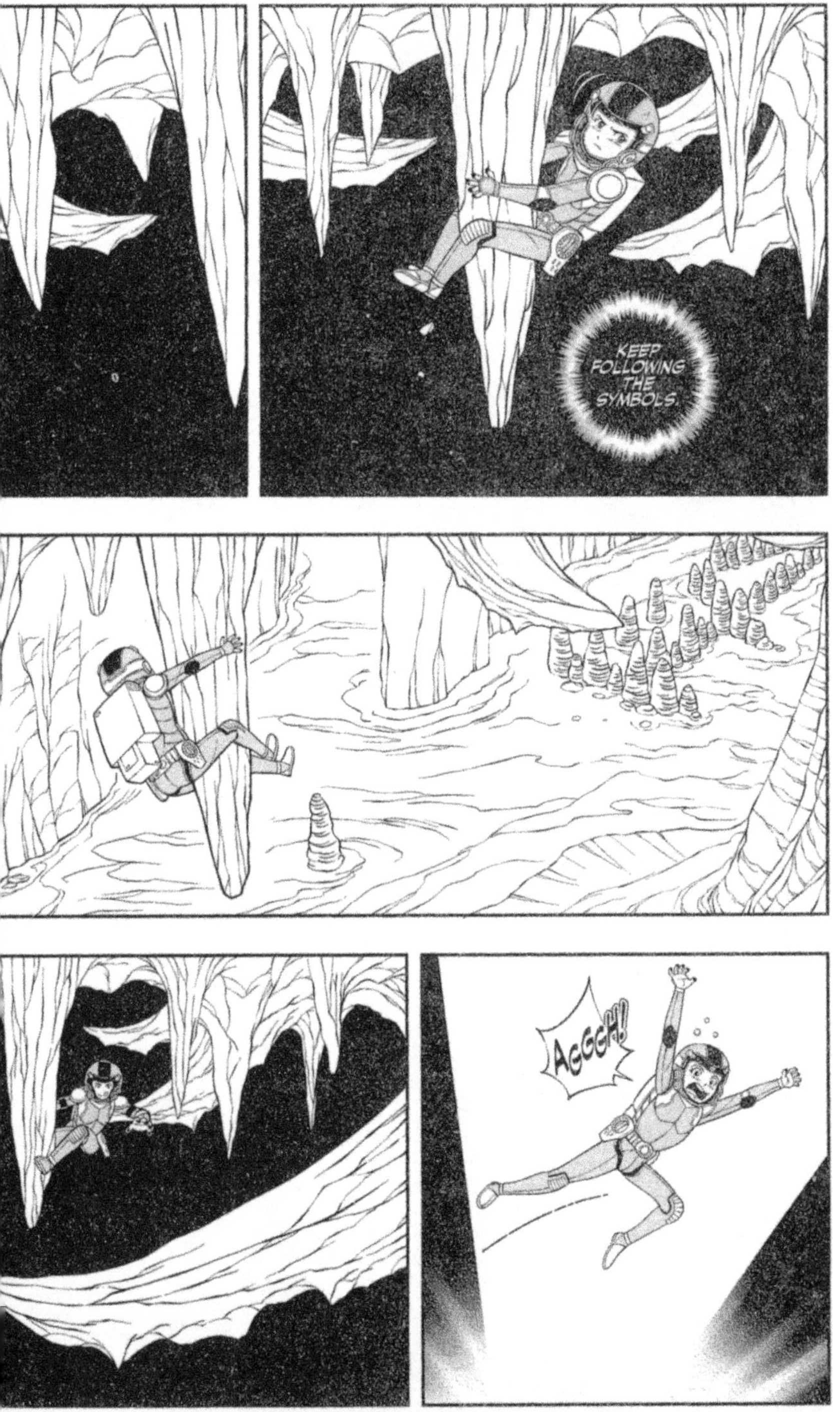
KEEP FOLLOWING THE SYMBOLS.
AGGGH!

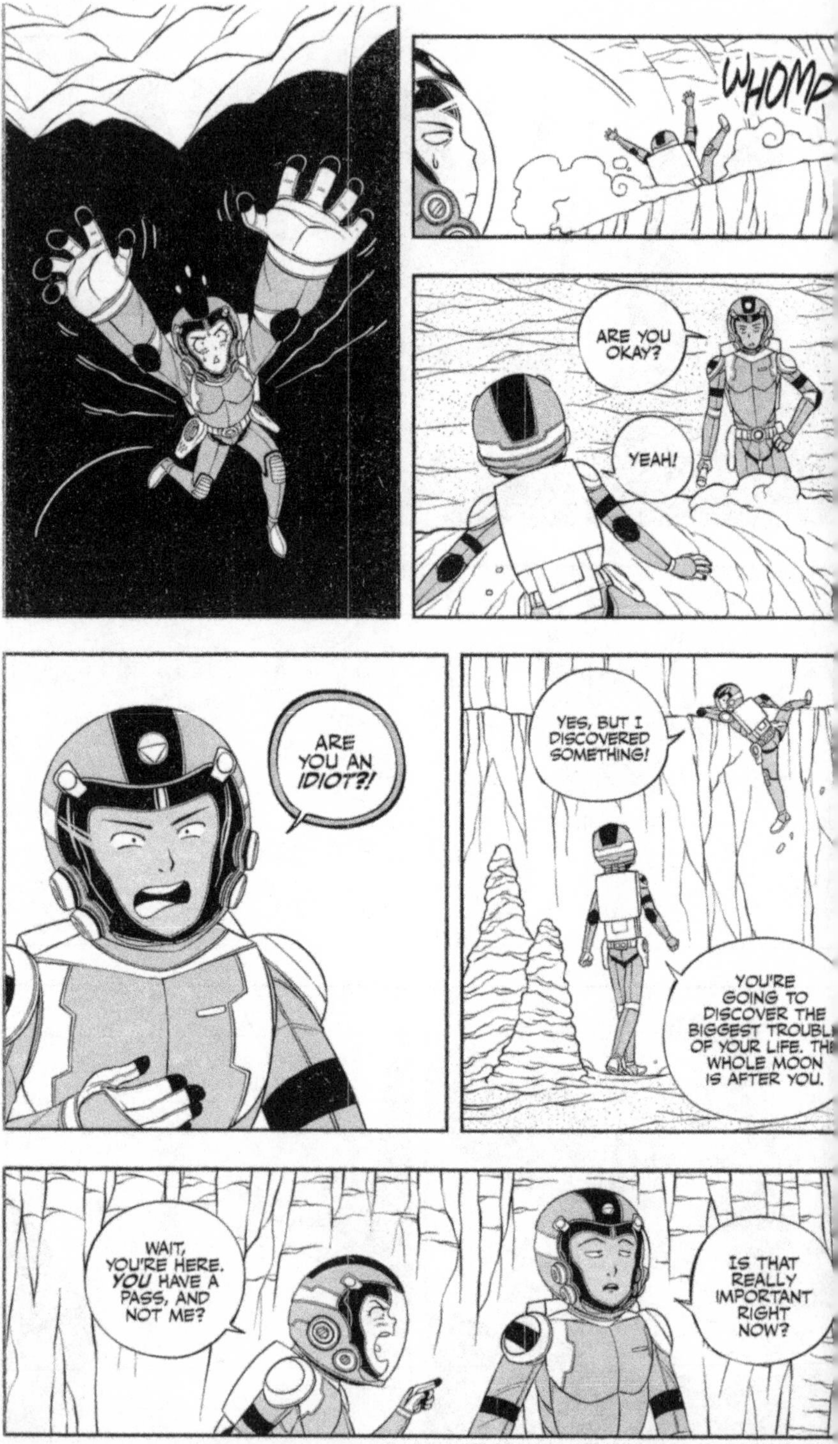
WHOMP
ARE YOU OKAY?
YEAH!
ARE YOU AN *IDIOT?!*
YES, BUT I DISCOVERED SOMETHING!
YOU'RE GOING TO DISCOVER THE BIGGEST TROUBL OF YOUR LIFE. TH WHOLE MOON IS AFTER YOU.
WAIT, YOU'RE HERE. ***YOU*** HAVE A PASS, AND NOT ME?
IS THAT REALLY IMPORTANT RIGHT NOW?

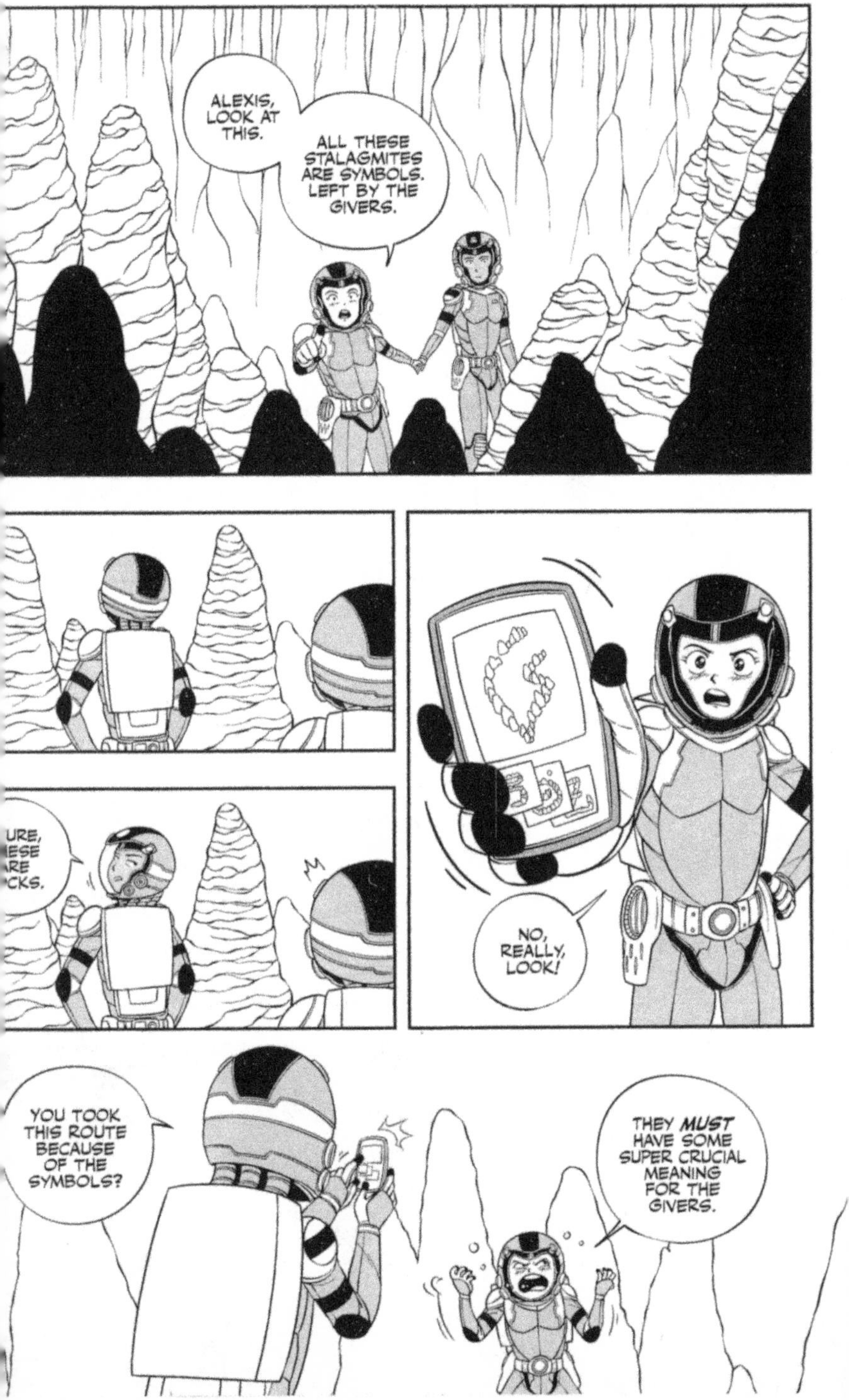
ALEXIS, LOOK AT THIS.
ALL THESE STALAGMITES ARE SYMBOLS. LEFT BY THE GIVERS.
URE, ESE ARE CKS.
NO, REALLY, LOOK!
YOU TOOK THIS ROUTE BECAUSE OF THE SYMBOLS?
THEY *MUST* HAVE SOME SUPER CRUCIAL MEANING FOR THE GIVERS.

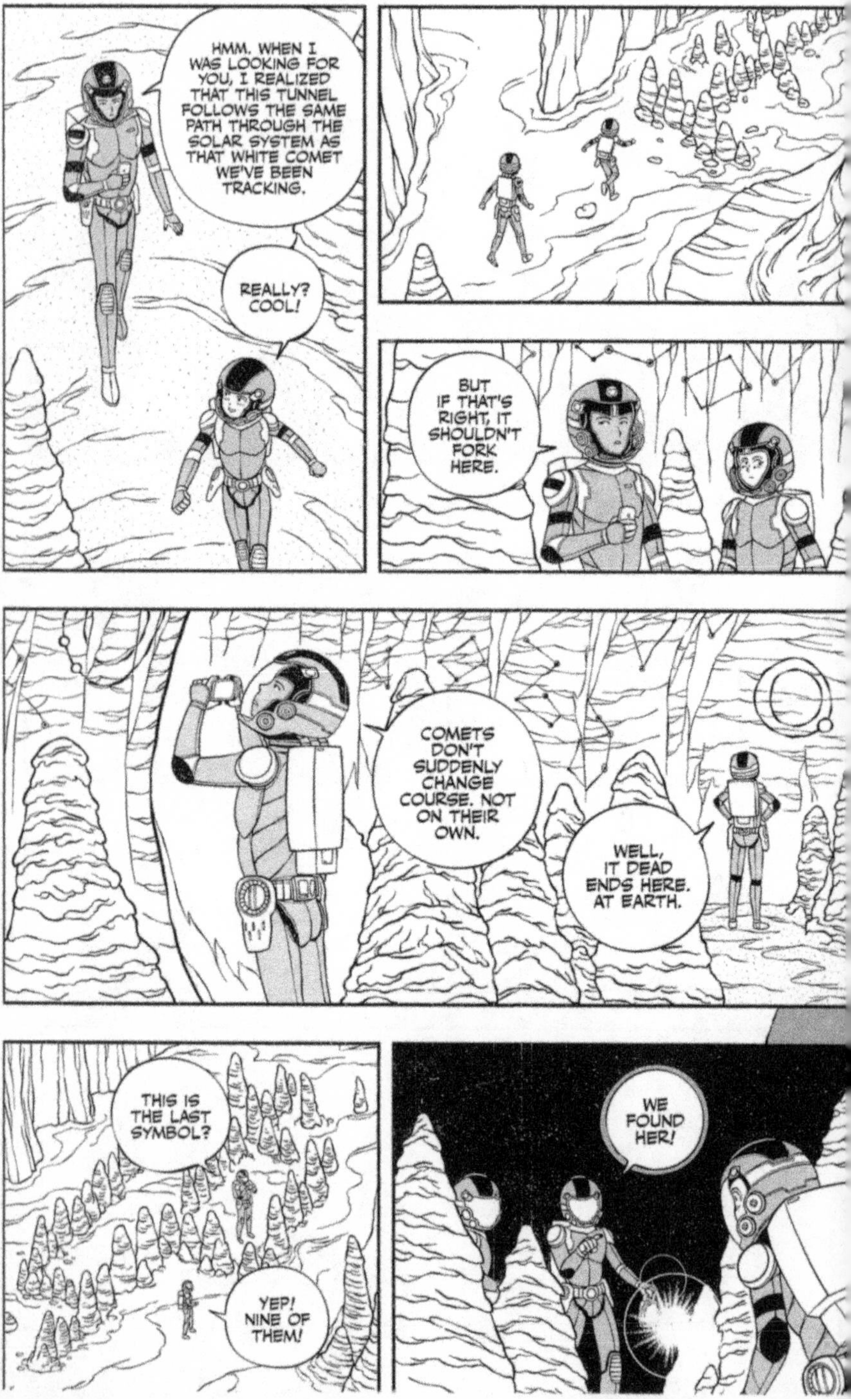
HMM. WHEN I WAS LOOKING FOR YOU, I REALIZED THAT THIS TUNNEL FOLLOWS THE SAME PATH THROUGH THE SOLAR SYSTEM AS THAT WHITE COMET WE'VE BEEN TRACKING.
REALLY? COOL!
BUT IF THAT'S RIGHT, IT SHOULDN'T FORK HERE.
COMETS DON'T SUDDENLY CHANGE COURSE. NOT ON THEIR OWN.
WELL, IT DEAD ENDS HERE. AT EARTH.
THIS IS THE LAST SYMBOL?
YEP! NINE OF THEM!
WE FOUND HER!

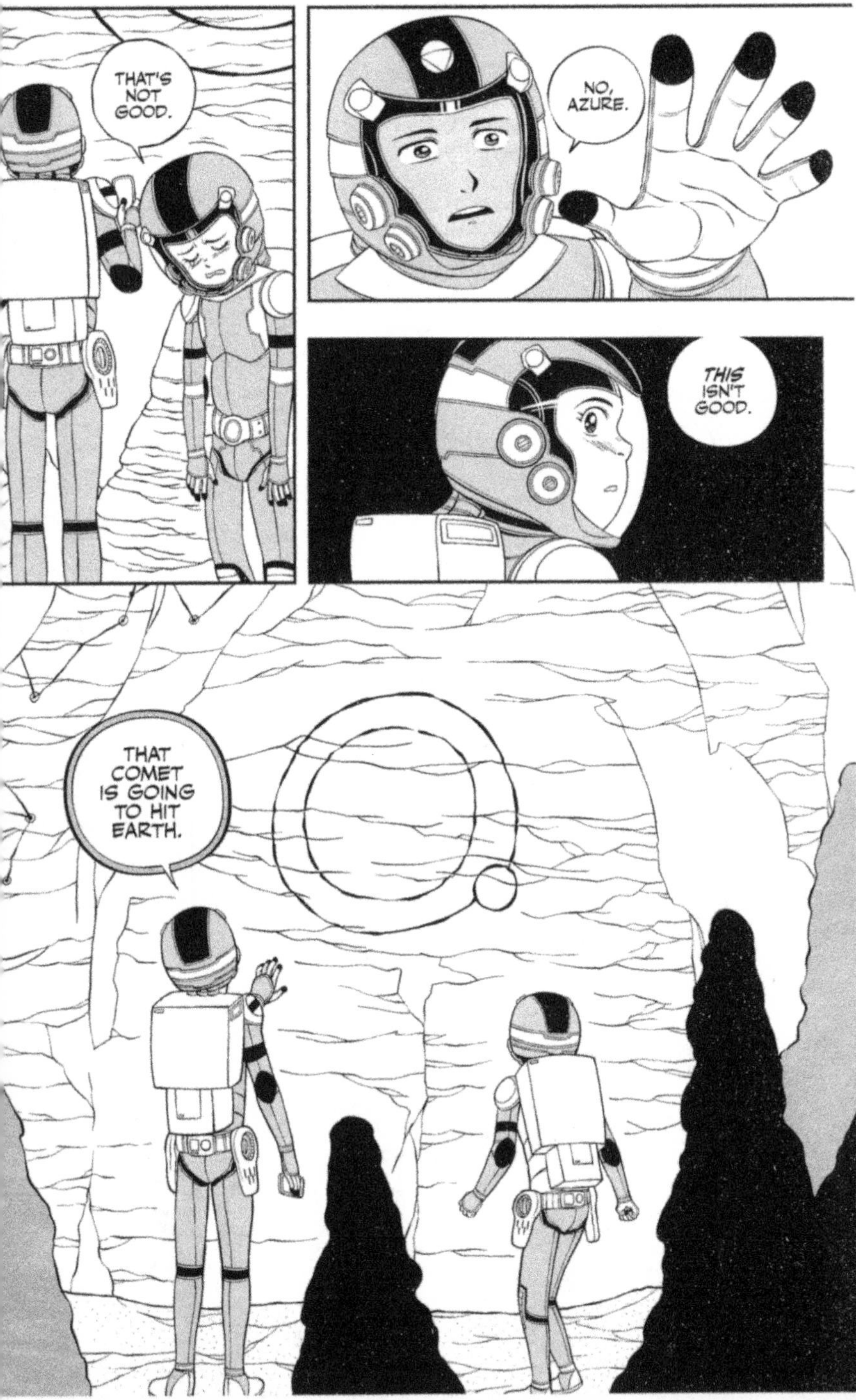
THAT'S NOT GOOD.
NO, AZURE.
THIS ISN'T GOOD.
THAT COMET IS GOING TO HIT EARTH.

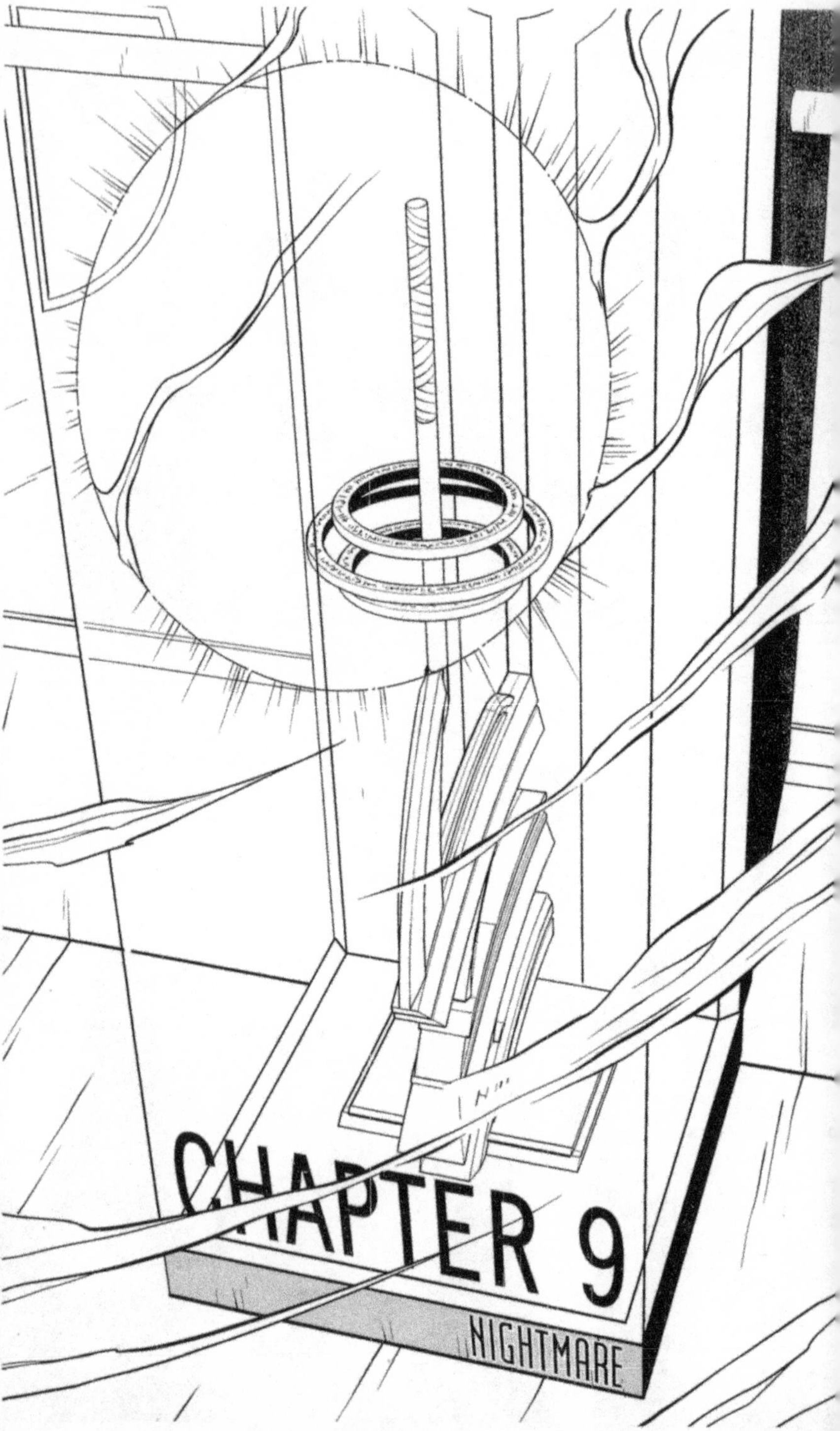
CHAPTER 9
NIGHTMARE

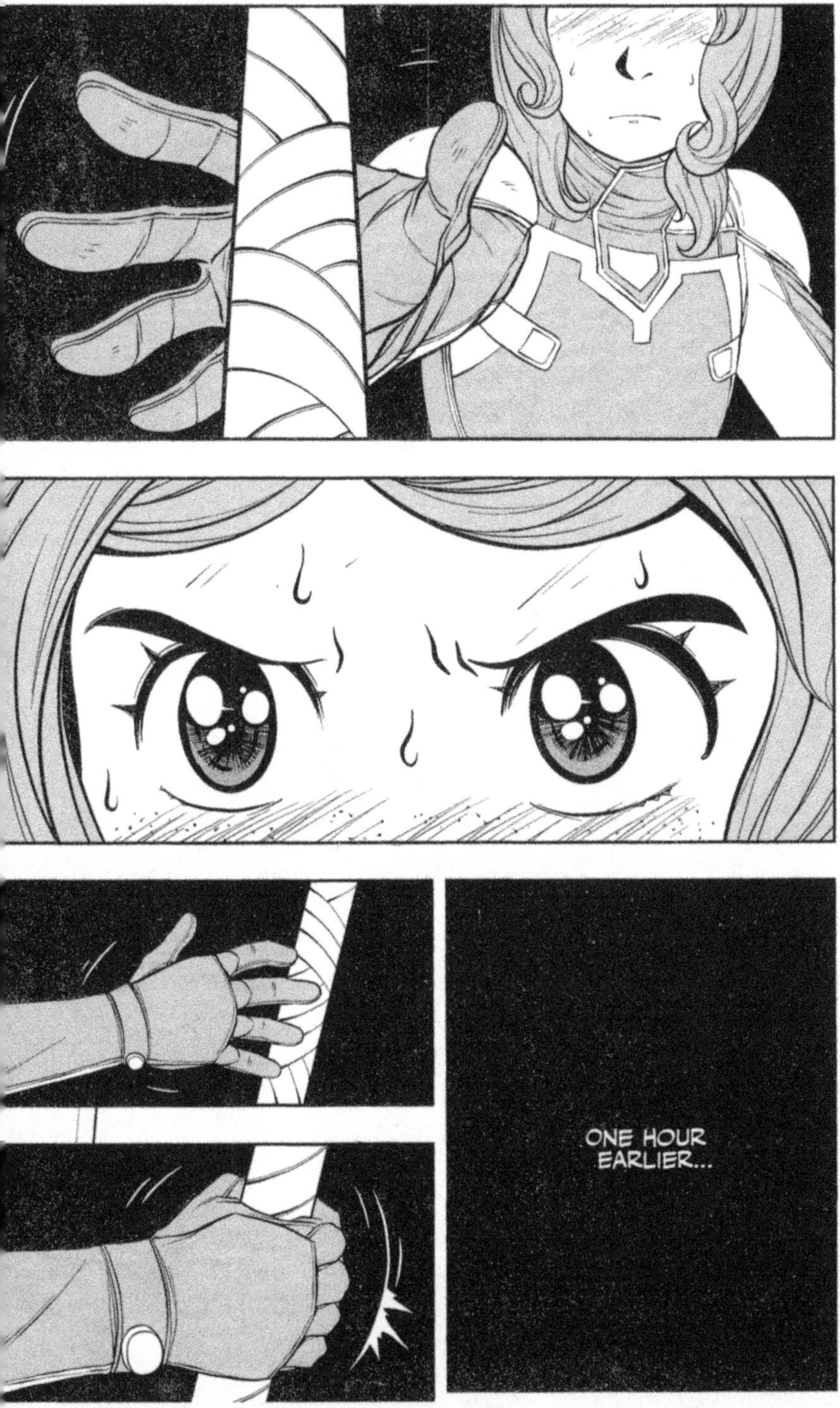
ONE HOUR
EARLIER...

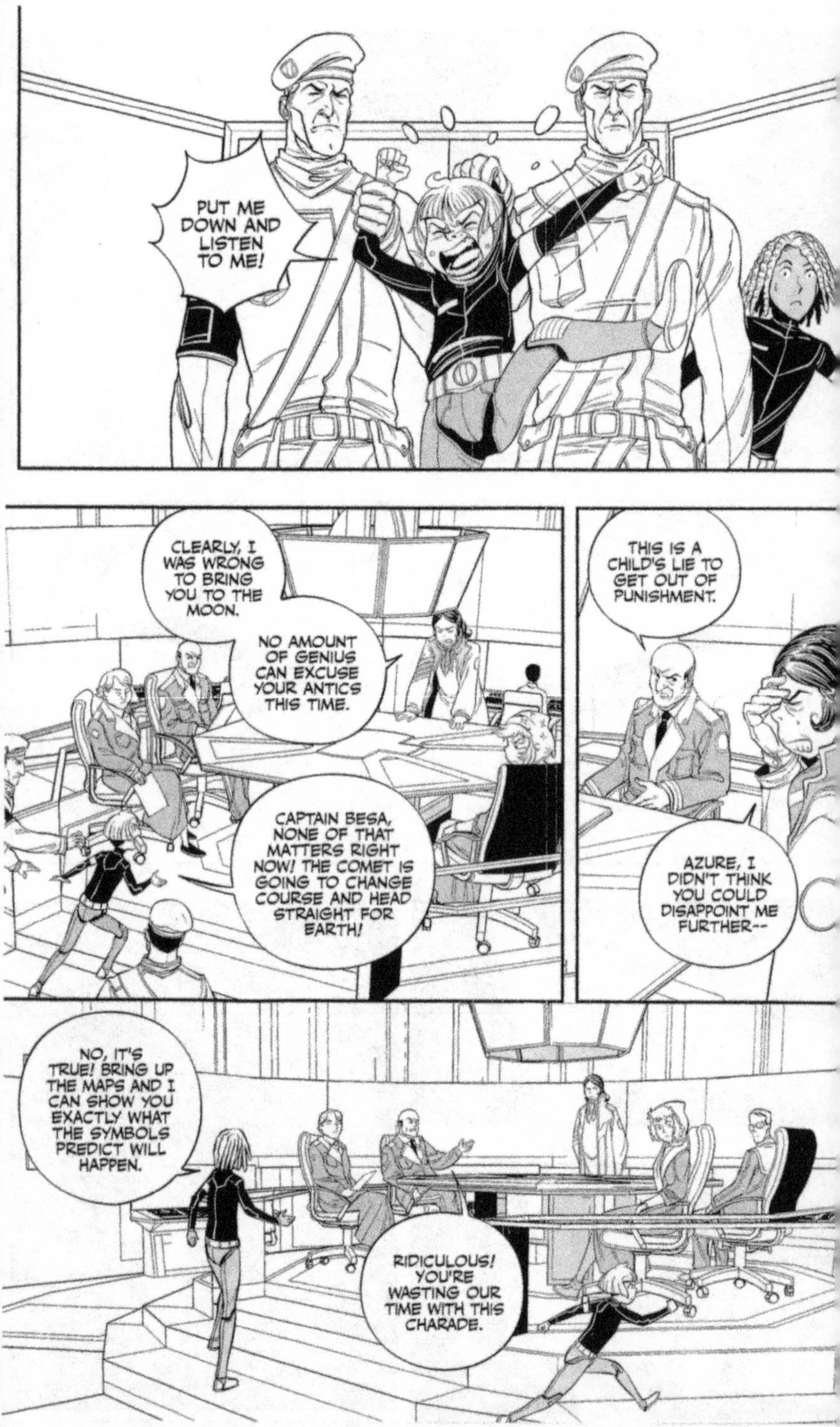
PUT ME DOWN AND LISTEN TO ME!
CLEARLY, I WAS WRONG TO BRING YOU TO THE MOON.
NO AMOUNT OF GENIUS CAN EXCUSE YOUR ANTICS THIS TIME.
CAPTAIN BESA, NONE OF THAT MATTERS RIGHT NOW! THE COMET IS GOING TO CHANGE COURSE AND HEAD STRAIGHT FOR EARTH!
THIS IS A CHILD'S LIE TO GET OUT OF PUNISHMENT.
AZURE, I DIDN'T THINK YOU COULD DISAPPOINT ME FURTHER--
NO, IT'S TRUE! BRING UP THE MAPS AND I CAN SHOW YOU EXACTLY WHAT THE SYMBOLS PREDICT WILL HAPPEN.
RIDICULOUS! YOU'RE WASTING OUR TIME WITH THIS CHARADE.

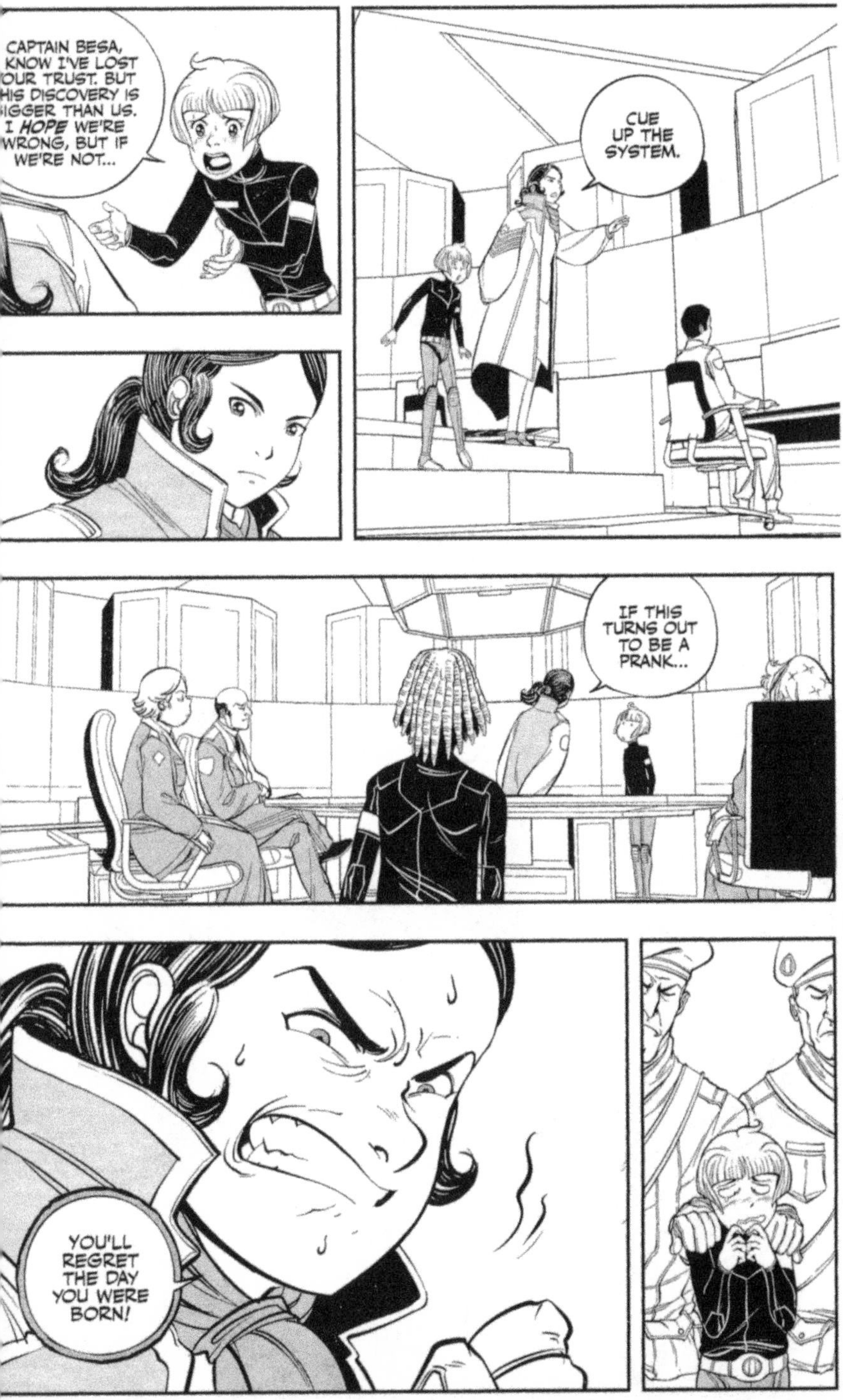
CAPTAIN BESA, KNOW I'VE LOST OUR TRUST. BUT HIS DISCOVERY IS IGGER THAN US. I *HOPE* WE'RE WRONG, BUT IF WE'RE NOT...
CUE UP THE SYSTEM.
IF THIS TURNS OUT TO BE A PRANK...
YOU'LL REGRET THE DAY YOU WERE BORN!

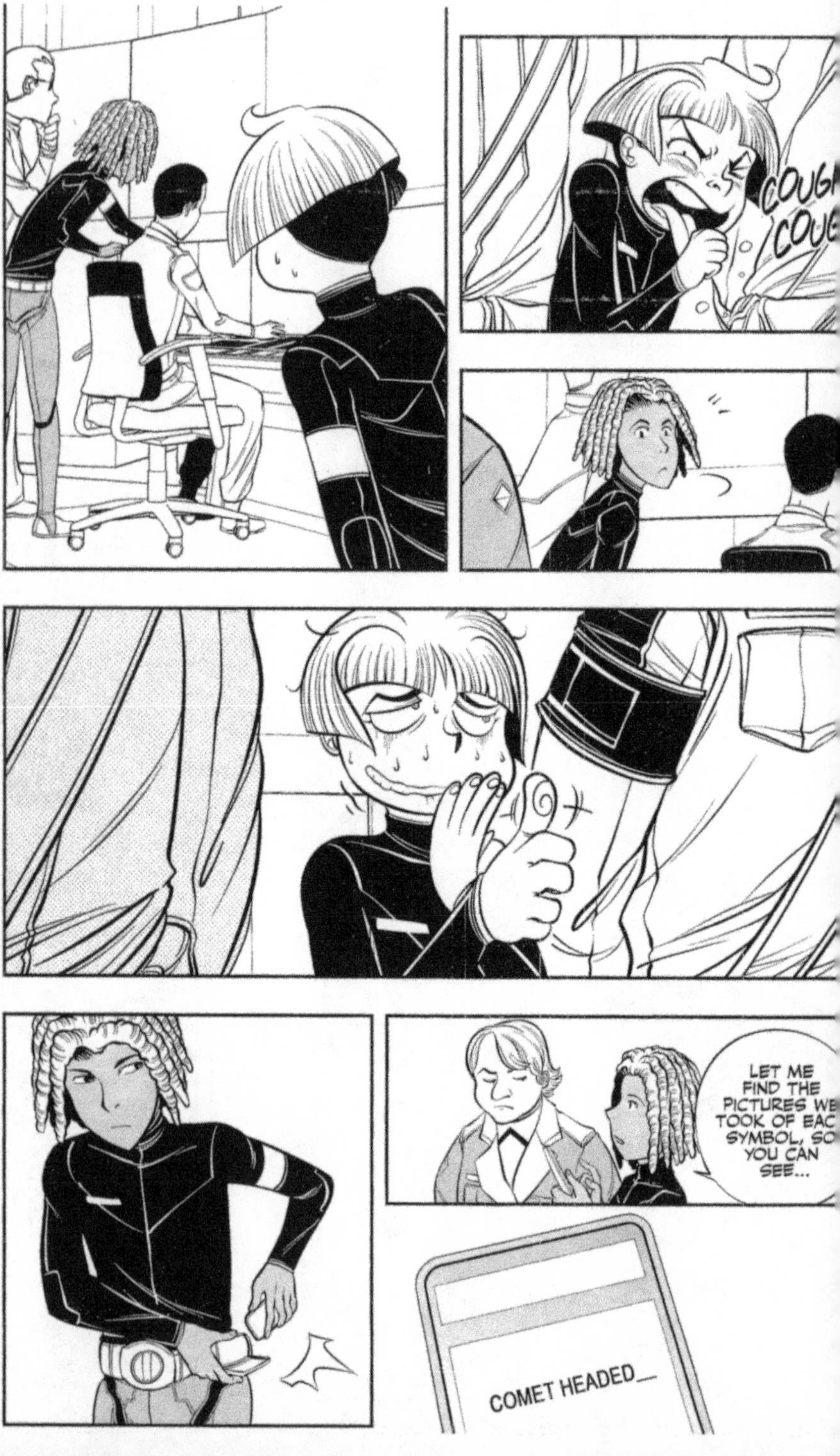
COUG
COU
LET ME FIND THE PICTURES WE TOOK OF EAC SYMBOL, SO YOU CAN SEE...
COMET HEADED_

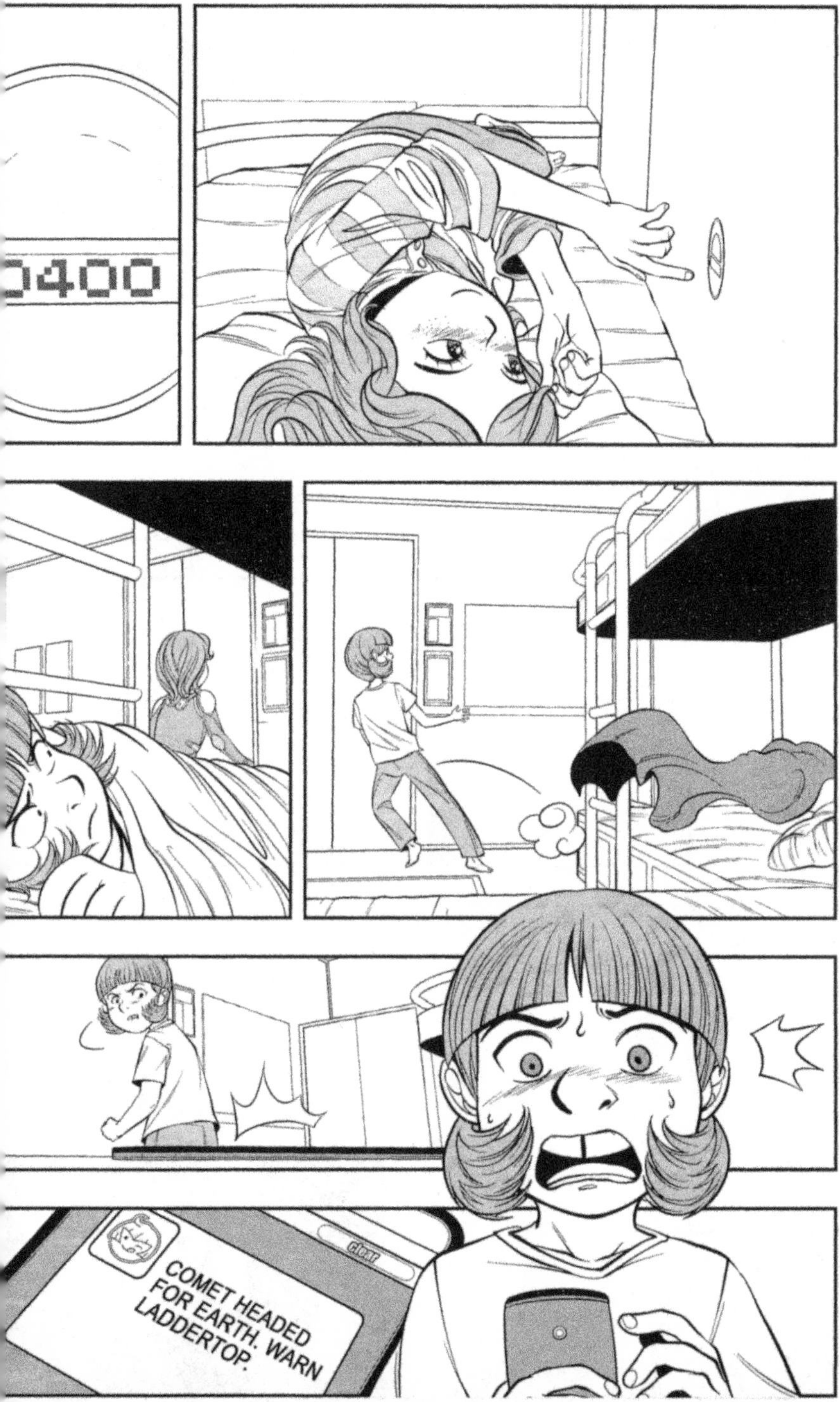
0400
clear
COMET HEADED FOR EARTH. WARN LADDERTOP.

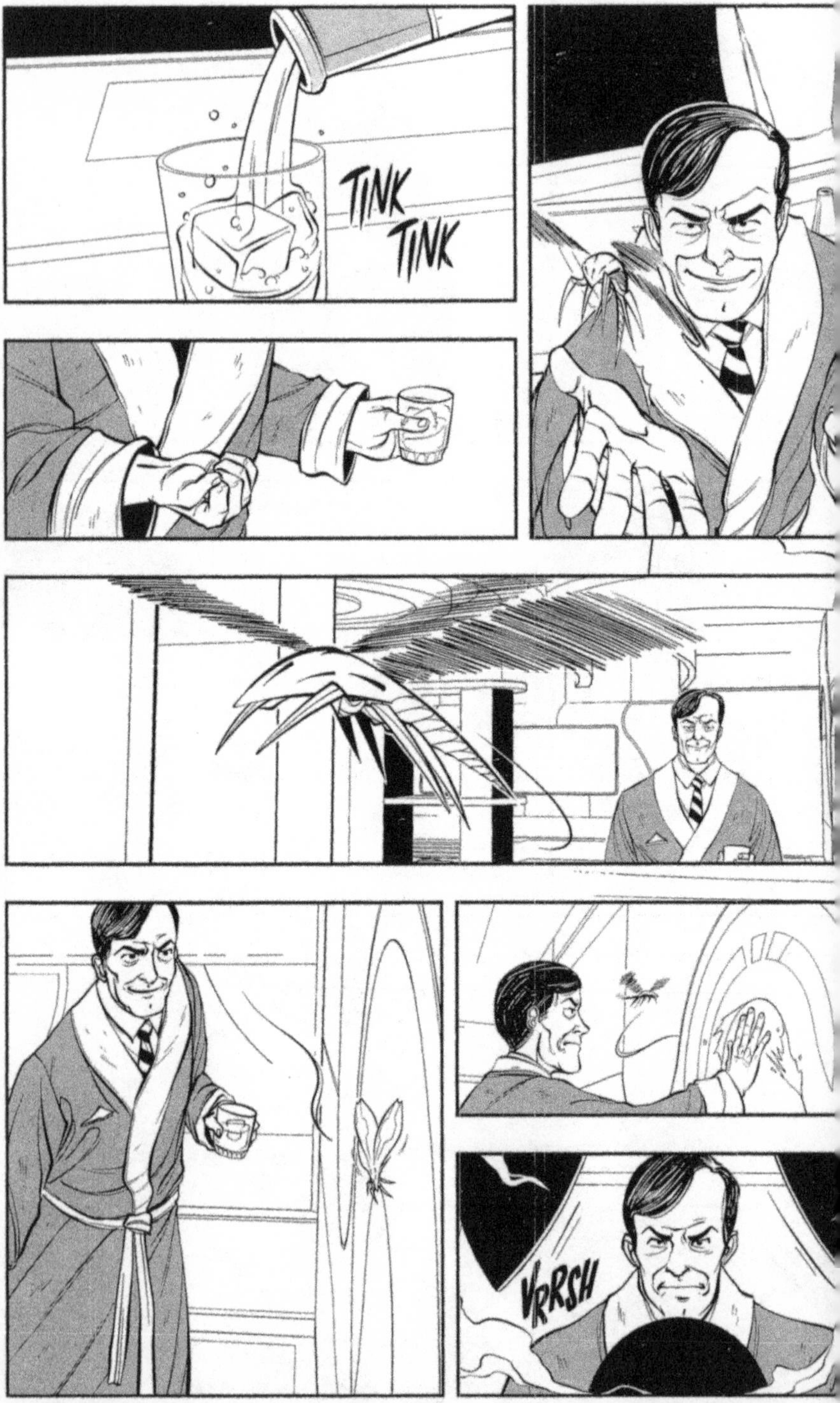
TINK
TINK
VRRSH

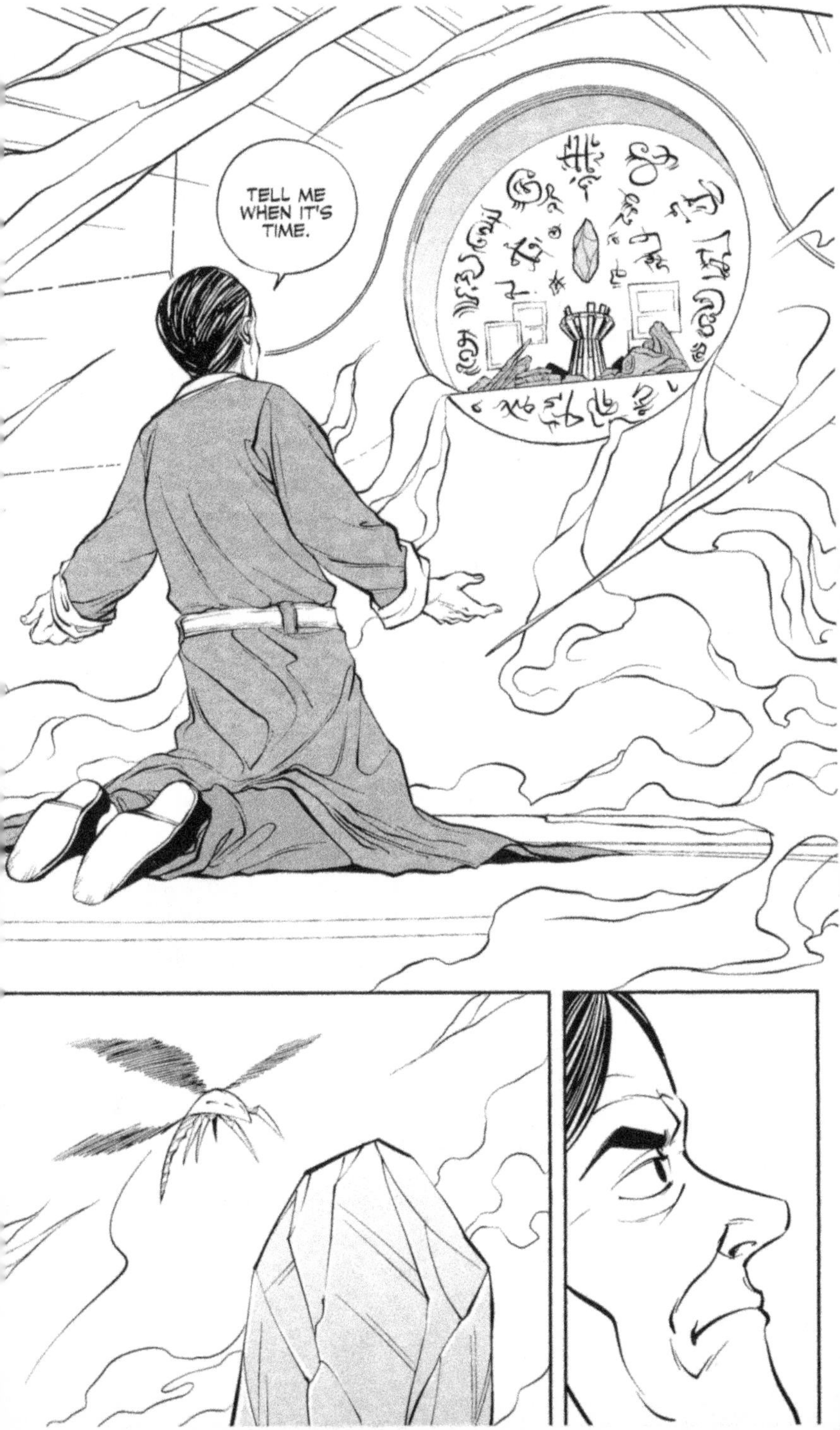
TELL ME WHEN IT'S TIME.

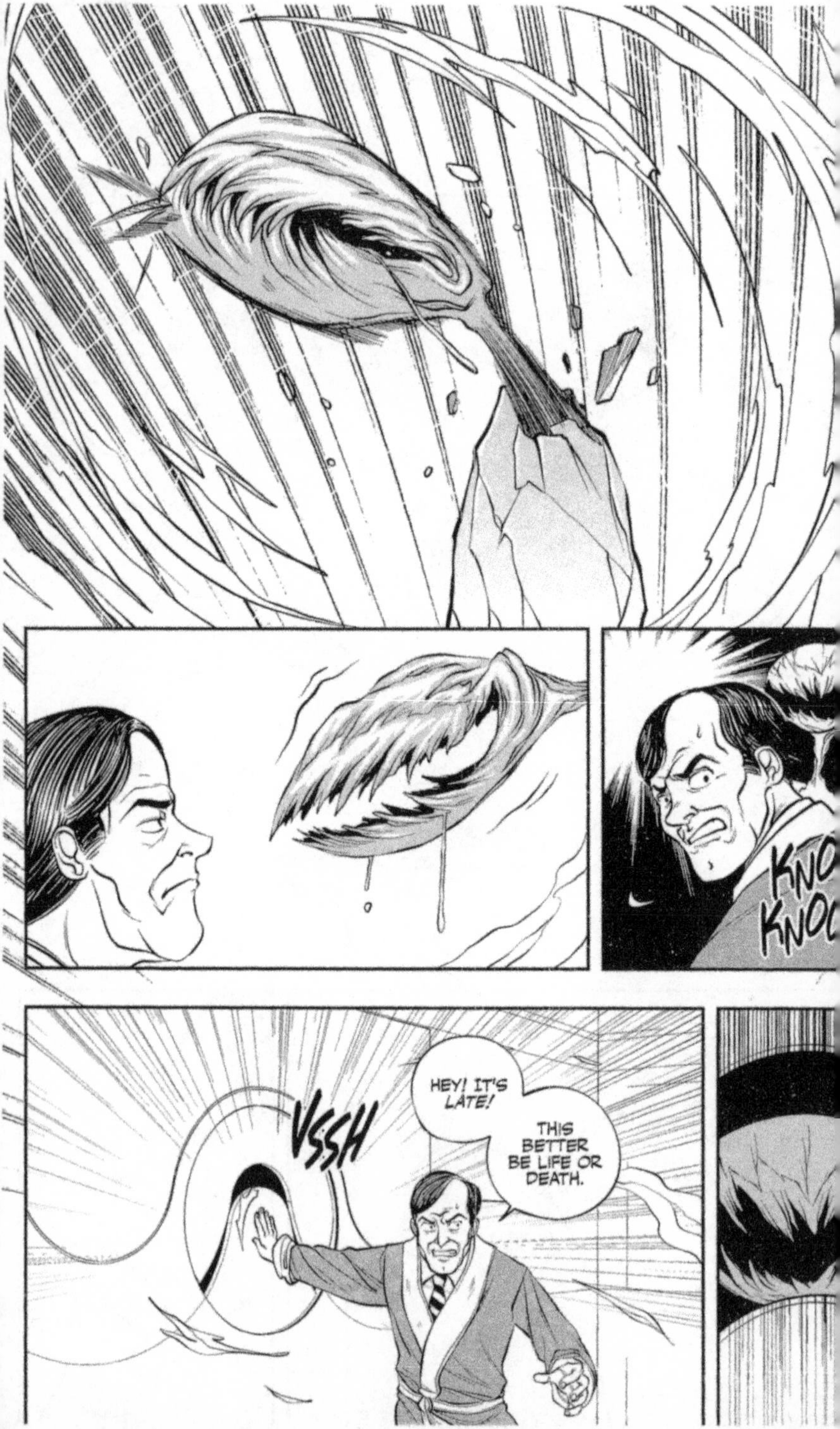

KNO
KNOC
VSSH
HEY! IT'S LATE!
THIS BETTER BE LIFE OR DEATH.

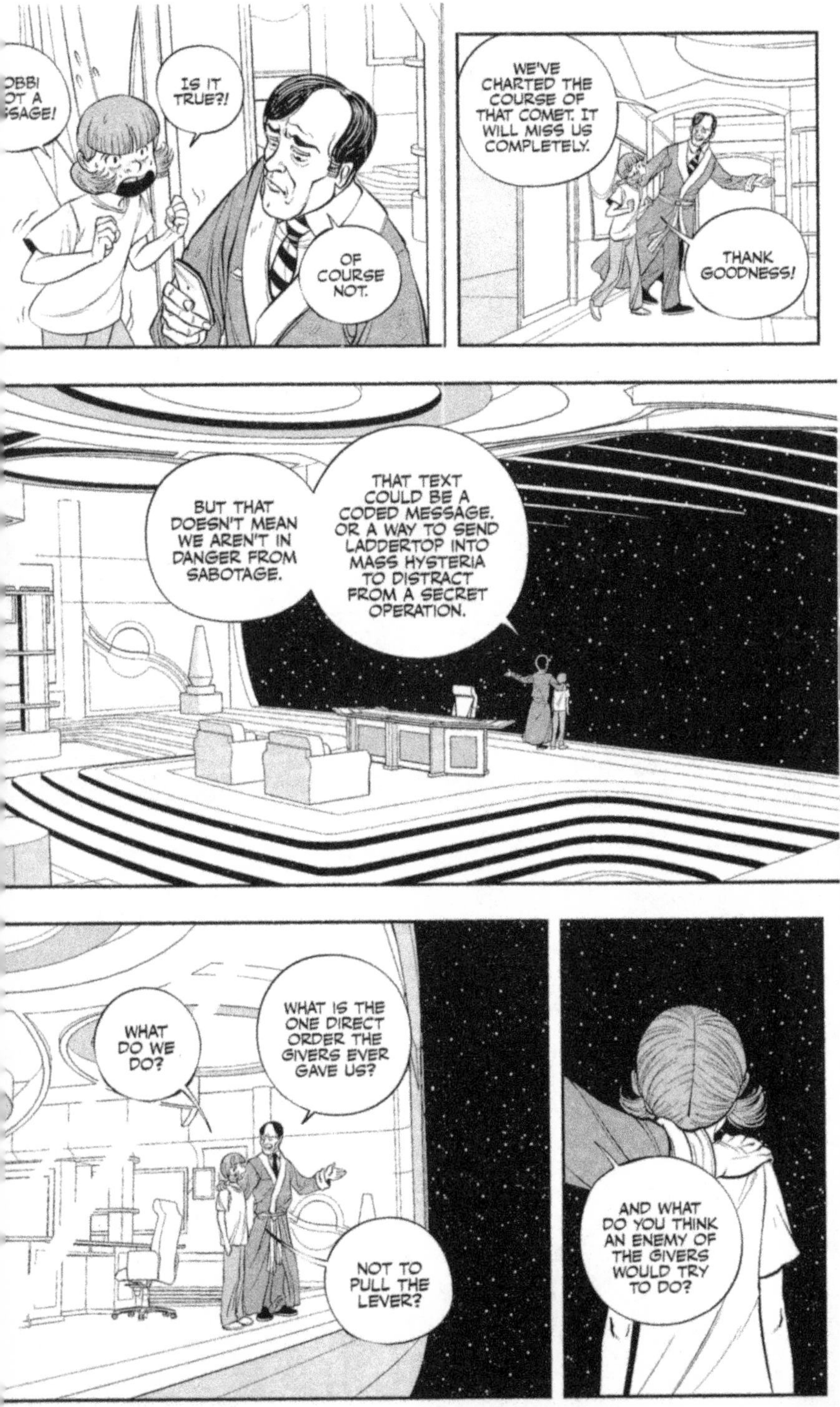
OBBI
OT A
SSAGE!
IS IT TRUE?!
OF COURSE NOT.
WE'VE CHARTED THE COURSE OF THAT COMET. IT WILL MISS US COMPLETELY.
THANK GOODNESS!
BUT THAT DOESN'T MEAN WE AREN'T IN DANGER FROM SABOTAGE.
THAT TEXT COULD BE A CODED MESSAGE. OR A WAY TO SEND LADDERTOP INTO MASS HYSTERIA TO DISTRACT FROM A SECRET OPERATION.
WHAT DO WE DO?
WHAT IS THE ONE DIRECT ORDER THE GIVERS EVER GAVE US?
NOT TO PULL THE LEVER?
AND WHAT DO YOU THINK AN ENEMY OF THE GIVERS WOULD TRY TO DO?

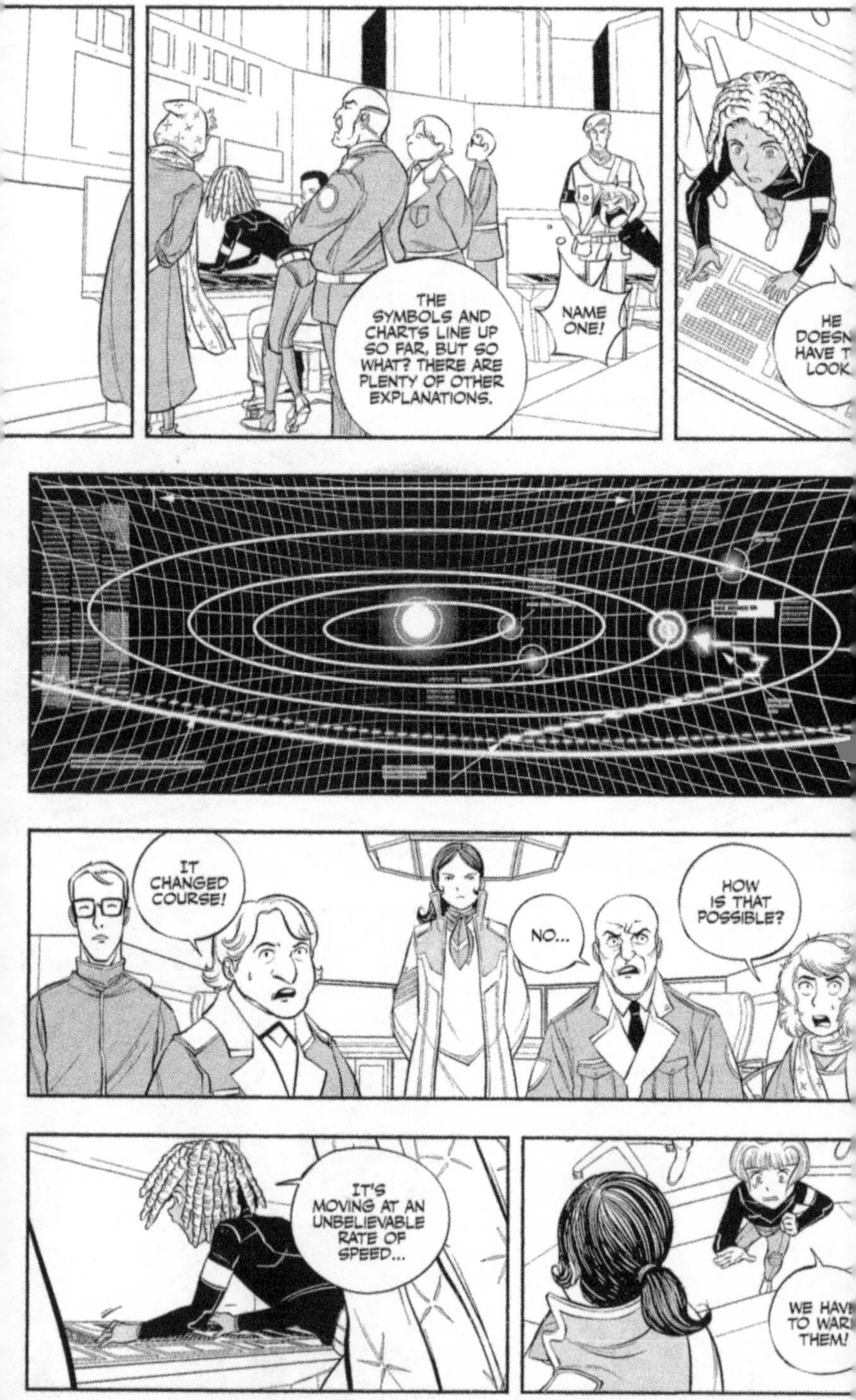
THE SYMBOLS AND CHARTS LINE UP SO FAR, BUT SO WHAT? THERE ARE PLENTY OF OTHER EXPLANATIONS.
NAME ONE!
HE DOESN HAVE T LOOK
IT CHANGED COURSE!
NO...
HOW IS THAT POSSIBLE?
IT'S MOVING AT AN UNBELIEVABLE RATE OF SPEED...
WE HAV TO WAR THEM!

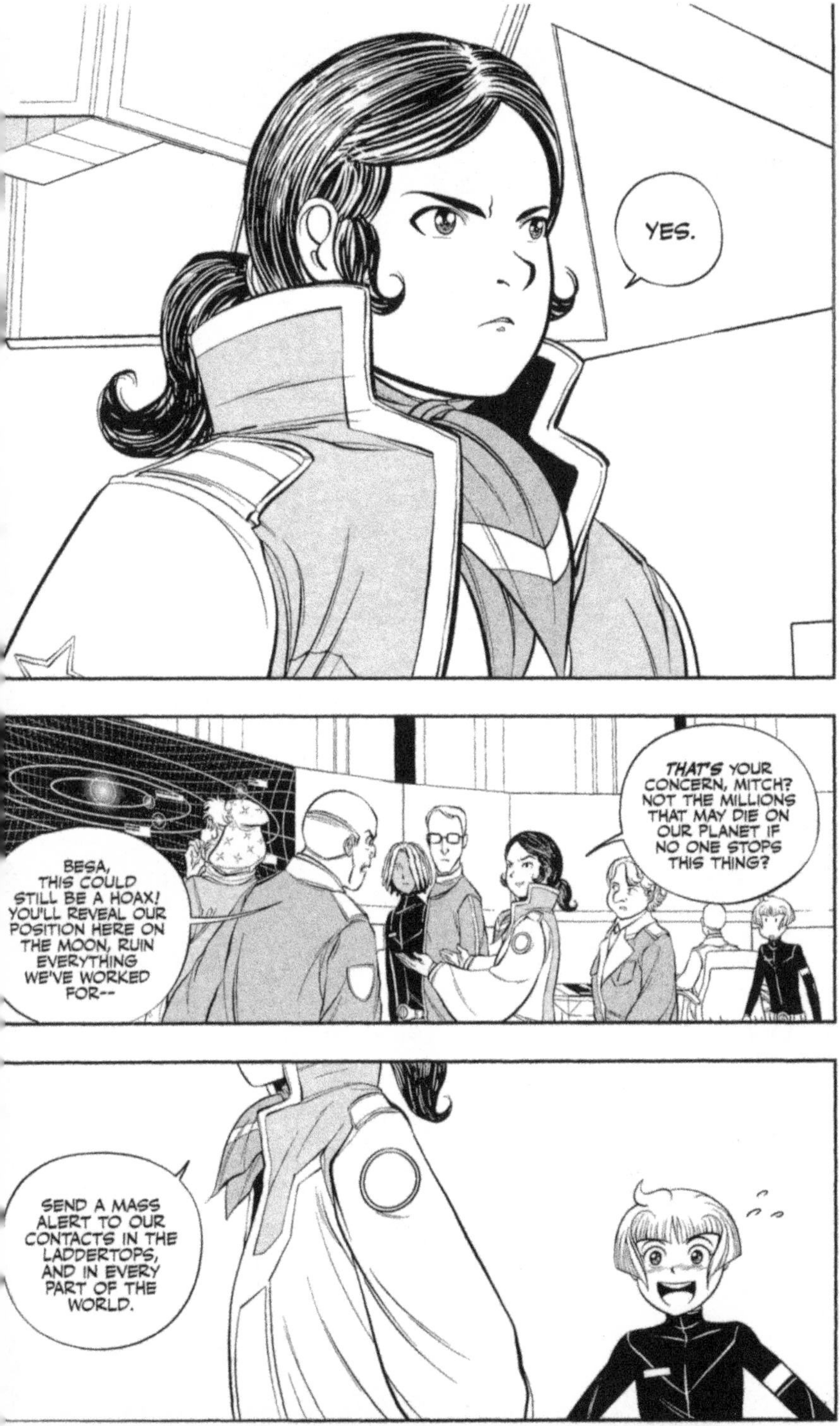
YES.
BESA, THIS COULD STILL BE A HOAX! YOU'LL REVEAL OUR POSITION HERE ON THE MOON, RUIN EVERYTHING WE'VE WORKED FOR--
THAT'S YOUR CONCERN, MITCH? NOT THE MILLIONS THAT MAY DIE ON OUR PLANET IF NO ONE STOPS THIS THING?
SEND A MASS ALERT TO OUR CONTACTS IN THE LADDERTOPS, AND IN EVERY PART OF THE WORLD.

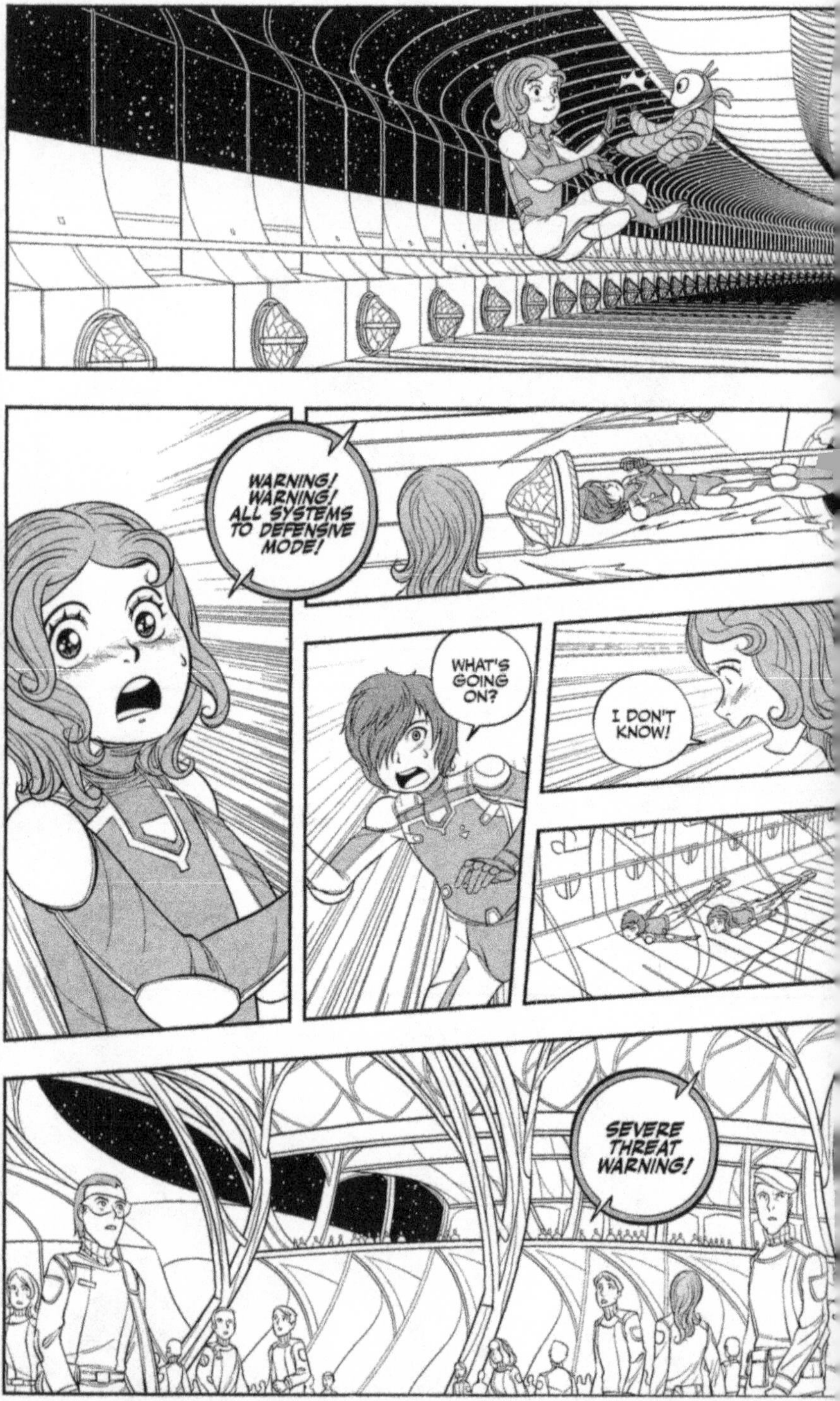
WARNING! WARNING! ALL SYSTEMS TO DEFENSIVE MODE!
WHAT'S GOING ON?
I DON'T KNOW!
SEVERE THREAT WARNING!

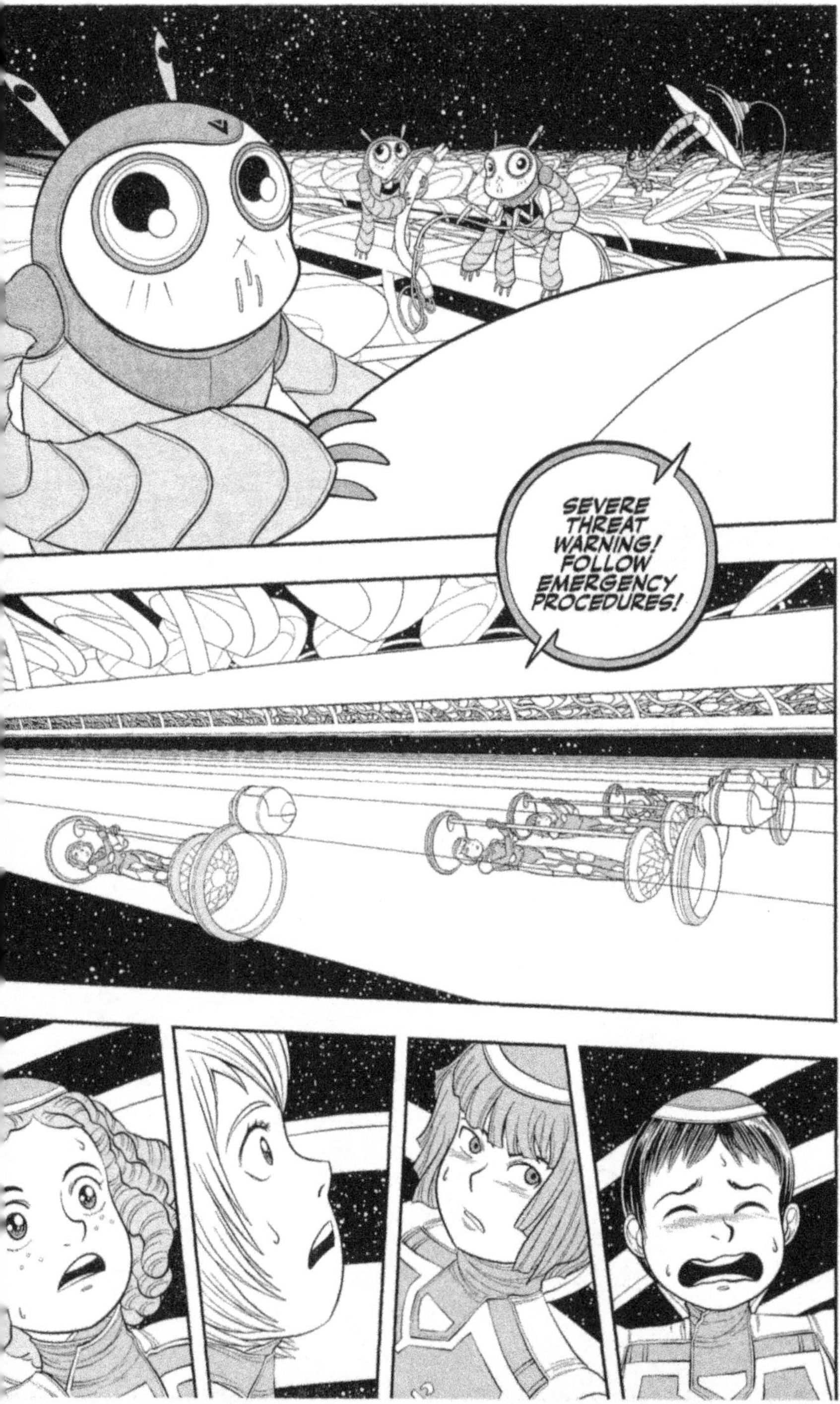
SEVERE THREAT WARNING! FOLLOW EMERGENCY PROCEDURES!

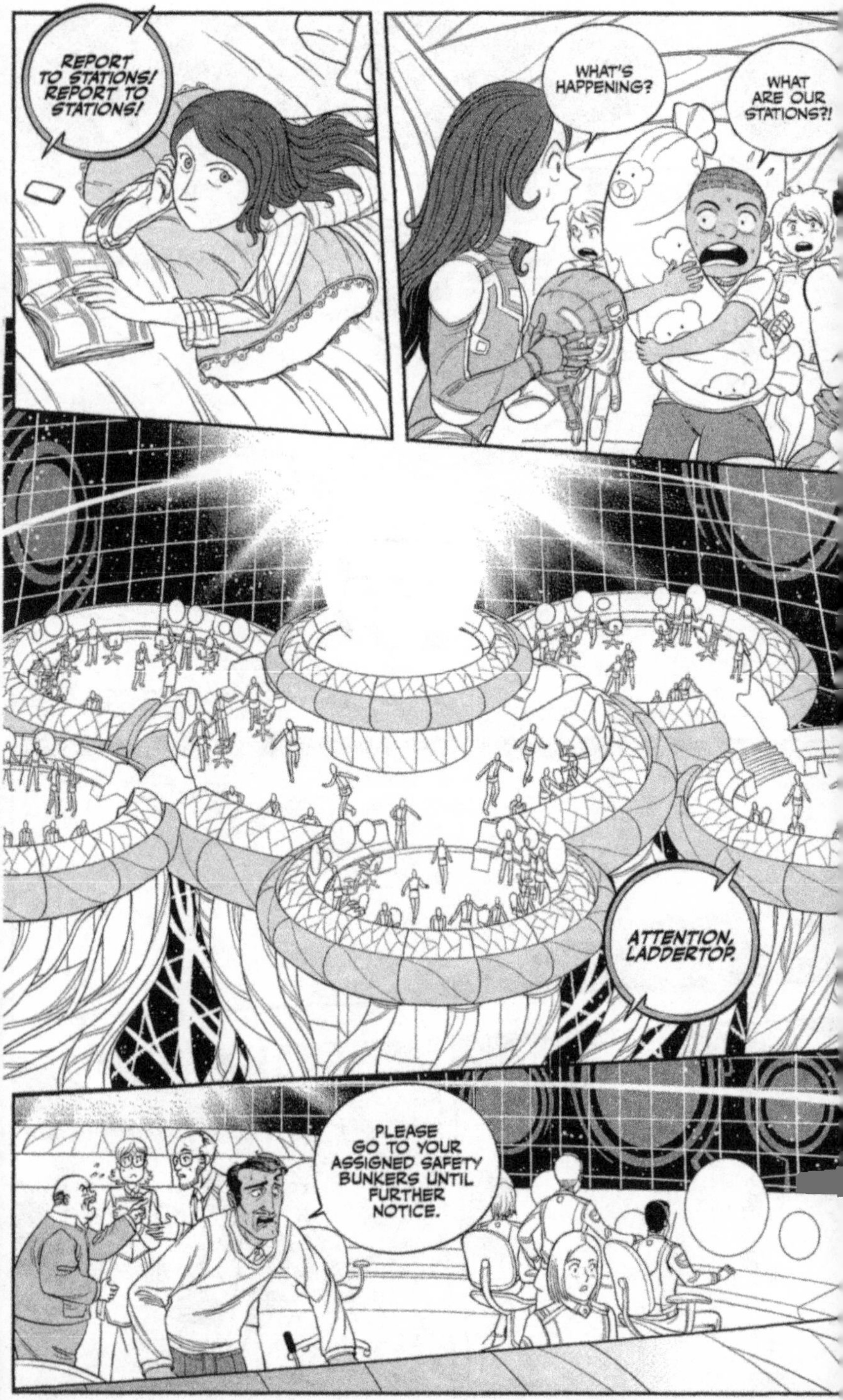
REPORT TO STATIONS! REPORT TO STATIONS!
WHAT'S HAPPENING?
WHAT ARE OUR STATIONS?!
ATTENTION, LADDERTOP.
PLEASE GO TO YOUR ASSIGNED SAFETY BUNKERS UNTIL FURTHER NOTICE.

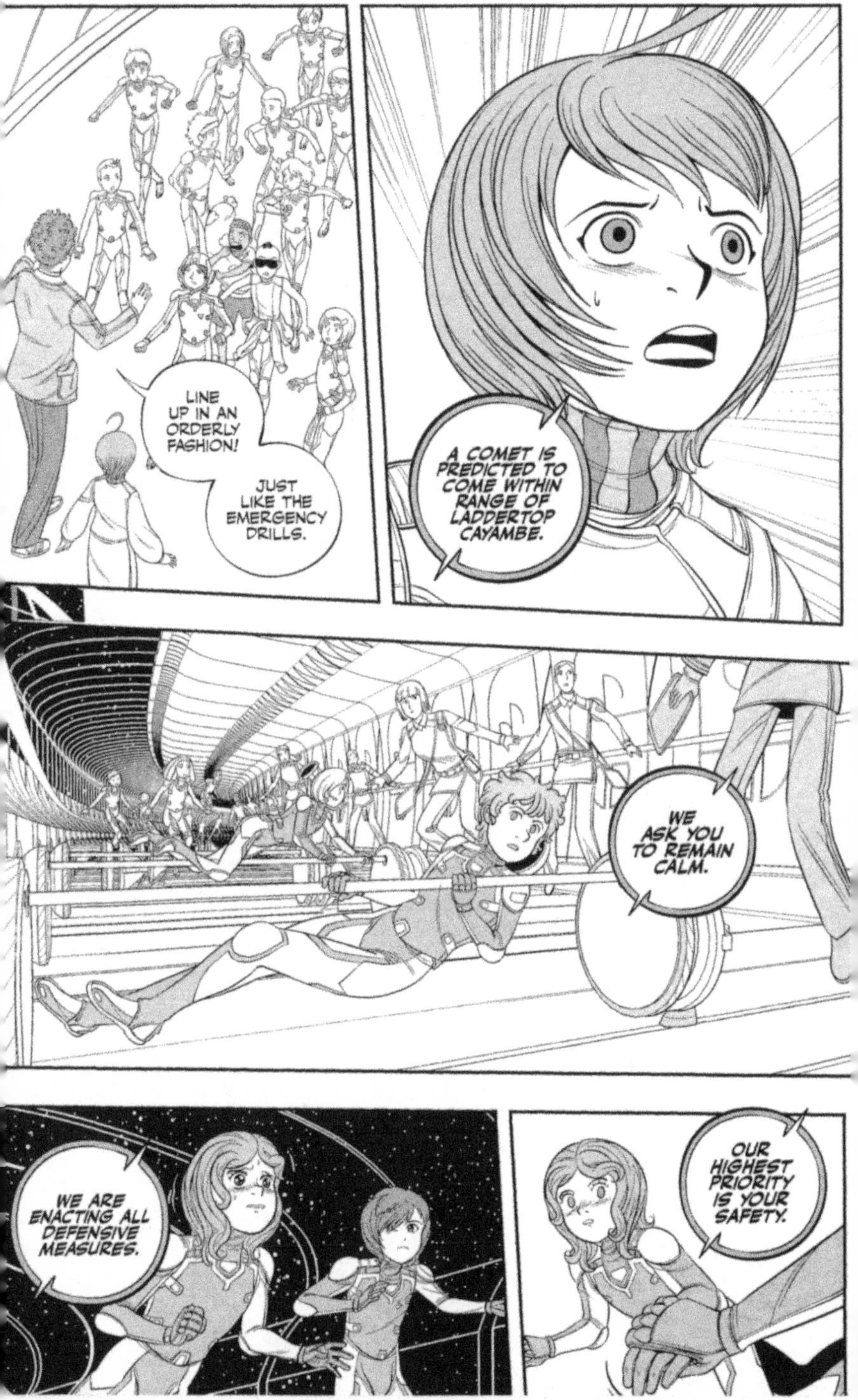
LINE UP IN AN ORDERLY FASHION!
JUST LIKE THE EMERGENCY DRILLS.
A COMET IS PREDICTED TO COME WITHIN RANGE OF LADDERTOP CAYAMBE.
WE ASK YOU TO REMAIN CALM.
WE ARE ENACTING ALL DEFENSIVE MEASURES.
OUR HIGHEST PRIORITY IS YOUR SAFETY.

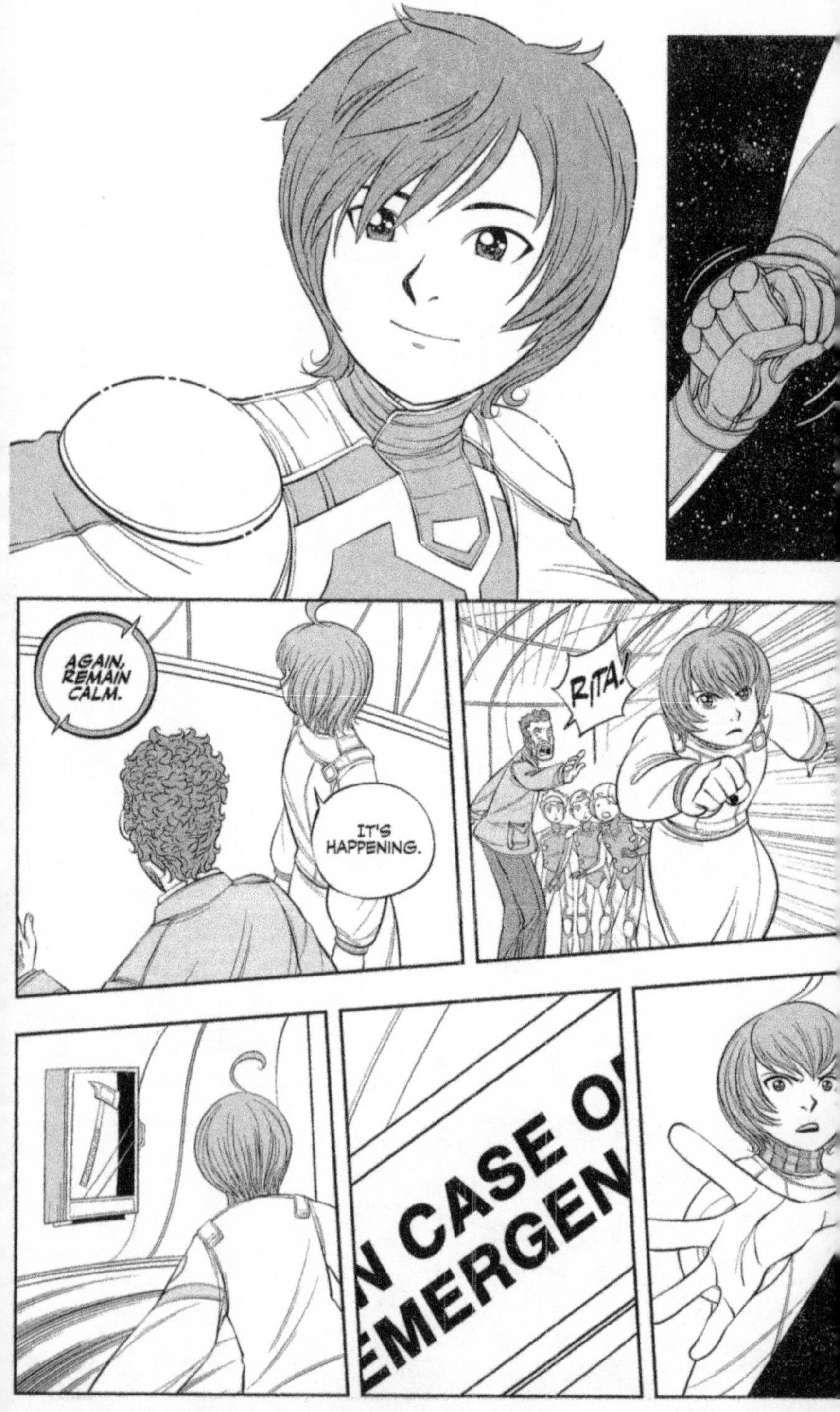
AGAIN, REMAIN CALM.
IT'S HAPPENING.
RITA!
N CASE O
EMERGEN

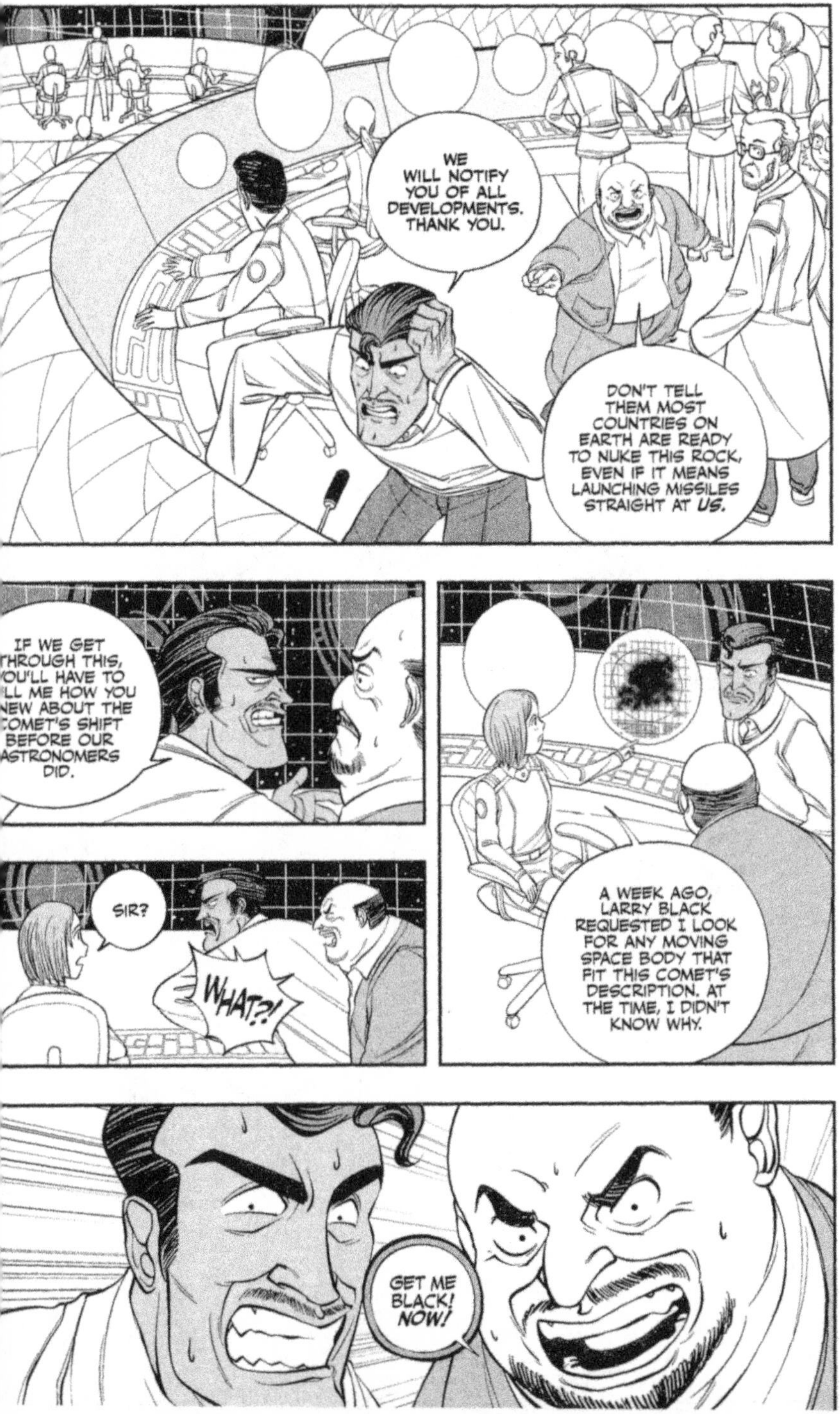
WE WILL NOTIFY YOU OF ALL DEVELOPMENTS. THANK YOU.
DON'T TELL THEM MOST COUNTRIES ON EARTH ARE READY TO NUKE THIS ROCK, EVEN IF IT MEANS LAUNCHING MISSILES STRAIGHT AT *US*.
IF WE GET THROUGH THIS, OU'LL HAVE TO LL ME HOW YOU NEW ABOUT THE COMET'S SHIFT BEFORE OUR ASTRONOMERS DID.
SIR?
WHAT?!
A WEEK AGO, LARRY BLACK REQUESTED I LOOK FOR ANY MOVING SPACE BODY THAT FIT THIS COMET'S DESCRIPTION. AT THE TIME, I DIDN'T KNOW WHY.
GET ME BLACK! *NOW!*

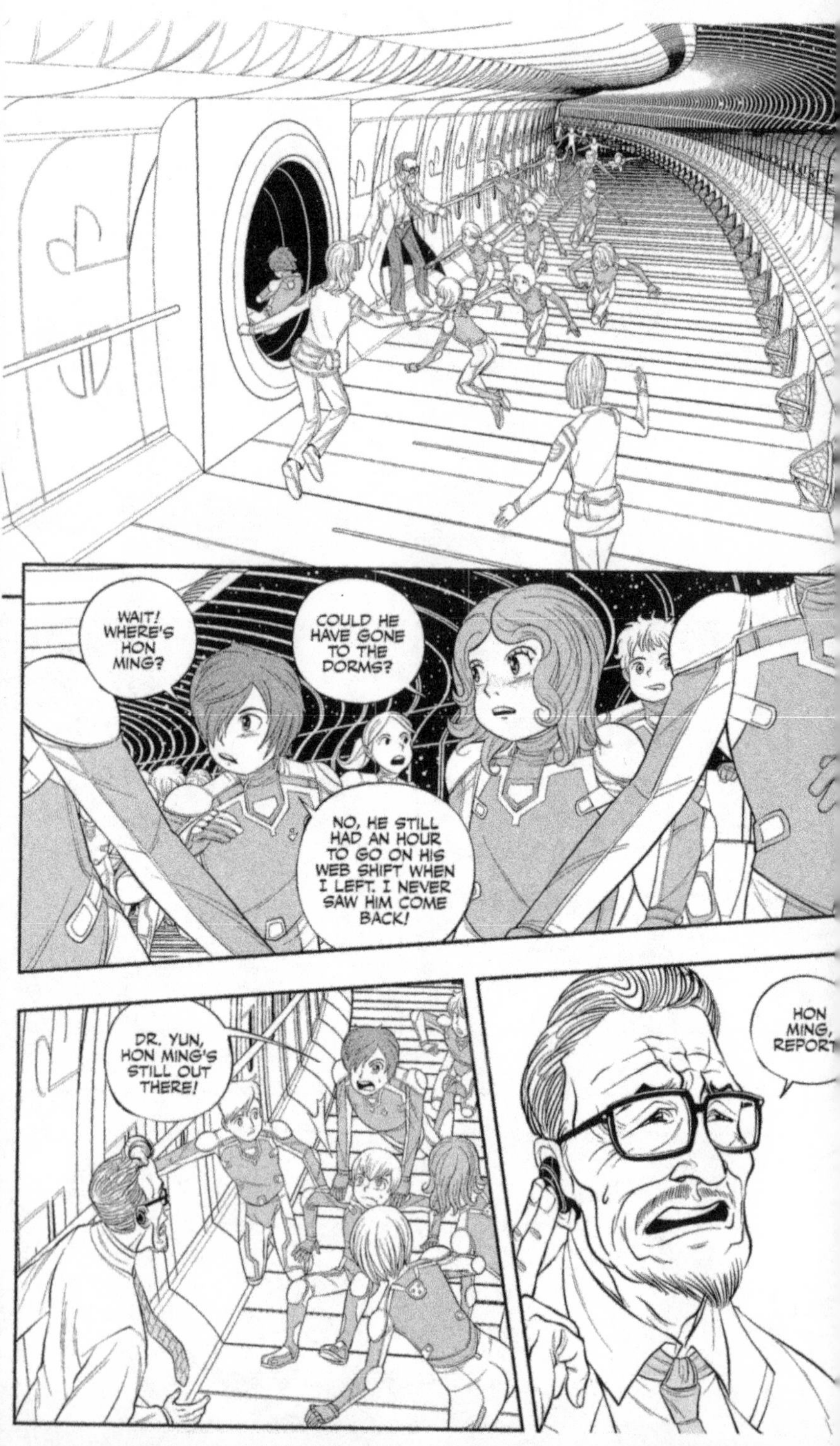
WAIT! WHERE'S HON MING?
COULD HE HAVE GONE TO THE DORMS?
NO, HE STILL HAD AN HOUR TO GO ON HIS WEB SHIFT WHEN I LEFT. I NEVER SAW HIM COME BACK!
DR. YUN, HON MING'S STILL OUT THERE!
HON MING, REPORT

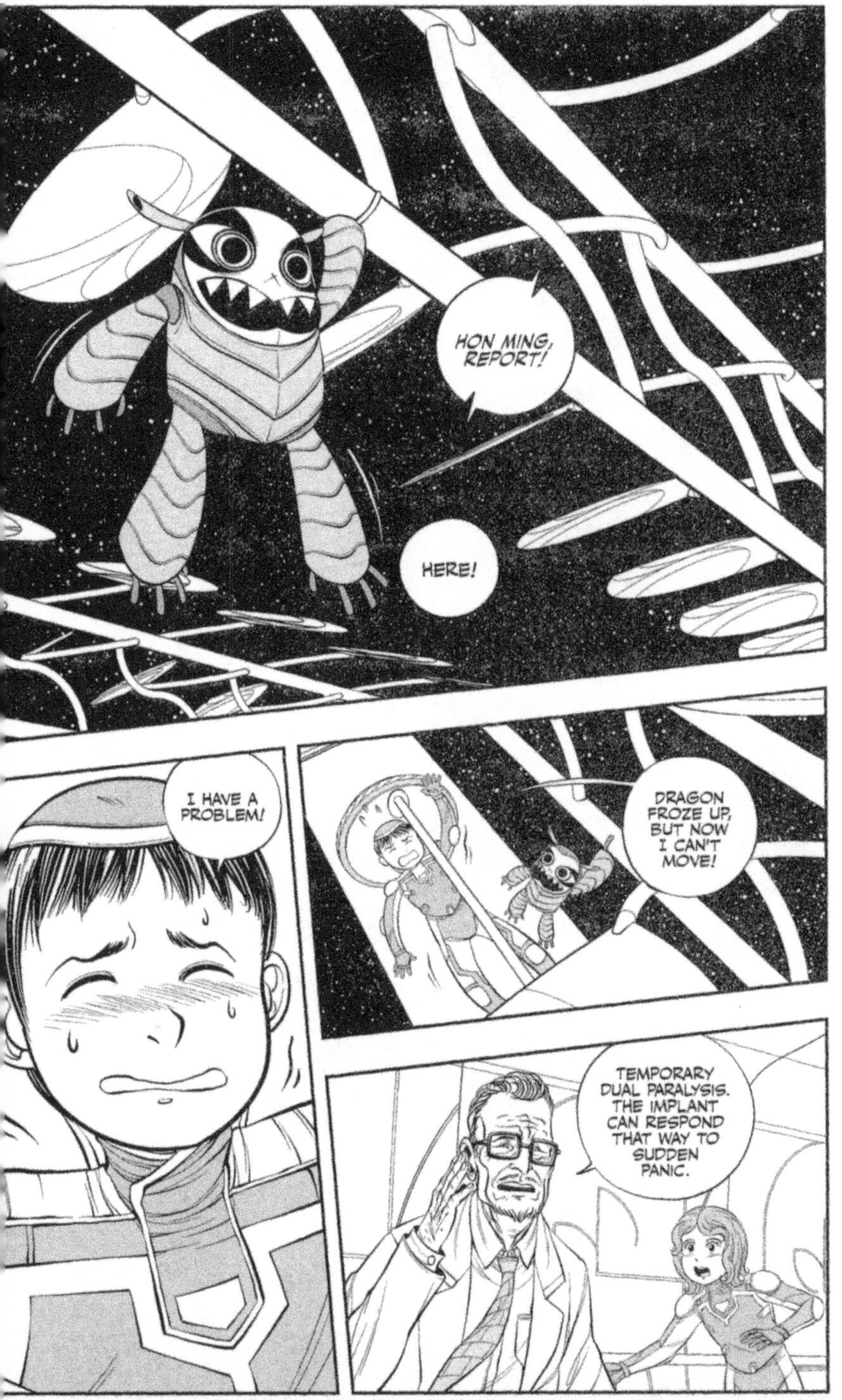
HON MING, REPORT!
HERE!
I HAVE A PROBLEM!
DRAGON FROZE UP, BUT NOW I CAN'T MOVE!
TEMPORARY DUAL PARALYSIS. THE IMPLANT CAN RESPOND THAT WAY TO SUDDEN PANIC.

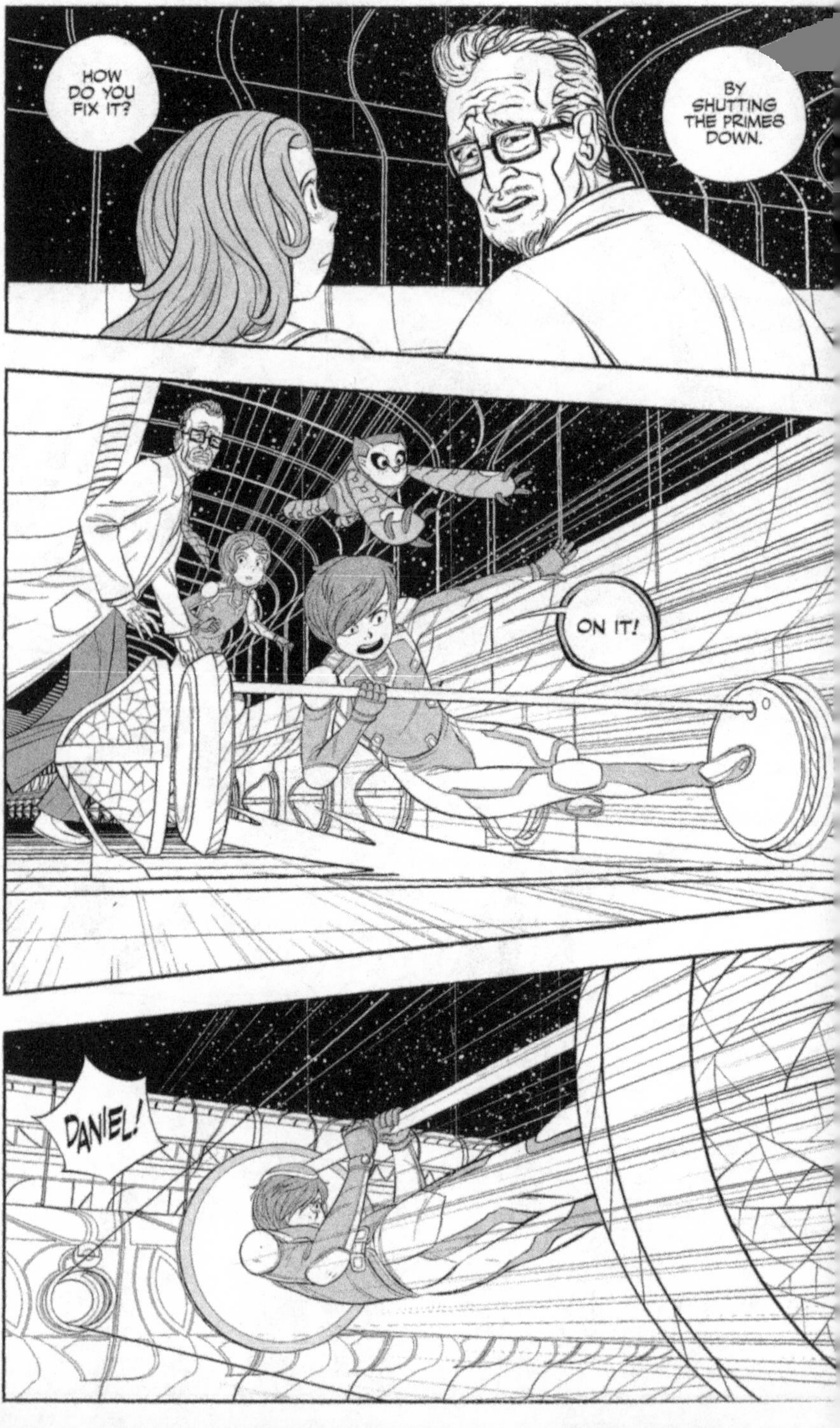
HOW DO YOU FIX IT?
BY SHUTTING THE PRIMES DOWN.
ON IT!
DANIEL!

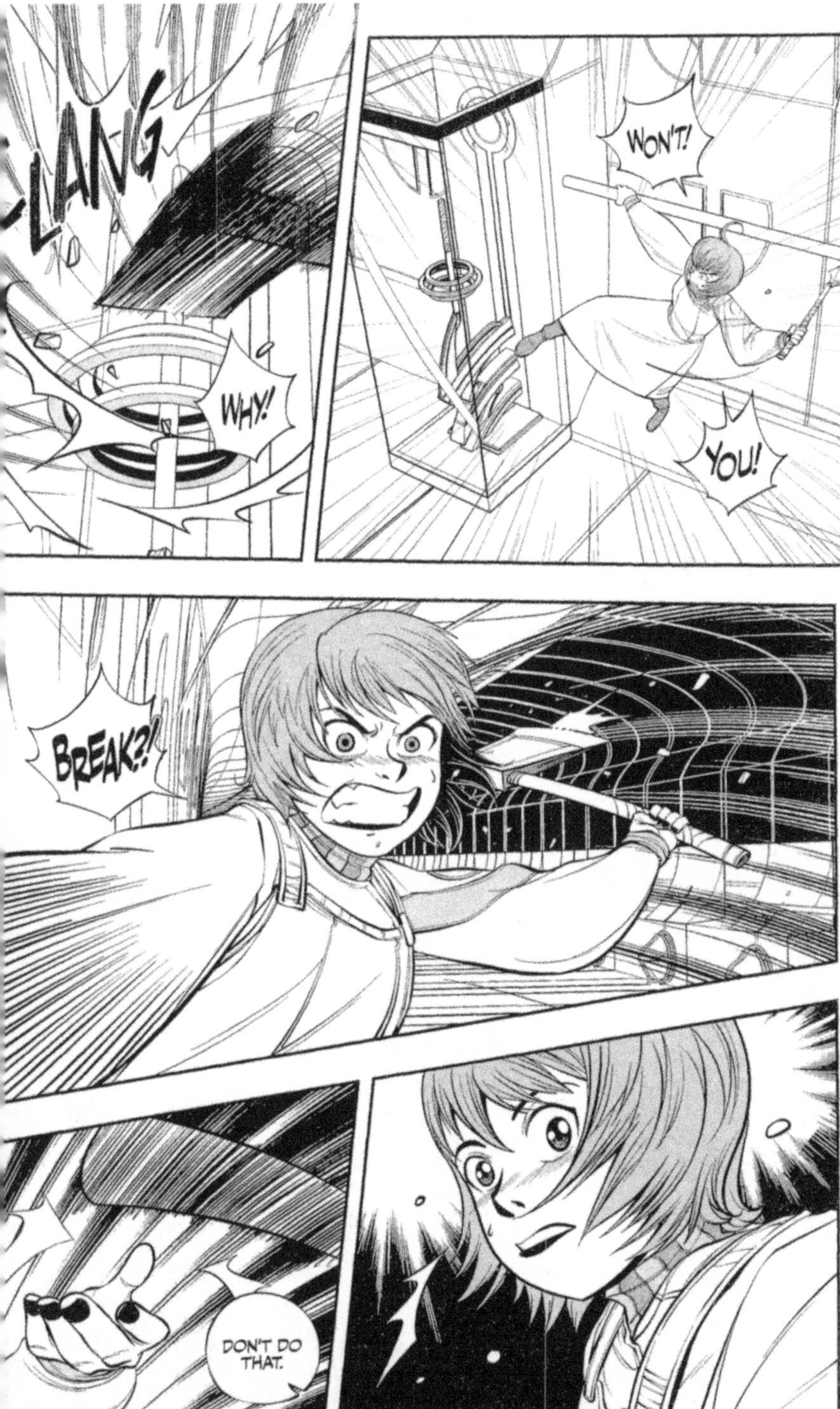
CLANG
WHY!
WON'T!
YOU!
BREAK?!
DON'T DO THAT.

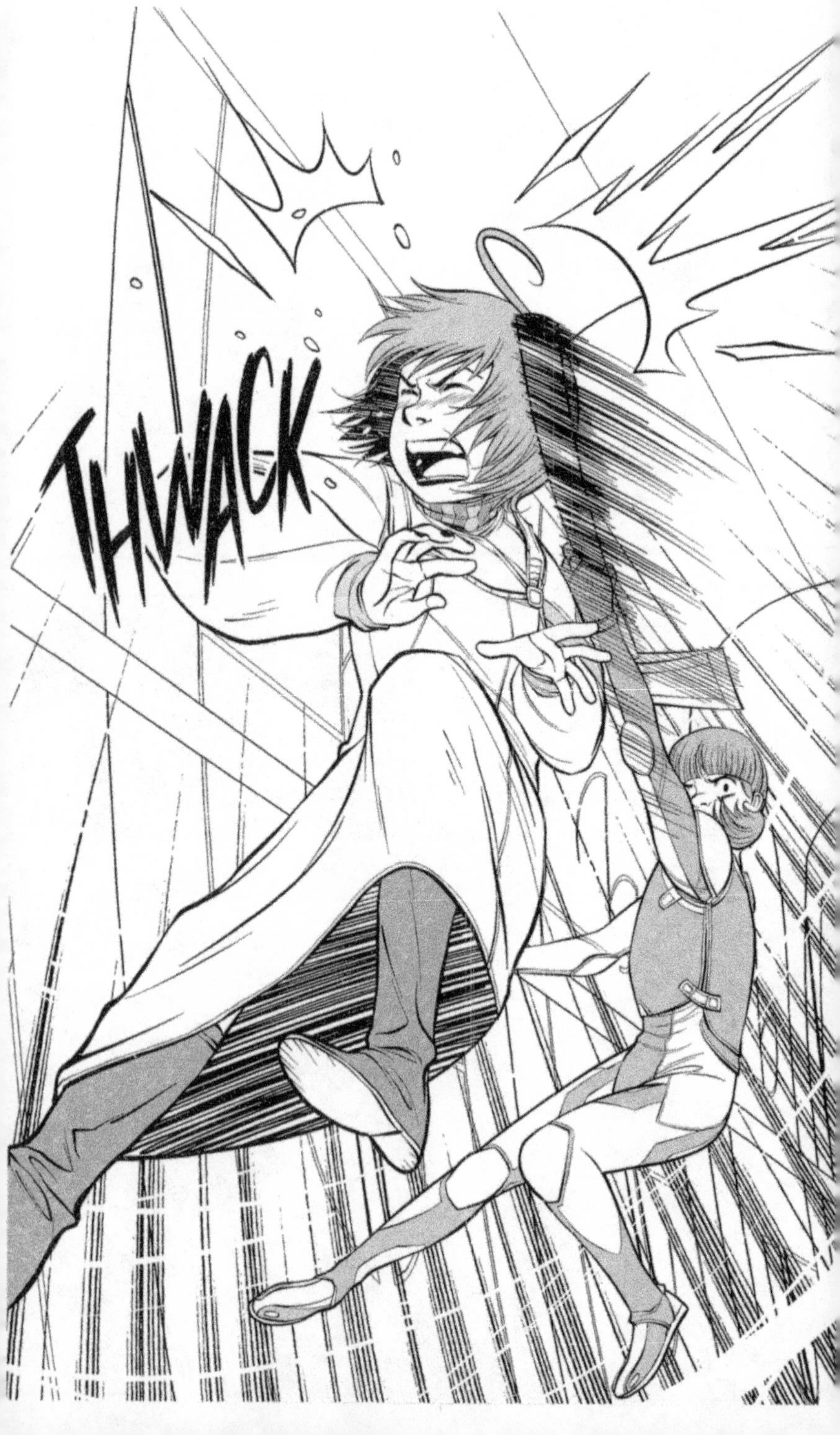
THWACK

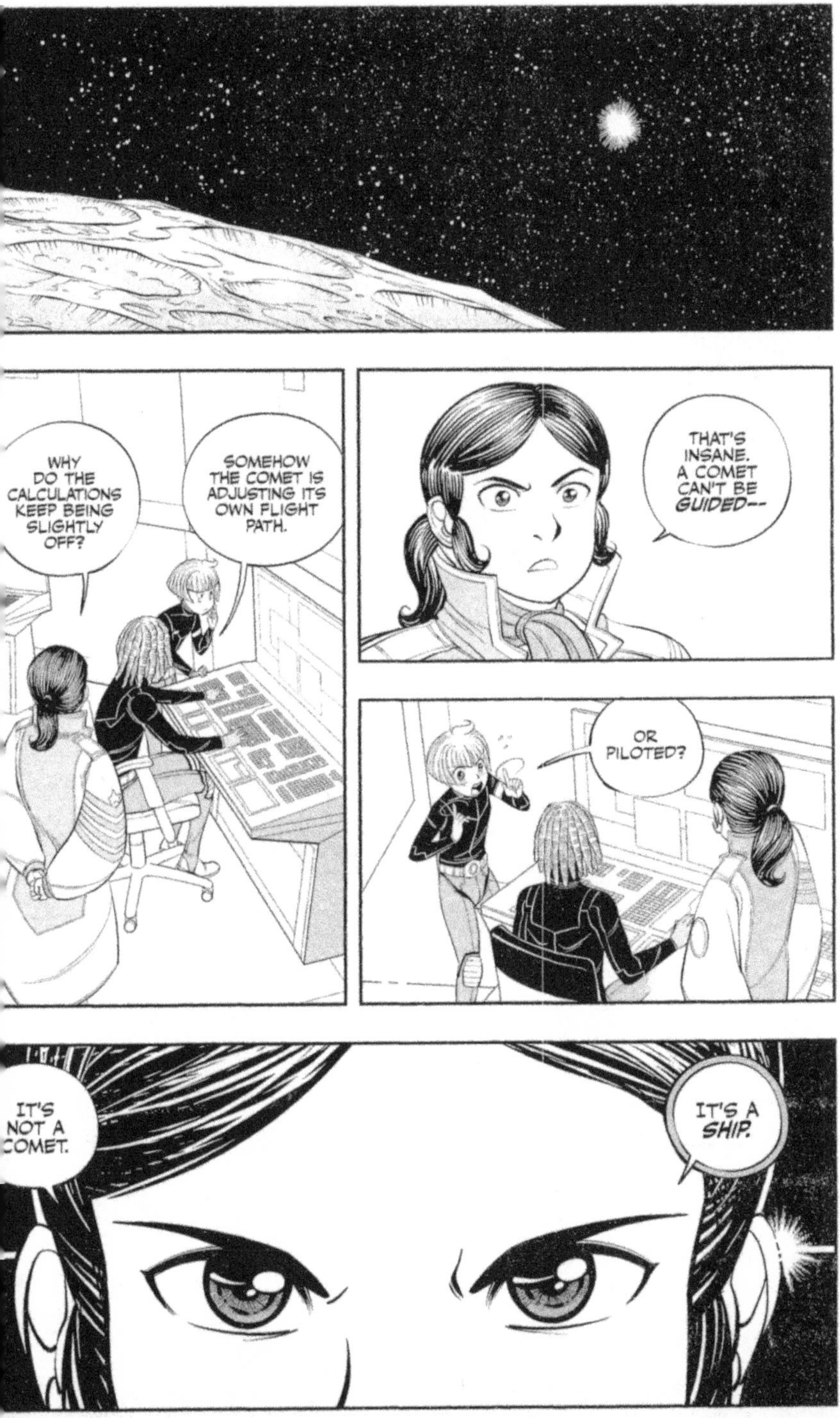
WHY DO THE CALCULATIONS KEEP BEING SLIGHTLY OFF?
SOMEHOW THE COMET IS ADJUSTING ITS OWN FLIGHT PATH.
THAT'S INSANE. A COMET CAN'T BE *GUIDED*--
OR PILOTED?
IT'S NOT A COMET.
IT'S A *SHIP.*

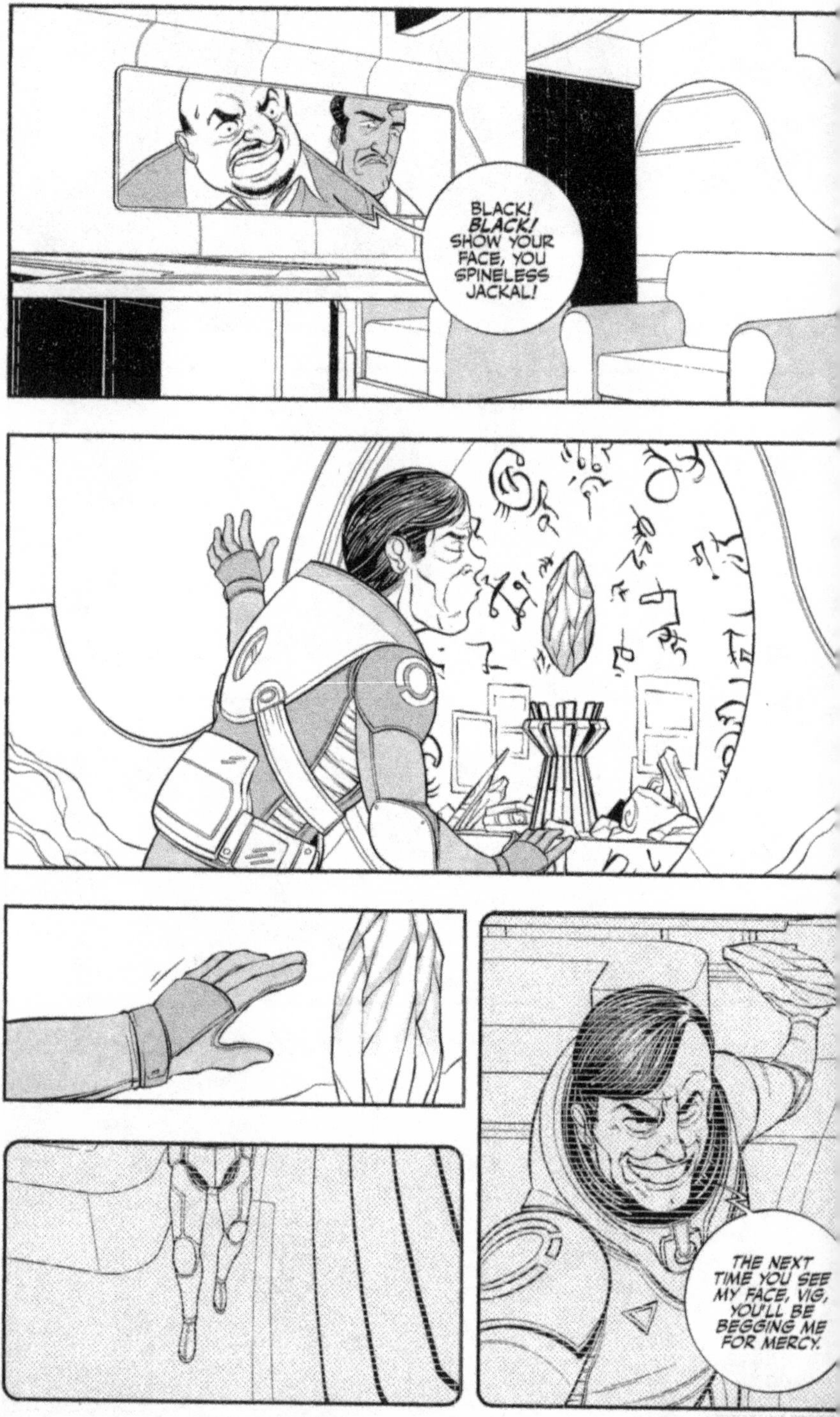
BLACK! *BLACK!* SHOW YOUR FACE, YOU SPINELESS JACKAL!
THE NEXT TIME YOU SEE MY FACE, VIG, YOU'LL BE BEGGING ME FOR MERCY.

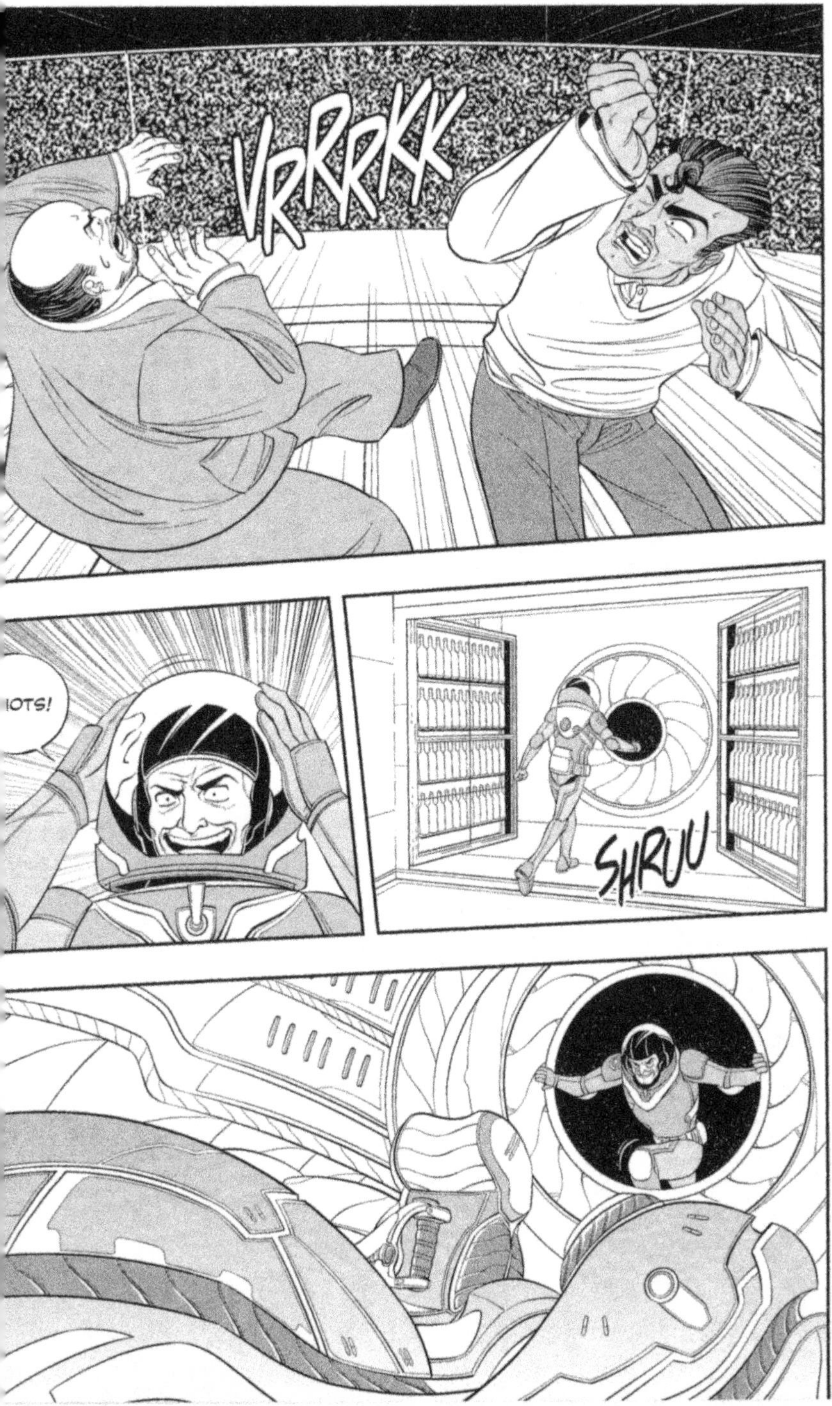
VRRRKK
IOTS!
SHRUU

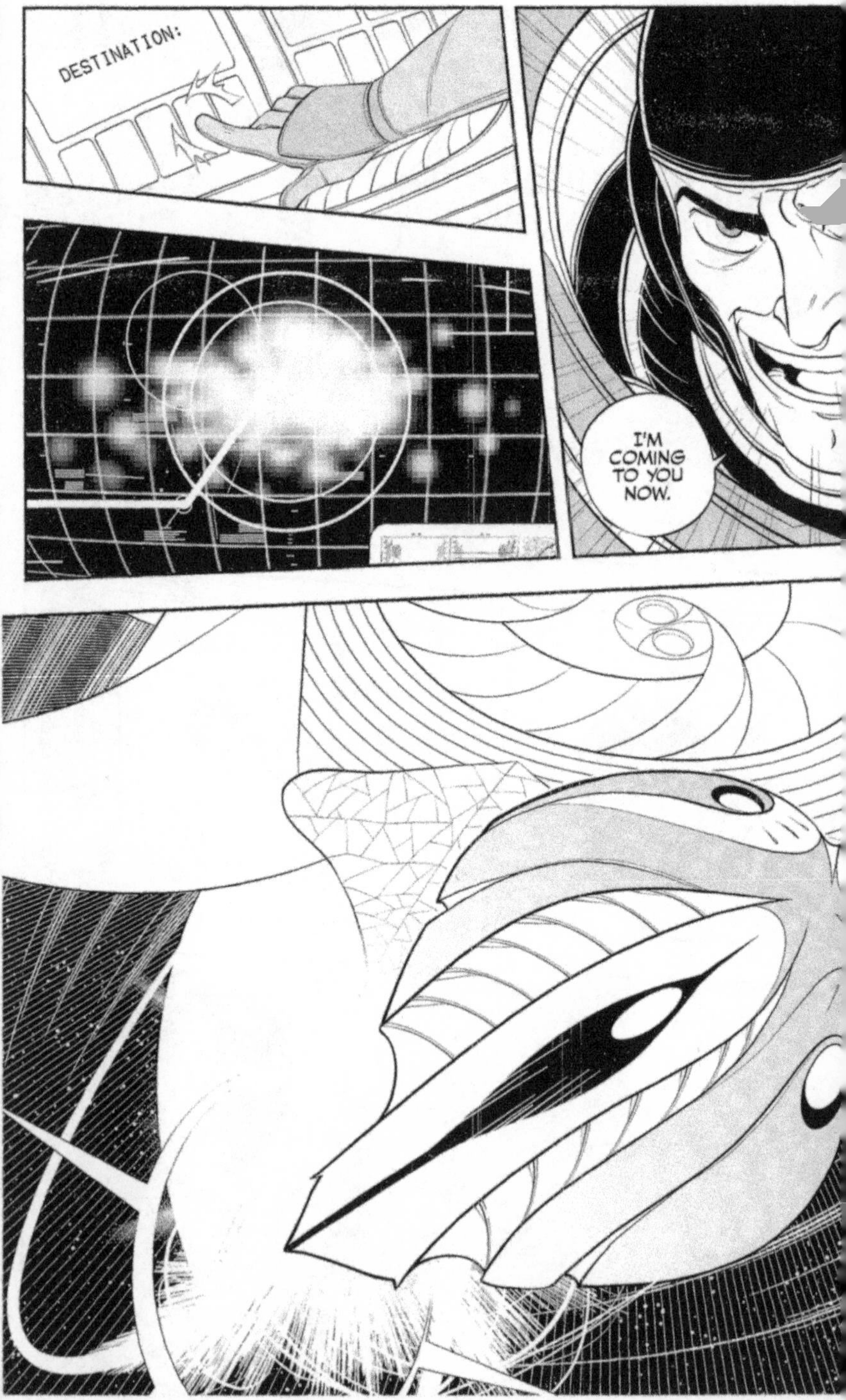
DESTINATION:
I'M COMING TO YOU NOW.

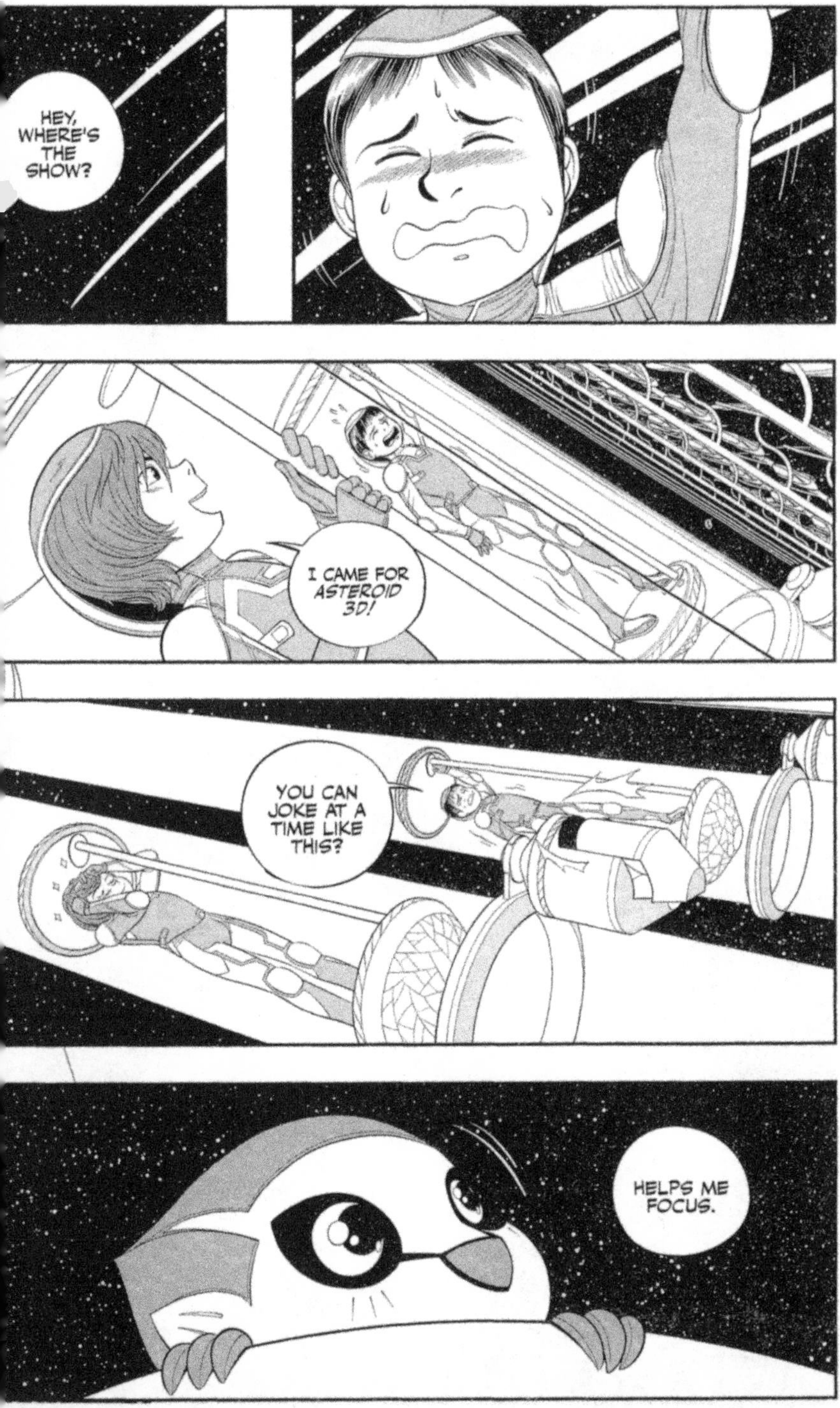
HEY, WHERE'S THE SHOW?
I CAME FOR *ASTEROID 3D!*
YOU CAN JOKE AT A TIME LIKE THIS?
HELPS ME FOCUS.

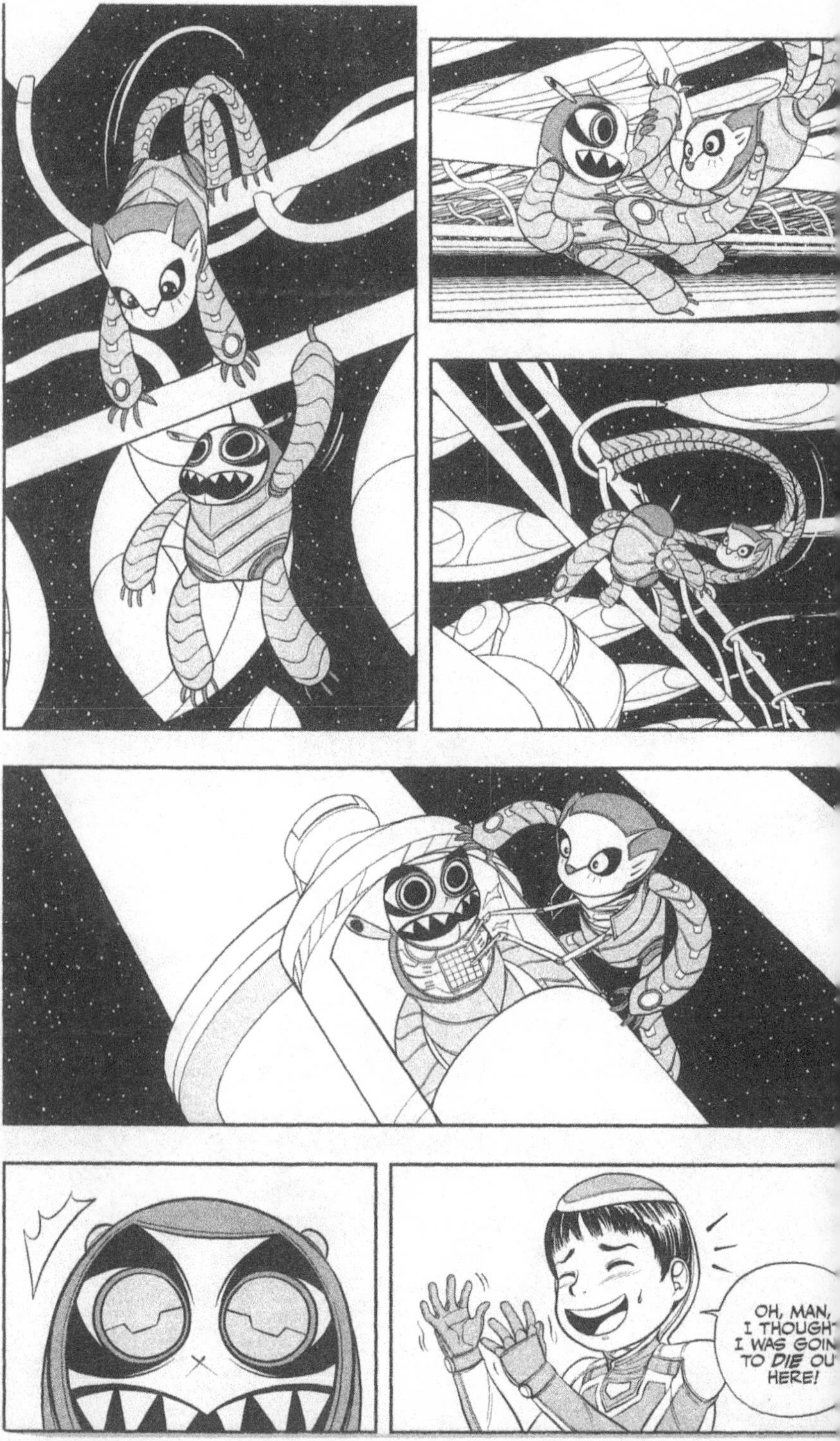
OH, MAN, I THOUGHT I WAS GOIN TO DIE OU HERE!

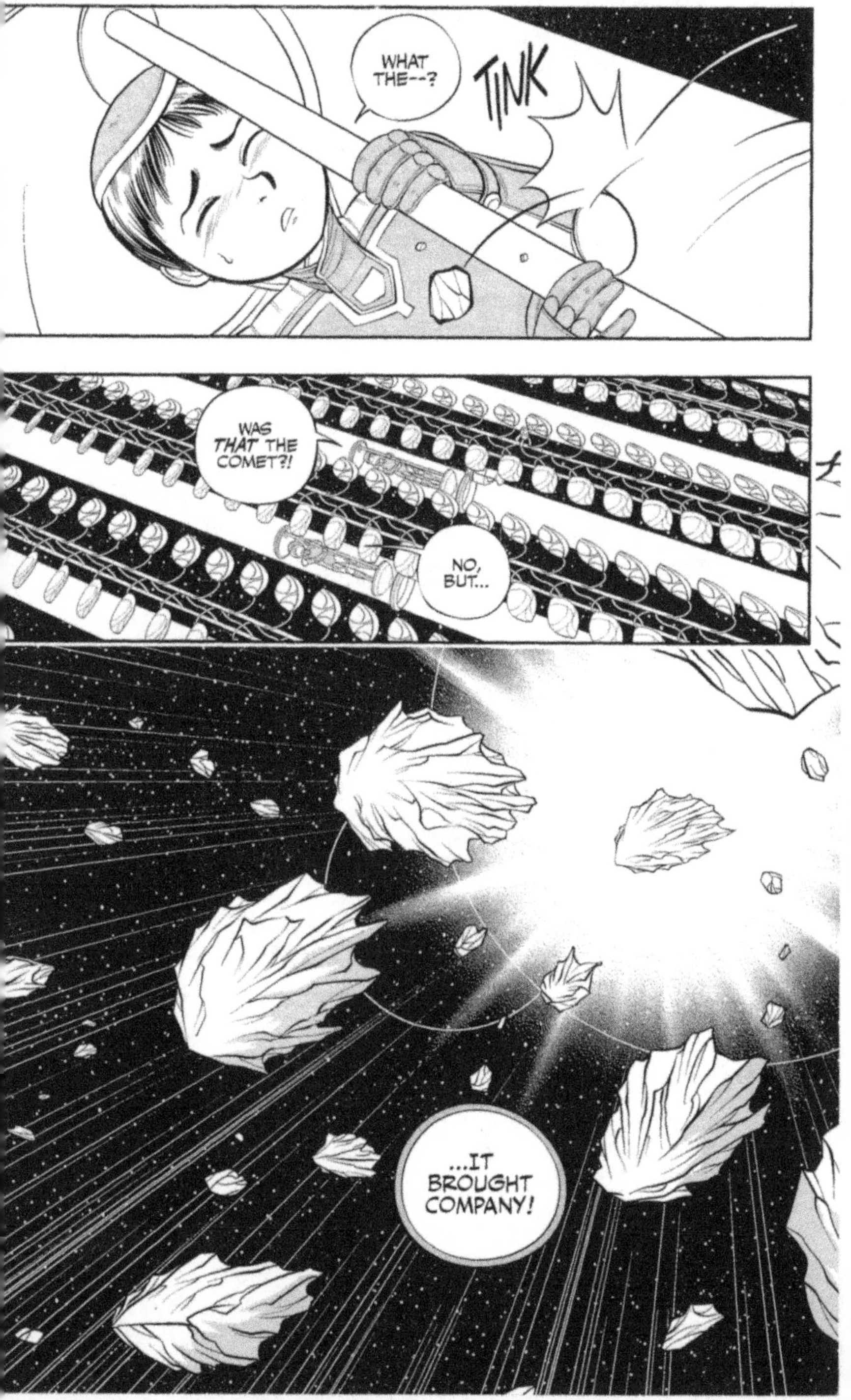
WHAT THE--?
TINK
WAS THAT THE COMET?!
NO, BUT...
...IT BROUGHT COMPANY!

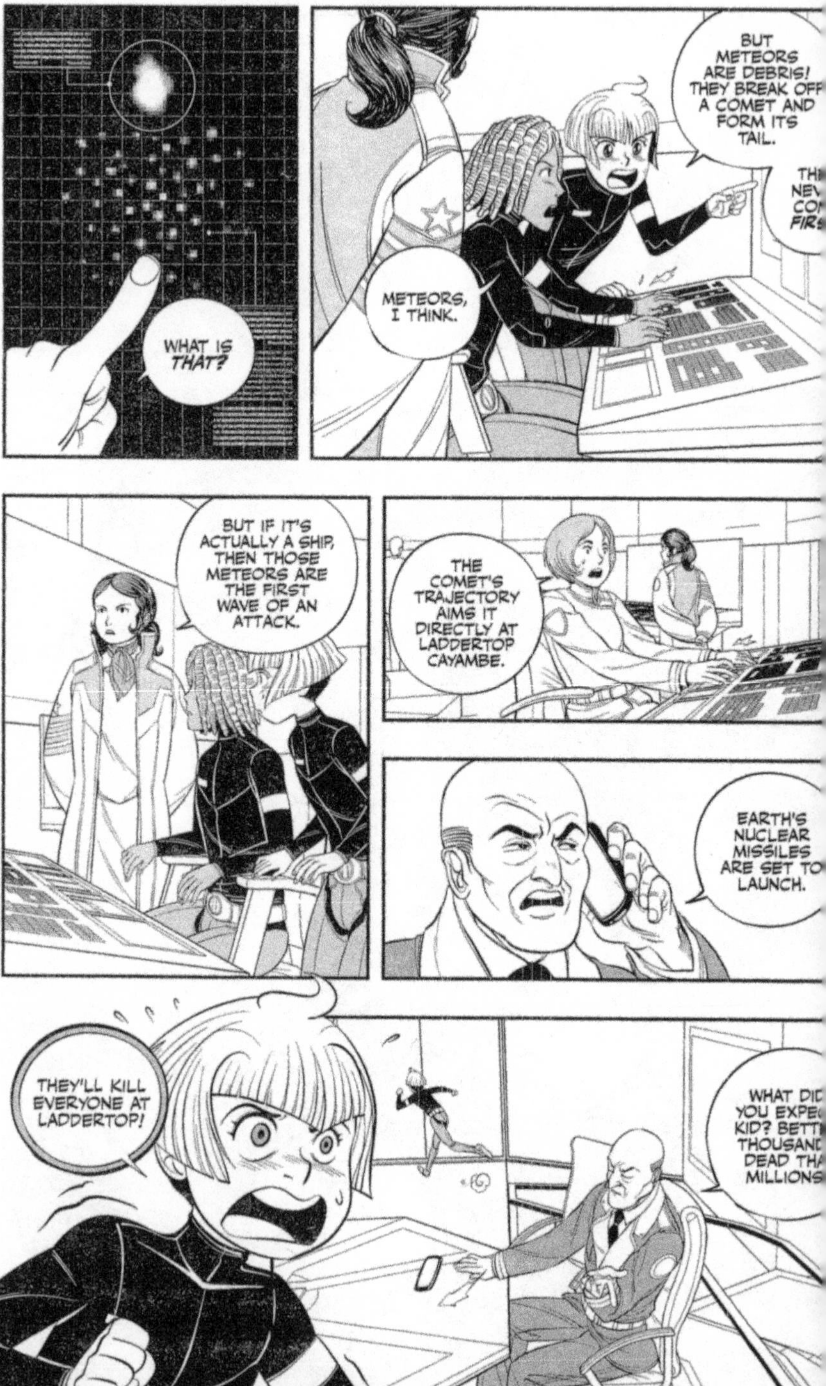
WHAT IS *THAT?*
METEORS, I THINK.
BUT METEORS ARE DEBRIS! THEY BREAK OFF A COMET AND FORM ITS TAIL.
TH NEV CO FIRS
BUT IF IT'S ACTUALLY A SHIP, THEN THOSE METEORS ARE THE FIRST WAVE OF AN ATTACK.
THE COMET'S TRAJECTORY AIMS IT DIRECTLY AT LADDERTOP CAYAMBE.
EARTH'S NUCLEAR MISSILES ARE SET TO LAUNCH.
THEY'LL KILL EVERYONE AT LADDERTOP!
WHAT DI YOU EXPE KID? BETT THOUSAN DEAD TH MILLIONS

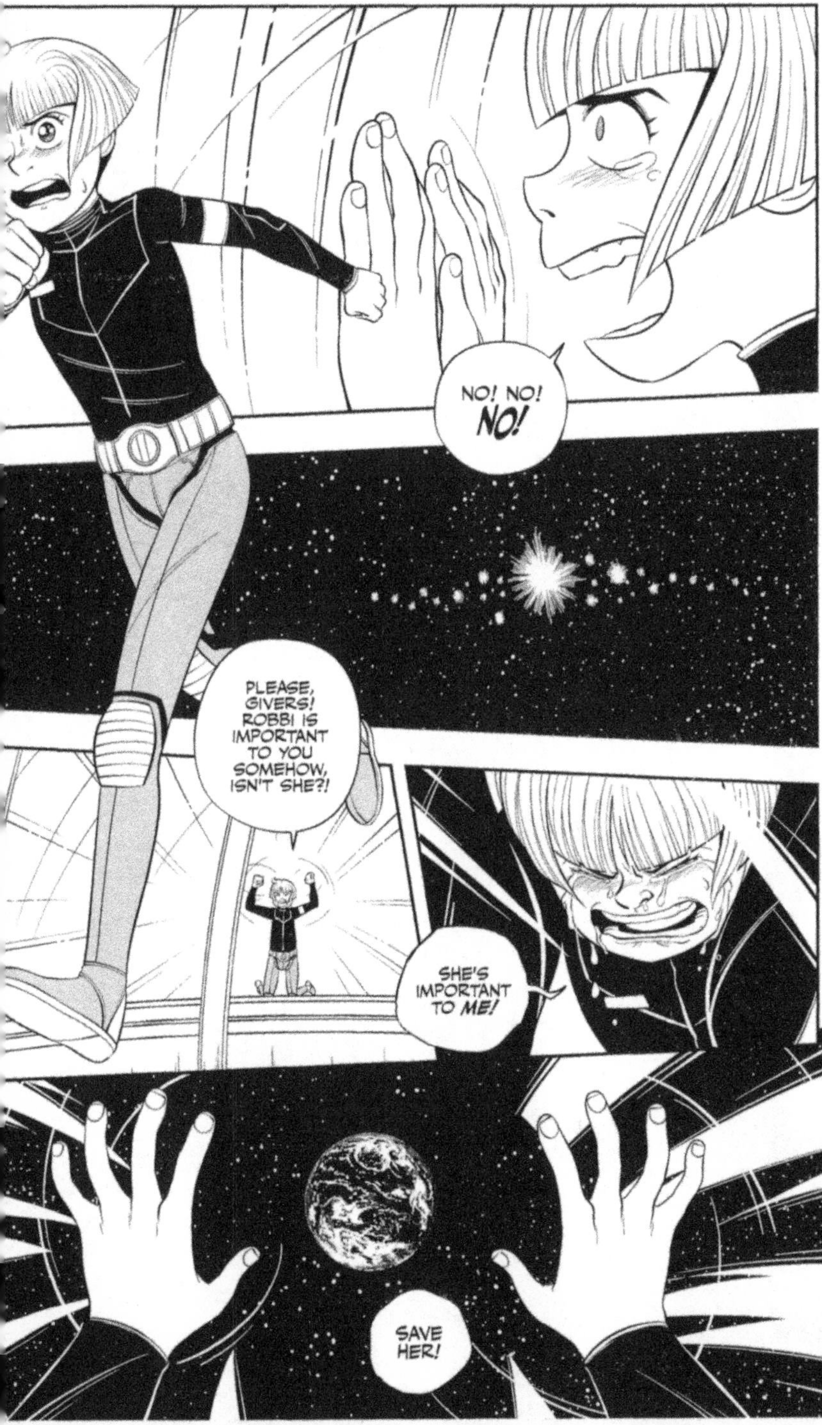
NO! NO! NO!
PLEASE, GIVERS! ROBBI IS IMPORTANT TO YOU SOMEHOW, ISN'T SHE?!
SHE'S IMPORTANT TO *ME!*
SAVE HER!

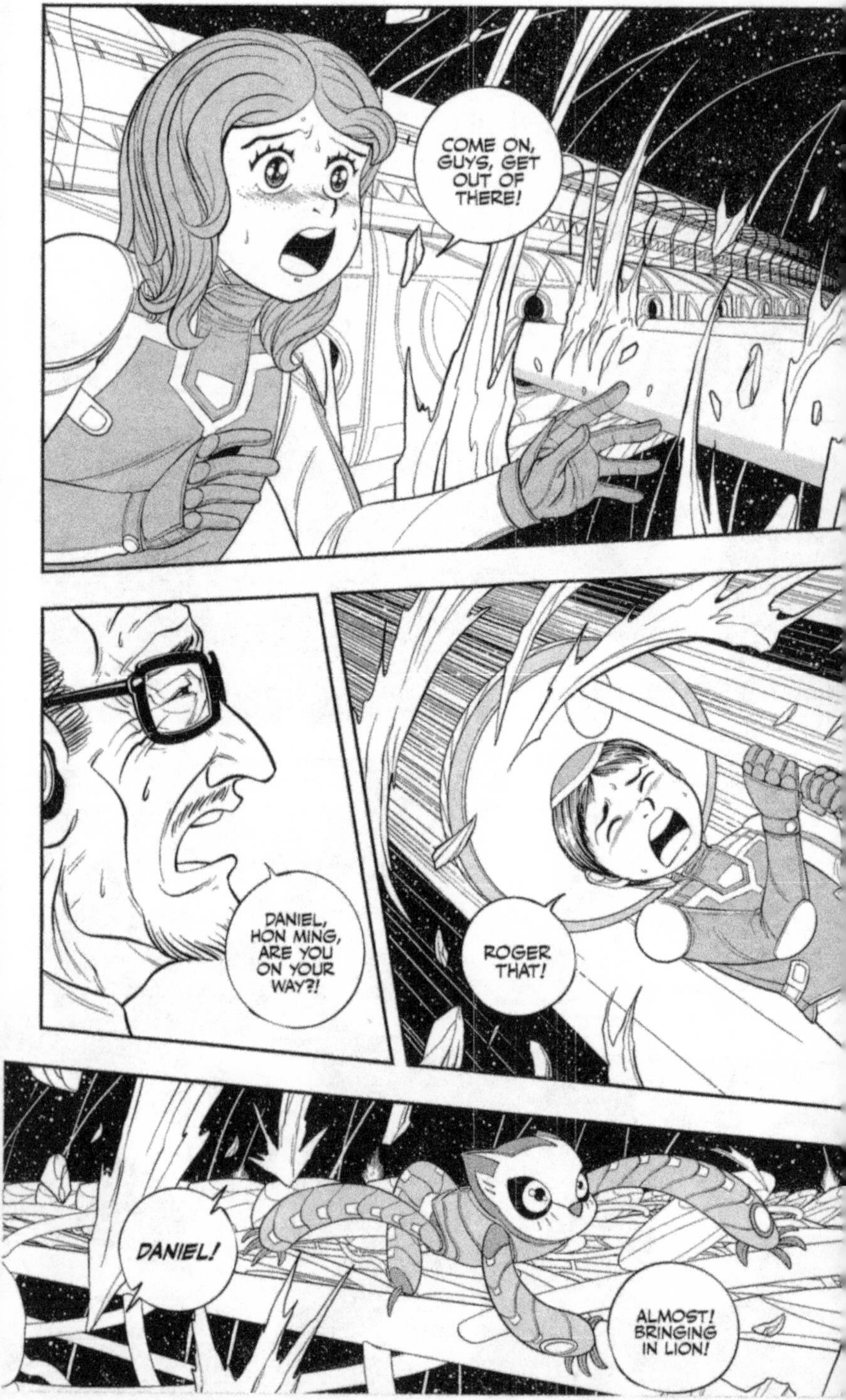
COME ON, GUYS, GET OUT OF THERE!
DANIEL, HON MING, ARE YOU ON YOUR WAY?!
ROGER THAT!
DANIEL!
ALMOST! BRINGING IN LION!

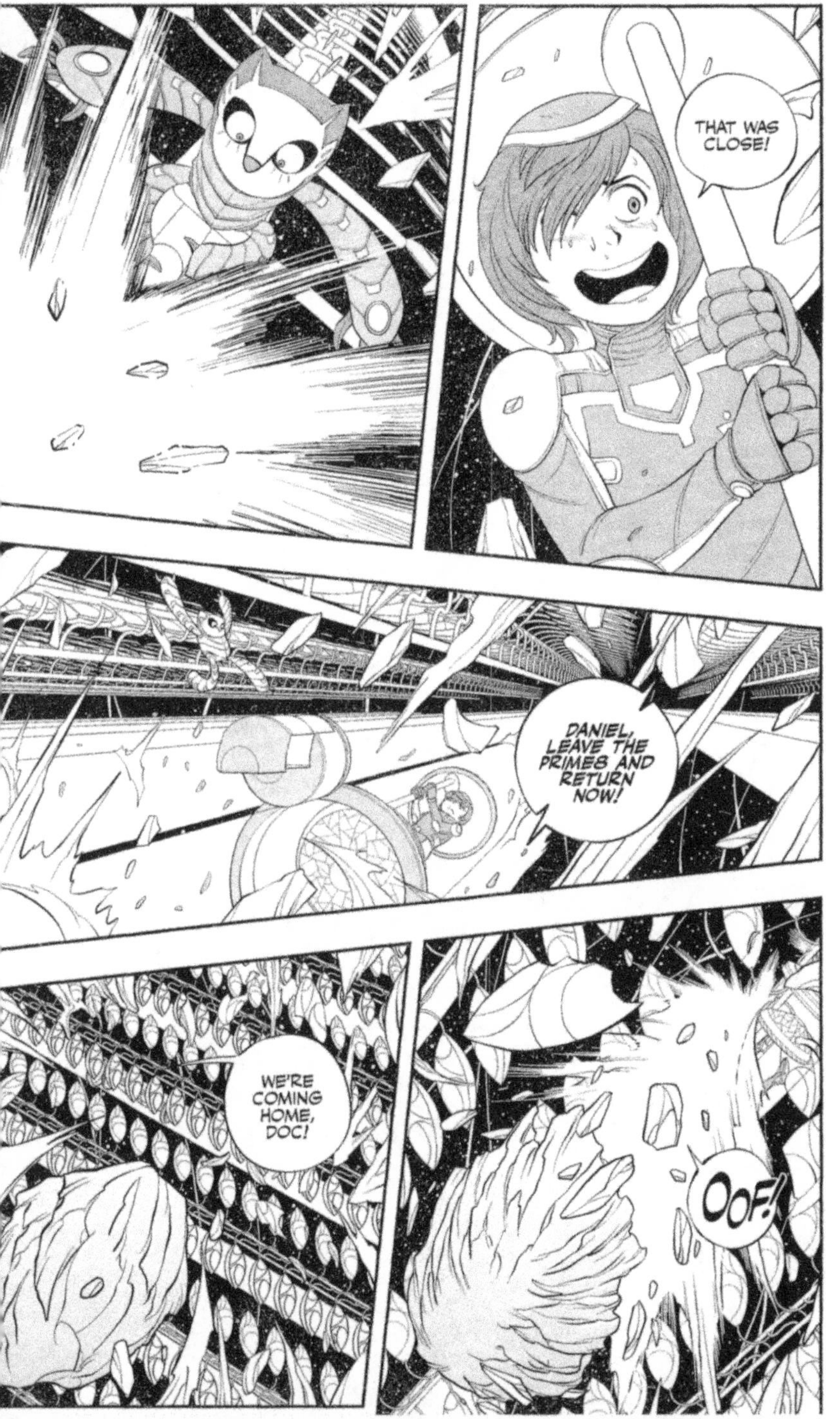
THAT WAS CLOSE!
DANIEL, LEAVE THE PRIME8 AND RETURN NOW!
WE'RE COMING HOME, DOC!
OOF!

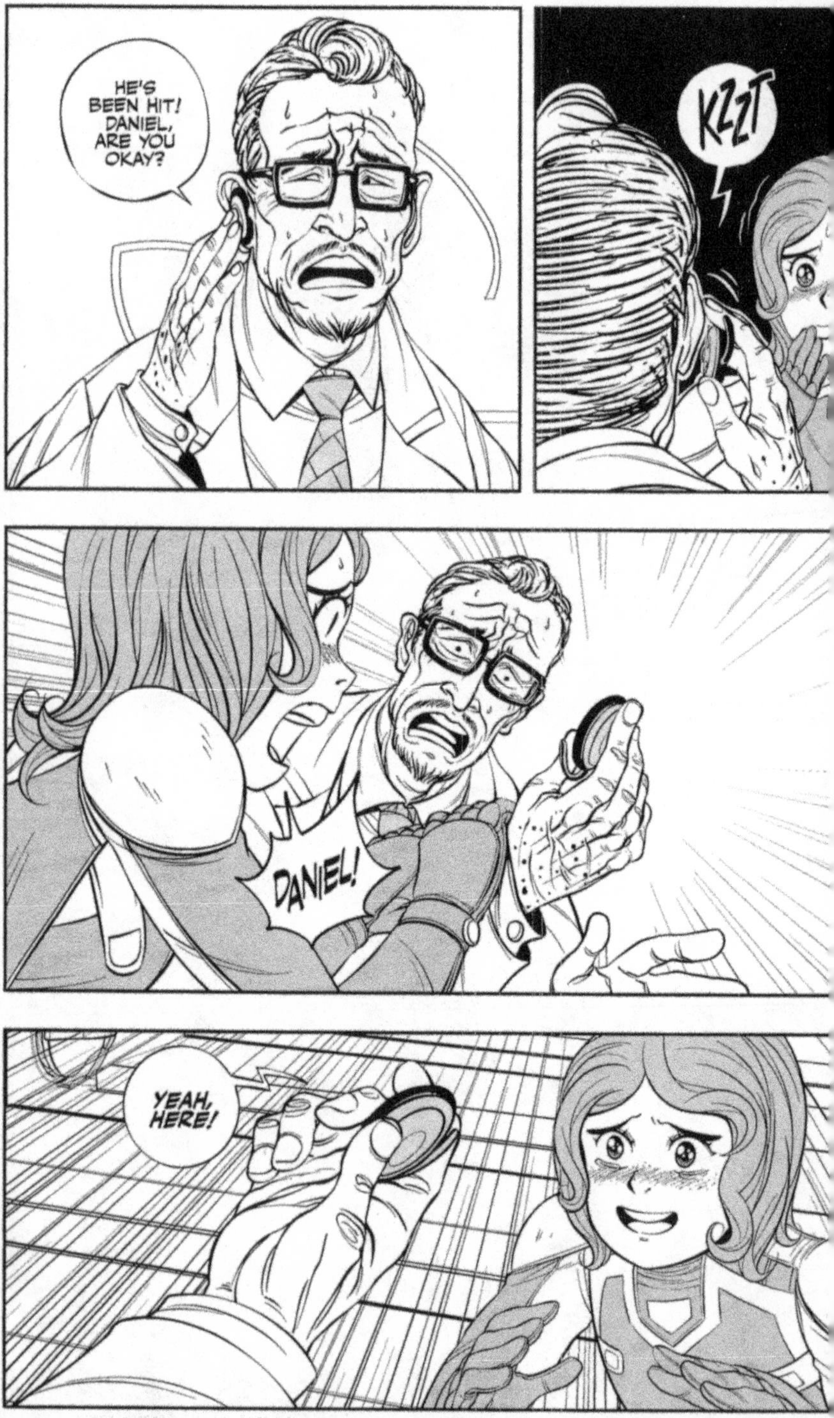
HE'S BEEN HIT! DANIEL, ARE YOU OKAY?
KZZT
DANIEL!
YEAH, HERE!

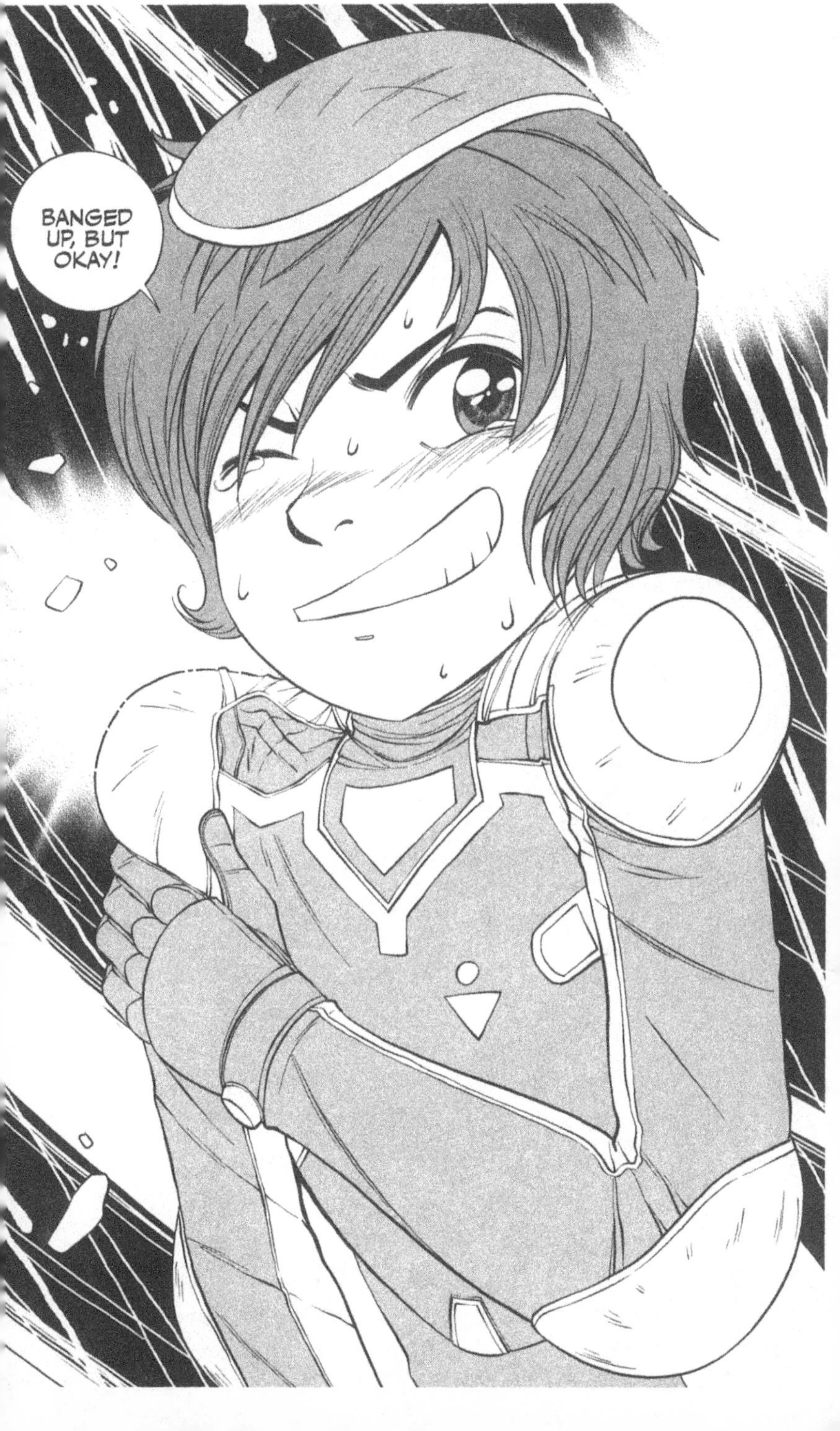
BANGED UP, BUT OKAY!

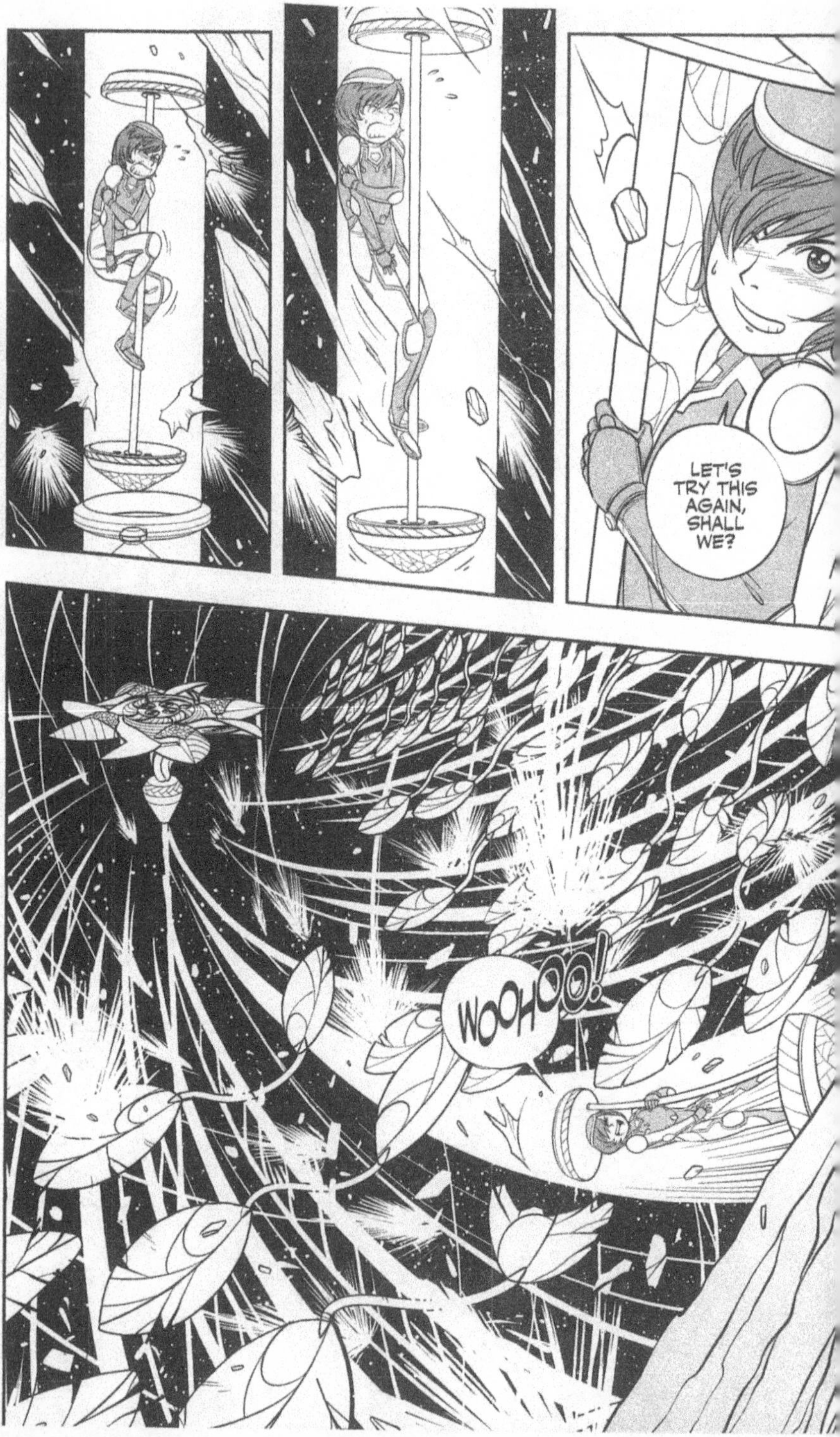
LET'S TRY THIS AGAIN, SHALL WE?
WOOHOO!

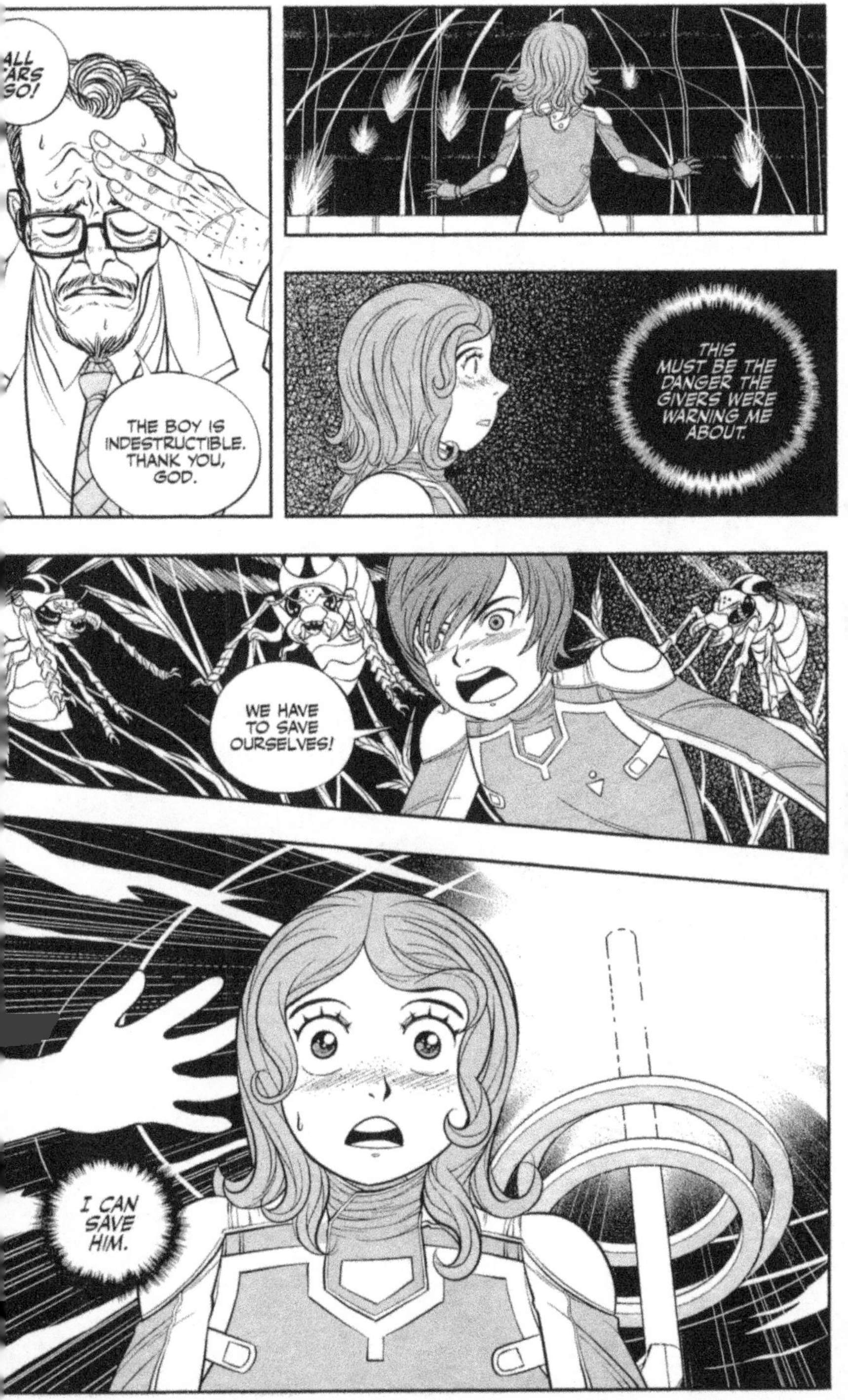
THE BOY IS INDESTRUCTIBLE. THANK YOU, GOD.
THIS MUST BE THE DANGER THE GIVERS WERE WARNING ME ABOUT.
WE HAVE TO SAVE OURSELVES!
I CAN SAVE HIM.

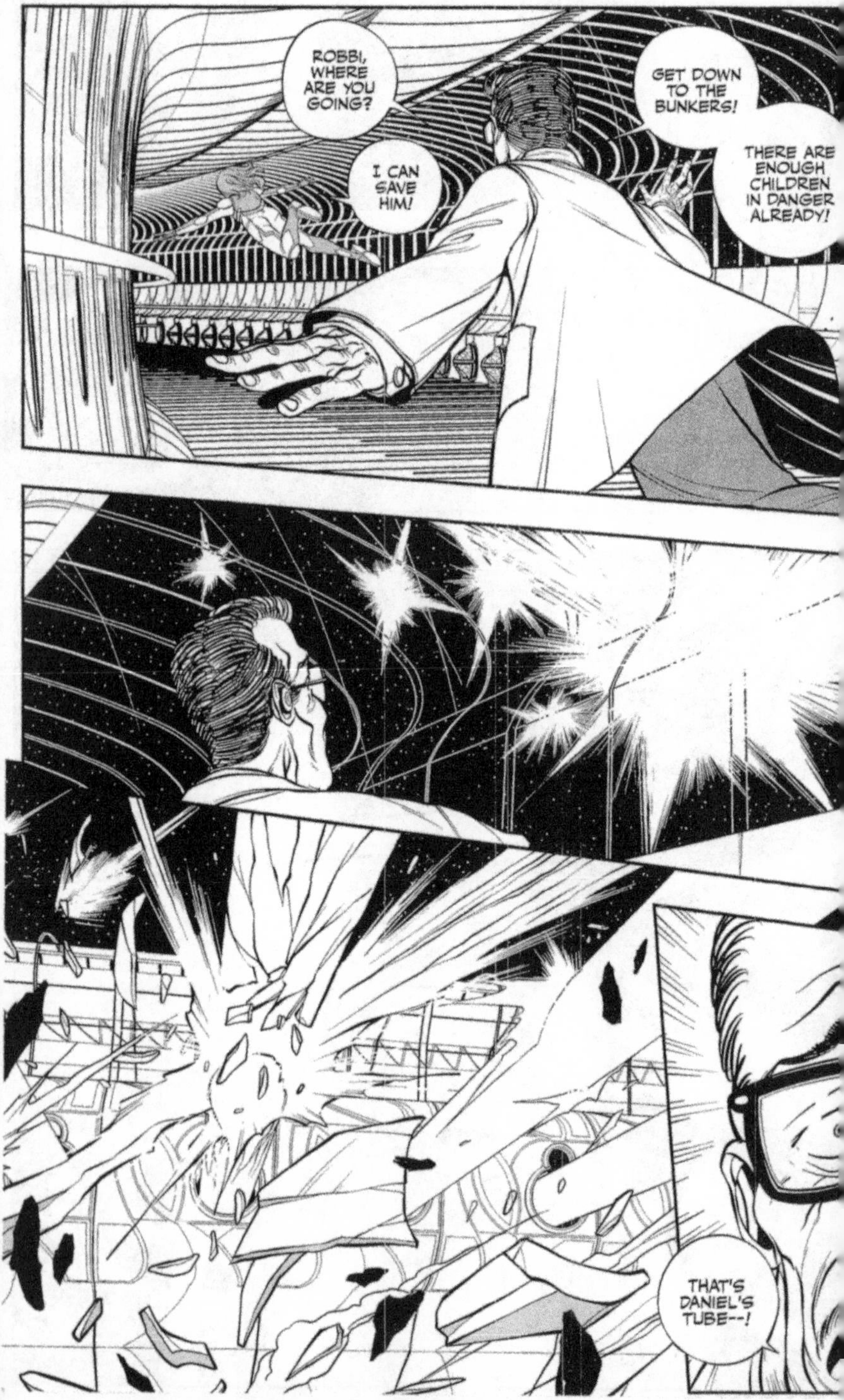
ROBBI, WHERE ARE YOU GOING?
I CAN SAVE HIM!
GET DOWN TO THE BUNKERS!
THERE ARE ENOUGH CHILDREN IN DANGER ALREADY!
THAT'S DANIEL'S TUBE--!

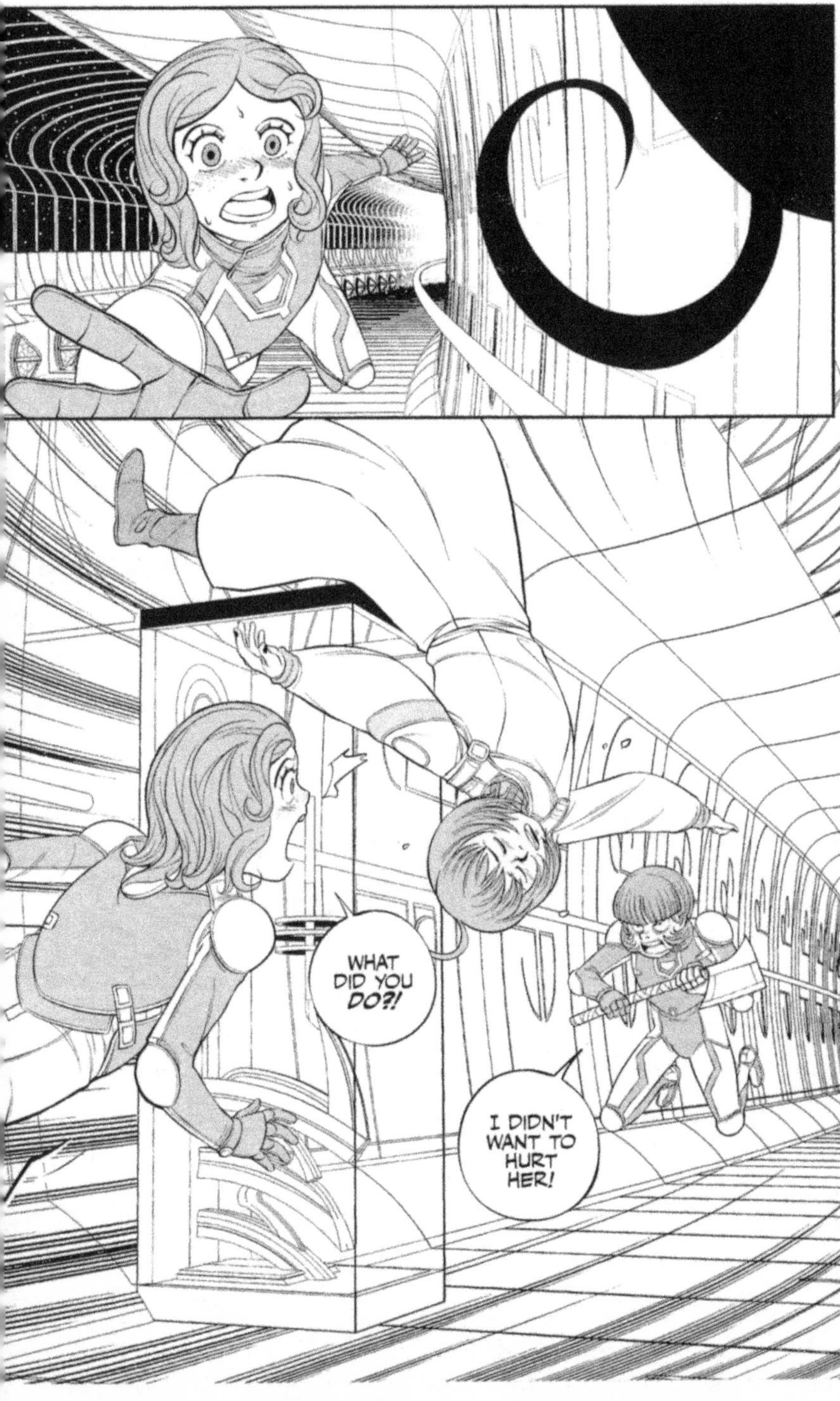
WHAT DID YOU DO?!
I DIDN'T WANT TO HURT HER!

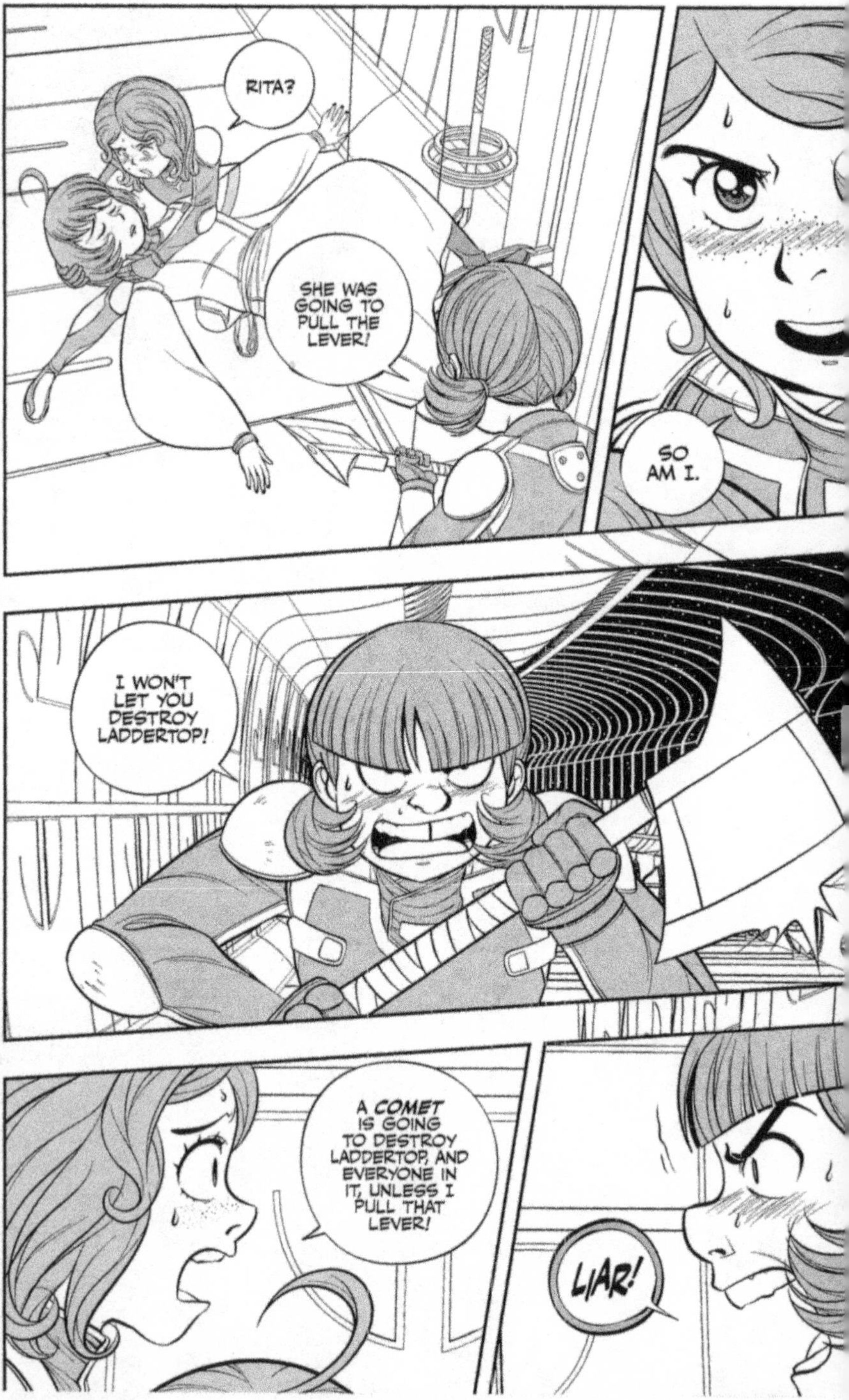
RITA?
SHE WAS GOING TO PULL THE LEVER!
SO AM I.
I WON'T LET YOU DESTROY LADDERTOP!
A *COMET* IS GOING TO DESTROY LADDERTOP, AND EVERYONE IN IT, UNLESS I PULL THAT LEVER!
LIAR!

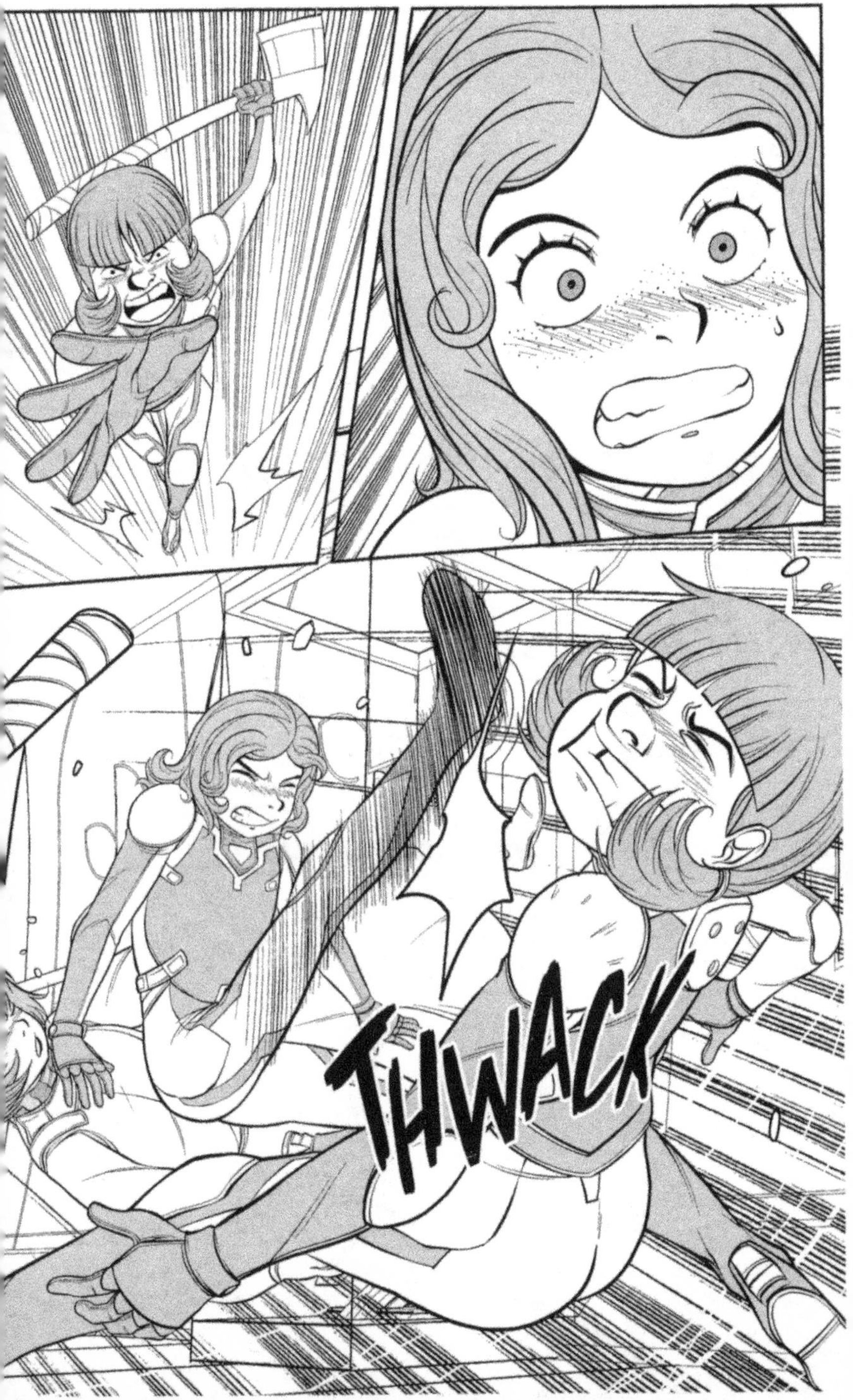
THWACK

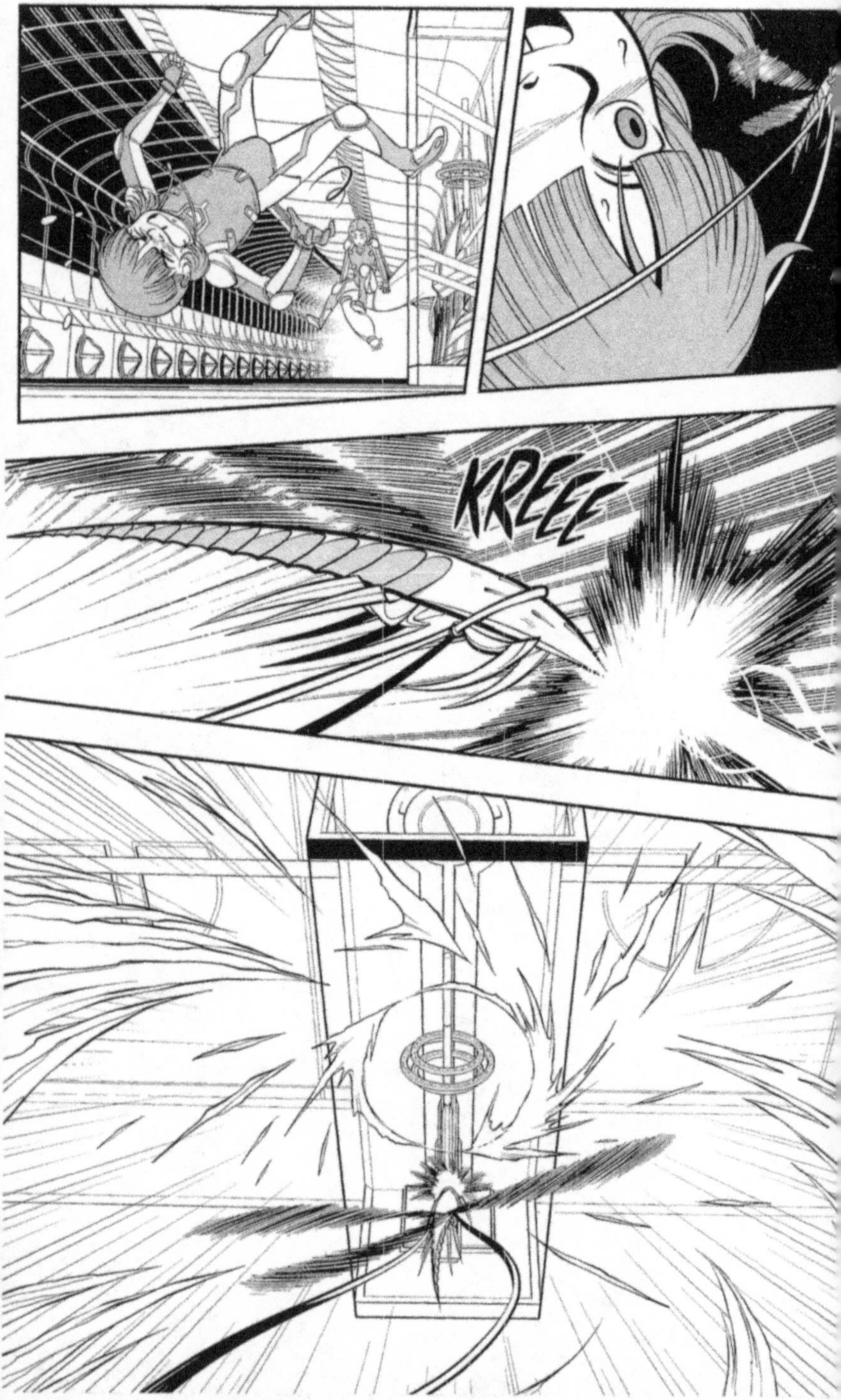
KREEE

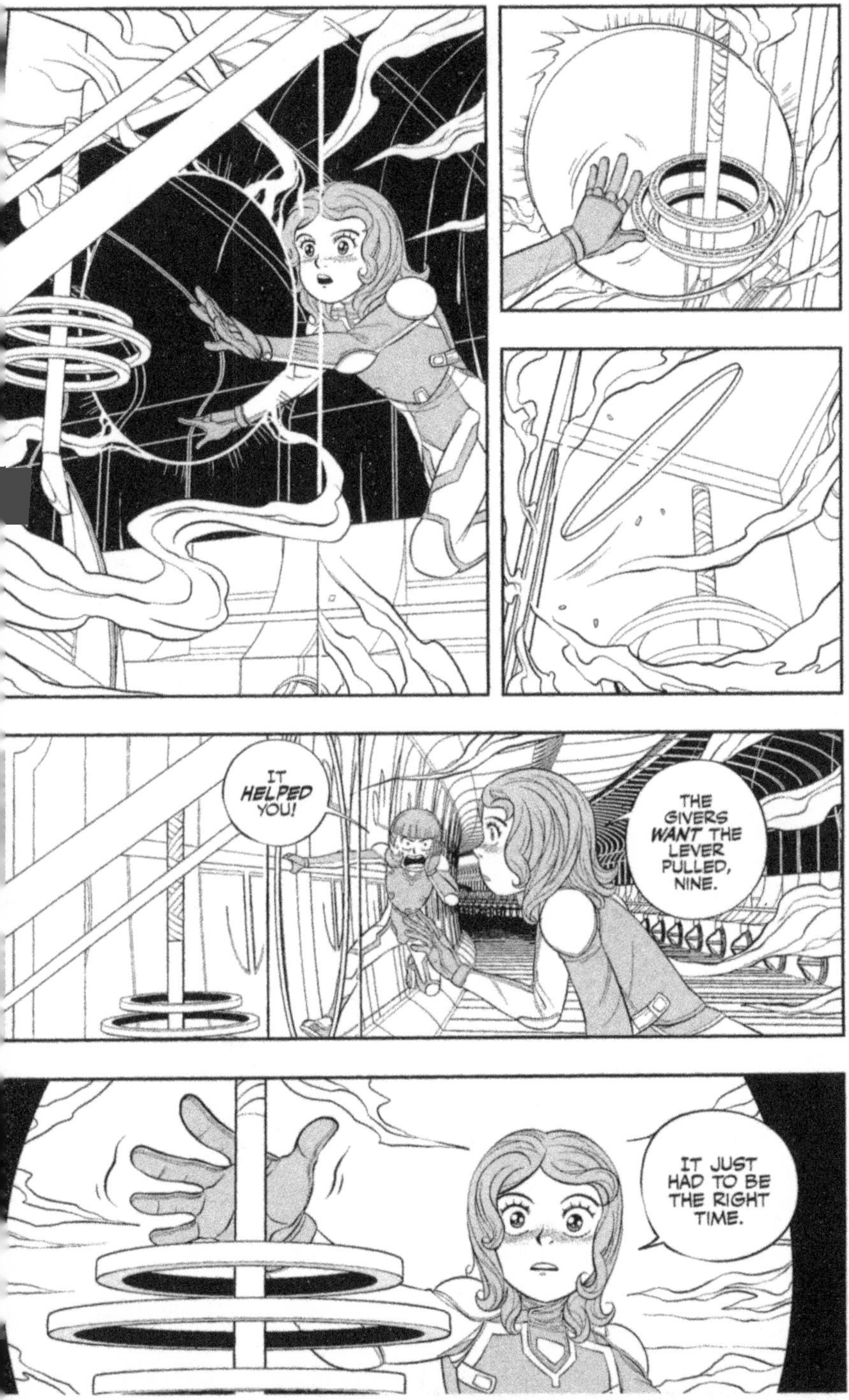
IT *HELPED* YOU!
THE GIVERS *WANT* THE LEVER PULLED, NINE.
IT JUST HAD TO BE THE RIGHT TIME.

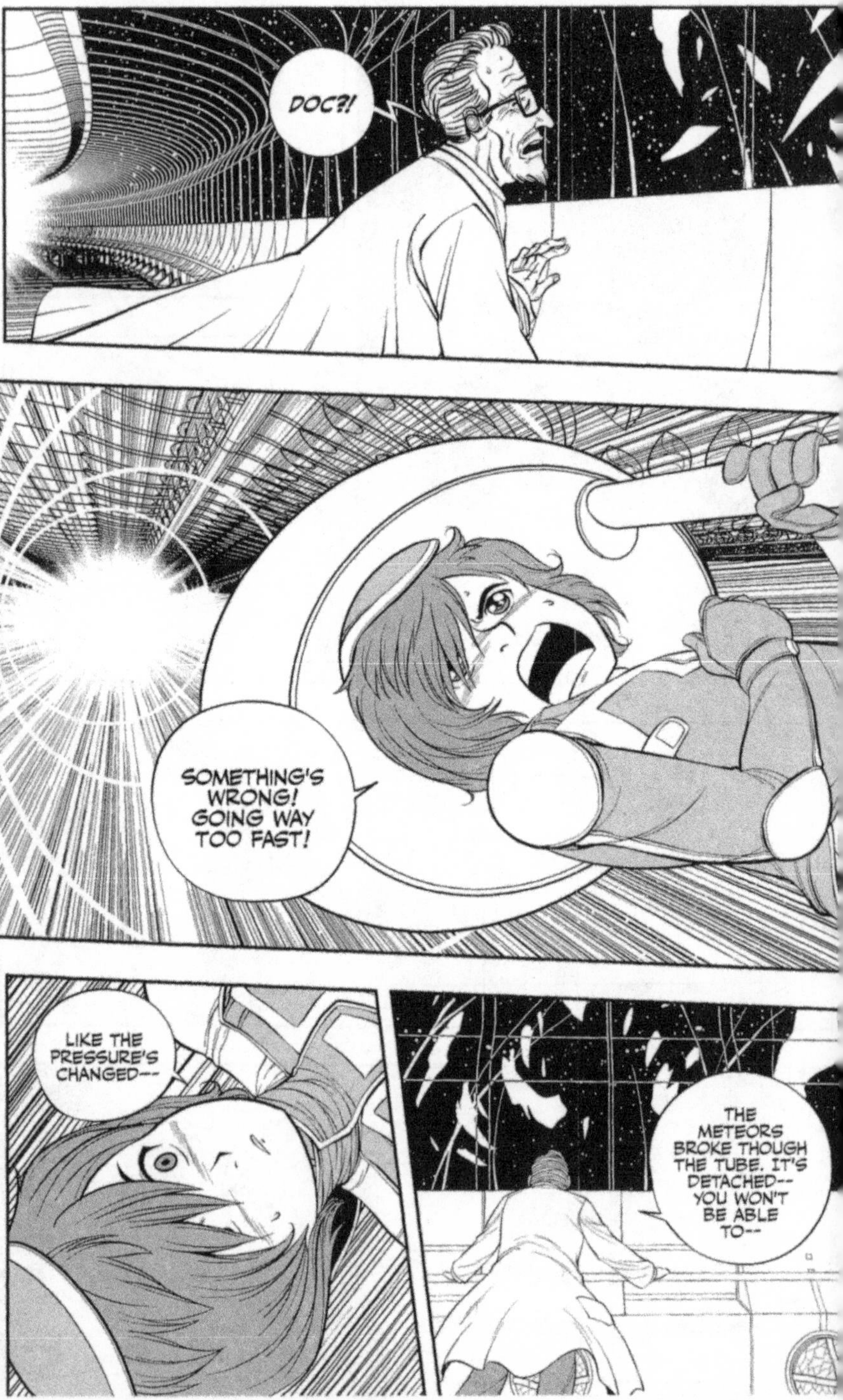
DOC?!
SOMETHING'S WRONG! GOING WAY TOO FAST!
LIKE THE PRESSURE'S CHANGED--
THE METEORS BROKE THOUGH THE TUBE. IT'S DETACHED-- YOU WON'T BE ABLE TO--

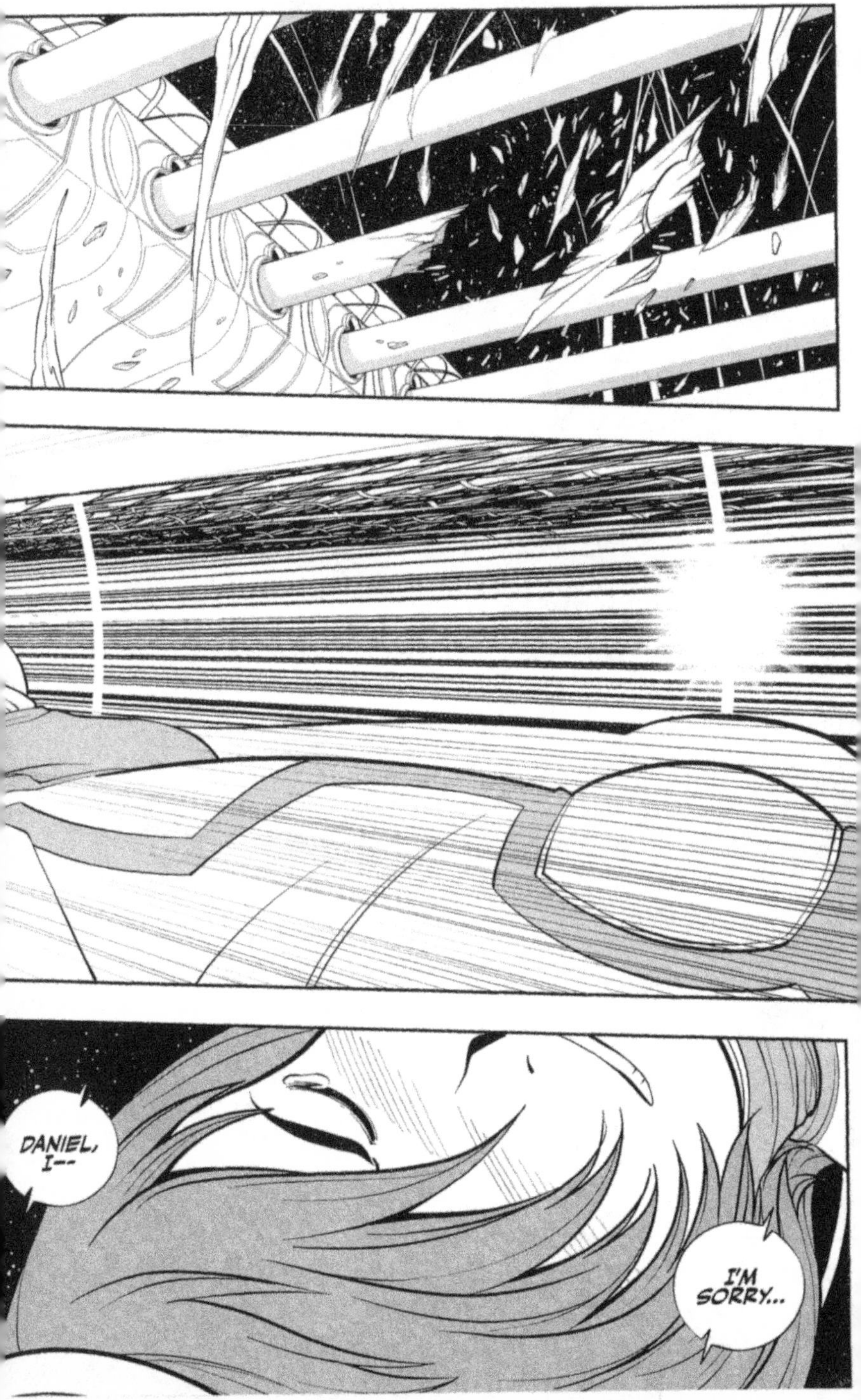
DANIEL, I--
I'M SORRY...

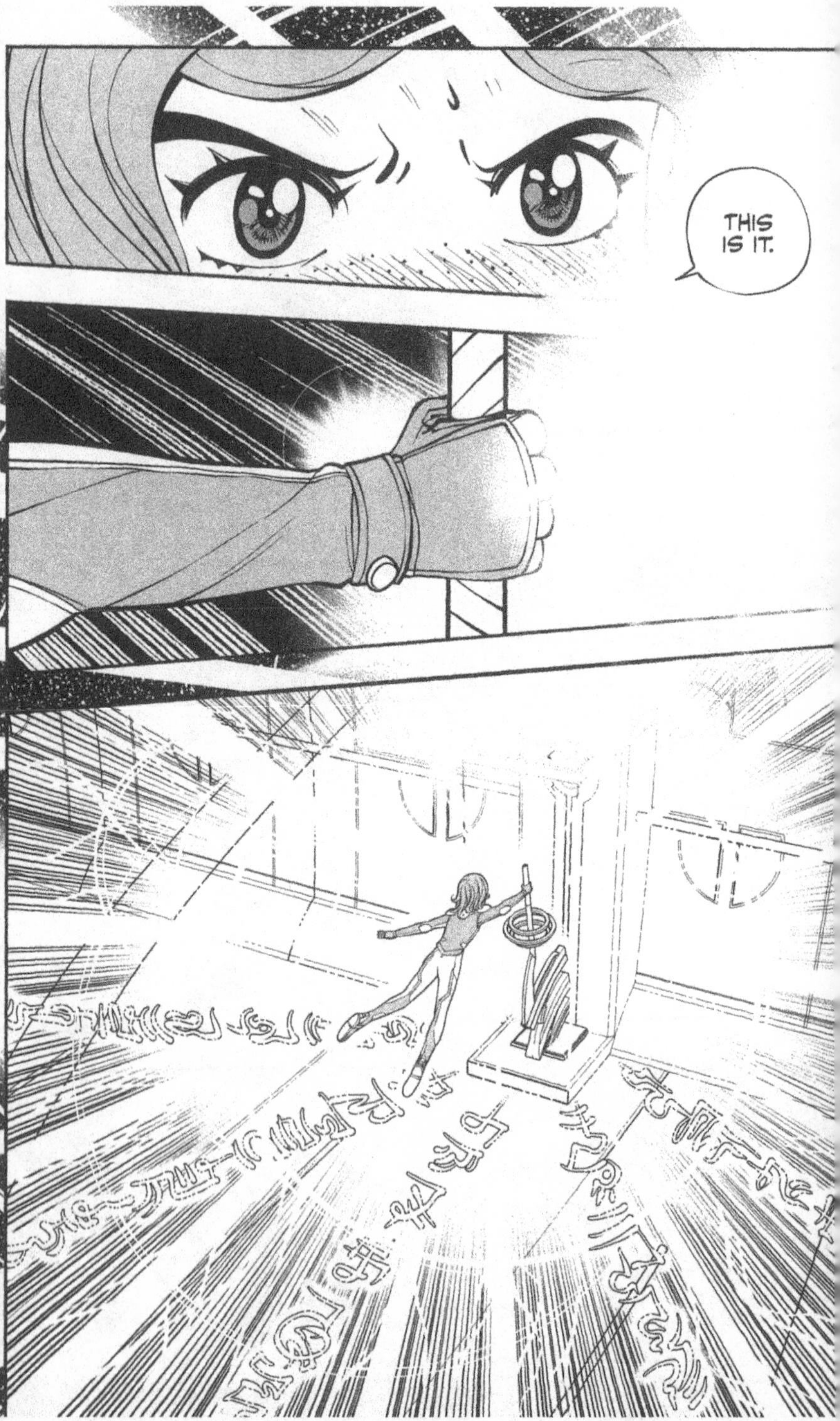
THIS IS IT.

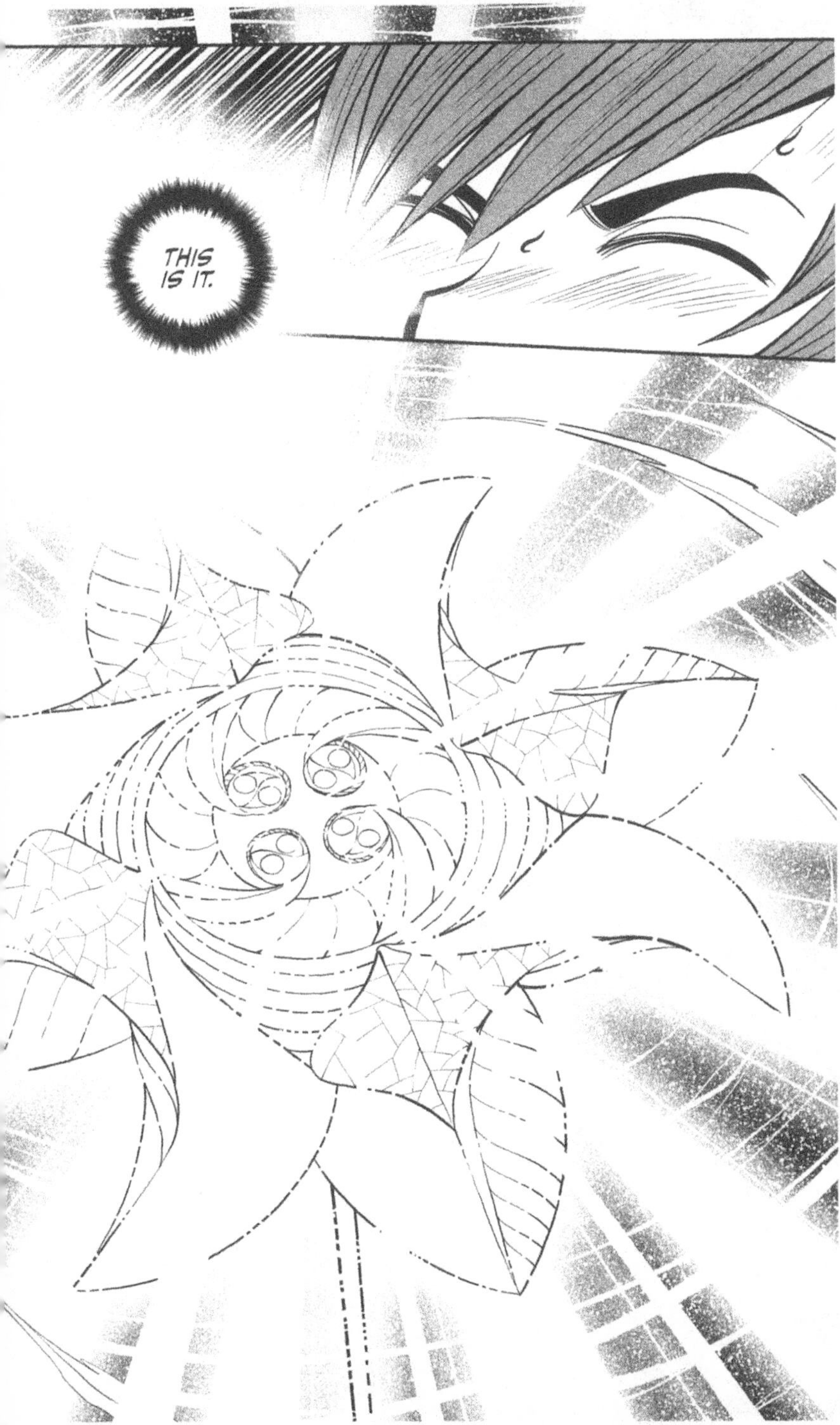
THIS IS IT.

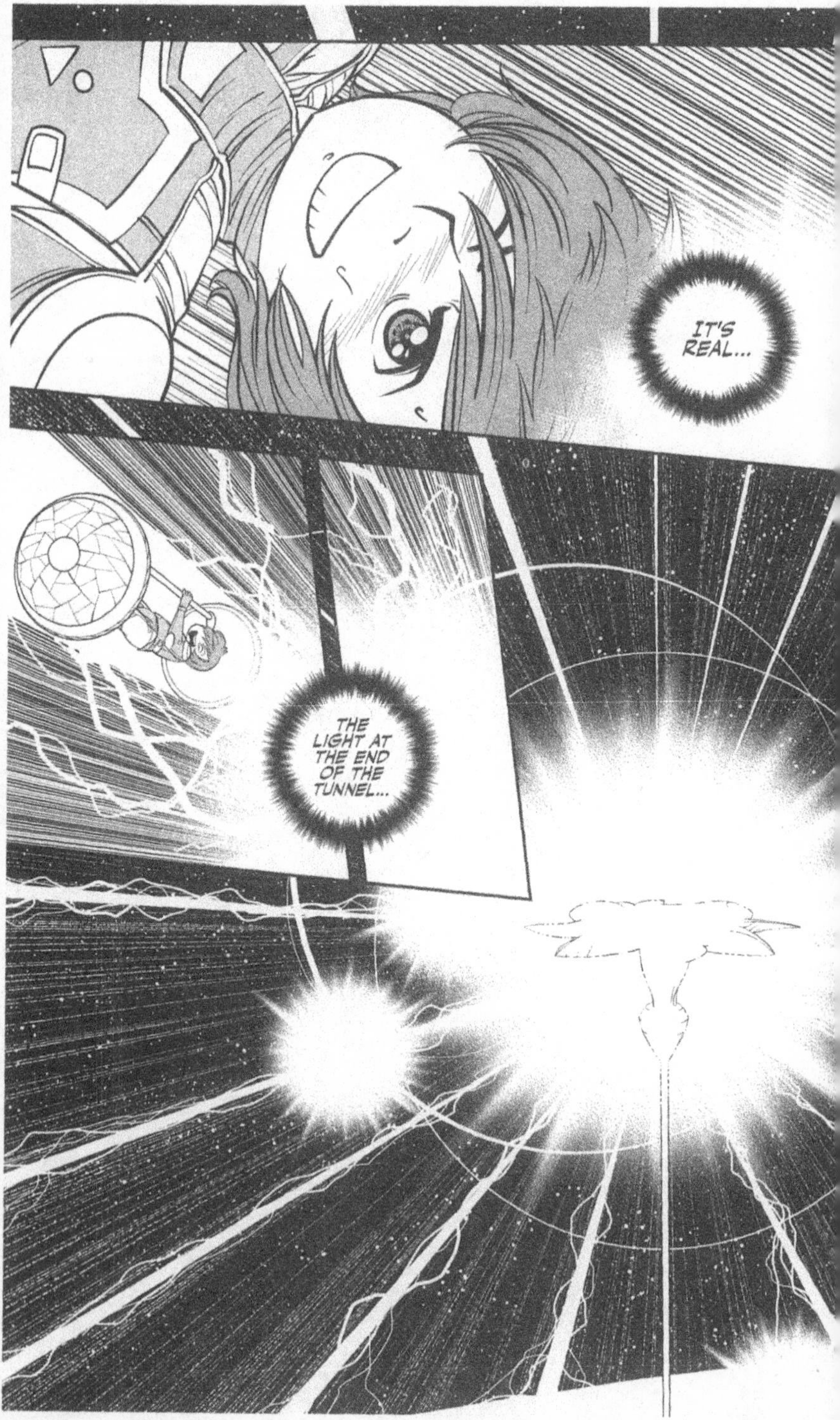
IT'S REAL...
THE LIGHT AT THE END OF THE TUNNEL...

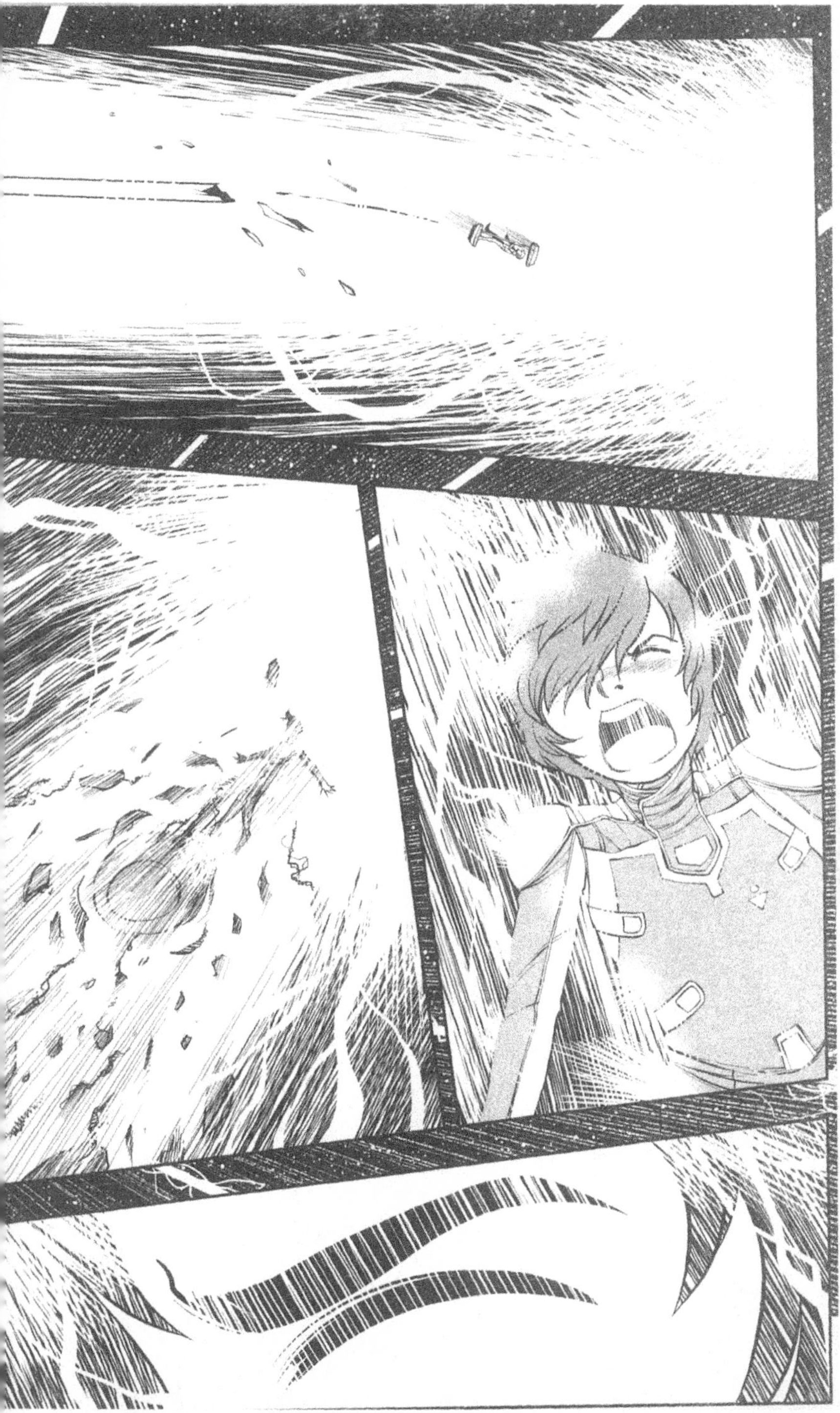

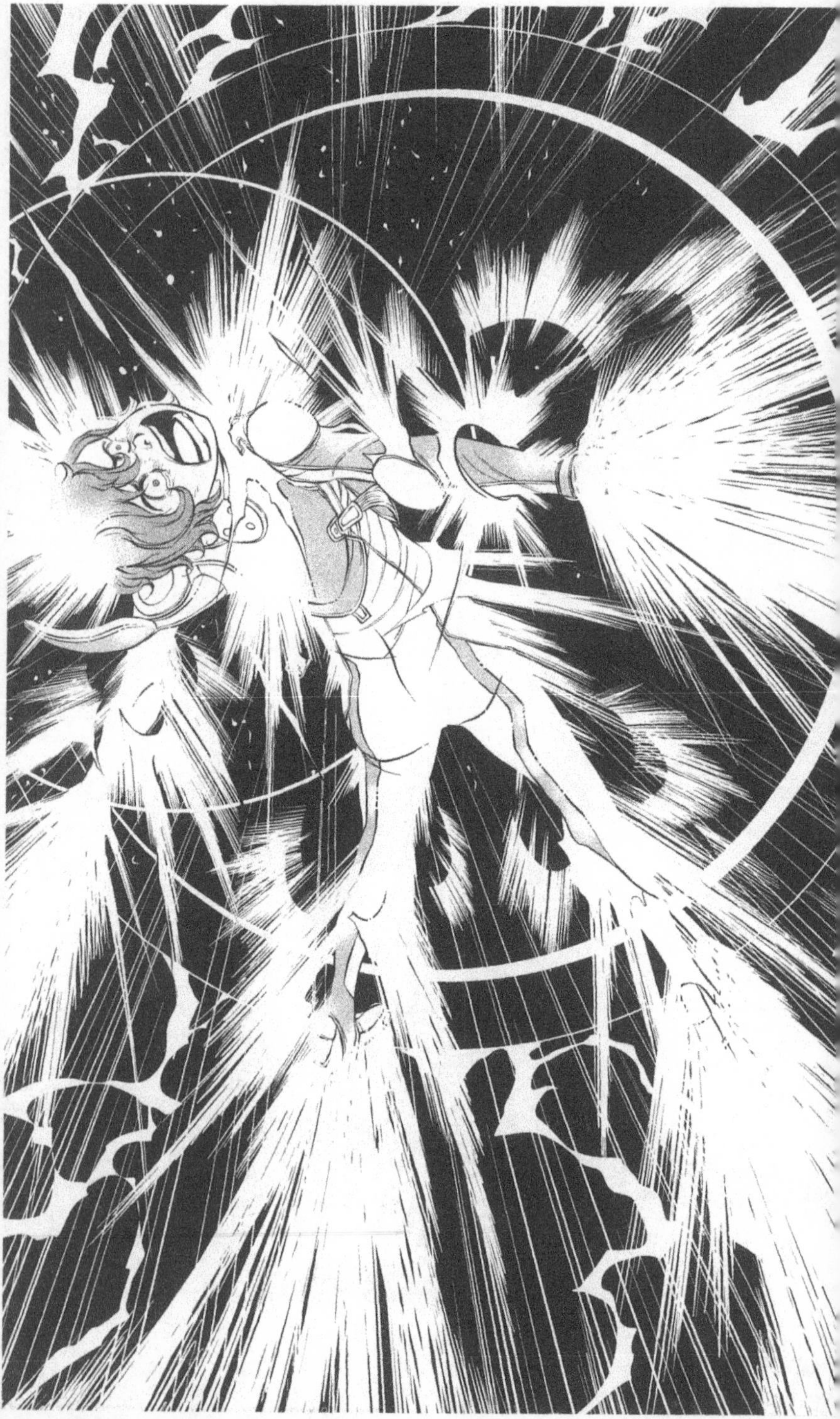

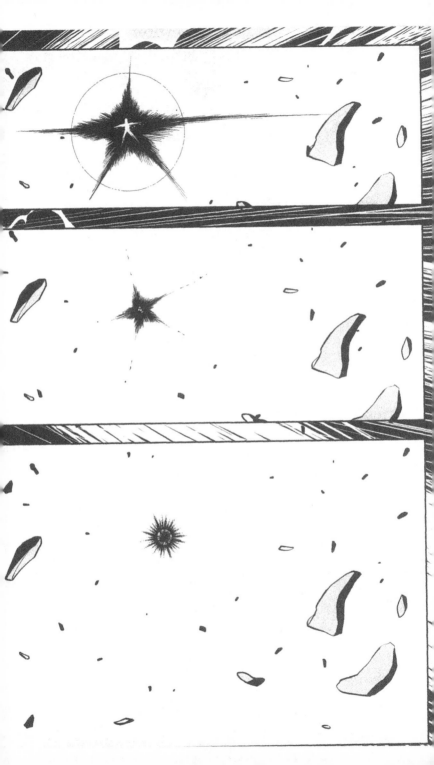

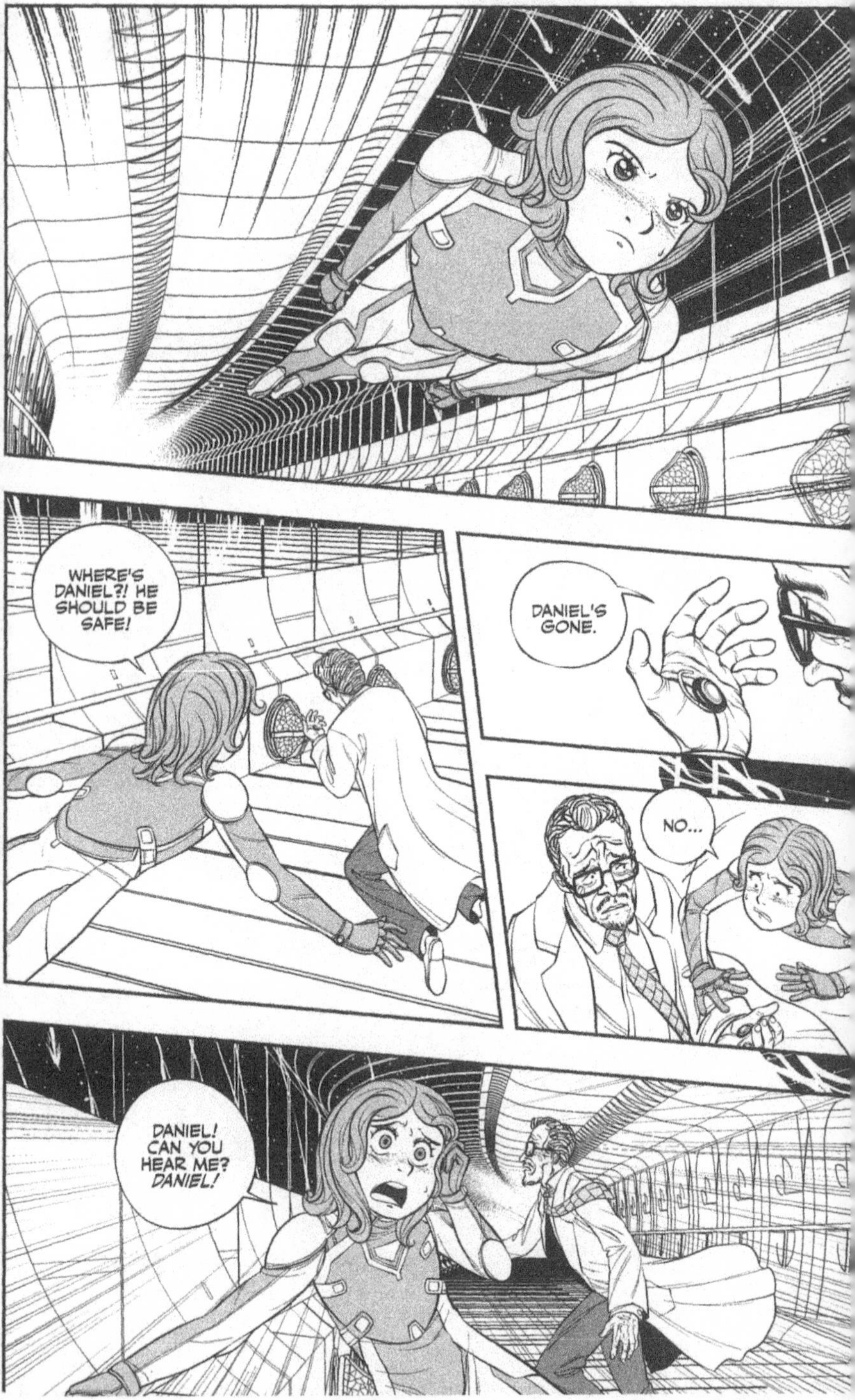
WHERE'S DANIEL?! HE SHOULD BE SAFE!
DANIEL'S GONE.
NO...
DANIEL! CAN YOU HEAR ME? *DANIEL!*

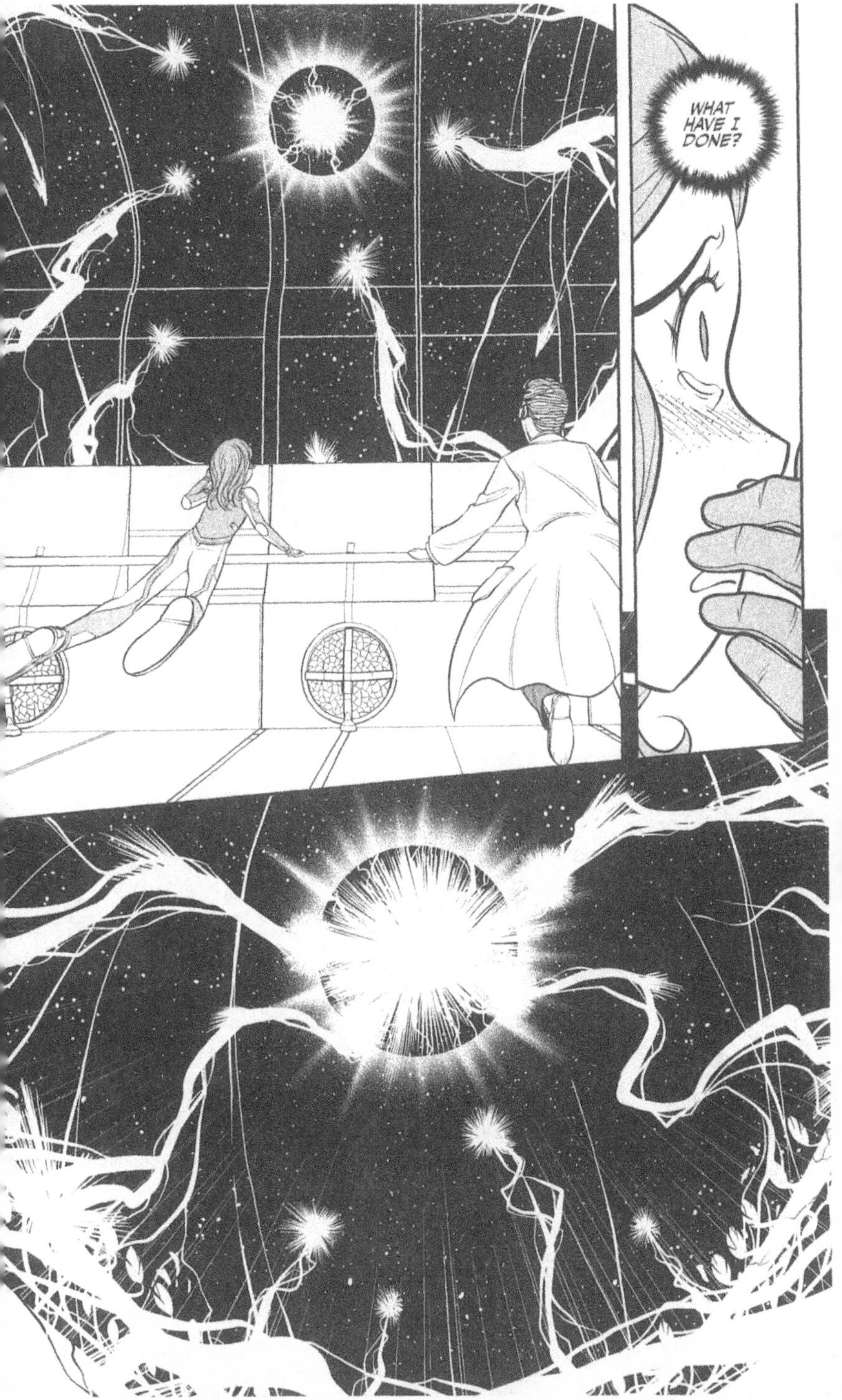
WHAT HAVE I DONE?

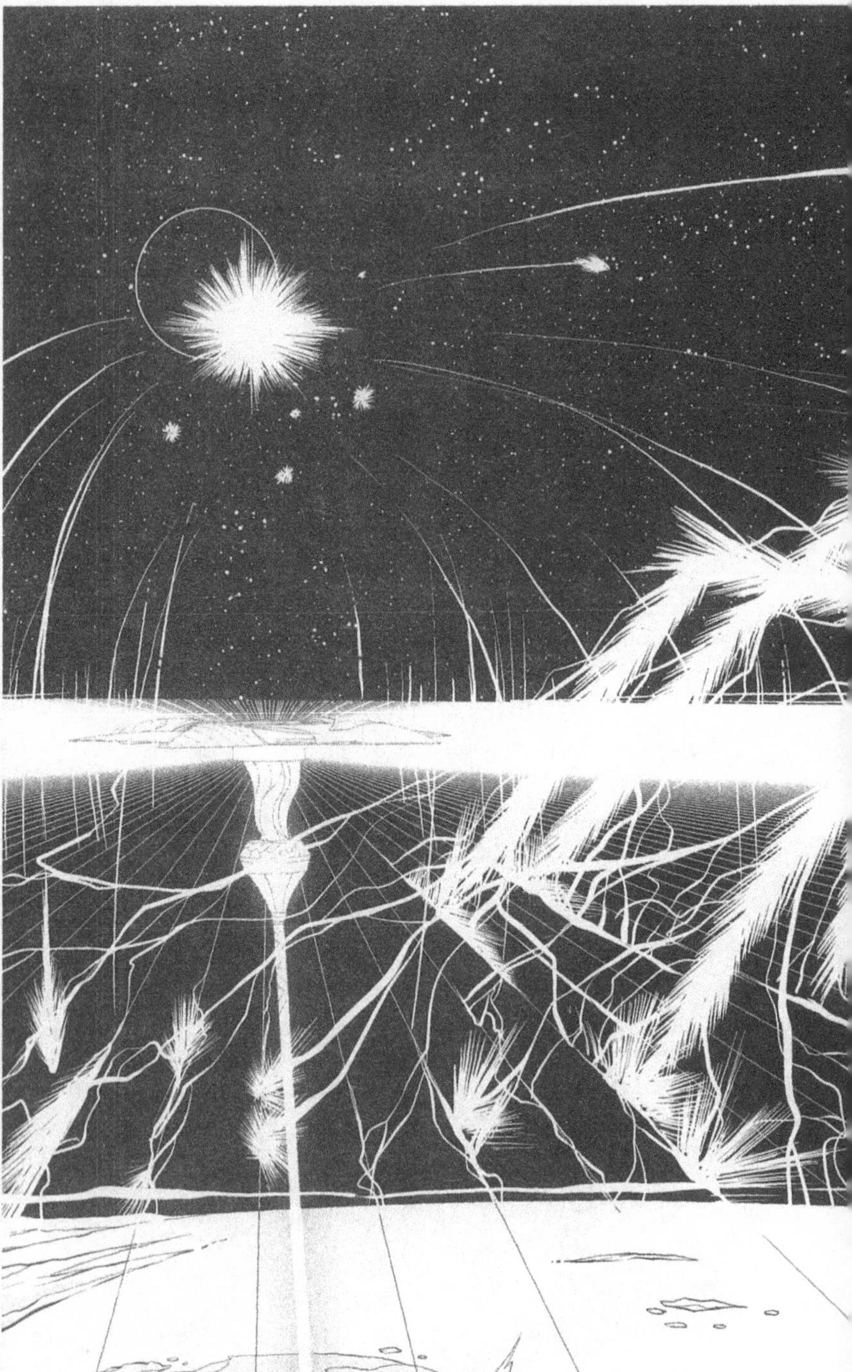

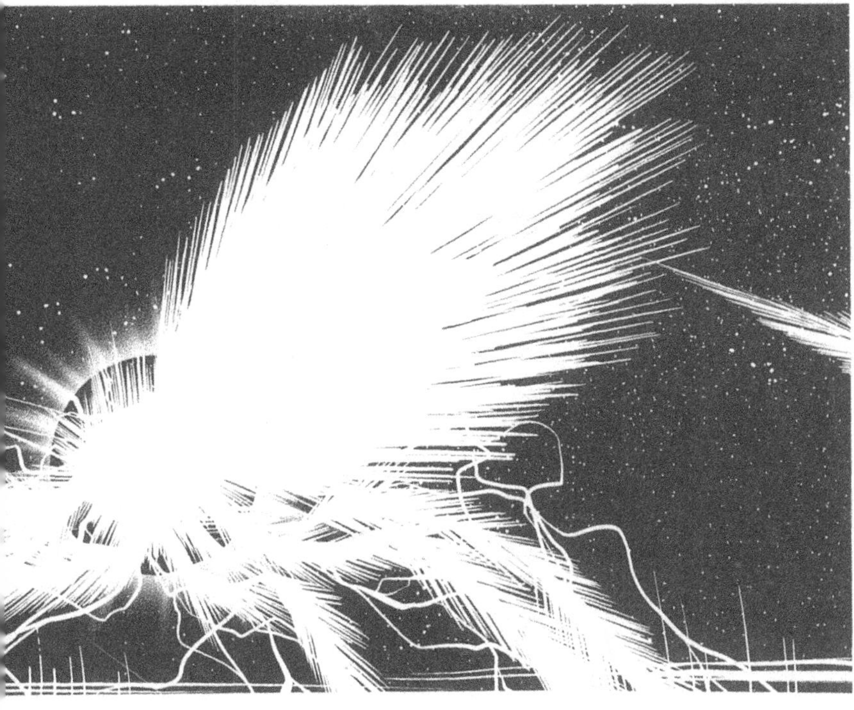

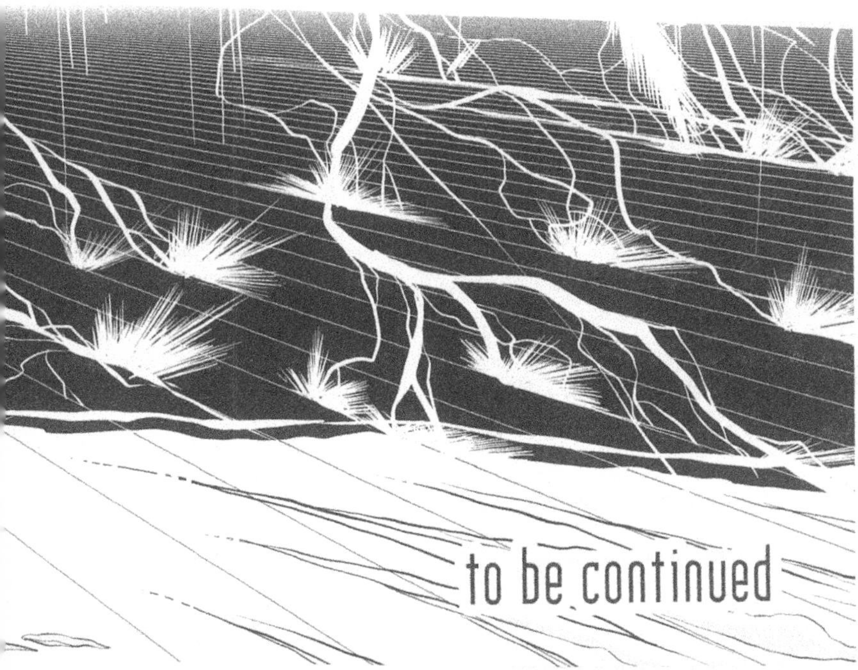
to be continued

Laddertop

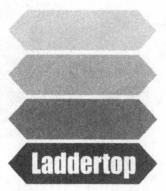

LADDERTOP
CHARACTER DESIGNS

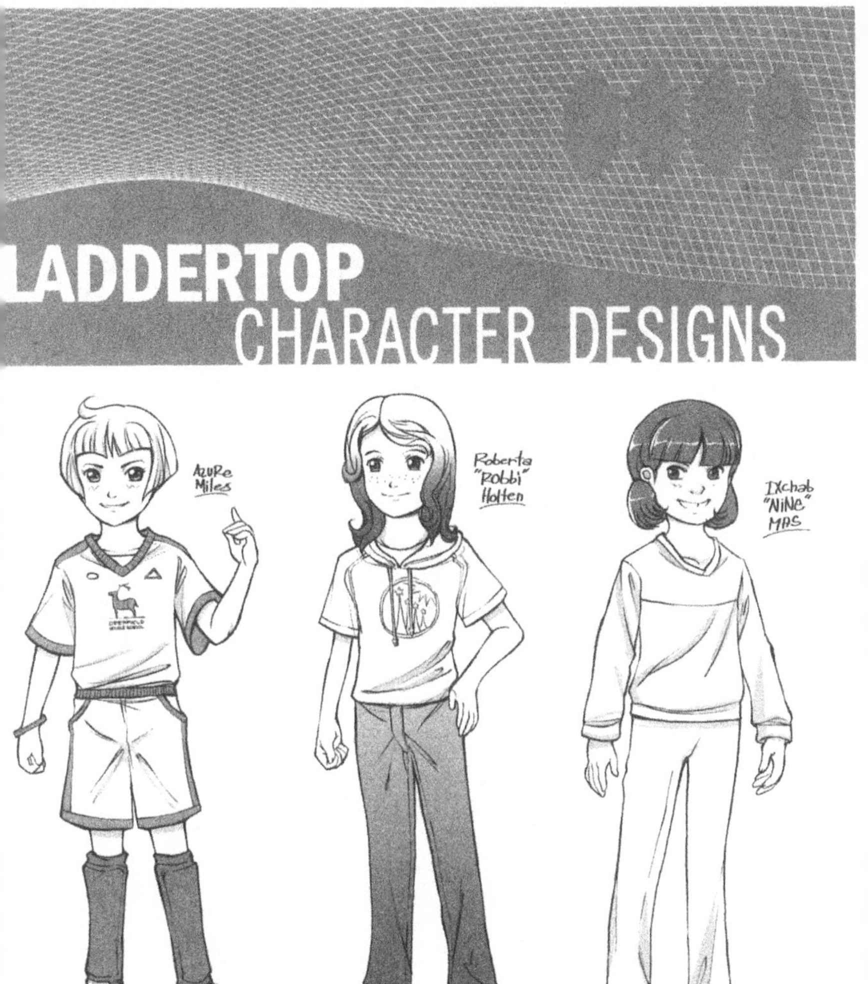
AzuRe Miles
Roberta "Robbi" Holten
IXchab "NiNe" MAS

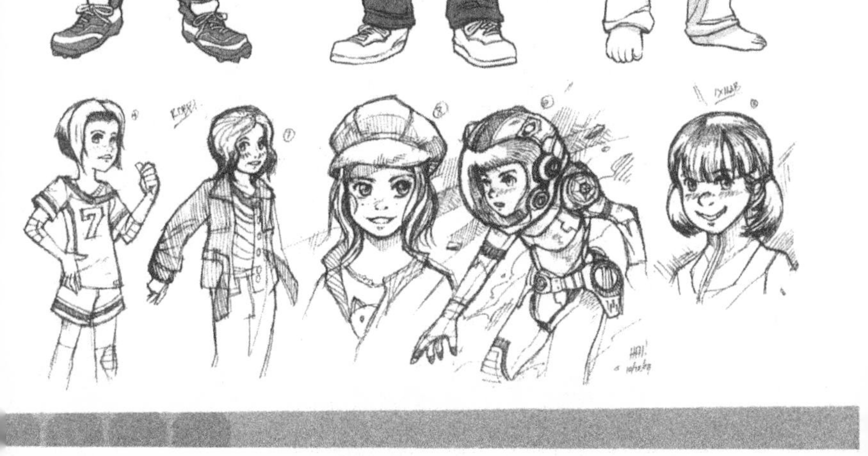

LADDERTOP

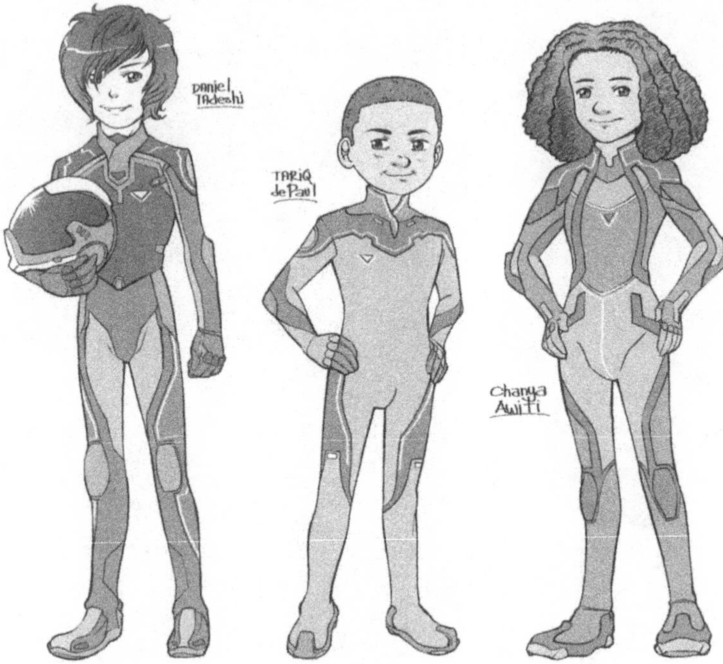
Daniel Tadeshi
TARIQ dePaul
Chanya Awiti

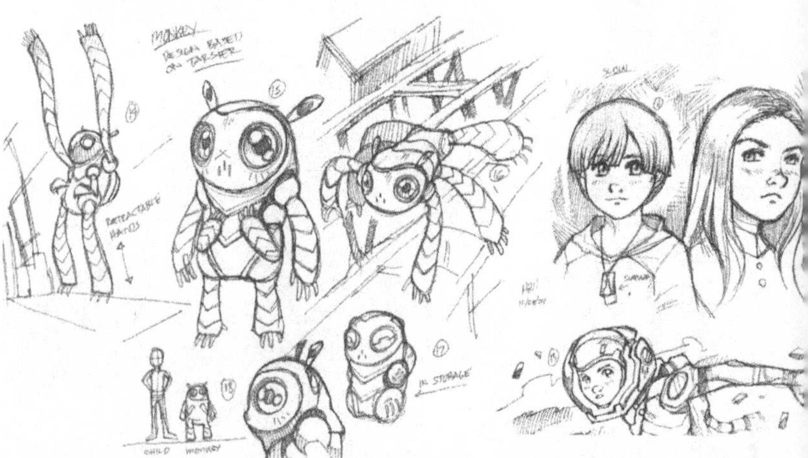
MONKEY
DESIGN BASED ON TARSIER
RETRACTABLE HANDS
IN STORAGE
CHILD
MONKEY

CHARACTER DESIGNS

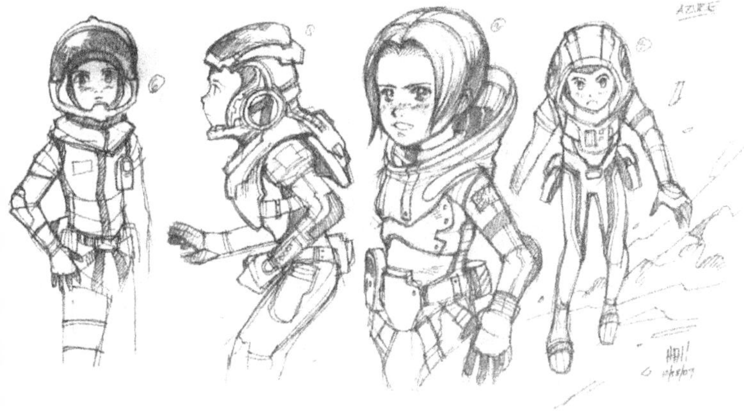

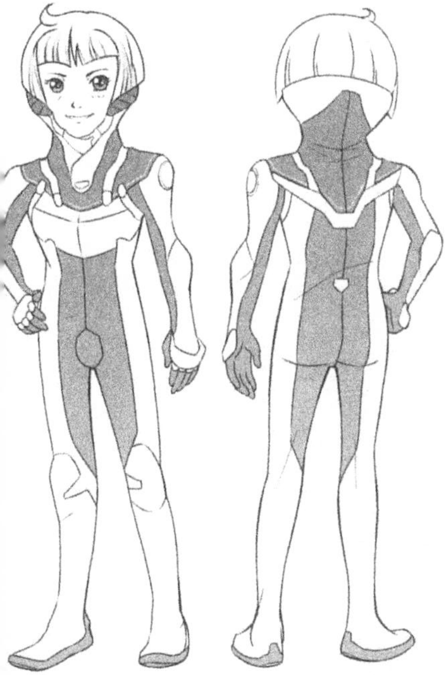

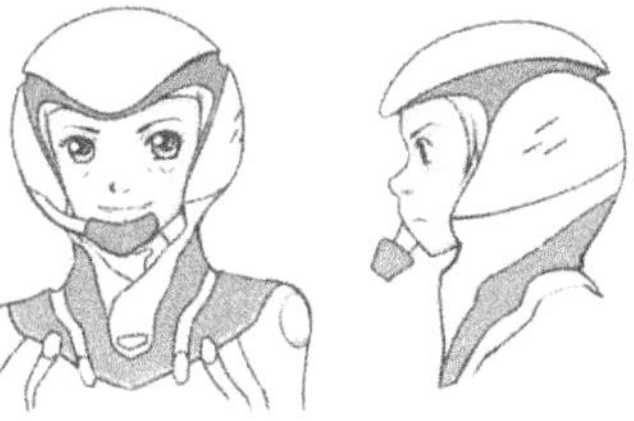

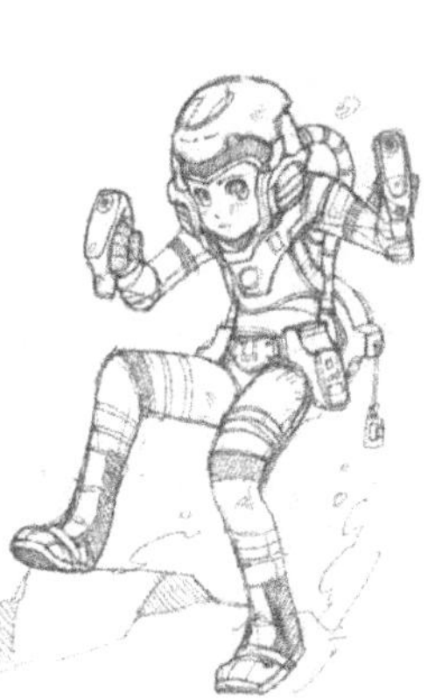

NULL-GRAVITY
TRAINING SUIT

LADDERTOP

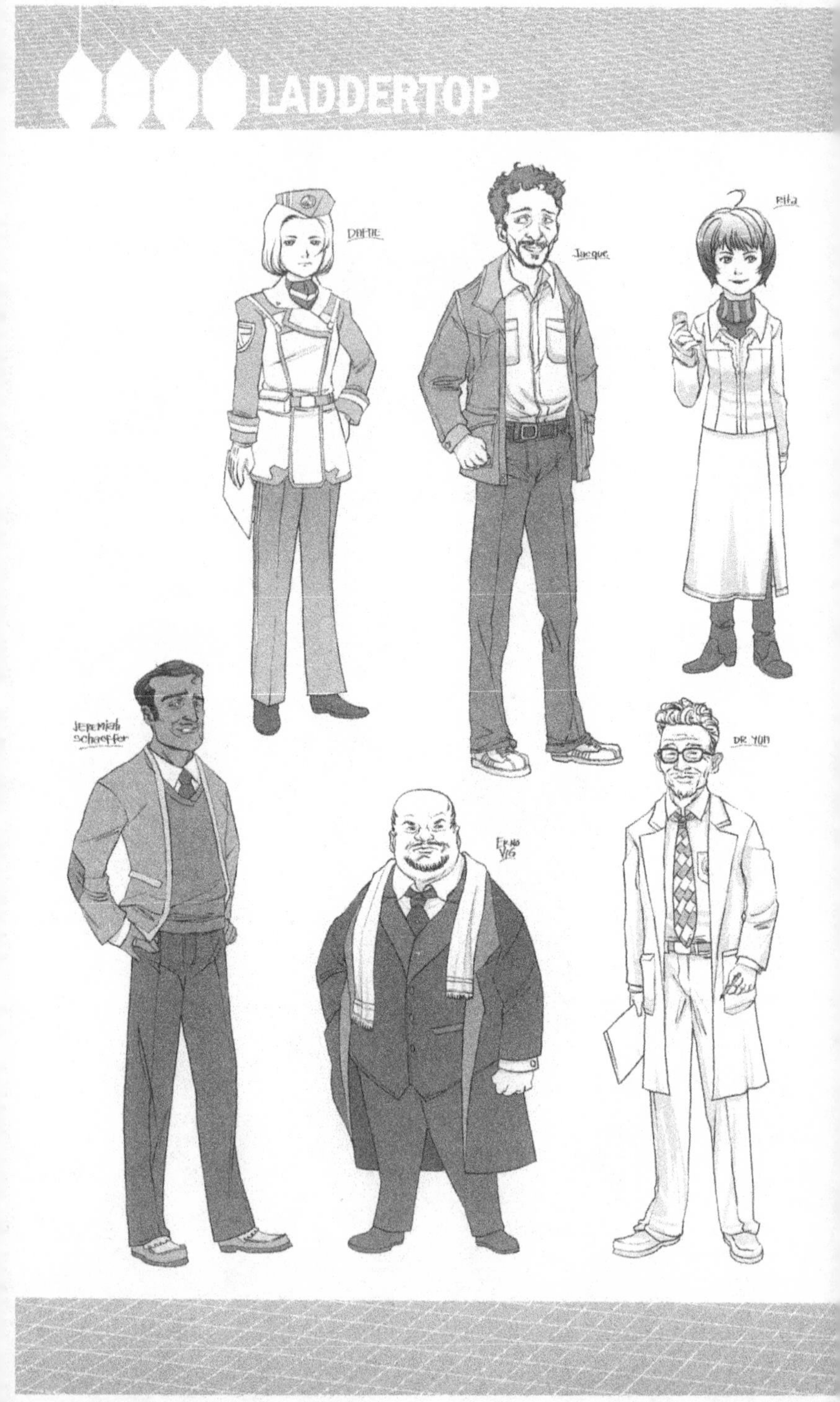
Jacque
Rita
Jeremiah
Schaeffer
Erno
Vig
DR YUN

CHARACTER DESIGNS

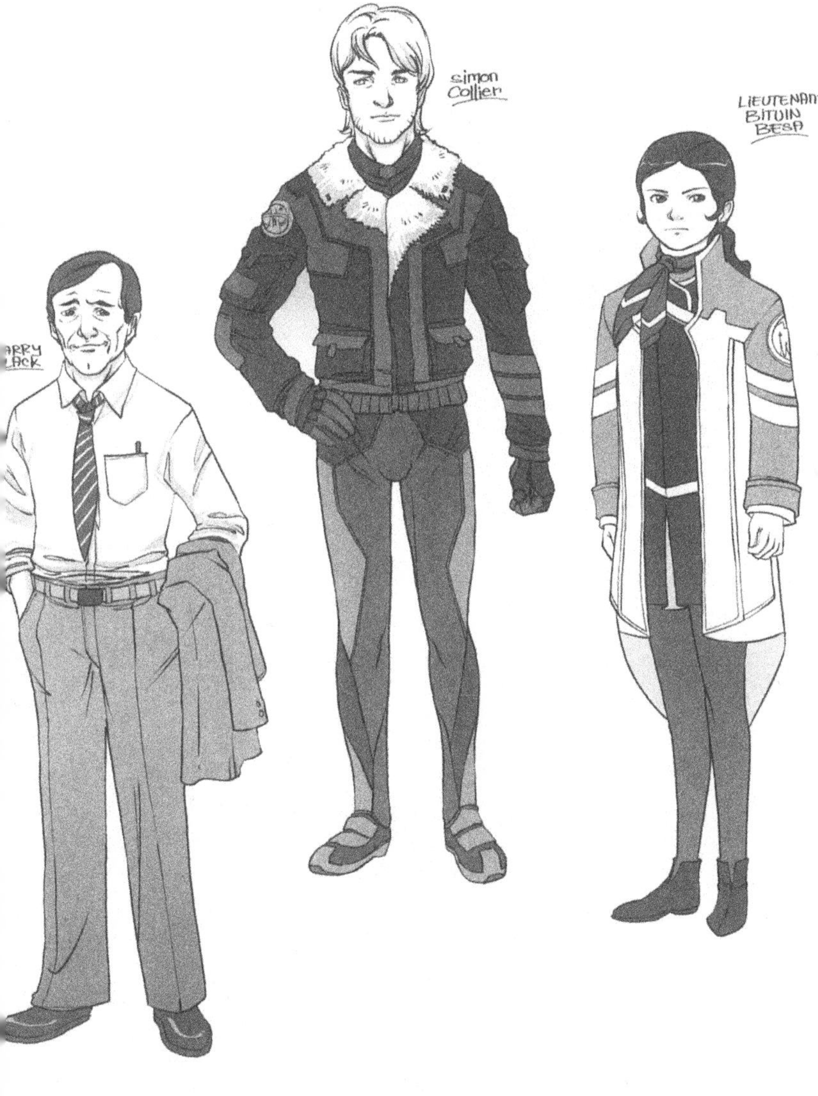
ARRY
LACK
Simon
Collier
LIEUTENANT
BITUIN
BESA

LADDERTOP

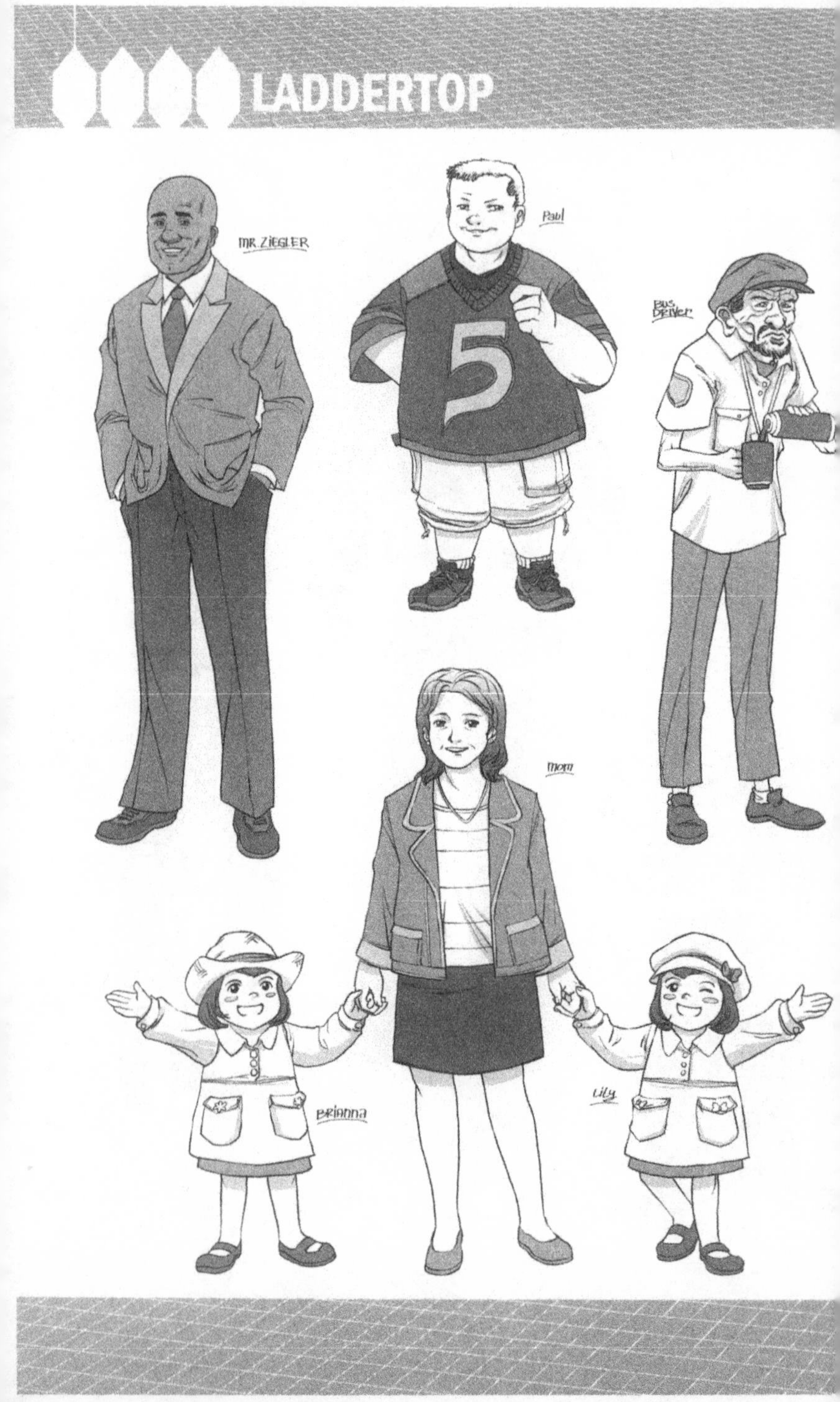
MR. ZIEGLER
Paul
5
Bus Driver
mom
Brianna
Lily

CHARACTER DESIGNS

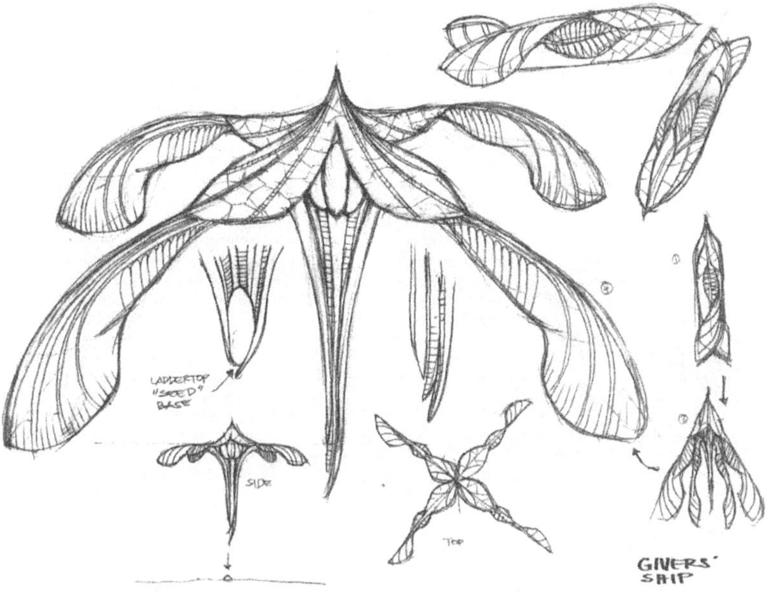
LADDERTOP
"SEED"
BASE
SIDE
TOP
GIVERS'
SHIP

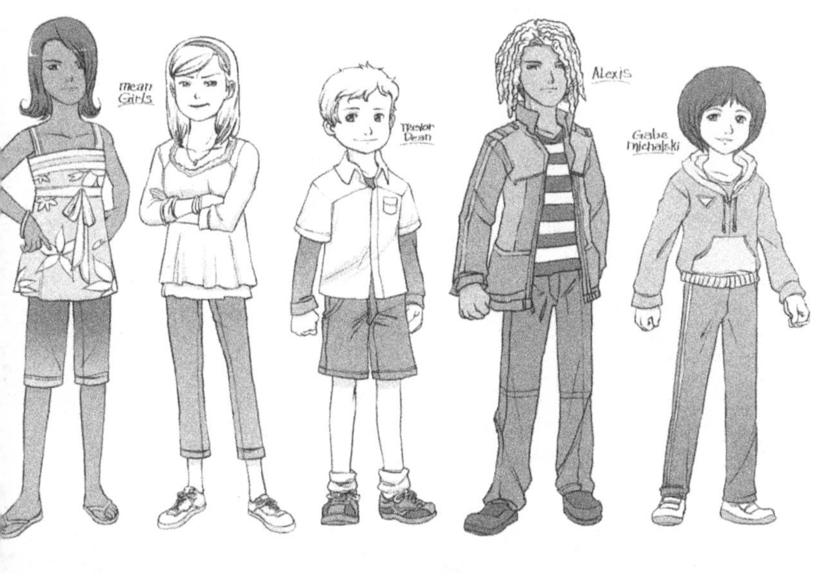
mean
Girls
Trevor
Dean
Alexis
Gabe
michalski

Orson Scott Card wrote every version of *Ender's Game* except the movie. He has written more than 60 books, but none of them were more fun to work on than *Laddertop*. He lives with his wife, Kristine, in Greensboro, North Carolina, where he feeds birds, squirrels, chipmunks, possums, raccoons, and fish, some of them on purpose.
www.hatrack.com

Emily Janice Card is an award-winning audiobook narrator, a director for Skyboat Media, and the creator of the popular web short *Jane Austen's Fight Club*. She lives with her husband and daughter in Los Angeles.

Zina Margaret Card is a theatre major at Brigham Young University with an emphasis in everything. While she is welcoming her transition into adulthood, a part of her is still waiting for a talking animal to awaken her powers as a magical girl.

Honoel A. Ibardolaza is an award-winning children's book writer and illustrator. He is also a manga and comic book artist whose published works include *Blade for Barter*. You can find him at www.honoel.com.

CPSIA information can be obtained
at www.ICGtesting.com
Printed in the USA
LVHW031715260819
628963LV00001B/57/P